1 MONTH OF
FREE
READING

at

www.ForgottenBooks.com

By purchasing this book you are eligible for one month membership to ForgottenBooks.com, giving you unlimited access to our entire collection of over 1,000,000 titles via our web site and mobile apps.

To claim your free month visit:

www.forgottenbooks.com/free923031

ISBN 978-0-260-02532-6
PIBN 10923031

NATIONAL

BANKRUPTCY REGISTER

REPORTS.

CONTAINING ALL THE

IMPORTANT BANKRUPTCY DECISIONS

IN THE

UNITED STATES.

EDITORS:

WILLIAM A. SHINN,   RAPHAEL J. MOSES, Jr.

VOLUME VI.

New York:

J. R. McDIVITT,

LAW BOOKSELLER AND PUBLISHER,

111 Nassau Street.

1874.

315072

LANGE, LITTLE & Co.,
PRINTERS, ELECTROTYPERS AND STEREOTYPERS,
108 TO 114 WOOSTER STREET, N. Y.

TABLE OF CASES REPORTED.

TABLE OF CASES CITED

AMENDMENTS TO THE BANKRUPT ACT.

A BILL

To declare the true intent and meaning of section two of an act entitled "An act to establish a uniform system of bankruptcy throughout the United States," approved March second, eighteen hundred and sixty-seven.

Be it enacted by the Senate and House of Representatives of the United States of America in Congress assembled, That the powers and jurisdiction granted to the several circuit courts of the United States, or any justice thereof, by section two of an act entitled "An act to establish a uniform system of bankruptcy throughout the United States," approved March second, eighteen hundred and sixty-seven, may be exercised in any district in which the powers or jurisdiction of a circuit court have been or may be conferred on the district court for such district, as if no such powers or jurisdiction had been conferred on such district court; it being the true intent and meaning of said act that the system of bankruptcy thereby established shall be uniform throughout the United States.

Approved June 10th, 1872.

·A BILL

To amend an act entitled "An act to establish a uniform system of bankruptcy throughout the United States."

Be it enacted by the Senate and House of Representatives of the United States of America in Congress assembled, That the first proviso in section fourteen of an act approved March second, eighteen hundred and sixty-seven, entitled "An act to establish a uniform system of bankruptcy throughout the United States," be amended by striking out the words "eighteen hundred and sixty-four" and inserting in lieu thereof "eighteen hundred and seventy-one."

Approved June 10th, 1872.

THE NATIONAL

BANKRUPTCY REGISTER.

VOLUME VI.

UNITED STATES SUPREME COURT.—December Term, 1870.

[Appeal from the Supreme Court of the District of Columbia.]

Where a party lays claim to a certain fund, the possession of the depositary is his possession, provided his claim is just and legal; therefore if the assignee in bankruptcy would divest him of the possession and control of the fund in question, he must do it by a suit at law or in equity, as provided in the third clause of the second section of the bankrupt act.

Strangers to the proceedings in bankruptcy not served with process and who have not voluntarily appeared and become parties to such a litigation, cannot be compelled to come into court under a petition for a rule to show cause, as the third clause of the second section of the said act affords the assignees a convenient, constitutional and sufficient remedy to contest every adverse claim made by any person to any property or rights of property transferable to or vested in such assignee.

Cause remanded for further proceedings in conformity to the opinion of this court.

SMITH v. *MASON, Assignee*

CLIFFORD, J.—Jurisdiction, power and authority in cases in bankruptcy, when the bankrupt resides in this district, are conferred upon and vested in the supreme court of the district, to the same extent and subject to the same rules, regulations, and restrictions as are enacted and prescribed in respect to the jurisdiction, power, and authority of the district courts of the United States, where the bankrupt resides in any one of the judicial districts within the several states. 14 Stat. at Large, 541.

By the terms of the act establishing the supreme court of the district the court consists of four justices, any three of whom may hold a general term, and any one of them may hold a circuit court or special term for the purposes and under the conditions therein prescribed, or may hold a district court of the United States, in the same manner and with the same powers and jurisdiction as are possessed and exercised by the federal district courts within the several states. 12 Stat. at Large, 763.

Enough appears in the record to show that one Frederick P. Sawyer, of the firm of Sawyer, Risher & Hall, was adjudged bankrupt by the supreme court of this district sitting in bankruptcy, and that Geoege Mason the appellee in this case, was appointed assignee of his estate by decree of the bankrupt court. He commenced the proceedings in this case by the petition exhibited in the transcript, in which he represents that George Taylor, as agent of that firm, had collected from the United States the sum of four thousand seven hundred and forty-four dollars and nineteen cents for the firm, and that other funds due to the firm, it was expected, would soon come into his hands; that Risher & Hall, the other two members of the firm prior to the bankruptcy of the senior partner, made an assignment of the claim, from which that amount was realized, to George E. Biddle & Co., as collateral security for the payment of a certain indebtedness of their firm to the said assignees, which indebtedness the petitioner believes has been paid; that the assignees of the claim afterwards made an assignment of their interest in the same to James R. Smith, as collateral security for their indebtedness to him, which, as the petitioner belives, has also been paid; wherefore he prayed that the said George Taylor might be restrained from paying out said money, or any other money which might come into his hands belonging to the same firm, pending the petition, and that the respondent might be required to give bond for the safe keeping of the money and for its production in court when ordered.

Such an order was issued, and the party holding the money was enjoined and required to give bond as prayed. Subsequently the petitioner presented another petition to the same court, in which he represented that James R. Smith also claimed an interest in the fund in question, and prayed that an order might be made requiring him to show cause on a day therein named why the fund should not be paid to the petitioner. Smith appeared and filed an answer to the rule, to the effect following : (1.) That the court had no jurisdiction to proceed against him in that mode. (2.) That the money enjoined came to him by regular assignment for a valuable considerarion before the senior partner of the firm was adjudged bankrupt, and that he was and is the *bona fide* owner of the claim. (3.) That neither the assignee of the bankrupt's estate nor his creditors have any right to any part of said funds.

Before the hearing the other partners of the firm, to wit, Risher & Hall, intervened, and alleged that the money enjoined rightfully belonged to them and not to the respondent in the rule, because the assignment of the claim, as they represented, was made by the senior partner of their firm merely as a security to the said assignees, to be applied by them to the payment of the debt due by their firm to those assignees ; that it was expressly understood that if the assignors paid the debt before the claim was collected from the United States the claim should revert to them, the assignors ; that they paid their entire debt to those parties before the claim was allowed at the treasury department, and that they as the representatives of the firm since the bankruptcy of the senior partner, are entitled to the money : wherefore they pray that an order may be passed directing the depositary to pay the same to them, or, if it be paid to the said assignees, that it be so paid to their use.

Evidence was introduced by the intervenors tending to show that the indebtedness of the original owners of the claim to the assignees of the same had been paid, and that the respondent in the rule held the claim merely as collateral security for his assignors. On the other hand the respondent in the rule was examined and he testified that he obtained the assignment of the claim in good faith and for

Smith v. Mason.

value, without notice that his assignors held it subject to any conditions, or that it was not their property in case the indebtedness ·of their assignors was discharged before the claim was collected. He produced the assignment duly executed by the original owners, directing the depositary to pay the amount to the assignees when collected at the proper department, and also introduced the deposition of the senior partner of the firm to which the claim was assigned, and he deposed that his firm transferred and assigned the same to the respondent in the rule with the knowledge and consent of ·the original owners; that they, the assignees, took the order or draft at its date in the regular course of business, and that they assigned the same for value to the respondent, and that the accounts of the original owners with his firm had never been settled, but that they are still largely indebted to his firm. Hearing was had, but the court was of the opinion that the respondent took the order or draft merely as collateral security ; that he was not a *bona fide* purchaser of the same ; that he was to credit the proceeds when collected to his assignors, and that they were to credit the same to the original owners.

Pursuant to that finding the court entered a decretal order that the depositary of the claim should pay the net balance in his hands to the assignee in bankruptcy for the benefit of the creditors of the original owners. Immediate application was made by the respondent for an appeal to the general term, which was granted on the following day. Due appearance was entered not only by the appellant but also by the intervenors, as well as by the assignee in bankruptcy, and they were again heard before all the justices of the court ; and the court being of opinion that there was error in the decree and that the intervenors, as the solvent partners of their firm, were entitled to the money, entered a decree dissolving the injunction and directing the depositary of the money to pay the net balance in his hands to those parties as the survivors of the original owners of the claim ; whereupon the respondent appealed to this court.

Smith v. Mason.

Instituted as the proceeding was to restrain the depositary of the claim from paying out the money which he had collected, or any which might thereafter come into his hands, it is quite clear that the alleged purpose of the petitioner was accomplished when the injunction was granted as prayed in the petition, as the party respondent in that proceeding never filed any answer and testified in the case that the order restraining him from paying out the money was procured by him so that he might not be required to act without the directions of the court.

Had the matters terminated there the appellant would not have had any right of appeal to this court, as he was an utter stranger to the proceedings. He was not made a party to the petition nor was he served with process, nor did he voluntarily appear. Whatever the purpose of the petition was or by whomsoever the injunction was procured the proceeding was commenced and terminated without the knowledge of the appellant and before any steps were taken by the petitioner or any one else to connect the appellant with the litigation.

More than a year and a half before the petition was filed the original owners of the claim had assigned and transferred the same to the assignors of the appellant, and had directed, in writing, the depositary in whose hands they had placed it for collection to pay the same when collected to their said transferees, and the record shows that the depositary of the claim accepted the draft or order at the time and agreed to pay the same as directed whenever the same should come into his hands, less expenses and commissions. None of these facts are contradicted and the appellant proved that the assignees of the claim, within a few days after receiving the same, assigned and transferred the same to him for full value in the usual course of business.

Beyond all doubt, therefore, the case is one where the appellant claimed absolute title to and dominion over the matter in controversy between him and the assignee of the bankrupt's estate. Absolute title to the matter in controversy is also claimed by the assignee in bankruptcy, as appears by his second petition, in which he prayed that the appellant might be summoned to show cause why the fund should not be paid to him as such assignee.

Suggestions may be made that the decree gives the fund to the intervenors, but the court will at present re-examine the case as between the parties first made in the second petition, before the solvent members of the firm to which the claim originally belonged were permitted to intervene in the litigation, as it is quite obvious that the whole proceeding subsequent to their intervention is irregular and that the decree must be reversed if it be held that the bankrupt court had no juisdiction to proceed and determine the right of property as between the assignee and the transferee of the same for value in that mode of proceeding.

Neither the depositary of the fund nor the appellant claimed anything from the estate of the bankrupt, and the appellant contends that the bankrupt court cannot take jurisdiction in such a case by a rule to show cause, served on a stranger to come in and answer in support of his title or claim to such a fund or to any other property over which he claims absolute dominion.

Power and jurisdiction in all matters and proceedings in bankruptcy are conferred upon the district courts, and those courts as courts of bankruptcy are authorized to hear and adjudicate upon the same according to the provisions of the bankrupt act. Examined separately the clause of the first section of the act, which provides that the powers and jurisdiction therein granted and conferred may be exercised as well in vacation as in term time, and that a judge sitting in chambers shall have the same powers and jurisdiction as when sitting in court, would seem to afford some support to the views of the assignee in this case, that all the powers and jurisdiction of the district courts, when sitting as courts in bankruptcy, may be exercised in a summary way without process, as by a rule to show cause, as in a motion to set aside a verdict in an action at common law, or in a collateral proceeding in a suit in equity.

Most matters and proceedings in bankruptcy may doubtless be heard and adjudicated by the district court in that way, but that general clause in the first section, which is referred to as supporting the unlimited scope of that power and jurisdiction, must be considered in connection with all the other provisions of the bankrupt act, as is expressly required by the preceding clause of the same section, in which it is enacted that the district courts shall hear and adjudicate upon all matters and proceedings in bankruptcy according to the provisions of the bankrupt act.

Superadded to that general clause, and as an exposition of the same, is another and more important clause, in which is given a specific enumeration of the cases and controveries to which that general jurisdiction extends, and it is plain that the enumeration does not include "suits at law or in equity which may or shall be brought by the assignee in bankruptcy against any person claiming an adverse interest, or by such person against such assignee touching any property or rights of property of said bankrupt transferable to or vested in such assignee." On the contrary, the third clause of the second section expressly enacts that circuit courts shall have concurrent jurisdiction with the district courts of all such suits at law or in equity, provided the suit at law or bill in equity shall be brought within two years from the time the cause of action accrued. 14 Stat. at Large, 518; *Morgan et al.* v. *Thornhill et al.* 5 N. B. R. 1.

Controversies, in order that they may be cognizable either in the circuit or district court under that act, must have respect to some property or rights of property of the bankrupt transferable to or vested in such assignee; and the suit, whether it be a suit at law or in equity, must be in the name of one of the two parties described in that clause and against the other, as appears by the express words of the provision. Such a suit, whether at law or in equity, may be commenced either in the district or circuit court, at the election of the party suing, and if in the former it is clear that the case, when it has proceeded to final judgment or decree, may be removed into the circuit court for re-examination by writ of error, if it was an action at law, or by appeal if it was a suit in equity, provided the debt or damages claimed amount to more than five hundred dollars and the writ of error is seasonably sued out or the appeal is claimed and the required notices are given within ten days from the rendition of the judgment or decree. *Knight* v. *Cheney*, 5 N. B. R. 309.

None of those regulations, however, apply to petitions for revision under the first clause of the second section, nor does the bankrupt act fix any precise limitation to the right of a party aggrieved by the ruling, decision or decree of the district court to file a petition for that purpose in the circuit court. Power to revise all cases and questions which arise in the district courts, in such a proceeding, "except when special provision is otherwise made," is conferred upon the circuit courts by the first clause of the same section, but the court is of the opinion that the power conferred by that clause does not extend to any case where special provision for the revision of the case is otherwise made, as where it is provided that an appeal will lie from the district court to the circuit court, or where a writ of error will lie from the circuit court to the district court in the manner provided in the laws of congress allowing appeals and writs of error. Id. 310.

Special provision is made for the revision in the circuit court of controversies like the one exhibited in this record, and the court is of the opinion that such causes cannot be commenced by a petition for a rule to show cause, as in this case, nor be determined in a summary way by the district court sitting in bankruptcy, without due process of law. *Ex parte* Bacon, 2 Molloy, 441.

Cases of the kind before the court fall directly within the third clause of the section under consideration, and must, in the judgment of the court, be determined by a suit in equity or an action at law, as the case may be ; and where an action

Smith v. Mason.

at law is the proper remedy the parties are entitled to a trial by jury if the value in controversy shall exceed twenty dollars. Concurrent jurisdiction in such cases, it must be conceded, is vested in the circuit and district courts, and it is equally clear that either party, where the proceeding is correct, may remove the cause, in a proper case, when it has proceeded to final judgment or decree, into the supreme court for re-examination, as provided in other causes outside of the bankrupt act.

Possession and control of the claim had been surrendered by the original owners long before the senior partner of the firm was adjudged bankrupt, and the depositary of the same had duly accepted the order or draft transferring the proceeds of the same to the assignors of the appellant, showing that the assignee in bankruptcy had neither the possession nor the right of possession to the same at the time the petition for the rule was filed.

Independent of the injunction, which was granted without notice to the appellant, he was apparently entitled, and if the evidence he introduced is believed, he was in fact entitled to demand and to receive the whole fund as his own property.

Suffice it to say, without expressing any opinion as to the weight of the evidence, the appellant claimed the fund as his own property, and if his claim is just and legal, the possession of the depositary was his possession, and if the assignee in bankruptcy would divest him of the possession and control of the fund he must do it by a suit at law or in equity, as provided in the third clause of the second section of the bankrupt act. Equity would certainly have jurisdiction in such a case, as in that mode of proceeding all the parties could be brought before the court.

Extended remarks in respect to the decree in the case appears to be unnecessary, as it is as clear as anything in legal decision can be that the intervenors could not claim to divest the appellant of his interest in the funds by becoming parties to a rule like the one before the court, nor in any other manner than by due process of law.

Objection is also made that the appeal is irregular, as having been prosecuted from the supreme court of the district, but the regulations of the forty-ninth section of the act afford a satisfactory answer to that objection, which is all that need be said upon the subject. Want of notice of the appeal comes too late after a general appearance, but the record shows that the appeal was duly claimed and that the appellant filed his appeal bond in open court and that the same was duly approved by the chief justice who presided at the hearing when the final decree was entered in the cause.

Strangers to the proceedings in bankruptcy, not served with process, and who have not voluntarily appeared and become parties to such a litigation, cannot be compelled to come into court under a petition for a rule to show cause, as in this case; nor is the exercise of such a jurisdiction necessary, as the third clause of the second section of the bankrupt act affords the assignee a convenient, constitutional, and sufficient remedy to contest every adverse claim made by any person to any property or rights of property transferable to or vested in such assignee.

Decree reversed and cause remanded for further proceedings in conformity to the opinion of this court.

UNITED STATES CIRCUIT COURT—RHODE ISLAND.

In the absence of fraud the assignee takes only such rights and interests as the bankrupt himself had or could assert at the time of his bankruptcy, and consequently they are affected with all the equities which would affect the bankrupt himself if he were asserting those rights and interests.

A mortgage executed in a state having no statute on the subject of record, or if record is not required between the parties, will not be defeated by the proviso in the fourteenth section of the United States bankrupt act of eighteen hundred and sixty-seven in relation to recording.

When the revisory jurisdiction of the circuit court is invoked over the decision of the district court upon a question of fact, the burden of proof is on the petitioner for review to show cause in the decision, and he must also show that the evidence cannot support the finding.

In re J. DOW.

SHEPLEY, J.—This is a petition under the first clause of the second section of the bankrupt act, for the exercise of the superviso ·urisdiction of the circuit court.

The first question presented for adjudication is whether, in the absence of fraud, the assignee takes only such rights and interests as the bankrupt himself had and could assert at the time of his bankruptcy, or whether he is to be considered as a purchaser for a valuable consideration in the proper sense of those terms.

Joseph Dow, the bankrupt, on the twenty-fourth day of December, eighteen hundred and sixty-seven, made a chattel mortgage to Potter, Denison & Co. in the common form, which was acknowledged on the same day and lodged for record on the twenty-sixth day of December in the same year. The property mortgaged was described as "the articles of personal property enumerated and described in the schedules and bills marked respectively A, B, C and D, hereto annexed and constituting a part of this mortgage."

These schedules, although attached to the mortgage and forming a part thereof, and although left with the mortgage at the office of the city clerk in Providence, *were not in fact recorded.* The mortgage which was recorded contained no enumeration or description of the articles conveyed, so that the record book gave to enquirers no other information than that contained in the general description referring to. the schedules.

While the mortgage and schedules were remaining in the city clerk's office unrecorded, after having been revived and entered by him, the originals of both could have been seen and examined, and were all which could be found in the office indicative of the claim of the mortgagee. But after the clerk had extended his record, it is that only which the law treats as the evidence required. *Sawyer* v. *Pennell*, 19 Maine, 173.

If, therefore, the assignee of the bankrupt, or as in this case, the trustee, is to be considered as entitled to the same rights as an attaching creditor or a purchaser for a valuable consideration without notice, he would take a good title as against Potter, Denison & Co., who claim under the unrecorded mortgage.

In re Dow.

Under the English bankrupt act, Lord Hardwicke, in *Bacon* v. *Heathcote*, 1 Atk. R. 160, 162, says : "The ground that the court go upon is this : that assignees of bankrupts, though they are trustees for the creditors, yet stand in the place of the bankrupt, and they can take in no better manner than he could." See also *Jewson* v. *Moulson*, 2 Atk. 417, 420 ; *Mitford* v. *Mitford*, 9 Vesey, 87 ; *Worrall* v. *Marlur*, 1 P. Will. 459, n.

Under the bankrupt act of eighteen hundred and forty-one, in the case of *Mitchell* v. *Winslow et al.* 2 Story, 630, 631, Mr. Justice Story says: "Now it is most material to bear in mind under this aspect of the case, that it is a well established doctrine, that (except in cases of fraud) assignees in bankruptcy take only such rights and interests as the bankrupt himself had and could claim and assert at the time of his bankruptcy, and consequently they are affected with all the equities which would affect the bankrupt himself, if he were asserting those rights and interests." See also *Winson* v. *McLellan*, 2 Story, 495; *ex parte* Newhall, 2 id. 363 ; *Fiske* v. *Hunt*, 2 id. 584.

But it is urged with much force and ability on the part of the petitioner, that the decisions of Mr. Justice Story above cited, having been made under the bankrupt act of eighteen hundred and forty-one are not applicable to the statute now in force. Reliance is placed upon the distinction in the phraseology of the respective sections of the act of eighteen hundred and forty-one and the act of eighteen hundred and sixty-seven, saving the rights of mortgagees.

The second section of the bankrupt act of eighteen hundred and forty-one provided "that nothing in this act contained shall be construed to annul, destroy, or impair any lawful rights of married women or minors, or any liens, mortgages or other securities on property, real or personal, which may be valid by the laws of the states respectively, and which are not inconsistent with the provisions of the second and fifth sections of this act."

The proviso in the act of eighteen hundred and sixty-seven is, "that no mortgage of any vessel, or of any other goods or chattels, made as security for any debt or debts in good faith and for present considerations, and otherwise valid and duly recorded pursuant to any statute of the United States or of any state, shall be invalidated or affected hereby." The fourteenth section of the act of eighteen hundred and sixty-seven vests in the assignee (with certain specified exceptions) all the property and estate of the bankrupt, and all the property conveyed by the bankrupt in fraud of his creditors, and authorizes him " under the order and direction of the court, to redeem or discharge any mortgage, or conditional contract, or pledge, or deposit, or lien upon any property, real or personal," etc.

It must be born in mind, in determining this question, that the statute of Rhode Island, like the statute of Maine, under consideration in the case of *Mitchell* v. *Winslow*, decided by Mr. Justice Story, expressly recognizes the validity of an unrecorded mortgage of personal property between the parties, so that if the assignee is to be considered as merely standing in the place of the bankrupt, he would, in contemplation of law, be one of the parties to the instrument, and as against him no record would be necessary. The literal terms of the proviso, it is true, only save mortgages which have been duly recorded, but can it therefore be inferred that those mortgages are not saved which are valid by the laws of the respective states, which need no record. Are mortgages which are good at common law, and mortgages otherwise valid, made in states where there is no provision for the recording of mortgages avoided by the bankrupt law, while those are upheld which are made and recorded in states requiring a record ? Such could not have been the intent of the statute or the object of the proviso. The proviso, as stated by judge Lowell *in re* Griffiths, 3 N. B. R. 180, " appears to have been inserted out of greater caution lest it should be supposed that valid chattel mortgages should be affected by the assignment and not with any view of construing the laws regarding record ; and so, if the mortgage be one that requires no record, as if it be executed in a state having no statute on the subject, or if, as in this case, record is not required between the parties the proviso will not defeat it."

The language of Mr. Justice Field in the opinion in the case of *Second National Bank of Leavenworth* v. *Hunt,* 4 N. B. R. 198, might seem at first glance to favor a different construction, but on more careful examination it will appear that the decision is placed upon the ground that the mortgage was not valid by the laws of Kansas and was fraudulent as against creditors.

Two other questions decided by the district judge are presented for revision, one a question of law on the construction of the statute, the other a question of fact upon the evidence in the case.

The district judge in effect decided that after the lapse of four months from the date of the conveyance, simple *preferences* of a *bona fide* creditor by an insolvent debtor not otherwise fraudulent, are to be held valid so far as the preferred creditor is concerned.

Prior to the passage of the bankrupt act, the acts described in the thirty-fifth and thirty-ninth sections were such as were not forbidden by the common law, or generally by the statutes of the different states. A preference by an insolvent or a person approaching insolvency, may sometimes be unjust to other creditors, and under other circumstances may be the dictate of the purest justice in reference to all concerned. Preferences are not in their essential nature, necessarily immoral or dishonest. The bankrupt act of eighteen hundred and sixty-seven gives priority to five classes of debts to be first paid in full in the order in which they are successively named in the act. Congress, therefore, has adopted a purely conventional rule to determine the validity of mortgages given as security for *bona fide* debts and which operate as preferences. The creditor who receives payment or security to the exclusion of other creditors, with the knowledge, express or implied, of the insolvency, does so at

In re Dow.

the risk that if within four months the debtor himself or his creditors shall invoke the aid of the law providing for an equal distribution, the transaction will be invalidated, and the property thus received must go into the common fund for distribution. This question of construction of the first clause of the thirty-fifth section, considered in connection with the second clause of the same section and thirty-ninth section, is so fully considered in the very able opinion of the circuit court of the United States for the district of Missouri, in the case of *Bean* v. *Bookmire et al.*, 4 N. B. R. 57, that we deem it unnecessary to say more upon this point further than to express our entire concurrence with the reasoning and decision in that case.

Sustaining therefore, as we do, the decision of the district judge, that the second clause, commonly called the six months clause, of the thirty-fifth section of the act, is not applicable to the case of a simple preference by a bankrupt of a creditor's claim, his decision upon the question of fact that the circumstances of the transaction between Dow, the bankrupt, and Potter, Denison & Co. did not, in point of fact, bring the case within the provisions of the second clause becomes comparatively immaterial.

Appellate courts, even in appeals, proceed upon the ground that the decree in the subordinate court was correct, and the burden to show error is upon the appellant. 8 Wall. 378.

Matters of fact as well as matters of law, may doubtless be revised in the circuit court, but it was not the intention of congress, in this form of proceeding, to give a party a second trial merely as such, but to secure to him an appellate tribunal for the re-examination and revision of the rulings, orders and decrees of the district courts, and for the reversal of the same in case they are found to be erroneous. *Littlefield* v. *Delaware & Hudson Canal Co.*, 4 N. B. R. 77.

When the revisory jurisdiction of the circuit court is invoked over the decision of the district court upon a question of fact, the burden is on the petitioner for review to show error in the decision. It is not sufficient merely to show such a condition of the testimony in the case, that different minds, with equal fairness, might possibly arrive at different conclusions, but to show more nearly in anology to the case of a motion for a new trial, that the evidence cannot support the finding.

After a careful revision of the testimony, we see no reason for disturbing the decision of the district judge.

Decree of the district judge affirmed with costs

UNITED STATES DISTRICT COURT—N. D. NEW YORK.

A court should not do indirectly what it has no power to do directly, therefore when a petition has been dismissed in the United States circuit court the parties considering themselves aggrieved by such decision cannot apply to the United States district court for a re-hearing of the original decree that they may, on an adverse decision being re-entered, again have the right to appeal to the circuit court, as this would be an attempt to extend the time fixed by the statute within which an appeal can be allowed.

In re TROY WOOLEN COMPANY.

HALL, J.—This case has again been brought before me by the petition of Shepard Tappen, the assignee of the bankrupt, for a re-argument or re-hearing upon the report of Worthington Frothingham, Esq., (sustaining claims of Cooper, Vail & Co. of New York, against the bankrupt to an amount exceeding sixty-seven thousand dollars) and the exceptions to such report filed by such assignee and by the First National Bank of Troy, a creditor of the bankrupt. Upon the application of the bank the claim of Cooper, Vail & Co: was allowed to be contested by such bank or any other creditor of the bankrupt, or by such assignee, and it was referred to Mr. Frothingham to take the proofs and accounts touching such claim, and to hear and determine the legality and amount thereof. The order for this purpose was entered November twenty-ninth, eighteen hundred and seventy, and after a laborious and protracted examination of witnesses, books and papers the referee made his report of the amount

In re Troy Woolen Company.

due to Cooper, Vail & Co. He also reported several hundred folios of the testimony orally given before him, together with about four hundred exhibits given in evidence upon the reference. To this report the bank and the assignee, jointly, filed twenty-one exceptions. The argument on this report and the exceptions was heard on the twenty-third and twenty-fourth of May last, the counsel on both sides speaking without limitation of time other than that imposed by their own sense of propriety. After several days spent in the examination and consideration of the report, exceptions and evidence and the points, statements and arguments of the counsel, and in writing an opinion, I directed the entry of an order or decree overruling the exceptions, and confirming the report, and allowing the claim of Cooper, Vail & Co. This order or decree was filed July thirteenth, eighteen hundred and seventy-one, and the bank and the assignee were on or about the fifteenth, informed thereof. The bank attempted to obtain a reversal of the order or decree by a petition to the circuit court asking that court to review and reverse the decision made here, and the assignee upon the request of a portion of the bankrupt's creditors, took proceedings for its review and reversal by an appeal to the circuit court, but too late to make his appeal effectual. Both the appeal and the petition were at the last October term dismissed by the circuit court.

The present application, though in form an application by the assignee for a re-argument or re-hearing, is, in substance and fact, an application to this court in the interest of the other creditors of the bankrupt who oppose the claim of Cooper, Vail & Co. for an order vacating the order or decree allowing the claim of Cooper, Vail & Co., that it may on being re-entered be subject to an appeal. It is an application to the court to do in this indirect manner, what it is conceded it cannot directly do—that is, to extend the time fixed by statute within which an appeal can be allowed—for there is not even a pretence that it is hoped upon a re-argument to show that the court, in its former laborious and careful examination of the case, overlooked or misapprehended any portion of the evidence having such materiality as would by any possibility change its conclusion. The application is based upon the fact that the counsel of the assignee and the bank were mistaken in their views of the law and practice of the bankruptcy courts in respect to the modes of proceeding to obtain the desired review, and it must be conceded that their mistake in regard to the right of the creditor to be heard upon petition for review should not be attributed to any unusual want of care, diligence or learning. . In respect to the time and manner of taking an appeal by the assignee there was certainly less and perhaps little, if any doubt; but the delay in bringing the appeal probably resulted in part, at least, from the mistake which was made in respect to the right of the bank to obtain a review of the case upon its own petition, and the consequent intention of the assignee to leave the further litigation of the claim of Cooper, Vail & Co. to the bank. The delay is then to some extent excused, and this has made it necessary to give the application under consideration a careful hearing and a deliberate and somewhat elaborate examination, the result of which, with some of the reasons which have influenced the decision will now be stated, although the giving of an elaborate opinion to set forth fully the grounds of the decision will not be attempted.

It was insisted by the counsel of Cooper, Vail & Co. that the court had no authority to grant the motion; and that if it had such authority, the motion ought, according to well established rules of decision and upon controlling authority, to be denied.

After an examination of the cases of *Waite* v. *Van Allen*, 22 N. Y. Rep. 319; *Cauldwell* v. *The Mayor of Albany*, 9 Paige, 572; *Bank of Monroe* v. *Widner*, 11 Id. 429; *Humphrey* v. *Chamberlain*, 1 Kernan, 274; *McMicken* v. *Perrin*, 18 How. 507; *Cameron* v. *McRoberts*, 3 Wheat. 519, I should hesitate long before granting this motion, even if I could reach the conclusion that there was serious doubt of the legal validity of the claim of Cooper, Vail & Co., and that aside from the strict legal rights of the parties their equities were equal, for the cases which hold that a court should not do indirectly what it has no power to do directly, should be adhered to, except perhaps in such extraordinary and extreme cases as ought to be considered as exceptions to an almost inflexible and absolute general rule.

The case of *Jellinghaus* v. *The New York Insurance Co.* 5 Bosw. 678, is probably a stronger case or one of more weight and authority in favor of the petitioner than any other cited upon the argument. In that case exceptions had been taken by the defendant at the trial, and a bill of exceptions and amendments had been proposed and settled; but in the meantime a judgment had been regularly entered so that the right of the defendant to a review at general term had been cut off. A motion was made for the purpose of enabling the defendant to be heard on his bill of exceptions. It was shown that the defendant's attorney acted in perfect good faith, and at no time suspected there was any doubt of his right to be heard on the exceptions, until long after that right was barred; and the attorney for the plaintiff seems not to have insisted upon a denial of the motion, except from a sense of duty in opposition to his inclination to relieve his professional brother from the consequences of his mistake. The report states that " the position taken by the plaintiff's attorney was, that although he was willing to oblige the defendant's attorney in every way possible consistent with his duty to his client; yet that judgment had been regularly entered and notice thereof given; the time to appeal had elapsed, and the case and exceptions could not be heard, and he was not at liberty and had no power to waive the rights which his client had thereby acquired." And the judge who delivered the opinion, says : " the plaintiff's attorney, in declining to waive the default now, does so only because he supposes he has not the power, authority and right to do it." And in deciding that, " as no injury can result to any party from granting the relief sought, while possibly the ends of justice may be promoted, the defendants should be permitted to be heard." The learned judge immediately added: "At the same time I deem it proper to say that to justify the granting of such relief the case should be one of unquestionable mistake, and evincing perfect good faith, and should be meritorious; *and even then to grant such relief is going to the extreme verge of judicial discretion.*

Even under the doctrines of this case the motion should be denied. It is fair to presume from the papers presented on the hearing, that the assignee did not intend or expect to appeal until he was urged and induced to attempt to do so by the creditors, under whose influence much expensive and unreasonable litigation has already been had in this case, to the great injury and loss of the parties interested; and this, and not any mistake in regard to the law and practice regulating an appeal by him, was the main, if not the sole cause, of the early delay which resulted in the failure to take and perfect his appeal in time.

The application is not meritorious to any such extent as to induce a court to go to the extreme verge of judicial discretion. The assignee and the bank have had a laborious and expensive examination and litigation of the questions involved, before a very careful and competent referee. That referee has made a report, evidencing full, careful and able examination and consideration, and fully sustaining the claim which it is now sought to overthrow. Numerous exceptions were taken to this report, and after full argument, and a careful and deliberate examination of the questions involved, this court confirmed the report of the referee. Scarcely a doubt of the justice or of the strictly legal validity of the claim of Cooper, Vail & Co. was then entertained, and the arguments made and the papers submitted on the hearing of the motion for a re-hearing have strongly confirmed, instead of weakening the confidence then felt in the justice and propriety of the referee's decision. It is of course possible that another judge might reach a different conclusion, and it is evident that the opposing creditors, in view of the fact that their own claims are very large and that the claim of Cooper, Vail & Co. amounts to about one-third of the aggregate amount of the debts proved against the Troy Woolen Co., are quite willing, if the expense of the litigation can be thrown upon the fund in the assignee's hands so that one-third must in effect be borne by Cooper, Vail & Co., even if their claim is established, to speculate further upon the possible chances and proverbial uncertainty of litigation.

But if there can be a possible doubt of the strict legal right of Cooper, Vail & Co., the equities of the case are not, in my judgment, in the slightest degree doubtful. To demonstrate that will not be attempted. To do so would require not only a full review of the evidence and exhibits before the referee, but also an elaborate statement of what has appeared before this court upon various applications made or opposed under the influences which have induced the assignee to make this application. The probable origin and purpose of the Gale mortgage; the applications in respect to the payment of fifteen thousand dollars on that mortgage by the assignee ; the petition for the sale of the premises mortgaged immediately afterwards and their sale and conveyance to the trustees; of a combination of creditors for scarcely a tithe of the value put upon them by the assignee in his sworn petition; for authority to make payment upon the Gale mortgage ; the strenuous opposition to the motion to set the sale and conveyance aside, and the appeal from the order setting aside the sale—a sale, the circumstances of which were such as to justify the circuit judge, in stating in his written opinion upon the appeal, that he thought it would "be a gross discredit to the administration of justice if the sale of the bankrupt's estate, made as was the one now in question, and at so great a sacrifice that real estate, mills, water-power and machinery of great value, have, in the administration of the assignee, been rendered worse than valueless, should be permitted to stand;" and many other facts and circumstances which might be stated, do not commend to the favor and discretion of this court an application for leave to use the assignee for the purpose of further unjust litigation at the expense of the bankrupt's estate, and to the certain and protracted postponement of any dividend.

The motion for a re-argument or re-hearing, or for an order vacating the former order and decree of this court, is denied. November 17th, 1871.

———•••———

UNITED STATES DISTRICT COURT—NEVADA.

The United States district court sitting in bankruptcy has power to enjoin the sheriff of a state court or parties litigant therein, from proceeding to sell property levied upon by virtue of a writ of execution issued out of such court upon a judgment obtained therein before proceedings in bankruptcy were commenced.

In re E. MALLORY.*

HILLYER, J.—On the twenty-third day of October, eighteen hundred and sixty-nine, Henry Vansickle obtained a judgment, by confession, against the bankrupt, in the state district court for the county of Douglas. Execution was issued thereon, levied on certain property of the bankrupt, and the sheriff of Douglas county had advertised the property for sale, when, on the fifth day of February, eighteen hundred and seventy, Mallory was adjudged a bankrupt in this court on his own petition. On the same day the bankrupt petitioned this court for an injunction restraining the said sheriff from selling the property levied on, which was granted.

Vansickle now files a petition praying that the injunction may be dissolved. Mallory's assignee answers, alleging that the judgment is not a valid lien, was procured in fraud of the bankrupt act, and prays that the same may be declared to be no lien upon the property, and that the property be ordered to be sold by the assignee free from any lien of the said judgment. As a matter of practice, it may be stated

* See 4 N. B. R. 38.

that it was unnecessary to file a petition in this case. A motion to dissolve the injunction would have been the correct way of proceeding.

The main question argued was as to the power of this court sitting in bankruptcy to enjoin the sheriff of a state court or parties litigant therein from selling property levied upon by virtue of a writ of execution issued out of the state court upon a judgment obtained therein before the proceedings in bankruptcy were commenced, with the understanding that the injunction should remain in force if the court should be of opinion that such power existed, leaving the question as to the validity of the lien of the judgment to be determined hereafter, in some other proceeding.

The question is one of utmost importance, involving the propriety of the exercise of a power by a federal court the effect of which is to restrain proceedings in a state court, and I feel that its decision imposes upon this court a great responsibility.

In September last, this same question was brought before me in the case of the Lady Bryan Mining Co., and a motion to dissolve the injunction denied; but as in that case there was no question raised as to the validity of the judgment liens, and the lien of the judgment creditors was transferred to the proceeds of the property, the point was not so fully argued as it has been now, and I was in this case not only willing but desirous of hearing further argument from the learned counsel who represent the present parties.

Upon this argument, the sections of the bankrupt act relating in any way to this question have been read and commented on by counsel, for the purpose of ascertaining the policy and object of the act and the extent of the power conferred to carry out the policy and effect the object; a great mass of authorities was cited and read on the hearing, and the whole, together with a careful examination on my part of the entire subject, has resulted in more firmly confirming me in the correctness of the opinion expressed in the Lady Bryan case.

Congress, in the enactment of laws upon the subject of bankruptcies, has complete and plenary power unrestricted save as to uniformity. It has, in legislating upon this subject, power to take from State courts the administration of remedies for the enforcement of liens. The passage by it of a bankrupt law, *ipso facto* abrogates all state insolvent laws. The bankrupt law is then the supreme law of the land, binding alike upon federal and state tribunals, and wherever by express words or by necessary implication it affects state laws, the power of state courts, or the remedies of suitors therein, it is paramount.

The jurisdiction of the courts of the United States in matters of bankruptcy is derived from and its extent must be determined by reference to the language of the bankrupt act; and before those courts restrain parties litigant in, or officers of state courts from prosecuting their remedies therein or executing the process of those courts, the power to do so ought to be found either in the express language of the act, or it must result as a necessary means for effecting the powers expressly conferred.

Section one of the bankrupt act constitutes the several district courts of the United States courts of bankruptcy, and gives them original jurisdiction in all matters and proceedings in bankruptcy. This jurisdiction is declared to extend to all cases and controversies arising between the bankrupt and any creditor or creditors who shall claim any debt or demand under the bankruptcy; to the collection of all the assets of the bankrupt; to the ascertainment and liquidation of the liens and other specific claims thereon; to the adjustment of the various priorities and conflicting interests of all parties; to the marshaling and disposition of the different funds and assets and to all acts, matters and things to be done under and in virtue of the bankruptcy until the final distribution and settlement of the estate of the bankrupt and the close of the proceedings in bankruptcy.

As reference will be made to the bankrupt act of eighteen hundred and forty-one, I quote that portion of it conferring

In re Mallory.

jurisdiction. It is declared to "extend to all cases and controversies in bankrupty arising between the bankrupt and any creditor or creditors who shall claim any debt or demand under the bankruptcy; to all cases and controversies between such creditor or creditors, and the assignee of the estate, whether in office or removed; to all cases and controversies between such assignee and the bankrupt, and to all acts, matters and things to be done under and in virtue of the bankruptcy until the final distribution and settlement of the estate of the bankrupt and the close of proceedings in bankruptcy." 5 Stat. at Large, 445. sec. 6. Under this section of the act of eighteen hundred and forty-one there was much diversity of opinion among courts and lawyers as to the existence of power to control by injunction upon the parties the proceedings in state courts. The changes made by the act of eighteen hundred and sixty-seven are very noticeable and important. The present law, unlike that of eighteen hundred and forty-one, extends the jurisdiction in plain terms to the collection of all the assets of the bankrupt, the ascertainment and liquidation of liens and other specific claims upon those assets, and to the adjustment of priorities and marshaling of assets so as to secure the rights of all parties, and this jurisdiction is original and exclusive. Now, when congress delegated to the district courts this equitable jurisdiction in bankruptcy, it must follow by necessary implication that it also delegated at the same time the power to administer such remedies, known to the law, as were absolutely indispensable to the complete exercise of the jurisdiction expressly conferred. One power directly given is the collection of all the assets. The means by which this result is to be reached are not enumerated, but power to accomplish the result is given, and the right to employ the proper legal process for effecting the result must follow by necessary implication.

The property levied on in this case is part of the assets of the bankrupt. It may be subject to a lien, but the legal title to the property was in the bankrupt when the petition was filed, and passed to the assignee. The judgment of Van-

In re Mallory.

sickle, if a valid lien by the laws of this state, are not impeachable under the bankrupt law as a fraud against it, is to be respected and protected by the bankruptcy court. But this statutory lien is neither a right in or to the thing, but is simply a charge thereon.

How now, I ask, could the assets in this case have been collected by the assignee without restraining the sheriff from selling them under his execution? It certainly would complicate the case exceedingly if the sheriff, after the legal title, by virtue of the bankruptcy, had passed out of Mallory to the assignee, had sold the property as the property of Mallory.

Closely connected with this power of collecting the assets is that of ascertaining and liquidating the liens which may be claimed to exist upon those assets.

If the validity of any lien upon the assets of the bankrupt is denied, or questioned, in what court is the question to be tried, the validity or invalidity of the lien ascertained, and if found valid, liquidated? The answer is, that by the express terms of the act this jurisdiction is given to the bankruptcy court.

Here, as in collecting assets, a specific result is to be attained, and can it be doubted that the means by which it is to be attained are also given.

The lien is to be ascertained and liquidated in the bankruptcy court, and this would be an idle proceeding if that court had not the power to preserve the property by restraining its sale until the lien is ascertained to be good or to be void; and of what use is it to say that this court shall liquidate liens if it cannot restrain parties from liquidating their liens without its intervention. The bankrupt law is highly remedial, and it ought to have a liberal construction for the purpose of effecting its aim and policy. The expediency and policy of bringing all the assets into the bankruptcy court, and ascertaining and liquidating there all liens and specific claims thereon is undeniable.

And while neither the expediency of exercising this power nor the inconvenience of not exercising it, can justify

In re Mallory.

its employment if not found in the statute in direct or neces-sarily implied terms, these considerations may be, and ought to be looked at in construing the law and arriving at the intention of the law-makers. Let us suppose that two persons, each have or claim to have a lien by judgment in the state courts, upon the property of the bankrupt at the time of bankruptcy, and that there is a dispute between them as to the priority of their liens or the validity of one of the judgments. One creditor comes into the bankruptcy court, proves his claim and asks to have his lien liquidated. The other proceeds in the state court. If neither court can restrain or control parties before the other, here will be a direct conflict of jurisdiction. Decisions as to priorities or validity of the liens may be conflicting, and each court pro-ceeding to take possession of the property through its process and officers, and satisfy the lien of the party before it. Such a state of things would be very much to be depre-cated if the bankrupt law was so lame and impotent as to have left the case unprovided for. But the law is not, I conceive, so defective. It gives the bankruptcy court an original and exclusive jurisdiction over all the parties to the bankruptcy proceedings, all the assets and all the liens thereon. Again, a lien may be good by the law of the state and void under the bankrupt law; thus a lien by attachment is avoided, and the state law creating it is so far abrogated if the attachment was made within four months next preced-ing the commencement of proceedings in bankruptcy; so a judgment lien may be void under the bankrupt law as an un-lawful preference to the judgment creditor. Hence, while the judgment might stand in a state court, the lien of that judgment might be avoided in the bankruptcy court; and so it was held under the law of eighteen hundred and forty-one, and that the creditor was liable to refund to the assignee the proceeds of a sale made under the judgment, such creditor having notice of the proceedings in bankruptcy. *Shawhan* v. *Wherritt*, 7 How. 626.

Let us see now how this question stands upon authority.

Where judgment had been obtained in a state court, execution issued and returned unsatisfied, and an order made on proceedings supplementary to execution for the examination of the judgment debtor, Judge Blatchford ordered a stay of all proceedings on the said order until the question of the discharge of the bankrupt should be determined by the bankruptcy court. *In re* Reed, N. B. R. Sup. i.

In an inventory proceeding before the same Judge, he, under the fortieth section of the bankrupt act, enjoined the sheriff of a state court from proceeding to sell property of the alleged bankrupt, and on motion refused to dissolve it until the question whether or not the debtor was to be adjudged a bankrupt was decided. *In re* Devlin & Hagan, N. B. R. Sup. viii.

The fortieth section of the act gives the district court power by injunction to "restrain the debtor and any other person" from making any transfer or disposition of any part of the debtor's property until the return of the order to show cause why the debtor should not be adjudged a bankrupt. On the hearing it was argued that the express grant of power to enjoin in proceedings *in invitum* was a denial of any such power in voluntary proceedings upon the maxim, *expressio unius exclusio alterius*. But it is to be observed that under section fourteen it is "in virtue of the adjudication of bankruptcy and the appointment of an assignee" that the property vests in the assignee. Now, in voluntary cases, the filing of the petition is an act of bankruptcy and the debtor at the same time surrenders all his estate and effects for the benefit of his creditors, and is forthwith adjudged a bankrupt. The district court is thus clothed at once in voluntary cases with jurisdiction over the debtor and his property. But where the proceeding is involuntary the debtor is not adjudged a bankrupt until the return and hearing of the order to show cause, and may not be then if he have a sufficient defence.

There is, therefore, good reason for giving the court power to enjoin between the time of filing the creditor's petition and the return of the order to show cause, as there is in these cases no voluntary surrender of the property and the title cannot vest in the assignee until after adjudication. If the argument of the petitioner is sound, the court would have power to enjoin in involuntary cases before adjudication, but must dissolve it immediately after, because the statute in express terms only provides for an injunction until the return of the order to show cause. So that the court might enjoin before it was certain the property of the bankrupt would ever come into its possession, and might not after the property was fully within its jurisdiction.

A bankrupt held under arrest by the sheriff of the city and county of New York, under order of arrest from the state court was discharged from arrest and proceedings on actions against the bankrupt in the supreme court of the state were stayed. *In re* Jacoby, N. B. R. Sup. viii.

In a case before Judge Benedict, E. D. New York, where judgment was obtained, execution issued and levied on property of the bankrupt prior to the commencement of proceedings in bankruptcy, that judge enjoined the creditors from enforcing the levy. On motion to dissolve, which was denied, although this question of power was not discussed, the judge said that the power seemed to be fairly included in the power to collect all the assets, to ascertain and liquidate liens and to adjust priorities. *In re* Schnepf, N. B. R. Sup. xii.

In a voluntary proceeding upon a bill filed to enjoin a sheriff from selling property of the bankrupt under an execution from a state court, Judge Hill, of the Miss. district, held that the bankrupt himself had a right to file the bill before an assignee was appointed; that if the sheriff had actually levied before the bankruptcy, he would be allowed to proceed without a showing that the sale would be injurious to the general creditors or to some one having a prior lien ; that the twentieth section, in connection with the first and twenty-fifth, gave the court jurisdiction of the subject matter, that the commencement of proceedings in bankruptcy transferred to the district court, jurisdiction over the bankrupt, his estate,

In re Mallory.

and all parties and persons connected therewith, and operated as a supersedeas of the proces in the hands of the sheriff and an injunction against all other proceedings than such as might thereupon be had by authority of the bankruptcy court. *Jones* v. *Leach*, 1 N. B. R. 165. A sheriff was restrained from selling goods under execution by the same judge, in *Pennington* v. *Sale*, 1 N. B. R. 157.

After judgment in a state court, execution, levy and advertisement for sale, the sheriff was restrained. *In re* Bernstein, N. B. R. Sup. xliii. The jurisdiction of a district court of the United States is superior and exclusive in all matters arising under the statute, and extends to a suspension of proceedings taken for the purpose of subjecting portions of the estate surrendered to a sale under state process. Until a sale is made, the bankrupt is not divested of his interest in the property under seizure. *In re* Barron, 1 N. B. R. 125. A preliminary injunction was issued restraining the plaintiff in an execution upon a judgment confessed in a state court, and he moved to dissolve it. The question was argued before two judges, Grier and Cadwalader, and the jurisdiction maintained, the court refusing to dissolve the injunction. *Irving* v. *Hughes*, 2 N. B. R. 20.

Where judgments were rendered after the bankruptcy, Judge Deady held the jurisdiction to restrain the enforcemen of the judgments was undoubted. *In re* Wallace, 2 N. B. R. 54. Parties proceeding, after the bankruptcy, to foreclose a mortgage on the property of the bankrupt in the state court, were enjoined. *In re* Kerosene Oil Co., 2 N. B. R. 164. A landlord was enjoined from distraining the bankrupt's property for rent, *Brock* v. *Tirrell*, 2 N. B. R. 190.

In a case where the bankrupt himself filed a petition to restrain certain persons, who had obtained judgments against him prior to the filing of his petition, from proceeding by execution, Judge Giles, of the Maryland district, in answer to an objection that the district court had no jurisdiction, but that the proceeding must be by bill and in the circuit court, said : " I am clearly of the opinion that the petition was properly filed in this court, and that this court has, by virtue of the first section of the bankruptcy act, full and adequate jurisdiction over all matters relating to the settlement of the bankrupt's estate, either at law or in equity, by way of petition or bill; and that whenever the relief sought is necessary to the protection of the general creditors, such relief will be granted." But as in the case before him there was no suggestion of fraud, and the judgments were admitted to be valid liens, he held that the jurisdiction of the bankruptcy courts was not exclusive, and permitted the judgment creditors to proceed in the state court. *In re* Bowie, 1 N. B. R. 185.

Upon the application of parties interested, the district court has jurisdicton to ascertain and liquidate a judgment lien, and while so doing to enjoin the judgment creditor from enforcing the same by execution out of the state court. *In re* Fuller, 4 N. B. R. 29. If creditors who assert a claim against the bankrupt are not barred by the discharge and are allowed to commence suit in the state court for the purpose of saving the statute of limitations or securing testimony, the suit, after this object is attained, can be stayed to await the decision of the question of the debtor's discharge. *In re* Ghirardelli, 4 N. B. R. 42. After the bankruptcy, creditors of the bankrupt having a lien by mortgage were proceeding to foreclose in a territorial court. The supreme court held that all the property, choses in action, effects, interests and equities of the bankrupt must be brought into the bankrupt court for settlement and distribution, and enjoined the creditors from proceeding in the foreclosure suit. *In re* Snedaker, 3 N. B. R. 155. Judgment was obtained in a state court, execution levied and property advertised for sale before the filing of the petition in bankruptcy. The sheriff was restrained from proceeding with the sale. *Beattie* v. *Gardner*, 4 N. B. R. 107. Under the law of eighteen hundred and forty-one an injunction was ordered against the assignee appointed under the state laws to stop his interference with the property of the bankrupt, and also to prevent certain creditors from proceeding with an execution. *Ex parte* Eames, 2 Story, 322.

In re Mallory.

For an instructive statement of the nature and extent of the equitable jurisdiction of courts of bankruptcy, see *ex parte* Foster, 2 Story, 131.

In re Campbell, N. B. R. Sup. xxx, after the property had been sold and the proceeds were in the hands of the sheriff, an injunction to restrain the state courts and their officers from proceeding, for the purpose of bringing the proceeds of the sale into the bankruptcy court for distribution, was refused. Judge McCandless based his refusal upon the ground that the courts of the United States have no power to enjoin proceedings in the state courts either directly or by restraining the officers of such courts or parties litigant therein.

This is the only opinion, so far as I can discover, directly denying this jurisdiction.

Upon my own convictions as to the proper construction of the bankrupt act, and upon the weight of authority, I hold that the court had jurisdiction to issue the writ. The prayer of the petition is therefore denied with costs.

Opinion of FIELD J., on petition for review of the foregoing decision:

When counsel closed their argument on the petition of Vansickle, for a review of the order of the district judge, I had no doubt of the correctness of that order, but I thought the case was one of sufficient importance to justify a written opinion giving at length the views of the court upon the questions raised. I therefore took the papers and reserved my decision. Since then I have read with care the opinion delivered by the district judge, when the matter was before him on the application of the petitioner to disolve the injunction, and I find that it covers every question in the case, and presents the law in a very clear and satisfactory manner. It renders any opinion from me entirely unnecessary. I could not add to it nor improve it. I concur both in its reasoning and conclusion. Petition denied.

UNITED STATES CIRCUIT COURT—W. D. MICHIGAN.

When the petition for review under the rules in the sixth circuit is demurred to, its statements, like those of any other pleading, will be taken as true and the appeal determined upon its averments. If the facts therein are sufficient, the demurrer will be overruled and the decree below reversed.

When an agent is sent by an insolvent debtor to compromise with creditors, and some of them, through him, return different terms than those submitted, such agent does not thereby become that of such creditors but remains the agent of the debtor, and his knowledges, mistakes and acts are those of his principal—the insolvent. The same effect would be produced if he were deemed the *common* agent of both parties.

When a debtor and a preferred creditor know of the insolvency, but erroneously suppose all other creditors have compromised for thirty-five cents in time paper, a transfer so securing the creditor as to create a preference financially is an act of bankruptcy. If insolvency is once known all parties act at their peril, when such condition actually exists, whether known or unknown.

When proceedings were pending in bankruptcy, and a preferred creditor and the insolvent settle the petitioning creditor's debt and employ the attorney who conducts such proceedings to compromise with the other creditors, authorizing him to pay some one price and others another, and it appears that such discrimination was in fact made, such scheme is *prima facie* fraudulent and the burden is upon the actors to show that all the creditors *consented* to such preferences. It will not be presumed. But if any one creditor does not consent it is a fraud upon him, although all the others are satisfied.

CURRAN et al. v. *MUNGER et al.**

EMMONS, J.—The petition of appeal is demurred to, and I infer from the perusal of the opinion of the district judge that its statements materially vary the facts from those which were before him. All the leading and more important conclusions upon which he dismissed the petition are fully negatived in the case as it comes before this court.

A separate outline of the very voluminous facts is unnecessary. The opinion will be understood by parties without it, and the rulings upon them are not important as precedents.

The court below held that the compromise was lawful, and that as the respondents believed it included all creditors save Colt, the transfer to him was not with the intent de-

* The facts appear more fully in the printed judgment of the court below, 4 N. B. R. 90.

manded by the statute to make it an act of bankruptcy. Upon this ground it dismissed the petition.

Upon the case as it stands in this court the compromise is clearly *fraudulent*. The respondents knew that representations had been made to some of the creditors, that others had settled for thirty-five cents, when in fact they were secretly to receive more. This ground alone would compel an entry of a decree against the respondents. ·

Hodges was the agent of the respondents only. He had no authority to represent the appellants. It is the common case of an agent bringing back the *replies* to his principal. His frauds, knowledge, negligence and misunderstandings are those of the men who employ him. This familiar general rule has been fully applied in many cases under this act. 4. N. B. R. 106; id. 92 ; id. 178; 2 id. 137. There are many other similar judgments.

But there is no necessity for a resort to a rule which might legally charge them with knowledge they did not in fact have, and so decide this appeal upon technical grounds at variance with actual truth. Upon the facts here there is no reasonable ground for any belief on their part, or that of Hodges, that petitioners had accepted their terms. All knew they had been rejected. They told Hodges they would receive thirty-five cents *cash*. He so told the debtor. Subsequently Clark, Colt's partner, wrote that they said *precisely the same thing*—that they would take thirty-five cents. There was nothing in this having the slightest tendency to encourage, much less justify, the extraordinary and sudden change of opinion that the rejected terms had been accepted.

The petitioners swear positively that Hodges was *not* their agent. He was not sworn, and nowhere is there a scintilla of proof of such fact. But grant the unwarrantable assumption that he was *alike* the agents of the debtors who sent him and the creditors who made replies. It is still but the case of a *common agent*, where his knowledge binds both alike.

And if this were not so, still there must be an adjudication of bankruptcy upon the case here, because the respondents had *all the facts* before them that Hodges had.

The ground is that Hodges represented that *he* had authority to accept the terms for the appellants. But all knew why he so said; that he interpreted the letter of Clark as they themselves professed to have done. They knew he had no *further* authority than what he fully reported as their agent on his return. It is not a case of reliance upon representations where the facts upon which opinion rests are unknown.

The case might well be disposed of upon the foregoing and other views which might be taken of the facts in the petition of appeal. But we place the reversal upon different grounds. From the argument made by the respondent's counsel we infer they misapprehend the practice or they would have answered the petition and procured a settlement of the facts. No rights are lost, however, for we hold that when debtors once know of hopeless insolvency they are in the law bound also to know whether that condition *continues;* and the belief whether well or illy founded, that· all other creditors have settled when they have not so done, is no justification for a transfer which in fact operates as a preference.

In a learned and most careful argument the counsel for the appellants has collected and analysed the judgments, holding that when insolvency is known and a preference is made, the intent is a presumption of law. They are useful as inducements to the conclusions arrived at, but the precise point here decided does not demand their citation and discussion at length.

I quite approve in this regard all that is actually decided in the recent judgment of Hopkins, J., 5. N. B. R. 182. He says substantially section thirty-nine has far less reference to the condition of mind of the insolvent debtor than in the condition of insolvency *as a fact.*

But whatever difference may exist in relation to the debtor's duty of knowing his financial condition originally, there should be none concerning the very different obligation,

Curran et al. v. Munger et al.

when he once knows his insolvency, of waiting before he se-
cures his relatives and endorsers, until he knows that his condition is changed, or that his creditors have consented to the
preference.

When a party with full knowledge of his insolvency makes
a preference, it seems but a play upon terms to say that he
did not in a legal sense *intend* it because he erroneously supposed his creditors had consented to it.

It is not even the case where there was a mistaken belief
of full payment, which though it could not justify the transfer,
would, we grant, in a literal but immaterial sense, disprove
an actual intention to prefer. A man who believes he has
but one creditor cannot intend to make a preference. While
on the one hand we do not assent to this merely formal argument to show no preference was intended within the meaning
of the law, so on the other we do not go on its literalisms,
which are satisfied if there was a preference *in fact* which in
the accidents of this case was contemplated by the parties.
This may strengthen the justice of the particular judgment
here, but is by no means necessary to sustain it. The sale
was unlawful, no matter what the actual intention of the parties may have been. It is held broadly as a general principle
to which there should be no exceptions, that where the parties
know the insolvency they must act at their peril if they appropriate the *trust fund* which the law devotes to the equal
payment of all, before they *know, also,* that creditors have
ceased to be such, or that they consent, after the most full
and fair disclosure of all the facts, to the discrimination which
is made. Without this it is an act of bankruptcy.

It is an irrelevant fact that they erroneously supposed the
creditors had consented. Their carelessness, rash and interested conclusions, or never-so-well warranted misapprehen-
sions, can give them no power over the statutory vested
rights of innocent and non-concurring creditors.

Establish the doctrine that an unjust preference is lawful,
because the debtor was ignorant of his insolvency; add, also,
that it is so when he knew it, but had reasonable ground to

believe he had compromised at thirty-five cents on the dollar in *time paper*, and go forward in the application of the principle in these rulings to all the analagous exigencies of failing business men, and the bankrupt law would require immediate and important amendments.

Some reliance was made upon the absence of the other creditors. Of course one, in principle, presents the same legal questions as if all *but* one were here. *In re* Williams, 3 N. B. R. 72. But *non constat* the other creditors are satisfied. There is no proof that they are, and no presumption of such fact arises upon such a record as this.

There is a mode of construing judgments by arguing from their implications and deducing conclusions of law because dissents are not uttered, that makes it proper to say further, that were it necessary in this case we should hold the entire scheme of this settlement, as set forth in the petition of appeal, a fraud upon the act, irrespective of the affirmative proof that misrepresentations were made to the compromising creditors.

The case here, and as set forth in the printed judgment of the learned district judge, with which we have been furnished by the appellant's counsel, substantially shows that a petition had been filed against the debtors; that the claim was settled by them, and the hostile attorney who conducted the proceedings in the district court, employed by the joint consultations of Colt the preferred creditor, and the debtors, to compromise with all the others. It was agreed by all that it would be necessary to pay some one price, and some another, as it has been done in the attempted settlement. Colt agreed if this could be brought about for forty cents in the aggregate, he would *then* buy the goods, give his note for the compromise money, and pay his endorsements *in full*. They all enter into the scheme of discrimination and *preference*. They withhold the assets from the bankruptcy court, where in law they belong the moment the debtor becomes insolvent and proposes liquidation, and attempt through the agent just what the law prohibits. *Hardy et al.* v. *Bininger*

& Co. 4 N. B. R. 77; and 3 N. B. R. 99; *Cookingham et al.* v. *Morgan et al.* 5 N. B. R. 16; *Driggs* v. *Moore,* 3 N. B. R. 149; *in re* Drummond, 1 N. B. R. 10; *in re* Smith, 3 N. B. R. 98; *in re* Silverman, 4 N. B. R. 173, and numerous similar judgments. That when the *act* is necessarily a preference, and insolvency is known, it is *per se* an intent to prefer, or to defeat the act.

In this case the *intention* was not actually to *consummate* these unlawful preferences until by their contemporaneous execution every creditor would be bound by the acceptance of the paper and so precluded from objecting to it. The *intention* was not to *abstain* from making preferences gross and unjust, but to secure such a settlement as would cut off the power of complaint. But the preference *has* been made just as was intended, and the creditors were *not* precluded. In these circumstances I think the proceedings relied upon to sustain the transfer to Colt are *themselves* acts of bankruptcy, because they show an intentional preference by an insolvent debtor.

There is another view upon which I think decree below should have been in favor of the creditors.

Hodges has not been sworn, and the proof is meagre in reference to misrepresentations to creditors; but he who is conversant with such matters, and knows the keen sense of wrong which every merchant feels when he learns that his liberality has been successfully appealed to for an acceptance of thirty-five cents, when his fellow-trader has unjustly gotten seventy-five or a hundred, will not fail to make the presumption that full disclosure was not made by the attorney here. We venture to say that such a thing as an unequal settlement, some receiving a hundred cents and others thirty-five, was never voluntarily made without fraud and misrepresentation, in the whole history of American business.

In the circumstances of this case a condition is presented where the *onus probandi* is upon the actors. We do not think it the duty of the appellants in a case like this to prove

Curran et al. v. Munger et al.

that creditors have not consented to the injustice which has been done them. There is none that the apparent fraud ever come to their knowledge, that they might complain. Every familiar principle in this department of the law compels the presumption that they did not assent. The letter of Clark, Colt's partner, saying he thought the scheme would fail because he feared the creditors had *learned* of the inequality, is by no means necessary to help this legal conclusion. 1 Phil. Ev. 615, n.; 3 Starkey, 48, and other similar authorities.

It is never necessary to prove affirmatively that a man has not assented to that which is to his disadvantage. The presumption of the law is that he has not. Nor is this at all at war with the rule that fraud shall not be presumed. It is the quite different doctrine that when such facts are presented as make it an irresistible inference of common reason the *law will* presume it, unless the apparently guilty actors do what any innocent man in his senses would do, if it were in his power—explain the suspicions. It is their duty to prove how a fact so extraordinary occurred as that creditors having equal rights in a common fund, turned by law into a trust for their benefit, were seduced into action so anomalous as the surrender of this right to Colt, and the other creditors receiving full pay. And when the agent in all this sits in court and is not examined by the respondents, a duty is omitted which the law casts even upon the criminal in similar cases. *U. S.* v. *Chaffee*, 11 I. R. R. 110; 4 How. 242; Starkey, Evd. 820.

Decree below dismissing petition reversed and adjudication of bankruptcy ordered.—December, 1871.

DON M. DICKINSON for creditors.

BATES & HODGES for debtors.

UNITED STATES DISTRICT COURT—E. D. OF MICHIGAN.

A. contracted with B. for the sale of certain scales, payment to be made by B's note on their delivery and after they were set up. They were delivered but not set up according to contract, and B's note was not given. Soon after this B. was declared bankrupt. A. petitioned to have his goods returned, which was granted, and an order entered accordingly.

In re A. PUSEY.

On the petition of Morris N. Rowley for an order requiring the assignee to deliver to him, the said Rowley, as his property, three certain scales, of which the assignee has taken possession as assets of the bankrupt. An answer was put in by the assignee denying Rowley's right to the scales, and proofs have been taken.

Mr. PALMER, (Ward & Palmer) for petitioner. Mr. DRIGGS, (Meddaugh & Driggs) for assignee.

LONGYEAR, J.—It appears by the proofs that some time in May, eighteen hundred and seventy-one, Rowley, by his agent, agreed to sell to the bankrupt three scales—two of three thousand five hundred pounds, each at one hundred and five dollars, and one at eight hundred pounds for thirty-six dollars, less five per cent. The scales were to be delivered and put up by Rowley, and the bankrupt was to give his note for the purchase price on six months' time. The time was to run from the time the scales were put up.

Thus far there is no conflict in the proofs. The agent who made the sale testifies that beside giving the note the bankrupt was to give security on the scales. He also testifies that in a subsequent conversation with the bankrupt he admitted such to be the fact, and this last statement is corroborated by the testimony of the petitioner. This is denied by the bankrupt.

Taking into consideration the further fact appearing by the proofs that such was the usage of the petitioner in making sales of this kind, and that we have the testimony of two against the one, standing equally fair, to say the least, with the one, the preponderance of evidence is decidedly in favor of petitioner's claim in this respect. It must therefore be considered that it was a part of the agreement that security was to be given.

The contract was entire, and no note or security could be demanded until the scales had first been all delivered and set up. It is equally clear that until so delivered and set up, and the note and security given, the property in the scales did not pass to the bankrupt, but remained in the petitioner, unless, as claimed by the assignee, there was a waiver of these conditions. Story on sales, sec. 196, *et seq.; Whitney* v. *Eaton*, 15 Gray, 225 ; *Riddle* v. *Varnum*, 20 Pick. 280 ; *Herschom* v. *Canney*, 98 Mass. 149.

Such is in fact conceded to be the effect of the contract ; but it is claimed in behalf of the assignee, that there was a waiver, on account of which the scales did in fact become the property of the bankrupt. Dates here become somewhat important, and it is to be regretted that they do not appear with more certainty in the proofs. The facts, however, out of which such waiver is claimed, are substantially as follows :

As we have seen, the contract was made some time in May, eighteen hundred and seventy-one. Some time in the June following, and in the latter part of the month, the scales were all taken to the premises of the bankrupt, where they were to be put up by the agent who made the sale ; and one of the large scales and the small scale were put up. The agent was then taken sick and left. Soon thereafter the bankruptcy proceedings were commenced, and the other large scale has never been put up, and the note and security were not given. James Pusey, a brother of the bankrupt, testifies as follows : " I helped him," (the agent) " to set the first set up, and he showed me where it was best to set the second set and told me I and the carpenter could do it just as well as he could. He was taken sick just as he got the first set up. He told me to put up the second set and he would pay brother for doing so, and marked the place for it. I took them out of the box and they stand there yet, never were put up. I was at work for brother at that time." This

In re Pusey.

was told to the bankrupt, as he testifies, two or three days afterwards, but nothing was done in pursuance of it further than as above stated in James Pusey's testimony.

If these facts had the effect to vary the contract so as to relieve the petitioner from his obligation to complete setting up the scales, then all that was to have been done on his part must be deemed to have been done, and he had the right to demand the note and security then, and not having done so he must be deemed to have waived the giving of them at the time, as a condition precedent to the passing of the property in the scales to the bankrupt, as is claimed on behalf of the assignee.

But can these facts be given any such effect? What the agent said to James Pusey was not a proposition to the bankrupt; and if it had been it would then be necessary to show that it was accepted by him, or that he had acted upon it. It was a mere request or suggestion to James Pusey for him and the carpenter to go on and set up the remaining scale, not for the bankrupt, but for the petitioner; and when this was told to the bankrupt it does not appear that he even assented that they might do it. Certain it is that neither he nor his men ever acted upon the request or suggestion.

I am clear, therefore, that the facts stated did not have the effect claimed, and hence that the property in the scales did not pass to the bankrupt, but remained in the petitioner. This being the situation at the time the bankruptcy proceedings were commenced, and as the assignee can claim no greater rights to the property than the bankrupt had, the prayer of the petitioner must be granted.

Ordered accordingly.—November 8, 1871.

In re Merchants' Insurance Co.

UNITED STATES DISTRICT COURT—ILLINOIS.

The object and intent of the United States bankrupt act of eighteen hundred and sixty-seven is to place the administration of the affairs of insolvent persons and corporations exclusively under the jurisdiction of the federal courts. Hence, the appointment of a receiver for an insolvent insurance company by a state court is an act of bankruptcy, being a "taking on legal process" within the meaning of the thirty-ninth section of said act; the United States courts sitting in bankruptcy having in such cases exclusive jurisdiction over the property.

The payment of rent in full by an insolvent corporation, in order to prevent the forfeiture of a valuable lease, is a technical act of bankruptcy.

In re MERCHANTS' INSURANCE CO.

BLODGETT, J.—The petitioning creditor in this case, the Singer Manufacturing Co., seeks an adjudication in bankruptcy against the Merchants' Insurance Co., on an alleged indebtedness existing upon a policy of insurance issued by the latter company, upon which loss was sustained on the ninth day of October last, and the chief act of bankruptcy alleged is that said insurance company, being insolvent, did, on the sixth day of November last, suffer its property to be taken on legal process, under certain proceedings instituted by the attorney general of this state in the circuit court of Cook county, pursuant to the twenty-third section of the statute of this state, approved March eleventh, eighteen hundred and sixty-nine, entitled, "An act to incorporate and govern fire and marine insurance companies," etc.

An answer is filed by the insurance company, admitting the substantial facts alleged in the petiton, and submitting to the court whether those facts constitute an act of bankruptcy within the meaning of the law.

The facts thus alleged and admitted are substantially these :

The respondent is a corporation, created under a special charter by the legislature of the state of Illinois in eighteen hundred and sixty-one, and since eighteen hundred and sixty-three, up to about the sixth of November last, said company has been engaged in doing a fire and marine insurance business, pursuant to the powers granted in its act of incorporation, having its principal office in the city of Chicago. By reason of the losses sustained in the great fire which occurred in this city on the ninth of October last, said company became insolvent, and on the thirty-first of October last the people of the state of Illinois, by the attorney general of the state, filed their bill of complaint in the circuit court of Cook county, pursuant to the twenty-third section of the law referred to, alleging in substance that said company had become insolvent and unable to pay its liabilities, and that its assets were insufficient to justify the continuance of said company in business, and praying that said corporation might be dissolved, and that a receiver might be appointed to take charge of its assets; and on the sixth of November last, the officers of said company, fearing that judgments might be obtained in certain suits then pending against the company, and the plaintiffs in such suits thereby obtain an undue preference over other creditors, consented to the appointment of a receiver by said court in accordance with said bill, and W. E. Doggett, Esq., was accordingly appointed such receiver, and the company has since delivered over to him all its assets and property. No charge of willful or intended fraud is brought against the corporation or its officers; it being conceded that its officers and managers are among the most upright and capable of our citizens, and that the present insolvency of the company results from circumstances beyond the control of those in charge of its affairs.

Upon these admitted facts we are called upon to adjudicate. There can be no doubt, or at least we have none, that this corporation is one of that class of corporations intended to be within the scope and provisions of the general bankrupt law. The thirty-seventh section declares that " *the provisions of this act shall apply to all moneyed, business or commercial corporations and joint stock companies.*" ·The business of insurance, for the carrying on of which this company was incorporated, and in which it has been engaged, is clearly included within the definitions given by the statute.

In re Merchants' Insurance Co.

The object and intent of the general bankrupt law is to place the administration of the affairs of insolvent persons and corporations *exclusively* under the jurisdiction of the federal courts of bankruptcy; and the enactment of the general bankruptcy law now in force suspended all actions and proceedings under state insolvent laws. *Perry v. Langley,* 1 N. B. R. 155; 2 N. B. R. 154 and 188.

It also seems clear to us that the appointment of a receiver by the state court to take possession of the property and assets of a person, firm or corporation, and apply the same to the payment of debts, is a "taking on legal process" within the meaning of the eighth clause of the thirty-ninth section of the bankruptcy act. The receiver of a court of chancery is its executive officer, as much so, to all intents and purposes, as a sheriff of a court of law; and the goods or property in his hands are as much in the custody of the law as if levied upon under an execution or attachment. And the purpose for which the receiver in this case takes the property is the same as that of a sheriff in making his levy, except that the scope of the receiver's warrant is more comprehensive, he being required to pay *all debts,* while the sheriff only seeks the payment of the specific debt mentioned in his execution or attachment.

Although I am not aware that this particular point has ever before been raised in this court, it has often been decided elsewhere. 2 N. B. R. 2.

But it is objected that the proceedings in the state court here complained of being in accordance with a general statute of this state and part of the organic law by which the respondent exists, and being predicated mainly upon the reserved right of the state to protect its citizens against irresponsible insurance companies, and the state court having acquired jurisdiction of the parties and subject matter, this court cannot now interfere as a bankrupt court and take charge of and administer the assets in question, although the insolvency of the respondent is fully conceded.

It seems enough to suggests in answer to this position

that, if correct, any state could effectually defeat the operation of any bankrupt law passed by congress by simply providing that any person or corporation, if deemed insolvent or incapable of doing business by a state officer, might, under the power of exercising and enforcing police regulations or enactments by the states, be wound up and its assets administered upon in the state courts, notwithstanding such person or corporation might be insolvent and guilty of all the acts of bankruptcy provided for in the general bankrupt law.

It is further urged that the proceeding in question does not come within the terms of the bankrupt act, because the state law under which it is instituted is not an insolvent law, inasmuch as it does not purport to discharge the debtor from its liabilities, but we fail to perceive how the treatment the debtor may receive at the hands of the state court can avail to sustain that court's control over the assets. If the *fact* of insolvency exists, and the person or corporation is within the provisions of the bankrupt law, the federal courts sitting in bankruptcy have *exclusive* jurisdiction of his property, and the fact that a state law does not purport or attempt to relieve the debtor from his debts, cannot, it seems to us, be urged as a reason why the state court should hold the assets and administer them after proper proceedings in bankruptcy have been instituted in the federal courts.

We might further answer this objection by the suggestion that a discharge of an insurance company's liabilities under this state statute and proceedings in the state courts would be in the nature of things superfluous and unnecessary, for the reason that the main object of the proceeding is to forfeit the charter and franchises of the corporation, and why assume to discharge from further liability a debtor whose legal entity is to be dissolved? If its corporate existence is to be terminated, it matters little what becomes of its unpaid balances.

It also seems clear to us that in so far as a state law attempts to administer on the effects of an insolvent debtor and distribute them among creditors, it is to all intents and

In re Merchants' Insurance Co.

purposes an insolvent law, although it may not authorize a discharge of the debtor from further liability.

We have no doubt that the proceeding in the state court, to forfeit the charter and corporate franchises of this company is entirely valid and within the powers and jurisdiction of that court—perhaps exclusively so. The state having created the corporation may undoubtedly dissolve it in its own way, consistent with the terms of the grant.

The fallacy of the respondent's argument seems to us to consist in the assumption that, because the state court had jurisdiction for the dissolution of the corporation, it can therefore hold jurisdiction under all circumstances for the distribution of the assets. If the fact of insolvency had not existed, the state court would probably have had the right to administer the assets, if once within its control, as an incident to the principal object of the proceeding, which was the dissolution of the corporation. But, as before stated, when insolvency intervenes so as to make the debtor a proper subject for the operation of the bankrupt act, the exclusive jurisdiction of the bankrupt court attaches, and the state court, and those acting under its mandate, must surrender the control of the assets, whatever may be the final decree in regard to the continuance of the corporation. When the corporation found itself insolvent, or was certified to be insolvent by the state auditor, acting under the state law, and proceedings were instituted for the dissolution of the corporation and the administration of its assets, it was the duty of the corporation at once to voluntarily file its petition to be adjudged a bankrupt in the federal court, and its failure to do so, and its acquiescence in the proceedings by which its assets were placed under the control of the state court, is in itself an act of bankruptcy.

This is not a case of concurrent jurisdiction between the state and federal courts. In all cases where the state and federal courts have concurrent jurisdiction, the court which first obtains control of the parties and property by judicial proceedings will retain it, and the authorities cited by the counsel from the 8 How. and later cases, are full in point, conceive they do not apply to this case, inasmuch as the court has exclusive jurisdiction in causes of bankruptcy. .

In our view, then, the admitted facts show the respondent guilty of the act of bankruptcy charged in the petition, and nothing in the proceedings had before the state court, tends to oust this court of its jurisdiction and authority to adjudicate the respondent a bankrupt.

The precise steps by which the officers of this court shall hereafter obtain possession of the assets of the bankrupt need not now be indicated, as the action of this court in that regard will be governed by circumstances as they may hereafter arise.

In thus announcing our conclusions we do not consider that we are adopting any new rule or making even a new application of an old one, as the pathway we are treading appears to us to be well beaten by precedents and authority. Nor should we have taken pains to so fully state our views, but for the fact that the overwhelming calamity which befel this city on the 9th of October last brought financial ruin upon a large number of insurance companies doing business here, and makes it seem desirable that a tolerably full exposition should be given of the law governing the rights and duties of insurers and insured.

It is also proper to add that the petition in this case charges a further act of bankruptcy : in that said insurance company, on or about the thirty-first day of October last, being then insolvent, paid one of its creditors in full, thereby giving such creditor a preference over other creditors. And it is admitted in the answer that after the company became insolvent a large sum of money fell due one Tuthill King for rent of the lot on which the company had erected a valuable building. And as this lease was deemed a valuable asset, and would be forfeited unless the rent was paid at maturity, the company paid the same, deeming that it was thereby subserving the best interests of its creditors.

We have no doubt but what the admitted facts applicable to this charge make out a technical act of bankruptcy. But no stress was laid upon it in the argument, as all parties seemed desirous of a decision upon the first charge.

The expenditure complained of seems to have been judicious and made in good faith, and this court would probably, on the facts stated, have authorized it, but this does not change the character of the act under the law.

DRUMMOND, C. J., sat with BLODGETT, J., on the hearing of this case and concurred in the decision.

ELDRIDGE & TOURTELOTTE for petitioner. SCAMMON, MC-CAGG & FULLER for respondent.—December 18, 1871.

------•••------

SUPREME COURT OF THE UNITED STATES—DECEMBER TERM, 1871.

[Appeal from the United States Circuit Court for the District of Arkansas.]

By insolvency, as used in the bankrupt act, when applied to traders and merchants, is meant inability of a party to pay his debts as they become due in the ordinary course of business.

The transfer by a debtor of a large portion of his property, while he is insolvent, to one creditor, without making provision for an equal distribution of its proceeds to all his creditors, necessarily operates as a preference to him, and must be taken as conclusive evidence that a preference was intended, unless the debtor can show that he was at the time ignorant of his insolvency, and that his affairs were such that he could reasonably expect to pay all his debts. The burden of proof is upon him in such a case, and not upon the assignee or contestant in bankruptcy,

A creditor has reasonable cause to believe a debtor, who is a trader, to be insolvent, when such a state of facts is brought to the creditor's notice respecting the affairs and pecuniary condition of the debtor as would lead a prudent business man to the conclusion that he is unable to meet his obligations as they mature in the ordinary course of business.

A transfer by an insolvent debtor with a view to secure his property, or any part of it, to one creditor, and thus prevent an equal distribution among all his creditors, is a transfer in fraud of the bankrupt act.

TOOF et al. v. MARTIN, Assignee.

FIELD, J.—This is a suit brought by the assignee in bankruptcy of Haines and Chetland to cancel certain conveyances alleged to have been made by them in fraud of the bankrupt act. As appears from the evidence in the case, Haines and Chetlain were, in February, eighteen hundred and sixty-eight, and had been for some years before, merchants, doing business under the firm name of W. P. Haines & Company, at Augusta, in the state of Arkansas. On the twenty-ninth of that month they filed a petition for the benefit of the bankrupt act, and on the twenty-eighth of May following they were adjudged bankrupts, and the complainant was appointed assignee of their estates. On the eighteenth of the previous January, which was about six weeks before the filing of their petition, they conveyed an undivided half-interest in certain parcels of land owned by them at Augusta, to Toof, Phillips & Company, a firm doing business as merchants at Memphis, in Tennessee, for the consideration of one thousand eight hundred and seventy-six dollars, which sum was to be credited on a debt due from them to that firm. At the same time they assigned to one Mahan, a member of that firm, a title-bond which they held for certain other real property at Augusta, upon which they had made valuable improvements. The consideration of this assignment was two drafts of Mahan on Toof, Phillips & Company, each for three thousand and thirty-four dollars, one drawn to the order of Haines and the other to the order of Chetlain. The amount of both drafts was credited on the indebtedness of Haines & Company to Toof, Phillips & Company, pursuant to an understanding to that effect made at the time. There was then due of the purchase money of the property, for which the title bond was given, about seven hundred dollars. This sum Mahan paid and took a conveyance to himself from the obligor who held the fee.

The bill of complaint charges specifically that at the time these conveyances were made the bankrupts were insolvent or in contemplation of insolvency; that the conveyances were made with a view to give a preference to Toof, Phillips & Company, who were the creditors of the bankrupts; that Toof, Phillips & Company knew or had reasonable cause to believe that the bankrupts were then insolvent, and that the conveyances were made in fraud of the provisions of the bankrupt act.

Toof et al. v. Martin.

The bill also charges that the assignment of the title-bond to Mahan was in fact for the use and benefit of Toof, Phillips & Company, for the purpose of securing the property or its value to them in fraud of the rights of creditors, and that this purpose was known and participated in by Mahan.

The district court, by its decree, ordered that the conveyances be annulled and that the title of the property be vested in the assignee, the latter to refund the amount of the purchase money advanced by Mahon to obtain the deed of the land described in the title-bond, less any rents and profits received by him or Toof, Phillips & Company from the property. This decree the circuit court affirmed, and from that affirmance the case is brought before us on appeal.

The bill presents a case within the provisions of the first clause of the thirty-fifth section of the bankrupt act. That clause was intended to defeat preferences to a creditor made by a debtor when insolvent or in contemplation of insolvency. It declares that any payment or transfer of his property made by him whilst in that condition, within four months previous to the filing of his petition, with a view to give a preference to a creditor, shall be void if the creditor has at the time reasonable cause to believe him to be insolvent, and that the payment or transfer was made in fraud of the provisions of the bankrupt act. And it authorizes, in such cases, the assignee to recover the property or its value from the party who receives it.

Under this act it is incumbent on the complainant, in order to maintain the decree in his favor, to show four things :

1st. That at the time the conveyances to Toof, Phillips & Co. and Mahan were made, the bankrupts were insolvent or contemplated insolvency ;

2d. That the conveyances were made with a view to give a preference to these creditors :

3d. That the creditors had reasonable cause to believe the bankrupts were insolvent at the time ; and,

Toof et al. v. Martin.

4th.' That the conveyances were made in fraud of the provisions of the bankrupt act.

1st. The counsel of the appellants have presented an elaborate argument to show that inability to pay one's debts at the time they fall due, *in money*, does not constitute insolvency within the provisions of the bankrupt act. The argument is especially addressed to language used by the district judge when speaking of the statement of the appellants in answer to one of the interrogatories of the bill, to the effect that at the time the transfers were made they did not believe the bankrupts were able to pay their debts *in money*, but were able to do so on a fair market valuation of their property and assets. The district judge held that this was a direct confession of a fact which in law constitutes insolvency, and observed that "if the bankrupts could not pay their debts in the ordinary course of business, that is in money, as they fell due, they were insolvent."

The rule thus laid down may not be strictly correct as applied to all bankrupts. The term insolvency is not always used in the same sense. It is sometimes used to denote the insufficiency of the entire property and assets of an individual to pay his debts. This is its general and popular meaning. But it is also used in a more restricted sense, to express the inability of a party to pay his debts as they become due in the ordinary course of business. It is in this latter sense that the term is used when traders and merchants are said to be insolvent, and as applied to them it is the sense intended by the act of congress. It was of the bankrupts as traders that the district judge was speaking when he used the language which is the subject of criticism by counsel.

With reference to other persons not engaged in trade or commerce, the term may perhaps have a less restricted meaning. The bankrupt act does not define what shall constitute insolvency, or the evidence of insolvency, in every case.

In the present case the bankrupts were insolvent in both senses of the term at the time the conveyances in controversy were made. They did not then possess sufficient property, even upon their own estimation of its value, as given in their schedules, to pay their debts. These exceeded the estimated value of the property by over twenty thousand dollars. And for months previous the bankrupts had failed to meet their obligations as they matured. Creditors had pressed for payments without success; their stock of goods had been levied on, and their store closed by the sheriff under an execution on a judgment against one of them. It would serve no useful purpose to state in detail the evidence contained in the record which relates to their condition. It is enough to say that it abundantly establishes their hopeless insolvency.

2d. That the conveyances to Toof, Phillips & Co. were made with a view to give them a preference over other creditors hardly admits of a doubt. The bankrupts knew at the time their insolvent condition. A month previous they had made up a balance sheet of their affairs which showed that their assets were insufficient to pay their debts. They had contemplated going into bankruptcy in December previous, and were then pressed by numerous creditors for payment. Their indebtedness at the time exceeded fifty thousand dollars, and except to Toof, Phillips & Co., they did not pay upon the whole of it over five hundred dollars during the previous fall and winter. Making a transfer of property to these creditors, under these circumstances, was in fact giving them a preference, and it must be presumed that the bankrupts intended this result at the time. It is a general principle that every one must be presumed to intend the necessary consequences of his acts. The transfer in any case by a debtor of a large portion of his property while he is insolvent, to one creditor, without making provision for an equal distribution of its proceeds to all his creditors, necessarily operates as a preference to him, and must be taken as conclusive evidence that a preference was intended, unless the debtor can show that he was at the time ignorant of his insolvency, and that his affairs were such that he could rea-

Toof et al. v. Martin.

sonably expect to pay all his debts. The burden of proof is upon him in such case, and not upon the assignee or contestant in bankruptcy.

No such proof was made or attempted in this case. But, on the contrary, the evidence shows that the conveyances were executed upon the expectation of the bankrupts, and upon the assurance of Toof, Phillips & Co. that in consequence of them they would continue to sell the bankrupts goods on credit, as they had previously done; and that no arrangement was made by the bankrupts with any other of their creditors, either for payment or security, or for an extention of credit.

The fact that the title-bond was assigned, and the property for which it was given was conveyed to Mahan alone, and not to Toof, Phillips & Company, does not change the character of the transaction. Mahan was a member of that firm, and the conveyance was made to him with the understanding that the sum mentioned as its consideration should be credited on the indebtedness of the bankrupts to them. Both of the bankrupts testified that such was the understanding at the time. The pretence that Mahan bought the lots as an investment on private account will not bear the slightest examination. It is in proof that the lots at the time were only worth four thousand dollars at the outside, yet the consideration given was nearly seven thousand. Toof, Phillips & Company might well have been willing to credit this amount on their claim against insolvent traders in consideration of obtaining from them the possession of property of much less value, but it is increditable that an individual, seeking an investment of his money, would be careless as to the difference between the actual value of the property and the amount paid as a consideration for its transfer to him.

3d. From what has already been said it is manifest not only that the bankrupts were insolvent when they made the conveyances in controversy, but that the creditors, Toof, Phillips & Company, had reasonable cause to believe that they were insolvent. The statute, to defeat the conveyances,

Toof et al. v. Martin.

does not require that the creditors should have had absolute knowledge on the point, nor even that they should, in fact, have had any belief on the subject. It only requires that they should have had reasonable cause to believe that such was the fact. And reasonable cause they must be considered to have had when such a state of facts was brought to their notice in respect to the affairs and pecuniary condition of the bankrupts, as would have led prudent business men to the conclusion that they could not meet their obligations as they matured in the ordinary course of business. *Scammon* v. *Cole*, 5 N. B. R. 257. That such a state of facts was brought to the notice of the creditors is plainly shown. Chetlain, one of the bankrupts, testifies that previous to the execution of the conveyances, he had several conversations with Mahan respecting their finances, and told him the amount or near the amount of their indebtedness, and that they could not pay it. Mahan advised them to get extensions, and said that he would help them to get through. Chetlain also testifies that such was the state of the finances of the bankrupts that on one occasion, in conversation with Mahan, they offered to turn over to him their entire assets if he would assume their liabilities and give them a receipt, and that he declined the offer.

It also appears in evidence that the levy by the sheriff upon the stock of goods of the bankrupts, already mentioned, which was made in January, eighteen hundred and sixty-eight, caused a temporary suspension of their business, and that Mahan was in Augusta at the time and had an interview with the bankrupts on the subject of the levy.

It also appears that about the last of December, eighteen hundred and sixty-seven, or the first of January, eighteen hundred and sixty-eight, Toof, Phillips & Company sent notes of the bankrupts which they held to an agent in Augusta for collection. The agent presented the notes for payment to the bankrupts and was told by them that they could not pay the notes at that time. The agent then wrote to Toof, Phillips & Company that they had better look to

Toof et al. v. Martin.

their interests, as his conviction was that it was doubtful whether they would be able to collect their debts. Shortly after this Mahan went to Augusta to look after the matter, and whilst there the conveyances in controversy were made.

It is impossible to doubt that Mahan ascertained, while thus in Augusta, the actual condition of the affairs of the bankrupts. The facts recited were sufficient to justify the conclusion that they were insolvent, or at least furnished reasonable cause for a belief that such was the fact.

4th. It only remains to add that the creditors, Toof, Phillips & Company, had also reasonable ground to believe that the conveyances were made in fraud of the provisions of the bankrupt act. This, indeed, follows necessarily from the facts already stated. The act of congress was designed to secure an equal distribution of the property of an insolvent debtor among his creditors, and any transfer made with a view to secure the property or any part of it to one, and thus prevent such equal distribution, is a transfer in fraud of the act. That such was the effect of the conveyances in this case, and that this effect was intended by both creditors and bankrupts, does not admit, upon the evidence, of any rational doubt. A clearer case of intended fraud upon the act is not often presented.

Decree affirmed.

[Mr. Justice Bradley was absent from the court when this case was submitted, and consequently took no part in its decision.]

UNITED STATES DISTRICT COURT—OREGON.

A debtor who seeks to make a composition of his debts by the payment of a part only of what he owes, is not bound to make any representations concerning his assets or resources; but he must act in good faith, and if he does make any such representations, he must make them truly or he will be guilty of fraud.

Creditors who have received more than the amount stipulated in the composition deed without the knowledge of the other creditors, are not thereby barred from bringing an action against the debtor on their original obligation when such action is brought on the ground that the composition deed was fraudulently procured.

A debtor cannot be allowed to have the benefit of a composition with his creditors which was confessedly procured by the false representations of his agent, upon the ground that the agent was ignorant of the truth and made the representations in good faith.

ELFELT et al. v. *SNOW et al.*

DEADY, J.—This action was commenced in the circuit court of the state for the county of Multnomah, on April fifth, eighteen hundred and sixty-seven, to recover from the defendants, H. H. Snow and D. M. Jessie, a balance of seven thousand and twenty-six dollars, with interest, from November eighth, eighteen hundred and sixty-six, alleged to be due the plaintiffs on a promissory note made by the defendants to J. Kohn & Co. on July twenty-eighth, eighteen hundred and sixty-two, for the sum of eight thousand three hundred and twenty dollars and twelve cents, and by the latter endorsed to the plaintiffs in eighteen hundred and sixty-four.

Defendant Jessie was not served and did not appear. On July thirty-first, eighteen hundred and sixty-seven, Snow filed a second amended answer to the complaint, in which he denied that the defendants were indebted to the plaintiffs in anywise; and alleged that on November nineteenth, eighteen hundred and sixty-six, the defendants being indebted to the plaintiffs and others, " and much embarrassed financially on account thereof," the plaintiffs and others, naming them, did then execute and deliver to defendants a certain writing by which such plaintiffs and others agreed to accept forty-five cents on the dollar, in gold coin, to be paid in two weeks, in full satisfaction of their several claims, which amounted in the aggregate to ten thousand six hundred and seventy-two dollars and seventy-seven cents; and that said defendants, in pursuance of said agreement, afterwards paid said plaintiffs and others said forty-five cents on the dollar, which sums plaintiffs and others accepted in full satisfaction of said claims, and discharged defendants from further liability thereon; and that the claim mentioned in said writing is the debt upon which the plaintiffs' action is brought.

On August first, eighteen hundred and sixty-seven, plaintiffs replied to the answer, alleging that in November, eighteen hundred and sixty-six, the defendants represented to the · plaintiffs that they were insolvent, and the only property owned by them or Snow was four thousand dollars' worth of gold dust and a train of mules, from which they could realize about three thousand dollars, and that seven thousand dollars would pay only about forty-five cents on the dollar " of the original amount they owed;" and that the plaintiffs, relying on and confiding in the truth of said representations, agreed to accept and did receive the sum of forty-five cents on the dollar of the original indebtedness due from the defendants, and in pursuance thereof delivered said note to defendant Snow; but that said representations were false and fraudulently made by said defendants with intent to deceive the plaintiffs; and that the said defendants fraudulently concealed from the plaintiffs a large amount of property then belonging to said Snow, over and above the said forty-five cents on the dollar to be paid plaintiffs and others, consisting of real estate and a stock of goods at Lafayette, Oregon, and a large sum of money, of which plaintiffs had no knowledge.

After three trials in the state court, in one of which there was a verdict and judgment for plaintiffs, which was reversed on appeal·for error in the charge of the court, and in the others the jury disagreed, the cause was removed to this court on July fifteenth, eighteen hundred and seventy, upon the petitition of the plaintiffs, who are non-residents of the state.

The cause was tried in this court before SAWYER, C. J., and DEADY, J., and a jury on May ninth, tenth and eleventh, and a verdict found for the plaintiffs for ten thousand one hundred and eighty-seven dollars and seventy cents, the balance due upon the note sued on. The defendants moved for a new trial upon the following grounds:

I. The evidence was insufficient to justify the verdict.

II. The verdict is against law.

III. For error in law occurring at the trial and excepted to by the defendant.

IV. For error of the court in giving and refusing instructions.

On May eighteenth the motion for new trial was argued and submitted, and taken under advisement. Before considering the first ground for a new trial it will be necessary to state the issue between the parties upon which the jury passed.

The pleadings substantially admit the making of the note as alleged, and that the composition deed was in fact signed by the plaintiffs and others, creditors of the defendants, and delivered to Jessie on November nineteenth, eighteen hundred and sixty-six, and that within two weeks thereafter, Snow, in pursuance of the terms of said deed, paid plaintiffs forty-five cents on the dollar of the principal of the note, and also a further sum, in pursuance of a private understanding between plaintiffs and Jessie, amounting in the aggregate to four thousand dollars; and that plaintiffs then accepted said sum in full payment and discharge of defendant's note and delivered the same to Snow.

The issue submitted to the jury arose upon the allegation of the replication, to the effect that the execution of the composition deed and the delivery of the note upon the receipt of the four thousand dollars was procured by the false representations of the defendants, as to their means of paying their debts, and that therefor the plaintiffs were not bound thereby.

If the evidence is sufficient to support this allegation, the verdict must be correct.

Elfelt et al, v. Snow et al.

It appears from the evidence that prior to July, eighteen hundred and sixty-two, Snow and Jessie had been engaged in the business of retail merchants at Lafayette, Oregon, and purchased goods of plaintiffs and their predecessors in business, J. Kohn & Co. About this time Jessie removed to the east of the mountains, in the Territory of Washington. Snow continued the business in Lafayette until the spring of eighteen hundred and sixty-five, when he sold the stock of goods and six lots in the town, including his store house, to one Allen, for six thousand dollars, for which the latter gave his promissory notes, with a mortgage upon the lots to secure one-half of them.

Soon after this, Snow went east of the mountains and engaged with Jessie in packing and trading between the upper Columbia and Idaho and Montana. Jessie lived at Walla Walla, and Snow appears to have been upon the road and in Montana. In November, eighteen hundred and sixty-six, Snow came into Walla Walla, bringing with him eleven thousand six hundred and sixty-four dollars in gold dust, and a young man by the name of Harris, in whose name he deposited his dust for assay, so as to prevent his creditors, including the plaintiffs, from knowing that he had it. Here Snow stopped and sent Jessie forward to Portland to effect a settlement with the Portland creditors. Upon his arrival at Portland, Jessie called upon the plaintiffs, the principal creditors, and entered into negotiations with one of them—Solomon Goldsmith—for a compromise.

According to his own testimony, Jessie then represented that Snow and Jessie, or Snow & Co., as they were called, were insolvent; that their assets consisted of only four thousand dollars in money and a train of mules worth three thousand dollars; and that with this amount—seven thousand dollars—he thought they could pay forty-five cents on the dollar of their indebtedness excluding accruing interests; that he, Jessie, had about five thousand dollars worth of individual property, and owed four thousand dollars of individual debts. When asked by Jessie how the proposed settlement would leave Snow, Jessie replied "that he knew but little about Snow's business—*that he had some means*, and that the property at Lafayette was sold;" to which Goldsmith replied "that he knew about that; that Snow had told him what he sold it for."

, According to Goldsmith's testimony, Jessie stated that Snow and Jessie were giving up all their property, and that Jessie did not state that he did not know what property Snow owned individually, but that he informed him about his own individual property, and for that reason no attempt was made to prosecute the action against Jessie.

The result of the negotiation was the execution of the composition deed of November nineteenth, Goldsmith writing it and procuring the other creditors who are parties to it to sign it. Jessie then returned to Walla Walla and gave the writing to Snow, who immediately came to Portland and proceeded to plaintiffs' store with two gold bars, worth about six thousand five hundred dollars, where he met Goldsmith and informed him that he was ready to settle upon the terms agreed upon with Jessie. Goldsmith said that in consideration of cash advanced by plaintiffs to defendents to help get their goods up the Columbia river, Jessie had promised to pay them something more than forty-five cents on the dollar —in all four thousand dollars. With some show of reluctance and surprise Snow assented to this arrangement. Goldsmith bought the gold bars, and retaining four thousand dollars for the plaintiffs and the sum due Wasserman & Co., one of the parties to the deed, gave Snow the promissory note and the remainder of the money to pay the other creditors, which he did. Before closing the transaction with Snow and handing him the note, Goldsmith testifies that he said to him, "Snow, the amount you are paying us is very small, and from the treatment you received from us we expected you would do better; but we make this settlement *only* upon the representation made to us by Jessie, that you are giving up all that you have;" and that Snow answered, "Jessie's representations are true; *we are giving up all that we have.*"

Goldsmith also testifies that he was aware of the sale of the Lafayette property to Allen, but not of the mortgage by him to Snow; and that he believed from the representations of the defendants that Snow was substantially giving up all his property, and that thereby he was induced to settle with them and accept forty-five cents on the dollar as he did.

Alfred E. Elfelt, not one of the plaintiffs, testifies that he was present at the conversation between Goldsmith and Snow, and that it took place as the former states it.

The defendant Snow was examined as a witness for the defence. His account of the transaction, so far as it went, did not differ materially from the foregoing. He stated that he told S. Goldsmith about the time of the sale to Allen that he got notes secured by mortgage for the real property in Lafayette, but was not certain that he informed him that he got Allen's notes for the stock of goods. He admitted that at the time the four thousand dollars was paid and the note returned, that T. Goldsmith said to him that the amount paid was small and that the plaintiffs were induced to make the settlement by the representations of Jessie that this was all that Snow & Co. could pay, and that he replied that he presumed that what Jessie said was correct; and also that at the same time he had in his possession of his own property six thousand five hundred dollars in gold bars and dust which he had brought with him from Montana, besides being the owner of a train of mules aforesaid, for which he ralized in cash and Allen's notes for six thousand dollars as aforesaid, which were worth three thousand dollars—in all, eleven thousand six hundred dollars over and above the seven thousand dollars of partnership funds paid to creditors.

Upon the argument of the motion the only point urged under this head was that upon the testimony of Jessie it did not appear that he had made any false representation or fraudulent concealment as to Snow's individual assets, because when asked how the settlement would leave Snow, he replied, "I know but little about Snow's business; he has some means," etc. Upon this answer it is maintained by

Elfelt et al. v. Snow et al.

counsel for defendant that Jessie disclaimed any knowledge of Snow's individual means, and that, therefore, in this respect the plaintiffs made the settlement upon their own knowledge, and not the representations of the defendants. It is admitted that the law applicable to the question was correctly given to the jury as follows : When a debtor seeks to make a composition of his debts by the payment of a part only of what he owes, he is not bound to make any representations concerning his assets or resources ; but he must act in good faith, and if he does make any such representations, either voluntarily or upon the request of his creditors, he must make it truly and completely, or he will be guilty of fraud.

Now, Jessie did not absolutely disclaim all knowledge of Snow's affairs; and under the circumstances the jury was warranted in inferring that he knew quite as much about them as he said he did. He said he knew but little about Snow's business—that he had *some means*. What was the impression that this remark was calculated to make upon Goldsmith? Certainly not that, while Snow was proposing to compromise his debts at forty-five cents on the dollar of the principal, with the sum of seven thousand dollars, he had of his own means, besides this, eleven thousand six hundred dollars in cash and cash values—enough when put together to have paid all the debts in full and left him at least two thousand dollars surplus. " Some means " is a relative expression, to be measured by surrounding circumstances. Ordinarilly, when we say that a man has something left after paying his debts or sustaining a loss, we do not mean, nor are we understood as asserting, that he has nearly twice as much left as he paid or lost. When it is said that a debtor will have some means or something left after settling with his creditors at forty-five cents on the dollar, it is necessarily understood that this *something or some means* is very small in proportion to the amount paid. In this case the aggregate amount paid the creditors was only seven thousand dollars, and it could not have been understood by Goldsmith or any person in like circumstances that the " some means " which the settlement was

Elfelt et al. v. Snow et al.

to leave Snow with, was more than one or two thousand dollars. The statement then that Snow had only " some means" left of his own after making this settlement was, under the circumstances, a false representation. Relatively he had *much* " means."

But this argument assumes that Jessie's testimony was all the evidence before the jury on this point, while the fact is that Goldsmith, corroborated by Elfelt, testifies that Jessie said that Snow and Jessie were giving up all their property, except the individual property of the latter. Neither of them state or admit that Jessie said he was ignorant of Snow's business or that the settlement would leave him with " some means." It was the province of the jury to determine from the testimony of these witnesses what representations Jessie did make. They have found by their verdict that the representation as to Snow's " means " was untrue, and I think they might reasonably have come to the same conclusion upon the testimony of Jessie alone.

Furthermore the jury were warranted in believing, from the conduct and declarations of Snow, from the time he left Montana to come to Walla Walla, that he intended to procure a settlement with his creditors for fifty or forty-five cents on the dollar, without reference to his ability to pay more, and that from the time he left the latter place to come to Portland to perform the agreement which his agent had succeeded in obtaining from his creditors, he was conscious that he had obtained, by such agreement, an unfair advantage over such creditors.

Snow persistently · concealed from the plaintiffs that he had in his possession the six thousand five hundred dollars in gold over and above the amount paid the creditors. He brought Harris with him from Montana to Portland as the pretended owner of the treasure he had for the purpose of deceiving his creditors in that respect. Although he deposited the six thousand five hundred dollars with the plaintiffs immediately on his arrival, and although their house had always been his headquarters in Portland, he did not take the six thousand five hundred dollars there, but took care to keep it out of their sight and knowledge. Now if Snow honestly believed that the settlement which he had procured was agreed to by the creditors, with the understanding, express or implied, that he would have six thousand five hundred dollars in cash left, besides the pack train and Allen's notes, he would not have taken this trouble to conceal from them the fact that he had it. His conduct in this respect reasonably admits of the explanation that he was conscious his creditors had been induced to sign the agreement to take forty-five cents on the dollar, upon the representations or understanding that · he was substantially giving up to them all he had, individually as well as otherwise. So when Goldsmith informed him that he was only induced to make this settlement upon the representations of Jessie, that he was giving up all he had, instead of replying, "you are mistaken, you must have misunderstood Jessie; I will have between eleven thousand and twelve thousand dollars, in cash and cash values left," he said that what Jessie said was correct, thereby directly adopting and affirming a representation of his agent which he knew to be grossly false in fact.

It is true that the compromise deed cannot be avoided by the plaintiffs on account of what was said or done by the defendants after it was executed; at least, so the court instructed the jury at the request of the defendant. But the conduct and declarations of Snow at the time of making the payment and receiving the note after he was informed of the representations upon which the plaintiffs were induced to sign the agreement, are pertinent to show that Snow authorized, intended or contrived, that Jessie should make such representations for the purpose of misleading and defrauding the plaintiffs.

Upon a careful consideration of the premises I am of the opinion that the verdict of the jury upon the issue arising upon the pleadings, is supported by the weight of evidence, if indeed there be any to the contrary. In my judgment, the facts and circumstances of the case all tend to prove that the defendant, Snow, intending to procure a settlement with his creditors at not to exceed fifty cents on the dollar, did, by his representations made through Jessie and his own conduct, concealments and declarations, cause the plaintiffs to believe that Snow and Jessie could only pay forty-five cents on the dollar of their indebtedness, after deducting the interest due on the same, and did thereby induce the plaintiffs to execute the composition deed, whereby they agreed to receive that sum in full of what was due them.

The remaining grounds of the motion are for alleged errors in law, and will be considered collectively. Upon the argument of this branch of the case, counsel for defendants made two points: First, That the plaintiffs cannot maintain this action, and the court erred in refusing to so instruct the jury, because the plaintiffs having induced their co-creditors to sign the composition deed, and having received from the defendants in pursuance of a secret arrangement to that effect, more than the per centum stipulated in such deed upon their demand, without the knowedge or consent of such creditors, did thereby commit a fraud upon them. Second, That the court erred in instructing the jury to the effect that Jessie, being Snow's agent to negotiate this compromise, if he through ignorance of the truth which was known to Snow, made a false representation as to the affairs or pecuniary resources of the latter, Snow is responsible for such representation, the same as if he made it in person.

Two authorities are cited in support of the first proposition, namely: *Breck* v. *Cole*, 4 Sand. 79, and *Wood* v. *Roberts*, 3 Eng. Com. Law, 411. Neither of these cases are in point. The first was an action brought by a creditor to enforce payment of a note given by his debtor, upon the execution of a composition deed, as a condition of the former's signing the same, for that portion of the debt not provided for in such deed. The court held that the arrangement was void as against the other creditors, upon whom it was a fraud, and also as to the defendant, upon the ground that it was obtained from him by moral *duress*. Now, in the case at the bar, the plaintiffs are not seeking to enforce or claim the the benefit of any secret arrangement with the debtor to the prejudice of their co-creditors in the composition deed, but on the contrary they repudiate the whole transaction as a fraud committed upon them by the defendants. This action is not brought to enforce the composition deed, nor any additional security secretly given to the plaintiffs in connection therewith, but upon the original promise of the defendants contained in this note to J. Kohn & Co.

The case of *Wood* v. *Roberts*, *supra*, was an action by a creditor for a balance of account after having accepted a portion of his demand in pursuance of an arrangement for a composition between the creditors, including himself, and the debtor. There was a verdict for the defendant, the court instructing the jury that to allow the plaintiff to·recover would be a fraud upon the other creditors who had in pursuance of the composition accepted the partial payment and discharged the defendant. In other words, the court held, as is now well established, that a debt may be discharged by the payment of a smaller sum, where it is made in pursuance of an arrangement to that effect among the creditors and with the debtor; and that therefore such composition and payment thereunder was a bar to an action by the creditor' for the remainder of his debt. The reason given by the court that to allow the creditor to maintain the action for the balance would be a fraud upon the other creditors, is not one upon which the courts have finally rested the validity and binding force of what are called composition deeds, or compromises between a failing debtor and his creditors. The general rule is that a simple agreement between a debtor and creditor that the latter will take a sum in payment of his debt less than the amount thereof is a *nudum pactum*, and therefore void for want of consideration. But when two or more creditors agree *with one another* and the debtor to take a part in payment of the whole amount of their several debts, and discharge the debtor from the remainder, it is held that the mutual promises of the creditors to and with one another is a sufficient consideration to support the agreement.

In support of the second proposition as above stated, counsel for defendant maintains that Snow is not liable for the misrepresentations of Jessie unless it appear that he expressly authorized or was cognizant of them or they were brought to his knowledge before the payment of the money and the delivery of the note.

The latter alternative of this agreement admits too much for this motion, because, as has been shown, the evidence warrants the conclusion and justified the jury in finding that Snow was aware of Jessie's misrepresentations concerning his "means," at least before he had paid plaintiffs the money and received his note. In support of the position that Snow is not liable for Jessie's misrepresentations unless he expressly authorized them, counsel cited Chit. on Com. 679, where it is said that "the mere fact of an agent having innocently made a misrepresentation of facts while affecting a contract for his principal, will not amount to fraud on the part of the latter, if the principal, though aware of the real state of the facts, was not cognizant of the misrepresentation being made, nor ever directed the agent to make it." Chitty cites *Cornfoot* v. *Fowke*, 6 M. & W. 358, which he states to have been an action for the non-performance of a written agreement to take a ready furnished house. The defence was fraud on the part of the plaintiff. The facts were that one Clarke, the agent of the plaintiff, let the house to the defendant, and that while the parties were making the bargain, the defendant asked Clarke "if there was any objection to the house," to which the latter answered, there was not, whereupon the defendant signed the agreement. Afterwards he discovered that the adjoining house was a brothel, and on that ground refused to fulfill the contract. It also appeared that the plaintiff knew of the existence of the brothel, but that the agent did not. The court held that the facts did not establish fraud on the part of the plaintiff; the Ch. B.

Lord Abinger, dissenting. In my judgment, the law of this case is doubtful, but be that as it may, the case itself is very different from the one at bar. That was a case of a misrepresentation by one of two strangers dealing with each other at arms length, about a matter which, so far as appears, was equally open to the observation of both of them.

The case at bar arises between a creditor and debtor. The latter is seeking a discharge from his debts upon the payment of forty-five cents on the dollar, on the ground that he was unable to pay more. In such case, the law very properly requires the utmost good faith on the part of the debtor. Here Snow asked to be discharged from fifty-five per centum of debts for which he was individually liable. It was natural and reasonable that the creditors should want to know what condition the proposed settlement would leave him in individually. Under these circumstances Jessie comes to the creditors to see what can be done. He was Snow's agent in this matter in a double sense: FIRST, By reason of their being partners; and, SECOND, Because Snow had specially authorized and requested him to negotiate this compromise with the creditors while he practically remained without their reach at Walla Walla. Snow spoke through Jessie, and it was his business to inform Jessie of the true condition of his affairs so that he could speak truly, if he spoke at all. If he omitted to do so either from negligence or design, and the agent made false representations concerning his means which misled the plaintiffs to their injury, he is responsible for it the same as if he made them in person. Snow cannot be allowed to have the benefit of a composition with his creditors which was confessedly procured by the false representations of his agent, upon the ground that the agent was ignorant of the truth and made the representation in good faith. If such were the law, dishonest debtors could cheat and deceive their creditors with impunity by means of honest but conveniently ignorant agents. Under the head of fraudulent concealment, it is laid down in Addison on Con. 130, that " If a debtor induces his creditors to

compound their claims and execute a deed of composition
for their several debts by concealing from them the true state
of his affairs, and withholding information which ought, in
good faith, to have been afforded, the deed will be void, and
the creditors will be remitted to their original rights,
and will be entitled to sue for the full amount of their
several debts." "If a principal * * * purposely employs an agent ignorant of the truth, in order that such
agent may innocently make a false statement, believing it to
be true, and may so deceive the party with whom he was
dealing, * * * he would be guilty of a fraud." Id.
130.

In *Stafford* v. *Bacon*, 1 Hill, 535, Cowan, J. says: "The
duty of a debtor who comes for a discharge on part payment is clear. If he willfully misrepresent or suppress any
material fact in the statement of his affairs, the accord and
satisfaction are void."

In 1 Par. on Con. 63, it is said, that "though there be no
actual fraud on the part of the agent, yet if he makes a false
representation as to a matter peculiarly within his own
knowledge or that of his principal, and thereby gets a better
bargain for his principal, such principal, although innocent,
cannot take the benefit of the transaction."

In Chit. on Con. 687, it is said "if it appear that there
has been a willful withholding by the debtor of information
respecting his estate, it will avoid the composition, and remit
the creditor to his right to sue for the whole."

In the light of these authorities, as well as upon the reason of the matter, there can be no doubt but that Snow is
responsible for Jessie's misrepresentations, though innocently
made and without his knowledge. There is no error in the
charge of the court on this point.

Indeed, after long and careful consideration, it appears
to me, both upon the law and the facts, that this verdict is
not only a just determination of the controversy between the
parties to this action, but that its effects will be wholesome
and promotive of good morals in the community upon the

subject of contracts. for the composition of debts between debtor and creditor.

The motion for a new trial must be overruled and the plaintiffs have judgment upon the verdict.

LOGAN & FRIEDENRICH, for plaintiffs; PAGE & DOLPH, for defendants.—October 30, 1871.

———•••———

UNITED STATES DISTRICT COURT—CALIFORNIA.

A creditor of an insolvent who has reasonable ground to believe him to be such, can assign his demand to a debtor of the insolvent whose debt is not yet payable, so as to enable the latter to offset the demand so assigned to him against the debt due from him to the insolvent, the latter debt having become due and payable at the time the offset is claimed.

In re CITY BANK OF SAVINGS, LOAN AND DISCOUNT.

HOFFMAN, J.—The question presented on the facts as developed by the evidence taken by the register, is whether a creditor of an insolvent who has reasonable ground to believe him to be such, can assign his demand to a debtor of the insolvent, whose debt is not yet payable, so as to enable the latter to offset the demand so assigned to him against the debt due from him to the insolvent, the latter debt having become due and payable at the time the offset is claimed.

The register was of opinion that the debts and credits which it sought to offset against each other were not "*mutual*" within the meaning of the statute, inasmuch as at the time of the bankruptcy the debt *owed* by the bank was due and payable, while the debt *to* it was not.

The question whether a debt payable *in futuro* could be set off against a debt payable *in præsenti* was one of the earliest which arose under the English bankrupt act. It was decided in the affirmative on the ground that though there might not be debts mutually payable between the parties, there were mutual *credits*, and that the case came within the equity of the statute. *Ex parte* Prescott, 1 Atk. 230; *Dobson* v. *Lockhart*, 5 T. R. 133; *Alsagn* v. *Currie*, 12 M. & W. 751; *ex parte* Wagstaff, 13 Ves. 65; *Sheldon* v. *Rothschild*, 8 Tamb. 156; *Atkinson* v. *Elliott*, 9 T. & R. 378; Robson on Bankruptcy, 265.

The same question has received a similar solution in the United States, under both the former and the present bankrupt acts.

In *Marks* v. *Barker*, it was held by Washington, J., that the acceptor or endorser of a bill of exchange who has paid the bill after the bankruptcy of the drawer, may offset the same against the bankrupt's assignees, the case being one of mutual credits given before the bankruptcy, although the money was not paid until after. 1 Wash. C. C. 178.

In the case of *Catlin* v. *Foster*, Deady, J., after a careful consideration of the whole subject, held that a party who has acted under a deed of trust declared void, as being contrary to the provisions of the bankrupt act, may set off the value of the services rendered by him under the deed, against the claim of the assignees for property of the bankrupt received by him. 3 N. B. R. 134.

In *Fort* v. *McCully*, 59 Barb., cited in A. L. Reg., it was held that deposits made with a private banker, subject to the call of the depositor, are not to be deemed *due* until demand, and, therefore, if the banker transfers the depositor's notes before demand, the latter *it seems*, cannot enforce a set-off against the holder, either at law or in equity. But that where the banker being insolvent, made a general assignment, including the notes of the depositor whose deposit was not yet due, and directed his assignee to pay his debts in the same order and manner in which the estate of a bankrupt is required to be used and applied for the payment of debts proved and allowed under the provisions of the bankrupt act, the depositor was entitled to his set-off, and the assignee could only recover the balance after deducting the set-off.

These decisions seem not only the unavoidable result of the express terms of the bankrupt act, but necessarily required by considerations of reason and justice.

By the nineteenth section, all debts existing, but not payable until a future day, may be proved against the estate (a rebate of interest being made when no interest is payable), and by the twentieth section, mutual debts and credits are required to be set-off against each other whenever the claim sought to be used as a set-off is "in its nature a debt not provable against the estate and has been purchased or transferred after the filing of the petition." A claim, therefore, for a debt provable against the estate, and transferred before the filing of the petition, falls within the very terms of the section.

The rule thus established seems indispensable to the attainment of justice. "Natural equity," says Lord Mansfield, in *Green* v. *Farmer*, 4 Barr. 2214–20, "requires that cross demands should compensate each other by deducting the less sum from the greater, and that the difference only is the sum which can be justly due. But positive law, for the sake of the forms of proceeding and convenience, has said that each must sue and recover separately in separate actions."

The civil law followed what Lord Mansfield declares to be the dictate of natural equity. 2 Evans Pot. on Oblig. 98. And in England and most of the states of the Union, statutes of set-off have been enacted, allowing cross demands to be used as set-offs in specified cases; and even courts of common law have long been in the habit of allowing judgment to be set-off against each other. But even in those where the counter claim cannot be set up as a defence *pro tanto* to the action, the party holding it can sue and recover judgment upon it. The refusal to allow him to use it as a set-off leaves his right to enforce his demand unimpaired.

But when a bankruptcy has occurred, the creditors' right of action is suspended. The whole estate of the debtor is taken possession of by the court, and the holder of an unsecured claim against it is entitled merely to his *pro rata* share of the assets. It would therefore be the height of injustice to compel a debtor of the bankrupt to pay to the assignee the full amount of his debt, while for a demand of equal or greater amount against the bankrupt he can only receive such dividends as the assets may afford.

A similar injustice would be done to the estate of the bankrupt, (if offsets were not allowed,) where the creditor has also become bankrupt. For the estate of the creditor might receive dividends on the debt due him, while it might be insufficient to pay dividends of a like amount on the debts due by him. To avoid these results, liberal and comprehensive provisions for the allowance of offsets have been made in the bankrupt acts of England and America ; but their object would be in a great measure defeated, if their operation were restricted to those debts only, which, at the time of the bankruptcy, were not only *due but payable*.

The objection therefore that the debt of the debtor who seeks the benefit of the set-off was not *payable* until after the filing of the petition, must be overruled.

The second objection urged has more force.

It is contended that the transaction was in its nature a fraud upon the bankrupt act ; that its object and effect was to hinder or defeat its operation and to evade its provisions, by preventing assets from coming into the hands of the assignee, and by indirectly enabling a creditor to obtain full satisfaction of his demand by selling to a debtor of the bankrupt a claim to be used by him as a set-off.

That such may be the effect of this transaction, if this set-off be allowed, I am not prepared to deny.

But I am unable to see what authority this court has to prevent it.

By the terms of the act, all mutual debts and credits must be set off against each other, and the balance only allowed or paid subject to two conditions : first, that the claim is in its nature provable against the estate ; and second, that it has not been transferred or purchased by the debtor claiming the benefit of it, after the filing of the petition. This latter proviso contains an obvious negative pregnant, and implies a declaration that the claim may be used as a set-off, if acquired even by purchase, at any time before the commencement of the proceedings.

Had congress seen fit to prohibit the acquisition of such claims, for the purpose of using them as set-offs by a debtor of a bankrupt who has reasonable cause to believe that the latter is insolvent, it would have been easy so to provide. But there is no such provision. And even if such a limitation upon the right to acquire or use a demand as a set-off had been imposed, it is reasonable to suppose that some period of time would have been fixed after which the transaction could no longer be questioned. By the thirty-fifth section, certain transfers intended to give a preference, or to hinder or delay the operation of the act, or to prevent the property of the bankrupt from coming into the hands of the assignee, are .declared void, *provided they have been made within four months and six months* respectively before the filing of the petition.

But if the court should declare in this case the transfer of the demand against the bankrupt void, and unavailable to the debtor as a set-off, for the reason that it would have the effect to give a creditor a preference, and to hinder and defeat the operation of the act, what period of time is it to assign within which the transfer can be avoided? Is it to adopt the period of four months, or six months, or some other arbitrary limitation?

That some period of time should be fixed after which transfers analogous to this, and which the act pronounces void cannot be assailed, congress has clearly indicated.

It seems an unavoidable inference that if it had been intended to prohibit transfers like that in the case at bar, or rather to render them unavailable for the object intended, the act would not only have so declared in explicit terms, but a definite period would have been fixed within which its provisions should operate upon them; and that the court in

In re City Bank of Savings, Loan and Discount.

the absence of any such provision, has no right to assume the legislative function by first declaring the transfer ineffectual, and then fixing an arbitrary period, after which it shall be held valid.

The bankrupt act, moreover, being a special statute, and to a certain extent in derogation of rights existing at common law, or under state legislation, its provisions ought not to be construed under suggestions of its probable object, policy or spirit, to embrace cases not provided for by its terms. By the law of this state, and I presume of that of the most of the states, the claim set up in this case could be used by the debtor as a set-off in action brought against him by the bank.

He who contends that it is made unavailable by the bankrupt act should point to some clear and unmistakable provision to that effect in the act.

It is also to be observed that by the amended insolvent law of Massachusetts, from which the provisions of the bankrupt act are in great part derived, the benefit of offsets acquired under circumstances like those of the case at bar was withheld.

Congress, therefore, in omitting to incorporate that provision into the bankrupt act may justly be deemed to have intentionally declined to adopt it. It would seem, on the contrary, as if it had been designed in this particular to follow the English bankrupt act.

The proviso in that act is as follows : "Provided that the party claiming the benefit of the set-off had not, when such credit was given, notice of an act of bankruptcy by such bankrupt committed."

Under this proviso it was held, in an action brought by the assignees of certain bankers, that a party had a right to set-off notes of such bankers, taken by him *after he knew they had stopped payment*, but before he knew they had committed an act of bankruptcy. *Hawkins* v. *Whittier*, 10 B. & P. 217 ; *Dickson* v. *Cast*, 1 B. & Ad. 343. And the act of bankruptcy must have been that on which the adjudication was founded, or one capable of sustaining it. . *Ex parte* Bickett, 2 Rose, 71; *ex parte* Sharp, 3 M. D. & D. 490; 8 Jur. 1,012; Robson on Bankruptcy, 272.

But a debtor of this bankrupt will not be allowed to set-off a debt transferred to him *after* the bankruptcy, for the debt is to a third person, and the creditor cannot, *after the bankruptcy*, by a transaction with a third person, vary the relation in which he stood to the bankrupt at the time of the bankruptcy. *Dickson* v. *Evans*, 6 T. R. 57; *Marsh* v. *Chambers*, Strange, 1,234.

The rule established by these cases seems to have been adopted by congress in framing the provisions of the bankrupt act with regard to offsets. A debtor of the bankrupt is allowed to set-off a debt due to him from the bankrupt, provided it has been purchased by or transferred to him before the filing of the petition, *i. e.* before the bankruptcy. I think that these provisions must receive a similar construction to that given by the English courts to the closely analogous provisions of the English law. The objection is therefore overruled.

It is also objected that the transfer of the debt sought to be set-off was not absolute, but conditional on the debtor's being allowed to avail himself of it. But I see no ground for this suggestion in the evidence. The claim of the depositor seems to have been regularly and formally assigned to the debtor of the bankrupt, and the latter appears to be the legal owner and holder of it.

My opinion is that the offset claimed should be allowed.

UNITED STATES DISTRICT COURT—S. D. NEW YORK.

[Before JOHN FITCH, Register.]

An assignee is an officer of the court and acts subject to its orders. The bankrupt is entitled to a certificate of the assignee giving the names and residence of the creditors who have proven their claims, as per form, in order to enable him to move the court for an order to show cause why he should not be discharged. &c. The register has the power to make such an order and it is the duty of the assignee to obey it. Motions to compel an assignee to do his duty are properly made before the register.

In re BLAISDELL et al.

This case is now pending before me. It is an involuntary proceeding. At the first meeting of creditors herein John Mackenzie was duly chosen assignee and accepted said trust, his appointment was duly confirmed and the usual assignment of the bankrupts estate and effects was made and delivered to him; that quite a large number of claims have been proven against the estate, which proofs of claims have been delivered to said assignee; that Alvah Blaisdell, one of said bankrupts on the twenty-seventh day of October, eithteen hundred and seventy-one, filed his petition for final discharge in the office of the clerk of this court in bankruptcy; that the said cause is before me in accordance with the rules and practice of this court. Whereupon said bankrupt applied to me for an order to show cause why he should not be discharged. I thereupon made and delivered to said bankrupt duplicate lists of all the debts proven against his estate, taken from my books, the record of this court; that it appears from the petition of said bankrupt, that said list of debts &c., were delivered to and left with said John Mackenzie, assignee as aforesaid, for his signature, on or about the twenty-ninth day of October, eighteen hundred and seventy-one; that said petition further states upon information and belief that said lists of debts were by said assignee delivered to one D. M. Porter, Esq., his attorney, who was called upon several times by one James J. Yates, Esq., on behalf of said bankrupt, for the purpose of obtaining said lists of debts, &c; that said D. M. Porter stated to him that he would examine said lists at his leisure, and if he found them correct he would send them to the register; that said Poter did not send said lists of debts &c. to me and said bankrupt on the eighth day of November, eighteen hundred and seventy-one, applied to me by petition duly verified, for an order to show cause why said John Mackenzie, assignee as aforesaid, should not sign said lists of debts, &c. and deliver the same to me. Whereupon I issued an order to show cause, directed to said John Mackenzie, assignee, requiring him to show cause before me on the fourteenth day of November, eighteen hundred and seventy-one, at twelve o'clock noon of that day, why he should not sign said lists of debts, &c.

That a copy of said petition and order to show cause, were duly served upon said assignee, on the ninth day of November, eighteen hundred and seventy-one, as appears by affidavit. That on the return day of said order to show cause, to wit, November fourteenth, eighteen hundred and seventy-one, said assignee failed to appear either in person or by attorney, neither did he sign or deliver said lists of debts, &c. to me or said bankrupt.

The bankrupt is, by the rules and practice of this court, entitled to an order to show cause and the certificate, as it is necessary to file with the petition for discharge a list of the creditors who have duly proved their debts, and it is also the duty of the assignee to certify the same, as notice to the creditors who have proven their debts must be sent by mail to all such creditors. Gazzam on Bankruptcy, 135. It has been the uniform practice in this district for the assignee to make such certificate, which certificate most certainly comes within the word " Instrument, " as per section eighteen of the bankrupt act, and it is but reasonable that he should do so, as many claims as are proven before the courts, other than of the district in which the cause is pending, and sent directly to the assignee in the case, instead of being first sent to the register in charge, to be by him adjudicated upon, entered upon the record of the court and then delivered to the assignee, as they should first be entered upon the records of the court. It has been the uniform practice in this district to have such certificate signed both by the register and the assignee, in order to enable the bankrupt to have a correct list filed with the clerk, so that all the creditors may receive the notice of the order to show cause, thus enabling them to oppose the bankrupt's discharge, and also freeing the bankrupt from any imputations of filing an incorrect list, or of withholding the name of any creditor, also leaving his discharge free from any taint of fraud, and avoids the appearance of any evil intent.

I hold it to be the duty of the register in the trial of the causes before them to see that the rules and practice of the court shall be complied with, and that the proceedings had before them should be in conformity with the rules of the court, the general orders and the bankrupt law. This doctrine is held by the court *in re* Bushing, 3 N. B. R. 167. This motion is properly made before the register as the register is the court before whom it must be heard. *In re* Carow, 4. N. B. R. 178; 41 How. 112; *in re* Heller, 5 N. B. R. 46; 41 How. 213.

The bankrupt has a right to make this motion, as the refusal of the assignee, or his neglect to give such certificate operates as a stay of proceedings, as the certificate is a necessary proceeding in the case in order to enable the bankrupt to obtain the order to show cause why he should not be discharged, and to notify the creditors entitled by law to such notice. This proceeding is *ex parte.* The bankrupt is entitled to the order as a matter of right. It is the duty of the register to grant it. It is an application to the court to require the assignee, who is an officer of the court, to do his duty. A creditor has no right to oppose it, and no notice of it is required to be given to any one but the assignee. Should the assignee be dissatisfied with the decision of the register, he has the right to appeal from the order at chambers to the special term the same as a creditor would have from the

In re Blaisdell et al.

decision of the register allowing amendments to schedules. *In re* Hill, N. B. R. Sup. iv; *in re* Orne, N. B. R. Sup. xviii; *in re* Jones, 2 N. B. 20; *in re* Levy, N. B. R. Sup. xxx; *in re* Patterson N. B. R. Sup. xxii; *in re* Morford, N. B. R. Sup. xlvi; *in re* Watts, 2 N. B. R. 45.

The decison of this motion necessarily involves the question of the duties of an assignee and the power of the courts over them and their proceedings. The law and practice of the courts give sufficient power to the courts for all practical purposes to compel the assignee to obey its orders. It arises in these proceedings before me to certify the same to the courts. The English authorities hold an assignee to be a person appointed by the court during the pendency of a suit to do and perform certain acts under the direction and order of the court, or under the provisions of some statutory enactment. Wyatt's P. R., 355 ; also, see Gazzam's American and English Bankruptcy Digest. He is an officer of the court, *in re* Burke, B. & B. 74, and cannot be disturbed by anybody without leave of the court. His appointment was provisional only, and was subject at all times, upon proper cause shown, to removal by the court. *Skipp* v. *Hamond*, 3 Atk. 564 ; *Cooke* v. *Gayur*, 3 Atk. 690. He was appointed by the court as an indifferent person and as an officer of the court to act on behalf of the parties interested.

The supreme court of this state at a general term, first judicial district, INGRAHAM, J., held that an assignee was an officer of the court, and it was the duty of the court to make all orders to secure the proper fulfillment of his duties, and such has been the uniform decisions of all our state courts. The rights, duty and power of the court to control the action of assignees is clearly given by section eighteen of the bankrupt act, and it is also in the inherent power of the court to exercise a sound discretion and controlling jurisdiction of its officers and suitors, as well as the subject matter of the action in any proceeding pending before it. 18 Wend 652 ; 1 Denio, 659 ; 11 Johnson, 254 ; 1 Gra. Pr., 3d. Ed. 661–675, Gazzam's American and English Bankruptcy Digest.

In re Blaisdell et al.

By rule nineteen of the general orders in bankruptcy, the duties of an assignee are defined and his actions governed by the orders of the court. In a recent decision by the supieme court of the United States, CHASE, C. J. in the opinion of the court, all the justices concurring, " That an assignee must do his duty," and it is but fair to hold that if he neglects or refuses to do his duty, the court will, on motion, compel him to do so which can be done by the judge or register as the circumstances of the case requires. In a case like this it is clearly the intention of the bankrupt act that the register should exercise this authority while the case is pending before him.

By section eighteen of the bankrupt act, " An assignee refusing or unreasonably neglecting to execute an instrument when lawfully required by the court, or disobeying a lawful order or decree of the court in the premises, may be punished as for a contempt of court.

. Any person interested in the acts of an assignee may apply to the court for an order requiring of such assignee the specific performance of any of his duties ; and that in this case the register has the power to grant the order asked for. *In re* Gettleson, 1 N. B. R. 170 ; American and English Bankruptcy Digest.

It was plainly the intention of congress to give the registers acting as assistant district judges the same power in all respects in cases pending before them that the district judges have ; such has been the uniform decision of all the district judges and the registers who have written on the subject. Such power was absolutely necessary to be given to the registers, in order to enable them to discharge the judicial duties devolving upon them. *In re* Kingon, 3 N. B. R. 113 ; 38 How. 392.

The assignee does not, either in person or by attorney, show any cause why this motion should not be granted, therefore admits the facts stated in the motion papers, and that the bankrupt is entitled to this specific relief. It is but reasonable and right that he should give the certificate, and

In re Blaisdell et al.

the refusal to do so, especially after the notice of this motion is improper, and a lack of good faith as assignee, the non-performance of a plain and imperative duty and calls at once for the imperative order of this court requiring him to do his duty.

I propose to grant the following order, and ask the direction of the district court thereon which order will be binding on the assignee, and it will be his duty to obey it or be punished for contempt of court.

At the request of the bankrupt I certify the fact of the non-performance of duty on the part of the assignee to the district court.

Upon the motion papers, proceedings in bankruptcy and application of Alvah Blaisdell, one of the said bankrupts, and upon all the proceedings under the order to show cause of November eighth, eighteen hundred and seventy-one, it is ordered that John Mackenzie, the assignee herein, furnish and deliver to Alvah Blaisdell, one of the above named bankrupts, a list of all the debts and claims proved against the estate of said bankrupts which have come into his hands, with the places of residence and post office addresses, when stated, duly signed by said John Mackenzie as assignee herein, within three days after the service of a copy of this order upon him.

First. Upon the motion papers and the proceedings in this case before me, I decide as a matter of law, that this motion to compel the assignee to perform a duty merely to give the usual certificate of the names of the creditors who have proved their claims herein is one which he has a right to make *ex parte*, and the regester the right to hear and determine, and that none but the assignee and bankrupt has a right to be heard upon the motion.

Second. That the bankrupt is by the rules and practice of this court and the bankrupt law, entitled to the usual certificate, giving the names of the creditors who have proved their claims, and that the assignee in this case sign a certificate setting forth the names of the creditors who have proved their claims as per form.

In this case the relief asked for by the bankrupt is necessary in his proceedings. It is the duty of the assignee to make the required certificate; he has been duly requested to make it. He has failed to do so. The motion of the bankrupt is granted.　　　　　　　　　JOHN FITCH, *Register.*

BLATCHFORD, J.—I think that the register has power to make the proposed order, and that it will be the duty of the assignee to comply with it.—December 1, 1871.

--- • ◦ • ---

COURT OF COMMON PLEAS—HAMILTON COUNTY, OHIO.

[NOVEMBER TERM, 1871.]

A discharge, unless impeached for fraud, is a bar to the continuance of a suit on a claim which was provable under the bankrupt law.
Granting a second trial has the effect of setting aside a judgment previously rendered. Case dismissed without prejudice, leaving the party to their remedy under the bankrupt law. Costs to be paid by plaintiffs.

HUMBLE & CO. v. *CARSON.*

This suit was commenced in eighteen hundred and sixty-nine. The plaintiffs sue for forty-two hundred dollars, balance claimed to be due them from defendant upon a contract for building two houses on Fourth street, in Cincinnati.

Carson answered over two years ago admitting the claim of plaintiffs, but claiming that he over paid them, and that they owe him nineteen hundred dollars.

The case was tried and resulted in a judgment for four hundred and twenty dollars; plaintiffs gave bond and took a second trial under the statute. Since that time James Carson, defendant, has been adjudged a bankrupt in the United States district court and has been discharged. He now pleads his discharge in bar to the further maintenance of this suit. The parties now submit the question to the court whether the discharge is a bar to further proceedings in this court or not.

J. H. CLEMMER' for plaintiffs; CARTER GAZLAY for defendant.

BURNETT, J.—The discharge, unless impeached for fraud, is certainly a bar to the continuance of this suit; the claim of the plaintiffs was provable under the bankrupt law. The judgment rendered has been set aside by the granting of a second trial.

This court could not render a judgment against the defendant in the face of his discharge, and could not render a judgment in his favo.* on his counter-claim, as that passed out of his hands and now belongs to his assignee in bankruptcy. The bankrupt act and the decisions clearly show that the discharge is a complete bar. *Ex parte* Foster, 2 Story, C. C. R. 132; *Odell* v. *Wootten,* 4 N. B. R. 46; *Fox* v. *Weed,* 21 La. An. R. 58.

The case will be dismissed out of this court without prejudice, leaving the parties to their remedy under the bankrupt law, the plaintiffs to pay the cost.

----•◦•----

UNITED STATES CIRCUIT COURT—W. D. MICHIGAN.

A suspension of payment of commercial paper for fourteen days under section thirty-nine, before the amendment of July fourteenth, eighteen hundred and seventy, was *per se* an act of bankruptcy.

The ommission to pay such paper for fourteen days, subsequent to that amendment, is a suspension within its meaning, although the paper fell due and was dishonored before its passage.

BALDWIN et al. v. *WILDER et al.*

EMMONS, J.—The only question necessary to notice is whether a suspension of payment of commercial paper for fourteen days, *subsequent* to the amendment of July fourteenth, eighteen hundred and seventy, and within six months from the filing of the petition, is *per se* an act of bankruptcy, when there has also been a suspension of payment of the same paper before that enactment.

The learned judge of the court below held that a suspension commencing before the amendment and continued afterwards, was not affected by it, but must be governed by the original act under which it commenced; holding, also, that under the act as it stood before the amendment a suspension for fourteen days, without fraud, was not an act of bankruptcy. He dismissed the petition.

We are unable to concur in either of these views. A suspension of payment for fourteen days, before the amendment, was *per se* an act of bankruptcy. If this were not so, we are clear that such suspension commenced before and continued after the amendment, for fourteen days, is so.

While section thirty-nine stood in its original form, a large majority of the adjudications held that under it a suspension of payment for fourteen days was *per se* an act of bankruptcy.

In re Wells, N. B. R. Sup. xxxvii, was a petition *in invitum* in the northern district of New York. The petition alleged that the respondent "being a merchant, &c., fraudulently stopped and *suspended, and had not resumed payment* of his commercial paper within a period of fourteen days." There was proof of the suspension, but no allegation or proof that it was fraudulent. HALL, J., says: "It was contended on the argument that this provision which authorises proceedings *in invitum* against any person, 'who, being a merchant, &c., has fraudulently stopped or suspended and not resumed payment within a period of fourteen days,' does not authorise such proceedings *unless the original stoppage or suspension of payment was fraudulent, no matter how long such suspension may be continued.*" He holds that such is not the true construction of the provision, but that "its true construction requires an adjudication if a merchant, &c., *who has suspended and not resumed payment of his commercial*

Baldwin et al. v. Wilder et al.

paper within a period of fourteen days, although such suspen sion or stoppage was not fraudulent."

"The provision," he says, "embraces two cases : the one of an original, fraudulent stoppage, in which proceedings may be instituted at once, and the other of a suspension of payment, not fraudulent, and not *per se* an act of bankruptcy, but which, if continued for more than fourteen days, becomes an act of bankruptcy by its continuance." He applies the same rule to a petition where there was an averment of fraud in the petition. *In re* Weikert *et al.* 3 N. B. R. 5 ; see also *in re* Cowles, 1 N. B. R. 42. *In re* Thompson *et al.* 3 N. B. R. 45, DRUMMOND, J., uses language which has been literally adopted by the amendment of July, eighteen hundred and seventy. Similar rulings are made *in re* Schoo, 3 N. B. R. 52, and *Doan* v. *Compton*, 2 N. B. R. 182. *In re* Noyes, LONGYEAR, J., in his charge, adopted and applied the doctrin.

I think the opinion of SHIPMAN, J., may be added to these. *In re* Ballard *et al.* 2 N. B. R. 84. Certainly he does not, as the respondents' counsel suppose, rule the other way.

A contrary construction makes the law read substantially as follows : If the merchant *fraudulently* suspends *at all*, if but for one hour, he shall be adjudged a bankrupt and the *same* consequence—no more, no less—shall issue if he continue this fraudulent suspension for fourteen days. All in reference to the fourteen days suspension is thus stricken from the law. Were it necessary to sustain this petition we should reject this latter construction of the original act, and say a fourteen days' suspension was sufficient without fraud.

A less number of judgments, with varying and somewhat contradictory reasons, decided that the petition must in all cases contain an averment that the stoppage was *fraudulent*. *In re* Leeds, 1 N. B. R. 138 ; *Gillies* v. *Cone et at.* 2 N. B. R. 10 ; *in re* Davis, 3 N. B. R. 89 ; *in re* Lowenstein, 2 N. B. R. 99 ; *in re* Dibblee *et al.* 2 N. B. R. 186.

But these same judgments, and others by the learned judge, hold that suspension by a *solvent* debtor is fraudulent; that the like act by an *insolvent* who neglects *himself* to go into bankruptcy is also fraudulent; and when it is added that he also holds that the omission to pay a single note at maturity is *evidence of insolvency*, it is not perceived that the least difference exists between the practical results of his judgments and those which simply affirm that suspension of fourteen days is *per se* sufficient. Substantially the same criticism may be made in reference to the decision by FIELD, J., *in re* Jersey Window Glass Co. 1 N. B. R. 113. Indeed, they who hold that the fourteen days' suspension is insufficient without fraud, create such severe tests in reference to *its existence*, that practically mere suspension becomes sufficient. We prefer the more direct and less technical mode of arriving at the same result, which gives all the clauses of section thirty-nine a rational meaning.

It was to terminate this apparent conflict, and enact in plain language the construction which had made the fourteen days' suspension an act of bankruptcy *per se*, that the amendment was passed. It is in the very words of several judgments declaring how the former clause *should* judicially be read. It provides that if the merchant, &c., has *fraudulently* stopped payment, "*or* has stopped or suspended and not resumed payment of his commercial paper within a period of fourteen days he shall be adjudged a bankrupt." Looking to the reading of the original enactments, its literal adoption by an amendment, and the canons of interpretation which nearly all tribunals which administer the statute have to it, as a remedial and benificent law whose spirit of equality should be extended by liberal constructions, I think no such exception to the operation of this clause should be set up by judicial implication. A suspension of payment should not be excluded because it had commenced before its passage. 2 N. B. R. 123; 3 N. B. R. 86; 2 Abb. 243.

I know of no precedent for giving a purely remedial statute a wholly prospective operation, unless there is some-

In re Dupee.

thing in its language or nature that imperatively demands it. The general rule is quite the other way.

It seems to us, however, that this case requires no retrospective application of the amendment. The suspension continued for months *after* it was adopted. It is none the less a suspension afterwards, because there was *also* one *before*.

Must a creditor commence proceedings within *six months* from the first suspension of commercial paper? Would not the petition be sustained by showing that the debtor had fraudulently suspended within six months, even though it *commenced* beyond that time? Is the suspension an indivisible act that once committed is not continuing? The law is full of analogies to the contrary. Every fourteen days' suspension, no matter how often repeated or how long continued, are but successive acts of bankruptcy, and the suspension by the respondents in this case, after the amendment, we must hold to be within it.

Decree below dismissing petition reversed and ordered that an adjudication of bankruptcy be entered.

DON M. DICKINSON, for creditors. EGGLESTON & KLEINHAUS, for debtors.—December, 1871.

UNITED STATES DISTRICT COURT—MASSACHUSETTS.

The district court sitting in bankruptcy has a right to recall a final decree granting a discharge to a bankrupt upon application made during the term of court at which the decree was passed.

It seems that the court has the power to do this after the term has ended. This power will be exercised in a case in which counsel opposing the discharge was prevented by a sudden and overpowering accident from being present at the hearing, if it shall be made to appear that the opposing creditors were in fact prevented by the accident from presenting their case, and if they believe they had, and have, a good case upon the merits, showing fraud in the bankrupt.

In re J. E. DUPEE.

In this case the firm of Stephen, Hill & Stevens, creditors of the bankrupt, filed specifications of objection to his discharge and a day was set, by notice of the debtor, agreed to by the creditors, for a hearing before the court, neither party having asked for a jury. On the day appointed, the debtor attended, and just before the adjournment of the court asked for his discharge, and made proof of the notice and agreement. The creditors not appearing, the order was passed and the discharge was issued in due form. Soon after, and within the same term, the creditors filed a petition setting forth that they were contesting and intending to contest the discharge, and that their counsel was unavoidably prevented from being present or from informing them in order that they might obtain a postponement. They therefore prayed that the order might be rescinded and the discharge recalled. The debtor appeared and opposed the motion.

W. W. WARREN, for petitioners; G. A. SOMERBY and W. N. MASON, for debtor.

LOWELL, J.—There is nothing in the bankrupt act which bears directly upon the case, excepting section thirty-four, authorising the court to set aside a discharge for certain causes and for certain circumstances, one of which is that the creditor asking for such reversal, had no knowledge of the facts before the discharge was granted, a circumstance which these petitioners cannot truly allege. They therefore invoke the power which they say every court has to vary or annul its decree when justice requires it.

This power is denied by the bankrupt. No decisions were referred to by either party, excepting those in the southern district of New York, in which the court had re-heard a case after refusing a discharge. The power of the court does not seem to have been brought in question in those cases; nor does it appear very clearly that any final decree had been made in them before the re-hearing. In this case a final decree was rendered under section thirty-two, and a certificate thereof was given, and the case in bankruptcy closed. This would seem to be the termination

In re Dupee.

of the jurisdiction which by section one is to last until the close of the proceedings in bankruptcy. Still, I think the court must have the same inherent power as all other courts to recall its own decrees,'or to vary or annul them as justice may require. All the courts claim and exercise this power when it is the only remedy for the party aggrieved. It has been admitted, in criminal as well as in civil cases, that the court may vary its judgment and impose a different sentence at any time during the same term. *Com.* v. *Weymouth*, 2 Allen, 144, and cases cited.

In admiralty; the time and mode of opening a final decree in a defaulted action are regulated by a general rule of the supreme court; but this is not understood to take away the right to re-hear cases not falling within the rule. 2 Conk. Adm. 360.

It is generally conceded that the judgments of a court of common law may be reversed, altered or amended during the term ; and the modern cases put no such limit upon the power but assert the right of any court to amend its decrees in its discretion, at any time. No matter how closely in the opinion of judges the exercise of this right ought to be confined, the discretion appears to be admitted. *Stickney* v. *Davis*, 17 Pick. 169; *Janvrin* v. *Smith*, 1 Sprague, 13; *Northwestern Insurance Co.* v. *Hopkins*, 14 A. L. Reg. 44; the Monarch, 1 W. Rol. 21; the Fortuna, 4 Rob. 278; *Chase* v. *Scales*, 10 M. & W. 488; the New England, 3 Sumner, 506; the Martha, B. & H. 171.

The power of the court appears to me to be clear, and whether it is limited to the term is immaterial in this case. It was admitted that a sudden and overpowering accident prevented the attendance of the creditors' counsel at the hearing, and this seems to me to present a case where if injustice has been done, and there is no other remedy, the court ought to reverse its own decree. It does not appear to be a case for the supervisory power of the circuit court, because this court has committed no error, and I do not see that there is any other remedy than the one now asked for.

In re Isaacs and Cohn.

If, however, no injustice has been done, or if the petitioners were not in fact prevented from trying their case by the accident referred to, they ought not to be permitted to litigate anew. If they shall file affidavits showing that they were prepared with evidence to substantiate the specific charges of fraud alleged by them, which I believe are two, and that they would have been ready to try those questions on the day appointed, and that they believe they have a good case on the merits in respect to these charges of fraud, I will re-open the decree so far as such frauds are concerned. I do not think I ought to do so for any mere technical matter, such as an inaccuracy in bookkeeping without fraud.

Ten days to be allowed the petitioners to file affidavits. April, 1871.

UNITED STATES DISTRICT. COURT—CALIFORNIA.

An agreement between two traders to unite their stocks in trade as the capital of a partnership to be formed between them, and to convert the separate business debts of either into joint debts of the firm, will not entitle a separate creditor who has not acceded in any way to the arrangement before bankruptcy, to prove his claim as a joint creditor of the firm against the partnership estate.

In re ISAACS & COHN.

HOFFMAN, J.—It appears by the statement of facts reported by the register and admitted by the attorneys for the respective parties, that on the seventh of March, eighteen hundred and seventy-one, the above bankrupts, by a writing under seal, entered into a contract of partnership, by which it was agreed that the parties who had previously been doing business on their individual accounts should unite their stocks of goods and uncollected book accounts, to form a joint capital for the partnership, and that the copartnership should assume and become liable for all the separate business debts of either partner, as shown by his books.

The firm having become bankrupt after incurring partnership debts, a creditor of one of the partners, (and who appeared by the books of the latter to have been such,) for goods sold before the formation of the partnership, offered to prove his debt as a joint debt with a view of sharing in the distribution of the firm assets.

No evidence was offered to show that the separate creditor acceded to the substitution of the firm liability for that of the partner by whom the debt was contracted. He does not even appear to have been aware of the terms and conditions of the agreement between the partners.

The register was of opinion that the proof offered should not be received, and the question having been fully argued, is submitted to the court for its decision.

The question thus presented, viz: Whether an agreement between two traders to unite their stocks in trade as the capital of a partnership to be formed between them, and to convert the separate business debts of either into joint debts of the firm, will entitle a separate creditor who has not acceded in any way to the arrangement, to prove in bankruptcy as a joint creditor of the firm, is closely analogous to that which arises, where, on the dissolution of the firm, the continuing partner takes an assignment of the joint assets, and agrees to be responsible for the firm debts; and after bankruptcy, a joint creditor who has not, before bankruptcy, assented to the conversion of his debt, seeks to prove it against the separate estate of the continuing partner.

Both of these questions have frequently been submitted to the courts and have received with one or two exceptions a uniform answer.

A joint debt may be converted into a separate debt, or a separate debt into a joint debt, either with or without *an extinguishment* of the original obligation.

In the former case the creditor can only rely on his debt according to its new quality, and is therefore entitled to only one mode of proof. In the latter case, as the old debt still subsists, he can take advantage of it in either its old or its new form, and is consequently entitled to an election of proof. Story on Part. 369 ; Collyer on Part. 767.

As no arrangement between debtor or debtors and third persons, or between themselves, can impair or destroy the liability of either or all of them to a creditor, without his consent, it is evident that to establish an *extinguishment* of the old debt, it must appear that he has accepted the new liability as a substitute for and in discharge of the old.

But when a conversion merely is set up, *i. e.*, the creation of a new liability without an extinguishment of the old, as this is ordinarily beneficial to the creditor, less evidence of an assent by him to the arrangement will be sufficient than in cases where it is sought to substitute a separate for a joint liability. Robson on Bankruptcy, 599, and cases cited.

But even where a mere conversion is set up, as in this case, evidence of the assent of the creditor before bankruptcy seems always to be required.

In the case of *ex parte* Williams, 1 Buck, 13, a trader, indebted, entered into a partnership and brought his stock in trade into the new firm, under articles by which the joint trade was to pay his creditors named in a schedule. It was held that a separate creditor named in a schedule did not by the articles become a joint creditor of the firm. In this case Lord Eldon says : "If it is meant to be said on the part of the petitioner, that a joint action might have been maintained by the creditors named in the schedule, against the partners immediately on the execution of the deed, and by force of the deed only, *independently of an accession to the agreement on the part of the creditors* named in the schedule, I cannot assent to the doctrine. * * * But I agree to the proposition that a very little will do to make out an assent to the agreement."

The same point was decided by Sir John Leach in *ex parte* Freeman, id. 471, though the question there arose in a case where a retiring partner had assigned the stock in trade to a continuing partner, who covenanted to pay the joint debts. The partners having become bankrupt, it was held that the joint creditors, not having previously to the bankruptcy, accepted the continuing partner as their sole debtor, could not prove against the separate estate of the continuing partner.

This case, although it was overruled by Lord Eldon, seems, nevertheless, observes Mr. Collyer, to be consistent with the most of those on the same subject which preceded it, and as the grounds of Lord Eldon's decision do not appear, and as Sir John Leach decided the subsequent case of *ex parte* Fry, 1 Glyn & J. 96, in the same manner, there seems just reason to suppose that the case of *ex parte* Freeman was rightly decided. Collyer on Part. 774.

In *ex parte* Lane, 1 De Gex, 300, it was held that a parol agreement to convert a separate debt into a joint debt is not within the statute of frauds if the former debt is extinguished, but an assent on the part of the creditor must be shown.

The case of *ex parte* Appleby, 2 Deac. 482, decided in eighteen hundred and thirty-nine, was nearly identical with *ex parte* Freeman, and it was held that a joint creditor could not prove against the separate estate of a continuing partner who had taken an assignment from the retiring partner of the joint assets, and agreed to indemnify against the partnership debts, there being no satisfactory evidence that there was no joint estate, nor that the joint creditor had *accepted* the continuing partner as his separate debtor.

So in *Kirwan* v. *Kirwan,* 1 Tyrwhett's R. 491, it was decided that mere knowledge of the dissolution of a partnership is not sufficient, although an account is continued with the new firm. The creditor must appear to have expressly, or by some act, accepted the substituted credit of the new partnership instead of the retiring partners.

Ex parte Parker, 2 Mont., Deac. & De Gex, 511, was a case where a trader indebted to a lunatic in the amount of the purchase money of a business and the machinery and stock in trade, entered into partnership under an agreement by which the stock in trade and property of the business were to belong to the firm, which was to assume the liabilities of the sole business. The firm tendered an annual account in its own name. in respect of the debt, to the committee of the lunatic, who made no objection to this form of account. It was held on the firm becoming bankrupt that the committee was not entitled to prove against the joint estate. It was even doubted whether the committee had power and whether the lord chancellor could have given him power to convert the separate into a joint liability. It will be observed that this case is much stronger than the case at bar. The debt was for the purchase money of the property transferred to the firm. The creditor was a lunatic incapable of personally assenting to the conversion, and there was some evidence tending to show that his committee had assented to it.

Ex parte Whitmore, 3 Mont. & Ayrton, 627, was decided expressly on the ground that the creditor had assented to the conversion before the bankruptcy. The court says: "The question is solely of fact. Did the creditor intend to substitute the firm for the separate liability?"

It is unnecessary, however, to multiply citations of cases on this point, for the authorities are with a single exception uniform that in proceedings in bankruptcy, at least the assent of the creditors to a conversion before the bankruptcy must be shown.

Story on Part. s. 370, states emphatically that "in order to produce any conversion at all, either with or without an extinguishment, there must be a sufficient consideration, and also a *deliberate and mutual assent of the creditors and debtors to such conversion.*" And for this he cites Collyer, *ubi sup.*; Gow on Part. 284; Watson on Part. 274. And the same doctrine is laid down by Robson in his treatise on the law of bankruptcy, 509, where the leading cases quoted above and many others are cited.

I have been referred to but one decision on the point under consideration by the courts of bankruptcy of the United States, but the principles above laid down have been adjudged by the courts of Massachusetts under the insolvent law of that state, from which, as is well known, the bankrupt act was in great part derived.

In *Wild* v. *Dean*, 3 Allen, 579, it was held that the partnership debt is not provable against the separate estate of one of the partners who had received an assignment of all the partnership property and executed a bond to his retiring partner to assume and pay the partnership debts, without evidence of an express agreement or assent by him to pay the same to the creditors as his private debt, and notice by the creditor of his election to treat it as a private debt is not sufficient.

In *Robb* v. *Mudge*, 14 Gray, 534, it was held that a *bona fide* transfer of partnership property to one partner in consideration of his assuming the partnership debts, makes it his separate property and not liable in insolvency to the creditors of the partnership who have not agreed to accept him individually as their debtor, until his separate debts are paid.

The case chiefly relied on as seeming to countenance a different rule, is that of *Colt* v. *Wilder*, 1 Edw. Ch. R. 484, decided by vice chancellor McCoun. In that case it was held that a private creditor of a partner, whose debt it had been agreed between them at the formation of the partnership to treat as a firm debt, could not take dividends under an assignment by the partners of all the partnership propety in trust for the benefit of the creditors of the concern.

With regard to this case it will be observed that the question was not as to the right of the creditor to prove his debt in bankruptcy as a joint debt, but whether he had under the circumstances any right in equity to come in under the assignment.

Second. The cases of *ex parte* Peele, 6 Ves. 602, and *ex parte* Clowes, 8 Ves. 540, on which the learned vice chancellor chiefly relies, have received a different interpretation, not only by the text writers, but by the courts by whom they were decided.

In *ex parte* Peele the contest turned upon whether the

partners had agreed between themselves to the conversion
of the debt. With respect to this case Mr. Collyer observes:
" On this subject of assent Lord Eldon's opinion may be
gathered from his observations in the cases of *ex parte* Peele
and *ex parte* Williams. In the former of these cases it was
scarcely necessary to advert to the question of assent by the
creditor to the consolidating of the debts, as it was a disputed point whether the partners themselves had agreed to
consolidate them. But in the latter, where a separate creditor sought proof as a joint creditor by virtue of an arrangement between the two partners for the conversion of separate
into joint debts, Lord Eldon required evidence of assent by
the creditor to such arrangement before the proof could be
allowed."

With respect to *ex parte* Clowes, Mr. Collyer remarks:
" It is true that in this case no evidence appears to have
been given of express consent by the creditors to the
arrangement of the partners. But as some years elapsed
between the arrangement and the bankruptcy, and as nothing
is said which leads to a contrary supposition, the consent of
the creditors to the conversion may, perhaps, be presumed.
Lord Eldon, speaking of this case, said it turned on peculiar circumstances." Collyer on Part. 771.

The cases of *ex parte* Williams, *ex parte* Freeman and *ex
parte* Fry, are admitted by the learned vice chancellor to be
opposed to the view taken by him, and he rests his decision
on the supposed authority of *ex parte* Clowes and *ex parte*
Peele. But we have seen that those cases are not regarded
as maintaining the doctrine for which the vice chancellor
cites them, while the cases of *ex parte* Williams and *ex parte*
Freeman have been followed in a large number of subsequent cases, and are accepted as law by Collyer, Story and
other text writers.

In re Downing, 3 N. B. R. 182, also cited by the counsel,
DILLON, J. undoubtedly expresses the opinion that the creditors may enforce by bill in equity a promise given by a
continuing partner to whom all the firm property has been

In re Isaacs and Cohn.

transferred, to pay off and discharge the firm's liabilities and that they may assent to and claim the benefit of this promise at any time before or after the bankruptcy. For this last position no authorities are cited, and the learned judge seems to have mainly rested his opinion on the second position taken by him, viz: that under the bankrupt act, where each of the partners has been separately adjudged bankrupt, and there are no firm assets, the joint creditors may prove against the separate estate of either. " This," observes DILLON, J. " in effect reaches the result which the English chancellors have felt bound on equitable principles to adopt." But it may be added that the rule is applied so rigorously that it was held that where a continuing partner received possession of all the partnership property, and continued the business on terms of paying all the firm debts, that the joint creditors could not receive dividends from the separate estate until the separate creditors were paid in full, although the joint estate amounted to only thirteen pounds. *Ex parte* Kennedy *et al.* De G., M. & G. 100.

On the whole, I feel bound on the authorities, to hold that the separate creditors not having before the bankruptcy assented to the arrangement between the partners, and not having been so far as appears even aware of it, are not entitled to prove their debts against the joint estate.

But while so holding I am obliged to confess my inability to discover the equitable principle upon which the rule rests.

The reason of the rule is stated by Sir John Leach in *ex parte* Freeman as follows: " I have always considered it to be essential that the bankrupt should be indebted to the party proving, at and before the bankruptcy. The engagement of one partner with the other to pay the debts of the firm can, as to the creditors of the firm, be considered only as a proposal that he is willing to become their sole debtor. If they accede to this proposal before the bankruptcy they are his separate creditors. But their acceptance of him as their separate debtor after the bankruptcy comes too late, for he is then incapable of contract."

That the assent of the creditor is necessary to any assignment by which his rights are impaired, is obvious. And if the conversion is claimed to have operated as an extinguishment, or as the substitution of a separate liability for a joint liability, or *vice versa*, it is plain that the creditor must be a partner to the arrangement.

But we have seen that there may be a conversion without an extinguishment, " in which case," says Story, " the creditors can take advantage of the debts according either to their new or their old form and quality. In other words, they may treat them as joint as well as separate debts, and have their remedy against the joint or separate estate accordingly, in their election." Story on Part. s. 369.

As, then, this arrangement in no way impairs the rights of the creditors, but is ordinarily greatly for their benefit, I see not why their assent may not be presumed ; as in a case where property is conevyed in trust for the benefit of a third person, the assent of the party beneficially interested is presumed. It appears now to be admitted that a third party may maintain an action on a promise, not under seal, made to another for his benefit, though he was not cognizant of it when made. 1 Parsons on Con. 467 ; 2 Greenl. on Ev. 109.

I am unable to see why a promise made by one partner to another, that he will hold himself jointly liable for the separate debt of the latter, may not on the same principle be availed of by the creditor. Why should evidence of the assent of the latter be exacted, (and it is admitted that slight evidence will be sufficient, as was the case in *ex parte* Kedie, 2 D. and C. 32.) when that assent would in no case be withheld, as the only effect of the arrangement would be to give to the creditor the security of the firm liability and that of the other partner, in addition to the liability of the partner with whom he had separately contracted. The hardship of the rule is apparent in those cases where the retiring partner transfers the partnership property to the continuing partners, and thus converts it into his separate property. In such cases it is held that after bankruptcy it cannot be treated in marshal-

In re Sands Ale Brewing Co.

ling the assets as joint estate or applied to the payment of joint debts. *Robb* v. *Mudge*, 14 Gray, 537; *Howe* v. *Lawrence*, 9 Cush. 553.

But whatever may be said of the justice of the rule, I consider it too firmly established for me at least to depart from.

In the passage already cited, STORY, J. unhesitatingly declares that " to produce any conversion at all, *either with or without extinguishment*, there must be sufficient consideration, and also a deliberate and mutual *assent* of the *creditors and debtors* to such conversion." Story on Part. 370.

Of course after bankruptcy there can be no mutuality of consent between creditors and debtors, for the latter are incapable of contracting.

If I have ventured to doubt the soundness of the rule thus laid down, it is because it has appeared to me that sufficient attention has not been given to the distinction between cases where the creditor is supposed to have relinquished the old liability and accepted a new and substituted liability in its stead, and those were a new and additional liability is created without impairing the old. In the former, his assent is evidently necessary; in the latter, it seems to me, it should be presumed and he should be allowed the advantage of the promise made between third persons for his benefit. And in this view I have at least the countenance of DILLON, J.

UNITED STATES DISTRICT COURT—ILLINOIS.

A creditor who has his debt secured by a valid trust deed containing a covenant to insure the buildings erected on the property to their full insurable value, has a clear and specific lien upon the proceeds of the insurance, to the exclusion of the general creditors in case of a loss by fire. The fact that the policies were not regularly assigned makes no difference, as in equity the assignment is executed the moment the insurance is effected; nor is the case altered on account of a clause in the said deed allowing the insurance company to be selected by the party loaning the money, because an insurance having been effected to the insurable value of the property the creditor has no power to insure further.

In re SANDS ALE BREWING COMPANY.

BLODGETT, J.—This is an application by petition of

In re Sands Ale Brewing Co.

Francis B. Peabody, as trustee, for an order on the assignee of the estate of the bankrupt to pay over to the petitioner the proceeds of certain policies of insurance. The material facts in the case, and in regard to which there is no dispute, seem to be as follows:

The bankrupt is a corporation created and existing under the general law of this state. On or about the first day of January, eighteen hundred and sixty-eight, the bankrupt corporation, then being solvent, borrowed the sum of sixty thousand dollars, and to secure the payment thereof executed to the petitioner, as trustee, its trust deed bearing date on said first of January, whereby it conveyed to the petitioners certain lots and parcels of land on which was situate the brewery and buildings occupied and used by the bankrupt for the purpose of its business. This deed contained among other covenants, one providing that the Sands Ale Brewing Co., its heirs and assigns, would at all times thereafter, until said principal sum of money and arrearages of interest thereon should be fully paid, keep all the buildings, outhouses excepted, fully insured against loss or damage by fire in some good and responsible insurance company, the selection of such insurance company to be left to the option of the party of the second part, or his successors in trust, in the fair insurable value of such buildings, and cause such insurance to be made payable to the party of the second part, or his successors in trust, and deliver to him or them the policies thereof, as soon as such insurance should be effected; and in default of so doing the party of the second part, or his successors in trust, at their option, might effect insurance in his or their name or names, or otherwise, and the premium money paid therefore should be a charge upon the premises and secured by this instrument, and such premium money should be paid by the heirs, executors or administrators of the first part on demand; and the said party of the second part, or his successors in trust, should hold such policies of insurance as collateral and additional security for said principal sum of money, and should have the right to collect all the money that might be collectable or receivable upon such policies, and apply the same in the same manner, as far as possible, as was hereinbefore provided for the application of the proceeds of the sale of said premises.

Soon after the execution of this deed, and in compliance with this covenant, the bankrupt caused insurance policies on the property to be taken out and assigned to the trustee, and when the policies expired, which was some time in December, eighteen hundred and sixty-eight, new policies were taken out, but probably not assigned or made payable to the trustee, and although policies to a large amount were taken out each succeeding year, they were not assigned or made payable to the trustee, although there is some proof that the policies or renewals for the second year were also so assigned, but this is not fully admitted.

On the ninth day of October last, all the buildings and improvements on said premises were destroyed by fire, and at that time the bankrupt held policies of insurance to the amount of about one hundred and twenty thousand dollars on the buildings on said lots and personal property situate therein, the total value of said buildings being about two hundred thousand dollars. The interest on the debt of sixty thousand dollars, secured by said deed of trust, has been regularly paid as it fell due, but no part of the principal sum has been paid. Since the loss occurred by said fire, said brewing company has been declared bankrupt for acts of bankruptcy committed since that time. Indeed, it is considered that said company was solvent at the time of said fire, and at the time the policies in question were taken out. The lots are admitted to be now inadequate security for the debt. After the adjudication in bankruptcy, an assignee was duly elected, and he has since collected a portion of the money due on said policies, and a dividend meeting had been held and dividends voted.

The petitioner claims that the covenant quoted from the trust deed gives him an equitable lien upon the proceeds of the insurance to the exclusion of the general creditors. While on the part of the assignee and the general creditors it is insisted that the policies in question, not having been assigned to the trustee, nor made specifically payable to him in case of loss, he has no higher right to them than the other creditors, and that the fund, therefore, belongs to the assignee. The bankrupt being a corporation, I do not conceive that any changes which may have taken place in the ownership of its stock since the trust deed was given, can affect the question at issue. No matter who buys or sells the stock, or who holds the offices or manages its affairs, the corporate entity remains the same. Its covenants to insure is binding on all stockholders and officers, and all persons in privity with it, and being on record, is notice to all its creditors. The assignee can hold nothing in this case which the grantor in the trust deed could not have held if bankruptcy had not intervened. His relation is purely representative. Creditors who have trusted the bankrupt must be held to have done so with full notice of the covenant to insure, and of the legal and equitable effect of that covenant. The covenant to insure runs with the land as much so as a covenant to repair or rebuild or for another term, because it is a charge upon the land. 5 B. & A. 1; 1 Smith's L. C. 136; Washb. on Real Estate, 425; 4 Kent, 558.

What then was the effect of that covenant so far as the right to this insurance money is concerned.

The bankrupt covenanted to insure to the fair insurable value of the buildings, and to cause the insurance to be made payable in case of loss to the petitioner or his successors in the trust. The insurance was effected but not assigned, or made payable to the trustee. Can this make any difference? This court must be governed in disposing of this question by substantially the same rules as a court of equity. In 2 Parsons on Con. 440, it is said: "There is authority, strengthened, as we think, by reason, that when a mortgagor is bound by the mortgage contract to keep the premises insured for the benefit of the mortgagee, and does, in fact, keep them insured by a policy which contains no statement that the mortgagee has any interest therein, the mortgagee, nevertheless, having an equitable interest in or even a lien upon the proceeds of the policy which a court of equity will enforce for his benefit." See also to same point, 6 G. & J. 372; Carter & Rockett, 436; 2 Am. L. C. 834; *Nichols* v. *Baxter*, 5 R. S. 491; *Norwich Fire Insurance Co.* v. *Boomer*, 52 Ill. 446; 24 Pick. 210; 9 Penn. 198; 7 Cush. 1; Flanders on Fire Ins. 367.

The principle announced in all these cases is but a practical application of the maxim that equity will consider as done what the parties have covenanted to do. But it is objected that the mortgagee under this covenant must first select or indicate the companies in which he wishes the insurance effected before the covenant becomes binding or effective to vest any right in him to the proceeds of the insurance. It would seem a sufficient answer to this objection, that the covenant being to insure to the full insurable value for the benefit of the mortgagee in this case, and the insurance having been effected, it does not lie in the mouth of the mortgagor to say that the mortgagee shall not have the benefit of it because he has acted without the selection or contrary to the selection of the mortgagor. Suppose the mortgagee had selected the companies and notified the mortgagor, and the latter, in disregard of the selection, had effected insurance in other companies, could such violation of his contract divest the mortgagee of his rights? I think not. But the mortgagor having effected insurance to nearly if not quite the insurable value of the property, has put it out of the mortgagee's power to further insure, because the property can only carry a limited amount; and, therefore, the mortgagee must hold what has been effected or none. But there seems another answer to this point arising from the facts in this case. Insurance was effected and assigned in compliance with the covenant the first year and probably the second. Was not this a sufficient selection, and was it not the duty of the mortgagor to renew the policies thus effected until notified otherwise by the mortgagee, and if the underwriters have since been changed by the mortgagor without the mortgagee's consent, this act of the mortgagor cannot be plead in equity to defeat the effect of his covenant.

My conclusion then is that the covenant by the bankrupt to insure operated to assign in equity to the petitioner the benefit of any insurance effected by the bankrupt on the mortgaged property. It is no answer to say that the mortgagee might have insured in default of insurance by the mortgagor, because the mortgagor had insured, and his insurance enured at once to the benefit of the mortgagee.

It is urged by way of argument in behalf of one creditor, the Union National Bank, that if all or part of these policies had been assigned to that creditor, it could have been held then as against the petitioner, and that the assignee holding for the benefit of all creditors occupies the same position ; but this argument is fallacious because it overlooks or ignores the fact that all creditors had notice of the petitioner's equitable right to this insurance money, and could acquire no valid interest therein as against him. Equity made the assignment the moment that the insurance was effected, if the mortgagor did not do it. It is true courts in this country and in England have said that all general liens infringe upon the bankrupt laws, the object of which is to distribute the bankrupt's estate equally—and *that equality is equity.* But if any one point is carefully guarded by the bankrupt law now in force, it is the protection of all fairly obtained leins, whether legal or equitable in their origin.

The authorities quoted, and many others I have consulted in the examination of this case, have no doubt in regard to the effect to be given this covenant. The lien is neither doubtful nor general, but is clear and specific. It is but carrying out the interest of the parties, and giving the mortgagee the security he had bargained for and given the whole world notice he was entitled to.

In re Alabama and Chattanooga Railroad Co.

UNITED STATES CIRCUIT COURT—S. D. NEW YORK.

A railroad company incorporated by the laws of a state for constructing, maintaining and operating a railroad, cannot be proceeded against in bankruptcy in a district court without the state or states where its railroad is to be built, maintained and operated, on the petition of a creditor charging an act of bankruptcy. Allegation and proof that such company kept an office in said district for six months next preceding the filing of the petition, where its officers acted, its board of directors met, and where it contracted debts, made loans, purchases and payments, does not give such court jurisdiction.

In what districts proceedings against a debtor in invitum may be instituted, described.

"Carrying on business," within the meaning of the eleventh section of the bankrupt law, as applied to a railroad corporation, does not mean the conduct of such transactions as are merely collateral or incidental to the purpose for which the corporation is created, whether they are conducted by agents or officers, and although an office is continously kept for the purpose.

The business of a railroad company, in the sense of the act, can only be carried on where the railroad is or is to be constructed, maintained and operated ; hence, the district court of the United States for the southern district of New York, has no jurisdiction to adjudge an Alabama railroad corporation a bankrupt on such a petition by a creditor.

In re ALABAMA & CHATTANOOGA RAILROAD CO.*

WOODRUFF, C. J.—On the petition of a creditor, the respondent, a corporation created and organized under and by virtue of the laws of the state of Alabama, and owning and operating a railroad in the states of Alabama, Georgia, Mississippi and Tennessee, was summoned to appear in the district court for the southern district of New York, to show cause why such corporation should not be adjudged a bankrupt. It was alleged in the petition that the corporation owned property in the state of New York and had for the largest period of time within the six months next immediately preceding the date of the filing of the petition had its principal office, place of business and domicile in the city of New York, in which the corporation had transacted the ordinary monied, commercial and financial business of a railroad corporation.

The corporation pleaded or answered specially to this petition, that the district court for the southern district of

* See 5 N. B. R. 97.

New York had no jurisdiction to proceed against the said corporation upon such petition, or to any adjudication in bankruptcy against the respondent.

After taking proofs touching the carrying on of the business alleged in the petition by the respondents, within the southern district of New York, this plea was overruled and the district court then proceeded to adjudge and did adjudge the said corporation a bankrupt.

The respondent, the corporation, now seeks a review and reversal of that adjudication. And it was stated by counsel on the argument that the question to be considered on the review was this: Had the district court jurisdiction to proceed against this railroad corporation upon a petition *in iuvitum* because such corporation transacted within this district the business alleged in the petition in this case?

If I were charged with the duty of legislating upon this subject, I should hesitate long before I exposed a corporation incorporated in Alabama or California for the construction of a railroad in those states and for maintaining and operating the same there, to a proceeding in a distant district for the settlement of its affairs, the disposal of its property and the distribution of the proceeds (operating practically as a dissolution thereof), as a bankrupt.

It would seem to me most inconvenient and disadvantageous to it; creditors most unsuitable, though not wholly impracticable, in respect of the closing of the estate, collecting, managing and disposing of the assets and transferring them under the direction of the court—which ought to be conveniently accessible to all who are interested—needlessly but inevitably most expensive, and presumptively bringing the parties ultimately interested in its affairs, whether as creditors or stockholders, to a great distance to protect their respective interests, following to this district the proceeds of the railroad and its equipments, which might well be administered at home. Difficulties will exist also in effectively reaching its officers to compel their furnishing accounts and details which the law requires for the settlement of the

In re Alabama and Chattanooga Railroad Co.

estate, and even if they can be compelled to send such information here or to attend here in person to give it, this must be needlessly expensive, troublesome and vexatious, and in case of resistance, will in general be very unsatisfactory in the mode of proceeding and in its results. Presumptively, at least, the property of such a corporation is invested in their railroad and its equipment and means of conducting the business for which it was incorporated, which are in the state or district where its railroad is built and is to be operated under its charter. And it seems to me wholly unfit that the district court for the southern district of New York should have the duty imposed upon it of administering the affairs of such a distant corporation. When the fact is recalled that probably no railroad company exists in the United States which does not habitually transact some business in the city of New York, the burthen and inconvenience of such a jurisdiction—liable to be invoked by any one creditor on a charge of bankruptcy—becomes apparent to a degree that makes it incredible that such a jurisdiction and the consequent duty to exercise it when invoked, have been imposed upon that court.

It is, however, no part of the duty of this court to legislate, but only to ascertain and apply the law as it is; and these suggestions can serve no purpose unless they shall aid in interpreting the statutes under which the proceedings have been instituted and which are claimed to sustain them.

The forty-eighth section of the bankrupt law declares that the word " person " in that law shall include " corporation." This must of course be qualified in any of the provisions which are necessarily inapplicable to a corporation, and by any provisions that are specially and expressly made for corporations only, if any such there be. But in respect of the question now before me, I find no such qualification, either express or implied, since no claim is made that the language of the thirty-seventh section of the act prevent its application to a railroad corporation as has sometimes been contended.

The eleventh section, providing for voluntary bankruptcy, may therefore be read as if the words " moneyed, business or commercial corporations or joint stock companies " were inserted therein, and it will then provide that such corporation owing debts * * * may apply by petition addressed to the judge of the judicial district in which such debtor has resided or carried on buisness for six months, or for the longest period during the six months next preceding the time of filing such petition. And jurisdiction is given to proceed on such petition to adjudge the petitioner a bankrupt.

Nevertheless, it is clear that a corporation can have no residence out of the state by whose laws it was created, and therefore in virtue of residence no jurisdiction can be acquired by any district court outside of such state; and in construing the words " carried on business," it may be proper to consider what, as applied to a corporation, they reasonably import.

Again, the thirty-seventh section declares that upon the petition of any creditor or creditors of such a corporation as is therein mentioned, * * * the like proceedings shall be had and taken as are in the act afterwards provided in the case of debtors. This in terms subjects the corporations named to a proceeding *in invitum* for an adjudication of bankruptcy as fully as other debtors are subjected thereto by the subsequent provisions of the act.

Following the act to its subsequent provisions, we find that by section thirty-nine, any person—and of course any such corporation as is before mentioned—who commits any of the acts specified, shall be deemed to have committed an act of bankruptcy, and subject to the conditions thereinafter prescribed, shall be adjudged a bankrupt on the petition of one or more of his creditors, &c.

Neither in the thirty-seventh nor the thirty-ninth section, nor in any other section relating to involuntary bankruptcy, is there any express designation of the judge or court to whom the petition shall be pre : ted or who shall have jurisdiction thereof. The first section of the act makes the several district courts of the United States courts of bankruptcy and confers on them jurisdiction in all matters and proceedings in bankruptcy in their several districts.

In which of the district courts, then, may proceedings be taken by a creditor, whether against a corporation or an individual? No express terms of the statute gives an answer to this question. Certainly it ought not to be open to creditors or to a creditor to select any district court of the United States at his or their option. It must be such court as upon the general rules governing jurisdiction of the district court can acquire jurisdiction, or such court as may seem to have been intended by congress, in analogy to the jurisdiction given where the proceedings are voluntary. The latter would seem to be the generally received opinion and in this district it has, I believe, been the practical construction of the act. The act having assimilated the proceedings in involuntary bankruptcy, after the respondent has been adjudged a bankrupt, to the proceedings in voluntary bankruptcy, it is not unnatural to infer that when congress by the thirty-ninth section authorised an adjudication upon the petition of a creditor, they meant upon a petition addressed to the court which by the previous eleventh section was authorised to adjudge a debtor a bankrupt on his own petition. The supreme court of the United States in framing the sixteenth of the general orders in bankruptcy, seem to have acted upon this construction of the act in providing for the contingency of two or more petitions against the same individual in different districts.

My own unaided examination of the act would have suggested the doubt whether, although congress has given to the debtor the opportunity to apply to the court of the district wherein he resides or to the court of the district in which he carried on business, they had not, when they provided for a hostile proceeding against him, intentionally omitted a similar provision and in that respect intended that the proceeding should conform by analogy to the eleventh section of the judiciary act of seventeen hundred and eighty-nine, which forbids that any civil suit shall be brought in either the district or circuit court against any citizen, except in the district in which he resides, or in which he may be found to be served with process. 1 U. S. Stat. at Large, 78, 79. All the provisions of the act concurring, involuntary bankruptcy may be harmonized with this construction, viz: If he reside within the district, then he may be served personally or by leaving at his place of abode; or if he have absconded, or be concealed, or his place of residence cannot be ascertained then by publication. Section forty.

Although it was the design of congress to enable creditors to compel a debtor who has committed an act of bankruptcy to do that which, in a state of insolvency, he ought to do voluntarily agreeably to the eleventh section, it does not follow that they intended to enable creditors or a creditor to call the debtor on a charge of having committed such an act thousands of miles from his residence to contest the charge, merely because he had carried on some business at such remote point. The great hardship of such a call is manifest, and the general tenor of the fortieth section indicates that it is where the debtor resides that the proceeding is in general to be conducted, his not being found by reason of his absconding, or being concealed, or having no known residence, being the excepted cases of service by publication.

And it does not occur to me that there is any greater fitness or propriety in compelling an alleged debtor to go to a remote district to contest, in the court of bankruptcy, the claim on the alleged indebtedness to a pretended creditor, as well as the truth of the charge of bankruptcy, (for both of these may be involved in the litigation,) than there is in compelling such supposed debtor to go to a remote district to defend an ordinary suit by the same party under precisely the same circumstances, which is by the judiciary act expressly prohibited. And there being no express provision of the bankrupt law to this effect, I should have been reluctant to indulge in construction not necessarily required by what is expressed so as to produce a result quite in conflict with the former law.

In view of the general construction given to the act, and the sanction such construction has received from the deliberate action of the supreme court of the United States, I do not feel at liberty to dispose of this case by giving weight to the doubt which I have thus expressed. I must yield that doubt and hold, until otherwise advised, that a proceeding in involuntary bankruptcy may be prosecuted in the district in which the debtor carries on business, although he resides and may be found in another.

The further conclusion above stated, that a corporation included in the provisions of section thirty-seven is in the like condition, in this respect, as a natural person, leaves only one question open, viz : When applied to a railroad corporation, what do the terms "in which such debtor has resided or carried on business" mean ?

FIRST. A corporation has and can have no residence except in the state by whose laws it exists. It cannot of its own mere motion change its residence. This has often been decided by the supreme court. This is claimed here by the counsel for the corporation and it is conceded by the counsel for the creditor. Hence also it is well settled that a corporation created by the laws of one state cannot be found in another judicial district of the United States to be served with process through its officers, in an action in the federal courts of such last named district. Jurisdiction for the district court cannot therefore be maintained in this case on the ground of residence of the debtor, nor on the ground that the debtor, being a corporation under the laws of Alabama, was found in this disrict.

SECOND. Do the facts here show that the corporation, the alleged debtor, carried on business in this district within the meaning of the said eleventh section of the bankrupt law ?

In its broadest sense, the term "business" includes nearly all the affairs in which either an individual or a corporation can be actors. Indulgence in pleasure, participation in domestic enjoyment and engagement in the offices of merely personal religion, may be exceptions in the case of an individual, but the employment of means to secure or provide for these would to him be business, and to a corporation these exceptions can have no application. The conduct of any and all of the affairs of a corporation is business.

Does then the doings of any act whatever, pertaining to the affairs of a railroad corporation, constitute carrying on business in the sense of the act? Has the term carrying on business the same meaning as transacting any of its business? If the necessities or interests of a railroad company require that an agent should be sent to a timber region to purchase or otherwise procure (*e. g.*, by cutting, sawing, &c.,) materials for its superstructure, is that carrying on business there? Or if it send an agent or agents to a city, the center of capital, to negotiate its bonds and raise money in aid of the construction of its road, and such agency be continued for that purpose and for receiving subsequent remittances and making payments of interest or other indebtedness at an office provided therefor, is that carrying on business in such city within the meaning of the act?

I am constrained not only by considerations already suggested, but by what, upon the words themselves, should be deemed their proper interpretation, to answer these questions in the negative. There are in the carrying on of a business many affairs which are merely incidental and which may be and often are transacted elsewhere than at the place where the business—that which is the real design and purpose or object in view—is located; and such transactions may be of such frequent and even daily occurrence as to require an agency of considerable duration. It would seem to me greatly unjust and unreasonable to regard such transactions as a carrying on of business in the sense of the law. "Carrying on business," looks to the scheme and purpose to which such transactions tend, and not to the incidental transactions themselves.

In re Alabama and Chattanooga Railroad Co.

Thus, the business of a railroad corporation is, by its charter, the construction, maintenance and operation of a railroad. That is its business. In aid thereof it may be necessary or expedient to employ agents and agencies—since it can only act by agents—in other places than those in which its business of constructing, maintaining and operating the road can be done; but the transactions of such agents are only collateral or incidental; they do not in a just sense. constitute the business of the railroad company; that business cannot be removed; the company itself cannot transfer it; agents or officers who are agents and only agents, may from a distance advise therein, give rules or directions to other agents for its management, but *the business of the railroad company* can only be done where the railroad is or is to be constructed, maintained and operated.

The petition herein states that the alleged bankrupt corporation has had its principal office, place of business and domicile in the city of New York—in part at least a. legal impossibility—in which place and during, &c., such corporation has transacted the ordinary moneyed, commercial and financial business of a railroad corporation, and there was evidence that what the officers of the corporation called its general office was in New York; that its officers were here and its board of directors were accustomed to meet at such office; and there the records and various accounts of its affairs and business were kept; and here the corporation procured loans or made purchases in aid of the construction of its railroad and its equipment.

Here is but an agency whether it be minor or major, special or principal. It does not affect the present enquiry that the agents embrace more or less in number or in authority. It is not here that the business is done or can be done for which the company was created although here are business transactions within the power of the Corporation, it may be but only in aid of its substantive business and incidentally necessary, perhaps, to its accomplishment.

Further illustrations might be drawn from the existence

of very numerous banks, manufacturing and other corporations in various states of the Union which, although carrying on the business for which they are incorporated within the states where they are created, nevertheless have, for very important and necessary incidental transactions, continuous agencies in one or more of our principal cities. It was not intended by reason of such transactions to subject them to ·proceedings in bankruptcy where those agencies were maintained, whether there conducted by agents under one name or another, either officers or clerks, or by whatever name or official relation designated.

In view of all the considerations which I have suggested, I am of opinion that in reference to a railroad corporation created by the state of Alabama for the building, maintaing and operating a railroad in that state, a construction of the act which subjects it to proceedings in bankruptcy in this district is not reasonable, not required by the language of the statute and not according to its intention. I do not fail to see that the contrary may be plausibly argued, as in fact it has been plausibly and ably by the counsel for the creditors. But the corporation cannot itself remove to this district. It cannot in this district carry on the business for which it was created. It can only out of sufferance do here such collateral or incidental things as are not in its substantive business, but only aids thereto or which facilitate its accomplishment.

It follows that the objection to the jurisdiction of the district court for the southern district of New York should have been sustained and the petition of the creditor dismissed.

Ordered that the adjudication declaring the company a bankrupt be reversed accordingly.

CLARENCE A. SEWARD, for the railroad company; E. L. FANCHER, for the creditor.—February, 1872.

UNITED STATES DISTRICT COURT—S. D. NEW YORK.

There is nothing in the general orders in bankruptcy or in the rules in equity prescribed by the supreme court, which authorises a marshal to serve a subpœna to appear and answer in an equity suit at a place outside of the territorial limit of the district for which he is appointed.

Service of subpœna and injunction set aside for irregularity.

JOBBINS, Assignee, v. *MONTAGUE et al.*

BLATCHFORD, J.—This is a bill in equity. The defendant Jackson and his copartner, Joseph P. Brouner, were on the twenty-second of January, eighteen hundred and seventy, adjudged bankrupts by this court on the petition of a creditor of theirs. The plaintiff was appointed to be their assignee on the eighteenth of February, eighteen hundred and seventy, and received the usual assignment, under which his title relates back to the thirteenth of January, eighteen hundred and seventy, the date of the filing of the petition. The assignment was recorded in the office of the clerk of Hudson county, New Jersey, on the twenty-fourth of June, eighteen hundred and seventy. On and prior to June fifteenth, eighteen hundred and sixty-nine, Jackson was seized in fee simple of certain real estate in Hudson county, New Jersey. On that day Jackson and his wife executed a mortgage to the defendant Montague, on such real estate to secure the payment of a bond for ten thousand dollars and interest, executed by Jackson to Montague. The bill alleges that the bond was given with the knowledge of Montague, to shield the property from the just claims of the creditors of Jackson, and that the ten thousand dollars was never due on the bond. On the twenty-fourth of November, eighteen hundred and sixty-nine, Jackson and his wife conveyed the said real estate, with other property, by deed, to the defendant Albertson, in fee simple, professedly for the consideration of fifteen thousand dollars. The deed was recorded in Hudson county on the fourth of December, eighteen hundred and sixty-nine. The bill alleges that the deed was made in contemplation of bankruptcy, and for the purpose of delaying, hindering and defrauding the creditors of Jackson, with the knowledge of Albertson. On or about the twenty-sixth of February, eighteen hundred and seventy, the plaintiff filed a bill in equity in this court, to set aside the said deed to Albertson and other conveyances made by Jackson, and to have a receiver appointed of the said property, and other property similarly conveyed, and to enjoin Jackson and Albertson and others, grantees of Jackson, who were made defendants to that bill, from disposing of said properties. On that bill this court granted an injunction to the foregoing effect on the twenty-eighth of February, eighteen hundred and seventy, which was duly served on Jackson and Albertson. On the twenty-third of September, eighteen hundred and seventy, the plaintiff was appointed receiver in that cause of the said real estate in Hudson county, and of other property. In opposition to the motion for the appointment of such receiver an affidavit made by said Montague was read. On the eleventh of October, eighteen hundred and seventy, a copy of the order appointing the plaintiff such receiver was served on the said Montague in person. On the seventeenth of October, eighteen hundred and seventy, Montague filed his bill of complaint in the court of chancery of New Jersey against Jackson and his wife and Albertson and his wife, for the foreclosure of the said mortage. On such bill a decree was taken by default for ten thousand seven hundred and ninety-five dollars and twenty-six cents, principal and interest on said mortgage, on the seventh of February, eighteen hundred and seventy-one, and thereupon an execution was issued out of the said court of chancery, directed to the sheriff of Hudson county, New Jersey, commanding him to sell said real estate in Hudson county to satisfy said mortgage. The said sheriff. advertised the property for sale at public auction on the fourth of May, eighteen hundred and seventy one, but the sale was adjourned from time to time until the twenty-first of September, eighteen hundred and seventy-one. The bill in this suit was filed on the nineteenth day of September, eighteen hundred and seventy-one. It sets forth the foregoing facts, and avers that the plaintiff was not made a party to the said proceedings in foreclosure, and had no notice thereof, and did not know that they were in progress until after the final decree for foreclosure had been made, and a few days before the day first fixed for the sale; that the foreclosure proceedings were instituted and carried on by collusion between Montague and Jackson and Albertson for the purpose of delaying, hindering and defrauding the plaintiff, as such assignee and receiver, in his pursuit of his rights and remedies against the property mentioned in the mortgage, and with the intent that, by a sale under the foreclosure proceedings, Montague, Jackson and Albertson, or some of them, might either acquire a title to the property, or realize more money than is justly due on the mortgage, in fraud of the plaintiff's rights; that, in the foreclosure proceedings, no proofs appear to have been taken as to the amount due on the bond and mortgage, other than their production; that the plaintiff, from the fullest examination of the circumstances of Jackson and the giving of the mortgage, believes that the bond and mortgage do not truly show the real amount due; and that Jackson and Albertson and his wife reside in the state of New York, and Montague and the sheriff of Hudson county reside in New Jersey. The bill prays for a discovery from all the defendants except the sheriff of Hudson county; and that the conveyance from Jackson and wife to Albertson may be decreed to be void and of no effect as against the plaintiff and the creditors of Jackson and of him and Brouner as copartners; and that an account may be taken of the amount due on the bond and mortgage to Montague; and that the plaintiff may be decreed to be entitled to redeem the mortgaged premises upon paying or tendering to Montague or his legal representatives the amount which may be so found to be due; and that Montague may be decreed to deliver up the mortgage to the plaintiff to be cancelled, upon payment or tender of said amount; and that Jackson and Albertson and his wife may be enjoined from selling, leasing, encumbering or otherwise disposing of or interfering with the mortgaged property, or its rents, is-

sues or profits ; and that Montague may be restrained from
proceeding further in his suit for the foreclosure of said
mortgage, and from instituting any other suit for its foreclosure, or for the sale or possession of the mortgaged property, and from taking any other proceedings for procuring the
sale or possession of said property ; and that the sheriff of
Hudson county may be restrained from proceeding further
in the execution of the writ for the sale of the property, and
from executing any other writ at the suit of Montague for the
sale of the property, until the further order of this court.
Montague, Jackson, Albertson and his wife, and the sheriff
of Hudson county, are made defendants to the bill.

On this bill, and affidavits accompanying it, an *ex parte*
injunction was issued by this court, restraining the defendants
as prayed in the bill. On the same day a subpœna to appear
and answer was issued, directed to the defendants and returnable on the first Tuesday of November, eighteen hundred
and seventy-one. The subpœna and the injunction were
served on Montague personally, at Hackensack, New Jersey,
on the twenty-fifth of October, eighteen hundred and seventy-
one, by a deputy of the marshal of the United States for this
district. Montague now moves this court, by solicitors who
appear for him only for the purpose of the motion, to set aside
the service of the injunction and the service of the subpœna
on him, and to declare such service void and of no effect, on
the ground that such service was irregular and unlawful.

The plaintiff, on the nineteenth of May, eighteen hundred
and seventy-one, filed a bill in equity in the district court of
the United States for the district of New Jersey, against the
persons who are defendants in this suit, making the same allegations made, and praying the same relief prayed for, in the
bill in this court, and in such suit procured an injunction
staying the sale under the foreclosure decree. Montague
answered the bill and then moved for a dissolution of the injunction. On that motion the counsel for Montague raised the
question of the jurisdiction of the district court for New Jersey
to entertain the suit, inasmuch as the proceedings in bankruptcy

against Jackson and Brouner were proceedings instituted and pending in this court and not in the district court for New Jersey. The court dissolved the injunction and dismissed the bill for want of jurisdiction, on the ground that the bankruptcy proceedings were not proceedings instituted and pending in the district court for New Jersey. After that decision was announced the bill in this case was filed.

The service of the subpœna in this case on the defendant Montague, in New Jersey, is claimed to be irregular and without force to compel his appearance in the suit on pain of having the bill taken as confessed against him, on the ground that such service was in violation of the provisions of the eleventh section of the act of September twenty-fourth, seventeen hundred and eighty-nine. (1 U. S. Stat. at Large, 79.) That provision is as follows: " No person shall be arrested in one district for trial in another, in any civil action before a circuit or district court; and no civil suit shall be brought before either of said courts, against an inhabitant of the United States, by any original process, in any other district than that whereof he is an inhabitant, or in which he shall be found at the time of serving the writ." It is contended on the part of the plaintiff, that this court has power, under the provisions of the first and second sections of the bankrupt act of March second, eighteen hundred and sixty-seven, (14 U. S. Stat. at Large, 517), to bring the defendant Montague into this court, to answer this bill, by process served upon him in New Jersey.

It is not contended that this court has not jurisdiction of the subject matter of this suit. It has such jurisdiction by virtue of the second section of the bankrupt act, which declares that this court, being the district court of the district where the proceedings in bankruptcy against Jackson and Brouner are pending, shall have jurisdiction of all suits in equity brought by the assignee in bankruptcy of the bankrupts against any person claiming an adverse interest touching any property or rights of property of the bankrupts, or either of them, transferable to or vested in the assignee. The sole question is as to the jurisdiction of this court over the person of Montague by means of such service of subpœna as has been made.

That this is a civil suit, and that Montague is an inhabitant of the United States, and of the district of New Jersey, and was not an inhabitant of this district, or found in it at the time of serving the subpœna, are facts not disputed. Nor can there, I think, be any doubt that the subpœna by which this suit is brought is "original process." So far as Montague ·is concerned, the bill prays for an account of the amount due on the bond and mortgage to him, and for a decree that the plaintiff is entitled to redeem the mortgaged premises on paying to Montague the amount so to be found due, and that Montague shall then deliver up the mortgage to be cancelled, and that all suits and proceedings by Montague now or hereafter to. foreclose the mortgage, or to sell or obtain possession of the mortgaged property, may be enjoined.

This is not a cross bill in any sense. Montague has no suit pending in this court. It is an original bill praying for original relief, and the subpœna issued on it is original process.

That this court, independently of any provision in the bankrupt act, could not acquire jurisdiction of the person of Montague in this suit, by such service of the subpœna as has been made in this case, is not doubtful. Independently of that act this court could make effective no service beyond the limits of this district, of process of subpœna, in equity, to appear and answer, issued by it. *Toland* v. *Sprague*, 12 Pet. 300, 330; *Herndon* v. *Ridgway*, 17 How. 424, 425; *Atkins* v. *The Fibre Disintegrating Co.* 7 Blatch. C. C. R. 555, 566.

Does, then, the bankrupt act make lawful such service of the subpœna to appear and answer as was made in this case? In *Toland* v. *Sprague*, before cited, it is said, in reference to circuit courts: "Whatever may be the extent of their jurisdiction over the subject matter of suits in respect to persons and. property, it can only be exercised within the limits of the district. Congress might have authorized civil process from any circuit court to have run into any state of the Union. It has not done so. It has not in terms authorized any original civil process to run into any other district, with the single exception of subpœnas for witnesses, within a limited distance. In regard to final process there are two cases, and two only, in which writs of execution can now by law be served in any other district than that in which the judgment was rendered; one in favor of private persons in another district of the same state; and the other in favor of the United States, in any part of the United States. We think that the opinion of the legislature is thus manifested to be that the process of a circuit court cannot be served without the district in which it is established, without the special authority of law therefor." These views being founded on the language of the eleventh section of the act of seventeen hundred and eighty-nine, are equally applicable to the service of original process issued by a district court.

The jurisdiction conferred by the second section of the bankrupt act on this court, is one over "all suits at law or in equity which may or shall be brought by the assignee in bankruptcy against *any* person claiming an adverse interest * * * touching any property or rights of property of said bankrupt, transferable to or vested in such assignee." But, notwithstanding this grant of jurisdiction as to subject matter, when the suit is brought against a defendant making a particular claim of interest touching certain specified property, it by no means follows that such jurisdiction must not be exercised in subordination to the provisions of the eleventh section of the act of seventeen hundred and eighty-nine. There is nothing in the second section of the bankrupt act dispensing with or repealing the provisions of the said eleventh section, and nothing repugnant to or inconsistent with them.

The only other section of the bankrupt act which it is supposed authorises the service of subpœna made in this case, is the first section. But that section only relates to the powers which the court is to exercise as a court of bankruptcy, in matters and proceedings in bankruptcy. It is now determined by the supreme court, (*Smith* v. *Mason*, 6 N. B. R. 1), that the general clause in the first section, conferring jurisdiction on the district courts, must be considered in connection with all the other provisions of the act; that the clause in such first section specifically enumerating the cases and controversies to which the jurisdiction of said courts shall extend, does not enumerate the "suits at law or in equity" enumerated in the second section; that a cause involving a controversy such as that exhibited by the bill in this suit, cannot be commenced by a petition followed by an order to show cause why the prayer of the petition should not be granted, or be determined in a summary way by the district court sitting in bankruptcy, without due process of law; and that such a controversy falls within the provisions of the second section, and must be determined in a suit in equity or an action at law, as the case may be. In *Morgan et al.* v. *Thornhill et al.* 5 N. B. R. 1, it is said by the supreme court, that the jurisdiction conferred on the district courts by the second section of the bankruptcy act, is of the same character as that conferred on the circuit court by the eleventh section of the act of seventeen hundred and eighty-nine; and that the jurisdiction intended to be conferred on the circuit courts by such second section is the regular jurisdiction between party and party, as described in the act of seventeen hundred and eighty-nine, and the third article of the constitution. The jurisdiction conferred by the second section on the circuit court for the district where the proceedings in bankruptcy are pending, over the suits therein mentioned, is conferred in the same terms in which it is conferred on the district court of the same district. In respect to each court it is an enlargement of its jurisdiction. But for such provision the circuit court would have no jurisdiction of a suit wherein one of the parties named in the second section is not a citizen of the state where the suit is brought while the adverse party is a citizen of another state; and but for such provision the district court would have no jurisdiction of such a suit as is mentioned in the second section. The conferring of the jurisdiction on the two courts concurrently, by the second section, in the same terms, indicates plainly that one of them cannot, under authority derived from the provision, exercise such jurisdiction to an extent or in a manner different from the other. If, therefore, it can be claimed that this court can make effective such service of process as has been made in this case, it follows that the circuit court of this district, if this bill were pending in that court, could make effective a like service of process. But it is entirely clear, I think, that the jurisdiction conferred on both courts by the second section of the bankrupt act is a regular jurisdiction between party and party, of the same character as that conferred on the circuit courts by the eleventh section of the act of seventeen hundred and eighty-nine, and is to be pursued, as to forms and modes of process, under the same rules which obtain as to suits brought in the circuit courts in pursuance of such eleventh section. There is nothing in the bankrupt act indicating an intention on the part of congress that process int he suits specified in the second section of the bankrupt act shall be served or made effective in any different manner from that required in suits brought in a circuit court under the jurisdiction in " suits of a civil nature at common law or in equity " conferred on such court by the eleventh section of the act of seventeen hundred and eighty-nine.

It by no means follows, because, in bankruptcy proceedings proper, pending in a district court, a summons, or order, or notice issued by such court may, in some cases provided for by the act, effectually bind a person on whom it is served, although such service is not made personally at a place within the territorial limits of the district, that original process in the plenary suits mentioned in the second section of the act can be effectively served out of the territorial limits of the court issuing said process. Indeed, the act, in my judgment, clearly indicates, in numerous places, an intention on the part of congress, that service other than personal intra-territorial service shall be allowed in bankruptcy proceedings proper, while there is not in the act any indication of any intention that extra-territorial service shall be allowed in the suits mentioned in the second section of the act.

The views thus suggested are confirmed by the language of general order No. thirty-two in bankruptcy, prescribed by the supreme court, which provides, that, "in proceedings in equity instituted for the purpose of carrying into effect the provisions of the act, or of enforcing the rights and remedies given by it, the rules of equity practice prescribed by the supreme court of the United States shall be followed, as nearly as may be." One of those rules (rule fifteen) requires that the service of all process shall be by the marshal of the district or his deputy, or by some other person especially appointed by the court for that purpose, and not otherwise, while rule thirteen requires that the service of a subpœna shall be made by delivery of a copy thereof by the officer serving the same to the defendant personally, or by leaving a copy thereof at the dwelling house, or usual place of abode, of the defendant, with a member of or a resident in the family. By the twenty-seventh section of the judiciary act of seventeen hundred and eighty-nine, it is made the duty of the marshal of the district to execute "throughout the disrict" in and for which he is appointed, all lawful precepts directed to him and issued under the authority of the United States. There is nothing in the general orders in bankruptcy, or in the rules in equity prescribed by 'he supreme court, which authorises a marshal to serve a subpœna to appear and answer in an equity suit, at a place outside of the territorial limits of the district for which he is appointed.

The service of the subpœna in this case having been irregular it must be set aside, and so also must the service of the injunction.

W. B Putney for the motion; D. McMahon opposed.—December 27, 1871.

UNITED STATES DISTRICT COURT—N. D. OF NEW YORK.

[Opinion of J. D. HUSBANDS, Referee.]

A creditor who accepts a chattel mortgage with a view to obtain a preference, having reasonable cause to believe at the time that a fraud on the act was intended and that his debtor was insolvent, will not be allowed to prove his debt in bankruptcy, and likewise loses the lien of his mortgage.

BINGHAM, Assignee, v. *RICHMOND & GIBBS.*

In this case a bill is filed on the equity side of the court to set aside a chattel mortgage made by David S. Wing, the bankrupt, September tenth, eighteen hundred and sixty-nine, to these defendants, filed in the proper office September eleventh, eighteen hundred and sixty-nine, to restrain the proof of the debt by these defendants.

The bill alleges the insolvency of Wing at the time, and the intent by its execution to give the defendants a preference over his other creditors, and to defeat and delay the operation of the bankrupt act; that the defendants accepted such mortgage with a view of obtaining such preference, and that at the time said defendants received such conveyance they had reasonable cause to believe that a fraud on such act was intended, and that said David S. Wing was insolvent. All this as matter of fact is admitted by the stipulation in this case, and the only saving clause is that, "said defendants believed that they were entitled to the preference obtained." In simpler Saxon, they believed that a fraud on the act was intended, and had reasonable cause also to believe in the insolvency of their debtor and that they *had a right to commit that fraud on the act* because they believed they could.

The brief of their learned counsel mistakes in my judgment, when he confounds corrupt motive with their admitted intent.

Section fourteen of the act preserves the lien of mortgages on chattels made in good faith for present considerations otherwise valid, and passes the title to the assignee of property fraudulently conveyed, who is authorised to assail the bankrupt's fraud. The stipulation necessarily admits that this mortgage lien is not thus preserved.

The debtor has been adjudicated a bankrupt and no question arises as to him.

These creditors intended what they did. See reasoning of WOODRUFF, J., in 4 N. B. R. 79. And so HALL, J., and other judges have repeatedly held. The belief of a man that he may do what the law forbids, does not cure the illegality of the act. It may, however, save him from the charge of corruption. Before the heavenly vision, Saul believed conscientiously that he might persecute and slay the disciples. On the way to Damascus he learned that this belief furnished no justification. *Kohlsaat* v. *Hoguet et al.* 5 N. B. R. 159, was, I apprehend, an action by the assignee to recover the amount of the preference. BLATCHFORD, J., after stating the intent and the doing or suffering by the debtor, says: the elements on the part of the creditor are the receiving or being benefited by such thing, the having reasonable cause to believe the insolvency of the debtor, and the having reasonable cause to believe that a preference is intended. These six elements must co-exist, but nothing else is necessary to make the transaction void, if challenged by the assignee in due time. The question submitted is, whether the defendants, having taken such a preference in this manner, have a right to surrender it after suit brought by the assignee to challenge it and before answer. No question is made as to the time in which this action is brought.

It must be observed in respect to involuntary bankruptcy that by section thirty-nine, what enables the assignee to recover the property conveyed, assigned or transferred, also in express terms declares that the creditor shall not be allowed to prove his debt in bankruptcy, *provided* such creditor had reasonable cause to believe that a fraud on the act was intended, and that the debtor was insolvent. This case is alleged in the bill to be involuntary, and the stipulation admits it. The stipulation also admits in the language of the section all the proviso requires or declares, and I can discover no escape from the consequence without assuming the function of legislation. It is a penal statute in this behalf, but its language is clear and unmistakable. I never discovered wisdom in attempts on the part of judicial tribunals to wrest the language of a statute to meet a real or supposed difficulty or hardship. I remember that at an early day in England, the statute of limitations was considered by the courts a hard statute. In the time of Croke James decisions were made frittering away some of its provisions. The cooler and wiser judgment of other judges in England and this country construed and gave effect to the statute as it was, and held it to be a statute of repose.

I pass on this section as I read it. It interprets itself. It applies in terms to such a creditor as the section itself defines, and relates to involuntary proceedings only. See section thirty-nine and *in re* Evans, 3 N. B. R. 62. Why this distinction exists in the act, it is neither my duty nor my prerogative to enquire. Statutes are arbitrary and when the language is free from all ambiguity and is within the power of the law giver, *ita lex scripta est* is the only answer the judicial mind can give to criticisms upon it.

I think the admitted allegations of the bill bring this case directly within the language and spirit of the act, and that these defendants are therefore not allowed to prove their debt in bankruptcy and the complainant is entitled to the relief he seeks. If they desire to surrender for any other purpose I see no objection to it. I return herewith a stipulation, which, in connection with the bill of complaint, is the testimony in this case.

Scott Lord for plaintiff; R. P. Wisner for debtor.—January 9, 1872.

UNITED STATES DISTRICT COURT—N. D. NEW YORK.

[Opinion of J. D. Husbands, Referee.]

The word conveyance in the bankrupt act is a generic term, including all proceedings to dispose of or encumber property in derogation of the equality of creditors, with intent by such disposition either to defeat or delay the operation of the act ; hence it includes mortgages on real estate which, if given contrary to the provisions of the thirty-ninth section, are void, and deprives the mortgagee of all right to prove his claim in bankruptcy, even though he should be willing to surrender his rights under the mortgage.

BINGHAM v. *FROST.*
Same v. *WILLIAMS.*

My opinion in the case of this plaintiff against Richmond & Gibbs* applies to these cases if a mortgage on real estate is included in the word conveyance, as used in and within the meaning of sections fourteen and thirty-nine of the bankrupt act.

These cases forcibly illustrate the hindrances and delay produced by mortgages. Section fourteen provides that all property conveyed by the bankrupt in fraud of his creditors vests in the assignee. Section thirty-nine enacts that the creditor receiving a conveyance contrary to the act shall not be allowed to prove his debt in bankruptcy.

If it be not a conveyance within the meaning of the act, the assignee is not vested with the title to the land under section fourteen as against the mortgages, because this section relates to fraudulent conveyances, and it is the provision that makes it his duty to *invoke* the aid of the court to annul the fraudulent proceedings. Bump, 3d Ed. 297, and cases cited.

In this state the title remains in the mortgagor and descends to his heirs and the interest of the mortgagee is a chattel interest. But the word conveyance, in the bankrupt act, is a generic term, including all proceedings to dispose of or encumber property in derogation of the equality of creditors, with intent by such disposition either to give a prefer-

* See page 127.

ence or to defeat or delay the operation of the act. Its elementary definition, therefore, is to be ascertained. Bouvier defines a legal mortgage of lands to be a conveyance of lands by a debtor to his creditor as a pledge or security, &c., with a proviso. See also 1 R. S. (marg.) 762, sec. 38. 4 Kent Com. 136, says : " A mortgage is the conveyance of an estate by way of pledge for the security of a debt, and to become void on payment of it." 1 Washburne on Real Property, 475, defines a mortgage to be an estate created by a conveyance absolute in its form, but intended to secure, &c.

Books of forms have a heading of conveyances by deed or mortgages. See Clerk's Assistant. The form of a mortgage is a grant, &c., and this conveyance is intended as a security. Such also is the definition in the United States courts.

MARSHALL, C. J., in *United States* v. *Hool et al.* 3 Cranch, 462, says: "The difference is a marked one between a conveyance which purports to be absolute and a *conveyance* which from its terms is to leave the possession in the vendor. If in the latter case the retaining possession was evidence of fraud no *mortgage* would be valid."

In *Conrad* v. *Atlantic Ins. Co.* 1 Pet. 441, it is said that "a mortgage is a conveyance of property and passes it conditionally," which is stated as a very plain proposition, and STORY, J., adds: "a mortgage is a lien for a debt and something more. It is a transfer of the property itself as a security for the debt." In *Williams* v. *Wright*, 6 McLean, 340, the court says that the distinction between a trust deed and a mortgage is somewhat technical.

I cannot divest myself of the idea that the word conveyance, as used in sections fourteen and thirty-nine of the act, includes mortgages, and therefore these mortgages to the defendants. It may be proper for me to say that I think there is a construction which can reconcile sections twenty-three and thirty-nine. Section twenty-three is negative, denying the right to prove a preferred debt *in any case* without a surrender ; but it nowheres declare that in all cases of surrender the debt may be proved. Then comes section thirty-nine in involuntary bankruptcy, which declares that in cases described in that section, the debt shall not be proved at all in bankruptcy. Where is the repugnance? Read together in this view as it is, in case of any preference whatever, a surrender must be made in order to prove the debt, but in cases specified in section thirty-nine, such creditor as is therein defined, "shall not be allowed to prove his debt in bankruptcy." Thus they are in harmony.

If section twenty-three had provided that in all cases of surrender the debt may be proved, this construction could not be given to it; but it has not. There is no case of preference out of section thirty-nine where the debt can be proved without a surrender. There is no case within it where it can be proved, because this section in so many words forbids it; the creditor in a certain sense being a party to the fraud on the act.

It is observable that in most of the cases stating that section thirty-nine is qualified by section twenty-three, the question was not involved, for the debt was held not provable for other reasons. I cannot allow myself to legislate where such a distinction may be given in order to follow the opinion of judges for whom I have great respect. My duty is done by taking the statute as I find it.

The complainant is entitled to a decree.—January 9, 1872.

————•◦•————

A debt contracted in whole or in part for spirituous liquors, being in violation of the laws of Michigan must be rejected, and the name of the claimant stricken from the list of creditors of the estate of the bankrupt.
Claimant ordered to pay the costs and an attorney's fee of ten dollars.

In re S. PADDOCK.

The issues arise upon the three several petitions of Theodore C. Etheredge, assignee of the estate of the said bankrupt, to reject the debts of certain creditors which have been proven before the register, viz: of Dyer & Wilder, of Toledo, Ohio, for one hundred and ninety dollars ; of Markscheffel Brothers, of the same place, for three hundred and fourteen dollars and seventy-nine cents, and of Marshall Brothers & Co., of the same place, for one hundred and forty-nine dollars and nine cents ; for the alleged reason that the said debts were contracted for spirituous and intoxicating liquors sold in violation of the statutes of the state of Michigan.

The said creditors put in their respective answers to the said petitions, admitting that the debts were contracted for spirituous and intoxicating liquors, but alleging that they were so contracted at Toledo, in the state of Ohio, and that by the laws of the latter state the same were legal and valid.

Proofs were taken, and the facts appear to be as follows : the liquors were furnished to the bankrupt upon his orders given by him at Coldwater, in the state of Michigan, his place of business. Each bill of liquors so furnished exceeded fifty dollars in amount. There was no note or memorandum made in writing and signed by the bankrupt, of any of the orders except two, and they were unstamped. All the orders were taken by traveling agents of the sellers except one of the unstamped written orders, and one taken by one of the sellers in person. The orders taken by agents were in all cases subject to the approval of the sellers. There does not appear to have been any express direction or agreement as to how the liquors were to be forwarded, but as matter of fact they were placed by the sellers on the cars of the Michigan Southern and Northern Indiana Railroad at Toledo, and thence carried on said cars to Coldwater, where they were received by the bankrupt, and this was the only means of transportation of freights by common carrier between those places.

The issues were argued by Mr. POND, of Newberry, Pond & Brown, for petitioner; Mr. AUSTIN, of Pike & Austin, for creditors.

LONGYEAR, J.— A preliminary objection was made on

behalf of the creditors to the jurisdiction of the court, "for the reason that they are entitled to have the validity of their said claims adjudicated, and determined in a court of law, and by a jury." I do not consider this objection tenable in the present form of proceeding, for two reasons : FIRST. Because the creditors stand before the court in the attitude of plaintiffs, themselves invoking the jurisdiction to which they object ; and, Second. Because by general order in bankruptcy number twenty-six, ample provision is made for adjudication and determination of their claim in a court of law and by a jury, of which the creditors may avail themselves by taking an appeal to the circuit court under section eight of the bankrupt act, in case they were dissatisfied with the decision of this court.

The question for decision is, whether these debts under the circumstances stated, are to be deemed as having been contracted at Coldwater, in the state of Michigan, or at Toledo, in the state of Ohio. If the former, then it is conceded that they are illegal and void under the prohibitory liquor law of Michigan, and must be stricken out. If the latter, then it is also conceded that they are valid and must remain as debts against the estate of the bankrupt.

On the one hand it is contended that because the orders were subject to approval of the sellers at Toledo, and that by the usual course of business between the parties the liquors were to be delivered on the cars at Toledo, that was the place where the contracts were completed, and therefore they were Ohio contracts. On the other hand, while it is conceded that such would be the legal effect in the case of a valid order, it is contended that the orders were themselves void by the statute of frauds, and that no debt could be created by virtue of anything done under them until the liquors were actually accepted and received by the bankrupt, and that such receipt and acceptance having taken place at Coldwater, that is the place where the debts were in fact contracted, and therefore they were Michigan contracts.

The orders upon which the liquors were furnished consist

of three classes : First, Those which were given verbally to agents ; Second. The one given verbally to a principal ; and Third. The two which were given in writing.

FIRST. As to the verbal orders given to agents.

The statue of frauds of Michigan (2 Comp. L. 944, section 3184) enacts that " no contract for the sale of any goods, wares or merchandise, for the price of fifty dollars or more, shall be valid unless the purchaser accept and receive part of the goods sold, or shall give something in earnest to bind the bargain, or in part payment, or unless some note or memorandum in writing of the bargain be made and signed by the party to be charged thereby, or by some person there-. unto by him lawfully authorised."

This is but a re-enactment of the English statute, and it has been held in England that a common order, like those here in question, given to the seller for the article required, is clearly equivalent to a contract for the purchase, and so within the statute. Brown on Stat. of Frauds, sec. 293 ; *Allen* v. *Bennett*, 3 Taunt. 169. I think the circumstance that the orders were taken by the agents subject to the approval and acceptance of the principals, whose place of business was in Ohio, does not prevent the application of the Michigan statute. The orders being approved and acted on by the principals, constituted the contracts on the part of the purchaser, and having been made in Michigan, the contracts were Michigan contracts so far as this question is concerned. The statute does not require that the contract should be signed by both parties to make it valid, but it does require that it must be signed by the party *to be charged thereby*. The bankrupt's estate is sought to be charged by virtue of the orders as constituting the contracts for the purchase on the part of the bankrupt. The orders were given in Michigan, and each purchase was for more than fifty dollars. The statute of Michigan, therefore clearly applies unless avoided by something in the case other than the circumstance that the orders were taken by the agents subject to the approval of the principals.

In re Paddock.

It is contended that although there was no express direction as to how the liquors were to be forwarded, yet the mode in which they were forwarded being the only means of transit, and that being according to the usage of the parties, it must be presumed to have been so intended, and that therefore the delivery on the cars at Toledo was the completion of the contracts, and hence they were Ohio contracts.

However that may be, in a case of a contract not within the statute of frauds, it is clearly not so in a case like the present of contracts which are within that statute. Here delivery alone is not sufficient. *Acceptance and receipt* of the goods by the purchaser are essential. The right of stoppage *in transitu* still remained to the sellers after such delivery, and the right to reject the goods still remained to the purchaser. In all such cases it is well settled that it is the actual acceptance and receipt of the goods by the purchaser alone that constitutes a completion of the contract, so as to take it out of the statute making it invalid if not in writing. Brown on Stat. of Frauds, sec. 916; Story, on Sales, sec. 276; Hilliard on Sales, 161; 2 Parsons on Con. 321-2; *Alderton* v. *Buchor*, 3 Mich. 322.

The acceptance and receipt of the liquors by the bankrupt took place at Coldwater, in the state of Michigan. The contacts for their purchase, by virtue of these orders, were therefore completed in that state, and of course were Michigan contracts, and as such subject to the laws of that state.

SECOND. As to the verbal order given to the seller in person.

This order was also given at Coldwater, in Michigan, and except that it was not subject to subsequent approval, it is in all respects like the verbal orders given to agents, and the same considerations apply to it as have been applied to them. It is therefore also a Michigan contract.

THIRD. As to the two orders which were given in writing.

As we have already seen, such orders are equivalent to contracts of purchase. As such they come clearly within the perview of the internal revenue law of the United States, and were subject to a stamp of five cents. 13 Stat. at Large 298. By this same law, as amended by the act of Congress of July thirteenth, eighteen hundred and sixty-six, it is provided "That hereafter no deed, instrument, document, writing or paper, required by law to be stamped, which has been signed or issued without being duly stamped, or with a deficient stamp, nor any copy thereof shall be recorded, *or admitted or used as evidence* in any court until a legal stamp or stamps, denoting the amount of tax, shall have been affixed thereto, as prescribed by law." 14 Stat. at Large 143-4.

Therefore, as to these two items there is no evidence before the court of any order or request of the bankrupt. No liability or indebtedness of the bankrupt can therefore be deemed to have accrued on account of these items until the liquors were actually received and appropriated by him, and as such receipt and appropriation actually took place at Coldwater, in Michigan, these must also be deemed Michigan contracts.

We see then that each and all the debts in controversy arose out of Michigan contracts, and as such it is conceded that so far as they were for spirituous liquors, in whole or in part, they are absolutely invalid and void by the provisions of the prohibitory liquor law, so-called, of Michigan.

The debts of Dyer & Wilder and Marshall Brothers & Co. appear to be wholly for spirituous liquors, and are therefore invalid and void.

The debt of Markscheffel Brothers appears to have been part for spirituous liquors and part for groceries. The items for liquors are first in point of time in the account. Payments had been made on the account from time to time, and the bankrupt's notes had been taken to balance the account. The debt, as proven before the register, was based upon these notes, except as to a small account wholly for spirituous liquors, purchased by the bankrupt after the notes had been given.

The payment, which had been made before the notes were given were more than sufficient to cover the items for liquors, and it was contended that inasmuch as the items for liquors were the older items in point of time, the payments must be deemed to have been made upon such items, and that therefore the balance of account for which the notes were given must be deemed to have been wholly for the groceries.

But here steps in another provision of the prohibitory liquor law of Michigan, as follows : "All payments for such liquors hereafter sold in violation of law shall be considered as having been received without consideration and against law and equity, and any money or thing paid therefor may be recovered back by the person so paying the same," etc.   The payments which were made cannot therefore be deemed as applying to the items for liquors; neither could they be, even if they had been made with that express direction, which, however, does not appear to have been the case.

There is, however, another complete answer to this claim. The balance for which the notes were given was of the whole account, of which the items for liquors constituted a part. The consideration, therefore, must be deemed to have been in part for spirituous liquors, and this makes the notes invalid and void, the same as if the whole consideration had been such.

Each of the debts in controversy is therefore held to be invalid and void by reason of its having been contracted in whole or in part for spirituous liquors in violation of the laws of Michigan, and the same must be rejected, and the names of the respective claimants must be stricken from the list of creditors of the estate of the bankrupt, and the said claimants must pay the costs of this proceeding, including an attorney's fee of ten dollars in each case.

A separate order as to each debt must be prepared and signed to carry out the above decision.—January 16, 1872.

UNITED STATES DISTRICT COURT—MASSACHUSETTS.

The district court has jurisdiction of a bill in equity by an assignee in bankruptcy to set aside a conveyance of land alleged to be fraudulent as to creditors, although there may be concurrent remedy at law.

Land conveyed in fraud of creditors passes to the assignee in bankruptcy of the grantor by virtue of section fourteen of the act, though conveyed more than six months before the bankruptcy, and is not within section thirty-five.

In Massachusetts a voluntary conveyance to a wife or child of the grantor by a person much indebted is *prima facie* fraudulent, as to existing creditors If such a deed is set aside by existing creditors, it seems that the land or its proceeds are assets for creditors generally. If it should be assets only for a certain class of creditors, yet the assignee is the proper plaintiff to impeach the deed.

Where the bill alleged that the grantor was much indebted at the date of his voluntary deed, and that some of the debts still remained unpaid, but did not allege facts enough to show the deed to be void as to subsequent creditors, a demurrer to the bill was overruled.

When such a bill made a purchaser from the trustees under the voluntary deed a party defendant, without sufficient allegations that he knew of or partook in the fraud, the bill was dismissed as to him, but retained as to the other defendants, who were the parties to the voluntary settlement.

PRATT, Jr. v. *CURTIS et al.*

Two bills in equity by the assignee of the firm of Curtis & Collamore asking that certain conveyances made by Mr. Curtis about fifteen months before the bankruptcy should be set aside, and for other relief.

The first suit related to certain lands in Charlestown, settled in trust for the children of the settlor, and alleged that the deed was voluntary; that Curtis at the time of the settlement was indebted to the plaintiff and others, who were still his creditors, and was embarrassed in his circumstances, and that the deed was made with intent to delay and defraud his creditors.

The second bill was similar, excepting that it related to land in Boston, and that the conveyance was alleged to be for the benefit of the wife of Mr. Curtis, and that a purchaser of the land from the trustees was made a party defendant.

Demurrers were filed to both bills.

H. C. HUTCHINS & H. H. CURRIER, for defendants.

FIRST. The bill does not allege the particular provision of the bankrupt act on which the plaintiff relies; nor does it allege title in the assignee. Both of these things are essential in good pleading. *In re* Broome, 3 N. B. R. 90; *Bean* v. *Brookmire et al.* 4 N. B. R. 57.

SECOND. A conveyance is not fraudulent or void simply because it is voluntary, nor because the grantor is more or less indebted. The bill should show that the property conveyed was unreasonable in amount; or that the remaining assets were not sufficient to pay the debts existing at the time of the conveyance, or some other kindred allegation. *Sexton* v *Wheaton*, 8 Wheat. 229; *Hinde* v. *Longworth*, 11 Wheat. 199; *Babcock* v. *Eckler*, 24 N. Y. 622; *Sedgwick* v. *Place*, 5 N. B. R. 158, and cases there cited; *Salmon* v. *Bennett*, 1 Conn. 525; *Thatcher* v. *Phinney*, 7 Allen, 150; *Lerow* v. *Wilmarth*, 9 Allen, 386; *Winchester* v. *Charter*, 12 Allen, 606; s. c. 97 & 102 Mass.

THIRD. The assignee in bankruptcy represents all the creditors, and there is nothing in the bills to show that many of the debts are not subsequent in date to the deeds. If they are, the allegations ought to be sufficient to avoid the deed as against the creditors who hold these debts, or the assignee has nothing to do with the fraud.

FIFTH. There is no allegation that Wiswall was not a *bona fide* purchaser without notice. If he was the action cannot be maintained against him. 3 Washb. on Real Prop. 226, 296-7; 1 Story Eq. secs. 432, 6, 434; *Enders* v. *Williams*, 1 Met. (Ky.) 345; *Salmon* v. *Bennett*, 1 Conn. 525.

FOURTH. The remedy is at law. *Woodman* v. *Saltonstall*, 7 Cush. 181.

M. F. DICKINSON, JR., for plaintiff.

LOWELL, J.—The case cited from Cushing's reports shows that in the courts of this state, an assignee in insolvency must proceed at law for lands conveyed in fraud of creditors. But the equitable jurisdiction of the courts of the United States does not depend upon the remedies given by the state courts. It is the same throughout the country, and is the same now that is was in seventeen hundred and eighty-nine;

and nothing is better settled than that this jurisdiction exists in those cases in which the chancery courts in England have concurrent jurisdiction with the courts of common law, and notably of bills by creditors to set aside deeds said to be voidable by them. *Skelton* v. *Tiffin*, 16 How. 163; *Bean* v. *Smith*, 2 Mason, 252; *Hagan* v. *Walker*, 14 How. 29.

In respect to the second bill it was admitted at the bar that the remedy at law might not be adequate, because if it turned out that Mr. Wiswall was a *bona fide* purchaser without notice, the trustees might still be held to account in equity for the purchase money, though the land would be beyond their reach. But the cases are so many in which the jurisdiction has been sustained without any such special circumstances, that it is not necessary now to examine the reasons and to apply them to both suits. Every one of the cases in the federal courts which I shall have occasion to cite in the course of this opinion, was a case in equity.

SECOND. The objection that the bill ought to point out the particular section of the bankrupt law which gives the plaintiff a right to set aside the deed is not sound. The plaintiff is to set out facts, and it would be bad pleading to allege the law. Perhaps the meaning of the objection is that the assignee in bankruptcy cannot avoid any transfer of property but such as come within section thirty-five, which these deeds do not, because they were made more six months before the bankruptcy. This is a mistake. That section refers only to frauds on the act itself; but the assignee can, as a general rule, avoid any conveyances which the creditors could avoid. Thus in *Carr* v. *Hilton*, 1 Curtis C. C. 233, it was decided that the assignee under the bankrupt act of eighteen hundred and forty-one, could maintain a bill of this kind relating to lands conveyed by fraud before the passage of the act, and this, although that act did not mention conveyances in fraud of creditors. That decision would govern this case, even if the law of eighteen hundred and sixty-seven were silent; but that law, at section fourteen, vests in the assignee " all the property conveyed by the bankrupt in

fraud of his creditors;" being intended, I suppose, to meet
any possible doubt that might remain, notwithstanding that
decision.

THIRD. Does the bill state a case of fraud on creditors?
The defendants very justly draw a distinction between creditors at the time of the conveyance and those who become
such afterwards. Under our laws, which require the recording of deeds for the very purpose of notifying creditors as
well as purchasers, this general distinction, which is admitted
even in England, is highly just and equitable. It has been
fully adopted by the courts of the United States in the cases
cited. It is however the statute of 13 Elizabeth as adopted
and construed in Massachusetts, which governs this case, and
I have therefore examined the decisions of this state with
some care. From them I derive the following propositions:

FIRST. A voluntary conveyance to a wife or child is not
fraudulent *per se*, but it is a question of fact in each case
whether a fraud was intended. ·

SECOND. Such a deed made by one who is considerably
indebted is *prima facie* fraudulent, and the burden is on him to
explain it.

THIRD. This he may do by showing that his intentions
were innocent, and that he had abundant means, beside the
property conveyed, to pay all his debts.

FOURTH. If the deed was not in fraud of existing creditors
the burden of proof is on the subsequent creditors to show a
fraud on them. *Thatcher* v. *Phinney,* 7 Allen, 146; *Lerow* v.
Wilmarth, 9 Allen, 382; *Winchester* v. *Charter*, 12 Allen, 606;
s. c. 97 Mass. and 102 Mass. The bills do not allege the
facts which would be necessary to show a fraud on subsequent creditors only; but the rule appears to be that if a deed
is avoided by antecedent creditors, the land or its proceeds
goes to creditors generally. *Walker* v. *Burrows*, 1 Atk. 94;
Townshend v. *Windham*, 2 Ves. Sr. 11; *Jenkyn* v. *Vaughan*, 3
Drew, 419; *Whittington* v. *Jennings*, 6 Sim. 493. The case last
cited went this length: that a creditor whose account had
been running when the voluntary settlement was made, might

set it aside, though the items of debt at the date of the deed had all been paid, the balance having always been increasing. I am not aware that the precise point has arisen in Massachusetts; but the *dicta* support of the plaintiff's view, that if a conveyance is fraudulent as to existing creditors, it is so as to all. *Winchester* v. *Charter*, 12 Allen, 609.

In England there appears to be another rule in equity, that if there be nothing to impeach the settlement excepting that it is voluntary, no secret trust and no intent to defraud subsequent creditors, they will not be permitted to impeach the deed without showing one or more antecedent debts outstanding when the bill is filed. *Halloway* v. *Millard*, 1 Mad. 414; *Lush* v. *Wilkinson*, 5 Ves. 384. This doctrine is not easily to be reconciled with the other, nor with prcinple, because it makes the validity of the conveyance depend on matters arising *ex post facto*. It probably gained a footing in the courts at a time when such conveyances were held to be absolutely fraudulent in law as against existing creditors, and was a sort of equitable mitigation of the rigor of that doctrine.

Whether this is the law here, I do not now inquire, because this bill alleges the existence of antecedent debts. Whether the grantor must be actually insolvent at the time, in order to render the conveyance fraudulent against existing creditors, has been mooted. In *Winchestor* v. *Charter*, 12 Allen, 609, BIGELOW, C. J., says that a voluntary transfer of property by a person deeeply indebted and whose property was inadequate " or barely sufficient " for the payment of his debts, would furnish strong presumptive evidence of fraud. At another place on the same page he says it is necessary to show that he was indebted beyond his probable means of payment. In *Parish* v. *Murphree*, 13 How, 100, McLEAN, J., says that in case of a merchant, insolvency need not be proved; it is enough to show that his situation was such that a prudent man with an honest regard for the rights of his creditors could not have made such a settlement. I am much inclined to believe that if insolvency were distinctly proved, as matter of fact, the intent to defraud existing creditors would follow as matter of law, because one who undertakes to make a voluntary conveyance must be presumed to know the state of his affairs. *Christy* v. *Courtenay*, 13 Beav. 96. It has been so held even in cases of preference ; but the argument applies much more strongly to a gift, because a trader may often make payments of just debts in the ordinary course of business without any thought of his standing in respect to other creditors ; but in making a gift he undertakes to say that he is in a position to make it with justice to them. On the other hand, if insolvency is not clearly shown, the true inquiry perhaps is that put by Mr. Justice McLean, whether a prudent man, having a just regard for the rights of his creditors, would have permitted himself to do the act.

These bills do not allege insolvency ; but all the cases agree that if the grantor is much indebted or is embarrassed, the burden of proof is on him to explain the transaction, if questioned by existing creditors, and these facts are alleged ; it follows that the bills are sufficient to require the respondents to answer, unless their objection that the deeds can be set aside only to the extent that may be necessary to pay antecedent debts, and that the assignee cannot work out this equity, is well taken. We have already seen that the doctrine of courts of equity in England appears to be, that if the deed is set aside, the property becomes assets. I do not decide this point, however, because in my opinion, the assignee in bankruptcy and he only has the right to impeach the deed in the interest of any class of creditors. Great confusion would arise from any rule which required creditors to follow the property on their own account and in the state courts ; and on the other hand full power is given to this court to set aside all fraudulent conveyances to which creditors are affected and to marshal all assets. Many cases might arise in which the only difficult point to be decided would be whether all the creditors or only certain of them were interested, and upon the theory of the defence it would depend upon the decision of that point whether the suit

Davis v. Anderson et al.

should stand or fall, though it was clear that the deed was fraudulent as to some creditors; while if the assignee can bring the suit in either event, that difficulty is obviated.

The second bill seems to be defective so far as Mr. Wiswall is concerned, in not alleging distinctly his participation or knowledge of the fraud. He is not a necessary party to the bill, because the other defendants may be required to account for the proceeds of the sale, although his title should be found or be admitted to be unimpeachable. Indeed MARSHALL, C. J., has said in such a case, that no decree ought to be made against a purchaser, so long as there were volunteers before the court who were able to pay the debt. *Hopkirk* v. *Randolph*, 2 Brock, 132.

The demurrer is sustained as to the defendant Wiswall, with costs, unless the plaintiff chooses to amend within ten days upon the terms of paying his costs up to this time.

The other defendants are to answer over in two weeks, their demurrer being overruled.

UNITED STATES DISTRICT COURT—E. D. MISSOURI.

Creditors of bankrupt having security, whether by judgment, mortgage or otherwise, must prove their debts against the bankrupt and foreclose their liens under the authority of the court in bankruptcy, or they may not only be barred of their debt, but may also lose the benefit of their securities.

A sale of the debtor's land by virtue of an execution issued and levied after the filing of the petition in bankruptcy, will not pass the title to the land as against the assignee, although the judgment was entered and the lien created prior to the bankruptcy.

After the commencement of the proceedings in bankruptcy, all the property and assets of the bankrupt are in *custodia legis*, within the control of the bankrupt court only, and no other tribunal can interfere with its process.

It is not essential to the title of the assignee that the assignment to him by the register should be recorded within six months from its date. The title of the assignee takes effect by relation from the commencement of the proceedings in bankruptcy, and the recording is not required for the mere purpose of giving notice to purchasers.

The limitation of two years in section two of the bankrupt act applies only to property held adversely to the bankrupt and his assignee.

Where the bankrupt fraudulently conveyed his lands to avoid a judgment, a purchaser under the judgment and a sale made under execution after proceedings in bankruptcy commenced, cannot defend on the ground that the assignee did not commence suit to set aside the execution, sale and deed within two years after the assignment. No cause of action accrued to the assignee against such purchaser until he acquired his title under the judgment and execution sale.

The bankrupt court may order a sale of the bankrupt's property free and clear of encumbrances, and the secured creditor will then have his remedy only against the fund in court. If the secured creditor fails to prove his debt and proceeds against the fund, he does so at his peril.

DAVIS, *Assignee*, v. ANDERSON et al.

TREAT, J.—This is a bill to set aside certain sheriff's deeds for bankrupt's property, the levy, sale and deeds having been made after adjudication had in bankruptcy.

On the fourth of April, eighteen hundred and sixty-seven, six judgments were rendered in the circuit court of Scott county in favor of said county against Archibald P. Lane and others.

On the first of February, eighteen hundred and sixty-eight, Lane filed his petition and was adjudicated a bankrupt. On the twenty-sixth of March following, the plaintiff was appointed assignee. On March thirteenth, eighteen hundred and sixty-eight, executions were issued on said judgments, and a levy made on a portion of bankrupt's real estate; and on April ninth, eighteen hundred and sixty-eight, the sale thereof was made to Joseph T. Anderson and William B. Anderson, and the deed therefor executed and delivered October sixth, eighteen hundred and sixty-eight. On September fifteenth, eighteen hundred and sixty-eight, a levy was made on another portion of bankrupt's real estate, and a sale had thereunder October seventh, eighteen hundred and sixty-eight, to said Anderson, to whom the sheriff's deed therefor was made and delivered November thirteenth, eighteen hundred and sixty-eight.

On March nineteenth, eighteen hundred and sixty-nine, another levy was made under said judgments, and a sale on April ninth, eighteen hundred and sixty-nine, of another portion of the bankrupt's real estate, was made to Joseph T. Anderson, and a deed therefor delivered. The price paid at the first sale was twenty-five dollars; at the second fifty-five dollars, and at the third twelve dollars. Said property is worth from five to eight thousand dollars. At the time of each of said sales, said Andersons were copartners in business, and on dissolution of their partnership, February fourteenth, eighteen hundred and seventy, Joseph T. conveyed to William B. all his interest in said real estate.

The assignee did not record in Scott county the register's assignment to him within six months from the date thereof, nor until the sheriff's sale had been recorded.

The several judgment debts were duly scheduled and notice of bankruptcy, &c. sent to the judgment creditor in February, eighteen hundred and sixty-eight; but he has never appeared to prove his demand or obtain any order of the court with reference thereto. Said Joseph T. Anderson was also scheduled as a creditor, and duly notified of said proceedings in bankruptcy in February, eighteen hundred and sixty-eight.

This suit was commenced November seventh, eighteen hundred and seventy.

It appears that soon after said judgments were rendered against him, the bankrupt entered into a fraudulent scheme to conceal his property from his creditors. By deed dated May first, eighteen hundred and sixty-seven, he conveyed for the pretended consideration of five thousand dollars, all the real estate in question to one Goodin, and on September seventeenth, eighteen hundred and sixty-seven, Goodin executed a deed of trust thereon to secure a fictitious note in favor of Schwank; and October seventeenth, eighteen hundred and sixty-seven, the trustee sold the property to Schwank for default in the payment of said note. That contrivance was suggested to Lane by an attorney, in order to enable Lane to escape payment of his surety debts—the other parties agreeing to aid in the scheme for covering the property for the benefit of Lane. None of the facts concerning that fraud became known to the assignee until about November seventh, eighteen hundred and seventy, when a bill was filed against the parties thereto to have said deeds

Davis v. Anderson et al.

adjudged void, which decree has been rendered. On the same day as above stated, this suit was brought. Lane received his discharge in eighteen hundred and sixty-eight, there being no assets reported.

The principal questions of law which arise on the foregoing facts relate to the duties of judgment debtors and assignees, and to the effect of the limitation of two years prescribed by section two of the bankrupt act.

Under the Missouri statutes, the judgments mentioned were a lien upon Lane's real estate in Scott county. The judgment creditor seems to have supposed that no necessity existed for proving his demand in the bankruptcy court, or for invoking the aid of that court. Although the judgments had been obtained in April, eighteen hundred and sixty-seven, no execution or levy was made until Lane had been adjudged bankrupt, when it was probably deemed necessary to enforce the lien through executions from the state court.

Under the bankrupt act all subsisting liens are fully protected, but all lien creditors are required to prove their debts, however evidenced. This is apparent from section twenty-two of the act, and from various other provisions thereof. Section twenty-two requires the creditor to prove his demand and disclose "whether any and what securities" he holds, and the act rests in the court "the ascertainment and liquidation of the liens and other specific claims." Secured debts may be paid, or the secured creditor may relinquish his security, or he may become a general creditor "for the balance of the debt after deducting the value of such property, to be ascertained by agreement between him and the assignee, or by a sale thereof, to be made in such manner as the court may direct;" or the assignee may, if the value of the property exceeds the debt, release to the secured creditor the equity of redemption on receiving the excess; or he may sell the property subject to the secured creditor's claim. Section twenty-two further provides that "in either case the assignee and creditor respectively shall

Davis v. Anderson et al.

execute all deeds and writings necessary or proper to consummate the transaction. If the property is not sold or
released and delivered up, the creditor shall not be allowed
to prove any part of his debt." It must be observed that
the creditor referred to is " a creditor who has a mortgage or
pledge of real or personal property of the bankrupt, or a
lien thereon for securing the payment of a debt owing to him
from the bankrupt."

In *Buckingham* v. *McLean*, 13 How. 167, it was held that
" whenever by the local law a judgment or an execution
operates to make a lien on the property, it is to be decreed
a security." That was a decision under the bankrupt act
of eighteen hundred and forty-one, and the act of eighteen
hundred and sixty-seven is still fuller and more explicit as
to secured creditors. Hence a judgment creditor's demand
is scheduled, and he must prove his demand in bankruptcy,
and may elect which of the many modes contemplated with
reference thereto he will adopt. While his lien may be
enforced in any of the prescribed modes, it must be enforced
through the bankrupt court under whose control the bankrupt's property and rights of property pass. All of his
property is held to be *in custodia legis*, subject to the order of
the bankrupt court; and if so, the principles laid down in
Taylor v. *Carryl*, 20 How. 583, apply and are decisive. (See
authorities cited *post*.)

The supreme court of Illinois in *Cole* v. *Duncan et al.* 3
C. L. N. 323, held that the mortgagee might forclose the
mortgage in a state court, after the mortgagor was adjudged
bankrupt, without reference in any way to the bankrupt
court. It is said that the supreme court of Pennsylvania
has intimated similar views.

That was a suit to forclose a mortgage and the mortgagor
appeared and pleaded his discharge in bankruptcy. His
plea was held bad, for the reason that his personal discharge
did not divest the lein; and the court directed an amendment of the bill to bring in the assignee. It also held that
the mortgagee was not bound to prove his lien demand in

the bankrupt court. The case seems not to have been well considered, and certainly is not in accord with the provisions of the bankrupt act and the decisions of the United States courts.

The bankrupt act does not divest the lien either of a mortgage or judgment, but provides the means of enforcing them through the bankrupt court. The assignee has vested in him all the property interests of the bankrupt, legal or equitable, for the benefit of all creditors, whether secured or unsecured. The administration of the estate demands that he should be a party to all proceedings affecting it in any way. Under section twenty, as has been seen, he may, under direction of the bankrupt court, redeem from a mortgage or release the mortgagee. If the mortgagee can forclose in a state court without reference to the assignee's rights and duties under the bankrupt act, then many of the mischiefs intended to be guarded against will prevail without serious " let or hindrance." A fraudulent cover of the bankrupt's property in the form of a mortgage can readily be made effective ; for when mortgagor and mortgagee combine, and the assignee as representing the creditors is not made a party to the suit of forclosure, how is the fraudulent scheme likely to be defeated?

The act contemplates that all suits affecting the bankrupt's estate shall be prosecuted in the proper United States court, unless the United States court in charge of the estate otherwise direct. If this was not so, it would be very easy to devour the estate with unnecessary costs and delay its final settlement by uncontrolled litigation in the various state courts of the country. Whatever reason exists for compelling unsecured demands to be litigated in the bankrupt court is as potential with respect to secured claims—nay, is often more cogent. The various statutory provisions to defeat preferences and frauds would be unavailing, if the validity of a pretended mortgage debt could not be investigated, nor the validity of a judgment fraudulently obtained.

If a mortgagee, without proof of the mortgage debt before

a bankrupt court, or if a judgment creditor, without proving his judgment debt, can, despite the bankrupt court, proceed to swallow up the bankrupt's estate, then there would exist no *uniform* system, and no adequate protection for the general rights of creditors.

The first inquiry is, whether a mortgage debt really and honestly exists. Who is to ascertain its existence? Is there any distinction in this respect between such a debt or any other, or any reason why a creditor of one kind should ignore the bankrupt court rather than another and interfere with property in its custody?

But it is not necessary to elaborate this point. The act does not attempt to divert a lien; but it does require those who possess them to enforce their claims through the bankrupt court, and in so doing does not interfere with the rights of such a creditor any more than it does with the rights of other creditors. If the act did not exist, an unsecured as well as a secured creditor could resort to state courts, yet it is not pretended that, after bankruptcy, an unsecured creditor can sue the bankrupt in a state court in violation of section twenty-one, and the other provisions of the act.

The question is not as to the rights of property or the existence of liens, but of jurisdiction for their ascertainment and enforcement.

The views expressed might be vindicated more fully if the second clause of section twenty-five, as to property in dispute, and sections twenty-seven and twenty-eight, as to settlement of the estate, and sections fifteen, sixteen and seventeen as to the rights and duties of assignees, with respect to suits pending or to be brought, were carefully analysed.

It is true the act is not always precise in its use of terms, and some of its provisions are seemingly inconsistent with others. Thus, it is not easy to determine the precise effect of sections twenty, twenty-one and twenty-two, and the course to be pursued under them, with respect to certain demands, and hence the conflicting decisions with respect thereto. By section twenty a secured creditor may prove the balance of his debt over and above the value of the security, or release the security and prove the whole of the debt, sharing *pro rata* with the unsecured creditors as to the amount so proved. The language is, as to a secured creditor: "He shall be admitted as a creditor only for the balance of the debt," seemingly excluding him as a creditor to the extent that he has ample security so long as he retains that security; but section twenty-two requires that "all proofs of debts against the estate of a bankrupt" shall be made before a register, &c., and that the claimant shall disclose what securities he holds. Those and other provisions show that the language just quoted means that the secured creditor shall prove his debt and disclose the securities, but shall not be admitted as a creditor against the general assets to share *pro rata* with unsecured creditors, except for the balance of the debt remaining unsatisfied after the securities have been exhausted.

By section eleven the bankrupt is required to place in his sworn schedule "*all* his debts," and "a statement of any existing mortgage, pledge, lien, judgment, or collateral or other security given for the payment of the same;" also in his inventory of assets, "whether there are any, and if so what encumbrances thereon." A public notice and special notice is given "to all creditors upon the schedule," stating that "a warrant in bankruptcy has been issued against the estate of the debtor;" that "the transfer of any property by him is forbidden," and that "a meeting of the creditors to prove their debts and choose one or more assignees, will be held." Thus section eleven includes secured as well as unsecured creditors, just as do sections twenty, twenty-one and twenty-two.

But section twenty-one evidently has reference, in its first sentence, to debts proved against the estate for *pro rata* distribution—that is, if a judgment creditor elects to abandon his unsatisfied judgment and prove his original debt, he can do so, thus availing himself of the benefit further provided for in section twenty-two as to preferences. The second sentence forbids creditors "from prosecuting to final judg-

Davis v. Anderson et. al.

ment in law or equity any suit against the bankrupt until," &c.; and the third sentence provides for the stay of proceedings in such suit, except by leave of the bankrupt court, &c. Very serious questions have arisen under section twenty-one, where such suits have been prosecuted without a stay of proceedings asked by the bankrupt. Inasmuch as the discharge of the bankrupt leaves him still liable for his debts created by fraud, embezzlement, defalcation, &c., suits for recovery on such demands, it has been supposed, might proceed to final judgment, though the debt had been proved before the register and dividends received, as the act expressly permits. But whether that be correct ruling or not, (and no opinion is now given on the point), it is obvious that all debts have to be scheduled, all creditors notified, and all who wish any proceeds out of the bankrupt's estate must prove their demands, whether the bankrupt is discharged and released from the debts or not. On no other ruling can the various provisions of the act be reconciled nor the estate properly administered. The bankrupt schedules the secured debt and states what the security therefor is ; the secured creditor proves his debt and discloses the security ; and the assignee is vested with the bankrupt's rights of property as they stood at the date of commencing proceedings. The assignee is in a more favorable condition than the bankrupt as to many questions ; for, representing creditors, he may cause conveyances to be set aside which the bankrupt could not himself avoid. Such evidently is the case with regard to preferences, voluntary conveyances, judgments suffered or procured, &c. Hence if the bankrupt court is not to intervene, creditors will be deprived of their rights and the act to that extent become a nullity.

This court has held uniformly that after adjudication of bankruptcy an execution and levy may be enjoined, so that the bankrupt court may proceed to dispose of the property in such manner as to secure and enforce the rights of all concerned in the bankrupt's estate—that the administration of no part thereof, whether a lien thereon exists or not, is to be taken from it. The assignee under the direction of the bankrupt conrt must reduce the assets to money and account therefor to the fullest extent. The title to real estate, though judgment lien thereon exists, is in the assignee. How is that title to pass from him? If he sells, releases or compromises, he does so by order of the bankrupt court. If an adverse interest therein is claimed, he may cause the same to be judicially settled, either by litigation or by reporting the facts and receiving the proper order of the court in the premises.

Without pursuing this branch of the subject further, it may suffice to say that bankrupt courts have invariably, as occasion demanded, granted injunctions or taken such other steps with respect to judgment and other liens, as indicated that no other view obtained than that the property of the bankrupt could not be reached without the intervention of the proper bankrupt court—or in other words, that such property, whatever might be the liens upon it or its condition, was *in custodia legis,* not to be interfered with by any process or proceedings from any other tribunal.

But it is said that the assignee did not file a copy of the assignment to him for record in Scott county during the prescribed six months, and therefore the purchasers at the sheriff's sale had no notice that the title had passed out of the bankrupt into the assignee. As a matter of fact, Joseph T. Anderson did have such notice before any of the levies or sales. At the first two sales he and his brother became joint purchasers, and at the third he was sole purchaser. Hence if it were important to charge the defendants with notice, they stand so charged by the proofs.

But what is the object of the requirement to record the assignment in the various counties where the realty is situated? The recording thereof is not essential to the title, for by the assignment and operation of the law, title, by relation, passed to the assignee as of the date of filing the bankrupt's petition. Of course the assignment, which cannot be made before the election of an assignee, cannot be recorded prior thereto, that is, before it exists. If its validity depended on its being duly recorded, then it could not relate back; and if the purchase from or under the bankrupt —as by direct conveyance from him, or by execution, levy and sale on judgment previously rendered—is to be held valid because the purchaser had no notice that his title was diverted, then the relation spoken of would be a nullity. Is it to be contended that sales made intervening the adjudication of bankruptcy and the election of the assignee, are valid unless actual notice of the adjudication is brought home to the purchaser and no constructive notice by a recorded assignment had been made? It is obvious that the requirement about recording is for other purposes. It has been held that it was not to give force or validity to the transfer to the assignee, or for the purpose of constructive notice within the ordinary interpretation of registry acts, but to enable the purchaser under the assignee to have in the proper county a record of his derivative title.

It was wise, however, for other reasons. As the county records should contain a complete registry of all instruments on which transfers of titles depend, it was eminently proper for the protection of all concerned that the assignment in bankruptcy should be there recorded—an instrument in writing which though not conforming in the usual particulars with conveyances from one party to another, or even with sheriff's deeds, yet by the paramount law is a complete transfer and conveyance of all the bankrupt's real and equi· table interests, with the exceptions named in the act. That instrument is not signed by the bankrupt, or acknowledged by him, but is signed by the register or judge. When the assignment is recorded, the record or duly certified copy thereof is by section fourteen made evidence of the assignment in all courts, notwithstanding very different rules as to instruments affecting realty may obtain under state laws.

It is to be remarked that the clause directing the assignment to be recorded gives no further effects thereto than that just stated. The assignment itself passes the property with relation back to the commencement of proceedings, and all subsequent purchasers are affected accordingly, whether they purchased before assignment actually made or afterwards, and consequently the recording of the assignment is not essential to the validity of the transfer, and is not designed to operate as under state registry acts. The purchaser from the bankrupt after adjudication in bankruptcy or commencement of proceedings, although he had no notice thereof, would take no title. The question of notice could not therefore arise. As held by the Iowa supreme court in the cases hereafter referred to, purchasers under the bankrupt, after the transfer of title to the assignee, bought nothing, because they took only what the bankrupt had, and after proceedings in bankruptcy the bankrupt had nothing to be taken. The purchase being of what the bankrupt debtor had at the time, and all of his interest having passed to the assignee previously, the purchaser acquired no title as against the assignee.

A more serious question pertains to the true construction of the limitation in section two and the proper application thereof to the facts before the court. So far as was disclosed by the bankrupt's schedule, and as the records of the county showed, the bankrupt had no interest in this real estate. Lane had conveyed it to Goodin some nine months previous to the time he was adjudged a bankrupt for what purported to be a valuable consideration, and therefore there was no need to record the assignment in Scott county, or to institute suits with reference to this property against any person. It was not until November, eighteen hundred and seventy, that the fraud as to the Goodin and Schwank deeds became known to the assignee or creditors, and consequently no one except Goodin had any interest in combatting the levy and sales by the sheriff. There was no apparent interest in the assignee to be effected.

Section two is in these words:

"But no suit at law or in equity shall in any case be maintainable by or against such assignee, or by or against any person claiming an adverse interest touching the property and rights of property aforesaid, [viz : of said bankrupt, transferable to or vested in the assignee], in any court whatever, unless the same shall be brought within two years from the time the cause of action accrued for or against such assignee."

If the sheriff's levies and sales were valid, unless set aside by direct proceedings had for the purpose, then the causes of action may be said to have accrued at the date of the respective sheriff's deeds, and the bar of the act to be complete as to the first two sales, if the terms of the act are to be followed without regard to the ordinary statutory and equitable exceptions, making statutes commence to run in cases of fraud only from the date of the discovery thereof, or of knowledge or information of facts inducing a reasonable belief that a fraud has been perpetrated. *Martin* v. *Smith, et al.* 4 N. B. R. 83. Whether section two is to be construed so as to admit such an exception, it is not now necessary to decide. The defendants were no parties to the Goodin fraud, and do not claim under the Goodin title. If that title be, as it has been adjudged, fraudulent and void, their title is in nowise affected thereby. The assignee not having discovered that fraud, had no reason for proceeding against the defendants unless that fraud existed ; for the bankrupt's case could not be benefited by setting aside the sheriff's deeds. If those deeds are merely voidable at the option of the assignee, and he cannot maintain a suit to avoid them after two years, then the fraud, so far as the bankrupt's estate is concerned, has effectively worked its purpose. It is, perhaps, wise that such a limitation should be made in order to compel a speedy settlement of the bankrupt's estate, and also to close the many vexing suits that might arise under sections thirty-five and thirty-nine after knowledge of the facts was lost. There should be as early an end to litigation as is consistent with the rights of parties.

It has been held that section two does not apply to ordinary money demands not barred by the state statutes of limitation. *Sedcwick* v. *Casen*, 4 N. B. R. 161.

But the full force and effect of that provision seem not to have been judicially determined. 5 N. B. R. 252. It has, however, been held by the United States circuit court here, that the *concurrent* jurisdiction vested by that section in the circuit courts does not reach actions of assumpsit. It would seem, therefore, that the limitation is to be confined to controversies about property rights, or legal and equitable titles to property. What titles? Those existing at the date of proceedings in bankruptcy, or those supposed to have accrued subsequently? The assignee must unquestionably bring his suit against an adverse possessor or claimant—that is, adverse to the bankrupt originally—within the time specified. But how is it with regard to suits which the bankrupt could not maintain, but his creditors could, as under the statute of frauds and fraudulent conveyances, wherein the statute begins to run only from knowledge or information first had of the fraud? However that may be, the question still remains, does section two cover cases of fraudulent concealment of assets from the assignee? Is a fraud, successfully concealed for two years, to ripen into a valid title, or the assignee to be barred from unravelling it? Such questions may arise and have to be decided hereafter; but the present case has its solution in the legal rule which this court holds to be the true one under the bankrupt act, viz: That all liens, whether of judgments or mortgages, or by pledges, &c., must, after proceedings had in bankruptcy, be enforced solely through the intervention of proper bankrupt courts, and that a subsequent sale, whether under judgment or mortgage, without the consent of that court, is subject to be set aside by the bankrupt court. In no other way can the property, which is in its custody or under its control, be preserved for the equal benefit of creditors. Nor is this rule any more variant from those ordinarily governing litigation in state courts, than the direct provisions of the bankrupt act concerning new or pending suits against the bankrupt. If it be the supreme law within the purview of the constitutional grant concerning bankrupts, it overrides state statutes, not only

Davis v. Anderson et al.

as to assignments, preferences, &c., but also as to proceedings under insolvent and other conflicting laws, not as to the legal rules governing such transactions, but as to the forum where justiciable. On what legal theory do United States courts enjoin proceedings in state courts affecting the interest of bankrupt estates, if not on the theory that such questions should be determined exclusively in the bankrupt courts or under its direction? The bankrupt act expressly provides that by its own operation attachments in the state courts, in prescribed cases, are dissolved and suspends all other suits in state courts against the bankrupt, except by leave of the court in bankruptcy, and when that leave is granted, the suit proceeds merely "for the purpose of ascertaining the amount due," but execution is stayed.

In re Kahley *et al.* 4 N. B. R. 125, HOPKINS, J. held: "Under sections one and twenty the bankrupt court has the right through its officers to take possession of the mortgaged property after a default in payment, and sell it free of the lien without first satisfying the lien, in which case the lien is transferred to the fund in court. It is a matter of discretion with the court to sell subject to or free from the encumbrance of the lien." He cites in support of his views, *Houston* v. *Bank of New Orleans*, 6 How. 846; *Foster et al.* v. *Ames*, 2 N. B. R. 14; *ex parte* Christy, 3 How 308.

And again *in re* Cook & Gleason, 3 C. L. N. 410, the same learned judge holds that the liens of mechanics and all others should be presented to and read by the bankruptcy court, and the parties claiming those liens have no right to proceed in such suits without first obtaining leave of the bankrupt court. In support of his view he cites *Angel* v. *Smith*, 9 Ves. 335, and *Wiswall* v. *Sampson*, 14 How. 52. He held further that parties who proceed in the state courts to enforce their lien demands without leave of the bankrupt court were guilty of contempt; that the principle is applicable to every interference with the possession of a receiver or custodian who holds property as an officer of the court, for his possession is in law the possession of the court itself.

. Edwards on Receivers, 129; 3 Paige, 199; 1 Hogan R. 216; Mad. R. 406; 5 Paige, 489; 14 How. 368; 20 How. 583. And therefore the bankrupt court was bound to insist upon its exclusive right to administer and distribute the bankrupt's property, and not permit anyone with impunity to interfere through state process with such property. *In re* Hanna, 5 N. B. R. 292; *Swope et al.* v. *Arnold*, 5 N. B. R. 148; *Beers* v. *Place*, 4 N. B. R. 150; *Shaffer* v. *Fitchery & Thomas*, 4 N. B. R. 179. There are many other cases to the same effect, and this court has never hesitated to act upon the foregoing principles. .

The levy and sale by the sheriff under the executions named were in violation of the well settled rules governing these cases—an interference with property in the custody of this court—and therefore could give no right or title thereunder. *Taylor* v. *Carryl*, 20 How. 583. As between the assignee and the defendants, the title is still in the assignee. The defendant, William B. Anderson, is in no better position than his co-tenant in common and subsequent grantor.

The decree of the court will therefore be that said sheriff's deed be set aside, and held for naught; that the assignee proceed to sell said real estate free from all encumbrances, reserving to defendants the right to proceed against the fund for any demand they may have.

If any question should arise concerning the residue of the fund, the court will determine it at the proper time and in the proper way.

To the case of *Davis* v. *Campbell*, which has also been heard, the foregoing views apply, so far as the sheriff's deed is concerned.

The facts are that an execution on a prior judgment was issued and levy was made and sale was had after bankruptcy proceedings commenced; that the defendant, who was assignee of a mortgage, became the purchaser at the sheriff's sale; that his deed, it is contended, was filed for record before the assignment, although it appears from the clerk's certificate it was filed afterwards, and that Campbell had no actual notice of the proceedings in bankruptcy when he purchased.

The lien demand of neither the judgment nor mortgage was ever presented to the bankrupt court, nor has any leave to proceed thereunder been granted. The property was sold for a sum far below its value. But in this case as the defendant is, perhaps, a mortgagee in possession, although his sheriff's title is valueless, the court will enter a decree to sell the property free from all encumbrances, reserving to the defendant the right to prove any demand he may have against the fund.

The following doctrines on this subject have been frequently held and have passed into some of the text-books as settled law : " The commencement of proceedings in bankruptcy operates as a *supersedeas* of all process in the hands of the officer of any other court, and as an injunction against all other proceedings than such as may afterwards be had under the authority of the court of bankruptcy until the case is closed. Thus the levy of an execution, or the filing of a bill to forclose a mortgage, or the filing of a libel *in rem*, or the issuing of a distress warrant, or the filing of a mechanic's lien claim, where the lien only exists from the time of such filing, or the issuing of a writ of replevin for the purpose of affecting the estate, are null and void when such proceedings are instituted in any other court after that time. Claims against the bankrupt's property can only be enforced in the court of bankruptcy during the pendency of the proceedings, and this principle extends not only to liens, but to all controversies concerning even the title to property which was in his possession at the time of filing the petition."

The supreme court of Iowa in *Stuart* v. *Hines et al.* 6 W. Jur. 22, and several other cases passed upon at the same time, quote the foregoing, and add that the several cases cited in support of the doctrines thus laid down fully sustain the text. Indeed, as previously shown in this opinion, no other rules are consistent with the bankrupt act. And the custody of the property, the title being in the asignee as an officer of the court, cannot be divested except under the direction of the court. Hence some ill-considered opinions to the effect that the lien creditors may wait until bankruptcy proceedings are closed, and then enforce their liens through the state courts or under powers to sell, can have no force.

The assignee may cite in the secured creditor so as to determine what shall be done with respect to the security, and it may be advisable so to do, yet it is none the less the duty of the secured creditor to prove his demand and obtain the aid of the court for its enforcement. The court has jurisdiction over both the bankrupt debtor and all his creditors, and also over all demands affecting the bankrupt's estate. If the lien creditor does not act, and the property is sold by the assignee under the order of the court, free from all liens or encumbrances, what recourse is left to the creditor after the fund has been fully distributed? If he thus sleeps on his rights, he does so at his peril. The estate must not be left open indefinitely, to the detriment of all other creditors, because some secured creditor will not assert his rights as the law requires. It may even be a serious question whether, under the limitation in section two, he can proceed to prove his demand after the expiration of two years, and have the same enforced. Whether that section will admit of such a construction or not, it is certain that such a creditor may, through his own laches, like unsecured creditors failing to act, lose whatever right of property or interest he had in the bankrupt's estate. This court has held from the commencement, that secured creditors could not enforce their demands except through the bankrupt court, and has never hesitated to set aside sales made without its action after bankrupt proceedings were commenced. It has now given its views more at large than was necessary, without, however, citing the numerous authorities which support the various propositions stated. The bankrupt reports are full of cases, and the text-books refer to them with sufficient fullness.

UNITED STATES DISTRICT COURT—NEW JERSEY.

A debtor made a transfer of real estate to his bro her-in-law, who on the same
    day re-conveyed the property to the wife of the debtor.
Held, That the transfer took place at the time of the actual execution and
    delivery of the deeds, and not at their date, and was therefore within the
    six months limited by the act.
An exemplified copy of an examination of the debtor, taken under the laws of
    the state of New York, under supplemental proceedings upon a judgment,
    was offered, for the purpose of proving admissions of the debtor.
Held, That under the act of congress approved May twenty-sixth, seventeen
    hundred and ninety, such copy was proper evidence, such examination
    being "judicial proceedings" within the meaning of said act.

In re C. J. ROONEY.

NIXON, J.—The petition in bankruptcy in this case was
filed October eleventh, eighteen hundred and seventy-one.
The petitioning creditor's debt is claimed to be two several
judgments obtained by the petitioner against the defendant
in the supreme court of the state of New York, on the
twenty-fourth day of April, eighteen hundred and seventy-
one, for the sum of four hundred and eighty dollars and
seventy-nine cents and four hundred and thirty-one dollars
and forty cents respectively.

The act of bankruptcy alleged was the transfer of certain real estate on the eighteenth day of April, eighteen
hundred and seventy-one, by the said debtor without consideration, with intent to delay, hinder and defraud creditors.

The debt is proved by exemplified copies of the said
judgments, supplemented by the oath of the petitioner that
they remained wholly unpaid and unsatisfied. To prove the
act of bankruptcy, copies of two deeds of conveyance were
produced, certified by the clerk of Hudson county according
to law, one from Cornelius J. Rooney and wife to John J.
Gaffney, her brother, dated March first, eighteen hundred
and seventy-one, acknowledged April eighteenth, eighteen
hundred and seventy-one, and deposited in the clerk's office
for record on the last named day; and the other from the
said Gaffney and wife to the wife of the debtor, bearing date

March first, eighteen hundred and seventy-one, acknowledged April eighteenth, eighteen hundred and seventy-one, and left for record as aforesaid May nineteenth, eighteen hundred and seventy-one, and also an exemplified copy of certain proceedings had and taken before Judge Cardoza, one of the judges of the supreme court of the state of New York, under the said judgments, by virtue of the law of said state, in which proceedings the said debtor was examined and admitted under oath that the consideration paid by the said Gaffney for said transfer and conveyance was his check for five thousand dollars, which deponent endorsed to his wife; that with said check she bought back the property from her brother, and that when the conveyance was made by him to the said Gaffney, the understanding was that Gaffney should re-convey the same to deponent's wife.

It was further proved by the testimony of John H. Platt, Esq., that the two deeds were acknowledged before him by the respective grantors on the eighteenth day of April, eighteen hundred and seventy one; that he witnessed the execution of the first named deed by Rooney and wife on that day, and after annexing the certificate of acknowledgment he delivered the same to the grantors.

In order to render the transfer complained of in this case an act of bankruptcy, it must have been made within six months before the petition in bankruptcy was filed. The deeds are dated respectively on March first, and the petition was filed on the eleventh of October following. In the absence of any evidence to the contrary, it may be presumed that the date was the time of the execution and delivery of the deeds of conveyance, but I am satisfied from the proof that they were not actually executed and delivered before the eighteenth of April, and that time brings the act within the six months.

The counsel for the defendant insisted at the hearing, that there was no evidence of a fraudulent intent; that the debtor's admissions in the supplemental proceedings in New York were not legally proved, and that the copy of the examination, authenticated under the act of May twenty-sixth, seventeen hundred and ninety, (1 U. S. Stat. at Large, 122,) was not the highest and best evidence that the petitioner could have produced.

It has been held that the statute is not restricted to the case of judgments. *Hopkins* v. *Ludlow*, 1 Phila. R. 272. "Judicial proceedings" are indeed included in the very terms of the law as proper subjects to be authenticated in the mode proposed. The laws of New York provide for such an examination of the debtor, after execution, as to the disposition of his property, and his testimony thus taken and placed upon file may be fairly treated in another court as of the nature and character of a judicial proceeding, and thus capable of authentication under the act of congress.

I am therefore of opinion that the admissions of the debtor, thus authenticated, are evidence against him in this proceeding; that they are sufficient to establish the fact of a fraudulent transfer of his real estate to hinder, delay and defraud his creditors, and that an adjudication in bankruptcy should be made, and it is ordered accordingly.—December 19, 1871.

———•◦•———

UNITED STATES DISTRICT COURT—S. D. NEW YORK.

It is not "out of the usual and ordinary course of business," for a corporation engaged in manufacture and which owns mortgages yet to become due, and desires to realize money thereon for use in its regular business, to sell such mortgages for their cash value. Hence a transfer made under such a state of circumstances will be adjudged valid as against the assignee in bankruptcy.

JUDSON, Assignee, v. KELTY et al.

BLATCHFORD, J.—This bill is filed under the six months' clause of the thirty-fifth section of the bankrupt act. The bankrupts were put into involuntary bankruptcy by a petition filed February sixth, eighteen hundred and sixty-nine. The bill alleges that on the fourteenth of January, eighteen hundred and sixty-nine, and within six months before the filing of such petition, the bankrupts then being insolvent, made an assignment and transfer to the defendants of two mortgages on real estate on Staten Island, with the bonds accompanying the same, given to secure ten thousand dollars with interest, the same being then the property of the bankrupts, with a view to prevent the same being distributed under the bankrupt act, and to defeat the object of and to impair, hinder, impede and delay the operation and effect of said act, and that at the time of making such assignment and transfer the defendants had reasonable cause to believe the bankrupts to be insolvent, and that the assignment and transfer was so made to prevent said property from being distributed under the said act, and to defeat the object of and to impair, hinder, impede and delay the operation and effect of said act. The prayer of the bill is that such transfer may be declared fraudulent and void, and that the plaintiff may be declared to be entitled to the possession of the said property as assets of the bankrupts, and may recover the same from the defendants, and that if necessary the defendants may be ordered to account for said property under oath to the plaintiff, and that if the said property or any part of it has been disposed of by the defendants, the plaintiff may recover from them the value of so much as has been disposed of.

The transfer of the mortgages was made under the authority of a resolution passed by the board of trustees of the bankrupts, who were a corporation, on the nineteenth of December, eighteen hundred and sixty-eight. That resolution authorised Henry D. Blake, who was then the vice president of the corporation, to negotiate a sale or effect a loan on the mortgages on the best terms possible for the interest of the company. He endeavored to effect a sale of them for some time but could obtain no offer for them as large as that which the defendants made. He finally sold them to the defendants for seven thousand dollars. The evidence is satisfactory that that was as large a cash price as they would bring. They were payable in eighteen months from the fifteenth of December, eighteen hundred and sixty-eight, one being for six thousand, and one for four thousand dollars. The defendants paid to Mr. Blake on this purchase one thousand dollars on the fourth of January, eighteen hundred and sixty-nine, and six thousand dollars on the thirteenth of January, eighteen hundred and sixty-nine. The written assignment of the bonds and mortgages was executed and delivered on the thirteenth of January, eighteen hundred and sixty-nine.

Even if it be assumed that the bankrupts were insolvent and that the defendants had reasonable cause to believe them to be so, as well on the fourth of January as on the thirteenth of January, yet I see no state of facts which would warrant me in the conclusion that on either of those dates the defendants had reasonable cause to believe that the transfer was made with a view to prevent the property from being distributed under the bankrupt act, or to defeat its object, or to impair, hinder, impede or delay its operation and effect, or even in the conclusion that the transfer was made with such view on the part of the corporation.

The fact was much commented on that the check given ·by the defendants for the one thousand dollars on the fourth of January, was made payable to the order of Blake, while that given by them on the thirteenth of January was made payable to the order of the corporation, and it was sought to be maintained that the one thousand dollars was a loan made to Blake individually, and that such loan was repaid on the thirteenth, by taking the amount out of the price to be paid for the mortgages, and giving the corporation only six thousand dollars. But on the whole evidence it appears that the one thousand dollars was paid on the fourth as a part of the purchase price of seven thousand dollars to be paid for the mortgages.

It was also a subject of remark on the hearing, that Blake, on the fourteenth of January, paid off to the defendants individual indebtedness of his to them amounting to three thousand six hundred and forty-six dollars and twenty-seven cents. But it appears that the transaction between the defendants and the corporation in reference to the sale of

Judson v. Kelty et al.

and the payment for the mortgages was fully closed on the thirteenth of January, without there being any agreement or understanding between the defendants and Blake that he should pay to the defendants out of the money paid by them for the mortgages, the amount of his individual indebtedness to them. Whatever claim the plaintiff may have to investigate and challenge as against the defendants and Blake, the disposition of the money received by Blake as the purchase price of the mortgages, no such question is presented in. the bill in this suit. It attacks only the transfer of the mortgages.

The point was taken that the transfer of the mortgages was not made in the usual and ordinary course of business of the corporation, and that that fact is *prima facie* evidence of fraud, under the thirty-fifth section of the Act, throwing on the defendants the affirmative to show that there was no fraud. To bring this clause of the thirty-fifth section into operation, it is necessary for the plaintiff first to show that the transfer of the mortgages was made out of the usual and ordinary course of business of the corporation. It is not enough to show that the general business of the corporation was to make and sell gas stoves, and that the sale of a bond and mortgage was not the sale of a gas stove. Without reference to the general business of the debtor, the transfer must be out of his usual and ordinary course of business in respect to an article of the description of that transferred. In this case the corporation had sold the stock, fixtures and lease of a store in the Sixth avenue, in New York, and received the mortgages in payment therefor. It cannot be said to be out of the usual and ordinary course of business for a corporation, whose general business is the making and selling of gas stoves, and which owns mortgages yet to become due, and desires to realize money thereon for use in its regular general business, to sell such mortgages for their highest cash value.

It results, that the bill must be dismissed with costs.

ALBERT ROBERTS for the plaintiff, WILLIAM H. ARNOUX, for the defendant.—October 27, 1871.

UNITED STATES DISTRICT COURT—MASSACHUSETTS.

A decree of a state court dissolving an insurance company incorporated under the laws of the state, and appointing receivers to take and distribute the property of the company. and enjoining the latter from the further prosecution of its business, which decree was founded upon the insolvency of the corporation, does not take away the jurisdiction of the district court of the United States to adjudge the corporation bankrupt.

The state laws do not extend to all the matters arising in bankruptcy, such as preferences and property out of the state, and even if it be granted that the state courts have concurrent jurisdiction of an insolvent corporation, they have not full jurisdiction of the subject matter.

In re INDEPENDENT INSURANCE CO.

A creditor of the Independent Insurance Co., a corporation established under the laws of Massachusetts, filed his petition in January, eighteen hundred and seventy-two, alleging that the company was insolvent and had made certain fraudulent preferences.

On the return day a suggestion was made by the receivers appointed by the supreme judicial court of the commonwealth, which suggestion afterwards took the form of a plea to the jurisdiction, by which it was alleged that in December the insurance commissioners applied to the state court to have the corporation enjoined from further prosecuting its business, on the ground of insolvency; that a preliminary injunction was issued and hearings were had; and that on the same day that the petition was filed in this court, a decree was entered in the state court making the injunction perpetual, appointing receivers to take possession of the assets of the company, and distribute the same equally among the creditors of the corporation, and to divide the surplus, if any, among the stockholders. This decree was entered before the petition had been filed here.

C. J. REED, for receivers.

There can be no doubt of the power of a state to dissolve a corporation of its own creation, and this has been lawfully done in the case of the Independent Insurance Co. The effect of such a dissolution is to stay all suits and to render all future judgments erroneous. It is in strict analogy to the death of a natural person. *Merrimac* v. *Potomac Co.* 9 Pet. 281 ; *Curran* v. *Arkansas*, 15 How. 308 ; *Bacon* v. *Robertson*, 18 How.; *Merrill* v. *Suffolk Bank*, 31 Maine, 57 ; *Greely* v. *Smith*, 3 Story, 657.

H. W. PAINE & J. O. TEELE, for petitioning creditor.

The supreme court of Massachusetts has denied the power of the supreme court of New York to dissolve a corporation under like circumstances with these, and under a statute which cannot be distinguished. *Folger* v. *Columbian Ins. Co.* 99 Mass. 267.

2. The insolvent laws of the state, whether general or special, are superseded by the bankrupt act, and the bill of the insurance commissioners which alleges merely the insolvency of this company is nothing but a sort of petition in bankruptcy. In whatever way we take it, the jurisdiction of this court is full and exclusive *Thornhill et al.* v. *Bank of Louisiana*, 5 N. B. R. 367 ; *The Merchants' Insurance Co.* 6 N. B. R. 43.

B. SANFORD, for the corporation filed an answer submitting to the jurisdiction and admitting the acts of bankruptcy.

LOWELL, J.—The questions necessarily presented by this case do not appear to be difficult of solution, and as the affairs of the company are said to need attention, I have determined to dispose of them without delay. The somewhat startling proposition is advanced, that by the decree of the supreme court of this commonwealth dissolving the corporation, the whole jurisdiction in bankruptcy is foreclosed, and the general creditors must be content to take such assets as remain within the reach of the state process and to leave all extra-territorial property to the mercy of attaching creditors, and all payments which would have been preferences under the bankrupt act, to be mere payments in full of so many debts of the company. The corporation is extinct, it is said, and its property has reverted to the state, which never owned it, or to those who happen to be in possession of it at the moment of the dissolution. This view would be equally fatal, of course, to the title of the receivers and to the suit under which they are acting, as to all other suits and proceedings. They felt the pressure of this situation, for the learned and able counsel who represented them said that he was not sure whether he occupied any other relation to this case than that of an *amicus curiæ*, suggesting the death of the supposed bankrupt.

The cases cited for this position do not support it. One of these cases is *Curran* v. *Arkansas*, 15 How. 308, in which CURTIS, J. cites with approval a note to 2 Kent Com. 307, that the doctrine now contended for is obsolete, and all the other cases, excepting two decisions at common law, lay down the rule that a corporation, however it may be dissolved, still exists for the purpose of paying its debts and of dividing its surplus, if any, among its shareholders, or of having this done by a court of equity acting on the property. Those two cases do say that a judgment at common law cannot be lawfully rendered against an extinct corporation; but I have yet to learn that a petition in bankruptcy is an action at common law. It is an equitable sequestration, as much so as the bill under which the receivers were appointed in this, but having a wider reach and a more effectual operation. If it were an action at common law it would make no difference, because the statute of Massachusetts agrees with the doctrine of chancery and extends it to cases at law by enacting that all corporations whose charters expire by limitation or are annulled by forfeiture or otherwise, shall nevertheless be continued bodies corporate for three years for the purpose of prosecuting or defending suits, etc. Gen. Stats. ch. 68, sec. 36. The charter of this corporation has either been annulled by forfeiture or otherwise, or else it still exists, and in either event it may prosecute and defend suits excepting as restrained by a court of competent jurisdiction.

I do not intend to enter into any race of diligence, nor into any controversy concerning jurisdiction. If I see the supreme judicial court-exercise a power, I shall assume it to exist though I may not have discovered its origin. Granting then, for the purpose of this hearing, that the state law by which insolvent insurance companies are wound up is not, so far as the mere winding up is concerned, superseded by the bankrupt law, not even at the demand of the creditors, and that the jurisdiction is co-ordinate, it is yet certain that the decree of the supreme judicial court was not intended by that court to operate, and does not operate, to take away the jurisdiction of this court in bankruptcy. I find in it no injunction against a petition in bankruptcy even by the corporation, and of course none addressed to creditors, and I do not suppose that court would undertake to enjoin such a proceeding. It simply forbids the company to carry on business except in ascertaining losses and cancelling policies. Nay, more, if the power of the receivers is as extensive as it is said to be, it would be their clear duty under the decree to put the corporation into bankruptcy, since they can in no other way carry out the true intent of the decree, which is that the property should be equally divided among all the creditors. If we adopt the bold metaphor of the argument, that the defendant is dead and the funeral rites alone remain to be solemnized, we shall find that only in this place can they be adequately performed.

The cases of *Taylor* v. *Carryl, Freeman* v. *Howe*, and others which establish that where the courts of one jurisdiction have possession of the *res*, no others can interfere with it, have no application, because from its constitution and powers the supreme judicial court cannot have full possession of the *res*, and does not profess to have it. It knows no such thing as a preference. It cannot deal with property out of the state nor with property attached even in the state before bill filed, and therefore remains and must remain in every case a possible *res* for this court to act on, even if the jurisdiction is concurrent or co-ordinate, and that *res* is shown to exist in this case. For these reasons I have not considered with care the question whether the assignees will be entitled to the property. If they are they can undoubtedly obtain it by application to the supreme judicial court, should the receivers be in possession, of which I am not advised, and should refuse to resign it, which I do not anticipate. If the decree there should be against the assignees, they can have a writ of error to Washington, or they may, I suppose, sue the receivers in a personal action, though not by replevin, in the courts of the United States. I cannot doubt that full and speedy justice will be done them in either jurisdiction.

Finding, as I do, that this corporation still exists for the purpose of being proceeded against here, and that its creditors have not been enjoined from proceeding, nor the corporation from defending or being defaulted, and that it admits the acts of bankruptcy alleged against it, I adjudge it to be bankrupt, and order a warrant to issue as provided by law.

January, 1872.

UNITED STATES DISTRICT COURT.—MASSACHUSETTS.

There is nothing illegal in endeavoring to produce all the claims against the estate of a bankrupt for the purpose of staying the bankruptcy proceedings altogether ; failing in this, the purchaser should nevertheless be allowed to prove the claims purchased as though he were an original creditor.

In re PEASE et al.

LOWELL, J.—The register has certified to me, by consent of parties, the question whether a claim offered for proof in the name of Clark & Smith, ought to be admitted. The case will decide many others pending in the same bankruptcy proceedings. After the petition in bankruptcy was filed, the father-in-law of one of the bankrupt firm, undertook to buy up all the debts in order to settle the case out of court and save the "name and disgrace" of bankruptcy. Failing in

In re Pease et al.

this, the case proceeded and the debt now offered for proof is one of those which had been bought. The original creditors made the deposition after the assignment was agreed on, and at the time it was completed, and handed it to the purchaser, together with an order for the dividends; and it is in the interest of the purchaser that it is now offered for proof. The form adopted is that which was usual in Massachusetts, when the insolvent law was in operation in that state.

In the absence of agreement by the opposing creditor, I suppose his objection to be, either that no such assignment can lawfully be made after the bankruptcy, or that this debt was procured for the purpose of influencing the proceedings. *In re* Murdock, 3 N. B. R. 36, I gave my views upon the first point, and I have seen no reason to change them. In my opinion an assignee of a chose in action can prove it, and for the reasons there stated. It is more regular and the true mode of proving, that the holder should himself make the affidavit; else the statement that the claim was not procured etc., becomes merely illusory, for it is not made by the party who has bought the claim, and might be entirely true in respect to the affiant, and false as to the real party in interest.

The other question is one of fact mainly; that is, whether the debt was bought for the purpose of influencing the proceedings. There is no evidence that it was, but abundant evidence that it was not bought for that purpose. It was bought for the purpose of staying the proceedings altogether if all could be bought, but there is nothing either illegal or immoral in this.

The debt is admitted to proof.—December, 5, 1871.

UNITED STATES DISTRICT COURT.—KENTUCKY.

A consigned goods to B with orders to sell them and take negotiable notes payable to his order. B. sold the goods to C. taking negotiable notes payable to himself instead of to A. At the time of the sale, C. was accommodation endorser for B to a large amount. B. discounted the notes above mentioned and paid the proceeds to C. to apply towards taking up the notes on which C. was endorser. B. was insolvent at this time, and shortly thereafter was adjudged a bankrupt. His assignee brought suit and recovered the amount thus paid to C. on the ground that he, C., had reasonable cause to believe B. was insolvent when he received the money. A. filed a bill in equity to recover the money in the hands of the assignee, claiming that as it never belonged either to B. or C. he ought to be allowed to assert his right to it. The court held that it was not *shown* that the money paid to C. by B. was the product of the sale of A's goods, that although the bill alleges the whole of it was thus derived, and the allegation is not denied by the answer, the allegation is not on this account to be taken as true, that it is only an allegation of some fact which is presumed to be within the knowledge of the party answering, that can be taken as true, simply because it is not denied. The court further held that the fund having been recovered not in virtue of any right in the complainant personally, but in virtue of the rights of the bankrupt's creditors generally and in virtue of the clear legal right of all the creditors, under the bankrupt law, it must be distributed among them generally and not given to one.
Bill dismissed with costs.

WHITE v. *JONES, Assignee.*

Some time prior to February twenty-seventh, eighteen hundred and seventy-one, the complainant, White, consigned to the bankrupts, Schickedantz & Sewell, one hundred and twenty-five barrels of whiskey, for sale, directing them to sell and take negotiable notes, payable to his order. Schickedantz & Sewell sold all the whiskey, between the twenty-seventh of February, eighteen hundred and seventy-one, and March fourth, following, to Boes & Lucking, taking negotiable notes payable to themselves instead of White. At the time of the sale, Boes & Lucking were accommodation endorsers for Schickedantz & Sewell to the amount of six thousand four hundred dollars. Schickedantz & Sewell caused all the notes which they had received on the sale of whisky to be discounted in bank, and sometime between the first and fifteenth of March, eighteen hundred and seventy-one, paid to Boes & Lucking six thousand two hundred dollars, with the understanding that Boes & Lucking would appropriate the same to the taking up of the bills on which they were endorsers, as mentioned above. Schickedantz & Sewell, at the time of the payment to Boes & Lucking, were insolvent, contemplated insolvency, and were, on the eleventh of April, eighteen hundred and seventy-one, on the petition filed against them by one of their creditors, John D. Harris, adjudged bankrupts. Afterward S. E. Jones, the defendant, as assignee of the estate of Schickedantz & Sewell, brought suit against Boes & Lucking, under the provisions of the thirty-fifth section of the bankrupt act, and recovered from them the six thousand two hundred dollars, on the ground that the payment had been made by Schickedantz & Sewell, at a time when they were insolvent, and that Boes & Lucking, who were their creditors, had reasonable cause to believe them to be insolvent, and that the payment made by them was a preference, and a fraud upon the bankrupt act. In this suit it did not appear that the six thousand two hundred dollars, which had been paid to Boes & Lucking, was the same money that was derived from the discount of the notes given by them on account of White's whisky, but it did appear that the money was for the most part withdrawn from the bank by Schickedantz & Sewell, and mingled with their other moneys. The bill, however, alleges that the money paid to Boes & Lucking was the proceeds of the sale of White's whisky, and this is not denied by the answer of the assignee. The complainant, White, seeks to recover the money in the hands of the assignee which was recovered from Boes & Lucking, claiming that, as it never belonged to Schickedantz & Sewell, or to Boes & Lucking, he ought to be allowed now to assert his right to it, the same as if it had been found by the assignee in the hands of Schickedantz & Sewell in trust for complainant. That the fraudulent transfer to Boes & Lucking did not confer any rights upon the assignee in regard to the fund, other than what he would have had if such transfer had not been made.

BALLARD, J.—I have reluctantly come to the conclusion

White v. Jones.

that complainant has not made out a case which entitles him to any relief. It is not *shown*, that six thousand two hundred dollars, paid by Schickedantz & Sewell to Boes & Lucking, were the product of complainant's whisky. I may conjecture that a part, nay, that a large part of this sum was derived, but the fact is not satisfactorily proven. The bill, it is true, alleges that the whole of it was thus derived, and the allegation is not denied by the answer, but the allegation is not on this account to be taken as true. The rule in Chancery pleadings is not that every allegation of a bill be taken as true, simply because it is not denied in the answer. If any allegation is to be taken as true, simply because it is not denied, it is only an allegation of some *fact which is presumed to be within the knowledge of the party answering.* Now there is no ground for presuming that Jones knew that the money which Schickedantz & Sewell paid Boes & Lucking was derived from complainant's whiskey ; and, therefore, if I have stated the rule of equity pleading correctly, the allegation of complainant's bill, that it was so derived, though not denied by Jones, is not to be taken as true.

But assuming the fact to be as alleged, still it is undeniable that complainant could not recover the money from Boes & Lucking without showing that they knew it. The moment the money was paid to them, under circumstances which were entirely lawful, but for the provisions of the bankruptcy statute, it was free from all trust and claim in behalf of the complainant. There is no allegation in the bill that Boes & Lucking knew whence the money paid them was derived, and, therefore, it must be assumed they were ignorant of the fact. Now, I think if complainant could not have followed the money into the hands of Boes & Lucking ; if his lien on the trust in it was destroyed when it was received by Boes & Lucking, then he cannot follow it into the hands of the assignee in bankruptcy who recovered it of Boes & Lucking, not on the ground that they received it knowing the complainant's right or claim, but on the sole ground that they received it contrary to the provisions of the bankruptcy statute.

It cannot be maintained that the assignee holds the money subject to the same trust and equities which attached to it when it was in the hands of the bankrupts. If he had received it from them, or had received it as their right, then he would have no better right to it than they, and if in his hands, it would be subject to every equity to which it was subject to in their hands. But he did not receive it from them or recover it on the ground of any right in them. They had effectually parted with their right. The assignee recovered it in spite of their effort to part with it, and not as their representative, or as the representative of complainant, but as the representative of the bankrupts' creditors. He recovered not because the bankrupts had defrauded complainant, but because they had committed what is made by the thirty-fifth section of the bankrupt act a fraud on their creditors generally. As I view the case, the fund having been recovered, not in virtue of any right in complainant personally, but in virtue of the rights of the bankrupts' creditors generally; not in virtue of any peculiar equity. in any particular creditor, but in virtue of the clear legal right of all the creditors under the bankrupt law, it must be distributed among the creditors generally, and not given to one. Let the bill be dismissed with costs.

UNITED STATES DISTRICT COURT-- N. D. NEW YORK.

The application of creditors other than the petitioning creditor in a bankruptcy proceeding for an order annulling the adjudication on the ground that there was an agreement of compromise preceeding the commencement of bankruptcy proceedings to which agreement the petitioning creditor was a party, must be denied.

The proceeding by a petitioning creditor to force his debtor into bankruptcy is a proceeding *inter partes* like an ordinary action at law or suit in equity, and until the adjudication is had, they are the only parties. No outside creditor has a right to resist the adjudication or to ask that it be annulled.

Want of notice to a bankrupt is a formal objection well taken—as the bankrupt has an interest in the continuance of proceedings which may result in his discharge. If assignments of policies of insurance belonging to a bankrupt prior to his adjudication, are valid, they can be maintained as against the assignee, to be appointed in bankruptcy proceedings, and if they are not legal and binding, they should not be made so as against non-assenting creditors by the dismissal of proceedings after the expiration of the time allowed to dissenting creditors to commence proceedings in order to avoid a preference has elapsed.

In re L. BUSH.

HALL, J.—This is an application by the firms of Claflin & Co. and Paton & Co. of New York, for an order annulling the adjudication of bankruptcy made in this case on the sixth day of June, eighteen hundred and seventy-one, upon the petition of Henry Dickinson, a creditor of the bankrupt, which petition was filed on the first day of May, eighteen hundred and seventy-one. Notice of the application has not been served upon the bankrupt, and the attorney of the petitioning creditor who had been served with notice and appeared to oppose the application, objected on the hearing that notice should have been given to the bankrupt as well as to the petitioning creditor.

The ground on which this application is urged is, that in December, eighteen hundred and seventy, "nearly all the creditors" of the bankrupt, including Henry Dickinson, the petitioning creditor, signed an agreement of which the following is a copy, viz :

" We the undersigned, creditors of L. Bush, of Elmira, New York, for and in consideration of one dollar to each of us in hand paid, the receipt of which is hereby acknowledged, and in further consideration of the assignment of L. Bush to J.

Arnot, Jr., of Elmira, New York, for the benefit of his creditors, of the policies of insurance amounting to nine thousand
five hundred dollars, due him by reason of loss he sustained
by fire, agree hereby to accept in full satisfaction of our respective claims set opposite to our signatures, forty per
cent. payable in cash as soon as this agreement is completed,
and the amount realized from the policies, the surplus remaining after this agreement is complied with, to revert back to
the said L. Bush;" and that by an agreement with the bankrupt,
and with the knowledge and assent of the said Henry Dickinson, the petitioning creditor and all the other creditors of said
Bush (except some whose debts in the aggregate did not amount
to two hundred and fifty dollars), the said policies of insurance
were assigned to Claflin & Co. and Paton & Co., to be
held and prosecuted under and pursuant to said agreement
for the benefit of the creditors of the bankrupt, and that they
had commenced suits on said policies and incurred expenses
in the prosecution thereof. The papers used on the motion
leave it doubtful whether the assignment of the insurance
policies was for the benefit of all the creditors of the bankrupt or for the benefit of those only who should execute the
agreement.

The application must be denied. The formal objection to
the want of notice to the bankrupt is well taken, as he has an
interest in the continuance of proceedings which may result
in his final discharge, and the objection that Claflin & Co.,
and Paton & Co., as outside creditors cannot be heard upon
a motion to set aside or annul the adjudication is also well
taken. The proceeding by a petitioning creditor to force his
debtor into bankrupcy is a proceeding *inter partes* like an ordinary action at law or suit in equity, and until the adjudication is had they are the only parties. No outside creditor
has a right to resist the adjudication or to ask that it be annulled. *In re* Boston, Hartford and Erie Railroad Company,
5 N. B. R. 232 ; *Hobson* v. *Markson*, 1 Dillon, 421.

If the assignments under which Claflin & Co., and Paton
& Co., have been acting are valid and binding, they can be

maintained as against the assignee to be appointed in these proceedings, and if they are not legal and binding they should not be made so as against the creditors of the bankrupt who have never assented to them, by the dismissal of these proceedings after the time allowed to dissenting creditors to commence proceedings in order to avoid a preference has elapsed. The motion must be denied with costs.

GEORGE GORHAM, for Claflin & Co. and Paton & Co.; AUDLEY W. GAZZAM, and GEORGE WADSWORTH, for petitioning creditor. February 6, 1872.

UNITED STATES DISTRICT COURT—E. D. MICHIGAN.

An injunction granted under section forty of the bankrupt act does not extend beyond the adjudication. Hence any proceedings to punish parties for contempt in violating an injunction after adjudication, must be dismissed with costs.

In re S. J. MOSES.

The injunction was issued under section forty of the bankrupt act, on filing the petition for adjudication of bankruptcy. The petition was filed and injunction issued November fifth, eighteen hundred and sixty-nine. An order was issued at the same time, requiring the alleged bankrupt to show cause, as required by said section forty, returnable November sixteenth, eighteen hundred and sixty-nine, on which day an order of adjudication of bankruptcy was made, and an assignee was appointed December eleventh, eighteen hundred and sixty-nine. The acts alleged to have been done by Lang in violation of the injunction, are alleged to have been done January twentieth, eighteen hundred and seventy, more than two months after the adjudication of bankruptcy. Those alleged to have been committed by Hanaw appear to have been committed also after the adjudication, although no specific date is alleged.

It is contended on behalf of Lang & Hanaw that by the express provisions of section forty, under which the injunction was issued, its operation and effect were limited to the period of time between the time of its service on them and the time when the hearing and adjudication were had upon the petitiou for adjudication of bankruptcy, and therefore the acts complained of, not having been done within that period, are not within the purview of the writ.

Mr. REILLY for assignee ; Mr. PECK for Lang & Hanaw.

LONGYEAR, J.—So much of section forty of the bankrupt act as is material to the consideration of the question presented, is as follows : "That upon the filing of the petition authorized by the next preceding section, if it shall appear that sufficient grounds exist therefor, the court shall direct the entry of an order requiring the debtor to appear and show cause, at a court of bankruptcy to be holden *at a time to be specified in the order*, not less than five days from the service thereof, why the prayer of the petition should not be granted; and may also, by its injunction, restrain the debtor, and any other person, *in the meantime*, from making any transfer or disposition of any part of the debtor's property not excepted by this act from the operation thereof, and from any interference therewith."

As a court of bankruptcy, this court possesses no general powers to issue injunctions. Its powers in that regard are derived solely from that portion of section forty above quoted, and such powers are of course limited strictly within the scope of its provisions. The restraining power of the court then is limited in point of time to the period of time expressed by the words " in the meantime," which I have italicized in the quotation, and those relate manifestly to the period of time between the entering of the order to show cause and the time specified therein for the hearing, as provided in the first part of the quotation. I think the most extended construction that can be given to these words is, that they are intended to cover the whole period up to such time as a hearing and adjudication shall be had upon the petition for adjudication of bankruptcy. I can see no warrant whatever for extending their meaning beyond that.

It is true that in this case the injunction is in the ordinary form and reads : " Until the further order of the court." But this clause must be read in the light of the authority under which the writ was issued, and being so read its meaning is as follows : " Until a hearing and adjudication shall be had upon the petition for adjudication of bankruptcy against Solomon J. Moses."

If creditors, on filing petition for adjudication of bankruptcy, desire to restrain parties from interfering with the debtor's property beyond the time when an adjudication may be obtained, they must do so by invoking the general powers of a court of equity. This court does not possess such power. See *in re* Metzler *et al.*, N. B. R. Sup. ix ; *in re* Irving & Hughes, 2 N. B. R. 21 ; *in re* Kintzing, 3 N. B. R. 52 ; *Creditors* v. *Cozzens, et al.*, 3 N. B. R. 73 ; *in re* Fuller, 4 N. B. R. 30.

The acts complained of in these cases having been done after the restraining power of the injunction had ceased to operate, the orders to show cause must be discharged, and the petitions and proceedings against the said Lang and Hanaw for contempt must be dismissed, with costs to the said Lang and Hanaw, including an attorney fee of twenty dollars (being ten dollars in each case), to be paid by the assignee out of the funds of the estate of the said bankrupt in his hands. January 16, 1872.

UNITED STATES CIRCUIT COURT—W. D. MICHIGAN.

A debt wholly or in part secured, either by levy under an execution, by pledge of personal property or mortgage upon real estate, will sustain a petition for an adjudication of bankruptcy. The better practice is, when the debt is *fully* secured, to waive the security in the petition, but this is not necessary to its support.

In re STANSELL.

EMMONS, J.—The only question which arises on this

appeal is, can one whose debt is *fully* secured become a petitioning creditor for an adjudication in bankruptcy?

The petition was dismissed in the district court upon the ground that he could not.

The creditor had obtained judgment for his debt and levied upon property so much encumbered that no bids could be procured. It is found that its value, beyond the encumbrances, exceed the amount of the judgment. Thec reditor, however, disagreed in opinion with the witnesses, and, *waiving his security* by an amendment of the petition, asks to be permitted to stand as favorably in court as if he had no judgment and levy. The particulars of the practice need not be mentioned, as these facts sufficiently present the point for judgment.

The reason why a secured creditor cannot petition, is said to be that his debt is not within the meaning of section thirty-nine " provable under the act." The last clause of section twenty-two, it is said, prohibits the proof in whole or in part of secured claims.

The learning and accuracy of the judge from whose judgment this appeal is taken, has caused me to go carefully over all the accessible judgments in reference to this question, and to review opinions I have before formed and expressed in regard to the sections involved. They have been so repeatedly analysed in printed judgments, it is deemed unnecessary to reproduce them here. I concur fully in the interpretation which reads section twenty and the forms twenty-one and twenty-five as requiring *all* creditors, secured and unsecured alike to prove their claims, and which construes the last clause of section twenty-two, prohibiting the proof of any part of a secured claim, to mean only that the creditor shall not be admitted *to share in the assets* except for the just balance beyond his security.

I should, however, deem the concurring judicial construction of the statute sufficient to constrain aquiesence in it if I did not wholly concur with its principle. In this circuit I think it has been uniform, with the exception of the judgments of the learned judge who decided this case. The following citations being part only of a still greater number, authorise a decision here on the ground that so many rulings ought to put the question at rest. An intelligent outline of the practice in proving this class of claims, and the argument which sustains it, is found in the opinion of register Hesseltine, *in re* Bridgeman, 3 N. B. R. 84, approved by ERSKINE, J. It rules the point directly raised upon an application to make proof by a secured creditor. *In re* Ruehle, 2. N. B. R. 175, decides the same question, and holds expressly the security need not be released before proof. In *Markson & Spaulding* v. *Heany*, 4 N. B. R. 165, DILLON, J. arguing a question of jurisdiction over the mortgage property of a bankrupt in another state, says : "The debt of the mortgagee *is provable*, and such proof does not waive his lien." In order to prevent the latter consequence, of course the lien should be stated, and this is implied in the opinion of BENEDICT, J., *in re* Bigelow, 1 N. B. R. 186, which has been the leading one on this subject. A corporation held stocks in pledge for a debt, and applied to have them sold that it might prove for a balance. He held that it must first prove its claim. He considers the apparently conflicting provisions of the law, and says the last clause of section twenty-two does not prohibit the proof of the claim before the register, but only the admission ultimately of the creditor to share in the assets beyond what is justly due. LOWELL, J., *in re* Alexander, 4 N. B. R. 45, has also had the question before him. The only point was whether a secured creditor might petition for a balance of over two hundred and fifty dollars, and as his reasoning in holding that he could, seemingly tended to *exclude* one *wholly* secured, he added that he did not wish to be understood as saying that such a creditor could not sustain a petition if he offered to *waive his security*. That where the lien was created by attachment, levy or otherwise by operation of law, the mere *proof* of the debt, without mentioning it, would be a sufficient waiver ; but that when it existed by *contract*, as in the case before him, it ought to be *expressly* waived. That a secured creditor could sustain a petition is fully said in the judgment in *Rankin & Pullin* v. *Florida, Atlantic & G. C. R. R. Co.* 1 N. B. R. 196. In that case the petitioning creditor held secured bonds. There was no offer, as in the case before us, to waive the security. FRAZER, J. sustained the proceeding. He said that a claim which might in any mode be proved, when the necessary steps had been taken to authorise it, was one provable under section thirty-nine. See also *in re* Winn, 1 N. B. R. 131. *In re* Bloss, 4 N. B. R. 37, LONGYEAR, J. made a similar ruling, holding *first*, that a secured debt, like an unsecured one, would authorise a petition, and *second*, that when the lien, as in this case, was created by levy, an original petition for adjudication will *per se* waive it as fully as an unconditional proof of the debt before the register. *In re* Snedaker, 3. N. B. R. 155, the supreme court of Utah, in a judgment of more than ordinary elaborateness in this class of cases, held that the secured creditor who was proceeding to foreclose his mortgage in another territorial court, must come in and *prove his claim* or abandon his rights. It is said that the statute and forms twenty-one and twenty-five so demand.

Bump's Law and Practice of Bankruptcy, 4th ed. 54, after citing the cases *in re* Bloss and *Rankin & Pullin* v. *Florida, Atlantic & G. C. R. R. Co.*, to the point that a *secured* creditor may petition, subsequently adds, that if the debt is *wholly* secured, or is contingent, it is *insufficient ;* and cites *Sigsby* v. *Willis*, 3 N. B. R. 52, decided by HALL, J. and *Avery* v. *Johann*, 3 N. B. R. 36, by MILLER, J. The first concerns a contingent debt only. The other did dismiss a petition which was in fact secured, not *because* it was so, but on the ground that in the peculiar circumstances of that case the remedy was ample at law. We should, with BIGELOW, J. *in re* Alexander, *disclaim* authority to reject a petition on any such ground. This, however, is immaterial here. Neither case in the slightest degree sustains Bump's intimation that a fully secured debt will not sustain a petition.

I find but one counter judgment, and that is *in re* High &

Hubbard, 3. N. B. R. 46, by the learned judge who decided this cause in the district court. That was an application by bill to have mortgaged property sold that the complainant might prove for a balance. This case is like *in re* Bigelow, 1 N. B. R. 186, in which a contrary ruling is made. *In re* High & Hubbard the bill was sustained upon the ground that the complainant had no remedy by proof before the register for a secured claim. While the difference between these judgments results only in varying modes of doing precisely the *same thing*, there is in it less of practical importance. The one demands a new suit by bill and answer, with separate references to examining masters for testimony by which the secured creditor's claim is proved, and by the court adjudicated without release, agreement with the assignee, or sale of the security. It is like the proof before the register, all preparatory to those things. The other, through the instrumentality of the register and the forms pointed out by the statute, and the orders of the supreme court, performs identically the same judicial functions resulting in a like order or decree. It is a mere matter of *practice*. I do not understand the decisions which hold that a bill like that sustained *in re* High & Hubbard should be dismissed, go upon any jurisdictional reasons which deny the power of proceeding in that mode; but as saying only that as the statute and forms clearly contemplate the proof before the register of secured as well as unsecured claims, and as this is the more simple and expeditious form, they reject the most expensive and circuitous proceedings by an original bill. But when this difference leads to a denial of substantial right, and excludes every secured creditor in the nation from the protection and benefits of this statute, while at the same time they are subjected to its power and their claims cut off by the discharge, it arises in importance second to no other single question I have had occasion to consider under it.

The exigencies of our commerce and business, it seems to me, demand a different reading, or an early amendment of the law. There are hundreds of millions of secured railroad and other corporate bonds afloat in the country. In many localities the great bulk of our bankers and brokers make loans in the aggregate of vast sums upon government bonds and stocks, and upon bills of lading and warehouse receipts as collaterals. The greater share of the more permanent debt of the whole country is secured by mortgage. To exclude this great mass of claims from the power of launching, and the protections and benefits of the proceeding, is so manifestly without the intention of the law, that we should go confidently forward to that limit where construction ends and interpolation and erasure commences in pursuit of a different meaning. We had occasion, in *Linn et al.* v. *Smith*, 4 N. B. R. 12, to show how universally this class of laws, both in England and here, had associated the right of *petitioning* for an adjudication with a subjection of the debt to discharge by a decree. To enforce the one and deny the other would be as impolitic and unjust as it would be anomalous.

Irrespective of these views I should sustain this petition upon the doctrines ruled by LONGYEAR, J., *in re* Bloss, 4 N. B. R. 37, and the case of *Steward* v. *Isidor*, 1 N. B. R. 129, cited and approved by him. BARRETT, J., of the supreme court of New York, goes carefully over the English and American cases, and holds that proof of the debt in bankruptcy, without mentioning the security, is a waiver of the lien, See also *in re* Brand, 3 N. B. R. 85, and *Wallace* v. *Conrad*, 3 N. B. R. 10, where the doctrine of implied waiver by proof in bankruptcy of the secured debt without stating the lien, is stringently applied.

Here there was an express waiver in the petition. This I think the better practice, when it is conceded that the security exceeds the debt, but by no means necessary upon principle to the support of the petition. Certainly it should *not* be required where it is inadequate. It would compel a release where the statute expressly authorises its retention.

Decree below reversed and adjudication ordered.

MR. ATWELL, for creditors; MR. BALLARD, for debtor.

UNITED STATES DISTRICT COURT—W. D. WISCONSIN.

The term assets in the thirty-third section of the bankrupt act as amended July fourteenth, eighteen hundred and seventy, is not used to express the net balance to be distributed among the creditors, but means the entire estate of the bankrupt, irrespective of the use to which it may be appropriated by the court. Hence, where the estate was originally sufficient to pay fifty per cent. of the debts proved, but a large part has been wasted by litigation, the bankrupt is entitled to his discharge without the assent of his creditors.

*In re KAHLEY et al.**

HOPKINS, J.—In this case the assignee received from the estate of the bankrupts, a sum exceeding fifty per cent. of the debts proven, without deducting the costs and expenses of the proceedings therefrom, but after paying the costs and expenses it did not equal fifty per cent. of the debts.

The debts were all contracted since the first day of January, eighteen hundred and sixty-nine. Mr. Kahley, one of the bankrupts, now applies (after having petitioned) for his discharge. He claims that he is entitled to it without the assent of his creditors, as the amount of his assets *received by the assignee* exceeds fifty per cent. of the claims proven. The creditors do not appear to oppose.

The determination of the question involves a construction of section thirty-three of the bankrupt act as amended by the act of July twenty-seventh, eighteen hundred and sixty-eight.

The counsel for the bankrupt contends that in all cases where the *value* of the *assets* "equals fifty per cent. of the debts proven," a discharge should be granted as a matter of right.

On the presentation of the question to me I thought it quite plain that such was the meaning, but upon an examination of the authorities, I found it not quite so clear as I at first thought. I found that NELSON, J., *in re* Frederick, 3 N. B. R. 117, and *in re* Graham, 5 N. B. R. 155, had held that the term " assets " in the thirty-third section of the bankrupt

* See 4 N. B. R. 125.

act meant "the proceeds of the debtor's property which are *applicable* to the payment of his debts," and that BLATCHFORD, J., *in re* Webb & Taylor, 3 N. B. R. 177, had concurred with NELSON, J., *in re* Frederick, and said "that the proceeds of the bankrupt's property in the hands of the assignee subject to be divided among the creditors at the time of the hearing of the application for discharge, must be equal to fifty per cent. of the debts proven."

These authorities being at variance with my first impression of the meaning of the section as amended, I have given the subject a more thorough consideration than I at first thought it required.

I dislike to differ from those eminent jurists, each of whom has done so much towards elucidating the bankrupt act, and in giving to it a harmonious and efficient operation. I should ordinarily do so with a good deal of distrust and hesitation, but upon the question now under consideration, I do not feel much embarrassment, for to me it seems exceedingly clear, although at variance with their views.

In re Frederick this question was not, it seems to me, fairly before the court or necessary to be decided, and the decision may therefore be considered as *obiter*. That was a case of voluntary bankruptcy, and the bankrupt, before any debts were proven or assignee appointed, petitioned to have his assets appraised to show that they exceeded fifty per cent. of his provable debts. The judge denied that application, as no debts had been proven or assignee appointed. The application was clearly premature, and what the judge said upon the construction of section thirty-three seems to me to have been unnecessary, and therefore not binding as authority. And *in re* Graham, the court had ordered certain property subject to lien, to be sold, discharged therefrom, and that the lien be transferred to the fund in court. The surplus of the proceeds, after paying off that lien, did not reach the required amount, and the question before the court was as to whether the amount of the fund applied in discharge of the lien was to be reckoned as a part of the

" assets " in determining whether they equalled fifty per cent. and the court decided that it could not be, which disposed of that case; so the portion of his opinion affirming his views *in re* Frederick as to the meaning of section thirty-three, was not strictly necessary.

In re Webb and Taylor, the facts are not stated, but from the opinion I should infer that the question was fairly before the court. BLATCHFORD, J., does not argue the question or present any reasons for his opinion, but simply states his conclusions.

In order to determine the question, it becomes necessary to examine the history of the legislation upon the subject. Section thirty-three, as originally adopted, declared that " no discharge shall be granted to a debtor whose assets do not pay fifty per cent. of the claims against his estate, unless, " &c. That clearly meant the proceeds of the bankrupt's property applicable to the payment of the proven claims. In other words " net assets." The ordinary definition of the term assets was qualified and limited by other parts of the sentence as much as if the word *net* had been placed before it.

But congress, by the act of July twenty-seventh, eighteen hundred and sixty-eight, amended that clause so as to make it read " no discharge shall be granted to a debtor whose assets shall not be equal to fifty per cent. of the claims proven " &c., 15 Stat. at Large, page 228. The judge says, *in re* Frederick, " the amendment of July, eighteen hundred and sixty-eight, although more favorable to the bankrupt, has not changed the meaning of the word " assets " in the section, and that as the section now stands it must be construed as if it read " *the proceeds of the bankrupt's property in the hands of the assignee and subject to be divided among his creditors must be equal*" &c.

To such construction I cannot yield my assent. I think before the amendment it was qualified by the context so that it meant " *net assets,*" as before stated. But I think the amendment was adopted for the purpose of removing that restriction, and that it should now receive its ordinary signification, which is as comprehensive as "estate" or "effects." We must presume that congress meant to make some change in favor of the bankrupt, if the amendment was made in his interest, as is admitted by the learned judge *in re* Frederick. But if they did not give him the right to a discharge based upon the gross value of his assets, then they certainly did not improve his condition at all, for before he was entitled to a discharge upon paying fifty per cent. and if he is not entitled to a discharge now unless *he has in the hands of the assignee* fifty per cent. to pay upon his debts, the only change made by it was, that before the amendment he would have to see that it was *actually* paid over, while under the amendment he must see that it is *in the hands of his assignee ready to pay over.* Certainly such could not have been the meaning of congress in adopting the amendment, and such a construction effectually deprives him of any substantial benefit or advantage conferred upon him or intended to have been given him by the amendment.

The clear intention of the amendment to my mind was to relieve the bankrupt of the costs and expenses of the proceedings. If his estate realised a sum equal to fifty per cent. he should be discharged whether it went to the payment of costs and expenses or to his creditors. The costs and expenses are often, as in this case, largely increased by litigation between the creditors and by suits brought by the assignee, over which the bankrupt has no control, and if the creditors are willing to waste the estate or permit the assignee, who is their trustee, to do so in expensive litigation, they shall be responsible for the consequences to that extent that it shall not be deducted from the proceeds of the bankrupt's estate in determining the amount his assets would pay if applied solely to the payment of his debts.

It seems to me that the ordinary meaning of the word "assets" comprises the whole of a decedent's or insolvent's estate, unless limited by some qualifying word or expression. I think as used in the section as amended it must receive its ordinary signification and be held to include *all* the estate of

In re Kahley et al.

the bankrupt, not that only which is applicable to the payment of debts, but that applicable to the payment of costs and expenses as well. In section forty-seven it is certainly so used. It is there stated "that if sufficient *assets* for the payment of *fees*, &c. showing that it may be used and is used in the act as meaning the "estate," applicable alike to the payment of debts and expenses. I cannot find any authority in the act or any sufficient reason outside of it for giving to it a more limited signification in that section than in the others where it is used. The word "estate" is used to express a like purpose in section thirty, and the supreme court of the United States has construed "*no assets*" in the twenty-ninth section as meaning that the assignee "has not received or paid out any money on account of the estate." (See form thirty-five.) The converse of the proposition would be, that if he had received or paid out money on account of the estate, he had received "assets."

Again the amount to be divided among creditors in section twenty-eight is called "estate and effects." I therefore think that the words "estate," "estate and effects," and "assets" are used synonymously in the act. The term assets in the section as amended is not, in my opinion, used to express the net balance to be distributed among the creditors as held by the judge in the cases referred to. But on the contrary it means the *entire estate* of the bankrupt, irrespective of the use to which it may be appropriated by the court; and as the assets of the bankrupts in this case exceeded fifty per cent. of the debts proven, the bankrupt is entitled to his discharge without the assent of his creditors; and in determining the question as to whether the assets do amount to such sum, the costs and expenses of the proceedings are not first to be deducted. I am aware that in the administration of the bankrupt act, the district courts occasionally differ as to the true meaning of some of its provisions. Such differences I think ought as far as possible to be avoided, for the good of the profession as well as of the parties, and I have, on questions of practice not involving any substantial right or principle, often yielded my opinion for the sake of conformity, but I cannot allow the convenience or advantages of conformity to control me when to do so would deprive a party of a valuable right secured to him by the act.

J. C. SLOAN, for bankrupt.—January 22, 1872.

- - - -

UNITED STATES DISTRICT COURT—S. D. NEW YORK.

The register in charge has power to order an assignee to furnish him with all necessary information as to funds in his hands.

A third meeting of creditors—not being a final meeting—should not be called except for cause shown, and if the register be satisfied that no such cause exists, he is justified in refusing to grant the order for such a meeting.

*In re CLARK & BININGER.**

I, the undersigned register in charge of the above entitled proceedings, do hereby certify to this court, that I did, on the twenty-seventh day of October, eighteen hundred and seventy-one, receive from the assignee in this case a request to call a third meeting of creditors. That, as the said request did not state the reasons why such a request was made, I applied to the said assignee by letter, dated the thirty-first day of October, eighteen hundred and seventy-one, to call at my office and confer with me upon the subject of such application. That I received in reply thereto a letter from Messrs. Bangs, Sedgwick & North, "attorneys for the said assignee, *pro hac vice*," bearing date first November, eighteen hundred and seventy-one, which is herewith submitted. That, upon an examination of the accounts of said assignee on file in my office, I find, so far as I can understand the same, that no funds have been received since the last dividend meeting of the creditors held on the twenty-ninth day of March, eighteen hundred and seventy-one, at which meeting a dividend of six per cent was duly declared and paid—save the sum of

*See 3 N. B. R. 99, 121, 122, 123, 129, 130; 4 N. B. R. 77, and 5 N. B. R. 255.

ninety-seven dollars and forty-one cents, which appears to be the amount of interest which has accrued upon the sum of eight thousand eight hundred and twenty-six dollars and seventy-six cents, which is now and was, as I understand, on deposit in the United States Trust Company at the time of the said last dividend meeting, and is not yet in a condition to be divided among the creditors. In doubt whether any further sums were in the hands of the said assignee and uncertain if the said sums so in the said Trust Company could yet be divided among the creditors, I did, on the sixth of November, eighteen hundred and seventy-one, issue an order to the said assignee for information on this subject. In reply to the said order, I received a letter from the said attorneys for the said assignee on the seventh day of November, eighteen hundred and seventy-one, and on the same day I also received from said attorneys a request to certify the point to the court as to whether I had authority to make the said order.

Upon the question of the power of the register to make such an order, I submit that section twenty-eight of the act devolves upon the register the exercise of a discretion in reference to " further dividend meetings." He should call them if " occasion requires." This makes it his duty to ascertain if the occasion does require it. What other means of information has he at command? If he cannot order this information to be given, he is powerless to execute the duty imposed upon him by statute. General Order 5 makes it his duty to " take proceeding for the declaration and payment of dividends." Dividend meetings are most generally called for at the request of creditors, or, in many cases, they would never be called. In such cases creditors often aver that the assignee has funds, &c.

The practice then is to order the assignee to file accounts from which this fact can be ascertained, or otherwise inform the register upon the subject. When the fact is ascertained the register exercises a discretion—calling or not calling a meeting as the facts may warrant. It is clear from section twenty-eight that the meeting asked for, not being the final meeting, should not be called except for cause shown. See *in re* Son 1 N. B. R. 58.

And I further certify that on the fourth day of November inst., I was served with a paper to which was appended divers printed papers, being accounts and so forth, raising the point that it is my duty by law to grant the order so applied for, and requesting me to certify the point so raised to the court; and I further certify that before I had sufficient time to prepare said certificate I was served—to wit, on the eighth day of November —with an order of this court requiring me to call a meeting of creditors or certify the point so raised as aforesaid. I have not been served with a copy of the petition upon which said order is founded, and am ignorant of what it may allege.

But in obedience to said order I certify that under rule six of this court, and the ruling *in re* Son, 1 N. B. R. 58, it is the duty of the register to ascertain for what purpose the meeting is asked, and whether there be any funds for distribution.

That without such information on the subject, I cannot be called upon to exercise the discretion, which the act devolves upon me the duty of exercising, upon an application of this character. I have therefore waited in the hope of receiving such information so that I might intelligently pass upon the application.

In re Littlefield, 3 N. B. R. 14, LOWELL, J., in speaking of the second and third meetings of creditors which had been held, says:

" The meetings in this case having been called by order of the court, it must be presumed that *good cause* was shown for the action of the court in the premises."

And I further certify that from my knowledge of this case, and from what has transpired before me, I do not understand that it is the purpose of the assignee or his counsel, that a further dividend should be declared at the meeting asked for. But if the contrary be shown, or if reasonable grounds of any character whatsoever for calling such meeting be made to appear, I shall most cheerfully grant the order asked for. All of which is respectfully summitted.

I. T. WILLIAMS, *Register*.

BLATCHFORD, J.—I think the register had the authority to make the order of November sixth, eighteen hundred and seventy-one, and I concur in his views in regard to the calling of a third general meeting of creditors in thiscase.

November 11, 1871.

• • •

UNITED STATES DISTRICT COURT—S. D. NEW YORK.

A register has power so to audit and pass the accounts of an assignee at a second meeting called only under the twenty-seventh section of the act, as to bind the creditors, even though no notice had been given under the twenty-eighth section or otherwise, that such accounting would be had, and though such accounts be not filed until the hour of the meeting. If the creditors omit to attend such meeting or fail to object to such accounts, it is the duty of the register to direct their payment.

The provision in section twenty-eight, for auditing and passing the accounts of the assignee at the meeting for the final dividend, cannot be regarded as in any manner implying that such accounts of the assignee as are presented at the second general meeting of creditors shall not then be audited and passed by the register.

In re CLARK & BININGER.

I, the undersigned register in charge of this case, do hereby certify that I was, on the thirty-first day of October last, served with a paper requesting me, among other things, to audit and pass certain accounts filed with me at an adjourned second meeting of creditors of said separate estate, held on the ninth day of October, eighteen hundred and seventy-one, and direct the payment of such of the outstanding claims as were not objected to. The said paper recites that the period of ten days had elapsed since the accounts were so filed, and that no creditor had objected to said accounts, nor to any of said outstanding claims, and that there had been filed with me consents of several creditors to the payment of said claims.

And I further certify that the said second meeting was so as aforesaid held after several adjournments, and that but one ·of the creditors of said estate attended this second meeting, to wit, Mr. Mortimore Addoms; that the accounts aforesaid were filed on that day, and a dividend declared of ten per cent. upon the claims proved; that at the close of the meeting checks were drawn and countersigned for the payment of all of said dividends; that the claims against the said assignee by his attorneys amounted to the sum of five thousand one hundred and eighty-nine dollars and nine cents; that believing the said assignee and his said attorneys all perfectly responsible for any overpayment that might be made, I determined to countersign checks for the payment of said claims of said attorneys upon receiving from them an affidavit that the services so charged for had in fact been rendered, and that they were fit and proper services, and that the sum charged therefor was reasonable and proper, and thereupon drafted such an affidavit for that purpose; that said attorneys refused to swear to the same, all of which proceedings will appear from the certified copy memorandum of said day and filed with the clerk of this court; that on the twelfth day of October aforesaid, I received a notification from said attorneys, addressed to the said assignee and myself, which is herewith submitted. Whereupon, on the same day, I wrote a note to the said assignee, in reply to which I received, on the fourteenth day of October aforesaid, a letter from the said assignee; also a letter from his said attorneys, both of which are herewith submitted. Unwilling to have any unfavorable consequences follow upon my omission to countersign checks for the payment of the said claims of said attorneys, I determined, as I deemed the said assignee as well as his attorneys perfectly responsible, to countersign the said checks in case the said assignee—with full knowledge of the fact that I believed the law to be such, that the said claims of said attorneys would be open to be objected to by the creditors at the final meeting in case they or any of them should elect so to object—

desired me to do so. I thereupon, on the sixteenth of October aforesaid, wrote him a note, in reply to which I received on the seventeenth of October a letter, which is herewith submitted. That on the same day I received a paper from several of the creditors protesting against the said bill of said attorneys. And having received from the said attorneys a note in which they say: "Under your extraordinary ruling that even the register's own check is no protection to an assignee on a final accounting, we should not permit him to pay us any money even if you ordered him to do so," no further steps in that direction have yet been taken.

And now, touching my duty to "audit and pass the said accounts" prior to the final meeting of creditors: I have been desirous to do so if it could be legally done. The difficulties that present themselves to my mind are as follows:

The fourth section provides that the register "shall audit and pass accounts of the assignee." Section twenty-eight provides that "preparatory to the final dividend the assignee shall submit his account to the court and file the same, and give notice to the creditors of such filing, and shall also give notice that he will apply for a settlement of his accounts and for a discharge from all liability as assignee, at a time to be specified in such notice; and at such time the court shall audit and pass the accounts of the assignee," &c. I find nothing in the act or general orders to modify or change this provision. It seems to be imperative as to time and manner. The creditors are relieved from objecting at any other time or under any other circumstances, and if so relieved they cannot be bound to object at any prior time, or forever after hold their peace.

The request to direct payment of such of the said outstanding claims as were not objected to, would seem to imply a duty on the part of the creditors to object at such second meeting or be precluded of all objection thereafter. But that meeting was called under the provisions of section twenty-seven, and no notice was given to creditors that the assignee would file his accounts and apply for a settlement of the same as required by section twenty-eight.   It cannot possibly be said, therefore, even if the register have power to audit and pass the accounts at any save at a final meeting, that he has power to audit and pass them at a meeting at which no notice to that effect was given to creditors.   The attempt therefore to bind the creditors thus without notice ought not to be urged upon the court.

The assignee ought not to be heard to object that the court may not, at the final meeting, allow him for sums paid as counsel fees.   This would be to impugn the honor and integrity of the court.   The presumption at least is that the court, as well as all officers of the law, will do its duty.

I have usually, in similar cases, attempted to protect the assignee as well as the fund, when paying claims against the estate, by taking an affidavit of the justness of the claim before countersigning the checks.   This would perhaps throw the burden of proof upon the creditor objecting at the final meeting, and require of him something that would be in the nature of a surcharging or falsifying of the claim. Had the attorneys in this case been able to swear to the affidavit as required, it is scarcely probable that the creditors would at the final meeting take upon themselves the burden of surcharging or falsifying their claim; certainly not unless they thought the claim grossly unjust.   All which is respectfully submitted.   I. T. WILLIAMS, *Register*.

BLATCHFORD, J.—Inasmuch as the register has, by section four of the act and general order number five, the general power to audit and pass the accounts of assignees, and by section twenty-seven, it is provided that at the second general meeting of creditors the assigneee must report and exhibit to the court and to the creditors just and true accounts of all his receipts and payments verified by his oath, and produce and file vouchers for all payments for which vouchers are required by any rule of the court, I think that the register has power, and that it is his duty to audit and pass any accounts so reported and exhibited.   Section

In re Clark and Bininger.

twenty-seven requires the assignee to exhibit at the same time a schedule of creditors and property and a statement of the whole estate as then ascertained, and of property recovered and property outstanding, and debts or claims undetermined, and moneys remaining in hand, and then and there the creditors, by a majority in value, are to determine what net sum shall be divided, retaining a sum sufficient to provide for undetermined claims not proved and for other expenses and contingencies.

The creditors are to have notice of this meeting and must therefore be prepared to object, if they desire, to such accounts as the assignee shall then report and exhibit under section twenty-seven. In order to arrive at the net sum to be divided, the outstanding claims not disputed or objected to, must be arrived at, and their amount deducted. If they are not disputed or objected to, it is the duty of the register to direct their payment, as part of the business of auditing and passing the accounts, even though they have not been actually paid by the assignee. They may properly come under the head of "other expenses," the amount of which is to be retained by the assignee, such retention being specifically authorised by the meeting and the register to meet the specific items as such expenses.

The provision in section twenty-eight for auditing and passing the accounts of the assignee at the meeting for the final dividend, cannot be regarded as in any manner implying that such accounts of the assignee as are presented at the second general meeting of creditors shall not then be audited and passed by the register.—November 16, 1871.

UNITED STATES DISTRICT COURT—S. D. NEW YORK.

When written objections to a proof of debt are filed with the register and testimony is taken thereon, it is his duty, if requested by either party, to certify the same to the district judge for decision, even though no proof whatever be offered tending to invalidate the debt so proved.

In re CLARK & BININGER.

I, the undersigned register in charge of the above entitled matter, do hereby certify that on the second of August, eighteen hundred and seventy, Thomas D. James made proof before me of his claim against the said estate in due form of law. That on the third day of April, eighteen hundred and seventy-one, the assignee, by C. W. Bangs, his attorney, objected in writing to said claim, and filed said objection with me. That on the second day of November inst. the said Thomas D. James voluntarily appeared before me in person, and the said assignee, by Mr. F. N. Bangs, his counsel, also voluntarily appeared and stated that they desired to take proof of said claim, whereupon the said James was by me duly sworn and proceeded to give testimony, that at the close of said testimony, the said Bangs stated that he desired to state a question and have it certified to the court. He then wrote and signed a paper and handed it to the said James, who thereupon, at the request of Mr. Bangs, signed the same.

And I further certify that in my judgment no "point or matter" is raised upon the said papers within the meaning of the sixth section of the act. The words "point or matter arising" in said section must be construed so as to harmonize with the other provisions of the act. It cannot be that everything that a register is required to do can, at the request of a party, be carried before the judge. The order of reference in this case directs the register "to take such proceedings therein as are required by the said act." The act requires the register, in addition to divers specified things, "to sit in chambers and dispatch there such part of the adminis-

In re Clark and Bininger.

trative business of the court and such uncontested matters as should be defined in general rules and orders, or as the district judge shall in any particular matter direct."

Now if, upon the papers herewith presented, any point or matter is raised which is not equally raised by every other act a register may do, such point or matter is not perceived by me. The proof of debt, filed the second day of August, eighteen hundred and seventy, established *prima facie* the right of Mr. James to be placed on the list of unsecured creditors for the sum of one thousand one hundred and twenty-nine dollars and sixty-three cents, principal and interest. The objection to this claim made it proper, and gave both him and the assignee an opportunity to submit such evidence as each might see fit to offer. They have had this opportunity; Mr. James has but repeated the testimony which he gave in his deposition of August second, eighteen hundred and seventy. The assignee offers nothing, but asks that the "point or matter raised" be certified to the judge. How, then, does the case differ from what it would have been had the assignee or any creditor asked to have the point or matter raised on the deposition of August second, certified to the court? Except, perhaps, that there is less reason for such a certifying up, as the deposition of November second gives the proof more circumstantially and more fully than the law seems to require in the deposition of August second.

It is perfectly plain that if this may be required to be certified, the register may be compelled to certify every deposition of a creditor proving his debt, when asked to do so by an assignee or a creditor. Such a practice, it is certain, would not be tolerated by the court. It is my custom, and I believe the custom of most of the registers throughout the country, under the decision of this court *in re* Orne, N. B. R. Sup. xviii, to examine upon my own motion, into claims upon which suspicion is thrown either by the assignee or by a creditor, giving to either party if not satisfied with the conclusion to which I have come, an opportunity to have it certified to the judge for decision. I therefore submit that this matter should be remitted to the register to proceed thereon according to law. Respectfully submitted.

-I. T. WILLIAMS, *Register*.

· BLATCHFORD, J.—I am of opinion that the facts set forth in the certificate of the register show a case within the provision of the fourth section of the act, that in 'all matters where an issue of fact or of law is raised and contested by any party to the proceedings before a register, it shall be his duty to cause the question or issue to be stated by the opposing parties in writing, and he shall adjourn the same into court for decision by the judge. In the present case the opposing parties have stated in writing the question or issue. I think on the evidence that all of the claim of Mr. James is allowable, except the item of ten dollars and fifty-six cents.—November 23, 1871.

UNITED STATES DISTRICT COURT—S. D. NEW YORK.

When the register gave notice at the second meeting of creditors called only under the twenty-seventh section of the act, that the accounts of the assignee filed at such meeting would not be audited or passed at such meeting, as no notice of such auditing or passing had been given to creditors, and as the amounts had not been on file ten days, as required by the twenty-eighth section of the act,

Held, on an application by the assignee to the district judge to compel the register to order the payment of such accounts, that the register was right in refusing to make such order.

In re CLARK & BININGER.

I, the undersigned register in charge of this matter, do hereby certify and report, that a petition was filed with me on the twentieth day of November inst., by the assignee in these proceedings, John S. Beecher, Esq., reciting that on the twenty-ninth day of March, eighteen hundred and seventy-one, a second general meeting of the creditors of the said bankrupts was held before me, at which time the

In re Clark and Bininger.

said assignee filed a report and an account; that at said meeting no objection was made to the said accounts or any item therein, and that at the said meeting a dividend of six per cent. was declared and ordered to be paid; that no order has been made auditing or passing said accounts, or determining or adjusting the balance of money with which the assignee was then chargeable and applying to the register in charge to make an order:

"First. That the said credit be allowed and the amount of the balance of money with which the said assignee is chargeable, after allowing him the said credits claimed by him, is fixed, determined and adjusted, at the sum of nineteen thousand three hundred and ninety-nine dollars and sixty-six cents, and the said account is audited and passed accordingly.

"Second. A dividend of six per cent. having been duly ordered to be paid by the creditors present at said meeeeting, it is further ordered that the same be paid by means of checks, to be countersigned by the said register, pursuant to a dividend list (form thirty-eight,) to be furnished to the assignee by the register."

The said petition further prays that if the register refuse to grant said application or decide not to grant the same, that then the petitioner, upon said application and upon said accounts to said petition annexed, raised the point that it is by law the duty of the register to grant said application, and requests the register to certify to the court the point so raised.

I, the said register, having decided not to grant said application, do, pursuant to said request, now certify: That the said second meeting so above referred to, was ordered under the provisions of the twenty-seventh section of the bankrupt act, and not under the twenty-eighth; that the notice of said meeting given to creditors was as follows: "This is to give notice that the second general meeting of the creditors of said bankrupts will be held at 27 Chambers street, in the city of New York, on the twenty-ninth day

of March, eighteen hundred and seventy-one, at one o'clock
P. M., at the office of and before Isaiah T. Williams, Esq.,
register in bankruptcy, pursuant to an order made by said
register, for the purposes named in the twenty-seventh section of the bankrupt act of March, eighteen hundred and
sixty-seven;" that no other or different notice was given to
said creditors of said meeting; that at said meeting the said
assignee presented his accounts for the first time; that the
register took said accounts and stated to the meeting in substance that the said accounts would then be filed and that
they could be examined thereafter by any creditors who
desired to examine the same, and that they would not be
audited or passed until the final meeting of creditors, and
thereupon made an entry to that effect, to which ruling no
one then or there in anywise objected; that said accounts
were not nor were any or either of them examined by the
register or by any creditors to his knowledge; that the same
were then filed in the office of the register where they have
ever since remained, and have since that time been examined
by several of the creditors, most of whom, so far as the
knowledge of the register extends, have objected to the same;
that on the nineteenth day of October, ult., written objections and a protest against said claims were filed with me.

And I further certify that it has always been and is now
the uniform practice, where it is proposed to ask to have the
accounts of the assignee audited and passed, to order the
meeting under the twenty-eighth section of the act, and to
require the assignee to file his accounts before such meeting
is ordered, and then under the order for such meeting to
give notice to the creditors ten days before such meeting
that such accounts have been filed with the register, and that
the assignee will apply at such meeting for a settlement of
the same under the twenty-eighth section of the act.

And I further certify, that in my opinion, the order asked
for in said petition would have the effect to mislead and
betray the said creditors touching their rights, and in my
judgment would be a violation of the letter and spirit of the

provisions of the bankrupt act in such case made. But I forbear to enter further into the discussion of the case, deeming it unnecessary to do so and for the further reason that I am informed that should the court desire to hear an argument upon the questions now raised, Mr. L. R. Marsh, of counsel for the Continental Bank, Mr. E. L. Fancher, of counsel for the Ocean Bank, and divers other creditors by their respective counsel, will submit either oral arguments or written points. Respectively submitted,

I. T. WILLIAMS, *Register.*

BLATCHFORD, J.—In view of the statements made by the register to the second meeting of creditors, I think he is correct in refusing to make the order applied for so far as the first direction therein is concerned. As to the second direction, I understand the certificate as not applying to it.

November 23, 1871.

———— • • • ————

UNITED STATES DISTRICT COURT—E. D. NEW YORK.

A petition was filed by a creditor to restrain the assignee in bankruptcy from prosecuting a certain action of law in the supreme court of New York state to recover the payment of money made contrary to the provisions of the thirty-ninth section of the bankrupt act, claiming to recover back the amount so paid. *Held,* that said act is the law of the state courts as well as of the national tribunals, and if by virtue of that act the state court has no jurisdiction in the action brought against the petitioners, it will so decide upon proper plea and that no reason appears to compel the assignee to resort to the national tribunals instead of those of the state.

In re *THE CENTRAL BANK.*

BENEDICT, J.—This case came before me on a petition filed on behalf of the Chatham National Bank, in which they seek to obtain from the court, an order restraining the assignee in bankruptcy of the Central Bank from prosecuting in the supreme court of this state, a certain action

In re the Central Bank.

of law which he has there commenced against the petitioners, to recover of them the amount of a payment of money which the assignee claims to have been a preferential payment, made contrary to the provisions of the thirty-ninth section of the bankrupt act, and which he therefore claims to recover back by virtue of the provisions of the bankrupt act.

The application is based upon the ground that the state tribunals are without jurisdiction to entertain such an action as the one referred to.

I do not so understands the law. The provision of the second chapter of the bankrupt act does indeed confer upon the district and circuit courts jurisdiction of certain actions, but I have never supposed the effect of that section to be to oust the jurisdiction of the state courts. Moreover, in such a case as the one under consideration, the bankrupt act is the law of the state courts as well as of the national tribunals, and if by virtue of that act the state court has no jurisdiction in the action brought against the petitioners, it will so decide upon proper plea.

I think the question of jurisdiction should be there decided, and that no reason appears for the exercising of the restraining power of this court over the assignee, to compel him in a case like this to resort to the national tribunals instead of those of the state.

A. W. GAZZAM, for Chatham Bank.

In re Boston, Hartford and Erie R. R. Co.

UNITED STATES CIRCUIT COURT—CONNECTICUT.

A petition in involuntary bankruptcy is not a mere suit *inter partes*, but rather partakes of the nature of a proceeding *in rem*, in which any actual creditor has a direct interest.

If a third party, claiming to be a creditor of the respondent, seeks to intervene in such a proceeding, it is not an indispensable pre-requisite to his admission that he should have proved his debt in the ordinary form ; provided he can satisfy the court that he is in fact a creditor, and that his purpose is a meritorious one.

Upon a petition in bankruptcy against the Boston, Hartford and Erie Railroad Company, it appears that the company owned a railroad situated partly in Connecticut and partly in Massachusetts ; that a company by that name was first chartered by Connecticut, with power to purchase and complete any railroads running through parts of both states, on the line between Boston and Hartford ; that such purchases were made ; that subsequently the Boston, Hartford and Erie Railroad Company was, by an act of the Massachusetts legislature, declared to be a corporation within that state ; and that the road in both states was owned by the same stockholders, conducted by the same directors and subject to the same debts, in the same manner as if it were wholly within one state. *Held*, that—whether this company were one corporation or two corporations chartered by different states, but united, and having in all respects a common interest, or an anomalous body, not precisely answering either of their descriptions—upon the filing of the creditor's petition in the district court of the district where the principal office and place of business of the road was situated, that court acquired exclusive jurisdiction over proceedings in bankruptcy against it, which could not be affected by a petition subsequently filed by another creditor in another district.

If the company be regarded as composed of two corporations, the case would be governed by the spirit if not by the letter of sections thirty-six and thirty-seven of the bankrupt act and general order sixteen, relating to partnerships, and to joint stock companies. In the absence of any such provisions in the act, the same rule would be deducible from the practice of courts of equity in analogous cases, where different parties apply to different tribunals, existing under the same general jurisdiction, for the distribution of the same fund.

As the same debtor, in substance, was before both courts, the title of the assignees appointed under the petition first filed, would cover all the assets owned by the bankrupt at the time of the filing of that petition, and it would therefore be useless to proceed upon any petition subsequently filed in another district, since there would be no assets left to be reached by it.

In this case, after the filing of a petition in bankruptcy against the company in Massachusetts, another creditor filed another petition against it in Connecticut, under a collusive agreement with the company that no defence should be made to the proceeding. The creditor who had petitioned in Massachusetts thereupon filed an application in the district court in Connecticut, stating the prior proceedings by himself and the collusion, and praying for leave to come in and defend. The court found this application insufficient in its force, and proceeded to an adjudication of bankruptcy, and the appointment of assignees, who were the same previously chosen in Massachusetts. *Held*, On a petition of review to the circuit court, that the application was legally sufficient ; that no adjudication should have been granted ; but that, under the circumstance of the case, it was sufficient, without reversing the decree, to order a stay of any further proceedings.

The proper course for the court in Connecticut would have been to admit the intervening creditor as a defendant, and then to stay further proceedings until the court in Massachusetts had made some adjudication on the petition then pending. Nor could an adjudication in bankruptcy then made necessarily require the Connecticut court to dismiss the second petition. It might be advisable to continue it in that court till that court to fall back upon, if the Massachusetts decree should for any reason, not applicable to the Connecticut proceedings, prove unavailing or erroneous.

In re BOSTON, HARTFORD AND ERIE R. R. CO.*

On the twentieth of December, eighteen hundred and seventy, a petition was filed in the district court by James Alden, an alleged creditor of the Boston, Hartford and Erie Railroad Company, alleging the insolvency of the corporation and the commission of an act of bankruptcy, and praying an adjudication declaring them bankrupt. To this petition another alleged creditor, the Adams Express Company, by leave of court, became a party as co-petitioner. Pending the proceedings, Seth Adams presented a petition to the district court, and afterwards filed a supplemental petition, by which it appears that before the filing of the petition of Alden in this district, he (Adams) had, on the twenty-first of October, eighteen hundred and seventy, filed in the district court for the district of Massachusetts, his petition against the same corporation, alleging insolvency and an act or acts of bankruptcy ; and that such proceedings were thereupon had, upon due notice, that on the second of March, eighteen hundred and seventy-one, the corporation was adjudged bankrupt. The petitioner also avers that the proceedings in the district court for Connecticut are collusive and intended to and will prejudice the petitioner and other creditors ; that various defences exist thereto, which the company will not interpose ; that if the proceeding is further prosecuted in Connecticut it will lead to great embarrassment, expense, conflict of title and jurisdiction, and consequent litigation, to the prejudice of the creditors and the reduction of the assets. The peti-

In re Boston, Hartford and Erie R. R. Co.

tioner thereupon prays that he, as a creditor upon whose application the company have been decreed bankrupts in the district of Massachusetts, may be permitted to appear and defend against the petition of Alden in this district, and for other and further relief.

The district court held these petitions of Adams to be insufficient on their face to warrant his admission as a co-defendant for the purpose of resisting that of Alden, and dismissed them. To reverse this decision, Adams brought the present petition of review before the circuit court. In this petition he set forth the facts already recited, and averred that the district court, after dismissing his petitions, adjudged the company bankrupts, and directed that a warrant issue to take possession of their estate; and that a meeting of the creditors had been called to choose assignees. He also averred that the alleged bankrupts were chartered under the name of the Boston, Hartford and Erie Railroad Company, by the State of Connecticut, in eighteen hundred and sixty-three, with the right to purchase from any persons or corporations interested, the franchises and property of any and all railroad companies located in whole or in part of the state of Connecticut, whose routes, or any part thereof, were on the railway lines running from the harbor of Boston, in Masachusetts, to Willimantic, in Connecticut, and from Providence, in Rhode Island, through Willimantic to Waterbury, in Connecticut, and thence to Fishkill, in the state of New York; together with the right to make joint stock with any of said other railroad companies located or having routes upon said railway lines; that said company was duly organised under that act, and that afterwards, and before the year eighteen hundred and sixty-eight, the state of Massachusetts granted permission to certain railroad companies in that state to sell and transfer their franchises and property to the said Boston, Hartford and Erie Railroad Company, and declared the latter a corporation within that state, vested with all the franchises and powers pertaining to such corporations. And that thereupon, under and by virtue of an act of Massachusetts, ap-

In re Boston, Hartford and Erie R. R. Co.

proved April twenty-ninth, eighteen hundred and sixty-eight, the said Boston, Hartford and Erie Railroad Company became and was incorporated and established a corporation in the last named state. He also averred that that corporation owned and operated a railroad in the states of Massachusetts, Rhode Island and Connecticut, owning other property also in said states, and had its principal office, place of business and domicile in the city of Boston, in Massachusetts, where the same were for more than six months before the petitioner filed his petition against the bankrupts in the district court for the district of Massachusetts. That the petitioner is in fact a creditor, and that the said company had committed an act of bankruptcy which is set forth.

SIMEON E. BALDWIN, for petitioner.

WOODRUFF, C. J.—The petition of review presented by Seth Adams, a creditor of the bankrupt corporation, was brought to a hearing upon an order to show cause, which was duly served upon the bankrupts and upon the petitioning creditors prosecuting the proceeding in the district court. No party appeared to oppose the application for a review and reversal of the order of the district court, or to deny the allegations in the petition entered for that purpose. They are, therefore, for the purpose of such review, to be taken as admitted.

The question therefore is, ought Adams, upon the facts alleged by him and not denied, to have been permitted to intervene in the district court for Connecticut for the protection of the interest he had in the estate of the bankrupt corporation, and take part either in arresting or controlling the proceedings in this district.

This may depend upon two questions:

FIRST. Whether a creditor of an alleged bankrupt is, in any case, entitled to be heard in the district court touching any order which that court may be asked to make by the bankrupt, or by a creditor petitioning that the debtor be adjudged a bankrupt, or is such a proceeding so strictly *inter partes* that no other creditor can intervene, for any purpose, prior to the adjudication.   And,

SECOND. Whether the present petitioner presented a case in which intervention was necessary or proper for the protection of the estate or his interest therein.

It has been said that no creditor is entitled to be heard until he has proved his debt in due form, so as to entitle him to share in the assets of the estate.   This may, perhaps, be true when the object of such intervention is simply to interfere with the distribution of the assets, though I am not willing to hold even that so broadly as to say that no proof short of that of the formal and technical character contemplated by the forms of procedure will be sufficient to justify the court in entertaining an application by an actual creditor. *In re* Troy Woolen Co. 6. N. B. R. 16, on review, I affirmed an order of the district court setting aside a sale of real estate by an assignee, on the application of creditors of the bankrupts, although such formal proof had not been made, and their claim was in ' fact contested.   I cannot admit that a creditor of the bankrupt can have no standing in court to be heard touching the proceeding in any case prior to the adjudication, if he show by proofs, satisfactory to the court, that he is in fact a creditor, and that his interests will be affected by the adjudication.   Formal proof of debt under the proceedings instituted, is, in some sense, a submission to the jurisdiction of the court, and an apparent admission, if not a claim, that the adjudication should be made and the estate administered upon the petition then and there pending.

At first view it is natural and agreeable to our ordinary ideas upon the subject, to assume that a petition by an alleged creditor against his debtor to compel a submission of his estate to the bankrupt court, is a contest between two parties with which a third person may not meddle.   But this is by no means a complete view of the scope and effect of the proceeding.   It is not a mere suit *inter partes ;* it rather partakes of the nature of a proceeding *in rem,* in which every actual creditor has a direct interest. The proceeding is summary and in a high degree informal, and it should be free from technical embarrassment. It is true that no one is entitled to be heard therein who has no interest to protect, but, it seems to me, that if the applicant does in fact show that he is a creditor and has an interest to protect, it is not in accordance with the spirit of the proceeding to compel him first to file that formal proof of his debt which would import a recognition of the jurisdiction of the court over the question of the adjudication, and the administration of the assets, which, by his application, he sought to contest.

It is also true that to justify such intervention, the object or purpose disclosed must be one which, in a legal sense, is meritorious, and not purely officious; therefore the facts alleged as ground of intervention must be such as entitle the applicant to consideration. The court must be able to see that the intervention may serve some useful purpose, either in protecting the rights of the applicant, or those of the creditors at large. On this subject the case of *Brewster* v. *Shelton*, 24 Conn. 140, furnishes no remote analogy. There the creditor made application to the proper court to compel the appointment of trustees of the estate of his alleged debtor under the insolvent law of Connecticut. By that law the appointment of trustees operated to defeat liens acquired by prior attachments of the debtor's property. Certain creditors who had made the attachments, intervened for the protection of their liens, and were successful in defeating the application. The objection that they were not parties, and that they were not entitled to be heard, was urged, but the supreme court of errors overruled this objection and fully established their right to thus intervene. If it be suggested that the parties intervening in that case had acquired a specific lien which was distinctly involved in the matter before the court, such suggestion brings into view the precise relation of Adams, the present petitioner, to the matter pending in this case before the district court for Connecticut.

Leaving the general question, in what cases and for what

purposes a creditor is entitled to be heard pending the proceeding, (one of which is provided for in the thirty-first section of the bankrupt act, under which the courts have repeatedly held that a creditor has the right to be heard in opposition to the discharge of the bankrupt, whether he has made formal proof of his debt or not. Bump on bankruptcy, 385, and cases there cited.) It is sufficient for us now to deal with the precise case presented by this petitioner. He is the petitioning creditor in the district of Massachusetts, and has there obtained an adjudication, declaring the debtors bankrupt. He has thereby acquired a clear, legal right to have their property applied to the payment of their debts, and, in a proper sense, has obtained an equitable lien on all the property and estate of the bankrupts (assuming, of course, for the purposes of this question, that the proceeding in Massachusetts is legal and operative,) and has an interest in protecting it from embarrassment, complication and waste, or withdrawal from the control of that court; and especially from having the administration of any part of the assets transferred, under the forms of law, by collusion with the debtor and other creditors, to another and distant forum.

But, nevertheless, as already observed, no intervention should be permitted, unless the case made by the petitioner shows that he is seeking a proper object, and presents the facts necessary to warrant the relief for which he asks. This leads to the consideration of the second question, and that is, whether the petitioner has shown a case which entitles him to intervene for the protection of his interest in this estate.

In determining this point it is not necessary that I should express any opinion on the question whether the Boston, Hartford and Erie Railroad Company is, under the laws of Connecticut and Massachusetts, one corporation or two corporations having a common stock, a common property, common powers, and identical corporations. Nor is it necessary to enquire here whether railroad corporations are amenable to the bankrupt act as bankrupt debtors. For the purpose of this case I might test that point on the opinion of the

learned justice of the supreme court, by which the jurisdiction of the bankrupt courts over such corporations was affirmed in the case against this company in the district of
Massachusetts; but the question is not material for the disposition of the case now before me. If such jurisdiction exists, then this case is to be considered in other aspects. If it
does not exist, then, surely, that fact should be no obstacle
to an intervention to stay its assumption and exercise.

The petition shows that the debtors are, either a single
corporation, exercising corporate powers by authority of Massachusetts, having their principal office and place of business
in Boston, in the district of Massachusetts, and, therefore,
are within the jurisdiction of the bankrupt court there; or
they are two corporations united, owning all their property in
common, conducting their business for the joint benefit, exercising like powers, having in all respects a common interest,
performing all their functions to compass one object for the
benefit of the same corporation and stockholders, and having
one set of creditors. In this aspect they may be something
more than partners; but they are so united that they are
plainly within section thirty-six of the bankrupt act relating
to partnerships, as well as within that relating to joint stock
companies (section thirty-seven), and are therefore liable to
be proceeded against in the district of Massachusetts. It is
no less true, that, in either view of the character of the company, they were equally liable to be proceeded against in
the district of Connecticut. The district courts of both districts had jurisdiction over these debtors as bankrupts.

In this state of the law, if no express rule were prescribed, no doubt would, I think, exist as to the proper practice
where the jurisdiction of both courts to adjudge the debtors
bankrupt and administer their estate was invoked. The familiar practice of courts of equity, acting under the same
general jurisdiction, would require them, when their jurisdiction should be invoked for the distribution of the same fund
by different complainants, to permit the court first obtaining
jurisdiction of the fund by the institution of a suit, to proceed

therewith to its full and complete disposal. For it will be observed that such a case is not analogous to that of two suits proceeding at the same time in different states, under different laws. Both the district courts here are federal tribunals, acting under federal laws constituting a single system, operating alike in both jurisdictions, and necessarily governed by the same rules and proceeding to the same identical result. It would be a mere act of comity for a state tribunal to stay its proceedings on the ground that a suit was pending in a court of another state, both suits being for the administration of the same fund; as, for example, in a case for the construction of a will and the proper distribution of the estate under it. Here there can be but one administration; there is but one bankrupt law, the authority and jurisdiction of the courts are derived from one source, and the reasons for confining the administration of the estate to a single tribunal are of greater fitness and force. I am therefore of opinion that, in the absence of any express provision, it would be the duty of the other district court to yield the control and direction of the entire proceeding to that one whose jurisdiction was first invoked, and whose power is ample to accomplish all the purposes of the law and protect the rights of all parties interested, under the authority of the same act which governs each of them. Without this it is difficult to see how the law can be safely, uniformly and legally administered. On the appointment of an assignee all the property of the bankrupt is, by express terms, vested in him by the assignment made, and such assignment relates back to the commencement of the proceedings. When, therefore, one court having jurisdiction has adjudged a debtor bankrupt, appointed an assignee, and executed the assignment, nothing of the property of the bankrupt remain in him to be taken or administered by another tribunal. All is vested in the assignee appointed by the other, as of the time when the first petition was filed. If, on a second petition, filed in another court, the latter were to proceed to appoint an assignee, it is difficult to perceive that the title of the latter would not be completely overridden. To use for illustration the present case. The petition to put the debtors into bankruptcy was first filed in the district court in Massachusetts, which clearly had jurisdiction, and that court had adjudged them bankrupt before any such adjudication had taken place in Connecticut ; if then, as the statute expressly provides the appointment of the assignee, and the assignment to him relate back to the commencement of the proceeding, how can any assignee appointed in Connecticut under proceedings commenced subsequent to the beginning of those in Massachusetts, acquire any title or right to intermeddle with the administration as against the assignee appointed in the latter district and by relation, if not by prior appointment, having prior and exclusive title.

The law, however, contains other provisions bearing on the subject, and the general orders of the supreme court made by express authority of the act shed further light for our guidance. In case of co-partnerships, where the co-partners reside in different districts, and therefore more than one court has jurisdiction, it is provided that the court in which the petition is first filed shall retain exclusive jurisdiction over the case. (Section thirty-six.) This provision is to prevent the complication which might arise if both courts were to attempt to administer the same estate, and furnishes an apt analogy, if not a rule, for this precise case ; it is possible that the same assignee might be chosen and appointed in each jurisdiction, but it is also possible that different ones might be chosen, and if the same were chosen in both, there is no fitness or propriety that there should be a double accounting, or a double series of orders with double costs.

The act authorises proceedings against a single debtor, either in the district where he resides, or in that in which he carries on business. Proceedings might therefore be commenced against him in both ; and I find in the terms of the act, no express declaration as to which court shall have priority of jurisdiction. The implication, however, resulting from the vesting in the assignee the title to all the property

In re Boston, Hartford and Erie R. R. Co.

of the bankrupt by relation back to the commencement of the proceedings, seem necessarily to involve the same rule as that prescribed in the case of copartnerships. But the supreme court, whose orders in cases not otherwise provided for, or, at least so far as they are consistent with what is provided by the act, are conclusive, by general order number sixteen, have directed that "in case two or more petitions shall be filed against the same individual in different districts, the first hearing shall be had in the district in which the debtor has his domicile, and in case of two or more petitions against the same firm in different courts * * the petition first filed shall be first heard * * and in either case the proceedings upon the other petitions may be stayed until an adjudication is made upon the petition first heard, and the court which makes the first adjudication of bankruptcy shall retain jurisdiction over all proceedings therein until the same shall be closed." Upon the facts stated in this petition of review, if the bankrupts be regarded as a single corporation and having a domicile within the meaning of this order of the supreme court, that domicile is as truly in Massachusetts as in Connecticut, the bankrupts having been incorporated by both states. If, however, they are to be regarded as composed of joint parties and in the nature of a copartnership, then the petition filed in Massachusetts was entitled to be first heard, and there as in the other case provision was made for staying the proceedings in Connecticut; and the court in Massachusetts having made the first adjudication of bankruptcy, retained jurisdiction over all proceedings therein until the same shall be closed.

But if the character of the debtors here is anomalous, not precisely answering either description, then the law and the order of the supreme court prescribe a rule which, from its obvious fitness and propriety, should be the guide of the court in these proceedings in order to avoid the complication, embarrassment and expense if not inevitable conflict, resulting from an endeavor to administer the same fund in two districts.

It may not follow that the court in which the latest petition is filed must, or ought to, dismiss the proceeding lawfully and regularly instituted, but it should at least, in my opinion, on proper application, stay the proceedings until some adjudication touching the bankruptcy be had in the tribunal in which the petition was first filed, or, if the debtor has been already adjudged bankrupt there, abstain from an apparent interference with the title of the assignee to the estate.

If these views are correct, then there was ground for the application to the court in Connecticut to stay proceedings, and yield to the already acquired and exclusive jurisdiction of the court in Massachusetts.   This ground was fully shown by the petitioner in his application to the district court, and it was further alleged that the debtors were in collusion with the petitioning creditor here and would make no resistance to his petition.

Who then was authorised to present these facts to the district court in this state, and assert the prior and exclusive jurisdiction of the court in Massachusetts?   The debtors would not.   The petioning creditors would not.   If they were acting in collusion, their purpose could only be to complicate and embarrass the proceedings to the prejudice of the creditors, and to produce conflict and litigation.   I feel no hesitation in saying that the petitioning creditor in Massachusetts was eminently the proper party to bring the state of this case to the attention of the court, and ask to be heard in resistance to further proceedings which tended to his prejudice as the prosecuting creditor, and which if permitted to have any operation, tended to defeat the rights he had acquired, and the effect of the adjudication in Massachusetts.   Unless this be so, then the neglect of the debtors to resist the latter proceedings defeats the express provision giving exclusive jurisdiction to the court in which the petition is first filed, or that which gives to the court making the first adjudication exclusive jurisdiction ; or, it leaves the court to proceed to an idle and useless form of adjudication and administration, after its jurisdiction has been, for the time at least, defeated, and when the property of the bankrupt is divested so as to leave nothing for the court to administer. I think, therefore, that the petition of Adams should have been entertained, and if the facts therein alleged were not controverted or were found true, the proceedings in the court below should have been stayed.

Since the argument of this petition of review, the crediors, proceeding under the adjudication of bankruptcy in the district court, have chosen the same assignees who were chosen by the creditors under the proceedings in Massachusetts, and they have been approved by both courts.

I find nothing whatever in the case to warrant the conclusion that the adjudication of bankruptcy in this state was an improper decree. Surely the petitioning creditor, who himself sought a like decree in Massachusetts, cannot deny that the debtors were bankrupts, and would be properly so adjudged; and as other assignees, they are duly appointed by the court in Massachusetts, and the further sanction of an appointment in Connecticut can by no possibility prejudice the petition. There is, therefore, in the present condition of the matter, no occasion for disturbing what has been done. All that can be said is that, according to the views I have here expressed, the petitioner was entitled to have the proceeding earlier stayed to avoid a possible result that cannot now happen. It may be suggested that these subsequent occurences are not regularly before me on this review. In technical strictness that is true, but I have ample power to permit them to be brought before me. Such supervision as is conferred on this court in these cases, summary in its nature, is not to be so hampered by technical rules as to prevent my. dealing with the case as it now exists. It seems to me, therefore, that unless the petitioner desires to deny that those subsequent proceedings took place as I have stated, all that is necessary is to stay the proceedings in the district court. It is not easy to see that there can ever be occasion to move further therein; but if the jurisdiction of the court in Massachusetts should in any way be defeated, or the proceedings therein be reversed or dismissed upon any grounds not also

In re Boston, Hartford and Erie R. R. Co.

applicable to those pending in this district, it may be of the utmost importance to all the creditors, and especially to the petitioner himself, that these proceedings be resumed and continued to the final close of the administration of this bankrupt estate.—September 19, 1871.

UNITED STATES CIRCUIT COURT—S. D. NEW YORK.

Where the district judge for the southern district of New York privately signed the form of an adjudication of bankruptcy, on the first day of March, and endorsed on the same the words and figures "Filed March 1st, 1871, S. B.," and on the second day of March granted a re-argument of the application of the petitioning creditor in another district for leave to intervene and oppose an adjudication in this district, and at such re-argument on the third day of March, a certified copy of an adjudication made in such other district on the second day of March having been produced and read, the district judge produced the paper which had been signed by him on the first of March, but which, during the interval, had been in the sole knowledge and possession of the said judge, and had neither been entered with the clerk nor promulgated as an adjudication of the court, Held, that the said paper operated as an adjudication only as of the time when it was so produced in court, and promulgated, to wit, as of the third of March, and that the adjudication which was regularly made and entered in the other district on the second of March, took precedence as the earlier adjudication.

In re BOSTON, HARTFORD AND ERIE R. R. CO.*

On the twenty-first day of October, eighteen hundred and seventy, Seth Adams, a creditor of the Boston, Hartford and Erie Railroad Company, filed his petition in the district court of the United States for the district of Massachusetts, alleging that the said company had committed an act of bankruptcy, and praying that the company be adjudged a bankrupt, &c.

On the twentieth of December, eighteen hundred and seventy, James Alden, also a creditor, presented his petition, with a like allegation and prayer, to the district court of the United States for Connecticut.

On the thirty-first of December, eighteen hundred and seventy, the said James Alden presented his like petition to the district court for the southern district of New York.

* See 5 N. B. R. 230, 232, 233.

To these several petitions the company appeared and answered, resisting the application for such adjudication.

Pending the petitions, Seth Adams, the petitioning creditor in Massachusetts, applied, both in New York and Connecticut, for leave to intervene and oppose the said applications there made.

On the twenty-eighth of February, eighteen hundred and seventy-one, the company withdrew its answer and objection in each of the said districts, and on the second day of March, eighteen hundred and seventy-one, the district court in Massachusetts adjudged the company bankrupt, by a formal decree of the said court, and issued its warrant to the marshal of that district, in accordance with the statute.

This decree was shown to the district court for Connecticut, by the supplementary petition of the said Seth Adams (the petitioning creditor in Massachusetts); but notwithstanding such decree, the district court for Connecticut refused leave to Seth Adams to appear to resist the proceeding in that court, and dismissed his petition, and thereupon proceeded to adjudge, and did adjudge, the company bankrupt. On a petition of review presented by Seth Adams to the circuit court, it was, at the September term, eighteen hundred and seventy-one, held, that he was entitled to be heard in the district court, and that his petition ought not to have been dismissed. The circuit thereupon proceeded, upon the facts alleged in his petitions, which were not controverted, to direct that all further proceedings in the district court for Connecticut be stayed, in order that the district court in Massachusetts might thereafter exercise exclusive jurisdiction, for the closing of the estate and distributing the same among the creditors of the corporation.

The like petition of Seth Adams was brought to a hearing in the district court, for the southern district of New York, on the twenty-fifth of February, eighteen hundred and seventy-one, and the district court decided on the twenty-seventh day of February, eighteen hundred and seventy-one, that the said Adams had no standing in court in that stage in the proceeding prior to an adjudication of bankruptcy, and that he be not permitted to intervene to resist or stay the proceedings pending in this district; and an order denying his motion was made. But on the second of March, on the application of the counsel for the said Adams, the court allowed a re-argument, and such re-argument was had on the third of March. On the re-argument, and in further support of his claim of title to intervene, the counsel for the said Adams produced and read in evidence the decree of the district court for Massachusetts, adjudging the said railroad company a bankrupt. At the close of the argument, the court refused to permit such intervention, and then the following facts appeared, namely : that, after the withdrawal (on the twenty-eighth of February) by the railroad company of its answer to the petition of Adams, praying that the company be adjudged a bankrupt, an order or decree adjudging such bankruptcy was drawn and delivered to the district judge, and on the first day of March he signed the same, but retained it in his personal keeping until after the said re-argument, without any notice to either of the parties, or their attorneys or counsel, or to the clerk of the court, of the fact of such signing. The district judge endorsed upon such order or decree the words " Filed March 1st, 1871. S. B."

On denying the said application of Seth Adams, after such re-argument, the said district judge announced these facts in open court, delivered the said order or decree, adjudging the company a bankrupt, to the counsel for Alden, the petitioning creditor, and the same was by him delivered to the clerk of the court to be entered in the minutes and records of the court.

The said Seth Adams thereupon presented his petition to the circuit court, praying a review and reversal of the said proceedings of the district court, and that all proceedings in bankruptcy against the said company in the said court be stayed, and for other or further relief.

Though not material to the questions considered on the review, it is proper to state that the Adams Express Company had, by leave of court, become a co-partner with James Alden, and the proceedings of Seth Adams had, by supplemental petition, been made to apply to the proceedings of both of such petitioning creditors.

The circuit court having, as above stated, heard the petition for the review of the proceedings in the district court in Connecticut, and, in September, eighteen hundred and seventy-one, decided the same, staying proceedings in that court, the petition of the said Seth Adams for a review of the proceedings in the southern district of New York was brought to a hearing.

Joseph H. Choate, counsel for Seth Adams.

Charles M. da Costa, counsel for the petitioning creditors, James Alden and the Adams Express Co.

J. Langdon Ward, counsel for the bankrupt.

Woodruff, C. J.—It is unnecessary, in disposing of this review, to repeat the observations which were made on deciding the very similar review of the proceedings between the same parties in the circuit court for the district of Connecticut, at the last September term of that court. 5 N. B. R. 230, 232, 233; 8 Blatch. R. Whatever considerations were then suggested, tending to show the embarrassment, inconvenience and unsuitableness of an endeavor to administer the estate of the Boston, Hartford and Erie Railroad Company, as a bankrupt, and bring the same to a close by collecting and disposing of its assets and distributing its effects among its creditors, by proceedings in several district courts, and, as the case may be, through the instrumentality of different assignees appointed by these courts; the impracticability of bringing the fund together for one general distribution; the possible, not to say probable, conflict of title between the assignees, the title of each of whom, if valid, must be recognized in all courts; the possible different results of contests in the several jurisdictions respecting debts offered to be proved by creditors whose claims may be disputed; the useless and vexatious trouble and annoyance to creditors if they be required to go into each jurisdiction and prove their claims; the useless and extraordinary expense and waste of the estate by subjecting its administration to such multiplied proceedings, these and other reasons, showing that it is not only unfit, but unreasonable to continue proceedings in more than one district, and that the case is eminently proper for the application of the general rule in courts of equity among courts of co-ordinate jurisdiction, that when one has first obtained jurisdiction of the subject matter and of the parties, other courts should stay their hand and permit such court to carry the proceeding to a consummation and final disposition of the matter in question; all these and, perhaps, other like considerations, were suggested in the opinion delivered on the review had in Connecticut.   Nothing is, I think, more certain than that congress, in enacting the bankrupt law, did not contemplate any such complication, and I deem it equally certain, that nothing in its provisions produces any such necessary result.   The several district courts of the United States are not acting under authority derived from separate sovereignties; they are not administering separate systems of laws; they are not charged with a duty to afford special protection to the residents within their local jurisdiction, all which circumstances sometimes lead to conflict of jurisdiction between tribunals of different states, and operate to secure unequal results among parties interested, but residing in different states, domestic or foreign.

The district courts act by one authority, they execute the same law; each, in the administration of the estate of a bankrupt, will do precisely what each other district court will do, governed by the same rules and to the same ends.

In the opinion referred to, the bankrupt law was examined, and the general orders in bankruptcy made by the supreme court, were considered, to ascertain first, whether such proceedings must necessarily, if begun, be continued in more than one district court; if not, then which district court should be deemed to have priority of jurisdiction and be permitted to go on and complete the administration; and finally, if the bankrupt, with a view to hinder and embarrass the winding up of the affairs, should lie by silently, or colluding with one or more of the parties to produce such embarrassment, would not take any measures to prevent the action of either court, nor call to the attention of either the fact that prior proceedings were pending in another district, can a creditor bring the matter to the attention of the court and ask that the proceedings, subsequently commenced, be stayed, in order to avoid the expense, embarrassment and litigation about to arise to the prejudice of creditors, and to the waste of the fund which creditors have a right to share?

The court did not affirm the broad proposition that whenever a creditor filed a petition against his debtor for a decree declaring such debtor a bankrupt, any other creditor was at liberty, and as of course, to appear and claim a right to oppose such adjudication, but it was held that the court was not hindered from entertaining the application for leave to oppose, by rigid technical rules, governing actions at law *inter partes*, and that cases might exist in which a creditor should be heard, and on sufficient grounds, his intervention might properly be effective.

It was accordingly held : that, it appearing to the district court in Connecticut, on the petition of Seth Adams, that he was the petitioning creditor in the district court of Massachusetts ; that his petition was there filed on the twenty-first of October, eighteen hundred and seventy ; that the petition in Connecticut was filed on the twentieth of December, eighteen hundred and seventy, and that the district court for the district of Massachusetts had, on the second of March, eighteen hundred and seventy-one, decreed the company a bankrupt, and issued its warrant to the marshal, as required by the act of congress ; the district court for Connecticut ought to have received the petition of the said Seth Adams and stayed its further proceedings.

Subsequent reflection, aided by the argument of the review here pending, have deepened the conviction that the order made in Connecticut was right and proper. The only question, therefore, which is open here, is whether the district court for Massachusetts should be accorded, either as matter of strict right, or in conformity to the practice of courts of equity having co-ordinate jurisdiction above adverted to, the same priority of jurisdiction over the district court for the southern district of New York, which was yielded by the court for Connecticut.

In partial review of some of the reasons for the former decisions, it is suggested that there is no express provision of the bankrupt law assigning to either court priority, when two or more petitions are filed against a *corporation* debtor; and that the sixteenth of the general orders of the supreme court in bankruptcy does not apply to corporations at all, but only to individual natural persons, or co-partnership firms composed of individuals.

If this were conceded, it would not prevent the conclusion which was there reached, for three reasons : first, all the considerations which should dispose the court to accord to the tribunal which first obtained jurisdiction of the subject matter and of the parties, the continuance of the proceedings to its close, would require that the district court for Massachusetts, in which the petition against this bankrupt was first filed, should be permitted to have the exclusive administration without the interference of any other district court ; second, by the express provision of the bankrupt law (section fourteen) the appointment of an assignee and the transfer of the assets to him relates back to the commencement of the proceedings, i. e., to the filing of the petition, and thus the filing of the petition operates not only to render acts done at an earlier period—within six months preceding (section thirty-nine)-—grounds of adjudication which would not avail in the other courts, but it also enables the assignee to impeach earlier transactions—within six or four months (sections fourteen, thirty five and thirty-nine,) e. g., preference to creditors, seizures or attachments, executions, &c., and other conveyances which could not be impeached under later proceedings, and consequently the estate to be divided to creditors may be very greatly less or even swept beyond their reach if the court in which the petition is first filed be not permitted to administer the estate; and, third, in the only instance in which the act of congress itself appears to contemplate the possibility of proceedings being begun in two different district courts (section thirty-six), where proceedings are instituted in different districts against co-partners residing in such different districts, it directs unqualifiedly that the court in which the petition is first filed shall retain exclusive jurisdiction over the case. It would, in the absence of express provision, be altogether fitting to regard this as a proper rule by analogy, whenever petitions are filed in two or more district courts, each having jurisdiction.

It was insisted on behalf of the petitioner, Seth Adams, that the sixteenth of the general orders in bankruptcy does apply to a corporation, and to this corporation, either as if it were an individual natural person, or as a joint debtor in the nature of a firm, it being incorporated in several states, and yet having a common stock, common property, common interests, and owning the same debts, by force of the same obligations. But that the bankrupt was not a corporation by the laws of the state of New York, and the district court here could have no jurisdiction to proceed against the bankrupt except on the ground that it carried on business in this state, having its residence or domicile in the state or states by which it was incorporated.

The bankrupt, by act of the legislature of the state of New York, passed April twenty-fifth, eighteen hundred and sixty-four (Sess. Laws of N. Y., chap. 385), was authorized to purchase the franchise and property of a certain corporation, organized under the general railroad laws of the state of New York, to construct a railroad in this state, from the town of Fishkill to the boundary of Connecticut, and the act declared that the sale and conveyance should be effectual in law to pass title to the franchise and property sold, and that on the filing and record of the certificate of sale and conveyance, the said Boston, Hartford and Erie Railroad Company should become possessed of the rights of charter and property .sold, conveyed and described, and might have, hold and use the same, in their own right, as a portion of their railway line and property, and have all the rights the corporation making the sale and conveyance, had at the time of such conveyance, to construct and operate a railway within the terminal points designated in the charter of the company making the conveyance, and subject to the laws of this state, passed, or that may be passed concerning railroad corporations. The purchase and conveyance contemplated by this act were made, and the certificate of conveyance appears to have been filed, and the respondent is alleged to have carried on business in this state in pursuance of the said act.

If the case of such a corporation is not provided for, either in the terms of the act, or by the general orders in bankruptcy, the propriety of giving to the court in which the petition is first filed the administration of the estate, has been sufficiently indicated.

If the sixteenth of the general orders in bankruptcy should be construed to apply, then also, so far as the proceedings here proceed upon the carrying on of business in this state as the ground of jurisdiction, the rule requires that the first hearing shall be had in the district in which the debtor has his domicile ; and if the peculiar fact of incorporation in more than one state creates an analogy to a firm or co-partnership, then also, the petition first filed shall be first heard.

In either aspect of the case neither the general orders in bankruptcy, nor the general principles governing like subjects, nor the fitness or propriety of the thing, requires or permits the continuance of two distinct proceedings and the consequent double administration of the bankrupt's estate. And once more, if, instead of regarding the act of the legislalature of the state of New York as a permission given to a corporation created by the states of Massachusetts and Connecticut to construct, maintain and operate a railroad in this state, it be held that the act and the conveyance in pursuance thereof operated to make the Boston, Hartford and Erie

Railroad Company, a corporation of New York, and liable to be treated as a corporation, created by the laws of New York, then the case now under review is the same in these respects as the case which was under review in the circuit court for Connecticut, for the company was in the very terms of the acts of the legislatures of Connecticut and Massachusetts, a corporation in each of those states.

There remains, therefore, no ground for withdrawing the case under review, from the operation of the case already decided, unless what took place in the district court in the southern district of New York, prior to the second of March, eighteen hundred and seventy-one, gives to the district court last named priority and precedence of the district court for Massachusetts, by which, on that day, the respondent was adjudged a bankrupt. Without here enquiring in view of all that has been suggested in this or the former opinion whether, if it be regarded as amounting to an earlier adjudication of bankruptcy, it should have the effect last above mentioned, it may be sufficient to consider the prior question. Was it an adjudication of bankruptcy in any legal sense, which gives such priority?

My conclusion upon this branch of the subject is, that it was not an adjudication prior in legal effect and operation to the adjudication in Massachusetts, if that was the sole test by which this review must be decided.

This conclusion rests upon two grounds : first, that it had no legal operation or effect until after the adjudication in Massachusetts ; and second, if it could be deemed of any significance that the district judge had set his signature to a decree, retaining it within his sole knowledge, possession and control, that significance was wholly suspended and rendered inoperative by the granting of a re-argument of the application of the petitioner herein, for leave to appear and oppose any adjudication in the district court.

1. In the progress of proceedings in bankruptcy and in proceedings in formal suits, both at law and in equity, it is a common practice for the judge to receive the papers on a

motion or on a final hearing, for consideration.   It is not to
be held that if on such consideration, he should, in the first
instance, in the privicy of his chambers or in his library, set
his hand to the form of an order or decree, his power over
the subject is *ipso facto* gone, and that act is final.

On the contrary, he may, beyond all question—judges
often do—prolong his consideration, and if he find reason to
conclude that his first impression was erroneous, he may
make the final decision conform to the result of his most
full and deliberate examination and reflection.   This alone,
if correct, shows that such mere subscription is not *per se* an
adjudication of the matter.

Nor can it be sustained as an adjudication, by the suggestion that it is an adjudication which, if he does not change
his conclusion, operates by relation back to the date of the
signing, or in other words, that it may be regarded as a provisional adjudication, to stand, if no sufficient reason occurs
to the judge for changing it.

Some observations pertinent to this question, in both
aspects, may be found in the opinion of the circuit court for
the northern district of New York, in the *American Wood
Paper Co.* v. *The Glens Falls Co.* 8 Blatch., in which an
attempt was made to give a precedent effect to a judicial
determination by the acting commissioner of patents, because, as he testified, he had made up his mind and endorsed
and signed a decision which he retained to abide the result
of further consideration, if a further opposing argument .
should be presented.

A fair and just test of the question may be suggested by
enquiring when does the time to appeal begin to run, where
it is limited to a specific period after the order or decree.
If the adjudication were to be deemed operative from the
signing by the judge, and while all knowledge thereof was
confined to the breast of the judge himself, the whole time
to appeal might elapse while he held the order or decree in
his own possession, and the right of appeal be thereby
wholly defeated.

In re Boston, Hartford and Erie R. R. Co..

I have no hesitation in saying that the draught of an order, though signed, remaining in the sole possession and knowledge of the judge, whether for the purpose of further consideration, or for any other reason, is subject to his control, it is not final so as to conclude him; and until it is in some manner notified to the clerk of the court, or to one of the parties, in such wise that his decision can properly be said to be promulgated or announced, it concludes no one.

Decisions of court announced in open court are often and properly held to affect parties charged thereby, although the formal order or decree has not been entered, but decisions lying in the breasts of the judges can have no such effect, and the mere fact that the latter have been set down on paper ought to give them no different operation. This is not to be taken to import that all orders must be announced formally in open court, or that orders which may be made out of court, must be formally proclaimed, but there must be something tantamount to promulgation or delivery, something of which the parties to be affected can have or can obtain knowledge before their rights can be said to have received adjudication, something which completes and authenticates the judicial act.

2. The practical construction given by the district court to this act of signing the order, given while the order remained within the sole knowledge and possession of the judge, was in conformity with the view last above suggested. A re-argument of the application of this petition was ordered. This can have but one meaning. The application of the petitioner was for leave to appear and oppose the proceeding of the district court to any adjudication touching the bankruptcy of this railroad company. Now, whether he had or had not sufficient grounds for his application, the re-argument proceeded wholly on the idea that as yet no such adjudication had been made.

3. The re-hearing operated to take away any possible significancy in this respect to such private signing of an order. Even when a final decree has been promulgated and

entered, a re-hearing was held, in *Brockett* v. *Brockett*, 2 How. 238, to operate to suspend its operation, and an appeal taken within ten days after the refusal on the re-hearing to open such decree, was on that ground held to operate as a *supersedeas.*

In a court of equity, the granting of a re-hearing operates to open the decree for further examination in whole or in part according to the nature and extent of the grounds for re-hearing. *Consequa* v. *Fanning*, John. Ch. R. 593 ; *White* v. *Carpenter*, 2 Paige, 262 ; *Ferguson* v. *Kimball*, 3 B. Ch. R. 616.

The result is that there is nothing in the case presented upon this review which withdraws it from the operation of the decision heretofore made, as above stated, in the district of Connecticut.

In that district it was not deemed necessary to reverse the adjudication of bankruptcy which had been made; the same assignees who had been chosen and approved in Massachusetts, had also been chosen and approved in Connecticut, and such double sanction could work no prejudice to any party in interest. It was deemed sufficient to stay any further proceedings.

Here I am informed that an additional assignee was appointed. That appointment does not appear by the papers before me. But that appointment would of course fall with a reversal of the adjudication in bankruptcy. I have no doubt of the power of the court to make such order herein as may best secure all interests, and if the facts occurring are not admitted, to make a proper enquiry to ascertain them. It will be sufficient to reverse all proceedings subsequent to or founded upon the adjudication of bankruptcy, and stay all further proceedings in the district court.

UNITED STATES DISTRICT COURT—E. D. MICHIGAN.

An assignee acting under an order of court directing him to sell the goods of a bankrupt for the highest price he could obtain above a certain minimum specified, must comply with the order, and if it is made to appear to the court that he has not obtained the highest price offered, the sale will be set aside and the assignee directed to refund the amount received, and hold the sale open for higher offers until a day specified, when it shall be closed for the highest offer in cash received up to that time.

Costs and attorney's fee of ten dollars ordered to be paid out of the funds belonging to the estate of the bankrupt.

In re RYAN & GRIFFIN.

LONGYEAR, J.—The assignee had been authorised by an order of the court to sell a stock of boots and shoes belonging to the bankrupts' estate, in bulk and at private sale, for the best price he could obtain, but in no event less than six thousand nine hundred dollars. Martin Brothers and Matthew J. Moynahan were competitors for the stock. Moynahan, on being applied to by the assignee to state the highest price he would pay for the stock, offered seven thousand two hundred and fifty dollars, and stated that that was the highest price he would pay. The assignee then informed Martin Brothers of Moynahan's bid, and that they could not have the stock unless they would make a better offer. They desired time to consider. The assignee gave them time, and agreed with them that if, by a certain hour, they should conclude to pay seven thousand three hundred dollars, they should have the stock. In the mean time, and before any further transactions had taken place between Martin Brothers and the assignee, Moynahan offered the assignee seven thousand five hundred dollars, and tendered five hundred dollars of the amount as earnest money. The assignee, honestly believing that he had the power to make the arrangement he had made with Martin Brothers, and that he was in honor bound to wait till the expiration of the time agreed on, and then to sell to them if they complied with the specified terms, declined to entertain Moynahan's offer, except on condition that Martin Brothers should not accept the terms specified by the time agreed on. Within the time agreed on Martin Brothers accepted the terms and agreed to pay the seven thousand three hundred dollars, and paid to the assignee five hundred dollars of the amount, as earnest money, and the assignee agreed that they should have the goods. Moynahan then paid the five hundred dollars he had tendered as earnest money into court, and application was made to set aside the sale to Martin Brothers, and that the assignee be directed to entertain Moynahan's offer, and a hearing was had.

The assignee in bankruptcy is an officer of the court, and is limited in his transactions in that capacity to the powers and authority conferred upon him by the bankrupt act and the orders of the court. Anything he may do outside, or in conflict with, or in violation of, such powers and authority is, of course, null and void. In this case he was acting under an order of court, authorising and directing him to sell for the highest price he could obtain above a certain minimum specified. By his arrangement with Martin Brothers it was left entirely optional with them whether they would take the goods or not, and of course that arrangement did not amount to a sale, nor even a binding agreement to sell. The assignee's agreement with them to wait till a certain time for them to make up their minds, and then if in case they concluded to purchase at the price named, he would sell the goods to them at all events, and his refusal on account of such agreement to entertain a higher offer actually made in the meantime, were in direct conflict with and in violation of his authority and duty as specified in the order under which he was acting. The following order was made in the premises :

" This matter coming on to be heard upon the order for the assignee to show cause upon the petition of Thomas Griffin, one of the said bankrupts, and the same having been heard accordingly, on consideration thereof it is ordered, adjudged and decreed that the sale to Martin Brothers by the assignee of the stock of boots and shoes heretofore authorised by an order of this court to be sold by the assignee, in bulk and at private sale, was unauthorised and in violation of the terms of the said last-mentioned order, in this, to wit: that the sale was so made to said Martin Brothers for the sum of seven thousand three hundred dollars, when a higher offer of seven thousand five hundred dollars had been made, and was then and still is pending, by one Matthew J. Moynahan; and that the said sale to Martin Brothers is therefore void and of no effect, and the same is set aside and al·together held for naught.

"And it is further ordered, adjudged and decreed that the said assignee be, and he is hereby directed to entertain the said offer of seven thousand five hundred dollars, so made by the said Matthew J. Moynahan, and hold the sale open for higher offers; and that he close the sale at twelve o'clock noon of the twenty-third day of February, eighteen hundred and seventy-two, for the highest offer in cash he shall receive up to that time.

"And it is further ordered that the assignee pay the taxable costs of this proceeding, (including an attorney fee of ten dollars, to Lyman Cochrane, Esq.,) out of the funds in his hands belonging to the estate of said bankrupts.

"And it is further ordered that the assignee return to Martin Brothers any deposit or payment of money they may have made to him on account of said sale."

February 21, 1872.

UNITED STATES SUPREME COURT—UTAH TERRITORY.

The publishers of a daily paper and proprietors of a book and job printing office are manufacturers within the meaning of the bankrupt act.

Payment of wages to employees though made in the regular course of business is an act of bankruptcy if done in contemplation of insolvency; for although the law prefers an employee to the amount of fifty dollars, this preference must be secured by and through the proceedings in bankruptcy, and not outside of them or independent of and in spite of the act The negotiable paper of a firm of manufacturers is commercial paper within the meaning of the act, regardless of the purpose for which it was given.

In re KENYON & FENTON.

The question before the court arises upon two separate demurrers filed by said several alleged bankrupts to the said petition for adjudication of bankruptcy against them.

The said petitioner, among other things, alleges that said firm are publishers of a daily paper in Salt Lake City, in said territority, known as the "*Salt Lake Daily Review*," and have also conducted a book and job printing office connected therewith, in which are manufactured cards, notes, bill-heads, blank books, posters, show bills and other articles, &c.; that said firm, within six months, to wit, on the twenty-sixth of December, eighteen hundred and seventy-one, in said territory, being manufacturers, have suspended and have not resumed payment of their commercial paper within a period of fourteen days, which paper is therein set forth; and that being in contemplation of insolvency said Kenyon executed a mortgage or transferred all his right, title and interest in the business, material, effects and assets of the said *Daily Review* and the said job office to the said Fenton, with the intent to delay the operation of said bankrupt act; and that being in contemplation of insolvency, and within six calendar months, to wit, on the seventeenth day of November, eighteen hundred and seventy-one, and at sundry other times since then, made payments of money to sundry persons therein named, with the intent to give a preference to their creditors; and that within six calendar mon hs, to wit, on the second day of November, eighteen hundred and

In re Kenyon & Fenton.

seventy-one, the said firm being manufacturers, suspended, and have not resumed payment of their commercial paper within a period of fourteen days, therein describing the same and showing it to be negotiable paper.

The said demurrers substantially charge that said petition is not sufficient in law, and in this :

FIRST. It does not aver that the alleged bankrupts are manufacturers within the meaning of the bankrupt act.

SECOND. It does not aver that the notes mentioned in said petition were the commercial paper of the said bankrupts nor that they were made in the course of their trade as manufacturers within the meaning of said act.

THIRD. There is not a sufficient allegation that said mortgage, and the said payments made by said bankrupts, were made with the intent to prefer any of their creditors.

FOURTH. That there is no allegation that said mortgage and payments were made in contemplation of bankruptcy, etc.

FIFTH. That there are not sufficient facts alleged to entitle the petitioner to the relief prayed for under the said act.

CHARLES G. LOEBER, solicitor for Kenyon ; D. COOPER, solicitor for Fenton ; JAMES L. HIGH, Petitioner, *pro se.*

McKEAN, C. J.—The respondents must be regarded as manufacturers, and the promissory notes set forth in the petition as their commercial paper. The petition contains all necessary averments, and, therefore, the demurrers should be overruled.

HAWLEY, J.—To understand the questions raised by said demurrers, it becomes necessary to enquire into the nature and extent of the character of a manufacturer and trader within the meaning of the bankrupt act.

The character of a trader embraces a wide field of operation. It is of no consequence in what one may trade, the only question is, does he buy and sell articles which are subject to trade and commerce? *In re* Cowles, 1 N. B. R. 42.

Selling horses or other stock or the products of a farmer does not constitute him a trader within the meaning of the act. But if a farmer buys horses or other stock or products of a farm to sell again, and this constitutes a part of his business, he then becomes a trader, and subjects himself to this provision of the bankrupt act. *In re* Chandler, 4 N. B. R. 66.

The term manufacturer, under the bankrupt act, has a legal meaning; and this legal meaning must be governed by legal rules. It is true, that every one who manufactures, is not to be embraced within the legal phrase. A farmer is not to be considered a manufacturer in the commercial sense, when he confines his business to the manufacture of the milk of his cows into butter and cheese; nor when he converts the products of his farm into beef and pork. But it does not follow, that when he makes it a part of his business to buy milk and manufacture the same into butter and cheese, or to purchase the products of other farms and other stock than those of his own, and manufactures the same into beef and pork, that he is not a manufacturer within the meaning of the act.

When the manufacturing becomes the principal part of even a farmer's business, which requires him to buy articles or products and to manufacture them for sale, he thereby becomes a manufacturer and trader within the meaning of the act.

A buyer of leather, who makes it his business, or a part of his business to manufacture the same into boots and shoes, or harness, and sells the same, though he be a nursery-man or a gardener or a farmer, is a manufacturer and a trader within the meaning of the act. If other construction than this should be given to the act, the spirit and the letter of the same could be destroyed by assumptions the most frivolous as well as those the most false.

If it should be admitted that the publishers of a weekly or daily paper were not manufacturers within the meaning of the act, yet if they should buy paper, ink and other material and make the same into cards or billheads, or blanks and blank books, and conduct a business of this kind, as in this case it is averred the bankrupts have done, they are manufacturers and traders within the meaning of the act ; for these articles so manufactured are not necessary parts of the business of publishing a newspaper.

The petitioner avers that said alleged bankrupts are publishers of said newspaper, and manufacturers of books, cards, billheads, etc. Though it is not necessary to decide that the printing and publishing of a daily newspaper is manufacturing in the strict sense of the law, yet my brother judges have expressed the opinion it would be, and I am inclined to the same conviction. A newspaper publication is as much the result of manufacture as that of books or cards or billheads. To make a distinction between them, when in fact there is no distinction, would seem to be an utter disregard of the objects as well as the legal intendment of the law ; for they buy, manufacture and sell.

The second cause of demurrer, to wit, that there is no allegation that said notes set forth were the commercial paper of the said firm, certainly has no foundation ; for the averment of the petitioner is explicit, that said firm within six calendar months, to wit, on the second day of November, eighteen hundred and seventy-one, being manufacturers as aforesaid, suspended and have not resumed payment of their commercial paper within a period of fourteen days.

This allegation is in the language prescribed by the thirty-ninth section, and fully sets forth the making and suspension and non-resumption of their commercial paper for a period of fourteen days. What other or further averment is necessary is not comprehended, and we must therefore hold this averment sufficient.

The third cause of demurrer in part, is, that the averment that said Kenyon mortgaged his said interest in the property named to his co-partner, Fenton, who is made a party defendant in the proceedings in bankruptcy, with the intent to prefer his said partner, seems to be well taken ; for a transfer of one partner to another, of a firm, is not such a transfer that puts the property out of the firm in the strict sense. The removal of the property by mortgage out of the hands of one and into the possession and ownership of the other partner does not remove the same in legal contemplation from liability to the firm's creditors.

But the other clause of this specification, that said payments made by said firm within six calendar months with intent to prefer creditors, is a sufficient charge under the act; therefore, this cause of demurrer, being good only in part and not obnoxious to the petition in another material point, it cannot be sustained.

The fact that said payments were made to the employees of said firm, in their said business, while other employees, with the petitioner, were not paid, does not relieve, against this act, or cause for proceedings in bankruptcy against them. They have no right to prefer one of their employees against the rights of other creditors whether employees or otherwise. The law prefers an employee to the amount of fifty dollars, but this preference must be secured, if at all, by and through the proceedings in bankruptcy, and not outside of them, or independent of, and in spite of the act.

Whenever a person or a firm find they are unable to pay his or their debts in full, or his or their commercial paper at maturity, it is his or their duty to apply to the court in due form of law under the bankrupt act, to distribute his or their assets among his or their creditors equally, without other preference than the said act provides.

But, counsel insist, that because the petitioner has embraced certain elements of section thirty-five, with those of section thirty-nine of the act, therefore his petition in these respects is obnoxious to the demurrer. The petitioner manifestly has a right so to do. These two sections must, as they uniformly have been, be construed by the courts together: for in effect, section thirty-five so provides, as follows: "And if any person, being insolvent, or in contemplation of insolvency or bankruptcy, within six months before the filing of the petition *by or against him*, makes any payment, sale, assignment, transfer, conveyance, or other disposition of any part of his property to any person who then has reasonable cause to believe him to be insolvent, or acting in contemplation of insolvency, and that such payment, sale, assignment," etc., " is made to prevent the same from being distributed under this act, or to defeat the object of, or in any way impair, hinder, impede or delay the operation and effect of, or to evade any of the provisions of this act," etc., the same "shall be void," etc. The thirty-ninth section provides, " that any person residing," etc., " and owing debts," etc., " being bankrupt or insolvent, or in contemplation of bankruptcy or insolvency, shall make any payment, gift, grant, sale, conveyance or transfer of money.or other property, estate, rights or credits, or give any warrant to confess judgment, or procured or suffered his property to be taken on legal process, with intent to give a preference to one or more of his creditors, or to any person or persons who are or may be liable for him as endorser, bail, surety or otherwise, or with the intent, by such disposition of his property, to defeat or delay the operation of this act; or who, being a banker, broker, merchant, trader, manufacturer or miner, has fraudulently stopped payment, or who has stopped or suspended and not resumed payment of his commercial paper within a period of fourteen days, shall be deemed to have committed an act of bankruptcy," etc.

From the recital of these parts of the said two sections, it is manifest that they must be construed together, particularly in proceedings in involuntary bankruptcy. To decide otherwise would be a violation of the letter as well as the spirit of the act.

The fourth cause of demurrer assigned that there is no sufficient allegation that the said payments were made in contemplation of insolvency, with intent to give a preference, etc., cannot be sustained ; for the averments in the petition are, that the said firm, within the period of six calendar months, within said territory, to wit, on the seventeenth day of November, eighteen hundred and seventy-one, being in contemplation of insolvency with intent to give preference, did make payments to sundry persons (naming them) and at sundry other times therein named, within said territory, and also averring that they were manufacturers, etc. A more specific compliance with the provisions of the act could not be made than is made by the petitioner.

The fifth cause of demurrer is a general one and goes to the whole petition; it, therefore, follows from what has already been said, that it cannot be sustained.

The assertion of counsel that the notes in said petition set forth, were given by said firm as publishers of said daily paper and not as manufacturers as aforesaid, is not borne out by the allegation and averments in said petition contained. The petitioner avers that said firm were manufacturers of books, blank books, cards, bill heads, etc., as well as publishers of said paper, and also avers that said firm made said notes and delivered them, etc., that is, they put them in circulation as commercial paper. Thereby the same became their commercial paper under the act and under the law merchant, and cannot be restricted in its character by the appliance of a technical construction such as counsel have sought to give it. Whether it was uttered by said firm as the publishers of said daily paper, or as manufacturers of books, blank books, cards, bill heads, etc., it matters not, for the same being negotiable and put into circulation, either as publishers as aforesaid or as manufacturers as aforesaid, or as publishers and manufacturers as aforesaid, it becomes their commercial paper within the meaning of the bankrupt act, as well as under the law merchant. A more restricted construction would be an utter disregard of the spirit and letter of the law, and do violence to the best interests of the business community. *In re* Chandler, 4 N. B. R. 66; *in re* Nickodemus, 3 N. B. R. 55 *in re* Hollis, 3 N. B. R. 82.

The term commercial paper, within the meaning of the bankrupt act, includes negotiable notes, bills of exchange, negotiable bank checks, certificates of deposit used in commercial transactions known as the law merchant. In this sense congress used the term in the act, and not in the restricted sense of counsel in the argument of this case. By usage and by statute, negotiable paper is to be regulated by custom and the law merchant. If a "banker, broker, merchant, trader, manufacturer or miner" allows his paper to go to protest and suspends payment for fourteen days, or if he has fraudulently stopped payment, in either case he has committed an act of bankruptcy. A frandulent stoppage of payment is an act of bankruptcy, and his creditors may proceed against him at once, without waiting fourteen days. But when there is only stoppage or suspension of payment, without fraud, then the same must continue without resumption, fourteen days, before the act of bankruptcy is complete.

This provision in the thirty-ninth section, is so clear, that it seems strange that counsel should insist upon a different construction. *In re* Jersey City Window Glass Co. 1 N. B. R. 113; *in re* Ballard & Parsons, 2 N. B. R. 84; *in re* Lowenstein, 2 N. B. R. 99; *Doan* v. *Compton*, 2 N. B. R. 182; *Davis et al.* v. *Armstrong*, 3 N. B. R. 7; *Heinsheimer et al.* v. *Shea et al.* 3 N. B. R. 46; *in re* Hollis, 3 N. B. R. 82.

Paper not given in the ordinary course of the business of a banker, merchant, manufacturer, trader or miner, it has been held, is not commercial paper within the meaning of the act. *In re* Lowenstein, 2 N. B. R. 99; *in re* McDermott Patent Bolt Mfg. Co. 3 N. B. R. 33. But *in re* Chandler, 4 N. B. R. 66, holds the contrary doctrine.

It is sufficient, however, if the debtor's commercial paper was incurred in his character of banker, merchant, trader, manufacturer or miner. It does not matter whether the same was given for a loan of money, for goods, or to his or their employees, or otherwise, nor whether the maker, acceptor or endorser, as principal debtor or otherwise, is liable thereon, if it appear in the petition that it is the debtor's commercial paper of the class enumerated in section thirty-nine of the act. In the case at bar it so appears with sufficient averments. We must, therefore, overrule the demurrer and grant leave to the bankrupts to reply to the allegations contained in the petition.

STRICKLAND, J.—The petition appears to be sufficient upon its face and the paper is negotiable paper. Then the only question remaining is: are these parties within the purview of the law—are they manufacturers? If so, the paper as a matter of course is their commercial paper. I believe them to be manufacturers. The demurrer is not well taken.

UNITED STATES DISTRICT COURT—RHODE ISLAND.

The assignee in bankruptcy can claim only such interest and right in any property as the bankrupt could have claimed at the filing of the petition by or against him. Hence where the bankrupt has made conveyances by which his books of account pass to an assignee of his own selection, the assignee in bankruptcy cannot claim them until such conveyances are shown to have been fraudulent and void.

To obtain possession of such books, an assignee must proceed by a bill in equity or action at law, in which the validity of said conveyances can be tested, and not by simple petition.

ROGERS, Assignee, v. WINSOR.

KNOWLES, J.—The questions raised upon this petition, though seemingly of a novel character, will be found, I incline to believe, virtually settled in this district, if in no other, by reported adjudications of both SHEPLEY, C. J., and CLIFFORD, J., of the supreme court. The facts to be kept in view are substantially these:

On the sixth of September, eighteen hundred and seventy-one, a creditor's petition in bankruptcy was filed by Daniel W. Ford, against Gardner S. Hall and Robert I. Getty, formerly copartners as G. S. Hall & Co., upon which the said Hall and Getty, both as co-partners and as individuals, were adjudged bankrupt on the seventeenth of January, eighteen hundred and seventy-two. In due course of proceedings Horatio Rogers, Esq., was appointed assignee of the bankrupts, who, on the nineteenth of February, presented to the court at chambers, the petition now under consideration, which was on the following day called for hearing. The party respondent thereto, with his counsel, appearing in opposition. The petition, which was verified by the petitioner's oath, (omitting the specifications of books and papers and merely formal portions) was in the terms following:

."Horatio Rogers, assignee in bankruptcy of Gardner S. Hall and Robert I. Getty, individually and as co-partners, under the name of G. S. Hall & Co., who have heretofore been adjudged bankrupts on creditor's petition by this honorable court, respectfully represents,

"That the books of account and papers of said firm of G. S. Hall & Co., viz.: * * * * * * are all now in the custody and possession of one James A. Winsor, of the city and county of Providence, in said district, a member of the firm of Parsons, Bugbee & Co.; that he has demanded from said Winsor, all of said books of account and papers; that said Winsor refuses to surrender possession of the same, pretending to have a right to retain the custody of the same against your petitioner as such assignee in bankruptcy, by virtue of two deeds of assignment (so-called) to him, copies whereof are hereto annexed, marked A and B respectively. One whereof is executed by said G. S. Hall, both in the name of the late firm of G. S. Hall & Co., as well as in his own proper name, said firm having, at the date of the execution thereof been dissolved; and the other whereof is executed by the said G. S. Hall, the first whereof was dated on the thirteenth day of May, eighteen hundred and seventy-one, and the other whereof was executed on the twenty-third day of May, eighteen hundred and seventy-one, and both being executed and dated less than four months before the filing of the petition against said bankrupts, upon which they were adjudged bankrupt, and which said so-called deeds of assignment your petitioner represents are void, having been made in fraud of the provisions of the act to establish a uniform system of bankruptcy throughout the United States, and of the creditors of said bankrupts, and of your petitioner as such assignee.

" Wherefore he prays that said Winsor may be required by the order of this honorable court to deliver up to him all of the aforenamed books of account and papers, and all other books of account and papers relating to the business or property of said G. S. Hall and Robert I. Getty, individually, or as copartners as G. S. Hall & Co.

" (Signed),   " HORATIO ROGERS, *Assignee*," &c.

The deed A. referred to purports to convey to said Winsor certain specified personal property of the firm, including in terms " all debts due the firm and the evidences thereof;" and the deed B. purports to convey to him all the said Hall's interest in the same property, and also certain other specified property belonging to him individually, including in terms " all books of account and other evidences of debt and credits of every name and nature pertaining to " the business of the firm.   The two conveyances are respectively, expressly " in trust," vesting the grantee with absolute power of disposal and prescribing to what purposes the proceeds shall be appropriated—a leading purpose in each being to secure and indemnify the grantee, Winsor, and his firm (Parsons, Bugbee & Co.) against loss on any claims then existing or that might thereafter, within two years, accrue in their favor against the said Hall & Co., or the said Hall individually.

Upon the facts stated in his petition, and shown or evidenced by the said deeds, the petitioner proffering no further or other proofs, contends that the order prayed for should be granted, in conformity (as argued) with the letter and spirit of the fourteenth section of the bankrupt act, citing as of signal pertinancy and of irresistible cogency, and independent and unqualified sentence therefrom in these words :—" No person shall be entitled, as against the assignee, to withhold from him possession of any books of account of the bankrupt, or claim any lien thereon."

The intent of the legislator in employing these emphatic words, was, he maintains, to assure to an assignee in bankruptcy the possession and use of the bankrupt's books of account, at as early a day as practicable, and to render it impossible, without violation of law, for a bankrupt by any form of conveyance, or by collusion or confederacy, or any conceivable desire, to conceal or withhold such books from him. Between books of account and property of any other species, he further maintains, this sentence of the act establishes a distinction which the court is bound to recognize, and in view of which it ought, as of course, to order any holder of a bankrupt's books of account to surrender them to an assignee upon his motion or petition merely in court or at chambers—and this, although for possession of property of any other description, in which an adverse interest is claimed by a stranger or grantee of a bankrupt, such assignee would be compelled to have recourse to " due process of law," *i. e.*, a suit in equity or action at law—under the reported adjudication in this district, and by the supreme court of the United States. *Knight* v. *Cheney*, 5 N. B. R. 305; *Smith* v. *Mason*, 6 N. B. R. 1.

In answer to this claim and this reasoning of the petitioner, the learned counsel of the respondent, proffering no proofs upon any point, says:

FIRSTLY. That the " deeds, books and papers," which pass to an assignee under the provisions of the first sentence of section fourteen of the bankrupt act, are simply and merely such as "relate to " the property and estate which vests in the assignee by virtue of the proceedings in bankruptcy; and that as the respondent Winsor claims, and is prepared to assert and maintain, that none of the property now in his hands, and to which the books and papers in controversy "relate " did, or could vest in the assignee, having for about four months prior to the commencement of proceedings in bankruptcy been in his possession, under conveyances claimed to be valid and unimpeachable, this demand for books, papers and deeds is manifestly not sustainable—even had the court the power, upon the mere petition of the assignee, to pass upon the antagonising claims of the petitioner and the respondent. But, if this position be adjudged untenable, they say :

SECONDLY. That by the settled law in this district, save in cases of attachment and cases affected by fraud, the assignee in bankruptcy can claim in any property only such interest and right as the bankrupt himself could have claimed at the filing of the petition by or against him—citing in support of this proposition, *Potter et al.* v. *Coggeshall,* 4 N. B. R. 19, and s. c. (revision by SHEPLEY, C. J.,) *in re* Dow, 6 N. B. R. 10, and other cases. And in view of this state of the law, contending that until the conveyances A. and B. shall be shown to have been fraudulent, and therefore void, the respondent's right to the books and papers in question is as perfect, to all intents as against the assignee, as his right to any chattels in his possession, inherited from his grandsire or purchased in open market fifty years ago. And furthermore they say.

THIRDLY. That whether or not books of account are distinguishable from other kinds of property as contended by the petitioner, an assignee is precluded from seeking to obtain possession of them under the circumstances of the case by a simple petition. The law, say they, as now settled by the decisions in *Knight* v. *Cheney,* 5 N. B. R. 305, and *Smith* v. *Mason,* 6 N. B. R. 1, forbids a court's assuming to pass upon the conflicting claims of the petitioner and the respondent to either the absolute ownership or the possession of the books in question, until its judgment shall have been invoked by a bill in equity or action at law, in which the validity of said conveyances, A. and B. can be tested upon bill, answers and proofs, or upon issues, to a jury. These conveyances, the respondent avers, are unimpeachable in any " Forum and under any law—vesting in him an unimpregnable title to all and singular the goods, chattels, books and evidences of debt enumerated and described in them, as he is confident will be made apparent whenever he shall be called on in the proper manner to assert or defend that title." Until then, he adds, as he is assured and believes, he can

Rogers v. Winsor.

securely rest upon the indisputable fact, that for a period of about four months prior to the commencement of proceedings in bankruptcy against his grantors, he was legally in the possession, undisturbed and unquestioned, of the books, papers and evidences of debt, which the assignee is now seeking to wrest from him, not by " due process ·of law," but by a course of proceeding never to be favored, nor even to be allowed save in cases wholly free from doubt, as well of the necessity, as of the regularity of such a course.

Upon the question presented, my judgment must be in· favor of the respondent, as I cannot but regard his second and third objections as tenable and insuperable, whatever may be said of the pertinency or tenableness of the first. On the other hand, to sustain the position and claim of the petitioner, were, in my view, to misconstrue the provisions of the fourteenth section of the bankrupt act, and to ignore or dissent from the well-reasoned opinions, as authoritatively promulgated, of the judges of this circuit to whose decisions I am bound to defer and conform, and to whom it is a satisfaction to remember the petitioner may, with little delay and at trivial expense, apply at any time, at chambers or in court, for a revision and reversal of this decision.

The petition is dismissed.

HORATIO ROGERS and B. N. LAPHAM, for petitioner ; GEO. H. BROWNE and JAMES TILLINGHAST, for respondent.—February 22, 1872.

UNITED STATES DISTRICT COURT—NEVADA.

An injunction was granted on an order to show cause before adjudications in bankruptcy had taken place, to restrain the sheriff and all other persons from selling the property of the alleged bankrupt, on a judgment obtained by default in a suit brought in the state court. The sheriff moved to dissolve the injunction on the following grounds :—

First, that said injunction is not addressed to any person, therefore does not include the sheriff and judgment creditor.

Second, that the court has exceeded its just power, and cannot lawfully restrain the judgment creditor from selling the property in question, the judgment not being impeachable for fraud or as preference under the bankrupt act, the judgment having been docketed before the filing of the petition.

Held, first, when the injunction was served upon the sheriff and judgment creditor, it plainly apprised them of what they were restrained from doing, and the fact that they were not named in the order can make no substantial difference. Second, that neither the judgment nor the levy of execution divests the alleged bankrupt of his property, and he would be bound to include such estate in his inventory if adjudged a bankrupt ; and further, that the bankruptcy court may, in the exercise of a lawful jurisdiction, restrain by injunction the sale of property under an execution issued from a state court, even before the commencement of proceedings in bankruptcy.

In re LADY BRYAN MINING CO.*

W. T. Cummings, sheriff of Storey county, and Ely Johnson, moved to dissolve the injunction issued herein upon the following state of facts:

On the twelfth day of August, eighteen hundred and seventy, said Ely Johnson commenced a suit in the first district court for Storey county, Nevada, against the Lady Bryan Mining Co., to recover the sum of about two thousand eight hundred dollars. Summons was duly served, and on the twenty-third of August, the defendant having failed to appear, judgment by default was entered against it, and docketed, and an execution thereon issued to the sheriff, who levied on the real property of the corporation and advertised it for sale. Subsequently, on the second day of September, eighteen hundred and seventy, Henry Donolly, a creditor of the corporation, filed his petition praying that it might be adjudged a bankrupt ; and thereupon an order to show cause was made ; and upon application therefor it was further ordered " that said Lady Bryan Mining Co., and all other per-

See 4 N. B. R. 36, 131.

sons be restrained in the meantime from making any disposition of said Lady Bryan Mining Co.'s property, not excepted from the operation of the bankrupt act, and from any interference therewith." This order was served September third on Johnson and the sheriff.

The first ground upon which the motion to dissolve is based is that said injunction is not addressed to any person.

Section forty gives this court power, upon making an order to show cause, to restrain by its injunction the debtor and any other person from transferring, disposing of, or interfering with the debtor's property—between the time of filing the petition and the hearing of the order to show cause. This order may be made without notice, and its office is to preserve the property of the debtor until the question of bankruptcy is determined. In the present case the injunction is in the form of an order, and is addressed to the Lady Bryan Mining Co. and all other persons who may attempt to transfer or interfere with the property of that company, and when served upon the sheriff and Johnson, as it was, it plainly apprised them of what they were restrained from doing. The fact that they were not named in the order can make no substantial difference. Any distinction between a *writ* of injunction and an order in the nature of one, has been disregarded in practice. Hilliard on Inj., 42 ; *Erie R. R. Co.* v. *Cary*, 26 Penn. 292.

The second ground is that this court has exceeded its just power, and cannot lawfully restrain the judgment-creditor, or the sheriff, from selling the property under the execution issued out of the state court.

Johnson having obtained a judgment, and it having been docketed before the filing of the petition in bankruptcy, the judgment, not being impeachable for fraud or as a preference, is a lien which this court must protect.

But it is only a lien, for neither the judgment nor the levy of execution divests the bankrupt of its property in the estate levied upon, and it would be bound to include such estate in its inventory as part of the assets.

I am fully satisfied that this court may, in the exercise of a lawful jurisdiction, restrain by injunction the sale of property under an execution issued from a state court before the commencement of proceedings in bankruptcy, and that this may be done by restraining the judgment creditor or the officer about to make the sale, or both. Looking at the first section of the bankrupt act, it is difficult to imagine how a more unrestricted jurisdiction over matters in bankruptcy could have been granted. All the assets and all the parties in interest are to be brought before the court, priorities adjusted, liens ascertained and liquidated, and the different funds and assets marshalled and distributed. The grant of these powers carries with it the right to employ such process, mode of procedure and remedies, as are indispensable to make the grant effectual. In this case the real estate levied on is assets, and power to collect the assets is given. But this power is of no avail in this proceeding, unless the court can preserve the assets until the question of bankruptcy is determined.

By section fourteen, the assignee has power under the direction and order of the court to sell encumbered property. Can it be doubted that the court may·make this provision effectual?

Section twenty gives the court power to direct a sale of property upon which a creditor has a lien, which can be wholly defeated if the position of the sheriff in this case is correct. The judgment creditor claims a lien upon the property under levy, but whether it is a valid lien or not, the law says the court of bankruptcy shall ascertain, and that if it is found valid it shall be liquidated in that court—provisions which would be rendered nugatory unless the sheriff can be restrained.

There may, no doubt, be cases where no good could be accomplished by issuing an injunction, but this is not such a case. Johnson's debt does not exceed three thousand dollars, for which he has a judgment bearing ten per cent. interest. His lien embraces property valued at some twenty thousand dollars, and it appears that it would be most advantageously sold in one parcel at private sale. The only damage to the judgment creditor will be a little delay, while the general creditors may suffer a serious loss by the forced sale of this large amount of property to satisfy so small a debt. Motion denied.—September 30, 1870.

UNITED STATES DISTRICT COURT—S. D. NEW YORK.

A register may order bankrupts to hand over to his custodian funds in their hands. Disobedience to such an order adjudged a contempt, for which an attachment was issued from the court.

In re F. & A. SPEYER.

The above named bankrupts filed their petition to be declared bankrupts on the fourth day of January, eighteen hundred and seventy-one. In their schedules they set forth that the sum of one thousand three hundred and ten dollars and five cents in money was in their hands.

The register in charge appointed Mr. LeRoy T. Gove custodian of the estate during the interim and until the assignee should be elected. The custodian thereupon demanded the said money of the bankrupts, and was informed by them that one of the bankrupts—having the money in his pocket—had been robbed of the same on the morning after filing the said petition. Whereupon the said custodian summoned the bankrupts before the register, and proceeded to examine them concerning the same. Upon this testimony so taken, the register made an order that said bankrupts hand over to the said custodian the said sum of one thousand three hundred and ten dollars and five cents within twenty-four hours after the service of said order on them. This order was duly served on the bankrupts; they failing to comply therewith, the said custodian moved the court before the district judge on notice to the bankrupts for an order that an attachment issue against them as for a contempt, for a disobedience to the order of the register. Whereupon the court referred the matter back to the register to take such testimony as the said bankrupts might offer by way of purging the alleged contempt. Testimony was then taken on the part of the plaintiffs, whereupon the register certified the case as follows :—

I, the undersigned register in bankruptcy, to whom the matter of the alleged contempt in this case was referred by the order of this honorable court, bearing date the fourth day of February, eighteen hundred and seventy-one, and hereto annexed, do hereby certify and report to this honorable court, That I have been attended by the said bankrupt, Abraham Speyer, and his counsel, Dubois Smith, Esq., and that I have taken all the testimony offered by him under said order, to wit : The testimony of the said Abraham Speyer, and Frederick Speyer, together with further testimony, of the said LeRoy T. Gove, Esq., all of which is hereto annexed, and herewith returned to this honorable court. And I further certify that upon a careful examination of said testimony, I am unable to accept the statements of the said bankrupts, as affording the true reason why the said sum of one thousand three hundred and ten dollars and five cents was not paid over to the said custodian on his demand, nor was there anything in the manner of either of the said bankrupts, while under examination calculated to inspire confidence in their statements. I cannot entertain the slightest doubt that the loss of said money is a mere pretence on the part of the said Abraham Speyer. I therefore certify to this honorable court, that in my opinion the order of the court should bo forthwith entered, committing the said Abraham Speyer to the county jail of the county of New York until he shall have paid over to the said custodian the said sum of one thousand three hundred and ten dollars and five cents, with interest thereon from the sixth day of January, eighteen hundred and seventy-one, besides the costs of this proceeding, to be adjusted before the register in charge of the said case.

BLATCHFORD, J.—Enter. an order herein in accordance with the conclusions of the register.

UNITED STATES SUPREME COURT—UTAH TERRITORY.

On a motion to dismiss a petition in bankruptcy for the reason that it was not signed or sworn to by the petitioning creditors or either of them, *Held*, that the general attorneys of creditors cannot make, sign and verify for such creditors a valid petition, as the debtor must be adjudged a bankrupt on the petition of one or more of his creditors, and not on that of their agent or attorney. Petition dismissed and all orders made thereunder vacated.

In re D. C. BUTTERFIELD.

The firm of Marshall & Carter as attorneys, &c., filed in this court on the twenty-third day of February, eighteen hundred and seventy-two, a petition against the said D. C. Butterfield, for adjudication of bankruptcy against him, in the name of the firm of "Babcock & Co.," averring certain causes of bankruptcy therein. It appears from the petition, as well as by the admission of Marshall & Carter, attorneys for Babcock & Co., in open court, that Marshall & Carter as the attorneys of Babcock & Co., made and signed the name of Babcock & Co. to this petition ; not as attorneys in fact or otherwise, but simply by virtue of being attorneys at law. The firm name of Marshall & Carter appears signed to the petition only as follows : "Marshall & Carter, attorneys for petitioners." The petition is verified by the oath of James M. Carter.

On the return day, D. C. Butterfield, by Earll & Smith, his solicitors, appeared and filed his motion to dismiss the said petition, because :

FIRST. The said petition is not signed by the said creditors or either of them.

SECOND. The said petition is not sworn to by the said creditor or by either of them.

There are other reasons assigned, but they are not regarded material to the disposition of this motion, and are therefore omitted.

EARLL & SMITH, solicitors for Butterfield ; MARSHALL & CARTER, solicitors for Babcock & Co.

HAWLEY, J.—This petition is made and filed by Marshall & Carter, in the name of " Babcock & Co.," with their names attached in the margin of the petition as "attorneys for petitioners," under the thirty-ninth section of the bankrupt act, and form number fifty-four. The only question to be considered is, can the general attorneys of creditors make, sign and verify for such creditors, a valid petition for adjudication in bankruptcy against their debtor?

The thirty-ninth section of the act provides, that a debtor for certain cause therein named, shall be deemed to have committed an act of bankruptcy, and subject to the conditions hereinafter prescribed, shall be adjudged a bankrupt, on the petition of one or more of his creditors, &c.

Form fifty-four contains the substance and the form of an involuntary petition for adjudication of bankruptcy, and in effect construes section thirty-nine to mean that the petition must be made and verified by the creditor. Form fifty-five, as well as section thirty-nine of the act, provides that the petition shall be made by the creditor, and his first proof of his claim shall also be made by him; and form fifty-six provides that the creditor shall file with his petition and his said proof of his debt, the affidavit of a witness to the act of bankruptcy.

This extreme caution and safeguard of the law, may, under many circumstances, throw great hardship upon a creditor, and even put his interests in peril; but this is no reason why a creditor should be allowed to obtain the benefits of the act without a strict compliance with the same.

The act being in derogation of the common law, must be followed or be complied with strictly. It is true, it, by its provisions is to be construed liberally; but that does not imply that a court can add to its terms in the interest of either debtor or creditor.

Bump, in his Law and Practice of Bankruptcy, says: " The petition must be made by the creditor, and in most instances can only be made upon information and belief." See Bump, 31. See also *in re* Muller & Brentano, 3 N. B. R.

86; *Orem & Co.* v. *Harley*, 3 N. B. R. 63. In *Hunt Tillinghast & Co.* v. *Pooke & Steere*, 5 N. B. R. 161, KNOWLES, J., said: "It is said, that the bankrupt act does not by its terms, require that the petition be verified by the oath of the petitioner or be subscribed by the petitioner himself. This (he adds) is true; but it also is true that the supreme court deemed it wise, in the exercise of the powers conferred upon them, to prescribe forms of proceedings to which parties are bound to conform as scrupulously as to the provisions of the act itself. That the petition, oaths and affidavits in this case are in conformity with those forms, is not pretended."

In concluding his opinion, he adds: "It is true no formal motion to dismiss the petition for substantial, incurable defects apparent on the record, was made by the respondents, but I cannot but hold that such a motion would have been in order on the moving of the hearing, entitled to immediate consideration, whatever the state of the pleadings, and of course cannot but hold that the objection is reasonably urged."

This is the only case, so far as I have observed, in which the question under consideration has been directly adjudicated. This court, taking substantially the same view of the law, must respect it. We will however remark, that we do not agree with this learned judge in saying, "that the bankrupt act does not, by its terms, require that the petition be verified by the oath of the petitioner, or be subscribed by the petitioner himself." For the thirty-ninth section of the act, by its terms provides, that a debtor liable to be adjudged a bankrupt, "*shall be adjudged a bankrupt on the petition of one or more of his creditors.*"

This language is emphatic and without ambiguity. He is to "*be adjudged a bankrupt on the petition of one or more of his creditors,*" and not on the petition of the creditor's agent or attorney. If it had been the intention of congress to allow an agent or attorney of the creditor to make, verify and file a petition against a debtor, as well as the creditor himself, the law would have so provided in terms. Such is the manifest construction placed upon this provision by the supreme court in prescribing under the power conferred upon them, forms fifty-four and fifty-five; we must therefore hold, that the motion of respondent to dismiss the petition must be sustained.

The clerk will therefore enter an order dismissing the petition filed in this case, and to vacate all orders of the court made thereunder.

--- · ◆ · ---

UNITED STATES CIRCUIT COURT—MASSACHUSETTS.

A corporation that has been dissolved by a decree of a state court, and a receiver appointed, still exists for the purpose of being proceeded against in bankruptcy; hence, an adjudication is valid if the corporation by answer admits the acts of bankruptcy alleged against it, although the receiver may not have been a party to the answer or given his assent to such adjudication.

No power exists to wrest from the jurisdiction of the courts in bankruptcy the assets of such bankrupt individuals and corporations, as are within the scope of the provisions of the United States bankrupt act.

In re INDEPENDENT INSURANCE CO.

SHEPLEY, J.—The constitution of the United States confers upon congress the power to establish uniform laws on the subject of bankruptcies throughout the United States. Unquestionably, congres is as competent to apply such laws to private corporations created by the states as to natural persons, or private corporations created by authority of congress. *Sweatt* v. *Boston, Hartford & Erie R. R. Co.* 5 N. B. R. 234.

Congress has exercised the power thus conferred upon it by the constitution, by the enactment of the bankrupt act, and "the provisions of this act apply to moneyed, business or commercial corporations." Having thus exercised this power by the enactment of the bankrupt act, and the constitution further providing that the laws of the United States, which shall be made in pursuance of the constitution, shall be the supreme law of the land, the inference is irresistible, that state laws on the subject of bankruptcy and insolvency must yield to the law of congress on the same subject, when the state law applies to the same subject matter; and when it differs in material respects from the law of congress, it appears clear that the state law is suspended, while the law of congress remains in force. *Ex parte* Eames, 2 Story, 323; *Sturgess* v. *Crowninshield,* 4 Wheat. 122, 196; *Ogden* v. *Saunders,* 12 Wheat. 213; *May et al.* v. *Buel et al.* 7 Cush. 40; *Griswold* v. *Pratt,* 9 Met. 23; *Thornhill et al.* v. *Bank of Louisiana,* 5 N. B. R. 372.

The Independent Insurance Company of Boston, is a corporation created by the laws of Massachusetts, to transact the "business" of insurance. It is clearly included in the class of "business or commercial corporations" to which the provisions of the bankrupt act apply. After the passage of the bankrupt act, it became insolvent and committed such acts of bankruptcy as clearly constituted it "one of those" corporations whose pecuniary condition brings them within the provisions of the act, entitled to the benefits which the act confers, and subject to all its obligations and requirements. *Sweatt* v. *Boston, Hartford & Erie R. R. Co.* before cited.

After this time, the operation of any state law, regulating the assignment and distribution of the property of the insolvent debtor corporation, and affecting the same persons, property and rights that would be affected by proceedings under the bankrupt act, was suspended. It was not the intention of the framers of the constitution, or of congress, when it enacted the bankrupt act, to have in existence two distinct and diverse systems affecting the same persons, property and rights, leaving it to the option of the debtor to elect one or the other at his pleasure.

In the language of the supreme court of Massachusetts, in *Cushing* v. *Arnold et al.* 9 Met. 23, "when the power is exercised by congress, and a bankrupt law is in force, it does suspend all state insolvent laws applicable to like cases, and this effect follows the enactment of such bankrupt law, and does not require the actual institution of proceedings in bankruptcy to produce such result."

On the ninth day of January, eighteen hundred and seventy-two, the firm of Joseph Nickerson & Co., filed their petition for adjudication of bankruptcy against the Independent Insurance Co. The petition sets forth, *inter alia*, the insolvency of the company, and alleges that the company committed acts of bankruptcy by fraudulent preferences, on the fourteenth day of October, eighteen hundred and seventy-one, to Edward Atkinson and to Henry Atkins & Co., who were creditors of the company and whose claims had long been overdue when the payment was made. Upon filing proofs sustaining the allegations in the petition, an order was issued by the district court to the insurance company, to show cause why the prayer of the petitioner should not be granted. On the return day of this order, Chester I. Reed and George Ripley filed a plea to the jurisdiction of the court, setting out that on the ninth day of January, eighteen hundred and seventy-two, they were, by a decree of the supreme judicial court of Massachusetts, rendered in a suit instituted on the second day of December, eighteen hundred and seventy-one, by the insurance commissioner in behalf of the commonwealth of Massachusetts, against said insurance company, appointed receivers of said company, and had accepted the trust and duly entered upon the performance of their duties.

The plea further avers that by the decree aforesaid of the supreme judicial court of the commonwealth of Massachusetts, the Independent Insurance Co., which was a corporation created and existing under and by virtue of a statute of said commonwealth, was dissolved, and an injunction, which had previously issued in said suit against any further prosecution of its business by said insurance company, was made perpetual. The record of the proceedings in the supreme court and of the decree is annexed to the plea and makes a part thereof. The decree of the district court then proceeds as follows :

"And it appearing that no denial of bankruptcy was made on the return day of the order tó show cause, and that said corporation, by its answer, admits the acts of bankruptcy alleged against it. And thereupon, and upon consideration of the proofs in said cause, and the arguments of counsel thereon, it was found that the facts set forth in said petition were true, it was therefore adjudged that the Independent Insurance Co. became bankrupt within the true intent and meaning of the act entitled, ' An act to establish a uniform system of bankruptcy throughout the United States,' approved March second, eighteen hundred and sixty-seven, before the filing of said petition, and it is therefore declared and adjudged bankrupt accordingly." A warrant in bankruptcy was accordingly issued. Within the time prescribed by the rules, the receivers filed in this court their petition for a revision and reversal of these orders and decrees of the district court in bankruptcy.

The errors assigned by the petition in the judgment orders and decrees of the district court are :

FIRST. That because of the proceedings in the supreme judicial court of Massachusetts, pleaded as aforesaid, and verified by the record aforesaid, and which record was not in any respect controverted, and because of the statutes of said commonwealth in relation to insurance corporations, the said district court had not jurisdiction to make said orders, adjudications and decrees.

SECOND. Because of said proceeding of said supreme court and said statutes, and upon the pleading and proofs aforesaid, said corporation had no right to appear in said court, except by said Reed and Ripley, the petitioners, and could not by any counsel, against the objection of said Reed and Ripley, appear, or admit the truth of any averment, plea or allegation, or matter of fact or law.

The petition then alleges, that the decree of said court basing its adjudication of bankruptcy wholly upon the admissions of said parties claiming to act as president and attorney of said company, was erroneous, and it avers that the corporation was dissolved on the ninth day of January.

In support of the petition for the exercise of the revisory power of this court, counsel contend that the corporation was the creation of the state, and existed merely at its pleasure ; that it was clearly in the power of the state to dissolve it, that this power has been exercised, that the corporation is defunct, and became so before the adjudication in bankruptcy ; that consequently the proceedings abated, there being no provision in the bankrupt act to the contrary, that the state law does not continue the corporation in being so as to change this result, and that, if the corporation is still living, it can only act through receivers, and therefore the decree of the district court was erroneous. Unquestionably, under ordinary circumstances, the sovereignty which has called a corporation into being, and which, by the terms of the charter or by the provisions of general law, has reserved the right to do so, may amend the charter or repeal it at will by the legislature, or acting through its judicial tribunals, it may declare the charter forfeited, or terminate the existence of the corporation.

Whether, subsequent to the exercise by congress of its constitutional power to establish a uniform system of bankruptcy, it would be within the power of a state, acting either through its legislature or its judicial tribunals, after an act of bankruptcy had been committed by an insolvent corporation, and all state insolvent laws applicable to such cases were suspended, to annul the existence of the bankrupt corporation, so as to prevent the commencement of process, or abate the proceedings after they had been commenced under the act of congress, may well be doubted. If this could be done, the operation of the bankrupt law upon insolvent corporations could be defeated, the whole jurisdiction in bankruptcy foreclosed, the general creditors could only reach the assets within the reach of state process, and all extra-territorial property would be left in the grasp of attaching creditors, and, so far as the extra-territorial assets were concerned, payments in full and preferences to favored creditors would be upheld. It is not necessary to decide this question in this case and at this time. The most cursory examination of the section of the fifty-eighth chapter of the statutes of Massachusetts, under which these proceedings were initiated by the insurance commissioner, will show that it does not contemplate or authorise any such decree as would annul the existence of the corporation. A careful examination of the record will show that no such decree was sought or prayed for in the petition, and the like examination of the decree will as conclusively show that no such decree was made by the court. Chapter fifty-eight, section six, of the Gen. Stat. of Massachusetts, provides as follows :

"If upon examination the commissioners are of opinion that a company is insolvent, or that its condition is such as to render its further proceedings hazardous to the public, or to those holding its policies, they shall apply to a justice of the supreme judicial court to issue an injunction restraining such company, in whole or in part, from further proceeding with its business until after a full hearing can be had. Such justice shall forthwith issue the injunction, and, after a full hearing of all parties interested, may dissolve or modify the same, or make it perpetual, and he may make such orders and decrees as may be needful to suspend, restrain or prohibit the further continuance of the business of the company; and may appoint agents or receivers to take possession of the property and effects of the company, subject to such rules and orders as are from time to time according to the course of proceedings in equity, prescribed by the court or a justice thereof, in vacation."

It is clear that this power to suspend, restrain or prohibit the further continuance of the business of the bankrupt corporation, no more authorised the court, in this form of proceeding, to annul the being of the corporation, than a similar statute power to suspend, restrain or prohibit the further continuance of the business of a bankrupt natural person would authorize the court to take the life of the bankrupt.

The insurance commissioner, in his petition, represented to the court that the corporation was insolvent and its condition was such as to render its further proceedings hazardous to the public and its policy holders. He prays for a writ of injunction commanding the corporation, its officers and agents, to refrain from further proceeding with the business of the corporation ; for the appointment of receivers to take possession of the property of the corporation subject to the order of the court ; and for notice to the corporation to show cause why such injunction should not be made perpetual and the receivers appointed as prayed for ; and for such further orders and decrees in the premises as may be needful. By the final decree of the court the injunction, previously issued in said cause as prayed for, was made perpetual. Receivers were appointed to take possession of the property and effects of said corporation ; to pay all debts due from said corporation, if the funds coming to their hands are sufficient therefor, and if not, to distribute said funds ratably among the creditors of said corporation who duly prove their claims, and if there is any balance left in their hands, after paying the debts as aforesaid, to pay and distribute the same among the persons legally entitled thereto, all under the direction of this court. "And to this end the said receivers shall have power to prosecute and defend suits in their own names, and do all other acts which might be done by said corporation if in being, for the purpose of settling any unfinished business thereof." The decree further commands all persons and corporations holding property or evidences of property of any kind belonging to said insurance company, to deliver the same to the receivers, and commands the receivers forthwith to take possession of the same. Then follows the portion of the decree upon which the argument of counsel is based. It is as follows : "It is further adjudged and decreed, that said corporation be, and the same is hereby dissolved."

By virtue of this decree, it is claimed that the corporation ceased to exist for any purpose before the adjudication of

In re Independent Insurance Co.

bankruptcy; that the bankrupt law does not authorise process to issue in bankruptcy against defunct corporations or deceased individuals, or undertake to administer on their estates; that it acts only on the living and has no dealings with the dead, unless they die after the decree in bankruptcy. In his view of the case it becomes important to consider whether this corporation is so far defunct, whether its charter is so annulled, and its franchises *to be* a corporation is so far taken away, by this decree, that it cannot be considered as having any being or existence for any purpose whatever. We have already seen that such an act of annulling the charter and destroying the life of the corporation was not provided for in the section of the statutes under which the proceedings were commenced, nor prayed for in the petition upon which the decree was founded. It is true, nevertheless, that the decree does adjudge the corporation "dissolved," but we are satisfied that by a fair construction of this language, as used in the concluding portion of the decree, it was the intention of the court only so far to dissolve the corporation as, in the language of the statutes under which they were acting, might "be needful to suspend, restrain or prohibit" the further continuance of the "*business*" of the company, and that it was not the intention of the court, by the use of this language, to make such a decree under the sixth section, on the application of the insurance commissioner, as by virtue of the eighth section, and under the other provisions of the general statutes of the state, they might make in a process of *quo warranto* instituted by the attorney-general, adjudging the charter forfeited and annulled. In the language of text writers of statutes, and not infrequently of judicial decisions, the phrase "dissolving a corporation" is used sometimes as synonymous with annulling the charter or terminating the existence of the corporation, and sometimes as meaning merely a judicial act which alienates the property and suspends the business of a corporation without terminating its existence. This is *paralysis*, not *necrosis*, a suspension of corporate action, not a cessation of corporate life. As a solvent liquid or heat dissolves a crystal by separating the parts and breaking the continuity of the atoms which compose it, leaving it formless and invisible to the eye, yet with the capacity of being crystallized anew into its pristine form and beauty; as "a figure, trenched in ice, which with an hour's heat dissolves to water and doth lose its form," and which an hour's cold may restore to its original form and substance; as a meeting, a parliament or assembly, dissolved so as to suspend for a time its unity of action, yet existing with the capacity for a new aggregation of its original constituent parts, a corporation may thus for certain purposes be considered as so far dissolved as to be incapable of injury to the public, and yet retaining all the vitality which may be essential for the protection of the rights of others.

This doctrine has been applied in several cases in the state of New York in the construction of a statute of that state, concerning manufacturing corporations, which provided that for all debts due and owing by the company at the time of its dissolution, the persons composing such company shall be individually responsible, &c. Under this statute, when an insolvent corporation suffered its property to be sacrificed and the annual elections were omitted, and no act was done manifesting any intention to continue the corporate functions, the court, for the sake of the remedy against the invidual members and in favor of creditors, presumed a virtual surrender of the corporate rights and "a dissolution" of the corporation. Yet, in these cases the courts in New York did not decide that the companies had lost all their rights or were defunct corporations, but only that even if they had a right to reorganize themselves, and were for certain purposes in being, the case had happened in which they were "dissolved" for the purpose of remedial action by their creditors. *Slee* v. *Bloom*, Johns. 456; *Penniman* v. *Briggs*, 1 Hopkins 300; s. c. Cowen 387; Kent Com. 311.

But in the learned and exhaustive opinion of GRAY, J., in the case of *Folger* v. *Columbian Insurance Co.* 99 Mass. 267, is to be found, perhaps, the most perfect compendium of the law on this subject. In that case the supreme court of New York had adjudged "that the Columbian Insurance Co. be, and it is hereby dissolved." But the supreme court of Massachusetts did not hesitate to inquire whether the judgment thus obtained in New York and relied on in Massachusetts, was rendered by a court having jurisdiction of the cause and of the parties, and to decide that to decree an absolute and final dissolution of a corporation at the suit of an individual, was no part of the general jurisdiction of a court of law or chancery, and can only be justified by express statutes; and then, after examining the express provisions of the statutes of New York, upon which the proceedings were based, to decide that notwithstanding the supreme court of New York had adjudged the corporation "dissolved" and Chancellor Walworth had decided that such proceedings had effected "a virtual dissolution of the corporation," yet the supreme court of Massachusett say, "It does not extinguish its franchise, terminate its legal existence, or render it incapable of being sued, at law or in equity. In the light of this opinion, it is not difficult to see the proper construction to be given to the words of the decree of the supreme court of Massachusetts ' dissolving ' this corporation as a dissolution adjudged by a court which had decided that such ' a dissolution of a corporation cannot deprive its creditors or stockholders of their rights in its property,' ' does not extinguish its functions, terminate its legal existence, or render it incapable of being sued at law, or in equity.' " See also *Coburn* v. *Boston Papier Mache Manufacturing Co.*, 10 Gray, 243; *Taylor* v. *Columbian Insurance Co.*, 14 Allen, 353; *Bacon* v. *Robertson*, 18 How. 485; *Lum* v. *Robertson*, 6 Wallace, 277; *Hunt* v. *Columbian Insurance Co.*, 55 Maine, 291.

This doctrine in relation to the extinction of a corporation is not a novel one, for in eighteen hundred and twenty-eight it was adjudged, upon the authority of earlier cases, in the case of *Hayward* v. *Fulcher*, Sir William Jones 166, " that a dean and chapter were not dissolved by a surrender to the king of all their possessions, rights, liberties, privileges and hereditaments, which they had in right of their corporation." See also *in re* Dean and Chapter, of Norwich, 3 Coke, 75, *a*. The court therefore entertains no doubt that this corporation still exists for the purpose of being proceeded against in bankruptcy. The petition also assigns, as error in the decree of the district court, that the corporation had no right to appear in said court except by the receivers, and could not, by counsel, against the objection of the receiver, appear, or admit by plea or otherwise, any matter of law or fact, and that the decree of the district court, basing its adjudication in bankruptcy wholly on the admission of Sanford, as counsel for the company, was erroneous. An examination of the record fails to convince the court that this assignment of error is sustained by the facts in the record, even if it were tenable in law. Granting, for the purpose of determining this question that which the court is not now called upon to decide, that the receivers were the sole and only proper persons to represent the corporation, yet the only plea or answer made by them was a denial of the jurisdiction of the court in bankruptcy.

This plea was heard, considered, and, as we have seen, properly overruled. No answer was put in by them, or any person, denying the acts of bankruptcy, and, after the plea to the jurisdiction was overruled, no cause was shown by them or any one, why a warrant in bankruptcy should not issue. If the president and attorney of the corporation, or those claiming to act as such, had no right to represent the corporation, then there was no denial of the allegations in the petition and no cause shown why the warrant should not issue upon the application of the petitioners in bankruptcy and the accompanying proofs. The decree of the court was well founded upon the fact recited in the decree itself,—" It appearing that no denial of bankruptcy was made on the return day of the order to show cause," without taking into consideration the other fact recited in the decree, that the corporation had by its answer admitted the acts of bankruptcy alleged against it.

It is not necessary to determine to what extent the receivers have the authority to represent the corporation itself. But it is clear that occupying the position they do, not as receivers under a mortgage or other lien or incumbrance on the property of the corporation which might take the property out of the operation of the bankrupt law, but as receivers appointed under a state law applicable to insolvent corporations and to the distribution among the creditors of the assets of an insolvent corporation, they have no power to withhold the assets of the company and to liquidate its liabilities and affairs according to the mode provided by state laws for the liquidation of insolvent corporations. As well stated in *Thornhill* v. *Bank of Louisiana*, 5 N. B. R. 375, "this cannot be allowed. No mode of proceeding authorised by a state law can be permitted to have this effect. If the forfeiture, under the state law, of the charter of the bank raises an obstacle to the jurisdiction of the federal courts, then the claim authorising the forfeiture of the charter is suspended by the federal law. To hold otherwise is to allow the states, by a particular form of liquidation, to override a law of congress, on a subject on which congress, by the constitution, has supreme power."

The sooner it is understood that, now, when a uniform law of bankruptcy is in operation under the authority conferred upon congress by the constitution of the United States, no power exists to wrest from the jurisdiction of the courts in bankruptcy the assets of such bankrupt individuals and corporations as are within the scope of the provisions of the bankrupt act, the more will the beneficent provisions of that act be felt and appreciated by the mercantile community. Nowhere is this doctrine in relation to the effect of a bankrupt law upon the operation of the insolvent laws of the states more clearly and ably enunciated than in the learned opinions upon this subject to be found in the reported decisions of the supreme judicial court of the commonwealth of Massachusetts.

Petition for revision and reversal of the decree of the district court dismissed with costs.

CHESTER I. REED and JOHN R. BULLARD, for receivers; H. W. PAINE, C. R. TRAIN and J. O. TEELE, for creditors; B. SANFORD, for bankrupt.—February 23, 1872.

———•◦•———

UNITED STATES DISTRICT COURT—S. D. NEW YORK.

A receiver appointed under an order of a state court cannot be one of the trustees appointed under section forty-three of the bankrupt act, for the reason that he must account, if at all, as receiver, to a trustee or assignee to be appointed by the United States district court, for the property as it stood at the date of the commencement of bankruptcy proceedings, and it is not proper that he should, as trustee, be plaintiff, and as receiver be defendant.   It appearing furthermore that the receiver does not intend, voluntarily, to surrender his receivership, when appointed a trustee by the court, but expects to have his acts as receiver and trustee confirmed by the respective courts, this court decides that his position is one of incompatibility, for if he is to be trustee under the bankrupt act, he must look to this court alone for authority and direction.   For the same reasons a receiver cannot be appointed assignee although three-fourths in value of the creditors whose claims were proven nominated him as trustee.

A creditor who claims a preference, which preference is contested by the other creditors, is an improper person to be one of the committee selected according to section forty-three of the bankrupt act.

In re THE STUYVESANT BANK.

BLATCHFORD, J.—Being of opinion, on the papers before me in this case, that the interests of the creditors of the bankrupt will not be promoted by the appointment of Mr. Archer as trustee, I must decline to confirm the resolution to that effect.

One of the grounds on which the bank was adjudged a bankrupt by this court was, that, being insolvent, it procured and suffered its property to be taken on legal process with intent, by such disposition of its property, to defeat and delay the operation of the bankrupt act, and suffered and procured a receiver of all its property and effects to be appointed by a state court, and surrendered possession thereof to such receiver. Mr. Archer was appointed such receiver and is such still. All the property which belonged to the bank passed into his hands as such receiver, he thereafter claiming the legal title to it, by transfer, and claiming to hold it as against all the world. Such as remains of it in his hands he claims to hold by the same title. The proceedings in bankruptcy were commenced on the twenty-third of December, eighteen hundred and seventy-one. If Mr. Archer is ever to account to this court, or to its proper officer, for what was the property of the bank, he must account for it as it stood on that day. It must be administered as of that day, and from that day, according to such principles of administration as may be determined by this court. It appears that Mr. Archer has, since that day, been dealing with the property which came into his hands as receiver, as having the legal title to it, collecting moneys and paying them out. For these acts he must, if he is to account to this court at all for them, account to a trustee or assignee to be appointed by this court. It is not proper that he should, as trustee, be plaintiff, and as receiver be defendant, in respect to these matters. Moreover, nothing can pass from him as receiver, of which he is now in possession, to any trustee or assignee to be appointed by this court, unless he voluntarily surrenders it or is compelled to do so by proper legal proceedings. It appears that he does not intend to so surrender it, nor does he intend, if confirmed as trustee, by this court, to cease acting as receiver. He announces that he intends to act both as receiver and as trustee, and have his acts authorised by the state court which appointed him receiver and by this court. This is a position of incompatibility which this court cannot permit one of its officers to occupy. If he is to be trustee under the bankrupt act, appointed by this court, he must look to this court alone as the source of his authority. If he is to hold and administer, as receiver, under the state laws, the property which he received as receiver, he must so administer it without

looking to this court for any authority or direction. If he is
to administer such property as a trustee appointed by this
court, he must so administer it without looking to the state
court, or to any other court but this court, for authority or
direction. The emphatic language of WOODRUFF, J., *in re*
Bininger, 4 N. B. R. 77; 7 Blatchford C. C. R. 262, 275,
276, shows how utterly impossible it is for this court to permit Mr. Archer to occupy at one and the same time the two
inconsistent positions of a receiver under the state law and a
trustee or assignee appointed by this court. He says : " The
design and purpose of the bankrupt law is, that the property
of insolvents shall be secured to their creditors in the very
mode pointed out thereby, with all the facilities for its appropriation, all the security for its administration, all the safe-
guards against fraud, all the protection against devices to
establish false claims, fictitious debts and illegal or inequitable preferences, which that act provides, and in the summary manner in which the proceedings may be conducted.
It is not, therefore, for the debtors or for the debtors and
some of the creditors to say, we can devise a better or safer
or more economical mode of reaching the same final result.
If it were true, it would be only saying we will resort to an
expedient to defeat the bankrupt law, and our reason therefor is, that we think our plan is wiser and better than that
which congress has seen fit to prescribe. But the administration of the property under a receiver in such a suit does
not necessarily accomplish the same result. It is not necessary to enlarge upon this to anticipate all possible differences,
but reference may be made to various provisions of the bankrupt law, such as requiring the surrender of securities as a
condition of participation in the bankrupt's estate, (section
twenty) ; excluding claims deemed fraudulent under the act
(sections twenty-two, thirty-nine) ; denying to creditors who
have received or taken securities, with reason to believe in
the insolvency of the debtor, and for the purpose of obtaining
a preference, any share of the estate (section twenty-three).
* * * These subjects would find no place in the adminis-

tration of the estate under the state laws through a receiver. There are, also, summary means of investigation and enquiry peculiar to the bankrupt law and not known to the other proceeding. So, too, the subject of making dividends from time to time is committed to the determination of creditors, (section twenty-seven) ; several classes of debts are declared entitled to a preference and to payment in full in priority to others, (section twenty-eight) ; and special modes of determining disputed claims are provided, (section six.) There are, doubtless, other differences between the administrations under the bankrupt law and by a receivership under the state laws, but the above are sufficient to show that the two are wholly inconsistent and that the latter defeats the former."

There is another objection to confirming the proceedings of the creditors in regard to a trustee. They have undertaken to select a committee consisting of three creditors. It is to be taken that they desire such committee to consist of three persons. Their action, under the act, is a unit, and their resolution must be confirmed as a whole, or not at all. One of the three persons they name to constitute the committee of creditors, is Mr. Bull, president of the New York Savings Bank. That bank claims, under a provision in the statutes of New York, to be entitled to a preference, and to payment in full in priority to others ; and by its proof of debt filed in these proceedings, it claims to have such statutes of New York applied in its favor, by preferring its claim, in distributing the assets of the bank under the bankrupt act. This claim of preference is contested by creditors of the bank who are unsecured and who claim no preference. Under these circumstances it is manifestly improper that Mr. Bull should be one of the committee of creditors under whose "direction," according to section forty-three of the act, the estate of the bank is to be wound up and settled.

The register certifies to the court that the first meeting of creditors herein has been finally closed ; that at such meeting there were some votes cast for an assignee, but there was no choice of assignee ; and that the register made no appointment of assignee, there being an opposing interest. It is provided by section thirteen of the act, that if no choice of assignee is made by the creditors at the first meeting, the judge, or, if there is no opposing interest, the register, shall appoint one or more assignees. The case, therefore, has arisen, where the resolution nominating a trustee not being confirmed by the court, it becomes the duty of the court to appoint an assignee. The objections to the confirmation of Mr. Archer as trustee apply equally to an appointment of him as assignee, although three-fourths in value of the creditors whose claims were proved, nominated him as trustee.

I appoint John H. Platt, Esq., as assignee of the bankrupt.

D. DUDLEY FIELD, for Mr. Archer; CHARLES TRACY and G. L. WALKER, oppos d.—March 20, 1872.

————•◦•————

UNITED STATES DISTRICT COURT—MASSACHUSETTS.

A person cannot commit an act of bankruptcy while insane; but if when *sane* he has committed such an act, he may be made bankrupt upon a petition *in invitum*, after he has become *insane*.
Whether he can obtain a discharge, *quære*.

In re D. PRATT.

LOWELL, J.—Pratt committed an act of bankruptcy and afterwards became insane. A guardian has been duly appointed for him under the laws of Massachusetts, and he appears and asks the court to make the adjudication. So far as any cases are reported which touch the standing of a lunatic in a court of bankruptcy, they decide that such a person cannot commit an act of bankruptcy while lunatic; but that if while sane he has committed such an act, he may be made bankrupt after he has become lunatic. Robson on Bankruptcy, 84; Anon. 13 Ves. 590, and Mr. Sumner's note *ex parte* Stamp, De Gex, 345; *in re* Marvin, Dillon, 178.

This appears to be a reasonable distinction, and conform-

In re Noyes.

able to the law in civil matters generally. It is highly important to the bankrupt's creditors that they should not be left to a race of diligence which has all the objections which can be found to a proceeding in bankruptcy, besides others of its own; and the rights of the bankrupt will be fully protected by his guardian. Whether he can obtain a discharge, if unable to take the oath prescribed by the statute and unable to submit himself to examination, I will not now say. If not, he will be no worse off than if he had not been made bankrupt, while his creditors generally will be much better off.

H. M. ROGERS for petitioner.

* * *

UNITED STATES DISTRICT COURT—E. D. MICHIGAN.

An assignee is not at liberty to charge the assets of the estate in his hands for professional and clerical services rendered him in the execution of his trust, until the same shall have been first duly allowed by the court.

Before incurring expenses for professional services and clerk hire, an assignee must apply to the court for proper authority; if, however, he has incurred and paid such expenses, or demands compensation beyond what he is entitled to by section twenty-eight of the bankrupt law, he must accompany his final account with a separate and distinct application for an allowance of the charges, and submit to such examination and furnish such proofs as may be required touching the necessity of such disbursements and services.

In re B. B. NOYES.

I, the undersigned register in bankruptcy, do hereby certify that in the course of proceedings in the above bankruptcy, at the fourth general meeting of creditors, the final account of the assignee of said estate was presented, under the provisions of the twenty-eighth section of the bankrupt act, to be audited and passed. On the day appointed the assignee filed satisfactory proofs that he had given the notice to the creditors as required by said section; that he had filed his account, and that he would, on the day specified in his notice, apply for a settlement of his account and for a discharge of his liability as assignee.

I further certify, that on the day appointed for the settlement of said account, of the one hundred and eighteen cred-

In re Noyes.

itors who have proved their claims against said bankrupt, not to exceed six, appeared at all, and none of them, so far as I know, examined said account nor made an inquiry concerning it, nor any objection to its allowance.

Proceeding, therefore, to the examination of the accounts, under the power and duty conferred by the fourth section of the bankrupt act, " To audit and pass the accounts of assignee "—I find that the assignee has received the gross sum of fifty-seven thousand five hundred and eighty-one dollars and thirty-seven cents ; that he has paid out on dividends to creditors the sum of fifty-one thousand one hundred and eighty-one dollars and twenty-seven cents, and for expenses the sum of three thousand four hundred and ninety dollars and one cent; making the gross sum paid out fifty-four thousand six hundred and seventy-one dollars and twenty-eight cents. Of the balance he claims two thousand six hundred and nineteen dollars and fifty-nine cents, for his commissions and services, leaving the sum of two hundred and ninety dollars and fifty cents for final distribution. The assignee furnishes satisfactory evidence that he has actually paid out the above mentioned sum of three thousand four hundred and ninety dollars and one cent stated as expenses. In this sum is included the sum of five hundred and twenty-six dollars and thirty cents, paid out for clerk hire, and also the sum of six hundred and ninety-seven dollars and eighty-nine cents, as follows:

To R. P. Toms, retainer and services in suits against Hill & Trollope, Dreher, Pate, Sales & Pilgrim, Danz, Whittle, Reichle, Streeter, Faughborn, Hemple, R. Gardner, Hertner, Kellogg Ladd, Priest &.Gray...... .... $150 00
R. P. Toms for taxed cost in Hemple, Whittle, Dreher & Pate.. 142 42
D. C. Holbrook, counsel fees, *in re* C. L. Noyes *et al.* examining bankrupt *et al*............................... .... 100 00
A. Russell *in re* Prentiss.............................:.... 15 00
R. P. Toms in suits v. Van Riper & Co., Cameron, Bathur, Trombley, St. Amoun & Waterfall......................... 50 00
Taxed costs in the above, and against Dantz, Faugborn & Donahue... 173 05
Taxed costs against L. Streeter............................. 37 42
Middaugh & Driggs, argument in District Court in opposition to claim of T. J. Noyes....................................... 30 00
————
$697 89

In 're Noyes.

· These items for clerk hire, counsel fees and taxed costs, amounting to one thousand two hundred and twenty-four dollars and nineteen cents, are, in my judgment, of a character that their allowance can only be claimed upon a proper showing of their necessity. If they had been considered at a creditor's meeting attended by a sufficient number to insure a fair representation of the creditor's interests, and had been affirmatively approved, or if they had, after such consideration, met with no objection, their allowance might have been justified without any further showing of their character or necessity.

The assignee presents his claim for services, under the general designation of "commissions and services," at two thousand six hundred and nineteen dollars and fifty-nine cents. The commissions are fixed by the statute (section twenty-eight), and amount as computed upon the sum "received and paid out," fifty-four thousand six hundred and seventy-one dollars and twenty-eight cents, to six hundred and ninety-six dollars and seventy-one cents. For the balance, one thousand nine hundred and twenty-one dollars and eighty-seven cents, no specification is given, nor any proof offered, that services entitled to this amount of compensation have been rendered.

The consideration of this account presents questions of very considerable importance, applicable not only to this, but to the settlement of every estate in bankruptcy, such as :

FIRST. Under what circumstances and to what extent is an assignee at liberty to charge the assets of the estate in his hands for professional services rendered him, in the execution of his trust?

SECOND. What circumstances will jutisfy the employment by the assignee of clerks, to be compensated out of the fund? And,

THIRD. Are the conditions implied above, on which expenses for professional services and clerk hire rest, to be determined by the assignee in the exercise of his judgment,· or is it his duty, before incurring the liability, to apply to the court for the proper authority?

I am unable, from any showing before me, or from any facts within my knowledge, to determine that the accounts as presented ought to be allowed; and deeming the subject to be one of sufficient practical importance to be presented to the court for a definitive settlement of the principles by which the practice in such cases is to be guided, I intimated to the assignee my purpose to certify the question of the allowance of his account into court for determination; at the same time inviting him to supplement his account by any statement or deposition of an explanatory nature that he thought desirable.

He prefers, however, to reserve them for the hearing which may be accorded to him on this certificate.

All of which is respectfully submitted, together with the accounts of the assignee, which are the subjects of consideration.   HOVEY K. CLARKE, *Register.*

LONGYEAR, J.—In answer to the three questions above certified, the court decides:

Section seventeen of the act provides that the assignee "shall be allowed and may retain, out of money in his hands, all the necessary disbursements made by him in the discharge of his duty, and a reasonable compensation for his services, *in the discretion of the court.*" Section twenty-eight makes a specific allowance to the assignee, of a certain·per centum "on all moneys received and paid out by him" *in addition* to the allowances authorized by section seventeen. (See *in re* Dean, 1 N. B. R. 26.) It is under these provisions, and these alone, that the right of assignees to charge the estate for disbursements and services must be determined.

The allowance provided by section twenty-eight is specific, and being a mere matter of computation, may be charged up by the assignee directly against funds in his hands, so soon as the "amount received and paid out by him" is ascertained; not so, however, with the allowances authorized by section seventeen. These allowances are *in the discretion of the court,*

In re Noyes.

and can be made only upon a specific application to the court, and a showing that the disbursements and services for which such allowances are asked, were necessary, and are reasonable in amount.

This is clearly contemplated by general order five, defining the powers of registers in bankruptcy, in which it is provided, among other things, that the registers may conduct proceedings where uncontested in relation to ordering payment of rates and taxes, "*and salary or wages of persons in the employment of the assignee*," and "*taking evidence concerning expenses and charges against the bankrupt's estate.*" Under this order the register may hear and determine such application when uncontested (*in re*, Lane, 2 N. B. R. 100). And it is preferable that such hearing should be had before the register, because, having the proceedings all before him, he is better able to judge of the exigencies upon which the necessity of the disbursements and services and the reasonableness of the amounts charged depend.

It would be difficult, and I think impracticable, to prescribe any general rule defining the circumstances under which, and extent to which, an assignee is at liberty to charge the assets of the estate in his hands for professional and clerical services in the execution of his trust. This must be left to be decided in each individual case according to its peculiar exigencies.

The answer to the first and second questions, therefore, must be that the assignee is not at liberty to charge the assets of the estate in his hands, for professional and clerical services rendered him in the execution of his trust, until the same shall have been first duly allowed by the court.

The answer to the third question is partly anticipated in what has been already said.

The assignee may, of course, apply to the court in the first instance, for authority to employ professional or clerical assistance, but in such case the court could do but little more than grant such authority in general terms, leaving the instances in and to which such assistance may be employed,

In re Noyes.

largely to the discretion of the assignee, as emergencies shall arise, making such assistance necessary. Such authority, I think, the assignee already possesses under his general powers, subject however, to the control of the court; such power must be used by him cautiously, and in the exercise of a sound discretion, and with the understanding that any abuse of it will be corrected by the court when applied to for authority to charge the estate for such assistance.

When the assignee desires to pay for any such assistance out of funds in his hands, belonging to the estate, before submitting his final account, he should apply to the court for the allowance of the same, or the person rendering the service may himself apply. In either case the assignee would be at liberty to charge the amount allowed to the estate at once, on payment of the same. If no such application is made, or if he has incurred liabilities or made disbursements for such assistance, or otherwise, in regard to which no allowance has been made, or if he makes a claim for services other than the per centum on moneys received and paid out by him allowed by section twenty-eight, then the assignee must accompany his final account with a separate and distinct application for an allowance of the same, and submit to such examination and furnish such proofs as may be required touching the necessity of such disbursements and services and the reasonableness of the amounts charged. The matter will then be heard and determined by the register, if uncontested, or by the court, if contested, and as the same shall be thus determined, the assignee will be at liberty to charge the estate in his final account, and not otherwise.

The application should contain a brief statement of the circumstances out of which the necessity for the disbursements, and the professional or clerical assistance, and the assignee's own services, arose, and from which the reasonableness of the amounts claimed therefor may appear, and it should be verified by the assignee.

In case the application accompanies the final account, it will, of course, be laid before the creditors at the same time, and if they assent or fail to object to the same, and the items and amounts appear to be just and reasonable, all further inquiry may be dispensed with.

In this case the assignee, laboring, no doubt, under a misapprehension as to his legal rights and duties in this regard, seems ·to have assumed to judge for himself, not only as to the necessity of the disbursements and services, but also as to the reasonableness of the amounts, and so charged the same directly to the assets of the estate in his hands, without first having obtained an allowance of the same. The register was, therefore, correct in refusing to audit and pass the account under the circumstances st..'ed by him in his certificate, without a proper showing by the assignee of the necessity of the professional and clerical assistance, and for his own services, charged in the account.

The assignee has, however, now supplemented his account with a particular statement as to the charges for clerk hire, and as to such portion of the charges for professional services as do not explain themselves, and has also submitted to an oral examination before me in relation thereto, and also in relation to his own services, and the particulars thereof, from all of which it satisfactorily appears that the professional and clerical services and the services of the assignee, charged in his account, were necessary in the execution of his trust, and that the charges therefor are reasonable in amount; the same must, therefore, be allowed.

It will be observed, that, in this particular case, the assignee has not been required to conform, in all respects, to the general rule above laid down; as, for instance, he has not been required to present a new account, omitting the charges for professional and clerical assistance and for his own services, other than his per centum, under section twenty-eight, and then to present a separate application for their allowance. This must be understood as an exception merely as to this particular case, and as in nowise qualifying the general rule.—January 2, 1872.

UNITED STATES CIRCUIT COURT—E. D. MICHIGAN.

That clause of section forty-four of the United States bankrupt act of eighteen hundred and sixty seven, which punishes by imprisonment any fraudulent disposition of the goods of a debtor, obtained on credit and remaining unpaid for, within three months next before the commencement of proceedings in bankruptcy, is constitutional and valid. Motion in arrest of judgment on this ground denied, and defendant sentenced to one year's imprisonment.

UNITED STATES v. PUSEY.

The defendant was tried and convicted on an information under that clause of section forty-four of the bankrupt act of eighteen hundred and sixty-seven, which provides, "That from and after the passage of this act if any debtor or bankrupt * * shall, with intent to defraud his creditors, within three months next before the commencement of proceedings in bankruptcy, pawn, pledge, or dispose of, otherwise than by *bona fide* transactions in the ordinary way of his trade, any of his goods and chattels which have been obtained on credit and remain unpaid for, he shall be deemed guilty of a misdemeanor, and, upon conviction thereof in any court in the United States, shall be punished by imprisonment, with or without hard labor, for a term not exceeding three years."

The ground of the motion in arrest is that the above clause of section forty-four is unconstitutional and void. There was another ground of motion stated, but it was not insisted on upon the argument.

The argument in support of the motion is: First, that the clause in question assumes to punish an offense committed before commencement of proceedings in bankruptcy, and is therefore not a law necessary and proper for carrying into execution the power of congress to establish uniform laws on the subject of bankruptcy; and second, that it is an *ex post facto* law.

MR. BROWN (Newberry, Pond & Brown) for the motion; MR. SWAN, Assistant United States attorney, opposed.

United States v. Pusey.

LONGYEAR, J.—Among the powers of congress enumerated in the constitution (article one, section eight), are, " To establish * * * uniform laws on the subject of bankruptcies throughout the United States," and, " to make all laws which shall be necessary and proper for carrying into execution the foregoing powers, and all other powers vested by the constitution in the government of the United States, or in any department or officer thereof. Under the first power named congress established the bankrupt law of eighteen hundred and sixty-seven. If, therefore, the clause of section forty-four in question, is a law " necessary and proper " for carrying the bankrupt law into effect, it comes within the latter power named, and is constitutional and valid ; otherwise it is not, because then it is a mere police regulation relating exclusively to the internal trade of the states, and does not come within the power of congress. *United States* v. *De Witt*, 9 Wall. 41.

Under the first proposition of the argument in support of the motion, it is important to bear in mind the distinction between the *subject matter*, bankruptcy, in regard to which congress is empowered to legislate, and the means, machinery or practice congress has prescribed for carrying that power into effect. It is with the former, the subject matter, we have to deal here, and not with the latter, any further than it may come in question incidentally.

What then is " the subject of bankruptcy ?" What does it include ? What realm do laws upon that subject occupy ? And what are necessary and proper laws for carrying such laws into effect?

The Federalist (No. 32) alludes to the constitutional power of congress to establish uniform laws of bankruptcy as a power intimately connected with the regulation of commerce, and for the prevention of frauds. 2 Story on the Constitution, sec. 1105. It is intimately connected with the regulation of commerce because it has for its subject the relation of debtor and creditor—a relation growing out of commercial transactions, and often, and it may be said to a very large extent, between citizens of different states, and, in fact, between citizens of the United States and those of foreign countries. That it is a power for the prevention of frauds on creditors has always been assumed whenever it has been exercised, and I believe has never been questioned. (See the former acts of eighteen hundred and eighteen hundred and forty-one, as well as the present act of eighteen hundred and sixty-seven.) To this end these laws are made to reach back of the commencement of proceedings to defeat frauds, and, in fact, to constitute acts frauds, which by the laws of the states, and but for the bankrupt law itself, were entirely valid.

Story on the Constitution, section 1,106, says: "It may be stated that the general object of all bankrupt and insolvent laws is, on the one hand, to secure to creditors an appropriation of the property of their debtors *pro tanto* to the discharge of their debts, whenever the latter are unable to discharge the whole amount; and on the other hand, to relieve the unfortunate and honest debtors from perpetual bondage to their creditors, either in the shape of unlimited imprisonment to coerce payment of their debts, or of an absolute right to appropriate and monopolise all their future earnings." A very compact and pointed description, or definition of a bankrupt law occurs in the debates on a bankrupt bill in the house of representatives in eighteen hundred and eighteen. It was there said: "Perhaps as satisfactory description of a bankrupt law as can be framed is, that it is a law for the benefit and relief of creditors and their debtors, in cases in which the latter are unable or unwilling to pay their debts. And a law on the subject of bankruptcies, in the sense of the constitution, is a law making provision for cases of persons failing to pay their debts." 4 Elliot's Debates, 282.

The "subject of bankruptcy," in a general sense, concerns the relation of debtor and creditor, and in a particular and no doubt stricter sense, concerns such relation in cases where the debtor is unwilling or unable to pay his debts.

Laws upon that subject have for their object the appropriation, either voluntarily or by compulsion, of the debtor's property to the payment of his debts, *pro tanto*, or in full, as t e case may be, and the relief of honest debtors. Tc accomplish this object these laws are made to operate upon, affect and control the relations of the parties, so as to limit and circumscribe the rights of the debtor in, and his control over, his property, and the rights of others dealing with him, in regard thereto, in many particulars, before any proceedings in bankruptcy shall have been commenced by or against such debtor. Of this nature are the provisions of sections thirty-five and thirty-nine, invalidating preferences under certain circumstances when made within four months, and certain payments, sales, transfers, etc., when made within six months before commencement of proceedings; and all assignments, gifts, sales, conveyances or transfers, with intent to delay, defraud or hinder creditors, *made at any time after the passage of the act.* There are other provisions of the same nature, but the above are sufficient for illustration.

The power of congress to enact the ̤provisions giving the act the operation and effect just mentioned (and I am not aware that their right to exercise that power has ever been questioned), is derived solely from their general powers under article one, section eight, of the constitution, to make all laws necessary and proper for carrying into effect their power to establish laws on the subject of bankruptcy. It is to this same general provision of the constitution that we must look for the power of congress to make the law in question. It must be found there or it does not exist at all.

One object to be attained by the enactment of a bankrupt law, as we have seen, is the appropriation of the debtor's property to the payment of his debts. And this may be said to be the principal or primary object of all such laws. The relief of the debtor, although an important consideration, is really but incidental to the other. Story on the Const. section 1106.

Is the provision in question a law " necessary and proper," within the meaning of those words as used in the constitution, for carrying into effect the bankrupt law, and the object and purpose of its enactment?

The meaning of the words "necessary and proper " has been judicially determined by the supreme court on full discussion and deliberation to be " *needful*," " *requisite*," " *essential*," " *conducive to*." *McCulloch* v. *Maryland*, 4 Wheat. 418. See also Story on the Const. sections 1248 to 1255, citing the above and other authorities, where the subject is very fully considered and the same construction maintained. In *McCulloch* v. *Maryland*, chief justice Marshall, in delivering the opinion of the court says : " we admit, as all must admit, that the powers of the government are limited, and that its limits are not to be transcended. But we think the sound construction of the constitution must allow to the national legislature that discretion, with respect to the means by which the powers it confers are to be carried into execution, which will enable that body to perform the high duties assigned to it, in the manner most beneficial to the people. Let the end be legitimate, let it be within the scope of the constitution, and all means are appropriate which are plainly adapted to that end, which are not prohibited, but consist with the letter and spirit of the constitution are constitutional."

Here, as we have seen, the end sought is the appropriation of the debtor's property to the payment of his debts. The clause in question is for the prevention of frauds by debtors on their creditors, by which that end may be defeated or impaired. It certainly does not need argument to show that the provision is a means clearly conducive, and plainly adapted, to the end sought.

But it is claimed in argument, first—that the provision in question purports to punish an offence committed before commencement of proceedings in bankruptcy, and that, therefore, it can have no connection with the bankrupt act ; and, second—that such offense (as is charged in the information in this case) is one committed by a debtor merely, one who may or may not become a bankrupt, and that, therefore, it has no connection with the act; and that for both reasons the offense concerns the internal trade of the States alone, and is not within the power of congress to be created or punished.

I think the ground occupied by the first objection is much too narrow. The proceedings in bankruptcy do not constitute the end to be accomplished by a bankrupt act. They constitute the machinery, so to speak, by which that end is to be obtained, viz.: the appropriation of the debtor's property to the payment of his debts. Therefore the prevention of the fraud denounced by the provision, being, as we have seen, conducive to that end, it can make no difference whether it relates to a fraud committed before or after the machinery provided for the accomplishment of the end is set in motion.

The second ground is more difficult of solution. The person who may commit the offense is described in the act as " any debtor or bankrupt," and in the case under consideration the defendant is described in the information as a debtor merely. In the English bankrupt acts, from which the provision in question was no doubt taken, the word " bankrupt " only is used, the word " debtor " having been added in our act. In order to be a bankrupt a person must first be a debtor. But a bankrupt, in the sense of the English act, as well as of our own, is a debtor, and something more. He is a debtor who has committed an act of bankruptcy, declared to be such by the bankrupt law. *Rex* v. *Jones*, 4 B. & Ad. 345; s. c. 24 Eng. Com. Law Rep. 71; *Reg.* v. *Lands*, 33 Eng. L. and Eq. 536; *Buckingham* v. *McLean*, 13 How. 167; *in re* Black *et al.*, 1 N. B. R. 81; *in re* Craft, 2 N. B. R. 44.

A " debtor " may or may not be a bankrupt. But, from the fact that both words, " debtor " and " bankrupt," are used, and in the disjunctive, it must be held that the former is used in the provision in question, as descriptive of a person who is a debtor, but who has not, at the time of committing the offense, become a bankrupt. And it is on this account, principally, that the difficulty arises. This difficulty, however, is only apparent, as we shall presently see. It grows less when we consider what, as we have already seen, is included by the expression "subject of bankruptcies," as used in the constitution—that in a general sense it concerns the relation of debtor and creditor, a relation existing largely between citizens of different States, and so, nearly related to, in fact constituting a branch of those great commercial relations over which the power of congress is also extended. True, the expression has a limited signification, that is, that it concerns the relation of debtor and creditor in cases where the debtor is unable or unwilling to pay his debts, yet it none the less concerns the relation of debtor and creditor, the limitation being in the instance only, and not in degree. And when we also consider that the leading object of a bankrupt law is the appropriation of the debtor's property to the payment of his debts, and to that end the prevention of frauds, reaching back of the commencement of proceedings, as the present law does (sections thirty-five and thirty-nine), and as the previous laws of eighteen hundred and eighteen hundred and forty-one did, and invalidating and annulling contracts and transactions on that ground (some of which, but for the bankrupt law, were valid when made), within certain specified periods of time, and, in some instances, at any time after the passage of the act; and this, so far as I know or can ascertain, without question, or even a doubt suggested as to the constitutional power of congress so to enact. And the difficulty grows still less, in fact vanishes, when the foregoing considerations are taken in connection with the fact that the ascertainment whether the act described constitutes a crime is made to depend upon the debtor's committing some act of bankruptcy, on account of which he shall be declared a bankrupt, within so short a time after doing the act specified as to afford a reasonable presumption that he contemplated bankruptcy (or committing an act of bankruptcy, which is the same thing, as we have seen), when he did the act specified. The time specified in the provision is "within three months next before the commencement of proceedings in bankruptcy." Commencement of proceedings in bankruptcy is the filing of a petition for adjudication of bankruptcy by or against a debtor, upon which such debtor shall be adjudicated a bankrupt. Section 38; *in re* Patterson, N. B. R. Sup. xxvii; s. c. Bt. 509. If the petition is filed by the debtor, then that is the act of bankruptcy whereby he acquires the legal status of bankrupt. (Section eleven). · If the petition is filed against the debtor, then the act or acts by which he acquired that status, and on account of which he is adjudged a bankrupt, must have been committed before the filing of the petition. So that in either case the debtor must have committed an act of bankruptcy within three months after the act specified in order to bring the case within the law.

Suppose congress had, in lieu of the present form of expression, provided that in order to constitute the specified act as an offense, it should be committed by a debtor contemplating, or in contemplation of bankruptcy; then I apprehend there could be no question of the constitutionality of the provision. But is not that the force and effect of the provision as it now stands? If congress had enacted as above supposed, it would have been left to courts and juries to determine what would constitute proof of contemplation of bankruptcy. Like all other questions of the intent or animus of the acts and conduct of persons, it would very rarely admit of direct proof, but in most cases would necessarily depend upon circumstantial evidence. There are provisions of the act by which the fraudulent character of transactions is expressly made to depend upon their having been had "in contemplation of bankruptcy." In such cases it has always been held that the fact that the transaction was had by a debtor at a comparatively recent period of time before becoming bankrupt, is presumptive evidence of the transaction having been had in contemplation of bankruptcy—stronger or weaker, as the time was more or less remote. But this leaves the matter to depend largly upon the uncertain and varying opinions of different judges and juries, and perhaps the fluctuating opinions of the same

judges—an element which ought not to exist in penal enactments. Congress has, therefore, seen fit in the enactment in
question, to withhold this question from courts and juries,
and by express enactment to establish a rule as to the time,
which shall be at once uniform and conclusive.

It was said in argument, that from the reading of the
provision in question, it is not the doing of the act specified
that constitutes the offense, but the commencement of proceedings in bankruptcy, by or against the offender. From
the views already advanced the answer to this objection is
obvious. If the debtor commits the act specified, and at
any time within three months thereafter, commits an act, on
account of which he is liable to be declared by the court to
be a bankrupt, he is, as we have seen, conclusively presumed
to have committed the act in contemplation of committing
an act of bankruptcy, and the offense is complete, upon
committing the former act, whether proceedings for adjudication of bankruptcy are commenced within three months or
not, except in the single instance where the act of bankruptcy is the commencement of such proceedings by the
debtor. But the offense *cannot be prosecuted* unless such
proceedings are commenced within three months. In this
respect it is a limitation merely.

It was also objected in argument that the limitation to
three months is purely arbitrary, that it might just as well
be three years, or thirty years. That would simply be an
abuse of power, which we have no right to presume any
congress would be guilty of. Story on the Const. section
1252, citing the Federalist numbers 33, 34, says: "There is
always some chance of error, or abuse of every power; but
this furnishes no ground of objection against the power. *
* * The remedy for any abuse or misconstruction of the
power, is the same as in similar abuses and misconstructions
of the state governments. It is by an appeal to the other
departments of the government; and finally to the people,
in the exercise of their elective franchises." And finally,
the same objection might be made to sections thirty-five and

thirty-nine, and to all limitation laws, which no one would think of making at this day.

From what has been said and written by early commentators, and by high authority, in regard to the power of congress over bankruptcies as well as from the nature of the subject itself, there is some ground for assuming that it extends to the regulation of all the relations of debtor and creditor, for the prevention of frauds, and otherwise, to the end of placing all creditors of the same debtor, not expressly preferred, upon one broad basis of equality, and of securing the honest appropriation of a debtor's property, not expressly exempted, to the payment of his debts, either with or without the commission of an act of bankruptcy, or whether bankruptcy was or was not in contemplation. But in this case it is unnecessary to go to that extent, and I therefore leave the point undecided.

Upon all considerations, I hold that the first ground of argument against the unconstitutionality of the law is untenable.

The second ground of the objection is, that the provision in question is an *ex post facto* law, and therefore unconstitutional, in this, that it purports to punish an act as an offense which was not such at the time it was committed. As we have already seen, the act which this provision purports to punish is an offense, when it is an offense at all, the moment it is committed. It is made necessary, it is true, to resort to the subsequent acts of the perpetrator, to ascertain the criminal character of such former act; but when thus ascertained, it relates back to the committing of it. Such subsequent acts do not invest such former act with any element it did not possess when it was committed, but simply ascertains what its elements were from the beginning.

An *ex post facto* law, however, is, in common acceptation, a law enacted after the fact. Here the law was in existence at the time the act complained of was committed. The objection, therefore, is not germane.

The second ground of objection is, therefore, also untenable.

While the powers of the general government are all derived from the constitution, the powers of each branch, the legislative, the executive and the judicial, are entirely separate and distinct from each other. And while the judicial branch, under its powers to expound the law, possesses the power to annul legislative acts on the ground of unconstitutionality, it will never exercise that power except in cases entirely free from all reasonable doubt. So that if I even entertained doubts in this case, which I do not, I should still be obliged to hold the law valid.

The law in question is one that strongly commends itself to favor. A proper and enlightened enforcement of it, must tend largely to strengthen credit and inspire confidence in commercial transactions—consummations highly worthy of the fostering care of the government, especially in a country like ours, where credit enters so largely in the business transactions between merchants and traders. The creditor, when he parts with his property, necessarily relies largely upon the honesty and good faith of his debtor—that the latter will do nothing intentionally which shall impair his ability to pay at maturity, or failing to do so, that shall interfere with the honest appropriation of his property to the payment of his debts. It is both a moral and a legal right of the creditor so to rely, and it is both a moral and a legal obligation and duty of the debtor to observe that right, and nothing in my opinion will conduce more to its observance than a rigid enforcement of the law in question. Let it come to be understood that it is a crime for a debtor wilfully and intentionally to violate the faith and betray the confidence placed in him, constituting as they do, in most cases, the very foundation of his credit, a crime for which severe and certain punishment will be inflicted, and I firmly believe that we shall have less of fraud, and fraudulent practices—that corrupt and debilitating disease with which the body commercial has always been afflicted.

This case was transmitted from the district to the circuit court, on account of the novelty and importance of the questions here involved, in the hope that a hearing of this motion might be had before a full bench. But on account of the extensive and laborious duties of the circuit judge on his too large circuit, the end sought was found to be impracticable without considerable delay. I have, therefore, by the consent and acquiesence of all parties concerned, heard the motion without his valuable aid. I have, however, availed myself of opportunities to consult with him, and have laid the views expressed in the foregoing opinion before him, and I am authorised by him to say that he fully concurs in the result at which I have arrived.

The motion in arrest of judgment must be denied, and judgment must pass upon the verdict.

The defendant was sentenced to one year's imprisonment.—March 5, 1872.

UNITED STATES CIRCUIT COURT—ILLINOIS.

A. and B. were copartners in trade, but A. owned most all of the property put into the firm, in his own individual right, and at the time of the formation of the partnership was in debt to some extent. This property was all he was worth and his individual debts were contracted on the strength of this property. The firm carried on business several years, when the bulk of copartnership property was sold out under a deed of trust given by the firm to secure firm indebtedness, but no formal dissolution took place. A short time afterwards A. filed his voluntary petition in bankruptcy; at this time the copartnership assets consisted of some personal property and a few outstanding accounts from which the assignee realized nothing. Held, that the individual and copartnership creditors should share equally.

In re GOEDDE & CO.

The assignee and Fink & Nasse agree that the following is a statement of the facts relating to the bankrupt and his estate, and business connections pertinent to the application of Fink & Nasse for a distribution of the estate to the creditors *pari passu* as their claims have been proved:

On the — day of May, eighteen hundred and sixty-five, Bernard Goedde and George Scheuneberg became copartners in business under the name of Goedde & Co., for the purpose of carrying on the flouring business. At this time, Bernard Goedde individually was, and until the bankruptcy, remained the owner of the property from which the moneys now in question were realised by the assignee. This was all he was worth at the time his individual debts were contracted, and they were contracted on the strength of this property. Most of the individual debts existed at the time of the formation of the copartnership. The firm continued to do business till January, eighteen hundred and sixty-eight, when embarrassments of a financial character led to a partial stoppage, that is to say, they ceased to manufacture flour, but the copartnership was never dissolved otherwise than as may result in law from the facts here stated.

On the second of May, eighteen hundred and sixty-eight, the bulk of the copartnership property was sold out under a deed of trust given by the firm to secure firm indebtedness other than that of Fink & Nasse.

On the twenty-second of May, eighteen hundred and sixty-eight, these proceedings began, upon the voluntary petition of Bernard Goedde. No proceedings by or against George Scheuneberg were had by copartnership or other creditors.

At the date of the bankruptcy proceedings, the copartnership assets consisted of some personal property and a few outstanding accounts, both of small value. From them the assignee has realised nothing. Scheuneberg at the date of the bankruptcy, had become and was insolvent, on account of the copartnership indebtedness, and so remains. He owed some individual debts, and had little individual property. The copartnership creditors, when their debts were contracted, knew of the ownership by Goedde of the individual property before referred to. Scheuneberg has resided during all the time mentioned in the southern district of Illinois. The individual creditors who have proved their debts are, John B. Livingstone, Clemens Charles Goedde and Clemens Goedde. The copartnership creditors

In re Norton.

who have proved their debts are, John Trendly, administrator, Sebastian Pfeiffer, deceased, and Fink & Nasse.

On the foregoing statement of facts, the assignee contended that the individual creditors were entitled to be paid in full, and that only the surplus remaining should be divided among the copartnership creditors. The district court ordered a dividend to be declared, in which the individual and copartnership creditors should share equally.

The question, on the application of the individual creditors, was certified to the circuit court for said district for review, and was submitted to the circuit court for review, as on petition, setting forth the facts, with the agreement that the order of the court below might be reversed or affirmed, as the court should see proper.

DRUMMOND, J.—It is ordered and adjudged that the judgment of the court below be affirmed.

LUCIEN EATON, for individual creditors; E. P. JOHNSON, for copartnership creditors.

----o◆o----

UNITED STATES DISTRICT COURT—N. D. NEW YORK.

There can be only one first meeting of creditors, and all adjournments are but continuance of the same, and if there appear any opposition or opposing interest to the appointment of a particular assignee, at any stage of the meeting, such opposition is to be considered as continuing until the termination of such first meeting, whether upon the day first appointed, or any other day to which such meeting might be continued, unless it affirmatively appeared that such opposition was withdrawn. In such cases it is the duty of the register to report the facts and return the matter for the action of the court.

In re C. H. NORTON.

Proceedings in bankruptcy case referred to register Comstock, of Utica. Notice of the first meeting being duly served, on the return day, the register being absent, the meeting was adjourned.

In re Norton.

On adjourned day the petitioning creditor appeared by attorney, and a number of other creditors appeared by another attorney. An informal *viva voce* vote was taken before the register, the attorney for petitioning creditor voting for one assignee, and the other creditors for another; the other creditors expressly opposing the selection of the assignee desired by the petitioning creditor. On application of petitioning creditor the meeting was adjourned by the register. At the adjourned session, by reason of telegrams, of the attorney of petitioning creditor, the attorney for other creditors was not present, and they were not represented, when the petitioning creditor, voting *viva voce* for the assignee which the other creditors had before opposed, the register made a report that at such meeting, there appearing no opposing interest, he had appointed the person so voted for as assignee. Such report being received in the usual manner, was approved by the court.

Motion made to set the appointment aside by the opposing creditors. *Held:*

HALL, J.—That there was no legal vote of the creditors for assignee ever had under the bankrupt act; that there can be only one first meeting, and all adjournments are but continuance of the same, and there appearing any opposition or opposing interest to an assignee, at any stage of such first meeting, that such opposition is to be considered as continuing until the termination of such first meeting, whether upon the day first appointed, or any other day to which such meeting might be continued, unless it affirmatively appeared that such opposition was withdrawn. On this ground the register could not properly return that there was no opposing interest, and as there was an opposing interest, the register had no authority to make any appointment under the bankrupt law; that in such case as this it was the duty of the register to have reported the facts, and returned the matter for the action of the court; that the appointment made in this case by the register was unauthorised.

Ordered : That the appointment of assignee be vacated, and the court will appoint.

G. W. ADAMS, for petitioning creditors ; C. D. PRESCOTT, for other creditors.

———•◦•———

UNITED STATES DISTRICT COURT—INDIANA.

When a man enters the commercial community as a merchant, trader, banker, broker, manufacturer or miner, he assumes all the responsibilities which attach to his calling. One of these is to take care of his commercial paper, whether made before or after he commenced business ; hence, if obligations, given before but falling due after he engaged in business, are allowed to remain unpaid for fourteen days after maturity, the maker can be adjudged a bankrupt.

In re W. CARTER.

GRESHAM, J.—This is a petition filed by the Hydraulic Woolen Mill Company of Columbus, Indiana, for an adjudication of bankruptcy against William Carter of the same place. Three distinct acts of bankruptcy are charged.

FIRST. That Carter sold and delivered to David Aiken personal property to the value of six hundred dollars, and received a credit for that amount upon a debt due from him to Aiken, he, Carter, being at the time insolvent, and intending by the payment to give Aiken a preference.

SECOND. That Carter, being insolvent and intending to give Francis J. Crump an unlawful preference, transferred to him, in payment of a debt, the promissory note of Harvey Daily for one thousand dollars.

THIRD. That Carter, being a merchant, trader and manufacturer, suspended payment of his commercial paper, and has not resumed payment within a period of fourteen days ; the said paper being Carter's promissory note for seven hundred dollars, made at Columbus, Indiana, on the seventeenth day of June, eighteen hundred and seventy, payable in one hundred and eighty days, to the order of the Hydraulic Woolen Mill Co., at the bank of McEwen & Sons, in the said city of Columbus.

I think the testimony shows that at the time of the sale and delivery of the personal property to Aiken, and that of the transfer of the Daily note to Crump, Carter was insolvent; but it is not so clear that in these acts he intended preferences in favor of Aiken and Crump. The question is embarrassing and I shall not undertake to dispose of it. It ceases to be important, inasmuch as Carter must be adjudged a bankrupt on the third ground specified in the petition.

Promissory notes payable to order or bearer, in a bank in this state, are by the statutes of Indiana placed on the footing of inland bills of exchange. The note described in the third ground of bankruptcy in the petition, and put in evidence, is, therefore, Carter's commercial paper. At the time the note was executed he was not in business; he was neither merchant, trader nor manufacturer, but at the time the note fell due and the obligation to redeem his promise to pay matured, he was the owner of a large flouring mill, and engaged in buying wheat and in manufacturing and selling flour. The precise question thus presented has never been passed upon by the courts, and is one of great importance to the commercial community.

It is argued with much force and earnestness by counsel for respondent, that the note is not commercial paper within the meaning of clause nine, section thirty-nine, of the bankrupt act, because when executed Carter did not belong to any of the classes designated in that clause, and did not, therefore, pledge himself to commercial promptness in its payment. I am referred to the cases in re Nickodemus, 3 N. B. R. 55; in re McDermott Pat. Bolt Manfg. Co. 3 N. B. R. 33; Davis v. Armstrong, 3 N. B. R. 7; Innes v. Carpenter, 4 N. B. R. 129, and in re Lowenstein, 2 N. B. R. 99, in support of the position that the statute, in naming commercial paper, means paper given by a merchant, trader, manufacturer, etc., in the direct course of his business. The authorities upon this point are not uniform, and I am therefore left free to follow those which seem best supported by reason.

The language of the statute is : "Who being a banker, broker, merchant, trader, &c., has stopped or suspended, and has not resumed payment of his commercial paper, within a period of fourteen days." The phrase "commercial paper," as here employed, was intended, it seems to me, to embrace all paper which by usage or statute is brought within the custom of merchants. I think with LOWELL, J., *in re* Chandler, 4 N. B. R. 66, that in saying that any person belonging to one of certain designated classes should be deemed a bankrupt if he failed to pay his commercial paper, congress simply referred to a well-known and conclusive test of insolvency. The language of the act above quoted is a legislative declaration of insolvency applied to the particular classes named on account of their relation to t:e commercial world.

In *Davis* v. *Armstrong*, above cited, HALL, J., held that the statute extended to one, who at the time he made the note was a merchant, but had gone out of business before it became payable. Such a construction, however, would not warrant the conclusion that one who is within the letter, is not also within the meaning of the act. To embrace the first class, the statute must be so extended as to include persons not within its language ; while to exclude the second class, is to adopt a construction which rejects those who are expressly within its terms.

If the construction for which the respondent's counsel contend is the true one, it becomes necessary to inquire into the origin of the debt or promise in whose proof it is offered ; and a merchant, trader or manufacturer may suspend payment of all his commercial paper, except such as he has executed in connection with his particular trade or business, and yet maintain his standing for solvency in the commercial world. The dishonor of the paper of a merchant, trader or manufacturer, given when not engaged in business, or, if he were in business, given in some transaction not immediately connected with his business, is not less damaging to his commercial reputation than the dishonor of commercial paper given in the usual course of his business. One affords no better test of insolvency than the other.

When a man enters the commercial community as a merchant, trader, banker or otherwise, he assumes all the responsibilities which attach to his calling. One of these is the obligation to take care of all of his commercial paper, whether made before or after he commenced business; and whether given by him as the result of his particular business, or as the result of some transaction not directly within the scope of that business.

The respondent is adjudged bankrupt, and the proper decree will be entered.

McDONALD, BUTLER & McDONALD, for the petitioning creditors; PORTER, HARRISON & HINES, for the respondent.

———•••———

UNITED STATES DISTRICT COURT—KENTUCKY.

A landlord's right to rent, against the bankrupt's estate, expires on the day of adjudication. If the assignee occupy the premises after that day, he, and not the estate, is liable for the rent; when, however, his occupancy is for the benefit of the estate, he will be credited by the rent he is obliged to pay.

In re WEBB & CO.

The bankrupt held a lease from Gustavus Schurman's estate, now in th: hands of Robert Cochran, as receiver, by order of the Louisville chancery court, at an annual rental of two thousand seven hundred dollars, which lease expires on the first day of July, eighteen hundred and seventy-two. J. C. Webb & Co. were forced into bankruptcy on the ninth day of October, eighteen hundred and seventy-one, and the assignee took possession of the leased premises, and held the same up to January thirteenth, eighteen hundred and seventy-two, for the purpose of selling off the stock on hand, at which time the assignee paid all rent to January thirteenth, eighteen hundred and seventy-two, and offered to surrender the premises to the landlord. which surrender the landlord accepted, with the express understanding that he claimed the rent for the full term of the lease up to July first, eighteen hundred and seventy-two. The landlord afterwards rented the premises to another tenant at four hundred and fifty-two dollars and fifty cents less than J. C. Webb & Co. had agreed to pay to July first, eighteen hundred and seventy-two.

The case came up in an agreed statement of facts. The landlord claimed a lien under the statute laws of Kentucky, which gives the landlord a lien on the property of the tenant or sub-tenant on the leased premises for twelve months rent, due or to become due. The assignee claimed that he had a right under the bankrupt act to surrender the lease, and that neither the assignee nor the bankrupts' estate were liable to pay the sum of four hundred and fifty-two dollars and fifty cents, claimed by the landlord.

· BALLARD, J.—I am induced to the opinion that under the bankrupt act the landlord's right to rent against the bankrupt's estate expires on the day of the adjudication. If the assignee occupy the premises after that day, he, and not the estate, is liable for the rent. But, of course, when his occupancy is for the benefit of the estate, and is in fact beneficial, he will be credited by the rent which he is obliged to pay. In this case the rent should be paid to January thirteenth, eighteen hundred and seventy-two, and no longer.

UNITED STATES DISTRICT COURT—MARYLAND.

Where a petition is dismissed the debtor is entitled to receive by law the attorney's fees on a hearing in equity twenty dollars. No fee can be taxed for petitioner's attorney.

DUNDORE v. COATES & BROS.

This was a case in involuntary bankruptcy. The debtors filed a denial and upon trial before the court without a jury were adjudicated not to be bankrupts, and the petition was dismissed. The clerk taxed an appearance fee of twenty dollars for the attorneys for both parties. The following exceptions were made :

Exception is taken to the taxation of any attorney's fees at all. The appearance fee is only allowed to the attorney of the successful party. *Gordon* v. *Scott*, 2 N. B. R. 28. It is not allowed unless there is a trial by jury. *In re* Mead & Co. 28 Leg. Intel. 277.

The ten dollars for judgment without jury trial and the five dollars for discontinuance, are only allowed in actions at law. 10 Stat. at Large, 161. A proceeding in bankruptcy is not an action at law within the meaning of the statute.

GILES, J.—Exceptions in this case overruled so far as respects the costs taxed for the defendant. By the thirty-first of the general orders in bankruptcy, in a case where the petition shall be dismissed by order of the court, the debtor is entitled to recover from the petitioner the same costs that are allowed by law to a party recovering in equity. By the act of eighteen hundred and fifty-three (the fee bill) the attorney's fee on a hearing in equity is twenty dollars. No fee can be taxed for petitioning attorney in this case.

CIRCUIT COURT OF THE UNITED STATES—CONNECTICUT.

On a petition for a compulsory decree adjudging the respondent a bankrupt, the latter may deny that the petitioner is his creditor, may maintain such denial, overcome the *prima facie* proofs given by the petitioner, and the court must in that case dismiss the petition.

One who holds a claim which is barred by the statutes of limitation of the state in which he and the alleged debtor reside, cannot maintain a petition for an adjudication declaring such debtor a bankrupt.

It was not the intent or purpose of the bankrupt law to abrogate state statutes of limitation, and such is not its effect.

Whether congress has power to do so. *Quere.*

The cases, *In re* Ray, N. B. R. Sup. xliv.; *In re* Shepherd, 1 N. B. R. 115 ; *In re* Kingsley, 1 N. B. R. 52, 66 ; *In re* Hawden, 1 N. B. R. 98, on the question whether a debt barred by the statutes of limitation can be proved so as to entitle the holder to share in the estates of the bankrupt. Commented upon. If it be held that such debt cannot be allowed against the estate, it does not follow that the discharges of the bankrupt will not be a defence thereto if the bankrupt is sued thereon in another state.

Where a debt is barred by the statute of limitations, a promise by the debtor to pay it when able, has been regarded as a conditional promise and not to operate as a revival entitling the creditor to sue until ability to pay appears; but where there is a present debt a promise to pay it when able does not destroy or postpone the right of the creditor to sue, nor does it in anywise hinder or prevent the running of the statute.

Nor does a promise to deposit the money in a savings bank, to the account of the creditor, convert the relation of the parties into that of trustee and *cestui que trust*, so as to prevent the running of the statute.

A prior gift constitutes no legal consideration for a promissory note, and the claim of the holder to be a creditor may be defeated on that ground.

Where a debtor whose property exceeds in value all that he owes, for the purpose of paying all his debts and of securing to himself a maintenance in the future, conveys all his property to another upon an agreement that the latter shall pay all such debts and support the grantor for the residue of his life, such conveyance is not *per se* fraudulent or void as against creditors, nor an act of bankruptcy.

In re D. CORNWALL. *

On the sixteenth of June, eighteen hundred and seventy, Nathaniel O. Cornwall, a resident of Portland, in the district of Connecticut, presented to the district court his petition under the thirty-ninth and fortieth sections of the national bankrupt law, alleging that he is a creditor of David Cornwall, (his father) also a resident of said Portland, averring that the latter has committed an act of bankruptcy and praying that he be declared a bankrupt, &c.

The act of bankruptcy, as stated in the petition is : that

*See 4 N. B. R. 134.

the said David Cornwall, being possessed of certain estate or property situated in Portland, real and personal, and being indebted to the petitioner and others, did, on the thirty-first day of March, eighteen hundred and seventy, with a view to insolvency and with intent to delay, hinder or defraud, as the case may be, his creditors, convey the property mentioned in the petition to Maria and Elizabeth Cornwall, of the said Portland, (his daughters and sisters of the petitioner,) the same being all the property, real and personal, which he possessed or which could be held as security for the payment of his, the said David Cornwall's, just and lawful debts.

The indebtedness claimed by the petitioner, to constitute him a creditor of David Cornwall, is stated to be upon a promissory note for money loaned to the said David, dated Portland, August twenty-ninth, eighteen hundred and sixty-nine, for five hundred dollars, payable to the petitioner or his order on demand with interest from its date, and also the sum of five hundred and twenty dollars and eighty-eight cents, loaned to the said David, July fourteenth, eighteen hundred and fifty-four, the receipt of which is acknowledged in writing with a promise to deposit the same for the petitioner's benefit in the savings bank, together amounting to one thousand and twenty dollars and eighty-eight cents, exclusive of interest.

The respondent, David Cornwall, appeared and answered the petition, and by his answer denied that he is indebted to the petitioner in any sum whatever.

He admits that he did, on the thirty-first day of March, eighteen hundred and seventy, execute the alleged conveyance of all his property to his daughters Maria A., and Elizabeth, but denies that the same was done with a view to insolvency, or with any intent to delay, hinder or defraud his creditors, and states that at the time of such conveyance he had no creditors except his two daughters, (to whom he was then largely indebted,) and except a few small bills in the neighborhood not amounting to three hundred dollars,

In re Cornwall.

and that his two daughters in consideration of such conveyance promised and agreed with him that they would support
him during life and would pay all his debts then existing,
and that they are ready and willing to pay all valid claims
existing against him, and that they informed the petitioner
before he commenced the proceedings that they would pay
all valid claims he had against his said father. The answer
also states the history of the apparent indebtedness of the
respondent to the petitioner, in detail, averring that the five
hundred and twenty-eight dollars and eighty-eight cents,
received from the petitioner in eighteen hundred and fifty
four, was given to him by his said son in consideration of
and in part repayment of advances which he had made for
the education of the p titioner at college, in order to which
he had been compelled to borrow money, and that afterwards
in his advanced years he was embarrassed by debts which
he had been unable to pay, while his said son had accumulated large wealth, and such sum was given and received to
relieve him from such embarrassment and without any expectation that the respondent was to repay the same or be
considered or treated as a debtor to his said son therefor.
And further, that more than six years have elapsed since the
said sum was so given to him by his said son, and if the
same constituted a debt it has been barred by the statute of
limitations of the said state of Connecticut. That the note
for five hundred dollars, dated August twenty-ninth, eighteen
hundred and sixty-nine, was made without legal consideration. Such sum (of five hundred dollars) was a voluntary
gift made by the petitioner for the especial relief and benefit
of his aged and infirm mother, to be expended and in fact
was expended in repairing a portion of their dwelling house,
which had become old and decayed, and which the respondent had not means then to repair; that such repairs were
proposed by the petitioner, the furnishing of the money for
the purpose was tendered by him, and the repairs were consented to and were made by the respondent in assent to the
petitioner's proposal, and on his agreement to give the money

to pay therefor; that when the petitioner requested a note therefor he reiterated that the money was a gift, but stated that, as the respondent was then embarrassed by endorsements for another, he desired to hold a note for the benefit of his sisters, so that if the respondent should fail or die, he could present said note against the respondent's estate and obtain something for his said sisters, and the respondent, in confidence in his said son, gave a note as requested; and afterwards, on the twenty-ninth of March, eighteen hundred and sixty-nine, upon the request of the petitioner and his statement, that such note was lost, he gave him another note for the same purpose, which is the note mentioned in the petition, and is without consideration and void.

Upon the petition and answer, and upon the proofs of the parties respectively, the matter was brought to a hearing in the district court and the petition was dismissed. The opinion of the district judge shows that without deciding other questions he deemed it sufficient to find that the petitioner is not, in fact, a creditor of the respondent upon two principal grounds:

FIRST, That the note mentioned in the petition was without legal consideration, the moneys advanced and alleged by the petitioner to be the consideration of the note having been in truth and in fact a voluntary gift by the petitioner out of his abundance to and for the relief and comfort of his aged and infirm parents, and accepted as such, and,

SECOND, That if the moneys furnished to the father in eighteen hundred and fifty-four, and applied by him to the repayment of moneys borrowed, ever created or constituted an indebtedness by the father to the son, the latter was by the statute of limitations of the state of Connecticut barred from having or maintaining any action therefor, and he therefore had no standing thereupon to ask as a creditor that David Cornwall be decreed a bankrupt. *In re* Cornwall, 4 N. B. R. 134.

Upon this appeal or review of the order of the district court, it is insisted that the order should be reversed on various grounds, the chief of which may be stated and considered in the following order :

FIRST, That the petitioner having, by his petitio:: and the proofs furnished in support thereof, shown himself to be apparently or *prima facie* a creditor, the respondent was not at liberty by putting that fact in issue to have a trial of the question and an adjudication dismissing the petition, but the cause should have proceeded to a decree upon the matter charged as an act of bankruptcy, and that being established, the petitioner, when he offered proof of his debt with a view to share in the distribution of the estate, would, if his claim was contested and disallowed, be entitled to a trial by jury before its final rejection.

SECOND, That the proofs do not warrant the finding that the five hundred dollars advanced for the repairs of the respondent's dwelling house were, a gift, but on the contrary they show that the money was sought as a loan, advanced as a loan and secured as a loan by the promissory note of the respondent upon the loss of which the note mentioned in the petition was given as a new or substituted security.

THIRD, That the state statutes of limitation have no application to proceedings in bankruptcy. That notwithstanding the lapse of time the debt still exists, and while it may be true that in one or even more states no action will lie for its recovery, an action may be maintained therefor in another state if the respondent is found therein, and unless it is shown that it cannot be recovered in any of the United States, it must be declared a debt, and the court of bankruptcy, as a national tribunal, must recognize as a creditor any one who has a cause of action valid in any state of the Union.

FOURTH, That if the statute of limitations in Connecticut be in general recognized by the federal court in bankruptcy as disabling the holder of a claim from proceeding against his debtor, the petitioner's claim in the present case is not barred thereby for two reasons : 1st, The promise made in eighteen hundred and fifty-four, as it appears by the proofs in writing, was that the respondent would, " as soon as it is in his power," deposit it in the savings bank according to the petitioners previous direction, so that the latter would be able to control it at pleasure. It has not been proved that six years have elapsed since it was in the power of the respondent to do this, and therefore it does not appear that six years have elapsed since the cause of action accrued, or, 2d, The respondent held the money of the petitioner upon a trust to deposit it in the savings bank to the account of the petitioner, and to such a trust the statute of limitations does not apply. and therefore the claim is not barred.

MR. SIMEON E. BALDWIN for the petitioner ; MR. CHARLES E. PERKINS for the respondent.

WOODRUFF, J.—The claim that in proceedings for a compulsory decree declaring a respondent a bankrupt, the latter may not deny that the petitioner is a creditor, or may not by proofs maintain such denial and thereupon dismiss the petition, is wholly untenable.

It is true that where a party has been adjudged a bankrupt, no one claiming to be a creditor can be excluded from a share in the distribution of the estate without having the opportunity furnished by the twenty-fourth section, to appeal, and on that appeal to have his claim tried as in an action at law in the usual manner in the courts of the United States; but this does not reach the question whether a party has been made by the law liable to be declared a bankrupt at the instance of one who has in fact no claim against him and no interest in the question whether the party has committed an act of bankruptcy or not.

Section thirty-nine of the bankrupt law declares what shall be deemed acts of bankruptcy, and makes him who has committed such an act liable to be " adjudged a bankrupt on the petition of one or more of his creditors, the aggregate of whose debts provable under this act amount to at least two hundred and fifty dollars, provided such petition is brought within six months after the act of bankruptcy shall have been committed."

In re Cornwell.

To the maintenance of the petition, or to give the petitioner any standing in court, several things must concur: The petitioner must be a creditor; the debt due to him must be provable under the act, and the amount thereof must be at least two hundred and fifty dollars. Unless all these concur he has no right to prosecute the petition, and however he may be able to prove or does prove the commission of acts of bankruptcy, he is not by the law clothed with the right or power to begin or sustain a prosecution, or ask a decree. It is nowhere expressly or impliedly said that one who can furnish proof which unexplained and uncontradicted would show *prima facie* that he is such creditor, may file such a petition, or that a party may be adjudged a bankrupt upon such a petition. The objection goes not only to the disability of the petitioner, but to jurisdiction of the cause, and this should be so. It would be monstrous injustice if parties were not only liable to be proceeded against, but must necessarily be adjudged bankrupt, submit to a warrant and be dispossessed of all their property at the instance of anyone and everyone who either dishonestly or by mistake was able to present by petition and affidavits *prima facie* evidence of a debt, when in truth none existed. It might often happen that the only act of bankruptcy alleged depended for its character upon the very question whether any debt was owing to the petitioner, and if a mere *prima facie* case, shown by the petition, precluded further inquiry on that question, a party might be declared a bankrupt, his property be subjected to administration under the law, and in the end it would appear that the petitioner having no debt, no act of bankruptcy had been committed, and the whole proceeding, injurious as it must be, was wholly groundless. Not only so, no other creditor appearing, the proceeds of the estate must be returned to the person groundlessly prosecuted. If, therefore, there were nothing further in the act bearing upon this point, I should not hesitate to say that a respondent called by the petition into the district court had the clear and full right to meet the petitioner at the threshold of the proceeding by denying and disproving any of the facts, without which the petitioner has no authority in the law to maintain the proceeding. But section forty-one gives this right in express terms, and makes it the imperative duty of the court to proceed summarily to hear the allegations of the alleged debtor, and as to the commission of the act of bankruptcy it must order a trial by jury if he demands it, and if upon such hearing or trial the debtor proves that the facts set forth in the petition are not true, "the proceedings shall be dismissed and the respondent shall recover costs."

What are "the facts set forth in the petition?" Obviously all those which are by the thirty-ninth section necessary to make it the duty of the court to adjudge the respondent a bankrupt; that is to say, there must be before the court a creditor, by a provable debt, to the required amount, and this being true there must be established an act of bankruptcy within six months before the filing of the petition. Let it be supposed that the petition did not state all these facts, it cannot be doubted that it would be the duty of the court to dismiss it. So if the respondent shows that any of these facts when alleged in the petition are not true, the statute requires that the proceedings be dismissed.

The enquiry in the district court whether in this case the petitioner was a creditor, having a debt against the respondent provable under the act, was therefore a proper enquiry; and if it was properly found in the negative, the order dismissing the proceeding was not erroneous.

2. Upon the merits of the case there is to my mind a difficulty in sustaining the petitioner's application in the point upon which no opinion was expressed in the district court. As already observed, to warrant the adjudication sought, it must appear that an act of bankruptcy has been committed. In the petition herein the precise act upon which the petitioner relies is stated, viz: that the respondent being indebted to the petitioner and others, conveyed his property to Maria and Elizabeth Cornwall with a view to insolvency and with intent to delay, hinder or defraud, as

In re Cornwall.

the case may be, his creditors. Now the proof is that the object of the conveyance was the payment of all the debts of the respondent and to make provision for his support by his daughters in his old age. This was not a purpose fraudulent as to any one.

So far from being a conveyance with a view to insolvency, it contemplated actual solvency and actual payment of all he owed, and his property, according to the proof, was fully adequate and more than adequate for the purpose, even conceding that the petitioner was a creditor to the full amount which, according to his own statement of the transactions, he could be allowed.

Unless then the transaction was *per se* fraudulent and void as against creditors, it could not, upon this proof, be pronounced an act of bankruptcy. This raises the question; when a person whose property exceeds in value all that he owes, with a view to the payment of his debts and to secure to himself a maintenance in the future, conveys that property to another on an agreement that the grantee shall pay all that he (the grantor) owes, and support him during the residue of his days, is such conveyance *per se* fraudulent and void as against creditors?

Such arrangements by aged and infirm parents to relieve themselves of care and labor in their declining years have not heretofore been unusual. They are commonly made with children or with some one selected, and in a sense adopted, to stand in that relation.

The facts that the grantor is aged, infirm and incapable of labor to make his estate productive; that the grantee is already a creditor and therefore has a claim to receive a portion of such property; that the grantor owes but little, besides; that the grantee is already (irrespective of such conveyance,) of sufficient ability to pay all the debts, and that he proceeds to do so and stands ready and willing to pay all that the grantor owes, may not give a transaction validity, which on its face must be held fraudulent, but they do utterly repel the suggestion of fraudulent intent or purpose in the minds of the parties thereto, and all these facts concur in the present case, and according to the proofs here the only reason why the petitioner has not been paid is that there is a question, and a very serious question, to say the least, whether there is any debt whatever due to him. The grantees here have always been ready and willing, and have declared to the petitioner that they are ready and willing, to pay him whatever, if anything, his father owes him. If in fact anything is due he could not (had no such conveyance been made) recover it in the face of his father's denial thereof, until he had established the indebtedness by an appropriate proceeding therefor. And there is now no existing difficulty in obtaining payment when he has so established a debt, the said grantees being ready and willing thereupon to pay it, and being compellable to pay it by proofs and proceedings adapted to such a state of facts. Under such circumstances the allegation in the petition savors more of bitter, not to say malignant, hostility provoked by the confidence reposed by his father in his sisters, or some unexplained family dissension, than of any sincerity or belief, even by the petitioner, that his allegation of fraud is true.

The court below having expressed no opinion upon his point,[*] it received little attention from the counsel on the argument of the review in this court; I have therefore deemed it proper to examine the other grounds upon which the propriety of the order was discussed, instead of resting the decision upon a failure to prove an act of bankruptcy.

3. Upon the question whether upon the proofs it was rightly held that the petitioner was not a creditor of the respondent, it is not insisted that if the advance of five hundred dollars for the repairs of the dwelling house, was in fact a free gift, made chiefly for the relief and comfort of the petitioner's aged mother, and in part, as the evidence tended to show, to provide a room which the petitioner might conveniently occupy on his visits to his parents, there

[*] 4, N. B. R. 134.

was any error in holding that such gift constituted no legal consideration for the note set forth in the petition, or the prior note, for which on the loss thereof, the said note first mentioned was given; and that it being without legal consideration, the petitioner could not be held a creditor by reason thereof.

That the advance was a gift, voluntarily made, and accepted as such; that the repairs were consented to by the respondent, and the money received and expended upon that understanding, is distinctly found as a fact by the district judge upon the trial of the cause, with the witnesses before him and with an opportunity to hear, observe and consider, not only what the witnesses testified, but their appearance and their manner while testifying. Such finding, it is true, is not conclusive upon this hearing; it is open to review; but it ought not to be lightly regarded, nor should it be overruled except upon a very decided conviction that it is erroneous. A careful study of the evidence, aided by the suggestions of the petitioner's counsel, has not produced that conviction. On the contrary, the preponderance of the testimony is that it was a purely voluntary contribution by the son, under the then influence of filial affection towards his mother, to render her latter days more comfortable; that it was received as such and mutually so understood; that there was on the part of the respondent neither intention nor willingness to run in debt for the purpose, and that it was in distinct response to the son's offer to bear the expense that he consented to make the repairs. True, the giving of the note for the amount is very strong persuasive evidence that the respondent regarded it as a loan. Unexplained it might override the evidence of the previous offer and acceptance; but the explanation makes the whole transaction consistent. Upon further reflection, and in view of the motive which had prompted his generosity, it occurred to the son that as his father was under some endorsement or endorsements to a third person, and might "fail" or die insolvent, it might happen that his purpose to benefit his

mother by the gift might be defeated, and that he might
better secure his whole purpose if he could induce his father
to execute a note to be held, and in such a contingency be
made a claim against his estate for the benefit of his mother
and sisters. Whatever might be said of such a design if the
contingency had happened and the attempt had been made
thus to withdraw a portion of that estate from creditors, it
is clear that such an arrangement was entirely consistent
with the original and actual intent of the petitioner to advance the money as a gift, and with its acceptance and
appropriation to the repairs, upon that understanding. So
that it not only remains true that the consideration for the
note was a gift, but the force of the evidence, which the
giving of the note involves, is weakened and in fact overcome
by the proof of the purpose for which it was solicited by the
petitioner and given by his father. And this view of the
subject is greatly strengthened by the fact that when, on the
representation that the first note was lost, another was given,
there was no claim for interest as upon a loan to the father.

If it appeared that upon all other grounds the note was
a valid note, I should hesitate at least in allowing parol
evidence of an agreement with the father, either prior or co-
temporaneous therewith, that he should not be held bound
to pay it, but on the question whether it ever had any legal
consideration, whether the money advanced was a gift which
neither party intended or expected would be repaid, or would
create any indebtedness by the respondent; the fact that it
was not treated as a debt, that the father was never called
upon to pay it, that when a note was given in apparent renewal thereof, it was not treated as if given for a loan and
no interest was charged, go very strongly in support of the
direct testimony to the point in controversy.

4. Whether, where the statutes of limitations of the state
in which the parties reside, have created a bar to the recovery of an alleged debt by action, the holder may nevertheless pursue the alleged debtor under the bankrupt law,
and by that means compel its payment, is a question of wider

and greater importance than the immediate effect of this particular litigation.

In the present case both parties reside in the state of Connecticut. If the advance secondly mentioned in the petition was a loan or created an indebtedness, it was for money received by the respondent in this state in the year eighteen hundred and fifty-four, he then and ever since residing here. For the purposes of this question it is assumed that such advance did create a debt, and therefore that the cause of action arose more than fifteen years before the filing of the petition in the district court, and is within the statute of the state which declares that no action "shall be brought but within six years after the right of action shall accrue."

In the construction of this statute and in declaring its effect the courts of the state hold that the statute does not merely prohibit the maintenance of an action technically so called, but it bars the claim in whatever form it may be asserted. They declare that it applies to the nature of the indebtedness as well as to the form of the action; that though in terms applicable to actions only, it applies to all claims which may be the subjects of actions however presented; that the lapse of time prescribed as a bar is regarded as furnishing a presumption of payment; that this presumption, when it is not overcome by a new promise withdrawing it from the operation of the statute, is conclusive, and that the presumption from the lapse of time, is that the defendant has lost the evidence which would have availed him in his defense if seasonably called upon for payment. Hence after the lapse of six years the claim can no more be used as a set-off than it can be made the subject of an action in form. Nor can it be successfully urged before commissioners appointed by a court of probate to receive and allow claims against the estate of a deceased with a view to the distribution of such estate. This construction and declaration of the effect of the Connecticut statute establishes fully that the claim of this petition is in their view and by force of the statute absolutely barred. The appropriation of the estate of a deceased to the payment of his debts by an auditing and allowance thereof presents a close analogy to the appropriation of the estate of a bankrupt, and in effect the Connecticut courts declare that no legal claim exists in favor of the petitioner, if the statutes of limitation of this state are to have their actual legal operation. See on this subject, *Robbins* v. *Harvey*, 5 Conn. 335, and Hart's appeal from Probate, 32 Conn. 520, and the cases there cited.

The federal courts sitting within the respective states regard their statutes of limitation, and give them the interpretation and effect which they receive in the courts of the state. This has been repeatedly declared in the supreme court of the United States, and is now the familiar practice. *Shelby* v. *Grey*, 11 Wheat. 361; *McCluny* v. *Silliman*, 3 Peters, 270; *Green* v. *Neal's Lessee*, 6 id. 291; *Ross* v. *Duval*, 13 id. 45, and cases therein cited.

In the case of *Ross* v. *Duval*, McLEAN, J., says: "These acts are of daily cognizance in the courts of the United States, and no one has ever doubted that in *fixing the rights* of parties they must be regarded as well in the federal as in the state courts." More than this, instead of regarding the nature and design of statutes of limitation as a mere withholding of the remedy, while a subsisting cause of action is nevertheless supposed to continue, the supreme court in recent cases regard them as proceeding on the presumption which, as above stated, the courts of Connecticut declare to lie at their foundation. Thus, in the *United States* v. *Wiley*, 11 Wallace, 513, STRONG, J., says: "Statutes of limitation are indeed statutes of repose. They are enacted upon the presumption that one having a well founded claim will not delay enforcing it beyond a reasonable time, if he has the power to sue."

In *Levy* v. *Stewart*, 11 Wallace, 249, CLIFFORD, J., says : "Statutes of limitation exist in all the states. * * * They are regarded as statutes of repose arising from the lapse of time and the antiquity of transactions. And they also proceed upon the presumption that claims are extinguished whenever they are not litigated in the'proper form within the prescribed period." See also the recognition of state statutes of limitation and their binding force in the federal courts, in *Stewart* v. *Kahn*, 11 Wall. 493, and *Hanger* v. *Abbott*, 6 Wall. 532.

It may be suggested that an act of congress (act of September twenty-four, seventeen hundred and eighty-nine, section thirty-four, 1 Stat. at Large, 92,) requires the federal courts, sitting in the respective states, to make the laws of such states the rules of decision in trials at common law, and that the recognition of state statutes of limitation is founded on that act. Doubtless the act so requires, but it does not follow that, looking to the grounds upon which statutes of limitation proceed, as above stated in repeated cases, the federal courts would not have recognized those statutes as a defence had there been no such act of congress. The reason of the statutes and the obvious justice of giving them due application, as well as consistency of adjudication, and the right of each state to prescribe the conditions and limitations of the liabilities of its citizens, all forbid that a plaintiff should be legally entitled to recover in the federal court against one whose defence is perfect in the state tribunals. The terms of the act of congress do not reach the federal courts when sitting as courts of equity, and yet it is certain that as courts of equity they do recognize and allow lapse of time as a defence in precise analogy to the statutes of limitation in cases where such analogy is appropriate. Besides this, if the act of congress be the ground of these decisions in the federal courts, it may be regarded, for the purposes of this question, as an adoption by congress of the statutes of limitation of the respective states within which the federal courts are held, and thereupon the same rules of interpretation and of application obtain, as are above stated to govern the state courts, and the foundation and scope of the statutes will be as also above stated. This leads to the same result. They will be held to apply to claims according to their nature and in whatever form asserted, they will be deemed statutes of repose, proceeding upon presumption of payment, and of loss of evidence, and will bar all claims which may be the subjects of actions at law however presented. And hence also their recognition by the federal courts when sitting as courts of equity, as furnishing the proper analogy.

With these declarations before us of the nature, foundation and effect of statutes of limitation by the courts of the state and of the United States, and in the face of the well settled recognition thereof by the latter in their several circuits and districts, at law and in equity, we are called upon to say that, when sitting as a court of bankruptcy in the state of Connecticut, the district court of the United States may and must disregard the statutes of limitation of the state, entertain a party alleging a claim long since barred as a prosecutor, upon his demand take possession of the estate of the respondent and actually appropriate such estate to the payment of such claim. And this is claimed notwithstanding section second of the bankrupt law requires this court, on a review of the proceedings, to determine all cases arising under that law as in a court of equity.

If there be any warrant for thus calling upon the district court to depart from the settled rule governing the federal courts on this subject, it must be sought in the express provisions of the bankrupt law, in its necessary construction, or in an evident intent of congress to produce this result, manifested in the act itself or in the circumstances of its enactment.

It is not claimed that there is any express declaration in the act forbidding the court, sitting in bankruptcy, from giving the same effect to the statutes of limitation of the state in which the court is held, which it would be bound to give in a litigation between the same parties in any other form, either at law or in equity. Nor in my judgment does its language in any respect, or its necessary construction as a system of bankruptcy, work such a result.

When it employs the terms debtor and creditor, debt, claim, demand and other like or kindred terms, as a guide to the court in the discharge of its duty within the jurisdiction where it is acting, it uses those terms in their usual accepted sense, and they are to be applied by the court within that jurisdiction and tested there. When the enquiry arises in the circuit or district court of the United States for the district of Connecticut; whether between two citizens of that state the relation of debtor and creditor exists, whether A. B. has a debt against C. D., it is to be answered by the enquiry; is C. D. under a legal obligation to pay money to A. B.? Has A. B. a claim which the law will recognize as entitling him to recover money from C. D.? The law of the jurisdiction answers the question.

It is suggested that the question in the federal court must be answered by enquiring, whether in any state of the United States such claim would be recognized as a debt entitling A. B. to a recovery from C. D., if he were brought within its jurisdiction; and if yea, then it must be so recognized by the federal court for the district of Connecticut, within the jurisdiction of which he is, and in which the question of his liability is to be determined; and, therefore, if it appear that should C. D. be found in Wisconsin, the courts of that state would treat him as a debtor, he must be so treated here. Or, in effect, the rights and responsibilities of a resident of Connecticut are to be determined by the laws of Wisconsin, and not by the laws of this state, though the matter arises here. The principle of this argument is nothing s ort of this: if he would be held a debtor anywhere, he must be held a debtor in the district court of the United States for the district of Connecticut. There is no ground for restricting the meaning of the words "debt" or "debtor," to a liability which would be enforced within the states of this Union. If, for the mere reason that by the laws of Wisconsin a resident citizen of Connecticut could be adjudged to pay what is claimed as a debt, provided he were found there, he must also in the district court for Con-

necticut be adjudged a debtor, it must be because, if anywhere such claim could be so enforced, it must be here; and
in short, whatever in any place on this globe could be recovered as a debt, if the parties should be subjected to its
jurisdiction, is a debt within the meaning of the bankrupt
law, and must be so treated by the federal courts, wherever
they are exercising their jurisdiction as courts of bankruptcy.

There is no law of the United States defining a debt or
describing a creditor, except as one to whom a debt is due.
The bankrupt law speaks of debts due and payable either
presently or at a future day. An alleged debt is not to be
deemed due and payable if the claimant cannot by law compel its payment. It is conceded by the argument that this
is true, if by the law of no state of the United States such
payment could be compelled, if the parties were there. No
reason can be assigned for this limitation, as already suggested, and if there is any foundation for the argument, the
proposition should be: If payment could be compelled anywhere on the habitable globe, were the parties there, then
it must be treated as a debt in this court and in this district.

In my judgment, the district court for Connecticut had
not, nor have I, sitting in this district, anything to do with
the question, what are the laws of Wisconsin, or what are
the laws of China, when considering the relation between
two resident citizens of Connecticut, growing out of transactions in this state. The parties to this controversy are not
and have not been in Wisconsin. The transaction did not
arise in Wisconsin. Neither the parties nor the subject
matter have ever been and are not under the jurisdiction of
that state, or affected by its laws; and whether, in the supposed contingency of the respondent's going to that state,
and being pursued there by the petitioner, the latter could
establish and recover a sum of money from him as a debt,
seems to me wholly irrelevant to the enquiry before the district court, and just as irrelevant as the same question would
be if applied to China. The respondent is not there; he is

in Connecticut. He is pursued in Connecticut, and here he is to be judged; not by the laws of Wisconsin, nor by the laws of China.

It may be that in some state of the United States, no statutes of limitation exist; or at least, for the purpose of testing this question, we may assume that to be possible. If so, then upon the argument the legislation of Connecticut, in all respects just, wise and entitled to favor, exercised for the protection of the citizens of that state and within its competent power, is to be defeated and rendered wholly inoperative, because some other state has no such enactment. It is using very moderate terms to say that such a view of the subject is unreasonable, and one of which the inhabitants of the several states within their respective limits might justly complain.

When the enquiry is permitted, what was the intent of congress, inferable from the terms of the act, or from any other considerations, or what should be deemed the true construction of the act, when it is open to construction, it is, as it seems to me, conclusive to observe, that the grounds taken by the counsel for the petitioner inevitably result in this: that congress, by the bankrupt law, has abrogated wholly all the statutes of limitation of the several states; not, it is true, in very terms, but in every case has destroyed their effect as a protection against stale demands. The enactment of such laws, as statutes of repose, as a protection against unfounded claims and debts presumptively paid, and to stand as a defence, when presumptively the evidence is lost which would have availed the defendant if the claim were seasonably prosecuted, is within the unquestionable sphere of state legislation. In regard to its own inhabitants and to transactions within its own limits, the state may properly insist upon its power in this respect, and the uncontrolled right to exercise it for the benefit of its citizens. If so, the congress of the United States is not to be deemed to have legislated in contravention of that power, or so as to destroy its efficiency, unless the terms or necessary construction of the act very clearly import such an intent. Indeed the question may pertinently be asked, has congress the power to pass an act which shall work such a result? It has power to enact uniform laws on the subject of bankruptcy throughout the United States. If power to pass such laws necessarily involved the power to abrogate all laws of a state designed for the protection of its inhabitants within its own limits for the purposes and upon the grounds on which statutes of limitation proceed; if bankrupt laws, as understood and constructed when the constitution was adopted, had the effect (notwithstanding statutes of limitation) to let in stale demands, and to permit the claimants to prosecute in bankruptcy, it might be claimed, at least, that power in congress was not wanting. But it was conceded on the argument herein, that the bankrupt laws of England have no such effect, and that the court of bankruptcy, like courts of equity, recognizes the statute of limitation as a bar. See 1 Arch. on Bankruptcy, ed. of 1867, 533; 2 Doria & McCrea on Bankruptcy, 787; *ex parte* Dewdney, 15 Ves. 478; 2 Rose R. 59; *ex parte* Roffey, 19 Ves. 468; *ex parte* Ross, 2 Glyn & J. 46; *Gregory* v. *Hurrill*, 1 Bing, 324; 8 Moore 190; *in re* Clendenning, 9 Irish Ch. R. 284; *ex parte* Woodward, 3 Deacon 294; *ex parte* Topping, 34 L. J., n. s. 44; *ex parte* Kidd, 7 Jur., n. s. 613.

The practical consequence of the claim here asserted by the petitioner also requires us to say, that congress in the enactment of the bankrupt law had no intention to override state statutes of limitation. Examples are numerous, of citizens who have for many years reposed in safety under the protection of those laws, and have been able from the earnings of careful industry to save some provision for old age, sickness, or the education of their children, and now, by the warrant of the bankrupt law, stale claims are produced; they are made the basis of prosecution in bankruptcy; acts otherwise wholly just and proper are called fraudulent, and deemed acts of bankruptcy by reason of such stale claims, now elevated to the character of debts; parties who could not, in any form, maintain a claim, in any court whatever having jurisdiction of the parties, become prosecutors; all the legal presumptions of payment or other defense, or loss of evidence, on which statutes of limitation are founded, are disregarded; and all that the now indeed unfortunate respondents have is swept away. Truly, if this be so, congress has provided a new way to collect old debts.

This was not the purpose or design of the law, and I cannot yield my assent to the argument which gives it such an operation. It is true that the consequences adverted to are not of such force as to control an express constitutional provision of an act of congress, but they are of great importance when an incidental effect is sought to be given to the act, which is not necessarily involved in its express words.

We are not left to the considerations which are above suggested as our sole guide to the determination of this question. The act itself, so far from declaring that the statutes of limitation shall not affect the prosecutor of the petition, contains a provision which seems very clearly to indicate that such statutes are to be regarded in the court of bankruptcy as fully as they have heretofore been recognized in the federal courts.

It was conceded by the counsel for the petitioner, that had the respondent been adjudged a bankrupt, the claim of the petitioner would nevertheless be open to contention; his debt must be established. This concession was clearly correct. The mere fact that he is a petitioner is not conclusive upon other creditors that he is to be allowed in the distribution of the estate just what he claims in his petition; nor is it conclusive upon the assignee. If this were not so, collusion between a debtor and a petitioner setting up a pretended but fictitious claim would work the grossest injustice. In the first instance the validity of claims and their title to allowance in the distribution of the estate are passed upon in the district court. (Sections twenty-two and twenty-three.) If rejected, an appeal lies to the circuit court; and here the claimant must file a statement setting forth his claim substantially as in a declaration for the same cause of action at law, and the assignee must plead or answer thereto in like manner, and like proceedings must thereupon be had in the pleadings, trial, and *determination* of the cause as in an action at law commenced and prosecuted *in the usual manner* in the courts of the United States. * * * Section twenty-four.

This section clearly imports that the assignee may interpose any legal defence whatever, which could be interposed in an ordinary action in the United States' courts, and the issue must on the trial be determined and judgment must be pronounced as in such an action. It has already been seen that, in actions at law in those courts, the state statutes of limitation are fully recognized as a defence, and they must, by the clear language of this section, be in like manner available on such an appeal, and the claim of this petitioner must in such case be rejected. The bankrupt act, therefore, not only does not abrogate the state statute of limitations, but here plainly warrants its interposition as a defence and requires the court to sustain it. That act has doubtless furnished some new defences, but it has deprived the party of none which were available in an ordinary action at law for the same cause.

This is also apparent from the provisions of the twenty-first section, which, although it provides for a temporary stay of pending suits, permits them to proceed to judgment. Clearly, therefore, the defence of the statute of limitations, whenever it has been interposed, must avail in all such suits.

These provisions seem to me to show conclusively, that nothing was further from the intention and effect of the bankrupt law than to deprive a party and his estate of the protection of such laws ; nor could language be better adapted to secure their benefit as a defence against stale claims. And this should be so. No equity pertains to a prosecutor in a court of bankruptcy to be allowed to enforce a claim which in a court of law and in a court of equity,

In re Cornwall.

(which proceeds in analogy to the statute of limitations,) would be rejected. He is in no worse condition than in either of those courts. All that can be suggested is, that if courts of bankruptcy recognize state statutes of limitation, and yet the discharge of a bankrupt operates against claims barred thereby, the claimants lose their chance of finding their alleged debtor in some other state and compelling payment. So far as this applies to the present petitioner, or any other prosecuting in this district, the answer is easy; if he prosecute the respondent in any other form, the effect is precisely the same ; the judgment in an action at law here' would forever bar any prosecution of an action in any other state.

The precise question in this case is whether one who alleges that he is a creditor by a debt which under the state law is barred can become a prosecutor in the court of bankruptcy, and demand that, on his petition and proofs, the respondent be adjudged a bankrupt. A conflict of opinion is found in the decisions of some of the district courts on the question whether after a debtor has been adjudged a bankrupt a debt barred by the state statute should be allowed to share in the distribution of the estate. *In re* Ray, N. B. R. Sup. xliv; *in re* Sheppard, 1 N. B. R. 115; *in re* Kingsley, 1 N. B. R. 52, 66 ; *in re* Harden, 1 N. B. R. 97.

Many of the views above suggested are ably presented in the discussion of that question. Incidentally to that discussion the question has arisen whether if such claims are not allowed, the discharge of the bankrupt would avail as a defence thereto, if he should afterwards be sued in another state. If it can be successfully insisted that a claimant can be permitted to prove his claim and share in the estate who could not have prosecuted the respondent and required the court to adjudge him a bankrupt, then the decision herein determines nothing on the question thus in conflict. It is, however, obvious that the views here expressed are quite pertinent to that question. It is therefore not irrelevant to add, that the apprehended consequence of leaving the discharged bankrupt exposed to prosecution and judgment for all claims barred by the laws of the state in which the discharge is granted, if he be found in another state, because they are held in the bankrupt court not to constitute the claimant a creditor, nor to entitle him to share in the distribution of the estate, is not necessarily the result of such a holding. True, it is declared (section thirty-four) that a discharge shall * * * "release the bankrupt from all debts, claims, &c., which were or might have been proved against his estate in bankruptcy," and in another form (section thirty-two) the order of the court must direct a discharge "from all debts and claims which by the said act are made provable against his estate." Whether a claim is provable or not is to be determined by its nature and not by enquiring whether it is possible to establish it. Provision is made in the act itself for the exclusion of many debts and claims which are in their nature provable; but it is not questionable that they are nevertheless released by the discharge; e. g., under section twenty-three, one who has accepted a preference contrary to the provisions of the act shall not prove his debt or claim nor receive a dividend, unless he has surrendered to the assignee the property received by him; the right of a mortgagee or pledgee to prove his debt is qualified by section twenty; by section thirty-five, one who obtains money or property as an inducement for forbearing to oppose or for consenting to the debtor's discharge, is excluded from any share in the estate; a creditor having reasonable cause to believe his debtor insolvent, &c., who receives a conveyance or payment as mentioned in the thirty-ninth section, is not allowed to prove his debt in bankruptcy. It is not at all doubtful that the discharge, if granted, is equally effectual as against such creditors to release the bankrupt as it is against any other creditor.

This is sufficient to show that a holding that an alleged debt is in the court of bankruptcy, as well as in a court of law or court of equity, barred by the statute of limitations, does not necessarily include a holding that the bankrupt cannot successfully plead his discharge as a defence thereto, should an action be afterwards brought against him in this or any other state.

The rejection of the claim by the court of bankruptcy proceeds upon the same ground as its rejection in a court of law, when there tried, whether in an ordinary action or on the appeal from its disallowance, (section twenty-four,) viz. : that it has no legal existence, that it is not a debt due and payable, and, therefore, if an action were afterwards brought therefor, it would stand just as a claim would stand, which on such an appeal and trial was found usurious, or to have arisen out of an illegal transaction, or to have been released or paid, or to be held by one who was forbidden to prove his debt by section thirty-nine. In either case the claim thus rejected is found not provable against the estate, and yet in such subsequent action therefor, the discharge would be a conclusive defence.

For the foregoing reasons I am clearly of opinion that a petitioner alleging a claim which is barred by the statutes of limitation, cannot maintain a petition in involuntary bankruptcy for an adjudication declaring his alleged debtor a bankrupt.

5. The suggestion that the advance of money made by the petitioner in eighteen hundred and fifty-four is not within the statute of limitations, because it was held as a trust, or, because the promise to repay it being conditional, six years have not elapsed since the cause of action accrued, is not sustained by a just view of the actual transaction.

Taking the account of the advance as given by the petitioner himself, (and therefore assuming that it was not made and received as a partial return of the money advanced by the father for the education of the son,) there has never been a moment when the son could not have maintained an action of assumpsit at law therefor. If treated as a loan, or as payable at all, it was payable whenever the lender saw fit to require it. Depositing it in the savings bank to the credit of the son was a mode suggested which would have been satisfactory; but the son could have required payment to himself personally at any moment, and the savings bank was merely constituted the agent to receive it.

The statement of the father in his letter, that he would deposit it as soon as in his power, called out no dissent; but there was no contract binding upon the son which required him to forbear; it was, therefore, payable on demand, and the statute began to run from the time the advance was made. The debt, if any, existed from that time. Where a debt is already barred by the statute of limitations, a promise by the debtor to pay it when he is able has been regarded as conditional and not to create an obligation, as a revival of the debt, until ability to pay appears, but where there is a present debt, a promise to pay it when able does not destroy the right of the creditor to sue, nor postpone such right, and it in nowise hinders or prevents the running of the statute.

I am inclined to say, also, that if the transaction were treated as a contract to pay when the respondent was able, and was binding as such upon both parties, the proofs show no change in the pecuniary condition of the father since that time ; he was able, in fact, to repay it when he received it, and ever since. True, he was embarrassed by the debts he incurred in providing for his son's education, and he wished to pay them, and did not wish to sell his farm for the purpose, but he was not insolvent. He wished to retain his property as a means of support for himself and family, but it is idle to say that, had his son brought an action of assumpsit at law for money lent, the father could have defended successful y on the ground of any inability to pay, shown by the proofs in this cause, or upon any idea of a trust cognizable only in a court of equity.

The order dismissing the petition herein was in no respect erroneous, and it must be affirmed with costs.

Affirmed accordingly.

UNITED STATES CIRCUIT COURT—ALABAMA.

On review of a motion in the United States court to appoint a receiver to take possession of the property of a corporation already ordered to be delivered to a receiver appointed by a state court. *Held*, That the jurisdiction of the two courts was concurrent; that the jurisdiction of the state court was first invoked and asserted, consequently no court of concurrent jurisdiction can or ought to interfere with it.

Motion continued, to allow the defendants to set up the facts in regard to the proceedings of the chancery court of Sumter county by formal answer.

BLAKE v. THE ALABAMA & CHATTANOOGA R. R. CO. *et al.*

WOODS, J.—I have listened with interest and attention to the re-argument of the motion for the appointment of a receiver in this case, and upon the points argued and decided at the first hearing have not been able to reach any different conclusions from those already announced.

On the re-argument, however, a fact in the case was stated and pressed upon the attention of the court, which was not stated in the first argument, or if it was, must have been overlooked. It is now stated, and the statement is supported by affidavits, that on the fourth day of September, eighteen hundred and seventy-one, a bill was filed in the name of the state of Alabama, complainant, in the chancery court of the state of Alabama for the county of Sumter, against the Alabama & Chattanooga Railroad Co. and others, defendants, seeking a foreclosure of the first mortgage executed by said railroad company upon its property and franchises, on account of interest due on the bonds secured by mortgage, which interest has been paid by the state of Alabama, in default of payment by the railroad company, and praying the appointment of a receiver of the property and effects of raid company. That upon the motion for the appointment of a receiver, said cause had been heard by the chancellor of the western division of the state of Alabama, who had sustained the motion, and appointed Charles Walsh, receiver, and that Walsh had accepted said trust and given bond. The interlocutory decree of the state chancellor, appointing a receiver, directs him to take possession of all the property both real and personal, within the state of Alabama, of said railroad company, and if the same is not delivered that a writ of possession be issued by the register of the court, and a writ of attachment against all persons refusing to deliver said property.

The bill in this case now on hearing was not filed until the twelfth day of September, eighteen hundred and seventy-one, eight days after the filing of the bill in the state chancery court. The motion is now to appoint a receiver to take possession of the property already ordered to be delivered to Walsh by the state chancery court.

On a motion addressed to its sound discretion, ought this court to make the order prayed for ?

The state court had jurisdiction of the subject matter of the suit before it and of the parties. Its jurisdiction was first invoked and asserted. It is too well settled to need citation of many authorities that as between courts of concurrent jurisdiction that which first acts is entitled to exercise its jurisdiction to the exclusion of the others. The courts of the United States and those of a state have concurrent jurisdiction in many cases, but when persons or property are liable to seizure or arrest by the process of both that which first attached is entitled to the preference. *Ex parte* Jenkins, 2 Wall. Jr. 521; *Smith* v. *McIver*, 9 Wheat. 532; *Shelby* v. *Bacon*, 10 How. 56; *Taylor* v. *Carryl*, 24 How. 583; *Mallett* v. *Dexter*, 1 Curt. 178; The Robert Fulton, 1 Pa. 621; *ex parte* Robinson, 6 McLean, 355.

In *Wiwall* v. *Sampson*, 14 How. 52, the supreme court held that when certain lands were held in the hands of a receiver appointed by the chancery court of Alabama in a case pending before it they could not be sold by the marshal upon process of execution issuing out of the circuit court of the United States for that district, although the judgment upon which the process issued was a lien upon the land, and the execution was laid before the receiver obtained actual possession of the property. In the same case the Court says: " When a receiver has been appointed his possession is that of the court, and any attempt to disturb it without leave of the court first obtained will be a contempt on the part of the person making it. This was held in *Angel* v. *Smith*, 9 Ves., 335, both with respect to receivers and sequestrators. When, therefore, a party is prejudiced by having a receiver put in his way the course has been either to give him license to bring an ejectment or to permit him to be examined *inter esse suo.*"

So in *Peale* v. *Phipps, et al.,* 14 How. 374, under note of the legislature of Mississippi, the charter of the Agricultural Bank had been declared forfeited, and the plaintiff in error appointed trustee. Commissioners, also, were at the same time appointed to audit the accounts, who rejected the claim sued on. Upon their refusal to allow it the defendants in error instituted proceedings in the circuit court of the United States for the eastern district of Louisiana. Upon these facts the court says: "We see no ground upon which the jurisdiction of the court can be sustained. The plaintiff in error held the assets of the bank as the agent and receiver of the court of Adams county, and subject to its order. He had given bond for the performance of this duty, and would be liable to an action if he paid any claim without the authority of the court from which he received his appointment, and to which he was accountable. The property in legal contemplation was in the custody of the court of which he was an officer, and has been placed there by the laws of Mississippi ; and while it thus remained in the custody and possession of that court, awaiting its order and decision, no other court had a right to interfere with it or to wrest it from the hands of its agent, and thereby put it out of his power to perform his duty."

The case of *Williams* v. *Benedict, et al.,* 8 How. 107, is also in point: By a law of Mississippi, if it appeared to the orphans' court that the estate of a deceased person was insolvent, it was made the duty of the court to direct the property to be sold by the executor or administrator, and to appoint commissioners to audit the claims of creditors, and to distribute the proceeds of the property among the creditors in proportion to the sum due them respectively. The appellant was the administrator of an intestate whose estate had been declared insolvent by the orphans' court. But the appellees had obtained a judgment against the administrator in the district court of the United States for the northern district of Mississippi, before the adjudication of insolvency by the orphans' court, and issued an execution, and laid it upon property upon which his judgment was a lien in case the estate was not insolvent. And upon a bill filed by the appellant to obtain an injunction staying proceedings upon this execution the appellees insisted that the estate was not insolvent, but had been wasted by the administrator, and that the proceedings in the orphans' court under the law of Mississippi were in bar to his recovering in a court of the United States, and the district court was of that opinion, and dismissed the appellant's bill. But the decree was reversed by the supreme court of the United States upon the ground that the jurisdiction of the orphans' court had attached to the amounts, and that they were *in gremio legis*, and could not be seized by process from another court.

The result of these authorities is, that when a court having jurisdiction has exercised and has taken possession of property rightfully, and is in the process of administering it, no court of concurrent jurisdiction ought to interfere with it, or can interfere. The chancery court of Sumter county is a court of general equity jurisdiction. It has obtained jurisdiction over the person of the defendant, the Alabama and Chattanooga R. R. Co, in a bill to foreclose a mortgage on property within its territorial jurisdiction. It has make a decree for the appointment of a receiver, and has directed him to take possession of and administer the property of the railroad company within the state of Alabama. Whether he has taken actual possession is a matter of no consequence. He has the right as the officer of the court, and it is his duty to take possession. How, then, can this court interfere with. his lawful authority, and the lawful ·powers of the court by whom he is appointed? Suppose this court appoints a receiver, as prayed, how is he to get possession of the property which is in course of administration in another court? Suppose the receiver of that other court resists, as is his duty, the authority of the receiver appointed by this court? We should have a scandalous spectacle of a contest between courts of concurrent jurisdiction, which it is the imperative duty of such courts to avoid, a contest in which this court would be clearly in the wrong. For in these matters *qui prior in tempore potior est in jure.*

, I have examined the cases cited by counsel for complainant. *Buck* v. *Colbath*, 3 Wall. 334; *Watson* v. *Sutherland*, 5 Wall. 74; *Payne* v. *Hook*, 7 Wall. 425; *Covington Bridge Co.* v. *Shepperd*, 21 How. 112, and can find in them no warrant for such action as is asked of this court. It is to be noted that the purpose of this bill is to obtain the appointment of a receiver to take possession of and administer property which is already in the hands of another court and in process of administration. This court could not even enjoin, on a bill filed for that purpose, the proceedings of the state court, much less can it interfere with its action in an irregular and forcible manner. For unless the proceedings in the Sumter chancery court are void, the question between that court and this on the appointment of the receiver here prayed for, would be a question of force to be decided by wager of battle. The Sumter court has this property in hand to be administered in a certain way for a certain purpose. Because this court desires to administer it in the different way it would not be authorized to interfere with the proceedings of the state court.

There is but one ground upon which this court would be justified in the action invoked, and that is, the want of jurisdiction in the state court, and as a consequence, the invalidity of its proceedings.

The state is authorized by section 3323 Revised Code, to sue a citizen of the state or a domestic corporation, in chancery, and the suit is to be governed by the same rules as suits between individuals. The state has a mortgage lien upon the property of a domestic corporation, the Alabama and Chattanooga Railroad Co. She may, under this clause, foreclose her mortgage by bill in equity. This is a right which all mortgagees have for default in payment of either principal or interest, secured by the mortgage. If it should turn out to be true that neither principal nor interest was due on the mortgage, that is a matter of defense which would not oust the jurisdiction of the court. It would have jurisdiction to try the question whether the principal or interest was due. And if the defendant should set up by way of defence that the state had, under a contract not to foreclose until the entire amount secured by the mortgage, both principal and interest, became due, such defense, even if established, would not oust the jurisdiction of this court. It would have jurisdiction to try the question whether the state had made any such contract. The proceedings to foreclose would not be void for want of jurisdiction, because the defendant might have a good defense.

But I am quite clear that the state has made no contract by which she has denied herself the right to foreclose her mortgage for non-payment of interest. The law authorizing her to sue in equity was in the statute book when the internal improvement act was passed. The remedies granted by that act appear to be merely accumulative, leaving the state her option either to follow them or to pursue her rights as a mortgagee.

I am satisfied that the state had the right to sue; that the chancery court of Sumter county had jurisdiction of the person of the defendant, and of the subject matter of the suit, and that this jurisdiction is not ousted by the fact that the defendant claims that the state cannot now maintain her action—in other words that her suit is premature. Whether the defence is a good one is for the decision of the court where the suit is pending.

There appears to be no obstacle to prevent the complainant in this case from making himself a party to the suit in the state court. The law authorises the state to file its bill in equity against a domestic corporation and the suit is to be governed by the same rules as suits between individuals. All persons, whether residents of the state or not, who are interested in the subject matter of the suit, may be, on petition, made parties defendant, and being made parties, they have the same right against the state as in a suit between individuals. They are authorised to make their defence according to the practice of court of equity, and if a cross bill is necessary to his complete defence, to file a cross bill. If this right were denied them the suit would not be governed by the same rules as suits between individuals.

The relief, then, for which the complainant seeks in this case, he may obtain by becoming a party defendant to the suit in the Sumter chancery court, which has first obtained jurisdiction of the subject matter. But even if he could get a larger and more satisfactory measure of relief in this court, that would not justify this court in an interference with the jurisdiction and proceedings of another court of concurrent power. I can find no authority for such action. No case has been shown where a court of chancery has undertaken to wrest property from another court of chancery of concurrent jurisdiction, because it, thought its own power better fitted to give complete and ample relief. If this court fails to respect the jurisdiction and proceedings of the state courts, how can it claim immunity for its process and proceedings from them. If the wise and salutary rule, that the court first obtaining jurisdiction shall have the preference, is disregarded, we shall have the unseemly spectacle often presented of violent conflicts between courts of concurrent jurisdiction, disgraceful to the administration of the law and promotive of conflict and disorder.

I find, therefore, in the action of the state chancery court for the county of Sumter, an insuperable obstacle to the granting of the motion for a receiver in this case, at this time, and the motion will be continued, to allow the defendants to set up the facts in regard to the proceedings of the chancery court of Sumter county by formal answer.

RICE, MORGAN & SOUTHWORTH for complainant; ELMORE, WALKER, BROOKS, O'NEIL, STONE & TROY for defendants.

UNITED STATES DISTRICT COURT—S. D. NEW YORK.

Under the thirty-ninth section of the bankrupt act, as amended by the act of July fourteenth, eighteen hundred and seventy, providing for putting into involuntary bankruptcy a person "who, being a banker, broker, merchant, trader, manufacturer or miner, has fraudulently stopped payment, or who has stopped or suspended and not resumed payment of his commercial paper within a period of fourteen days," a person who is not a banker broker, merchant, trader, manufacturer or miner, is liable to be put into involuntary bankruptcy, if he has stopped or suspended and not resumed payment of his commercial paper within a period of fourteen days.

Under the section, as so amended, a person cannot be put into involuntary bankruptcy for the fraudulent stoppage of payment, unless he is a banker, broker, merchant, trader, manufacturer or miner ; but if he is in one of those classes, he may, for the fraudulent stoppage of the payment of his debts, be put into bankruptcy at once, without waiting fourteen days, and without his stoppage being a stoppage of the payment of commercial paper.

Under the section, as so amended, "commercial paper" means bills of exchange, promissory notes, bank checks and other negotiable instruments for the payment of money, which, by their form and on their face, purport to be such instruments as are by the law merchant recognized as falling under the designation of "commercial paper."

A corporation, incorporated for the transaction of the business of life insurance, and not inhibited from borrowing money for the legitimate purposes of its business, and from giving notes, as evidence of such indebtedness, may, although not expressly authorized to do so, borrow money for use in its legitimate business, and give a time engagement to pay the debt.

The clause in the thirty-ninth section in regard to the stoppage of the payment of commercial paper, ought not to be used to enable a creditor to collect an ordinary debt on commercial paper, where there has been no stoppage or suspension of payment of the commercial paper of the debtor.

Such stoppage or suspension has not taken place, when a sufficient excuse is shown why the paper was not paid.

Even though the suspension may have continued for fourteen days, yet a bona fide denial of liability on the paper is such an adequate legal excuse, that a person ought not to be adjudged a bankrupt solely for suspending for fourteen days on the paper, even though, on investigation, the bankruptcy court may be of opinion that, in fact, the debtor was liable on the paper.

A debtor may, under certain circumstances, be considered as really having suspended payment generally of his commercial paper, although but a single piece of paper is shown to have lain over unpaid for fourteen days. Petition dismissed with costs.

In re THE HERCULES MUTUAL LIFE ASSURANCE SOCIETY OF THE UNITED STATES.

BLATCHFORD, J.—This is a petition by Rosalie Libline for an adjudication of bankruptcy against the Hercules

Mutual Life Assurance Society of the United States, a corporation organized under the laws of the state of New York providing for the incorporation of associations for transacting the business of life insurance. It is undoubtedly a business corporation, within the purview of section thirty-seven of the bankrupt act.

The indebtedness alleged by the petitioner is a promissory note made by the corporation in its corporate name, and signed by its president and by its assistant secretary, dated May sixteenth, eighteen hundred and seventy-one, for the sum of one thousand dollars, payable six months after date to the order of the petitioner. The act of bankruptcy alleged in the petition is, that the corporation "has stopped and suspended and not resumed payment of its commercial paper within a period of fourteen days, to wit, from the nineteenth day of November," eighteen hundred and seventy-one, " to the present time," (January sixth, eighteen hundred and seventy-two;) that a large amount of its commercial paper has been issued, while the said corporation was insolvent, which said commercial paper is past due and remains unpaid, and which the said corporation could not be able to pay in the ordinary course of its business, being insolvent at the time of making the same; that the corporation has property which it has fraudulently refused and neglected to appropriate towards the payment of its indebtedness."

The thirty-ninth section of the bankrupt act of March second, eighteen hundred and sixty-seven, as originally enacted, (14 U. S. Stat. at Large, .536,) provided, that "any person residing and owing debts as aforesaid," that is, (§11,) "residing within the jurisdiction of the United States," and "owing debts provable under this act exceeding the amount of three hundred dollars," " who, being a banker, merchant or trader, has fraudulently stopped or suspended and not resumed payment of his commercial paper within a period of fourteen days, shall be deemed to have committed an act of bankruptcy," &c. There was no doubt that the person to be proceeded against under this clause must in all cases have been a banker, merchant or trader. But various inter-

pretations were given by the courts to the words "fraudulently stopped or suspended and not resumed payment of
his commercial paper within a period of fourteen days"—
that, (*in re* Wells, N. B. R. Sup. 37, and *in re* Cowles, 1 N. B.
R. 42, and *in re* Compton, 2 *id.* 182, and *in re* Weikert, 3 *id.* 5,
and *in re* Thompson, *id.* 45, and *in re* Schoo, *id.* 52,) the word
"fraudulently" did not qualify the whole sentence, but an
adjudication could be had where the suspension continued
for fourteen days, although such suspension was not fraudulent, and also at once, where the original suspension was
fraudulent; that, (*in re* Jersey City Window Glass Co., 1 N.
B. R. 113, and *in re* Leeds, *id.* 138, and *in re* Cone, 2 Bt. 502,
and *in re* Hollis, 3 N. B. R. 82, and *in re* Davis, 3 Bt. 482,)
the suspension and non-resumption must in all cases be
fraudulent; that, (*in re* Ballard, 2 N. B. R. 84, and *in re* Shea, 3
id. 46,) a suspension for fourteen days was *prima facie* evidence of fraud ; and that, (*in re* Davis, 3 Bt. 482,) a suspension for fourteen days was not *prima facie* evidence of fraud.

In this condition of the statute and the decisions, congress
passed the act of July fourteenth, eighteen hundred and seventy (16 Stat. at large, 276,) which provides, that the clause
in the thirty-ninth section, " or who, being a banker, merchant
or trader, has fraudulently stopped or suspended and not resumed payment of his commercial paper within a period of
fourteen days," shall be amended so as to read as follows : " or
who, being a banker, broker, merchant, trader, manufacturer or
miner, has fraudulently stopped payment, or who has stopped
or suspended and not resumed payment of his commercial
paper within a period of fourteen days."

It is contended for the respondent, in this case, that it is
not a banker, broker, merchant, trader, manufacturer or
miner, and that, therefore, it is not within the clause in the
thirty-ninth section, as amended. This corporation is, undoubtedly, not a banker, or a broker, or a merchant, or a
trader, or a manufacturer, or a miner.

The view on the part of the respondent is, that the words
" banker, broker, merchant, trader, manufacturer or miner,"
qualify the whole of the clause as it now reads, as well

that part of the clause which follows the second "who" therein, as that part which precedes the second "who." In the clause, as it stood before it was amended, there was but one "who," and it was followed by only one "has." In the clause as it now reads, each "who" is followed by its own "has," and each "has" has its own "who" preceding it. If the clause now read, "or who, being a banker," &c., "has fraudulently stopped payment, or has stopped," &c., omitting the second "who," and leaving the "who" preceding the words "being a banker," &c., to be the nominative to the second "has," as well as to the first "has," there could be no doubt that the words "being a banker," &c., would qualify all the provisions of the clause. So, also, if the clause now read, "or, being a banker," &c., "who has fraudulently stopped payment, or who has stopped," &c., the words "being a banker," &c., would qualify all the words of the clause. In the preceding part of the section the first time the word "who" occurs, it is nominative to the word "shall," as that word recurs, five times, before the word "who" recurs again, and each time the word "shall" precedes the declaration of a distinct act of bankruptcy. The second time the word "who" occurs, it is nominative to the words "has been," as those words recur, twice, before the word "who" recurs again, and each time the words "has been" precede the declaration of a distinct act of bankruptcy. The third time the word "who" occurs, it is followed immediately by the qualifying words, "being bankrupt or insolvent, or in contemplation of bankruptcy or insolvency," which apply to and qualify all the enumerated acts of bankruptcy which follow in the section down to the fourth "who." Those words qualify the words "shall make," &c., "or give," &c., "or procure or suffer," &c. It is, therefore, apparent, that congress was, at the time the act of eighteen hundred and seventy was passed, cognizant of the use, in the section, of qualifying words to qualify various acts of bankruptcy expressed in a clause containing but a single "who." And, when it came to amend the clause containing the fourth "who," with   words in it, "being a banker," &c., which manifestly qualified the whole clause, it divided the clause, as distinctly as language can divide it, into two parts—(1.) A person, residing and owing debts as aforesaid, who, being a banker, broker, merchant, trader, manufacturer or miner, has fraudulently stopped payment; (2.) A person, residing and owing debts as aforesaid, who has stopped or suspended and not resumed payment of his commercial paper within a period of fourteen days. It repeats the word "who;" and, the second time, without the qualifying words given to it the first time. The words "stopped payment" do not require the aid of the words "commercial paper" to give them meaning. Fraudulent stoppage of payment by a banker, &c., is, in such a statute, predicable only of the fraudulent stoppage of payment of debts. Congress seems to have taken up the whole subject of the stoppage of payment of debts, as an act of bankruptcy, in the act of eighteen hundred and seventy, and enacted that brokers, manufacturers and miners, as well as bankers, merchants and traders, shall, if they fraudulently stop payment of their debts, be liable to be adjudged bankrupts at once, and that any person who makes commercial paper, and then stops or suspends payment of it, and does not resume payment of it within a period of fourteen days, shall be liable to be adjudged a bankrupt. In respect to those classes of persons who are more immediately connected with commercial transactions, namely, bankers, brokers, merchants, traders, manufacturers and miners, the clause, as amended, provides, that, if they fraudulently stop payment of their debts, they shall be adjudged bankrupts. In respect to all persons, as well those more immediately connected with commercial transactions as all other persons, it provides, that, if they so far voluntarily enter the field of commercial transactions as to give out their commercial paper, then, if they stop or suspend payment of such paper, and do not resume payment of it within a period of fourteen days, they shall be adjudged bankrupts. This is a reasonable and consistent view of the relations of debtors, in respect to the stoppage of payment of debts. If a person, be he who he may, wishes to be free from the lia' lity of being put into bankruptcy for the stoppage or suspension and non-resumption for fourteen days of the payment of commercial paper, let him keep out of the domain of commerce, by not giving commercial paper. If he is not a banker, broker, merchant, trader, manufacturer or miner, and has given no commercial paper, he is not within this clause at all. If he is a banker, broker, merchant, trader, manufacturer or miner, and has fraudulently stopped payment, he may be adjudged bankrupt at once, without the delay of fourteen days. If he is a banker, &c., and has stopped payment without fraud, he cannot be adjudged a bankrupt, unless he has stopped or suspended for fourteen days the payment of commercial paper given by him. Whoever gives commercial paper is considered as, *pro tanto*, engaged in commerce, and, in the interests of commerce, must not permit it to lie over for more than fourteen days. But a direct fraudulent stoppage of the payment of debts is made an act of bankruptcy only when committed by a person belonging to one of the six specified classes. They are selected as the classes most directly engaged in the business of commerce. And these views are consistent with the only grammatical reading of the clause.

Another suggestion is of force. In order to make the words, "being a banker," &c., qualify the words which follow the second "who," it is necessary that the second "who" should be eliminated, so that the structure of the sentence shall be, "who, being a banker," &c., "has fraudulently stopped payment, or has stopped or suspended and not resumed payment of his commercial paper within a period of fourteen days." But, there is as much warrant for eliminating, in addition, the second "has," as there is for eliminating the second "who" only. If the second "who" and the second "has" are both of them eliminated, the clause will read, "who, being a banker," &c., "has fraudulently stopped payment, or stopped or suspended and not resumed payment of his commercial paper within a period of fourteen days." This would not only make the words, "being a banker," &c., qualify the whole clause, but would also make the word

In re Hercules Mutual Life Assurance Society.

"fraudulently" qualify the whole clause, so that the two
classes of persons subject to the clause would be; (1.) " a
banker," &c., who "has fraudulently stopped payment " of his
debts, and who could be adjudged a bankrupt at once ; (2.)
" a banker," &c., who has fraudulently " stopped or suspended and not resumed payment of his commercial paper within
a period of fourteen days." On such reading, there would
be such an expression of an intention to confine a fraudulent stoppage or suspension on commercial paper to one
continued for fourteen days, as to make it necessary to confine the meaning of the words " fraudulently stopped payment," in the first branch of the clause, to a fraudulent
stoppage of the payment of debts other than commercial
paper ; otherwise, the second branch of the clause would be
comprehended within the first, and would have no meaning.
All this indicates, that the only proper rule of construction
is to give the usual grammatical effect and meaning to every
word in the clause, when, as here, the resulting interpretation
is one which makes the clause not only sensible and consistent in itself, in all its parts, but reasonable and natural, in
view of the subject matter to which it relates.

I am aware, that, *in re* Chandler, 4 N. B. R. 44, it is said
by LOWELL, J., that, by the act of eighteen hundred and
seventy, any person is liable to be adjudged a bankrupt, who,
being a banker, &c., has stopped and suspended and not resumed payment of his commercial paper within a period of
fourteen days. But the question I have considered did not
necessarily arise, because he found that the debtor in that
case was a manufacturer. So, also, in *Baldwin* v. *Wilder*, 6
N. B. R. 85, the question here discussed did not arise,
although EMMONS, J., in the course of his opinion, says, that
the act of eighteen hundred and seventy provides that, " if
the merchant, &c., has fraudulently stopped payment, or
has stopped or suspended and not resumed payment of his
commercial paper within a period of fourteen days, he shall
be adjudged a bankrupt." In *in re* Kenyon & Fenton, 6 N. B.
R. 238, the expression is used, that, if a banker, &c., allows his

paper to go to protest and suspends for fourteen days, or if he has fraudulently stopped payment, in either case he has committed an act of bankruptcy. This is undoubtedly true, but the question raised in the present case was not considered. There is an absence of adjudication on the direct point involved. But with the view I take of the statute, I must hold, that the fact that the debtor in this case is not in one of the six specified classes, forms no objection to adjudging it a bankrupt, if it has stopped or suspended and not resumed payment of its commercial paper within a period of fourteen days.

It is to be noted, that an interpretation of the clause, as amended, which would give to it the same meaning it would have if it read thus, " who, being a banker, broker, merchant, trader, manufacturer or miner, has fraudulently stopped payment of his commercial paper, or has stopped or suspended and not resumed payment of his commercial paper within a period of fourteen days," requires, not only that the grammatical effect of the second " who " in the clause shall be disregarded, in order to make the words, " being a banker," &c., qualify the words which follow the second " who," but that the words, " of his commercial paper," shall be adopted from the second branch of the clause and inserted in the first branch, after the word " payment." All doubtful and tentative constructions of the clause are avoided, if the natural and ordinary construction of the language is adhered to, and full effect given to every word.

So much of the petition as alleges that the corporation has property which it has fraudulently refused and neglected to appropriate towards the payment of its indebtedness, must be regarded as an allegation of a fraudulent stoppage of payment. This is no allegation of any act of bankruptcy in respect to this corporation, for the reason that it is not a banker, broker, merchant, trader, manufacturer or miner.

The remaining allegations are, that the corporation, while insolvent, issued a large amount of its commercial paper, which paper is past due and unpaid, and which it could not be able to pay in the ordinary course of its business, and that it has stopped and suspended and not resumed payment of its commercial paper from the nineteenth of November, eighteen hundred and seventy-one, being more than a period of fourteen days.

The commercial paper shown to have been issued by the corporation consists of negotiable promissory notes, in the usual form of such notes, payable to order at specified times after date, and running in the name of the corporation, and signed by its proper officers. The only consideration shown for such notes was loans of money to the corporation. On this it is insisted that the notes are not commercial paper of the corporation, within the act. One point taken is, that the corporation has no express power to make notes. But it is not shown that it is inhibited from borrowing money for the legitimate purposes of its business, and from giving notes as evidence of such indebtedness. In general, an express authority is not indispensable to confer upon a corporation the right to borrow money, or to become a party to negotiable paper. (Angell & Ames on Corporations, section 257.) A corporation, in order to attain its legitimate objects, may deal precisely as an individual may, who seeks to accomplish the same ends, and this includes the power to borrow money for use in its legitimate business, and the power to give a time engagement to pay the debt, in any form not prohibited by statute. (*Curtis* v. *Leavitt*, 15 New York, 9, 62; *Smith* v. *Law*, 21 *id.* 296, 298, 299.) In the present case, the evidence shows that the notes spoken of in the petition as commercial paper, were given, either originally or by renewal, for loans of money made to the corporation for its use, and used, by it, for the legitimate purposes of its business.

In the view I take of the clause in question, the decisions before the act of eighteen hundred and seventy in regard to the meaning of the term "commercial paper," in the clause as it then read, to the effect that it must be commercial paper given by a banker, merchant or trader in the course of, or in connection with, his business as such, and not merely commercial paper in form given for loans of money, have no application to the term as found in the clause as amended by the act of eighteen hundred and seventy. There can be no doubt that, where the act declares that any person who gives his commercial paper and then stops or suspends payment of it, and does not resume payment of it for fourteen days, may be adjudged a bankrupt, it means, by "commercial paper," bills of exchange, promissory notes, bank checks and other negotiable instruments for the payment of money, which, by their form and on their face, purport to be such instruments as are by the law merchant recognized as falling under the designation of "commercial paper." Under this definition, the notes in this case were commercial paper, within the act.

The allegation that the corporation issued this paper while insolvent has no relevancy in this case, except as bearing on the allegation that it has stopped and suspended and not resumed payment of such paper for fourteen days; and the same remark is true of the allegation that the corporation could not be able to pay such paper in the ordinary course of its business, the paper being overdue. The question then comes to this sole point—whether the corporation has stopped or suspended and not resumed payment of such paper within a period of fourteen days, within the true intent and meaning of the act.

One of the points most seriously contested, in this case, in the evidence and on the hearing, was, whether the corporation was really liable to the petitioning creditor on the note set forth in the petition. I think its liability on that note is established by the evidence. The one thousand dollars which she loaned on the note of Mr. Homberg, for one thousand dollars, endorsed by Mr. Reymert, of the sixteenth of November, eighteen hundred and seventy, was really loaned to the corporation, through Mr. Reymert, its president, and was used for the business of the corporation, the note being a note made to raise money for the corporation, and being one of three notes made by Homberg for that purpose, and loaned to the corporation in exchange for its note of the same date, for three thousand five hundred dollars, the aggregate amount of such three notes. This note for three thousand five hundred dollars was afterwards returned to the corporation, and the three notes of Homberg were extinguished, the note in the petition being given to the petitioner in exchange for the one thousand dollar note of Homberg, on which she loaned the one thousand dollars. In so giving its note to the petitioner, the corporation did what in justice it was bound to do, as respected both the petitioner and Homberg and Reymert—to give to the petitioner its liability for the one thousand dollars; and, if she chose to take that and give up any liability of Homberg and Reymert, it was at her option to do so. She did so, and the corporation gave her the evidence of what was in fact a debt of its own to her.

This note set forth in the petition was not paid at its maturity, November nineteenth, eighteen hundred and seventy-one, and it had not been paid when the petition was filed, January sixth, eighteen hundred and seventy-two. Several other notes of the corporation were due when the petition was filed; but in regard to all of them, as well as to the note held by the petitioner, I do not think that the evidence makes out a case of stoppage or suspension and non-resumption of payment of the notes, within the sense of the act.

When a person fails generally to meet his commercial paper according to the usual course of business, and suffers, not some, but all of it, as it matures, to go to protest, and so comes to a general suspension, because unable to proceed further with his business, he is undoubtedly within the clause, the suspension continuing for fourteen days. But on the other hand, the clause ought not to be used to enable a creditor to collect an ordinary debt on commercial paper, where the circumstances show that, although the paper is not paid, though due, there has been no stoppage or suspension of payment of the commercial paper of the debtor, within the meaning of the clause. In such case, the ordinary remedy furnished through a suit to collect the note, is all that the creditor is entitled to. *In re* Compton, 2 N. B. R. 182. It is not a stoppage or suspension within the clause, when a sufficient excuse is shown why the paper was not paid, and even though the suspension may have continued for fourteen days, yet a *bona fide* denial of liability on the paper in respect to which the suspension occurs, is such an adequate legal excuse, that a person ought not to be adjudged a bankrupt solely for suspending for fourteen days on the paper, even though, on investigation, the bankruptcy court may be of opinion that, in fact, the debtor was liable on the paper. (See *Davis* v. *Armstrong*, 3 N. B. R. 6; *in re* Thompson, *id.* 45; *in re* Hollis, *id.* 82.) The true view on this subject is, in my judgment, that laid down in *McLean* v. *Brown*, 4 N. B. R. 188, by TREAT, J., that the suspension referred to in the act is a general suspension of commercial paper, not the refusal to pay paper in respect to which liability is denied; that the bankrupt court will not sit to try the validity of the reasons alleged for the non-payment of the paper in respect to which the liability is denied; that it is not a court for the mere collection of debts; that each case must be considered by itself, in connection with the circumstances surrounding it; but that, when a party fails to pay his paper for want of means, and continues unable to pay it; he has suspended within the meaning of the act. It by no means follows, that a debtor may not, under certain circumstances, be considered as having really suspended payment generally of his commercial paper, although but a single piece of paper is shown to have lain over unpaid for fourteen days. On the other hand, the court must guard against being imposed upon by a denial of liability which is altogether sham and not made in good faith. The denial of liability may, however, be founded on reasons which are not valid, and which would fail as a defence in a direct action on the paper, and yet the denial may be made in good faith, in such wise, that the non-payment cannot be regarded as a stoppage or suspension within the act.

In the present case, it is not shown that the corporation failed, for want of means, to pay the note held by the petitioner, and the other paper referred to, nor is it shown that it was insolvent when the petition was filed. It is not alleged to have preferred any creditor, when insolvent, nor is it alleged to have committed any other act of bankruptcy than the suspension of payment for fourteen days of its commercial paper. Although subject to the supervision of the authorities of the state created for the purpose of investigating the affairs of insurance corporations and winding them up when insolvent, no proceedings had been taken against it, as an insolvent institution, by the state authorities. Within a week prior to the maturity of the note held by the petitioner, the former president of the corporation resigned and a new president took his place. The affairs of the corporation seem to have been in much confusion, and its books were not kept in such form as to afford the information which they ought to have afforded in regard to its business. Its accounts had not been kept separate from the accounts of its former president, and, without imputing any misfeasance or malfeasance to any person, it is not too much to say, that the information, and want of information, on the part of the new president, in regard to all the commercial paper referred to, and its consideration, and his views and those of his associates, honestly entertained, as the proof shows, in regard to the liability of the corporation to pay the same, were such that the failure to pay it, and the continuance of such failure down to the time of the filing of the petition, cannot be regarded as a stoppage or suspension and non-resumption of its payment, within the act.

The petition is dismissed with costs.

J. D. REYMERT for the petitioner; A. R. DYETT for the debtors.

UNITED STATES CIRCUIT COURT—E. D. PENNSYLVANIA.

The receipt by a creditor of part of his claim does not preclude him from petitioning to have his debtor adjudged a bankrupt if the creditor offers to bring this payment into the registry of the court.

In re J. F. MARCER.

CADWALLADER, J.—The thirty-ninth section of the bankrupt law enacts, not only that a payment or transfer by an insolvent person to a *creditor*, with intent to give a preference, shall be an act of bankruptcy, but also that a payment, gift or transfer, made by the insolvent with such intent, to any person or persons liable for him as sureties, shall be an act of bankruptcy. Therefore, if any other creditor than the city of Philadelphia had been the petitioner, the payment or transfer made by this debtor to the persons who were sureties on his bond to the city, would unquestionably have constituted an act of bankruptcy.

The fund which was the subject of this preference was paid in money to the city by the sureties with other money of their own, in discharge of their liability on the bond. The whole sum thus paid, being the amount of the penalty of the bond, was not more than, say one-fourth, of the alleged bankrupt's debt to the city. The question is, whether such receipt of the part of the debt secured by the bond precludes the city from suing here as the petitioning creditor.

If the city had actively promoted the payment and appropriation of the fund in question to the indemnification of the sureties, in order that this very fund might become a specific part of what should be received from the sureties in discharge of the bond, or if the sureties had paid the whole amount of their liability on the express condition that this fund should be received as part of such payment and it had been *so accepted*, there would in either case have been such an election as to preclude the city. But nothing of the kind is alleged. Whether the city or its officers knew of the source from which the payment was, in part, derived, is immaterial to the question of election. To constitute an election it is not enough that the party to be precluded shall know the fact on which the question of election depends. He must also be made to understand that the question has arisen and that he is put to his election.. 11 H. L. Ca. 588, 602, 603, 611–613. The money, as it was offered in this case, could not have been refused. The payment has discharged the bond at law, leaving open all equities under questions of preference and of election.

But the fund in question having found its way into the possession of the city, the petition, as originally framed, was not sustainable, because it contained no offer to bring this fund into the registry of the court, or otherwise make it a part of the estate in bankruptcy. This difficulty has been removed by the averment and offer contained in the amendment of the petition. If there should be no other creditor than the city, and a bill in equity at the suit of the assignee in bankruptcy should be hereafter sustainable against the sureties, they will be entitled to a deduction or credit equal to what would have been their dividend of the fund in question.

What might have been the course of procedure if the city had not been a creditor to an amount exceeding that of the bond, or if the excess had not been so great as to make the question one of mere deduction or credit, need not be considered. For the present, the rule that a party, asking equity must do equity, or offer to do it, has been complied with.

The debtor is adjudged a bankrupt. The usual bond of the petitioning creditor is dispensed with.

GEORGE D. BUDD and W. J. McELROY, ESQS., and C. H. T. COLLIS, ESQ., City Solicitor, for the city of Philadelphia.

DAVID W. SELLERS, ESQ., for bankrupt.

UNITED STATES SUPREME COURT.
[Appeal from the U. S. circuit court for the northern district of Illinois.]

A confession of judgment entered before the first day of June, eighteen hundred and sixty-seven, but after the enactment of the bankrupt law, is a fraudulent preference, when both parties knew of the insolvency of the debtor.

A creditor who has obtained judgment is not a necessary party in a suit between the assignee in bankruptcy and a subsequent judgment creditor.

An assignee has the right to proceed against a creditor in the federal court for the proceeds of a sale on an execution issued out of a state court, where the judgment on which it is founded is alleged to be in fraud of the bankrupt act.

The assignee has the right to recover from the judgment creditor, (a bank) although it has given no receipt to the sheriff, but only a certificate of deposit.

Receiving money in its capacity as a bank from collections due the bankrupt, by the creditor, and handing the same to the sheriff, who applies it to the payment of the bank's judgment, is a fraudulent preference ; so too, taking a check from the bankrupt for the amount on deposit and crediting the amount of the check on the bankrupts' note the day before taking judgment, is a preference, and void, hence, the question of set-off does not arise.

TRADERS' NATIONAL BANK OF CHICAGO v. CAMPBELL, Assignee.

MILLER, J.—This suit was brought in the district court of the United States for the northern district of Illinois, by Campbell, assignee in bankruptcy of Hitchcock & Endicott, against the Traders' National Bank of Chicago, and Hotchkiss & Sons, to recover money received by them of the bankrupts by way of fraudulent preference.

Hitchcock & Endicott were, on the thirteenth day of July, declared bankrupts by the district court, at the suit of their creditors, Doane & Co., commenced on the twenty-fifth day of June.

On the twenty-eight of May preceding this, the bank brought a suit against Hitchcock & Endicott, in which, on an allegation of fraud, a capias was issued for the arrest of Hitchcock. To avoid this arrest, the bankrupt firm gave the bank a demand note with warrant of attorney to confess judgment, and on the next day the bank entered a judgment for the debt less three hundred and twenty-five dollars and twenty cents, the amount of the bankrupts' deposit account with the bank, on that day, which was endorsed on the note as a credit. Execution was immediately issued on this judgment and levied on the bankrupts' stock of goods.

On the thirtieth of May, Hotchkiss & Sons obtained a judgment against the same parties for a much smaller debt, on which execution was also issued and levied on the same goods.

It is not asserted by counsel here that the defendant acquired any rights to the property levied on by its execution. It would be useless to do so, for the president of the bank acknowledged that he was aware of the insolvent condition of Hitchcock & Endicott, and had instituted his proceeding after taking the opinion of counsel, that the bankrupt law did not affect such cases until after the first day of June, the earliest time at which proceeding could be commenced under that law.

We are of opinion that the proviso to the fiftieth section of the bankrupt act, which declares that no petition or other proceeding under it shall be commenced before the first day of June, eighteen hundred and sixty-seven, is limited in its effect to such commencement, and that any act done after its approval, March second, eighteen hundred and sixty-seven, in fraud of the purpose of the statute, was within its prohibitions.

We will consider the objections to the decree in favor of the plaintiff, in the order in which they are assigned in appellant's brief.

1. It is said that Hotchkiss & Sons were necessary parties, without whom the court could not proceed. They were not within the jurisdiction of the court, and, though made defendants by the bill, never appeared in the case, and it was dismissed as to them without prejudice.

Their interest, as asserted by appellant's counsel, was that they also had a judgment against the bankrupts, on which execution was levied, on the same property, and that, as it was sold under both executions, Hotchkiss & Sons have a right to be heard as to the validity of that sale.

In the case of *Barney* v. *Baltimore*, 6 Wall. 280, this court, after reviewing the former decisions on this subject, remarks that there is a class of persons having such relations to the matter in controversy, merely formal or otherwise, that, while they may be called proper parties, the court will take no account of the omission to make them parties. There is another class whose relations to the suit are such that, if their interest and their absence are formally brought to the attention of the court, it will require them to be made parties, if within its jurisdiction, before deciding the case. But, if this cannot be done, it will proceed to administer such relief as may be in its power between the parties before it. And there is a third class, whose interests in the subject matter of the suit, and in the relief sought, is so bound up with that of the other parties, that their legal presence as parties in the proceeding is an absolute necessity, without which the court cannot proceed.

Hotchkiss & Sons manifestly belong to this second class, and not the third. The bank is sued for its own wrong in procuring judgment and selling the property, and for the proceeds now in its vaults. Hotchkiss & Sons may, or may not, be in the wrong in procuring their judgment and levy, but it is not alleged that they have received any of the money. If they are entitled to any of it, they will be at liberty to bring any suit they may be advised, after this suit is disposed of, against the assignee, or any one else, and their rights will not be precluded by the present decree; nor have they any such interest in the subject matter of this suit, that their presence is necessary to the protection of the bank. A complete decree can be made between the bank and the assignee without touching the rights of Hotchkiss & Sons, or embarrassing the bank in its relations to them. The organization of the federal courts have always required them to dispense with parties in chancery not within their jurisdiction, unless their presence was an absolute necessity, which it clearly is not in this case.

2. It is said that the assignee should have applied to the

State court for an order on the sheriff to pay over the proceeds of the execution to him.

But it cannot be maintained that the assignee, who is pursuing the assets of the bankrupt in the hands of third parties, is bound to resort to the state courts, because there is a litigation there pending. The language of the fourteenth section, that the assignee may prosecute and defend all suits pending at the time of the adjudication of bankruptcy, in which the bankrupt is a party, does not *oblige* him to seek a remedy in that way. The second section of the act declares that the circuit courts of the United States shall have concurrent jurisdiction with the district courts of all suits at law or in equity, which may or shall be brought by the assignee against any person claiming an adverse interest touching any property or rights of property of said bankrupt.

The decree in the present suit is founded on the idea that the bank, by the means of its illegal and collusive proceedings in the state court, has received the proceeds of property which ought to have come to the assignee. He has a right to proceed against the bank directly in the federal court for those proceeds, and is not obliged to resort to the state court, where the matter is substantially ended, for relief.

3. The third objection is, that the bank has not received from the sheriff any sum whatever in satisfaction of the judgment which is recovered against the bankrupts.

The facts of the case are simple and undisputed. The goods of the bankrupt were sold under the execution in favor of the bank, and the sheriff, after deducting the costs of the proceeding, deposited the remainder with the defendant. This suit being then pending, the defendant, instead of giving the sheriff a receipt for the amount as paid on the execution in his hands, gave him a certificate of deposit. This transparent device can deceive no one, and does not vary the legal character of the transaction. The sheriff, under the direction of the bank, levies upon and sells the property of the bankrupt, after the title has passed to the assignee, and in violation of the law. He deposits the proceeds of sale with the party whose agent he was in this illegal appropriation of the goods. The assignee electing to assert his right to the proceeds of the sale instead of the goods themselves, sues the party who caused the seizure and sale, and who has their proceeds in his possession. His right to recover under such circumstances cannot well be doubted.

4. The fourth objection is that the decree rendered against the bank is far too large a sum.

This assignment of error has regard to certain sums coming to the hands of the defendant as bankers of Hitchcock & Endicott, and which they claim a right to retain by way of set-off.

The amount of nine hundred and forty-three dollars and twenty cents was received on the twefth day of June, some days after their judgment had been recovered in the State court, and after the execution had been levied on the stock of the bankrupts' goods.

It was received as collections made by the bank, from drafts placed by the bankrupts in their hands in the ordinary course of business, and if they had retained it and appropriated it as a set-off against the debt of the bankrupt to them, an interesting question might have arisen as to their right to do so. But, instead of doing this, they handed it over to the sheriff, who levied on it as the property of the bankrupt, by virtue of the same execution under which he levied on and sold the goods. By the act of the bank it was thus placed in the same category with the goods, and instead of exercising their own right of set-off by directing the sheriff to credit the execution with the sum received by them on the debt, they delivered it to him to be treated as the goods of the bankrupt and subjected by him to their illegal judgment.

This amount then must be treated in the same manner as the other money received by them from the sheriff on the sale of the goods.

There was in the bank on deposit to the credit of Hitchcock & Endicott on the day they gave the judgment note, the sum of three hundred and twenty-five dollars and twenty cents. This sum was not computed or deducted when the note was given. On the next day, before the bank caused the judgment to be entered up, they credited this amount on the note, and took judgment for that much less. They now claim that this was what they had a right to do, and that it should remain a valid set-off. But this does not appear to have been really what was done. It appears that Hitchcock & Endicott gave the bank a check for the sum, and by virtue of that check it was endorsed on the note as a payment. Now as both the bank and the bankrupts knew of the insolvency of the latter, this was a payment by way of preference, and therefore void by the thirty-fifth section of the bankrupt act. In this case, as in the other, if they had stood on their right of set-off, it might possibly have been available, but when they treat it as the bankrupts' property, and endeavor to secure an illegal preference by getting the bankrupts to make a payment in the one case, and seizing it by execution in the other, when they knew of the insolvency, both appropriations are void.

We see no error in the decree which was rendered in the district court and affirmed in the circuit court on appeal, and which is again affirmed by this court.

UNITED STATES CIRCUIT COURT—MISSOURI.

A., who was insolvent at the time, wrote to his brother-in-law, B. at St. Louis, to come and buy him out. In response to this letter, B. came to the residence of A., and arranged to take the whole of his stock at twenty-five per cent. below cost. B., leaving the stock in possession of A. during his absence, went to Chillicothe, Missouri, and offered to sell the whole stock to C. at twenty per cent. below cost. Thereupon, B. and C. went together to the residence of A.; C. examined, paid for and shipped the goods away. The assignee in bankruptcy sued C. for the goods and recovered a verdict, which was set aside on appeal and the case remanded. On the second trial he obtained a judgment from which defendant again appealed. This time, however, the judgment was affirmed. Defendants then appealed to the United States court, on the ground that the jury were improperly charged. *Held*, That the charge was perfectly proper, as the judge of the court below had distinctly informed the jury, that notice of the fraud or participation in it, on the part of the defendants, was essential to the recovery on the part of the assignee. Judgment affirmed.

BABBITT, *Assignee*, v. WALBRUN & CO. *

TREAT, J.—In order that the views of the court upon the errors assigned, may be stated briefly, and that they may be understood, a succinct statement of the case is necessary.

Mendelson, doing business in Kingsville as a merchant, wrote to his brother-in-law in St. Louis to come and buy him out. Mendelson was insolvent at the time. The brother-in-law, Summerfield, went to Kingsville, and learning that Mendelson wished to sell out because the competition was so sharp that he could not make a living, bought out Mendelson at twenty-five per cent. off the cost of the stock.

Immediately, Summerfield, leaving the stock in possession of M. during his (Summerfield's) absence, went to Chillicothe, Missouri, and offered to sell the whole stock to defendants at twenty per cent. off, whereby Summerfield would apparently make five per cent. on the trade.

Defendants, by one of their partners, went to Kingsville with S., stopped over night at Mendelson's house, in the morning went to the store where the stock of goods was, commenced an examination of them, and upon learning that S. must leave in consequence of the alleged sickness of his wife, and upon the assurance of S. that he would make all

* See 4 N. B. R. 30.

right if the inventory was found defective, defendants paid the full inventory price at the rate agreed, and immediately shipped the goods away.

In connection with the alleged sale from Mendelson to Summerfield, and the subsequent sale by Summerfield to defendants, there were many facts and circumstances provoking inquiry, inducing suspicion, and represented differently in the sworn testimony of the respective parties thereto.

The case is one where, in an effort to unravel a supposed web of fraud, the parties implicated have to be successively examined under oath; thus seeking to ascertain from unwilling witnesses what they designed to conceal, and what their interest is to keep unrevealed.

In this case, as in most others of a supposed scheme of fraud cunningly devised, it was necessary to pursue the inquiry searchingly into all the facts and circumstances surrounding the two-fold transaction, and, consequently, to permit the testimony to take a wider range than in ordinary suits at law.

In doing so, many statements, voluntarily or otherwise made by the adverse witnesses who are the alleged parties to the fraud, should be carefully scrutinized, and admitted or rejected in the light of the developments made in the progress of the trial and the attitude of the witnesses. It does not follow that the plaintiff is concluded by every statement made by such a witness when called by him, nor is he precluded from proving directly the reverse to be the truth.

Hence it was proper to admit the testimony objected to under this head, and to charge the jury as to the credibility of witnesses in the manner the court did, instead of doing so in the language of the instruction asked, the latter being inapplicable to the course pursued.

Applying the rules of evidence correctly, the only doubtful point is as to the admission of Mendelson's statements concerning his loss of the money alleged to have been paid to him by Summerfield. But that statement by Mendelson had to be taken in connection with the various aspects the case might assume during the trial, and especially with the testimony that Summerfield did not have the means to pay what he and Mendelson say he did pay for the stock of goods; and the fact thus stated by him, whether true or not, was not made the basis of any suggestion or instruction, and at most was treated as an irrelevant and immaterial matter from which none of the parties could be-prejudiced, and least of all the defendants.

Without analyzing in detail the various facts concerning which evidence was given, and the instructions asked and refused, and the different portions of the charge, the main propositions of law controlling the controversy will give all needed light as to the views entertained by this court.

It is apparent that the case throughout had two aspects, viz. :

FIRST. Whether there had been an actual or mere sham sale to Summerfield.

SECOND. Whether the sale to *defendants* was *actually* by Summerfield, or through a mere sham contrivance ostensibly by him, but really by Mendelson.

Hence each aspect of the case had to be borne in mind, and what would not have been strictly admissible in evidence in one aspect, would be in the other.

It was not for the court arbitrarily to determine which aspect the jury might under the evidence find to be the true one.

It appeared that Mendelson, because he could not make a living at the business, (as he and Summerfield both swear,) sends for his married brother-in-law to buy out, for cash, a losing business; and that immediately his brother-in-law, destitute of means, perhaps, appears on the scene, pretends to buy out the concern, leaves it in charge of Mendelson, immediately proceeds to a distant town, negotiates with defendants to sell to them, and one of the defendants accompanies Summerfield, without delay, to Kingsville, closes the bargain and ships the goods away at once. Now the inquiry was a natural one, whether the part Summerfield played was not merely a contrivance between Mendelson and himself to sell the goods to defendants nominally through Summerfield as Mendelson's vendee, but actually from Mendelson direct to defendants. That branch of the subject matter had to be thoroughly investigated. The plaintiff was not bound to accept the pretenses set up as true, but had a right to go behind them in pursuit of the facts.

The instructions asked and the charge by the court relate largely to the hypothesis of an actual sale by Mendelson to Summerfield, as the consequent relation of defendants to the case as second vendees; yet the charge looked to each of the two aspects, and did not, as did the instructions which were refused, wholly ignore the other view of the case.

Treating the case in the light of the law governing a second vendee, the main proposition would be: Were defendants innocent and *bona fide* purchasers for value?

To ascertain their status it was necessary to learn whether they paid anything on the purchase, and how much, and whether they had notice of Summerfield's title as it stood affected by his dealings with Mendelson.

Necessarily, if the title was good in Summerfield, the controversy was at an end; and hence the first step was as to *that* title; therefore the inquiry under the bankrupt act into the alleged sale to Summerfield.

As it was out of the usual course of business, it was presumptively fraudulent and void as to him, if he knew Mendelson to be insolvent, (and the insolvency was admitted,) because, as held by this court during this term, in the case of *Lawrence* v. *Graves*, it is impossible to conceive how a person buying from a known insolvent all of his stock of goods (which the law presumes *prima facie* evidence of fraud) could be in a position other than to be put upon inquiry where reasonable cause existed to believe that the transaction was a meditated fraud.

In that view the court gave the instruction most complained of. Now if Summerfield bought the goods under such circumstances the sale to him was fraudulent, unless shown by rebutting evidence to have been *bona fide*. and honest.

If no such rebutting evidence was offered, the next step was to ascertain whether defendants had notice of the previous fraudulent transaction, or participated in it in such a way as was designed to aid the· fraudulent purpose intended by Mendelson.

In *Clements* v. *Moore*, 6 Wall. 312, the legal principles governing such cases are succinctly stated :

" A sale may be void for bad faith, though the buyer pays the full value of the property bought. This is the consequence where his purpose is to aid the seller in perpetrating a fraud. upon his creditors, and where he buys recklessly with guilty knowledge. When the fact of fraud is established in a suit at law, the buyer loses the property, without reference to the amount or application of what he has paid, and he can have no relief, either at law or in equity. * * * The cardinal principle in all such case is that the property of the debtor shall not be diverted from the payment of his debts, to the injury of his creditors, by means of the fraud."

Applying the doctrine thus laid down to the case at bar, the sale to defendants would be void if defendants had notice that the sale to Summerfield was fraudulent, or, there being no actual sale to Summerfield, if they really took title directly from Mendelson, knowing all the facts charged and the relation of Summerfield to the transaction. It was proper, therefore, to admit or exclude testimony, and to instruct the jury with reference to both hypotheses. True, the whole law applicable might have been more distinctly and formally unfolded, if each hypothesis had been separately stated, and the legal rules pertaining thereto arranged under each specific head ; yet it often happens that such an elaborate exposition of legal rules serves to confuse rather than aid juries.

The charge put to the jury, the essential. inquiries upon which the case was to turn, was first, as to the transactions between Mendelson and Summerfield, and next as to the *bona fides* of defendants. As to the second inquiry, the language was :

"It is not, however, sufficient in this case to find the sale from Mendelson to Summerfield to have been either void or fraudulent. In order to find the issues against the defendants you must be satisfied that they participated in the fraudulent sale, or at least had reasonable cause to know the sale to have been fraudulent."

Thus both hypotheses were included, so that notice of the fraud or participation in it was declared essential to a recovery. It was not, therefore, necessary to repeat that proposition, it having been once distinctly announced.

The views expressed by the plaintiff's counsel are not broad enough to cover the case of a second vendee. The first sale being void as between the parties thereto in consequence of fraud, a second vendee being a *bona fide* purchaser for valuable consideration is not affected by the technical rules which obtain as to the original parties alone.

Thus a purchaser from Mendelson who knew Mendelson to be insolvent, if the sale was out of the usual course of business, might have reasonable cause to believe the fraud to exist ; but a purchaser from the first vendee who knew merely that it included the whole stock of Mendelson was not thereby charged with notice that the first sale was fraudulent, for other elements are essential to make the sale fraudulent and void. A sale by an insolvent person, though known to be insolvent, is not therefore necessarily void, otherwise an insolvent person could not lawfully dispose of any of his property. But it is not necessary to go again over the ground already under this head fully stated during this term in the opinion delivered in the case of *Darby's trustee* v. *the Boatmen's Savings Institution.*

As previously decided in the case at bar, the purchasers from a first vendee must, in order to invalidate their title, be affected by notice of or participation in the original fraud. That is, must have been purchasers without valuable consideration or *mala fide.*

An examination of the record shows that the proceedings in bankruptcy were offered in evidence, including the bankrupt's schedules, and certainly that record was admissible to show the fact of adjudication and appointment of the plaintiff as assignee. It appears that so much of the bankruptcy record was introduced as included all proceedings of record up to and including the appointment of assignee; and though the schedules were thus introduced as a part of that record, no use was made of them, inasmuch as the fact of Mendelson's insolvency at the time of the sale was admitted. Thus the question presented by the counsel in that respect does not arise.

Juries have twice passed on this case upon the merits; and, therefore, more technical points are to be received with less favor, when the whole testimony is in the record and an examination thereof shows that the verdict was obviously for the right party. Affirmed.

------ • ◆ • ------

UNITED STATES DISTRICT COURT—W. D. TEXAS.

A debtor made an assignment of his stock in trade and notes of hand to one of his creditors within six weeks of the filing of a petition in bankruptcy against the debtor. Assignment held void under section thirty-five of the bankrupt act; and assignee in bankruptcy entitled to recover from the preferred creditor the value of the goods and notes thus transferred to him.

NORTH, Assignee, v. HOUSE, et al.

DUVAL, J.—This was a suit brought on the law side of the United States circuit court for the western district of Texas, by W. F. North, assignee of the involuntary bankrupt, W. A. Rawlings, for the recovery of eighty thousand dollars, the alleged value of certain goods, wares, etc., and certain notes, accounts, etc., which the plaintiff charged the defendant with having converted to his own use. The plaintiff claimed to recover their value as part of the assets of the bankrupt's estate.

The defendant answered, denying the allegations in the petition and joining issue.

The facts were, that the bankrupt, W. A. Rawlings, was a merchant in Huntsville, Texas, and had been for three or four years prior to this suit.

That the defendant, Thomas W. House, did a forwarding and commission and wholesale business in Houston, Texas, where, in connection with his mercantile and commission business, he also conducted a banking, exchange and collecting business; that the defendant, House, had been for several years prior to this action the correspondent of the bankrupt at Houston; that he had sold him large bills of goods and that the bankrupt had shipped him a large amount of cotton; that the bankrupt's commercial paper was (or at least the greater part of it) payable at the counting rooms of Thomas W. House; that in September, eighteen hundred and seventy, when the bankrupt was north, purchasing goods, that the defendant, House, was with him; that at that time a portion of the bankrupt's paper, being a note to Sheldon & Company for about twenty-five hundred dollars, was past due, and Buckley, a member of that firm, tried to induce the defendant, House, in whose hands the paper was, to pay it. He declined to do so, but promised to see it paid out of the first shipments of cotton which would come to his hands from the bankrupt. He never paid it and it is still unpaid. The defendant, House, also informed Messrs. Evans, Gardner & Company, that he considered the bankrupt solvent, (the bankrupt had referred them to House,) and on this assurance, they, in September, eighteen hundred and seventy, sold him goods.

That the bankrupt's paper, to the amount of thirteen thousand dollars, matured in January, February, and early in March, eighteen hundred and seventy-one, and was presented at the counting house of the defendant for payment. None of it was paid, and a considerable amount of it was protested and remained unsettled in the hands of House.

That while this state of affairs existed, on the twenty-

North v. House et al.

eighth of March, eighteen hundred and seventy-one (Rawlings, the bankrupt, having made on the last of February
an ineffectual effort to borrow about three hundred dollars
of House, and having then past due and in House's hands
over fifteen thousand dollars of paper, and being then, besides,
indebted to House himself in the sum of forty thousand
or fifty thousand dollars,) came to Houston and attempted
to induce the defendant or his agents to make him a further
moneyed advance, (House was then temporarily absent from
Houston,) but his agents refused. The bankrupt then proposed to sell them his storehouse, his stock of goods, valued
at about twenty-five thousand dollars, and his notes and accounts, valued at about fifteen thousand dollars. This offer
was accepted, and a deed was made to House on March
twenty-eighth, eighteen hundred and seventy-one, expressing a consideration of about forty-three thousand dollars.

That the payment was made by House assuming and paying certain debts and obligations of the bankrupt.

That not a dollar was paid to the New York creditors,
whose paper was endorsed to House for collection, and a
large part of which was at that very time in his hands.

That on receiving intelligence of the execution of this
deed House made no objection to it, but took possession
of the bankrupt's store, retained his clerks and placed one
of his own in charge, and sold the goods in his own name.

That four days after the transfer he paid, for the bankrupt,
six thousand dollars to one Thomason, a creditor, and to Gibbs
& Co., also creditors, about thirteen hundred dollars.

That on May ninth, eighteen hundred and seventy-one,
and within six weeks of the above transfer, Jehial Read &
Co., for themselves and other New York creditors, filed a
petition in bankruptcy against Rawlings, alleging said transfer to be an act of bankruptcy, charged it to be fraudulent,
made House a party, and sued out an injunction. Rawlings was
adjudged a bankrupt on June twenty-eighth, eighteen hundred and seventy-one ; the injunction dissolved as to House,
it being admitted that he was solvent and able to respond in

damages; the plaintiff elected assignee September fourteenth, eighteen hundred and seventy-one; and this suit instituted by him on December fourth, eighteen hundred and seventy-one.

The cause was tried before Judge Duval at the January term, eighteen hundred and seventy-two, when he charged the jury as follows:

" *Gentlemen of the jury* : This suit is brought by W. F. North, as the assignee of W. A. Rawlings, who, on the petition of certain of his creditors, was adjudged a bankrupt on the twenty-eighth day of June, eighteen hundred and seventy-one. This adjudication, however, related back and took effect on the ninth of May, eighteen hundred and seventy-one, when the creditors' petition was filed. After such adjudication, to wit: on the fourteenth day of September, eighteen hundred and seventy-one, a deed of assignment was made to said North by the register in bankruptcy, whereby all the estate, real and personal, of the bankrupt, including all the property conveyed by him in fraud of his creditors, vested in his assignee, and gave to the latter the right to bring and maintain suits for the recovery thereof.

"The petition in this case avers that on the twenty-eighth day of March, eighteen hundred and seventy-one, (though it seems from the evidence to have been a few days earlier,) the bankrupt being then insolvent and being also in contemplation of insolvency, and well knowing that such was his condition, fraudulently assigned and made over to T. W. House, one of his creditors, a stock of goods, wares and merchandise of the value of about fifty thousand dollars; and also notes, accounts, book accounts and debts, due said bankrupt, to the amount of about thirty thousand dollars. The petition further alleges, that at the time of such assignment the said House well knew that Rawlings was insolvent and in failing circumstances, and that he was in contemplation of insolvency and of bankruptcy, and that all of the property thus assigned to House was so done with a view to give him a fraudulent preference over his other creditors,

North v. House et aL

and to hinder, delay and defraud them in the collection of their just debts.

"So much of the bankrupt law as applies to this case provides as follows: 'That if any person, being insolvent, or in contemplation of insolvency, within 'four months before· the filing of the petition by or against him, with a view to give a preference to any creditor or person having a claim against him, or who is under any liability for him, makes any pledge, payment, assignment, transfer or conveyance of any part of his property, either directly or indirectly, absolutely or conditionally, the person receiving such payment, pledge, assignment, transfer or conveyance, or to be benefitted thereby, having reasonable cause to believe such person is insolvent, and that the same is made in fraud of the provisions of said act, the same shall be void, and the assignee may recover the property, or the value of it, from the person so receiving it, or so to be benefitted.' The act further provides: 'That if such· sale, transfer, assignment or conveyance is not made in the usual and ordinary course of business of the debtor, the fact shall be *prima facie* evidence of fraud.'

"In this case the questions for the jury to determine are :

"FIRST. Was Rawlings insolvent or in contemplation of insolvency at the time of his assignment to House, and did he make said assignment with a view to give a preference to him over other creditors?

"SECOND. Did House have *reasonable cause* to believe that Rawlings was then insolvent, and that said assignment was made in fraud of the provisions of the bankrupt act?

"If the jury believe, from all the evidence in the case, that they should give an affirmative response to both these questions, then they must find a verdict for the plaintiff. And, to satisfy themselves on these points, the jury can look to all the facts and circumstances disclosed by the evidence, and draw such reasonable conclusions therefrom as they . deem just and proper.

"The great object of the bankrupt act is to do away with all 'fraudulent preferences, by which one creditor in the collection of his debt obtains an unconscientious advantage over another, and to provide for a just and equal distribution of the bankrupt's assets among all his creditors.

"In order to render a transfer or conveyance fraudulent and void under the thirty-fifth section of the act, it is not necessary to bring home to the person receiving such transfer or conveyance actual knowledge that the party making the transfer was insolvent or intended a fraud upon the bankrupt act; it is sufficient to render the deed fraudulent and void as to such person, if he had sufficient knowledge of the financial condition of such party to put a man of ordinary business capacity on enquiry as to the condition of the debtor; and if, in this case, you believe that the evidence shows the bankrupt, Rawlings, to have been insolvent on the twenty-eighth of March, eighteen hundred and seventy-one, (the date of the transfer,) and that the defendant, House, either knew, or had from his knowledge of the bankrupt's business, reasonable cause to believe him insolvent, and unable to pay his commercial paper and his debts as they fell due, then the deed of assignment is fraudulent and void, and conveys no right to the party in whose favor it was made.

"And if the jury believe that the transfer under consideration was not made in the usual and ordinary course of business of the debtor, then that fact is *prima facie* evidence that it is fraudulent, and unless rebutted or controlled by other evidence in the case, is sufficient to establish knowledge, on the part of those dealing with him, of the bankrupt's insolvency.

"If the jury believe, from the evidence and under the instructions given them, that the transfer in question is fraudulent and void, they will return a verdict for the plaintiff, and allow him such amount as you believe from the testimony was the value of the goods and notes on the twenty-eighth of March, eighteen hundred and seventy-one, with interest thereon, at eight per cent., per annum, down to the time of this trial. Nor, if the deed is fraudulent, is the defendant, House, entitled to credit for the amount he may have paid to certain creditors of Rawlings, for the payments themselves would be in fraud of the bankrupt act, and give an undue preference to those paid over the other creditors, if the bankrupt was then insolvent and the defendant had reasonable cause so to believe.

"If the jury find for the defendant they will so say by their verdict."

(Signed.)   T. H. DUVAL, U. S. Judge.

"The jury, if they find for the plaintiff, will state in their verdict against which of the defendants the same is rendered."

And, at the instance of the plaintiff, he gave the following additional instructions:

"In determining the question as to whether or not the defendant, House, had reasonable cause to believe that the bankrupt, Rawlings, was insolvent at the date of the transfer, you have a right to look at all the facts in evidence bearing on this point; the business and personal relations of the parties; the connection, if any, the defendant had with the commercial paper of the bankrupt, and his opportunities and means of knowing his financial condition, and if from these and other facts in evidence you believe that the defendant had reasonable cause to believe the bankrupt insolvent, then the deed is void and you will find for the plaintiff.

HANCOCK & WEST, *Plff's Att'ys.*

Given.

(Signed.)   T. H. DUVAL.

"The mere fact that the defendant was not present when the deed was made, and knew nothing of the transaction, does not affect its character. If, when informed of it, he did not repudiate it, but accepted benefits under it, then he is as much bound by the acts of his agents in accepting the deed

In re Howard, Cole & Co.

as if he had accepted it himself. It was, under the law, the privilege of the defendant to have surrendered the property and repudiated the deed, had he desired to do so."

HANCOCK & WEST, *Plff's Att'ys.*

Given.

(Signed.)　　T. H. DUVAL.

"The mere fact that the defendant may have paid a valuable consideration or advanced money on the deed in·question will not validate it, if he had reasonable cause to believe the party insolvent at the time of its execution, and he was so insolvent." 　　HANCOCK & WEST, *Plff's Att'ys.*

Given.

(Signed.)　　T. H. DUVAL.

The defendant asked no instructions.

The jury returned a verdict for the plaintiff for the sum of thirty-nine thousand one hundred and sixty-five dollars and sixty-five cents.

UNITED STATES DISTRICT COURT—MARYLAND.

A. sent certain notes to B., which were endorsed by C., to be discounted and the proceeds placed to his (A's) credit. He drew against them by certain drafts in favor of C., which B. failed to pay. C. was subsequently adjudged a bankrupt, and B. sought to prove his claim against the bankrupt for the notes sent to him by A., but the assignee refused to allow it.

On the petition of B. to review the action of the assignee in refusing to allow the claim to be proved, the court held, that inasmuch as the drafts were not paid, B. had no right to retain the notes, and, therefore, there was a failure of consideration. Claim rejected.

In re HOWARD, COLE & CO. *

GILES, J.—The petition of F. Skinner & Co., of Boston, to review the action of the assignee in refusing to allow the claim of the petitioners as proved, and for an order allowing the same, &c.

To this petition the assignee files an answer, stating that

* See 4 N. B. R. 185.

In re Howard, Cole & Co.

the claim of the said petitioners is not a valid claim against the said bankrupt estate, because the said notes, on which it is founded were passed by Howard, Cole & Co. to J. S. Barry & Co. under a special agreement, and were only to be used for a particular purpose, and without any consideration passing from Barry & Co. to Howard, Cole & Co.; that under this special agreement, they were sent to the said petitioners by Barry & Co., by letter of the twentieth of November, eighteen hundred and sixty-nine, to be discounted by said petitioners, and out of the proceeds sight drafts to the amount of ten thousand dollars, in favor of Howard, Cole & Co., were to be paid, which was not done, but said petitioners placed the proceeds of said notes to the credit of Barry & Co. on their general running account, without any further payment or credit being given by them to Barry & Co.; and that therefore the said petitioners have no valid claim to hold the said notes, or prove them against the bankrupt estate of Howard, Cole & Co.

Two commissions have been issued in this case, one to Boston and the other to New York, under which much testimony has been taken. But the question in this case lies within a very narrow limit, and depends entirely on the circumstances under which these notes were passed by Barry & Co. to the petitioners, F. Skinner & Co.

Are they such as to render them the *bona fide* holders of the said notes for a valuable consideration?

Now, the evidence shows clearly that these notes were drawn and endorsed by said Howard, Cole & Co., and by them passed over to Barry & Co., under an agreement that said Barry & Co. were to get them cashed, and to divide the proceeds equally between the two houses. There is no evidence to show that this agreement was known to the petitioners when they received the said notes. We have the evidence of John S. Barry, of the firm of Barry & Co., and the evidence of Edward F. Cutter, of the firm of F. Skinner & Co., and also the letter from Barry & Co. to the petitioners, enclosing the said notes. Does the evidence show that petitioners received these notes under circumstances which makes them the *bona fide* holders of the same, free from any equities between Howard, Cole & Co. and Barry & Co.? The letter of the twentieth of November, eighteen hundred and sixty-nine, must settle this question, for although Cutter swears that he understood that these notes were to be discounted, and the proceeds credited to the house of Barry & Co., on their running account, yet, as it is not pretended, that, outside of said letter of the twentieth of November, there was any special agreement to that effect, can such agreement be found in the terms of the said letter? What are they? "We beg to advise our drafts on you direct, in favor of Howard, Cole & Co., five thousand dollars; ditto, five thousand dollars; R. Mickle, ten thousand dollars, in all twenty thousand dollars, which please honor and oblige. We enclose, herewith, a batch of good paper, amounting to twenty-six thousand seven hundred and six dollars, which please pass for us. Against this, and the former lot of one hundred and nine thousand and forty-two dollars and seventy-five cents, our total drawings to date, including the above named drafts (and draft advised to-night in another letter, in favor of your New York house) amount to one hundred and twenty-five thousand dollars in all, and all duly advised." To this letter, petitioners reply: "November twenty-second, eighteen hundred and sixty-nine: Your favors of the twentieth are at hand, covering notes amounting to twenty-six thousand seven hundred and six dollars and four cents."

This was a clear adoption of the terms of the letter of the twentieth November. Petitioners could not set up afterwards any claim inconsistent with it. Is not the true construction of the letter of the twentieth November this: "We send you a batch of good paper, amounting to the sum of twenty-six thousand seven hundred and six dollars, to be discounted by you, and against the proceeds of which we have drawn on you three drafts at sight, two for five thousand dollars each, and one for ten thousand dollars." Now the

In re Howard, Cole & Co.

evidence shows that the petitioners never paid these drafts, but that they were protested and returned. What claim can they now set up to retain these notes?

To sustain their claims, I am referred by their learned counsel to three decisions of the supreme court: To the case of *Swift* v. *Tyson*, 16 Pet. 1; *Bank of the Metropolis* v. *New England Bank*, 1 How. 234; and *Goodman* v. *Simonds*, 20 How. 343. The case of *Swift* v. *Tyson* decided, that where a party took a negotiable instrument before its maturity in payment of a pre-existing debt without any notice of facts which impeach its validity as between the original parties to the same, he holds it unaffected by these facts, and could recover on it, although, as between the antecedent parties, the note was without any legal validity.

In the case in 1 How. 234, the supreme court held that where there have been for several years mutual and extensive dealings between two banks, and an account current kept between them in which they mutually credit each other with the proceeds of all paper remitted for collection when received, and accounts regularly transmitted from one to the other and settled upon these principles, and upon the face of the paper transmitted, it always appeared to be the property of the respective banks, and to be remitted by each of them on its own account; there is a lien for general balance of account upon the paper thus transmitted, no matter who may be its real owner. And to show why it is so, TANEY, J., in delivering the opinion of the court, says: "If an advance of money had been made upon this paper to the Commonwealth Bank, the right to retain for that amount would hardly be disputed. We do not perceive any difference in principle between an advance of money *and a balance supposed to remain upon the faith of these mutual dealings.*"

The evidence in this case shows that no further payment or credit was given by the petitioners to Barry & Co. for or on account of these notes.

In the case of *Goodman* v. *Simonds*, the supreme court affirmed their ruling in the case of *Swift* v. *Tyson*, with this addition, that the surrendering of collateral securities, previously given, and affording increased indulgences as to time, furnish a sufficient consideration for the transfer of the paper, and passes it to the party unaffected by any prior equities between the original parties to the same. There must be some present consideration at the time of the transfer. The petitioner must show *that he paid value when he took it, or incurred some responsibility, or relinquished some right, or granted some indulgence, or discharged a precedent debt, upon the faith and credit of the paper.*

For this principle see the following cases: *Sweeney* v. *Easter*, 1 Wall. 166; *Farrington* v. *Frankfort Bank*, 31 Barb. 183; *Fenorlle* v. *Hamilton*, 35 Ala. 319; *Roseborough* v. *Mezick*, 6 Ohio n. s. 448; *Trustees* v. *Hill*, 12 Iowa 462; *Jenkins* v. *Sehaut*, 14 Wis. 1; *Ruddick* v. *Loyd*, 15 Iowa 441.

These cases have been decided since the case of *Goodman* v. *Simonds* and seem to answer the question propounded (but not decided) by the learned judge who delivered the opinion of the supreme court in that case, to wit: "Whether the same conclusion, (viz.: to hold the transfer unaffected by any equities between the original parties) ought to follow, where the transfer was without any other consideration than what flows from the nature of the contract at the time of delivery, and such as may be inferred from the relation of debtor and creditor in respect to the pre-existing debt?" On this question there had been much conflict in the decisions up to that time. The necessity for a present consideration to sustain the transfer and render it superior to any equities between the original parties to the paper, seems to be recognized as the law of this state in the case of *Gwynn & Co.* v. *Lee*, 9 Gill, 138.

I will therefore sign an order rejecting the said claim of the petitioners against the bankrupt estate of Howard, Cole & Co.

MAINE SUPREME JUDICIAL COURT.

A. sued B. in assumpsit on a promissory note. Defendant pleaded his discharge in bankruptcy in bar. Plaintiff replied that he ought not to be barred, for the reason that the defendant's schedule of indebtedness did not contain a statement of his debt, and that plaintiff had no notice of the proceedings in bankruptcy. *Held*, The omission of a creditor's name from the schedule of indebtedness of a bankrupt is not sufficient ground for annulling and setting aside a discharge, unless such omission is shown to have been fraudulent.

SYMONDS v. BARNES.

On exceptions to the ruling of GODDARD, J., of the superior court for Cumberland county.

Assumpsit on a promissory note, dated April twenty-one, eighteen hundred and fifty-three, given by the defendant to the plaintiff.

The defendant pleaded his discharge in bankruptcy, dated June five, eighteen hundred and sixty-nine.

The plaintiff replied that he ought not to be barred, because, that at the time of filing his petition in bankruptcy the defendant's schedule of debts annexed to his petition, or any amendment thereto, did not contain a statement of the debt in controversy as required by section eleven of the United States bankrupt act; that the defendant, at the time of filing his petition, or at any time afterwards, did not give to the marshal of the district, as messenger, the name of the plaintiff as one of the defendant's creditors; that the marshal did not serve written or printed notice by mail or personally upon the plaintiff; that the plaintiff has never received notice of the pendency of the proceedings in bankruptcy set forth in the plea; and that he never proved his said debt against the estate of the defendant in bankruptcy.

To this replication there was a demurrer and joinder.

The judge sustained the demurrer and adjudged the replication bad; whereupon the plaintiff alleged exceptions.

SYMONDS & LIBBY for plaintiff; J. D. & F. FESSENDEN for defendant.

APPLETON, C. J.   By the bankrupt act of eighteen hundred and forty-one the discharge of a bankrupt might be impeached for fraud in any court in which it was pleaded in bar to a pending suit.

By the bankrupt act of eighteen hundred and sixty-seven, section thirty-four, it is enacted, "that a discharge duly granted under this act, shall release the bankrupt from all debts, claims, liabilities, and demands which were or might have been proved against his estate in bankruptcy," unless his creditors should "see fit to contest the validity of said discharge on the ground that it was fraudulently obtained." This must be done in the court in which it was granted, within two years, for some of the fraudulent acts of omission or commission particularly set forth in section twenty-nine. Such was the construction given by this court to the act in *Corey* v. *Ripley*, 4 N. B. R., 163, and upon examining the debates, when the bill was under discussion, it will be seen that the effect there given to the discharge, unless set aside and annulled by the federal court granting it, was in strict conformity with the intention of congress.

The defendant pleads a discharge. It is in due form of law, "An order of discharge will be sufficient evidence of bankruptcy and of the validity of the proceedings thereon." Robson, on Bankruptcy, 458. The order proves itself. 1 Deacon on Bankruptcy, 800.

The plaintiff replies that his claim was omitted in the schedule of debts sworn to by the defendant. If the bankrupt "has willfully sworn falsely in his affidavit annexed to his * * * schedule or inventory," the court, granting the discharge, may, upon proceedings duly had before it, " set aside and annul the same."

But the plea contains no allegation of fraudulent conduct or willful false swearing. The court granting the discharge would not be authorized by the act " to set aside or annul the same," much less would any other court.

Under the act of eighteen hundred and forty-one it was held that a plaintiff could not avoid a discharge of his bankrupt debtor by merely showing that the defendant, in his petition in bankruptcy, omitted to insert the plaintiff's name, etc., to the sworn list of creditors, and that by reason of such omission, the plaintiff had no notice of the proceedings in bankruptcy, and could neither prove his claims against the defendant nor oppose his discharge. To avoid the discharge, by reason of such omission, if must be shown to be willful and fraudulent. *Burnside* v. *Brigham*, 8 Met., 75 ; *Mitchell* v. *Singletary*, 19 Ohio, 210.

The accidental omission of a creditor's name in the schedule of indebtedness is not made a ground for annulling and setting aside a discharge. The omission, to have that effect, must be fraudulent. The affidavit annexed to the schedule must be willfully false. Indeed, the act assumes that the schedule of debts may not be complete, for, by section eleven, the marshal is directed to serve " written or printed notice, by mail or personally, on all creditors upon the schedule filed with the debtor's petition, or whose names may be given to him in addition by the debtor. Exceptions overruled.

KENT, WALTON, BARROWS, and DANFORTH, JJ., concurred.
TAPLEY, J., concurred in the result.

UNITED STATES DISTRICT COURT—KENTUCKY.

Assignees under the state law cannot receive allowance for attorneys' fees, nor compensation for their own services where the debtor has been adjudged a bankrupt.

In re J. S. COHN.

BALLARD, J.—On the twenty-first of February, A. D. eighteen hundred and seventy, J. S. Cohn made an assignment to Louis Sechel of all his property, for the benefit of all his creditors.

On the seventh of June, eighteen hundred and seventy, a petition for adjudication of bankruptcy was filed against him by his creditors, and on the eighteenth of June, eighteen hundred and seventy, he was adjudged a bankrupt.

On the twenty-fifth of June, eighteen hundred and seventy, R. M. Mosby was appointed assignee in bankruptcy of said bankrupt, and accepted the trust.

Mosby sued out a rule from the United States district court against Sechel, to show cause why he should not surrender to Mosby, assignee in bankruptcy, the property conveyed by Cohn on the twenty-first of February, eighteen hundred and seventy, to Sechel.

Sechel responds that he has sold said property, and realized therefrom the sum of seven hundred and fifty-one dollars and six cents; that the expenses of said sale were thirty-nine dollars and seventy cents; attorneys' fees paid, fifty dollars; attorney's fee for which suit was brought and costs, &c., seventy-five dollars—one hundred and sixty-four dollars and seventy cents; that he paid taxes, internal revenue, sixty-four dollars and four cents; paid county and state taxes, forty-one dollars and twenty-five cents—one hundred and five dollars and thirty-one cents : total, two hundred and seventy dollars and one cent.

He says, also, that he is ready to pay over to the assignee in bankruptcy the amount received by him from the sale of the bankrupt's property, less the above items of expense of two hundred and seventy dollars and one cent, in administering his trust, and the cost of this proceeding.

The attorney for Mosby asks that Sechel be ordered to pay over to Mosby the full amount of money received from the sale of the estate of said Cohn, less the United States, state and county or city taxes, paid by Sechel, making no contest about the two last items in Sechel's account as above stated, because he considered that liens existed on the bankrupt's estate for the payment of taxes, and the assignee in bankruptcy would have to pay them at any rate.

The only remaining questions then are, shall Sechel be allowed credits in his account for expenses of sale of bankrupt's estate,.for the attorney's fee paid, and for another attorney's fee which he thought he might be adjudged to pay? Three items, amounting to one hundred and sixty-four dollars and seventy cents. The attorney for the assignee in bankruptcy says, "no; the assignment to Sechel on the twenty-first of February, eighteen hundred and seventy, was void," and cites *Langley* v. *Perry*, N. B. R., 155, to show that such an assignment is void.

The question before the court in that case was not whether the voluntary assignment was void or voidable, but whether it was an act of bankruptcy. The court in that case says: "It results conclusively that if the provisions of the bankrupt act were in force on the twenty-fifth of May, eighteen hundred and sixty-seven, the date of the assignment, and that the assignment was within the scope and intent of the law, and, as an act of bankruptcy, altogether null and void, the probate court of Gallia county had no jurisdiction of the assignment, and the acts of that court in regard to it are altogether invalid."

I have failed to find any case where the question, "whether an assignment of all the property of the assignor for the benefit of all his creditors was void or voidable?" came up directly before the court, and such assignment was decided to be void.

In *Pearce* v. *Holbrook*, 3 N. B. R. 62, CADWALADER, J., says: "Even where the assignment has been the sole foundation of the proceedings in bankruptcy I have considered it not a void act, but an act voidable by the assignee in bankruptcy by a bill in equity filed for the purpose of avoiding it." The questions before the court in that case were, whether a voluntary assignment was an act of bankruptcy if proper proceedings were instituted in six months, and whether such an assignment is a bar to a discharge under section twenty-nine of the bankrupt act, in the absence of actual fraud. *Catlin* v. *Foster*, 3 N. B. R. 134, decided by DEADY, J., in district of Oregon, is cited by the attorney for Sechel, to show that the credits claimed by S. in his account should be allowed.

In re Cohn.

In that case the voluntary assignee set up two counter claims in his answer; one for two hundred and fifty dollars, to pay an attorney's fee for which he said he was liable, and two hundred and fifty dollars for his own services under said assignment.

On motion, the first of these counter claims was stricken out, as it did not appear that the defendant had ever paid the amount to the attorney, but only that they claimed that he was liable for it.

The second, for services of the assignee under the voluntary assignment, to the extent of one hundred dollars was allowed, under the twentieth section of the bankrupt act, as a "mutual credit."

It appears to me that this section refers only to creditors of the bankrupt before the act of bankruptcy. It is the theory of the bankrupt law, that a balance is struck between the bankrupt and his creditors at the time he files a voluntary petition in bankruptcy, or a petition is filed against him in an involuntary proceeding in bankruptcy, upon which he is adjudged a bankrupt. All settlements with a bankrupt's estate must be made precisely as though they were made *at the moment* in which such petitions were filed.

I do not suppose it would be contended that a "payment, sale, assignment, transfer, conveyance, or other disposition of his property," made by a bankrupt "to any person who has reasonable cause to believe him insolvent, or to be acting in contemplation of insolvency," and that such "sale," &c., "is made with a view to prevent his property from coming to his assignee in bankruptcy, or to prevent the same from being distributed under this act, or to defeat the object of, or in any way impair, hinder or delay the operation and effect of, or to evade any of the provisions of this act," could stand after adjudication of bankruptcy, and proper proceedings to recover the bankrupt's estate. How, then, can it be argued that in committing the very act of bankruptcy itself, the bankrupt may incur a liability which shall be paid in full out of his estate to the prejudice of his other creditors?

Section thirty-five forbids a bankrupt or insolvent in any way to dispose of his property, yet does not this decision, by permitting him to incur a debt to be paid in full, and to the prejudice of all other creditors, allow him, to that extent, to dispose of his estate? He cannot pay any debt, even where the debt is of the most sacred character; and this section, by making a difference of two months in favor of creditors in the limitation, shows that creditors are to be preferred, at least to that extent, to strangers or persons not creditors. Can we, then, believe that a proper construction of sections twenty and thirty-five would forbid a bankrupt to pay the most sacred obligation, and at the same time permit him to at once create and to pay in full a new obligation to a person who knows that the bankrupt and himself are then acting in open violation of the bankrupt law?

The question whether an assignment like the one under consideration is void or voidable, appears not to have been directly decided by any court since the passage of the present bankrupt act.

The question whether a voluntary assignee, under such an assignment, should receive compensation for services and expenses under such assignment, has been decided both ways, depending, it appears, upon the merits of the particular case under consideration.

We have the above case by DEADY, J., allowing the assignee to have one hundred dollars for his services. On the other hand, we have Fox, J., *in re* Stubbs, 4 N. B. R. 124, in a similar case, who says: "The proceedings under the state law were had in fraud of the act, and the court in bankruptcy cannot allow a party the expenses incurred by him in his attempt to defeat the provisions and operations of the bankrupt law." Also in *Burkholder* v. *Stump*, 4 N. B. R. 191, in the eastern district of Pennsylvania, it is said: "every person receiving one of these assignments ought to know that the assignment is liable to be set aside if a bankruptcy follows; and the allowance to him of his charges and expenses ought to be refused where it cannot be so guarded as to prevent any injurious duplication of charges. In some of the judicial districts of the United States the allowance is refused wholly, and occasional precedents of contrary directions here will not be followed, if to follow them would result in any injustice to creditors.

The decisions on this point being thus variant, since the passage of the present bankrupt law, we must examine the authorities upon the relative subject of *fraudulent conveyances.*

In the case of *Hastings* v. *Spencer*, 1st Curtis, 504, "Where an assignment, made by an insolvent debtor, was held voidable, as actually fraudulent against creditors, and the assignee either had knowledge of the extraneous facts, which rendered the assignment voidable by creditors, or the means of knowing them, and was put upon inquiry, it was held, that he had no lien as against an attaching creditor, upon the proceeds of the property assigned for his services in partially executing the trust, or for retainers paid to counsel." "If the assignees were themselves participators in the fraud, or, in other words, if they undertook to execute the trusts, knowing that they were fraudulent and unlawful, the law cannot recognize such services as ground for a legal claim for compensation, and cannot treat them as creditors of the assignor."

In *Harris* v. *Sumner*, 2 Pick., 129, and *Burlingame* v. *Bell*, 16 Mass., 318, it was held, "That an assignment, fraudulent on its face or actually fraudulent, could confer no lien on the assignees, so as to enable to hold the property against the attachment thereof specially by a creditor."

The case of *Bartlett* v. *Bramhall*, 3 Gray, 257, is referred to by attorneys for Sechel, in which it is decided that an assignee under the insolvent laws of Massachusetts may sue an assignee under a voluntary assignment and recover the money and property of the insolvent, "deducting his expenses for collection, which the plaintiff must have incurred if the defendant had not, but deducting nothing for his labor and services, which are shown by the events that have occurred, to have been unwarranted and illegal. The deduction for expenses of collection is not allowed as compensation to the defendant for collecting, but because the claims collected were not worth more to anybody than the sum which the claimants could obtain therefrom, after incurring the necessary expenses of collection."

Is an assignment like the one under consideration, void or voidable?

I think it is not void but voidable.

The thirty-fifth section only says such an assignment is void, if it is made "within six months after the filing of the petition by or against" the bankrupt.

Then if a petition is not filed "within six months by or against" a bankrupt, such an assignment would stand. It then has virtue or vitality enough to live if not attached within six months. This must be in it from the first, for it continues good unless the petition is filed "within six months."

It is in the nature of a conditional conveyance, the condition being that no petition in bankruptcy shall be filed "within six months." It continues to exist, and is good if such petition is not filed within that time. It is then only voidable by the filing of such petition in said time. This is my construction of this section.

Shall the assignee under the state law be paid for his services, and reimbursed his expenses out of the estate of the bankrupt?

The thirty-fifth section of the act plainly forbids all such assignments. Their effect is to defeat the operation of the bankrupt law. The assignee, Sechel, must have contemplated the natural results of his own acts, and is presumed to know the law. He was then acting in fraud of the law, in the language of *Hastings* v. *Spencer* above cited. "The assignees knowing that they (his acts) were fraudulent and unlawful, the law cannot recognize such services as ground for a legal claimf or compensation and cannot treat them as creditors of the assignor."

If such assignees cannot be treated as creditors of the

assignor, the foundation for the decision *Catlin* v. *Foster* is gone, and the principle of "mutual credits" or the twentieth section of the bankrupt act does not apply.

I therefore conclude that the second item of Sechel's account, (amount paid attorney, fifty dollars,) and the third item, (for which he is sued by Phelps & Son, seventy-five dollars,) cannot be allowed him as credits in the settlement of his accounts. On the principle laid down in *Bartlett* v. *Bramhill* above, which appears to me equitable, I allow him the item of thirty-nine dollars and seventy cents for the expense of sale of property, as it appears from the affidavit filed with Sechel's answer that the sale was a good one.

The account will then stand thus:

LOUIS SECHEL, Dr.—To proceeds of sale		$751 06
Cr.— By taxes paid	$105 31	
By expenses of sale	39 70	
		145 01
Balance due		603 95

All of which is respectfully submitted.

J. H. WARD, *Register.*

BALLARD J.—I approve the foregoing opinion and report of the register.

* * *

UNITED STATES DISTRICT COURT—E. D. MICHIGAN.

On the return of an order to show cause why the bankrupt should not be attached for contempt in disobeying an order requiring him to appear and be examined under section twenty-six of the bankrupt act, he put in an answer that he was fully discharged before the issuing of the order, and therefore not subject to the orders of the court. *Held,* That after a discharge has been granted, the power or means to discover assets by the examination of the bankrupt, under section twenty-six, no longer remains, and that the power of examination will not be revived until the discharge has been set aside. Proceedings for contempt discharged.

In re G. C. JONES.

This matter came on and was heard on an order on the bankrupt to show cause why an attachment should not issue against him for contempt in not obeying an order made November twenty-second, eighteen hundred and seventy-one, requiring him to appear and be examined under section twenty-six of the bankrupt act.

For cause the bankrupt sets up that he was fully discharged July eighteenth, eighteen hundred and sixty-eight, and claims that he was therefore not subject to the orders of the court at the time said order was made.

Mr. ATTERBURY, assignee, in person; Mr. POND for bankrupt.

LONGYEAR, J.—The provision contained in the first clause of section twenty-six, "that the court may, on the application of the assignee in bankruptcy, or of any creditor, or without any application, *at all times* require the bankrupt, upon reasonable notice, to attend and submit to an examination," etc., must be read and interpreted in connection with, and as qualified by, the subsequent provision of the same section, that "the bankrupt shall, at all times *until his discharge*, be subject to the order of the court," etc.

The bankrupt cannot be required to submit to an examination under the former provision except by *an order of the court*. But by the latter provision he is subject to the order of the court only until his discharge. Clearly, therefore, he cannot be so required after his discharge. *In re* Dean, 3 N. B. R. 188.

Ample time is allowed for the examination of the bankrupt before he can even apply for a discharge, (see section twenty-nine,) and the power to subject him to such examination remains until the discharge is granted. *In re* Solis, 3 N. B. R. 186.

After this time has passed, however, and a discharge has been granted, the power or means to discover assets by the examination of the bankrupt, under section twenty-six, no longer remains. But the assignee and the creditors are not therefore necessarily remediless. The ordinary process and means for the discovery and the recovery by the assignee of property which ought to come to his hands remain the same after as before discharge, and I apprehend that the functions of the assignee for that purpose remain so long as there are any assets, the title to which passed to him, remaining uncollected, subject only to the limitations and actions as fixed by the act or by the general laws. They may also, under section thirty-four, contest the validity of the discharge at any time within two years after its date, and if they succeed in setting it aside, then the case will again stand as it did before any discharge was granted, and the power of the court to require the bankrupt to submit to an examination, under section twenty-six, will be revived.

The order of November twenty-second, eighteen hundred and seventy-one, for the examination of the bankrupt being, as we have seen, unauthorized, the same is invalid and void. The order to show cause why the bankrupt should not be attached for disobeying the said order of November twenty-second must therefore be discharged, and the proceedings, as for a contempt, must be dismissed.—February 6, 1872.

UNITED STATES DISTRICT COURT—LOUISIANA.

A. gave his bond to the United States as security for a certain claim against a vessel. The cause was tried and a decision adverse to the United States rendered. Additional evidence was produced in the circuit court, on appeal, and the decision of the district court was reversed, and a decree of condemnation rendered on the twenty-seventh of May, eighteen hundred and seventy.

While proceedings were pending in the circuit court, A. filed his petition in bankruptcy, and was, on the thirtieth day of June, eighteen hundred and sixty-nine, discharged from all his debts dischargable under the bankrupt act. On the eight of June, eighteen hundred and seventy, the circuit court overruled A's plea of discharge in bar of the claim, and gave judgment against him on the release bond.

On the twenty-first of April, eighteen hundred and seventy-one, the secretary of the treasury, for a valuable consideration, transferred the judgment to B., who, on the twenty-seventh of May, eighteen hundred and seventy-one, filed a petition to set aside A's discharge.

Held, That when the United States elected to take judgment upon the bond they parted with all right to prove it as a debt due and payable from the bankrupt at the time of the adjudication of bankruptcy, and as a debt to be proved against the estate ; that it is *res judicata* that this debt is not affected by the discharge, as the judgment is subsisting and operative. Exception sustained and the petition dismissed.

In re A. S. MANSFIELD.

DURELL, J.—On the twenty-third day of March, eighteen hundred and sixty-five, a suit entitled "the United States v the steamboat *Rob Roy* and cargo," was instituted in the then United States district court for the eastern district of Louisiana, wherein it was sought to forfeit said steamboat and cargo of one thousand one hundred and forty bales of cotton as enemies' property, because said property had been sought for, obtained, and brought on board said steamboat from within territory held in occupation by armed enemies of the United States, "declared to be in a state of insurrection." The boat and cargo were seized, and subsequently released on bond to one A. S. Mansfield, the claimant thereof.

The cause was tried in this court, and a decision rendered therein adverse to the United States. Additional evidence having been produced in the circuit court, on appeal, the decision of the district court was reversed, and a decree of condemnation rendered on the twenty-seventh day of May, eighteen hundred and seventy.

In the meantime, and while said proceedings were being had in the circuit court, to wit: on or about the first of June, eighteen hundred and sixty-eight, said Mansfield filed his petition in this court, praying to be adjudged a bankrupt, and was so adjudged on 'the ninth day of June, eighteen hundred and sixty-eight. On the thirtieth day of June, eighteen hundred and sixty-nine, said Mansfield was, in due course of law, discharged from all debts dischargeable under the bankrupt act.

On the third day of May, eighteen hundred and seventy, said Mansfield filed in the circuit court the following plea, in bar to the suit of the *United States* v. *the steamboat Rob Roy and cargo*, then pending in said court, to wit:

And the said A. S. Mansfield, by his attorneys, avers that, on the thirtieth day of June, eighteen hundred and sixty-nine, a discharge was granted him in the words and figures set forth in the duly certified copy of the decree hereto annexed, and made part hereof; and he pleads said discharge as a full and complete bar to this suit wherefore he prays judgment, if the said United States ought to have or maintain the aforesaid action against him."

In re Mansfield.

On the twenty-seventh day of May, eighteen hundred and seventy, the judgment of the district court was reversed, the libel sustained, and the *Rob Roy* and cargo condemned as forfeited to the United States. This judgment fixed the liability of Mansfield under the release bond. On the eighth day of June, eighteen hundred and seventy, the circuit court overruled Mansfield's plea in bar, and gave judgment against him upon the release bond for the sum of two hundred and four thousand nine hundred and eighty-two dollars and twenty-nine cents, with five per cent. interest thereon from the twenty-fourth of March, eighteen hundred and sixty-five, till paid, and cost of suit. On the twenty-first day of April, eighteen hundred and seventy-one, George S. Boutwell, secretary of the treasury of the United States, for and in consideration of the sum of twenty thousand dollars paid into the treasury of the United States, transferred this second judgment in favor of the United States to Stewart Q. Cochrane, who, by motion, entered and filed in the circuit court, on the twenty-seventh day of May, eighteen hundred and seventy-one, caused himself to be subrogated to all the right, title, and interest of the United States in and to said judgment.

On the same twenty-seventh of May, eighteen hundred and seventy-one, Cochrane filed a petition in this court in the matter of Asahiel S. Mansfield, a bankrupt, to set aside Mansfield's discharge.

It is not necessary to enumerate the many allegations made and contained in said petition, nor to notice the exceptions taken and answers filed by Mansfield in avoidance of and responsive thereto, except as to the one question: Was the debt set forth in the petition of S. Q. Cochrane provable in the bankruptcy of A. S. Mansfield?

Section thirty-four of the bankrupt act provides, " that any creditor or creditors of said bankrupt, whose debt was proved or provable against the estate in bankruptcy, who shall see fit to contest the validity of said discharge on the ground that it was fraudulently obtained, may, at any time within two years after the date thereof, apply to the court which granted it to set aside and annul the same." Under this section Cochrane's petition was filed.

Section nineteen provides, " that all debts due and payable from the bankrupt at the time of the adjudication of bankruptcy, and all debts then existing, but not payable until a future day, a rebate of interest being made, where no interest is payable by the terms of the contract, may be proved against the estate of the bankrupt."

Mansfield was adjudicated a bankrupt on the ninth day of June, eighteen hundred and sixty-eight. A decree was entered granting him his discharge on the thirtieth of June, eighteen hundred and sixty-nine. During all this time, the suit of " the United States against the *Rob Roy* and her cargo," was pending in the circuit court. It is to be remembered that judgment was rendered in the district court against the United States and in favor of Mansfield, the claimant restoring to him the property libelled, and that said judgment was reversed in the appellate court, on the production of evidence not produced in the lower court. Certainly, during the pendency of the appeal in the circuit court, and until the *Bob Roy* and cargo were adjudged forfeited to the United States, on the twenty-seventh day of May, eighteen hundred and seventy, there was no semblance of any indebtedness due from Mansfield to the United States, which could have been proved against Mansfield's estate, on the ninth day of June, eighteen hundred and sixty-eight, the day on which he was adjudicated a bankrupt.

Further, the judgment rendered on the twenty-seventh day of May, eighteen hundred and seventy, was not a personal judgment against Mansfield, condemning him to pay any certain sum of money, but a judgment against the *Rob Roy* and cargo, as forfeited to the United States. In order to obtain a judgment against Mansfield, further proceedings were to be had ; and, accordingly, the conditions of the release bond not being complied with, further proceedings were taken upon the bond, which proceedings ripened into a judgment·rendered against Mansfield and his sureties in favor of

In re Mansfield.

the United States, on the eighth day of June, eighteen hundred and seventy, for two hundred and four thousand nine hundred and eighty-two dollars and twenty cents. It is this judgment which the petitioner, S. Q. Cochrane, holds by assignment from the United States, and which he alleges to be a debt provable in bankruptcy against the estate of A. S. Mansfield, on the ninth day of June, eighteen hundred and sixty-eight. It will be seen that Cochrane is not the assignee of the release bond given by Mansfield to the United States, but the assignee of the judgment rendered thereon in favor of the United States, which are two very different things.

The nineteenth section of the statute says : " If the bankrupt shall be bound as drawer, indorser, surety, bail, or guarantor upon any bill, bond, note, or any other specialty or contract, or for any debt of another person, and his liability shall not have become absolute until after the adjudication of bankruptcy, the creditor may prove the same, after such liability shall have become fixed, and before final dividend shall have been declared." Now, if we concede that under this clause of the nineteenth section of the statute the liability of Mansfield, as the maker of the release bond, became fixed on the rendition of the judgment of condemnation and forfeiture of the *Rob Roy* and her cargo, and the non-compliance with the conditions of the release bond, and that the United States might have proved the same against the estate of the bankrupt, yet such concession does not involve the application of the same proposition to the subsequent judgment obtained upon the bond, on the eighth of June, eighteen hundred and seventy, and now held by the petitioner, Cochrane.

Mansfield filed in the circuit court, on the eight of May, eighteen hundred and seventy, a plea in bar founded upon his certificate of discharge. The court, for reasons orally given, overruled the same. Certainly the plea was not a good one if it was intended to bar the right of the United States, under the clause cited from the nineteenth section of the statute, to fix Mansfield's liability upon the release bond given by him March twenty-fourth, eighteen hundred and sixty-five. Neither was the plea in bar a good plea in bar of a judgment sought to be obtained upon the bond, where the creditor elects not to proceed under the clause cited from the ninteenth section of the statute, but to enforce his claim against the bankrupt personally as a debt due upon a liability, which has become fixed long after the bankrupt's surrender and adjudication thereon. The United States elected to pursue the latter course. Let us now see what are the legal consequences of such election.

"When a creditor obtains from his debtor a security of a higher nature than he had before, the original debt is merged in the higher security, and can no longer be made the foundation of any action or suit, or of proof in bankruptcy or insolvency." Lindly on Partnership, 368 ; 10 C. B. Rep. 561 ; Wells & Leovy, 3 McM. & G. Rep. 378.

This doctrine has been repeatedly held in Louisiana. In *Oakey* v. *Murphy*, 18 An. 372, the court said : " In this case, which is an action by the holder of a promissory note against the maker, the plaintiff filed a supplemental petition, in which he alleged that a judgment had been rendered in his favor, at the time of the institution of his suit, on the note sued on in the circuit court of the United States for the southern district of Mississippi. On a judgment by default being taken, it was confirmed on the evidence of this judgment rendered in Mississippi. So far from this judgment proving the right of the party to recover on the note, it establishes the reverse, inasmuch as it is a merger of the note. The plaintiff has lost his right of action on the note, and he has no right to amend his petition by an allegation which extinguishes it." The court refers to 9 L. R. 419 ; 2 M., N. S. 599 ; and 3 Blackstone. See also 7 An. 334 ; 12 An. 738.

In re R. Williams, 2 N. B. R. 79, the learned judge for the district of Connecticut held, "That a debt, upon which a judgment of law is founded, is merged in the judgment. and extinguished by it," citing 27 Maine, 441 ; 32 Maine, 418 ; 2 Cush. 173 ; 2 Denio, 72 ; 17 and 11 Cush. 25 ; 17 Conn. 580.

The authorities cited sustain the learned judge in the conclusion to which he arrives. See also 6 Hill, 255, where the court says : "The defendant has been discharged, under the bankrupt law, from all debts which he owed at the time he presented his petition. Subsequent to that time the cognovit was given, and the judgment recovered. The original debt has been merged and extinguished by the judgment. The judgment is a new debt, which is not affected by the discharge."

Bacon says: "If a bond creditor obtains a judgment on the bond, or has judgment acknowledged to him, he cannot afterward bring an action on the bond, for the debt is drowned in the judgment, which is a security of higher nature than the bond." [Extinguishment (D), citing 6 Coke, 40.] The authority cited is Higgins' case, wherein Lord Coke says: "It was objected that if a man recovers debt on a bond, or rent on a lease for years, it is at the plaintiff's election to sue execution on that judgment, or to have a new action." But it was resolved "that so long as the judgment remains in force he cannot have a new action on the same bond, for, as he who has a debt by simple contract, and takes a bond for the same, or any part of it, the contract is determined, so when a man has a debt on a bond, and by ordinary course of law has judgment thereon, the contract, by specialty, which is of an inferior nature, is by judgment of law changed into a matter of record, which is of a higher nature." The latest authority of the highest court of our country is to be found in 6 Wall. 234, in the case of *Mason* v. *Eldred et al.* FIELD J., the organ of the court, there says :

"If the note in suit was merged in the judgment, then the judgment is a bar to the action, and an examplification of its record is admissable, for it has long been established that, under the plea of the general issue in assumpsit, evidence may be received to show, not merely that the alleged cause of action never existed, but also to show that it did not subsist at the commencement of the suit." And again, at page 238 : "The general doctrine maintained in England and the United

States may be briefly stated. A judgment against one upon a joint contract of several persons bars an action against the other, though the latter were dormant partners of the defendant in the original action and this fact was unknown to the plaintiff when that action was commenced. When the contract is joint, and not joint and several, the original cause of action is merged in the judgment. The joint liability of those not sued with those against whom judgment is recovered being extinguished, their entire liability is gone." Indeed, the whole opinion there reported is an able review of the decisions of the state and United States courts upon this most interesting question or doctrine of the law. Counsel for the petitioner, Cochrane, has cited in his brief, opinions adverse to the conclusion at which I have arrived. Opinions to be found in 3 N. B. R., 145 171.

But however great may be my respect for my brothers of the eastern and western districts of Michigan and of the southern district of New York, I cannot readily yield a doctrine which is supported by a long line of decisions, commencing with the year books cited by Lord Coke, and coming down to this day. When, therefore, on the eight day of June, eighteen hundred and seventy, the United States elected to take judgment upon the bond, they parted with all right to prove the bond as a debt due and payable from the bankrupt at the time of the adjudication of bankruptcy, and as a debt to be proved against the estate of the bankrupt. Cochrane, the petitioner, and assignee of the judgment, cannot be held to be conditioned otherwise than was his assignor with regard to the same. It is *res judicata* that his debt is not affected by the discharge. It has been pleaded, and the decision made in his favor. This judgment is subsisting and operative. What title, then, has he to impeach an act of the court in which he was no wise concerned, and by which he is in no manner injured. The exception must be sustained and the petition dismissed.

J. S. WHITTAKER for petitioner; R. DE GRAY and J. A. CAMPBELL for Mansfield.

UNITED STATES DISTRICT COURT—E. D. MICHIGAN.

When a creditor presents his claim for probate, he at once subjects himself and his claim to the power and jurisdiction of the court, and becomes subject to its orders within the provisions of the bankrupt act; among which is the provision that the court may examine such creditor concerning the debt sought to be proved. He is, therefore, so examined as a party to the proceedings, and is in no sense a "witness;" hence the refusal of the assignee to pay witness fees under such circumstances must be sustained.

In re S. PADDOCK. *

I, Hovey K. Clarke, register, do hereby certify that on the twelfth day of September last, the deposition of Horace G. Miller, taken before Cephas R. Dresser, one of the commissioners of the United States circuit court for this district, was filed in my office, to prove the claim of said Miller against the estate of said bankrupt; and on the twentieth day of September last the deposition of John G. Gistivit, taken before the same commissioner, was filed in my office, to prove the claim of said Gistivit against the said estate.

I further certify that on September twenty-sixth, on the petition of the assignee of said estate, a copy of which is hereto annexed, I made an order requiring the attendance of said Miller and Gistivit before me, to submit to an examination of their said claims, as required by the twenty-second section of the bankrupt act; that on this sixth day of October, said Miller and Gistivit appeared and submitted to the examination required by such order.

I further certify that after such examination the said Miller and Gistivit asked for the allowance and payment to them by said assignee of the regular witness fees, to wit: to the said Miller, for one hundred and thirty miles travel, at ten cents per mile, thirteen dollars; one day's service, one dollar and fifty cents; and to the said Gistivit, for ninety-five miles travel, nine dollars and fifty cents, and one day's service, one dollar and fifty cents; which the assignee insists ought not to be allowed, for the reason that creditors who

* See 6 N. B. R. 132.

have proved their claims are required by the bankrupt act to attend for such examination and are not entitled to fees as witnesses; and an issue of law thereon arising, I have caused the question to be stated in writing, and herewith adjourn the same into court for the decision of the judge, as required by the fourth section of the bankrupt act.

Hovey K. Clarke, Register.

Longyear, J.—When a creditor presents his claim for probate, he at once subjects himself and his claim to the power and jurisdiction of the court, and both thereby become subject to the orders of the court, under and within the provisions of the bankrupt act, among which is the provision that the court may examine such creditor concerning the debt sought to be proved (section twenty-two.) He is so examined as a party to the proceedings, and is in no sense a "witness" in the sense in which that word is used in the act of congress allowing fees to witnesses. BLATCHFGRD, J., has held expressly that witness fees cannot be allowed in such case. Bankrupts examined under section twenty-six are clearly not entitled to witness fees. In re Okell, 1 N. B. R. 52; in re McNair, 2 N. B. R. 77. BLATCHFORD, J., bases his decision, and, I think, with entire correctness, on the analogy of the claim to witness fees in the two instances, "The language of section twenty-two, in regard to the examination of the bankrupt and of a creditor, and the language of section twenty-six in regard to the examination of the bankrupt, being substantially identical."

The assignee was therefore correct in refusing to pay to the creditors, Horace J. Miller and John D. Gistivit, fees as witnesses on their examination before the register concerning their respective claims, and such claim for witness fees must be disallowed. —October 6, 1871.

UNITED STATES DISTRICT COURT—E. D. NEW YORK.

A petition was filed against an assignee in bankruptcy to have him removed
for the reason that he attacked two mortgages upon the bankrupt's property
without sufficient cause, and that he delayed a sale of the property for
the purpose of obtaining the rents in order to spend them in litigation.
Held, That the assignee was fully.justified in his attack upon the mortgages,
and that there was no evidence to show that he ever collected any rents,
or how much he has spent in litigation.   Petition dismissed, with costs
to be paid out of the fund.

In re *SACCHI*.

BENEDICT, J.—This case comes before the court upon a
petition for the removal of an assignee, chosen by the creditors of the bankrupt.   The petition is filed by Gustavus A.
Sacchi, who, since the adjudication of bankruptcy, has become the sole creditor by a purchase of all the debts.

If the petitioner had sought an order for the substitution
of an assignee of his own choosing, in place of the one originally chosen by the creditors, upon the ground that he had
become the sole creditor, I should have felt disposed to grant
the order; but such an order is declined, and the retention
of the present assignee made dependent upon the decision
of the court on the charges of misconduct made against him
in the petition.

The complaint against the assignee is that, without sufficient cause, he attacked two mortgages upon the bankrupt's
property, known as the " Brooklyn market;" one of fifteen
thousand dollars, held by Henry Mill; the other for thirty
thousand dollars, held by the petitioner, and that he has
delayed a sale of the property for the purpose of obtaining
the rents in order to spend them in litigation.   I have examined with some care the circumstance under which the assignee interposed a defense to the mortgages in question, and
stopped the foreclosure proceedings taken in the state court
to procure a sale of the property in question, and I find
nothing to support a charge of misconduct against the

assignee—but, on the contrary, much to justify his attack upon the mortgages. I am confirmed in this opinion by the fact that none of the creditors, except the petitioner, appear to have complained of the action of the assignee; that Mill, whose mortgage of fifteen thousand dollars was attacked for usury, does not appear here to complain, and that when the mortgage of thirty thousand dollars, held by the petitioner, who is the father of the bankrupt, was attacked, he bought up all the creditors interested to push the attack, at a loss of four thousand dollars, as he says. In view of all the circumstances, I am inclined to think that it would have been good ground for an application for the removal of the assignee if he had omitted to attack the mortgages. Nor is the method adopted by him, in his endeavor to release this property from the mortgages, open to criticism. The charge that he delayed the action of the mortgagees, in order to collect rents to spend in litigation, is wholly unsupported by the evidence. The proofs do not show that he ever collected any rents, or how much he has spent in litigation. The assignee admits that he has paid or is become liable for fees in the defence of the suits brought to foreclose the mortgages referred to, but no amount is stated or proved, and, so far as the evidence shows, there is no fact which will warrant the inference that the defense of the suits was interposed for any other reason except to protect the property from what he supposed to be illegal demands. It is true that the assignee might have applied sooner than he did for an order directing the sale of the property, but when he did apply the petitioner opposed, and, moreover, it is by no means clear that the property could, with due regard to the interest of the creditors, be sold earlier than even the present time. If the petitioner desired for his own interest to realize upon his mortgage, proper proceedings on his part in this court would have given him relief. 1 Dillon, 511. The petitioner failed to apply to this, and took proceedings in the state tribunal, thus compelling the assignee to resort to injunctions in order to stop his proceedings there, and save the property for distribution among the creditors in this court, where its distribution properly belongs.

The prayer of the petitioner is therefore denied, with costs of the proceedings to be paid out of the fund.

A. C. MORRIS, for petitioner; TRACY, CATLIN & VAN COTT, for assignees.—March 27, 1872.

———•◆•———

UNITED STATES DISTRICT COURT—MARYLAND.

An exemption, in accordance with the provisions of the fourteenth section of the present bankrupt act, cannot be allowed to an individual partner out of the partnership estate, as such exemption can only be allowed in case there is a surplus after paying the partnership creditors.

In re J. S. & J. PRICE.

The state law allows an exemption of one hundred dollars. John S. Price applied for this allowance out of the partnership assets. GILES, J., passed the following order upon the petition, to wit :

Ordered, this third day of January, eighteen hundred and seventy-two, that the within petitition be and the same is hereby dismissed, as it appears from the report of the register that the partnership assets are not sufficient to pay the partnership debts.

By the thirty-sixth section of the bankrupt act, it is provided that after deducting out of the whole amount of the partnership assets *the whole of the expenses and disbursements,* the net proceeds shall be appropriated to pay the partnership creditors, and if there be any surplus, it shall be appropriated to the separate estate of each partner, and then only *this surplus* becomes liable to the provisions of the fourteenth section of said act, in reference to exemptions under state laws.

UNITED STATES CIRCUIT COURT—VERMONT.

An assignee obtained an order of the district court, requiring the bankrupt and certain other parties to deliver to him property belonging to said bankrupt. From this order an appeal was taken to the United States circuit court, in form and manner prescribed by the eighth section of the bankrupt act. The assignee moved to dismiss the appeal on the ground that the proceedings in the district court were summary, and could only be reviewed by summary petition, and, therefore, not a case for an appeal under the eighth section of the bankrupt act. *Held,* That although the appeal might be irregular, the district court had jurisdiction, and from the evidence was justified in making the decree appealed from. Decree affirmed with costs.

SAMSON, Assignee, v. *BLAKE et al.*

WOODRUFF, J.—This proceeding was commenced by a petition of the assignee that the respondents deliver to the assignee certain property alleged to be of the bankrupt, and which it was alleged had been subjected by him, through the form of a sale under executions against him, to an apparent transfer to the respondents or some of them, not only in fraud of the bankrupt law, but in part also to cover and conceal the property to defraud his creditors ; and praying that the respondents show cause why the property mentioned should not be delivered to the assignee.

The respondents severally showed cause by answers to the petition, denying most of the allegations tending to show fraud, and issue was joined by the assignee upon those answers, and the questions in dispute were tried before the Hon. W. D. Shipman, district judge for Connecticut, holding the district court temporarily in the place of the resident judge. He made an order or decree, requiring the bankrupt and Lester M. Clark and Blake, to deliver the property in question to the assignee.

The parties last named have appealed to this court, in the form and manner prescribed by the eighth section of the bankrupt law.

The assignee moved to dismiss the appeal, on the ground that the proceeding in the district court was summary and could only be reviewed by summary petition to this court for a review of the proceedings, and that it was not a case for an appeal under the eighth section. The appellants insist that, although not formally commenced by process of subpœna as a suit, yet the defendants could and did appear and answer without such process, and the petition and the proceedings on showing cause and on the trial and order thereupon were in all material characteristics a suit in equity, and that the proper mode of bringing the matter before circuit court was by appeal under the said eighth section.

The motion was argued and reserved, and the case was heard upon the merits, reserving the question raised by the motion.

Upon examination of the case upon the allegations and proofs, I am so fully satisfied that the conclusions of the judge of the district court were correct, that I deem it quite unnecessary to say anything upon the point of form raised by the motion to dismiss.

Nor do I deem it necessary to discuss the subject at length. The opinion delivered by SHIPMAN, J., presents it with great fullness and particularity, and I should do little more than repeat his views, if I were to state more fully my own. Giving to the appellants the full benefit of their claim on this appeal that the proceeding in the district court should be regarded as a bill in equity, proceeding upon pleadings and proof to final decree, the transfer to the defendant, Blake, was in both the aspects presented by the district judge void as against the assignee. The appellants are, therefore, in this court in this dilemma: if the proceedings below be regarded as summary and in professed exercise of the summary power conferred by the first section of the act, then they have not brought the matter into this court for review as a summary proceeding; and whether the order of the district court was in that form of proceeding a legal and proper order is not before me. If, on the other hand, the proceeding below was, as the appellants insist it was, a suit in equity under the second section, then their appeal is regular, but in that view of the proceeding the jurisdiction and power of the district court in the premises is unquestionable, and, as above stated, the proofs in my judgment warranted the decree.

The decree should, therefore, be affirmed with costs.

***

UNITED STATES CIRCUIT COURT—VERMONT.

The United States district court has ample power to restrain a claimant of a lien, obtained by collusion with the bankrupt, from proceeding elsewhere to enforce his lien, and this power may be summarily exercised without a formal suit. When necessary, for the protection of the bankrupt's estate, or in furtherance of justice, an order once made may be revoked.

A petition to enjoin a party from making use of a certain agreement which he holds is not a formal suit but a summary proceeding.

The examination of witnesses orally before the court is no ground for reversal of an order. Order affirmed.

SAMSON, Assignee, v. *CLARK & BURTON.* *

WOODRUFF, J.—On a like petition, setting out some of the matters alleged in the petition of the assignee herein, the district court in June, eighteen hundred and seventy, made an order enjoining Oscar A. Burton from making any use of an agreement entered into between him and the bankrupt, upon the ground that it was a collusive and fraudulent arrangement for the purpose of securing to Burton a preference over other creditors in respect of certain claims which had already been merged in a judgment or barred by such judgment, and for which so long as such judgment was in force Burton had no security. But the order then made did not go so far as to invalidate or impeach the previous reversal of that judgment, although entered by consent, because it did not then sufficiently appear that the fraudulent and collusive arrangement was entered into prior to such reversal, or that the reversal was a part of the scheme devised to se-

* See 4 N. B. R. 1.

cure to Burton a preference. It is unnecessary to recite here all the details of the controversy on that former petition. It will suffice to say that Burton being sued by Clark, had interposed a counter claim, by way of set-off, to the amount of one hundred thousand dollars. Pending this suit Burton also commenced an action of " book debt," or an action " on book," claiming to recover from Clark one hundred and fifty thousand dollars, and attached property of Clark to be held to satisfy the judgment therein if he should recover. The suit against Burton proceeded to judgment, and Burton recovered under his counter claim forty-six thousand dollars, which judgment Clark had taken on bill of exceptions to the supreme court of the state for review.

In this state of things, Clark's pecuniary embarrassment increasing, other attachments of his property being made, and judgments recovered against him, Clark was proceeded against in the district court and adjudged a bankrupt in February, eighteen hundred and seventy.

At the January term of the supreme court, eighteen hundred and seventy, the judgment in favor of Burton was reserved by consent, and shortly thereafter the written agreement was entered into which provided for the discontinuance of all suits but one, and if carried into execution would permit Burton, without regard to form of action or statute of limitations, to prove all claims which he had or alleged in the one action on book account wherein Burton had attached Clark's property, and thus secure to him an apparent lien and possibly an actual lien for the amount due to him upon the claims, to the amount of one hundred thousand dollars, which had been set up in the former suit, and for which, so long as the judgment therein was in force, Burton had no security.

By the order of the district court then made, Burton was left to such right to prove his claim last mentioned as the laws of Vermont might give him.

That order was brought into this court for review, and in January, eighteen hundred and seventy-one, it was affirmed, but leave was given to the assignee to renew his application for other and further order in the premises upon new or additional evidence.

Thereupon, a further petition was presented to the district court, which was answered by the respondents, Clark and Burton, and the same was brought to a hearing, and witnesses were examined orally and proof taken in the district court, and an order was made on the eighteenth of July, eighteen hundred and seventy-one, restraining Burton from further prosecuting his said action on book account, wherein he had attached the property of the bankrupt. From that order the respondent, Burton, has appealed to this court by a formal appeal taken in the manner prescribed by the eighth section of the bankrupt law, treating the proceedings under the last named petition of the assignee as a suit in equity, proceeding upon pleadings and proofs to a judgment or decree, and to be reviewed only by appeal under that section.

The case was brought to a hearing at the October term of this court, and at the same time a motion was made to dismiss the appeal, on the ground that the proceedings in the district court were summary and in exercise of the summary jurisdiction given to that court by the first section of the bankrupt law, and can only be reviewed in this court in accordance with the provisions of the second section. The appeal provided for in the eighth section, therefore, not being applicable to the case.

The opinions delivered in the district court and in this court on the former petition, and the very elaborate opinion of SHIPMAN, J., on the present petition, render it unnecessary to go over the details of the evidence, which in the present proceeding was deemed to establish that the fraudulent scheme or contrivance between Clark and Burton, to give the latter a preference was entered into before the reversal of the judgment above mentioned; that the reversal of that judgment by consent was in execution of that scheme; that its design and object was to remove an obstacle to proving in the action on book account the matters claimed as a set-off

and determined by that judgment—and so by letting them
into the action on book account to bring them within the scope
of the attachment lien, whereas, in truth and without such reversal, Burton had not and could not gain any security therefor. And I probably should not overstate the conclusions of
the district judge, if I should say that from a period shortly
before that reversal of that judgment, Burton and Clark,
who are brothers-in-law, were acting throughout in collusion
and with the fraudulent design to make use of the attachment lien acquired in the action on book account, as a drag
net to sweep into the hands of Burton so much of the bankrupt's estate as could possibly be done by the use of claims
theretofore unsecured, claims collusively exaggerated or fictitious, and not to be seriously contested by Clark; and so
pervert the action to a fraudulent use, to the prejudice of his
other creditors, if not wholly to deprive them of any share
of the estate.

In the conclusions of the district judge upon the questions of fact I concur.

I shall, therefore, content myself with stating the questions raised on this appeal, and very briefly my conclusions
thereon.

The appellant's counsel,

FIRST. Deny the power of the district court to proceed
summarily in such a case.

SECOND. They insist that the assignee is concluded by the
former order.

THIRD. Insist that this proceeding is in substance a suit
in equity—and that an appeal under the eighth section was
proper.

FOURTH. That it was irregular and erroneous to try the
questions of fact by examination of witnesses in open court.
But the testimony should have been taken and reduced to
writing before an examiner, which is claimed to be prescribed
by the rules of the supreme court in equity.

FIFTH. That neither the proofs nor the law applicable
thereto warranted the order, in any form of proceeding.

I. I have no doubt whatever of the power and jurisdiction of the district court, under the first section of the bankrupt law, to assume the entire administration of the estate of the debtor, to determine all questions touching the existence of liens thereon—to ascertain and settle the amount of such liens, and make provision for the liquidation and settlement thereof. And, as incidental to this, it has ample power to restrain a claimant of such lien from proceeding elsewhere to enforce his lien.

Language more comprehensive can hardly be suggested than is employed in the act giving power to collect all the assets, to ascertain and liquidate the liens and other specific claims thereon, adjust the various priorities, and marshal and dispose of the different funds and assets so as to secure the rights of all parties. To this end power is given to compel obedience to all orders by process of contempt and other remedial process. The entire estate is brought within the reach of these comprehensive powers by vesting it in the assignee appointed by the court to administer it under the direction of the court. Nor can it make any difference with the power of the court over this subject, that the lien or alleged lien is inchoate and incapable of execution until the amount secured thereby is ascertained and settled; ascertainment and liquidation are expressly authorized, and the subsequent provisions of the act relating to creditors having mortgages, liens or other security, show how fully the whole administration of the estate is confided to the court. True, it does not necessarily follow that in all cases the court must prohibit any proceeding in the state court for the benefit of a creditor having a lien. There is, however, no want of power. Often it is quite convenient, and ordinarily it may be quite desirable, to permit pending actions to proceed so far as to ascertain the amount due. In one case a foreclosure of a mortgage in the state court was permitted, though begun after petition filed in the district court, and under the special circumstances of the case I deemed it proper, on review in this court, to affirm the order.

But the power to control the creditors in this respect is, I think, clearly given. Two considerations illustrate the importance of the power, which are especially applicable to liens by attachment. First. Without such power there is no adequate protection to the other creditors against collusion between the bankrupt and the claimant, not even aided by the authority given to the assignee to defend. And second, the early settlement of the estate may sometimes require that the court in bankruptcy should take the determination of claims which are in dispute into its own hands.

I deem it equally clear that this power, conferred by the first section, is to be summarily exercised, and does not require a formal suit. Indeed, whatever powers are given by the first section are designed to be exercised summarily.

There are cases in which in order to bring the property pursued by the assignee within the control of the court or its assignee, or to remove obstacles to its administration, it may be necessary for the assignee to prosecute an action at law or suit in equity, and such cases are provided for in the second section. But when the property affected by a lien is confessedly the property of the bankrupt, and has passed to the assignee, and it only remains to ascertain and liquidate the alleged lien, the summary jurisdiction of the district court is entirely adequate.

II. The suggestion that the decision upon the former hearing was final and conclusive as *res adjudicata*, is without foundation. Even in a formal suit in equity, the court may qualify the decree so that it shall not operate to prevent a new suit, and nothing is more common in disposing of motions, than to give leave to renew or apply upon new or further evidence for additional relief. The highly equitable and remedial powers conferred by the court in bankruptcy are not less free from restriction, nor are they hampered by such technical rules as will prevent the doing of what is just and for the protection of the estate, even if it required the revocation of an order once made.

III. The proceeding in question was not a formal suit,

Samson v. Burton et al.

but was a summary proceeding. It does not conform in the manner of its institution, the manner of its prosecution, nor in its form, to a suit in equity. True, the facts stated and the relief sought were like in some of their features to bills for analagous relief in suits in equity, but that proves nothing; these same facts were the proper ground of a summary application, and for the relief it was competent for the court summarily to grant. If these proceedings are compared with the rules presented to the courts of the United States in equity, relating to the commencement of suits, the form of bills, appearance therein, &c., &c., no question will, I think, remain on this point.

It would seem to follow that the mode adopted to obtain a review of the order of the district court was not warranted. It will, however, be more satisfactory to the parties, if the case is disposed of upon grounds which import that no error was committed in the order appealed from, and also upon grounds alike applicable to the proceeding, if it were regarded as a suit in form, and I, therefore, observe upon the other points:

IV. It was not ground for a reversal of the order that the witnesses were orally examined before the court; the rules of the supreme court have not taken away the power which the court has, as a court of equity, to have the testimony of the witnesses taken in open court. That power is expressly reserved in the seventy-eighth rule, which implies its existence and its perpetuation. It is there left to the discretion of the court.

V. I have, perhaps, already sufficiently expressed my views of the merits. The conclusions of the district judge were, I think, warranted by the evidence. The power of the court over the subject I have already stated. Independent of any question of actual corrupt design, the arrangement to remove the impediment of an actual adjudication, and bring the claims therein determined under the operation of the attachment in the action on book account, was an attempt to give an illegal preference in fraud of the bankrupt law. On that subject I have already expressed my opinion, on the former review above mentioned. It is not enough to say that if the debt were permitted to be established in the pending action, the court could control the execution of the judgment. I would not express any doubt of that; but it will save embarrassment, expense, and any apparent effect of a formal judgment, to be avoided by the assignee, to arrest the execution of the fraudulent scheme. And this is especially true, in view of the evidence of actual fraudulent collusion, which is deemed established. The order should be affirmed.

UNITED STATES CIRCUIT COURT—VERMONT.

An assignee applied by petition to the district court to compel the return to him of certain property of the bankrupt, which had been taken from his possession by the sheriff, by virtue of a writ of replevin, issued in the name of A. against D.

A. appeared, and without objection to the form of proceedings, answered the petition, denying that the property was ever the property of the bankrupt.

A trial was had, and the court adjudged that D. had no title or interest, but that the property belonged to the bankrupt's estate.

A. then brought his petition of review in the circuit court. The assignee moved to dismiss it on the ground that the value of the property in question was not sufficient to give the court jurisdiction; that the petition alleges no error of law, assigns no specific error, in fact.

Held, That in summary proceedings there is nothing in the law to limit the jurisdiction of the court, on review, to the value of the property in controversy; that the neglect to assign any specific error was one that might be cured by amendment, and no delay should happen to the creditors through mere defect in the formal proceedings.

The power of review is given the court as a court of equity, and on appeal it is not bound to reverse on strictly legal grounds, if satisfied that the facts are correctly found and that no injustice has been done.

The declarations of the bankrupt were admissible as evidence, as the declarations of a co-conspirator in the attempt to defraud and as part of the res gestæ. Decree affirmed, with costs.

SAMSON, assignee, v. BLAKE et al.

On petition of Blake and Clark to review an order or decree of the district court.

WOODRUFF, J.—Amos J. Samson the assignee of Alanson M. Clark, in bankruptcy, applied by petition to the district court to compel the return to him of certain property, which he alleged to be part of the personal estate of the bankrupt, of which he had taken possession and which had been taken from his possession and delivered by the sheriff to William H. Blake, by virtue of a writ of replevin issued in the name of the said Blake against one La Crosse.

Blake appeared, and without objection to the form of the proceeding, answered the petition, denying that the property was in the possession of the assignee, averring title to the property in himself, denying also that the property was ever the property of the bankrupt, and praying the court to adjust and settle the right to the said property, as between himself and the assignee, and to direct the assignee to interfere no further therewith. A trial of the issues thus raised was held in the district court, on which it appeared that the assignee of Clark, after his appointment, entered upon a farm of which the title at the time of the adjudication in bankruptcy was in the bankrupt, and which was occupied by one La Crosse, under an agreement with Clark (the bankrupt) for the purchase thereof, but for which the consideration was to be paid at a future day, upon notes which had been given therefor by La Crosse. The property in question was upon this farm. La Crosse made no claim to this personal property, yielded the possession thereof to the assignee as the property of the bankrupt, and agreed to take care of the same for him. After this the property was taken by Blake through the writ of replevin, out of the state court to which La Crosse alone was made defendant.

Evidence was given tending to show that the personal property, prior to the proceedings in bankruptcy, belonged to Clark, the bankrupt, and remained on his farm.

On the other hand, evidence on the part of Blake tended to show that the property in question belonged to La Crosse, and that prior to the proceedings in bankruptcy an execution on a judgment against La Crosse was levied thereon, and the same was sold by the sheriff and purchased by the said Blake.

Other evidence tended to show that the sale on the execution and the purchase by Blake were part of a fraudulent scheme by the bankrupt, Clark, when wholly insolvent and on the eve of the proceedings against him in bankruptcy, by the aid of Blake, to cover and conceal his property by the form of legal proceedings, wherein the property was levied upon and sold as the property of La Crosse, though in truth belonging to Clark himself : that Blake bid off the property by the procurement of Clark : and that the purchase money was furnished or repaid by Clark to Blake; the design being to prevent the property from being thereafter taken by his creditors; and that the possession of the property was not changed, but the same remained on the farm of Clark.

The district court found and adjudged that the said Blake has not and never had any right, title or interest in the property ; that the same was the property of the said bankrupt until the filing of the petition against him in bankruptcy, and the same became vested in the assignee and came lawfully into his possession. And the court thereupon ordered and decreed the restoration of the said property to the possession of the assignee, or in default thereof payment by the said Blake of its value, one hundred and seventy-eight dollars, with costs.

The said Blake has brought this petition of review, stating the proceedings above detailed, and that it was adjudged and decreed by the district court, as also above recited, and then alleging " that he is aggrieved by said adjudication and decree." Wherefore he prays a review and reversal, and that this court will make such adjudication and decree as shall seem meet, &c., &c., without pointing out any errors or supposed errors in law or in fact, or specifying any ground or reason for a reversal of such decree, except the sweeping statement that he is aggrieved.

The respondent, the assignee, moved to dismiss this petition on the ground that the value of the property is not sufficient to give this court jurisdiction ; and second, that the petition alleges no error in law, assigns no specific error in fact, and contains only an allegation that the petitioner is aggrieved.

At the hearing the court reserved the consideration of this motion, and directed the argument to proceed on the merits.

I find no warrant for limiting the jurisdiction of this court to review summary proceedings in bankruptcy by any measure of the value of the property involved, and no statutory provision nor any decision of the courts was referred to prescribing or affirming any such limitation. If therefore, the proceedings below ought to be regarded as summary proceedings, this court has jurisdiction to review them. If, on the other hand, though informal, they were in substance a suit as upon bill and cross bill, then no proper appeal was taken; upon which, however, it will not be necessary to rest any conclusion.

As to the other ground on which the motion to dismiss was urged, it is sufficient to say; that, although I shall dispose of this case, when I hold that there is no sufficient ground for reversing the decree of the district court I do not design to sanction so loose a practice as this petition of review pursues. Nevertheless, as the defect might be cured by amendment, and as no prejudice can come to the assignee or to the estate, under the conclusion which has been reached on the other branch of the case, it is better for all interested as creditors or otherwise that no further delay should happen, through mere defect in the formal proceedings.

The proofs, I think, warranted the conclusion of the court below that the property in question came to the possession of the assignee as part of the estate of the bankrupt, and was in his possession when Blake took it by his writ of replevin. The district court would have failed in its duty had it suffered that possession to be forcibly displaced by a third person, although using the form of process of the state court, to which the assignee was not a party, and in which the title of the assignee was not in question, but the property was to be subjected to such fate as a contest between two strangers to the proceedings in bankruptcy might involve. The district court

was open to the application of such third party if he desired
to assert title and claim a delivery of the property by the
assignee to him, or a suit at law or in equity, as the case
might require, could have been brought against the assignee
by such third party, in that or in this court.

As to the title to the property itself; that depended upon
questions of fact, in respect to which there is no such preponderance of evidence against the conclusion of the district court
as calls for a reversal; on the contrary, my own conviction concurs with that of the district judge. If it were otherwise, a finding of fact, upon an examination of witnesses in the presence
of the court, where the opportunity for judging correctly of
the credibility of the witnesses and weight of the testimony
is better than can ordinarily be afforded by an inspection of
the testimony when reduced to writing, should not be reversed without a very clear and decided conviction that it is
erroneous.

It was strenuously insisted that error was committed in
the admission of declarations of the bankrupt in evidence.
On this point, three observations are pertinent.

First, this review is given to the court as a court of equity,
and there, on an inquiry into questions of fact, the court on
appeal are not bound to reverse upon strictly legal grounds,
if satisfied that the facts are correctly found and that no injustice has been done.   Second, the declarations in question
were in aid and in partial execution of, or at least, while Clark
was engaged in the alleged scheme to cover and conceal his
property to which Blake was a party; they were therefore
admissible as the declaration of a co-conspirator in the attempt
to defraud; and third, for the reason last stated, they were
properly regarded as a part of the *res gestæ*, when title in
La Crosse was set up by Blake, and the fraudulent sale and
pretended purchase by Blake were relied on.

It was not objected on the argument of this review, that
the proceedings on the petition of the assignee were not regular and proper, or that the order or decree sought to be reviewed was not within the summary jurisdiction of the dis-

trict court. Blake, the petitioner in review, appeared in the district court and answered the petition. He not only raised no objection to the form or substance of the proceeding, or the jurisdiction of the court therein, but submitting to the jurisdiction, he invoked its exercise in his own behalf, by filing an answer in the nature of a cross bill in equity, alleging his own title, and praying the court to adjust and settle the right to the said property, as between him and the assignee, to give to him the control thereof, and to restrain the assignee from interference therewith. Upon the issues of fact the parties went to trial, and with the results above stated. This court is therefore not called upon to consider whether the determination of the question of title to this property should have been sought by a summary proceeding in the district court or by a proceeding formally commenced by a process. Jurisdiction of the subject matter and question existed in the court, and both parties submitted themselves to its exercise, and indeed invoked it in the form and manner stated. Nor does the petitioner in review raise any objection in this court, that there is any defect or error in the decree or order, founded on the mode of procedure in the district court. Besides, the court having found as matter of fact that the property was in the possession of the assignee, the court had power to protect that possession against interference, except by resort to a proper legal proceeding to which the assignee should be a party ; and therefore, when Blake, the claimant, by his cross petition invoked the controlling power of the court over the assignee, as its officer, and submitted to a trial of the questions which he asked the court to determine, no question arises whether a more formal suit would or would not have been proper.

The judgment or decree must be affirmed with costs.

R. C. BENTON for the petitioner in review ; EDWARD J. PHELPS for the assignee.

SUPREME COURT—IOWA.

After the filing of a petition in bankruptcy no valid lien can be acquired upon property of the bankrupt by proceedings in a state court ; and an assignee is not bound to go into a state court to defend such a suit, the action being a nullity as to him. The order to show cause, as required by section forty of the bankrupt act, may be served personally outside the district in which the petition is filed by any one authorized by the solicitor for the petitioner to make it. This rule is not altered where one or more of several partners file their petition in bankruptcy, in which several members of the partnership refuse to join: the parties so refusing may be proceeded against as involuntary bankrupts, and the order to show cause may be served on them outside the territorial jurisdiction of the court, and by a person duly authorized by the solicitor for the petitioner.

STUART, assignee, v. *HINES et al.*

On the twenty-eight day of September, eighteen hundred and seventy, the plaintiff filed in the Muscatine district court his petition, claiming that, as assignee of the estate and effects of Thomas M. Isett, a bankrupt, he was the absolute owner, for the uses and purposes set forth in "an act to establish a uniform system of bankruptcy throughout the United States," of certain real estate in the petition particularly described, and that the defendants George R. Hines and David W. Eames, and Jacob Butler as their trustee, made some claims to said premises adverse to the estate and title of the plaintiff. Plaintiff prayed that his title and estate in and to said premises be established and quieted ; and that the defendants be barred and estopped from claiming or asserting any right or title therein.

The defendants, Hines and Eames, and Jacob Butler, filed their answer, denying that plaintiff was the owner of the premises described, and averring that Jacob Butler, as trustee, was the owner thereof in fee. For further answer, they alleged that all the proceedings in bankruptcy against Isett were without jurisdiction and void, and that the assignment to plaintiff was void. Subsequently the defendants filed a further answer, alleging, "that the said defendant, Jacob Butler, as trustee for defendants Hines and Eames, purchased said premises at sheriff's sale, made under an execution issued from the office of the clerk of this court upon a judgment regularly obtained at the June term of this court, in the year eighteen hundred and sixty-nine, as will more fully appear from an inspection of the records and papers of the case, entitled ' Hines & Eames, v. Isett, Kerr & Co.,' in which a writ of attachment was issued against the defendants, Thomas M. Isett, John Kerr, and Watson B. Farr, and the said premises were, on the thirteenth day of February, eighteen hundred and sixty-nine, attached as the property of defendants. That this court, before any other legal proceedings were had, obtained full and exclusive jurisdiction of the parties and the subject matter of the action. That neither the said defendants nor the said John M. Stuart appeared or made defence in said action ; and defendants aver that said defendants, Isett, Kerr & Co., and the said plaintiff in this action, are estopped from asserting any claim or title to said premises, so long as said judgment remains unreversed, and is not cancelled or set aside."

The cause was tried by the court, and judgment was rendered for the plaintiff.

The defendants appealed.

CLOUD & BROOMHALL, for appellants; CHARLES A. PEABODY, of New York, and RICHMAN & CABSKADDEN, for appellee.

DAY, C. J.—On and prior to August thirteenth, eighteen hundred and sixty-eight, Thomas M. Isett, John Kerr, and Watson B. Farr, were copartners, under the name of Isett, Kerr & Co., doing business as bankers and brokers, at the city of New York, in the southern federal district of New York. On the thirty-first day of December, eighteen hundred and sixty-eight, Kerr and Farr filed their petition in bankruptcy in the United States district court of that district, asking that they and their copartner, Isett, be declared bankrupts, alleging that Isett refused to join the petition with them. On the twenty-seventh of March, eighteen hundred and sixty-nine, Isett, Kerr and Farr were adjudged

bankrupts.   On the twenty-fifth of October, eighteen hundred and sixty-nine, the plaintiff, John M. Stuart, was regularly chosen to be assignee of the estate and effects of the
said bankrupts.   On the twenty-eighth day of October, eighteen hundred and sixty-nine, the proper register in bankruptcy executed a deed of assignment, conveying to said John
M. Stuart all the estate, real and personal, of which the said
Thomas M. Isett was seized, or in which he was interested,
on the thirty-first of December, eighteen hundred and sixty-
eight.   This deed was filed for record in Muscatine county,
Iowa, on the ninth day of November, eighteen hundred and
sixty-nine.   Thomas M. Isett owned the real estate in controversy, situated in Muscatine county, Iowa.   Hines and
Eames caused an attachment to be levied on said property
on the thirteenth day of February, eighteen hundred and
sixty-nine.   They obtained judgment on the fourteenth day
of June, eighteen hundred and sixty-nine.   The property
was purchased by Jacob Butler, as trustee of Hines and
Eames, on the twenty-fifth of June, eighteen hundred and
seventy.

Appellants discuss the points made in their assignment of
errors under two general heads.

FIRST. Did the judgment of the state court estop the
plaintiff from proceeding in this suit?

SECOND. Had the bankruptcy court jurisdiction over either
the person or property of Thomas M. Isett?

We will pursue the same order in our consideration of
the case.

1. *As to the effect of the judgments against Isett, Kerr & Co.,
in the Muscatine district and circuit courts.*

Appellants claim that by these proceedings valid and
subsisting liens have been created in favor of the defendants.
In support of their position they cite numerous authorities,
all of which we have examined with a care commensurate
with the importance of the questions involved in this appeal.

None of them, in our opinion, support the position they
are cited to sustain.   *In re* Houseberger, 2 N. B. R. 37; *in re*

Campbell, N. B. R. Sup. xxxvii; *ex parte* Burns, id. 105; *in re* Kerr, 2 N. B. R. 124; *in re* Schnepf, N. B. R. Sup. xli; *in re* Clarke & Bininger, 3 N. B. R. 123; *Clarke* v. *Bininger* 3 N. B. R. 129; *The United States* v. *The Judges of the Superior Court*, 9 Am. Law Reg. 279; *Samson* v. *Burton*, 4 N. B. R. 1; *in re* Davis, 2 id. 125; *Bowman* v. *Harding*, 4 id. 5; *Bates* v. *Tappan*, 3 id. 159; *Armstrong* v. *Rickey Bros.* 2 id. 150; *Sedgwick* v. *Minck*, 1 id. 204; *Hawkin's Appeal*, 8 Am. Law Reg. 205; *ex parte* Donaldson, 7 id. 213; *in re* Wallace, 2 N. B. R. 52.

Thus we have reviewed all the authorities cited by appellants. Not one of them is a case where an attempt was made in a state court to acquire a lien against the property of the bankrupt after the filing of the petition in bankruptcy. Not one of them even by implication or analogy sustains the validity of such a lien. Indeed the last case, *in re* Wallace, 2 N. B. R. 52, is a very strong one against the position of appellants; for if an attachment levied within four months *prior* to the filing of the petition in bankruptcy will in another court be held void, and execution for the enforcement of the judgment be stayed by injunction, what becomes of an attachment levied many months *after* the petition in bankruptcy is filed?

In the case at bar the petition for an adjudication in bankruptcy was filed on the thirty-first day of December, eighteen hundred and sixty-eight. The filing of this petition constituted the commencement of the bankruptcy proceeding. "The filing of a petition for adjudication in bankruptcy, either by a debtor in his own behalf, or by any creditor against a debtor, upon which an order may be issued by the court, or by a register, in the manner provided in section four, shall be deemed and taken to be the commencement of proceedings in bankruptcy under this act." Section thirty-eight.

"Where an adjudication of bankruptcy is made following the filing of a petition, then it is judicially established that the proceedings in the case commenced when the petition was filed:" *In re* Patterson, N. B. R. Sup. xxvii.

Section fourteen of the bankrupt act provides : " That as soon as said assignee is appointed and qualified, the judge, or where there is no opposing interest, the register shall by an instrument under his hand, assign and convey to the assignee all the estate real and personal of the bankrupt, with all his deeds, books and papers relating thereto, and such assignment shall relate back to the commencement of said proceedings in bankruptcy, and thereupon, by operation of law, the title to all such property and estate, both real and personal, shall vest in said assignee, although the same is then attached on mesne process as the property of the debtor, and shall dissolve any such attachment made within four months next preceding the commencement of said proceedings. The date of the filing of the petition in bankruptcy becomes the date from which the assignee takes all the property of the bankrupt which was his property at that date." *In re* Patterson, *supra.*

"The commencement of proceedings in bankruptcy operates as a *supersedeas* of all process in the hands of the officer of any other court, and as an injunction against all other proceedings than such as may afterwards be had under the authority of the court of bankruptcy, until such case is closed. Thus the levy of an execution, or the filing of a bill to foreclose a mortgage, or the filing of a libel *in rem*, or the issuing of a distress warrant, or the filing of a mechanics' lien claim where the lien only exists from the time of such filing, or the issuing of a writ of replevin, for the purpose of affecting the estate, are null and void, when such proceedings are instituted after that time. Claims against the bankrupt's property can only be enforced in the court of bankruptcy during the pendency of the proceedings, and this principle extends not only to liens, but to all controversies concerning even the title to property which was in his possession at the time of filing the petition :" Bump's ·Law and Practice of Bankruptcy, citing *Pennington* v. *Sale and Phelan*, 1 N. B. R. 157 ; *in re* Kerosene Oil Co., 2 id. 164 ; s. c. 3 id. 31 ; *in re* People's Mail Steamship Co. 2 id. 170 ; *in re* Wynne, 4 id.

5; *in re* Day, 3 id. 81; *in re* Vogel, 2 id. 138; s. c. 3 id. 49, which fully sustain the doctrine of the text.

The conveyance to the assignee was made on the twenty-eighth day of October, eighteen hundred and sixty-nine, and related back to the thirty-first day of December, eighteen hundred and sixty-eight, and vested in the assignee all the property of the bankrupt owned by him at that date. The attachments under which the defendant's claim were all levied after the petition in bankruptcy was filed. The authorities cited, clearly settle the doctrine that after a filing of a petition in bankruptcy, no valid lien upon the property at that time owned by the bankrupt can be acquired by proceedings in a state court, and are conclusive in favor of the assignee against these defendants. And if this were not so, the requirements of the bankrupt act might easily be ignored, and its provisions nullified. It can have force and efficiency, and can accomplish its purposes by no other construction.

There is another view of this case, which is equally conclusive against the title of these defendants.

The sale of the land upon execution to Jacob Butler, under the Hines and Eames' judgment, occurred on the twenty-fifth of June, eighteen hundred and seventy. On the ninth of November, eighteen hundred and sixty-nine, the deed of conveyance to the assignee was recorded in Muscatine county, and by the provisions of the bankrupt act, section fourteen related back to the thirty-first day of December, eighteen hundred and sixty-eight, the date of filing the petition in bankruptcy. It was apparent of record, then, at the time of the sale upon execution, that the judgment debtor had no title to or interest in the property sold. Hence, under the doctrine of *Norton et al.* v. *Williams*, 9 Iowa 528, the purchaser at sheriff's sale acquired no title. See *Bell* v. *Evans et al.*, 10 Iowa 353.

Appellants claim that the allegation that they are the owners of the premises in dispute by virtue of the proceedings in the state courts, makes a counter-claim of title, which, not being denied by plaintiff, must be taken as admitted.

This position is not tenable. The allegation of title is made merely as a defence to plaintiff's claim. No affirmative relief is sought against the plaintiff. A counter-claim is a cause of action in favor of the defendants or some of them, against the plaintiffs or some of them. Revision, Sec. 2889.

It is further claimed that it was the duty of the assignee to appear and defend in the state courts in place of the bankrupt, and that, having failed to do so, he is estopped from asserting any claim to the property. This position is equally unsound. The bankrupt act authorizes the assignee to prosecute and defend for the bankrupt, causes *pending* at the time of filing the petition in bankruptcy. Sec. 16.

We find no provision of the bankrupt law, nor any adjudged case, which requires the assignee to go into a state court to defend an action commenced against the bankrupt subsequently to the date of filing the petition in bankruptcy. Such a determination would be in direct conflict with the whole current of the authorities, which hold that all proceedings instituted against the bankrupt after the filing of the petition, in any other court than the court of bankruptcy, are invalid. Besides, the judgments in all the cases which have been prosecuted to judgment were rendered before the assignee was appointed. We conclude that the first position assumed by appellants cannot be maintained.

II. *As to the jurisdiction of the bankruptcy court over the person and property of Thomas M. Isett*—This question may be briefly considered. Appellee claims that the deed of assignment is, in this case, *conclusive* that such jurisdiction existed. In the view which we take of the case, we need not determine as to the soundness of this claim.

The petition in bankruptcy was addressed to the Hon. SAMUEL BLATCHFORD, judge of the district court of the United States for the southern district of New York. The order upon Thomas M. Isett to show cause why the prayer of the petition should not be granted was served in Jersey City, State of New Jersey, by Fisher A. Baker, one of the solicitors of Farr and Kerr, the petitioners.

Appellants claim : First. That personal service cannot be made out of the district in which the petition is filed. Second. That service must be made by the United States marshal, or by a messenger, as provided by statute.

1. The first position is not sound. Section thirty-six of the bankrupt act provides that a partnership may be declared bankrupt upon the petition of any one of its members. Rule eighteen, promulgated by the supreme court of the United States, (Gazzam on Bankruptcy 367,) provides that notice shall be given to any partner refusing to join in the petition, in the same manner as provided in the case of a debtor petitioned against. Section forty of the bankrupt act provides that upon the filing of the petition in bankruptcy, the court shall direct the entry of an order requiring the debtor to appear and show cause why the prayer of the petition should not be granted. "A copy of the petition and of such order to show cause shall be served on such debtor by delivering the same to him personally, or leaving the same at his last or usual place of abode ; or if such debtor cannot be found, or his place of residence ascertained, service shall be made by publication in such manner as the judges may direct." Bump on Bankruptcy 449. The act is entirely silent as to the place of service, the mode only is designated. Under section eleven of the bankrupt act, any member of a firm may file his petition to have the firm declared bankrupt in any district where the partnership business has been carried on for the longest period of the six months immediately preceding the filing of the petition. In such case, if the other members of the firm reside out of the district where the business is carried on and the petition is filed, efficiency can be given to this provision only by service out of the district. We do not, however, understand appellants to deny the power to obtain service out of the district. They contend that such service can be made only by publication. But the act authorizes service by publication only when the party to be served cannot be found, or his place of residence ascertained. The fact that Isett *was found* and

Stuart v. Hines et al.

personally served, shows that he does not come within the exception authorizing service by publication. Hence, if any service outside of the district in which the petition is filed is proper, personal service must be.

2. The second position is, in our opinion, equally untenable. The act nowhere provides by whom this service shall be made. Section eleven of the act provides that the judge or register shall issue a *warrant* directed to the marshal; and section forty provides that the court may issue a *warrant* to the marshal of the district commanding him to arrest the said bankrupt. The fact that the act makes special provision for the service of certain processes by the marshal and remains entirely silent as to the person by whom the order to show cause shall be served, is a strong argument against the position that such order can be served by the marshal only. *Expressio unius est exclusio alterius.*

In *Gordon* v. *Scott and Allen*, 2 N. B. R. 28, the question was raised whether a *subpœna* could be served by the party. In determining the question, McCANDLESS, J., holds this language: "It is true that the marshal is the executive officer of the court, and may be directed by the court to serve it, but the mandate of the writ is not to him but to the witness who is commanded to appear and testify. As there is no legislation of congress directing the service of a *subpœna* by the marshal, we do not feel disposed to depart from the practice of the state courts, which has always permitted the party to serve the precept and allowed him costs for the same. The first section of the act of September twenty-fourth, seventeen hundred and ninety-nine, requires the marshal "to execute throughout the district all lawful precepts *directed to him,* and issued under the authority of the United States. But the *subpœna* is not directed to him, but to the witness, and the marshal might legitimately refuse to serve it unless commanded so to do by an order of the court." The order to show cause in like manner is not directed to the marshal but to the debtor, and in the absence of legislation upon the subject, we know of no reason why another may not serve it.

III. Some objection is urged in the argument to the sufficiency of the averments of the petition in bankruptcy. It is averred that the petitioners for the six months next preceding the application have been residents of the judicial district in which the petition is filed, and that they and said Isett within said time were partners in trade in said district. Whilst it may have been more formal if the petition had averred that during the past six months they had been engaged for the longest period in business in said district, thus negativing the idea that as to the said firm the proper jurisdiction was elsewhere, yet as the court to which it was directed has treated it as sufficient, and it does not appear that the firm did business for a longer period in any other district, we must, for the purposes of this proceeding, regard the petition as containing enough to confer upon the court jurisdiction of the application.

We discover no error in the judgment of the district court, and it is affirmed.

UNITED STATES DISTRICT COURT—E. D. VIRGINIA.

A was residuary legatee of B, and took the real estate subject to the payment of a certain sum to C in trust for the benefit of three of B's children, to be paid at the expiration of three years from B's death. A enjoyed the possession of this real estate some thirty years. became insolvent, was adjudicated a bankrupt in January, eighteen hundred and seventy-one, and the estate in question was sold by his assignee. C did not receive the sum which was to have been paid to him by A according to the terms of the will. On the question of distribution the court held, that A was not an express or direct trustee, and that the statutory bar was a complete defence to any claim for the amount to have been paid to C as trustee.

In re A. G. O'NEALE.

UNDERWOOD, J.—Thomas L. O'Neale, the ancestor of Albert G. O'Neale, died in eighteen hundred and thirty-five, leaving a last will and testament, by which he devised a large estate to his widow and children, giving to the former a life estate in certain real and personal property, including slaves. To the children, four in number, he gave, under various conditions, property of different kinds. After these bequests and by another clause of his will, he declared : " I give to Albert G. O'Neale the whole balance of my estate, embracing Lindsey Hall—subject to the payment of three thousand dollars to D. W. Pitt and B. D. Pitt, in trust for the support of my son Robert Johnson O'Neale and of my daughters Mary Lindsey Andrews and Sarah J. Jones, and their children, to be paid to the said trustees at the expiration of three years from my death."

The will was duly probated in the proper county. On the death of the ancestor, Albert G. O'Neale went into possession of " Lindsey Hall" under the devise to him, and has continued to occupy it to the present time, a period of more than thirty years. Sarah J. Jones, now Sarah J. Dobyns, and Albert G. O'Neale have lived in the same neighborhood during all the period. O'Neale was a man of large wealth and undoubted responsibility until the close of the war, when he became insolvent and was adjudicated a bankrupt in June, eighteen hundred and seventy-one. His estate, Lindsey Hall, was sold by his assignee, and this controversy arises on the question as to how the proceeds of that sale should be distributed.

Sarah J. Dobyns claims a prior lien for part of the money bequest of three thousand dollars, which was to have been paid to the Pitts, for the use of herself and her children.

One Baylor claims priority under a judgment recovered in April, eighteen hundred and seventy, for about two thousand three hundred dollars. Smith, as guardian, claims priority under a trust deed executed March twelfth, eighteen hundred and seventy, but not recorded until May tenth, eighteen hundred and seventy, for about two thousand three hundred dollars.

It is admitted that the bequest of three thousand dollars, if treated as a right of action in suit before a court of law, is barred, more than the longest period for bringing civil actions having elapsed since the debt became due. It is also admitted the courts of equity apply the analogies of common law limitations, and will not enforce stale demands, and that no new promise has been made nor any act done to take this case out of the statute of limitations, but the claimant, Dobyns, insists that this is a trust, and that trusts are not within the statute of limitations. This general proposition is also conceded, but Smith and Baylor reply that the rule "that the statute of limitations does not apply between trustee and *cestui que trust*" extends only to direct or express trustees, and does not apply as between a *cestui que trust* and an *implied* trustee. There is some conflict of testimony as to whether the charge of three thousand dollars on Lindsey Hall has not been paid, but it is not necessary to consider that question now, nor to determine whether the whole or every part of the bequest, principal or interest, has been paid in fact to Mrs. Dobyns, or to her children, all of whom have been of age for many years, for in the view taken by the court the statutory bar is complete.

It is manifest that O'Neale was not made a trustee for Mrs. Dobyns by the *terms* of his father's will. Pitts and Pitts were the persons in whom the trust was reposed. They were the *direct* trustees, made so by the act and choice of the devisor. If Albert G. O'Neale took the character of a trustee at all, it was that of an implied or resultant trustee. That character was imposed upon him either by operation of law or by matters of evidence. He was changed into a trustee, if he ever became one, by matters of evidence or construction of law. When did that relation first attach? Certainly not when he entered into possession of the property under the will, for he took the estate in his own right, nor could it attach for three years thereafter, because the charge did not become due until the expiration of that period. The answer to the question must be, that if he ever became trustee it was because Pitts and Pitts failed to act as trustees, and Mrs. Dobyns and himself dealt with the estate and with each other as though he was the trustee, but it is not material when or how he became trustee, if he took the character, not by the appointment of the will, but afterwards by matter of evidence or construction of law.

The distinction between direct and implied trustees is important, and not to be overlooked. The former enters, takes and holds the estate not in his own right, but in the right and for the benefit of .another. It would be against conscience for such an one to claim, as against his *cestui que trust*, any title adverse to him, until by open and notorious act of disavowal the trust estate had been terminated. As between such a trustee and his *cestui que trust* no time runs, and the statute would not be a bar.

But as between the implied trustee, he who has entered into possession of the property in his own right, and who holds for his own benefit, but whose title is subsequently by matter of evidence or construction of law, turned into that of a trustee for the use and benefit, in whole or in part, of another, time does run, and the statute of limitations does apply, and that, in the opinion of the court, is the precise relation in which Albert G. O'Neale and Mrs. Dobyn stand, if in fact he ever became her trustee at all. This distinction as to the rights of express or implied trustees under the statute of limitations, is not new in this country nor in England. It is laid down by Story, 2d Story Eq. sec. 1520, b. Lewin on Trusts, sec. 774; Perry on Trusts, 778 ; *Ellendorf* v. *Taylor*, 10 Wheat. 168, 177 ; 23 How. 207 ; *Deeanche* v. *Saviter*, 3d Johns. C. R. 190 ; *Walker* v. *Walker*, 16 Sergt and R. 170; Angel on Limitations, sec. 471, 167, 178 ; *Shepard* v. *Turpin*, 3d Grat. 394 ; *Beaubien* v. *Beaubien*, 23 How. 207 ; *King* v. *Bloodgood*, 7 John., ch. R. 91, and very many other authorities.

The court is, therefore, of opinion that Albert G. O'Neale was not an express or direct trustee. That the statute of limitations does apply between Sarah J. Dobyns and Baylor and Smith, that this is, in fact, only a controversy between Dobyns, Baylor and Smith, rival lien holders and claimants to priority, and that both Baylor and Smith are entitled to priority over the claimant Dobyns. No opinion is, however, expressed at this time on the question of the relative rights of Baylor and Smith to priority of payment, but that question is left for future consideration.

In re Stowe, ex parte Godfrey.

UNITED STATES DISTRICT COURT—MAINE.

A creditor advanced money to his debtor, within four months of proceedings in bankruptcy, and took a mortgage of the debtor's stock in trade, first, as security therefor ; secondly, included in the same mortgage, another (antecedent) debt due to himself, which was secured by a prior mortgage on the same property, held by and given to the bankrupt's (debtor's) former copartner ; and, thirdly, for convenience, and to save writing an additional mortgage, an overdue note taken up and held by the endorser, by whose request it was inserted in the mortgage. Subsequent to proceedings in bankruptcy, the stock in trade was sold, with the consent of the several mortgagees, who proved their claims before the register as secured debts, and joined with the assignee in submitting to the register their rights under the mortgage. The register held that the mortgage was void as against the assignee, because intended to secure a pre-existing debt, &c.—the overdue note—according to the principle of the decision in *Denny* v. *Dana,* 2 Cush. 160.

Held, On appeal by the mortgagee, (the endorser withdrawing therefrom and surrendering all rights under the mortgage,) that the mortgage could be severed and sustained in part, and denied as to the rest. The court also disapproved the mode of presenting the case. It should be presented by a petition of the mortgagee against the funds in court.

In re STOWE, ex parte GODFREY.

The bankrupt applied, within four months of the proceedings in bankruptcy, to Godfrey for a loan of money, and agreed to give him a mortgage, as security, on his stock in trade in his store in Oldtown. He needed the money to pay off some overdue notes held by one Smith, which were secured by a mortgage of stock in trade, executed by the firm, Stowe & Waldron, composed of the bankrupt and Waldron, previously doing business at the same place then occupied by the bankrupt, and to whom he was successor.

Godfrey was also the owner of a note of Stowe & Waldron, secured by another mortgage, given by Stowe to Waldron at the dissolution of the firm, as indemnity against partnership debts, and which it was agreed should also be included in the mortgage to secure the loan then being negotiated.

While the negotiation was pending, Dillingham, another creditor, who had as an accommodation endorser been compelled, a few days before, to pay a note of the bankrupt, learning that Stowe was about making the mortgage in question, called upon Godfrey and informed him of the circumstances, and requested him as favor, and to save multiplying papers, to include his claim in this mortgage. A mortgage was accordingly made, including Dillingham's claim, which was evidenced by a note of the bankrupt, payable to his own order, endorsed in blank, and dated the same day as the mortgage, and a new note given to Godfrey, embracing his two claims.

Shortly after, Stowe failed, and proceedings in bankruptcy having been commenced against him, his stock in trade was sold under section twenty-five, with the consent of the mortgagees, and the funds arising from the sale were deposited in court, subject to the rights of the mortgagees; and, thereupon, by agreement between the assignee and the secured creditors, their rights under the last mortgage were submitted to the register in charge of the cause. Both Godfrey and Dillingham claimed before the register that they held a valid lien upon the funds in court, by virtue of the mortgage to Godfrey; and each filed "proofs of debt with security," accompanied by their examinations, taken on application of the assignee. No evidence was offered to show whether any of the Stowe and Waldron stock at the dissolution of that firm was in existence at the date of the mortgage to Godfrey. The register decided the mortgage was void as against the assignee, under section thirty-five, for several reasons, but principally because it was a preference of the Dillingham claim—that the mortgage was an entirety as presented by Godfrey, and being void in part, according to *Denny* v. *Dana*, 2 Cush. 160, was void in whole. On the issues of fact and law thus arising the register, at the request of the parties, adjourned the same into court for the decision of the judge.

At the hearing before the judge, and upon the suggestion of the court, that the proceedings were irregular, the parties withdrew their proofs, and Godfrey presented instead a petition against the funds in court, claiming payment only of his own demand; Dillingham making no further claim under the mortgage.

In re Stowe, ex parte Godfrey.

Fox, J., (*orally*).—I find the consideration of Godfrey's note was in part money *then* loaned and the balance was received in discharge of a note upon which he then had full security, *first* by the partnership of Stowe & Waldron and *second* by and through the mortgage on Stowe's stock, held to be sure by Waldron, but which in equity would inure to Godfrey's benefit as the holder of the liability thereby protected.

Under these circumstances, it does not appear to me that Godfrey and Stowe can be deemed to have intended a fraudulent preference of *this* demand; under the provisions of the bankrupt law there was a full present consideration for this mortgage *qua* this note, and the estate has not been in any way defrauded thereby.

Whether the Dillingham claim is equally pure and protected it is not in my view necessary to determine, as Dillingham makes no claim to payment from the mortgaged property, and the case of *Denny* v. *Dana* 2 Cush. 160, I think is not to control the rights of Godfrey. If Dillingham had taken the mortgage charged with a fraudulent motive and preference of his debt, under the bankrupt law, it may be that this case would control, but Godfrey himself is found by me entirely innocent, and so far as he is concerned, is a *bona fide* holder for present value.

I think the case falls within that class of which *United States* v. *Bradley* 10 Pet. 360 is an illustration, that a contract may be good in part and void for the residue, where the residue is founded in *illegality*, but not *malum in se*. Now *extra* the provisions of the bankrupt act Dillingham had a perfect right to take this security, and as all proceedings in bankruptcy are based on principles of equity, I think we are justified in severing the conditions of the mortgage and sustaining it so far as one of the claims in behalf of the sole mortgagee, entirely innocent of all violation of the law, is concerned.

The following decree was subsequently entered by the court :

In re Stowe, ex parte Godfrey.

Fox, J.—The assignee named in the foregoing petition having acknowledged notice, and the case having been argued by counsel in behalf of the respective parties, *it is by the court now ordered, adjudged and decreed,* that the security by mortgage of September twenty-seventh, eighteen hundred and seventy, on the bankrupt's stock of goods and merchandise, as set forth in said petition, for the payment to said Godfrey of the note of said bankrupt for seven hundred and ninety-three dollars and seventeen cents, on six months with interest, (said note being in part for a present consideration than advanced by said Godfrey to said bankrupt, and the residue thereof being in payment of a demand held by said Godfrey against said bankrupt, payment of which before that time had been and then was fully secured to said Godfrey,) constituted a valid and legal incumbrance on the property mortgaged to the extent of the amount due upon said note and was not in fraud of any of the provisions of the bankrupt act, and that said stock in trade passed to said assignee in bankruptcy, charged with and subject to said lien and incumbrance. And it is therefore further ordered, that said assignee pay to said Godfrey, forthwith, from the net proceeds of the sale of said mortgaged property, if the same shall be sufficient for that purpose after satisfaction of any previous liens, if any there be, the amount due upon said note with legal interest at six per cent. from the time said note became due and payable.

H. C. Goodenow, Esq., for assignee; C. P. Stetson, Esq., for Godfrey.—July 3, 1871.

U. S. DISTRICT COURT—W. D. MISSOURI.

A finding himself unable to meet his liabilities, compromised with all his creditors, except B, whom he proposed to pay in full if he would give a large extension of time ; to this B agreed, and received, as security, an assignment of two judgments, and also a deed for a lot, which together were supposed to exceed in value the amount of B's claim. At the time of this transfer an agreement was entered into, in effect that whatever was paid on the judgments should be credited on the claim, and the lot was to be returned within twelve months from the date of the transfer, providing the indebtedness was all liquidated. The claim was not paid, however, and more than six months after the assignment a petition in bankruptcy was filed against A by B, alleging that he had made a disposition of his property out of his usual and ordinary course of business, with intent to hinder and delay his creditors.

Held, 1. That B's claim was an existing indebtedness provable in bankruptcy.
2. That A made a disposition of his property with the intent to delay, hinder and defraud his creditors, and that he had committed an act of bankruptcy.

ÈCFORT & PETRING v. *GREELY.*

KREKEL, J.—This case calls for the determination of two questions :

FIRST. Did Ecfort & Petring have a claim or debt provable under the bankrupt law ? and

SECOND. Did Greely make a transfer, sale, or conveyance of his property with intent to delay, hinder, or defraud his creditors ?

The evidence as to the first question is, that Greely was a partner of a mercantile firm (Brutsche & Greely) which, in the fall of eighteen hundred and sixty-seven, became embarrassed and asked an extension of time, which was granted by their creditors, of whom Ecfort & Petring were the largest, they having a claim of upwards of thirty-two hundred dollars.

In the spring of the year eighteen hundred and sixty-eight, the firm, finding that they could not meet their liabilities, entered into a composition agreement with their creditors, by which they were to pay fifty cents on the dollar, and which was paid to all except Ecfort & Petring, whom they proposed to pay in full, if they would give a large extension of time. This proposition was accepted by Ecfort & Petring, on condition that they would secure them as far as they were able.. This the debtor firm agreed to do, and afterwards assigned two judgments, which amounted, when collected, to thirteen hundred and forty dollars. They also made a conveyance of a lot in Jerome, a station on the present Atlantic and Pacific railroad, at its crossing of the Gasconade river, which was estimated at two thousand five hundred dollars. As to the nature of this conveyance a controversy arises, Greely claiming that the assignment of the judgments and conveyance was in full satisfaction of the Ecfort & Petring indebtedness, while it is claimed by the latter firm that the conveyance, though in form absolute, was collateral only. The extension above referred to was granted on the twentieth day of September, eighteen hundred and sixty-seven, as shown by the notes executed on that day ; the compromise with the creditors the spring following, eighteen hundred and sixty-eight, and the assignment of judgments and deed on the sixteenth day of March, eighteen hundred and sixty-nine.

On the day of the assignment of the judgments and the making of the deed, two papers were signed by Ecfort & Petring and delivered to Greely, who produces them in court, one receipting for the judgments, closing with these words: " And the amounts realized on said judgments to be placed to their credit as soon as received by us ;" the other stating that they had received Brutsche & Greely's warranty deed for lots eleven and twelve in block twenty-four in Jerome, with the improvements thereon, valued at two thousand five hundred dollars, and proceeding to say : " And we hereby agree with Messrs. Brutsche & Greely to return them said property within twelve months from date, provided they shall by that time have liquidated their indebtedness, " and setting out that the deed was in the name of Kleinschmidt. Construing these papers together, it is difficult to arrive at the conclusion that a final settlement and payment of the indebtedness of Ecfort & Petring was thereby intended. The assignment of the judgment shows, upon its face, that the amount realized therefrom should be credited on the indebtedness. But, aside from this, the amount of the judgments and the estimated value of the Jerome property is far greater than any claim Ecfort & Petring had against Brutsche & Greely, and it is not to be supposed that they would pay more than their debt.

The peculiarity of the language of the receipt for the deed is easily understood when examined in the light of the evidence. Greely was deeply interested in Jerome, and hoped to be able to control the influence of the railroad company to again make it the terminus, for a time, at least, of the railroad then building, and hence his desire to have the right to possess the property he had improved and occupied at one time. The witnesses, except Greely, are unanimous in declaring the Jerome property valueless in eighteen hundred and sixty-nine, the time it was conveyed. The receipt itself speaks of a then existing indebtedness, and only when that had been paid was it to be effective. If any doubt as to the nature of the conveyance could still exist, a letter of February one, eighteen hundred and seventy, addressed by Ecfort & Petring to Greely, and the response thereto, would solve it. Among other matters, Ecfort & Petring write : " We also request you to come forward and settle off the old affair, as we are informed that you are amply able to do so," to which a response comes, dated February seventh, saying : " As soon as I can manage to pay the balance due on B. & G.'s debt I will do so, meantime it is secured by the judgment assigned to you, which will be paid. * * * * I must beg pardon for not calling on you before this, upon this matter, but will do so shortly and explain to you my situation financially." There never was a claim that a final settlement and payment had been made with Ecfort & Petring set up by Greely until about the time of the suits that E. & P. instituted. The notes were never given up by E. & P., and the attempt by Greely to explain why this was not done is unsatisfactory. Besides all this, the evidence in t'. cause greatly preponderates in favor of the deed being intended as collateral.

The difficulty which might arise in holding that the possessor of collaterals is entitled to sue without having exhausted his security, is removed by the concurring testimony of all the witnesses that the Jerome property is comparatively valueless.

Attention has been called to the course E. & P. saw cause to pursue in first having instituted suit in the circuit court of the county in which Greely resides, and that when Greely appears and puts in a plea of payment the plaintiffs dismiss their suit and make the present application. The causes assigned by the petitioning creditors as acts of bankruptcy on the part of Greely, the disposing of his property with the intent to hinder, delay, or defraud his creditors while the suit in the circuit court was pending, would seem to explain what caused the petitioning creditors to move in the bankrupt court. Be that, however, as it may, their right to do so is beyond dispute.

The first question must be solved in favor of petitioning creditors, as having an existing indebtedness provable in bankruptcy.

The second question—did Greely make a disposition of his property with the intent to delay, hinder, or defraud his creditors?—presents more difficulty ; and in order to arrive at a conclusion it becomes necessary to carefully examine the evidence. We find Greely, in eighteen hundred and sixty-seven, engaged as a merchant, partner of the firm of Brutsche & Greely, doing business on the line of the present Atlantic and Pacific railroad. In the fall of eighteen hundred and sixty-seven they became embarrassed, obtained an extension of time, and in the spring of eighteen hundred and sixty-eight compromising with their creditors at fifty cents. The same partners continue business for about eighteen months, to September, eighteen hundred and sixty-nine, when they dissolve, Greely undertaking to settle up the affairs of the partnership. Greely testifies that out of the affairs of said partnership there remained to him about two thousand dollars, but this statement comes in conflict with his partner, who swears he never got more than three hundred dollars out of the assets of the firm, which he himself collected. The Ecfort & Petring debt remains unsettled. Greely commences business in the fall of eighteen hundred and sixty-nine, on his own account, insures, is burned out in eighteen hundred and seventy, and commences anew soon after the fire.

He had purchased his homestead in the fall of eighteen hundred and sixty-nine, and improved it afterwards by expending from three to five thousand dollars, as variously estimated by wi'nesses. He also builds a store-house on one of his lots, expending about two thousand dollars, in the meantime carrying a stock of from five to ten thousand dollars. He estimates his property at the time these proceedings were instituted in round numbers as worth twenty-one thousand five hundred dollars, consisting of store goods, six thousand dollars; homestead, eight thousand dollars; Jerome property, one thousand dollars; notes and accounts, three thousand dollars; mining stock, one thousand dollars; store, one thousand five hundred dollars (after deducting mortgage of one thousand six hundred dollars); Verona real estate, one thousand dollars, making up the amount. When he is asked how he has accumulated so much property in so short a time, under such adverse circumstances, he accounts for it by large profits, which he claims to have made, without in any way supporting this affirmation. The evidence shows that the three thousand dollars of accounts, and one thousand dollars mining stock are utterly valueless. Add to this a one thousand five hundred dollar homestead, and the assets, as estimated by himself, are reduced to sixteen thousand dollars. Of debts, he recounts from memory, six thousand dollars due to various merchants, add one thousand eight hundred dollars to Ecfort & Petring, and three thousand five hundred dollars obtained of his father-in-law, and mortgaged on homestead four hundred dollars, and we have nearly twelve thousand dollars of liabilities, all due, except the three thousand five hundred dollars obtained from his father-in-law, of which, he says, he does not know whether that is a debt or not, but that he gave a paper acknowledging the receipt of the money.

Witnesses estimate the Greely property variously at from twelve to fifteen thousand dollars. All agree, that if the property, situate as it is, had to be sold within say six or nine months, it would not bring over one-half of their estimates. It will thus be seen that by very careful management Greely might be able to pay his debts, provided his own time were given him. But to be solvent, when a merchant, does not mean that he can pay his debts in the manner suggested.

In a late case, (*Toof et al* v. *Martin et al.*, 6 N. B. R. 49,) the supreme court of the United States, December term, eighteen hundred and seventy-one, with precision defines insolvency, when applied to merchants and traders. The court says : " It is sometimes used to denote the insufficiency of the entire property and assets of an individual to pay his debts. This is the general and popular meaning. But it is also used in a more restricted sense, to express the inability of a party to pay his debts as they become due in the ordinary course of business. It is in this latter sense that the term is used when traders and merchants are said to be insolvent, and as applied to them, it is the sense intended by the act of congress." Applying this definition to the case before the court, Greely may well be said to be insolvent, with more than eight thousand dollars of debts due, and unable to pay two comparatively small claims presented to him, at the very time he was making such large and sudden changes in his property. It is true that this question of insolvency is not directly in issue, but the effect it has upon determining what a debtor may do or not do with his property, under such circumstances as are shown, is too obvious to need elucidation. We find Greely merchandising with a stock of goods estimated by him at near six thousand dollars, exchanging the one-half thereof, the shelf goods and broken packages, for small pieces of realty, and two second-hand billiard tables, a transaction plainly shown to be out of his usual and ordinary course of business. He disposes of another part of his goods, drawing an order for the pay thereof in favor of one of his creditors. He turns in and sells his store-house, (which he had before rented for a year,) the purchaser assuming a mortgage of one thousand six hundred dollars, and giving him a note for one thousand five hundred dollars, "payable at any bank in St. Louis," for the balance. When payment of the note is enjoined, under the bankruptcy proceedings, he tells the payee that it is in the hands of an innocent purchaser, and that he will have to pay it. The attempted explanation made by Greely of the conversation, in which he is charged to have said this, leaves at least a very unfavorable impression as to what he meant by it. We find the note, after it becomes due, in his hands, with no design to transfer it to his creditors, as far as known, certainly with no effort on his part to turn it into the channel of paying his debts. When asked whether he was going to continue in business in Marshfield, he empathically asserts that he is, while he himself testifies that he was preparing to go to Mississippi to engage in railroad enterprises. The question of intent to hinder, delay, or defraud his creditors, must be solved by looking at what Greely said and did, and the effect thereof. That the effect of the disposition which Greely had in part made of his property when he was stopped by the bankruptcy proceedings was to hinder and delay his creditors, this court has not the least doubt. That he must have known this to be the case, may readily be inferred from what he said to Potter, that goods could be more readily made available to pay debts than real estate. If there were any doubts as to Greely's intention to hinder or delay his creditors generally in the collection of their debts, there can be none as to Ecfort & Petring. From the moment they instituted suit he declared his intention not to pay them, and the reason he assigns for so doing is by no means satisfactory to the court. The plea put forth, that they had received payment by the assignment of the judgments and the Jerome deed, has so little to support it in evidence that it must be rejected as conclusive, or persuasive even. The fact that Ecfort & Petring were the largest creditors of Brutsche & Greely, and headed the composition agreement entered into by them with their creditors, and without which they could not have succeeded in obtaining the terms they did, and afterwards trying to secure and now claiming their whole debt, arrested the attention of the court, and had there been anything in the testimony showing bad faith on their part toward the other creditors, the court would not be slow in ordering them not to come here without clean hands. But not the least testimony tending in the direction of bad faith has been given by any one, and hence the transaction must be looked upon as made *bona fide*. In compromises of this character, it may be well to remark, there should not only be the utmost good faith among the creditors, but it would be well to avoid everything calculated to throw the shadow of a doubt upon them.

The first question, as to an existing, provable debt, having been answered in favor of petitioning creditors;

The second question—Did Greely make a disposition of his property with intent to hinder and delay his creditors?—being also answered in the affirmative;

Greely is, therefore, declared a bankrupt, and adjudged accordingly.

LUEBKE & PLAYER and JUDSON, for creditors; PHELPS & McAFEE, for defendant.

———•◦•———

UNITED STATES CIRCUIT COURT—LOUISIANA.

A sheriff who levies upon property by virtue of an order to sell under a mortgage foreclosure suit, before the debtor is adjudicated a bankrupt, has a valid lien and may sell the property after the adjudication. Injunction to restrain purchaser from meddling with the property refused, but leave given the assignee to redeem it within three months if he thinks it worth more than the mortgage debt, interest and costs.

GODDARD, *Assignee* v. WEAVER.

BRADLEY, J.—The assignee of Fisk, a bankrupt, brought a bill in chancery to set aside the sale of certain property, made under a mortgage held by Weaver, by the sheriff of

Goddard v. Weaver.

Orleans. The sale was advertised on the twenty-seventh of November, eighteen hundred and seventy-one, and Fisk filed his petition to be declared a bankrupt on the twenty-seventh of December, eighteen hundred and seventy-one, and the sale took place on the sixth of January, eighteen hundred and seventy-two, Weaver becoming the purchaser for sixteen thousand two hundred dollars. The bill also asks for an injunction to prevent Weaver from intermeddling with the property.

The first question arising upon the case is " whether, as mere matter of law, all proceedings of the sheriff taken and had after the petition was filed were null and void." I cannot agree to the proposition that they are null "because repugnant to that exclusive control of the bankrupt's property vested in the bankrupt court." I cannot subscribe to the doctrine that the bankrupt's petition renders an honest execution, levied upon his property before the filing of his petition, and all proceedings under it null and void.

The assignee of a bankrupt is not the assignee of his creditors, nor of all the judgments, executions, liens and mortgages outstanding against his property. He takes only the bankrupt's interest in property, nor has he right, title or interest which other parties have therein; nor any control over the same further than is given expressly by the bankrupt act as auxiliary for the preservation of the bankrupt's interest for the benefit of his general creditors. It would be absurd to contend that the assignee becomes *ipso facto* seized in entirety as trustee of every article of property in which the bankrupt has any interest or share. This would give him the king's prerogative, which brooks not a divided domain in property in common with a subject. " The assignee succeeding to the bankrupt's possession of property, subject to certain fixed laws, may discharge them and sell the property, or he might dispose of it before discharge of the liens. It is not necessary to decide in all cases whether he could do this."

I know of no authority which the assignee has to take property possessed by a bankrupt, except as bailee, out of the sheriff's hands without paying the debt or seeking the aid of courts sitting in bankruptcy, and if the sheriff proceeds to sell, I am unable to see anything in the bankrupt act which renders void his acts done after the commencement of proceedings in bankruptcy.

The possession of the sheriff is lawful. He has a species of property in the thing; his right to sell extends to the entire interest of the debtor, and no assignment of that interest can divert the right of the sheriff.

The court will interfere in case of the exercise of the right of the sheriff, if its exercise would materially affect the interest of the general creditors. When divers persons have divers interests in the same thing, neither has a right to do what will injure the other, and each must submit to judicial restraint for the protection of other interests. Upon this principle courts are authorized to interfere with rights otherwise lawful, in regard to property situated as I have supposed. But I cannot regard, while having no doubt of the authority of the court to stay sheriff's proceedings in such a case, and even to set aside the sale, I cannot regard the sheriff's acts as void in law nor as voidable or subject to control, except upon cause shown in a court having bankruptcy jurisdiction.

The bankrupt court is the appropriate tribunal to investigate where any question is made as to the validity of the judgment, and proceedings under it may be restrained. But in the proceedings before us, no question is made as to the *bona fides* of the act in which executory process issued. The answer disposes of every charge of bad faith.

I do not think I ought to appoint a receiver, or to issue an injunction. Hence the motion is refused.

I will allow the assignee to pay the defendant's demand, and take the property at any time within three months from date, if he really thinks the same is worth more than the mortgage debt, interest and costs.

Order issued in accordance with the decision and the amendment.

In re Belden.

UNITED STATES DISTRICT COURT—S. D. NEW YORK.

A. filed his petition in bankruptcy on the thirtieth day of October, eighteen hundred and sixty-nine, and on the twelfth day of May, eighteen hundred and seventy, filed his application for a discharge. On the fifteenth of June, eighteen hundred and seventy-one, B., one of his creditors, commenced an action in a state court, to recover for goods delivered to A., shortly before the filing of his petition in bankruptcy. A. filed an offer in writing to allow judgment to be entered for the amount claimed with costs, and then presented his petition to the United States district court of that district, stating that the debt to B. arose prior to the filing of his petition in bankruptcy, and that it was a provable debt, and praying that he might be allowed to take judgment for the amount claimed, and that further proceedings in the action might be stayed to await the determination of the court on the question of his discharge, whereupon an order to that effect was granted. On application of B. to discharge the order of stay, on the ground that there had been unreasonable delay on the part of the bankrupt in endeavoring to obtain his discharge, *Held,* That there had been unreasonable delay, for the reason that the bankrupt had, on the seventeenth day of November, eighteen hundred and seventy, presented his petition to the circuit court, to review a decision of the district court, on questions arising in reference to a discharge, returnable on the nineteenth, with a stay of proceedings on such decision, and there was no evidence to show why he had not, for fourteen months, brought the matter to a hearing. Order entered vacating the stay of proceedings.

In re W. BELDEN. *

BLATCHFORD, J.—The petition for adjudication in this case, a voluntary one, was filed on the thirtieth of October, eighteen hundred and sixty-nine. The adjudication was made on the first of November, eighteen hundred and sixty-nine. On the twelfth of May, eighteen hundred and seventy, the bankrupt filed his application for a discharge. Between the first and the eighth of September, eighteen hundred and sixty-nine, the firm of L. Marcotte & Co. delivered to the bankrupt furniture and merchandise to the amount of two thousand four hundred and thirty-five dollars. On the fifteenth of June, eighteen hundred and seventy-one, they commenced an action against him in a state court to recover the said sum. He appeared in the suit and served a verified answer denying that he had ever bought or received the property, or was indebted to the plaintiffs in the suit in any sum. Thereupon they obtained an order to examine him,

* See 4 N. B. R. 57.

as a party before trial, which order was served on him. He then served an offer in writing to allow judgment to be entered against him for the two thousand four hundred and thirty-five dollars with interest and costs, and the offer was accepted. On the seventeenth of October, eighteen hundred and seventy-one, he presented to this court, a petition verified by him on the sixteenth, setting forth that the indebtedness to L. Marcotte & Co. arose prior to the presentation of the petition in bankruptcy, and was a provable debt, and praying that they might take judgment for the amount claimed, with costs, and that all further proceedings in the action might be stayed to await the determination of this court on the question' of his discharge from his debts. An order to that effect was made by this court on the seventeenth of October, eighteen hundred and seventy-one. The judgment was entered in the state court on the twentieth of October, eighteen hundred and seventy-one. The debt has never been proved in bankruptcy. L. Marcotte & Co. now apply to this court to discharge the order of stay, on the ground that there has been unreasonable delay on the part of the bankrupt in endeavoring to obtain his discharge.

On the filing of the application for a discharge, an order of hearing was made, returnable June ninth, eighteen hundred and seventy. Prior to that day, and in May, eighteen hundred and seventy, orders had been made, referring to the register for investigation, on the application of the assignee, certain claims of S. R. Jacobs, William Reed, Charles T. Yerks, Jr. and Jay Cooke & Co., as creditors, proofs of which claims had been postponed by the register prior to the meeting for the election of an assignee. On the eighth of June, eighteen hundred and seventy, Jay Cooke & Co. applied to the register for an order to examine the bankrupt and the assignee and others, to enable Jay Cooke & Co. to file specifications against the discharge. On the ninth of June, eighteen hundred and seventy, Reed and Yerks filed specifications against the discharge. On that day the bankrupt objected before the register to the application of Jay

Cooke & Co., and to the specifications of Reed and Yerks, on the ground that they had not proved their debts, and had no standing in court, and could not be permitted to show cause against a discharge. A motion before the register on that day, by Jay Cooke & Co., to adjourn the hearing on the application for a discharge, was opposed by the bankrupt on the same grounds, and on the further ground that no such examination as Jay Cooke & Co. had applied for could be allowed to enable a party to file specifications. The motion was denied by the register, on the ground that Jay Cooke & Co. had not proved their debt, but their claim had been referred to him for investigation and no proceedings had been had on such reference. This decision of the register, was, at the request of Jay Cooke & Co., certified to this. court. This court held that the register had power to adjourn the hearing until after the investigation into the disputed claims should be had. Thereupon, the hearing on the discharge was adjourned to the twenty-third of June, eighteen hundred and seventy.

On the sixteenth of June, eighteen hundred and seventy, Jay Cooke & Co. had subpœnaed the assignee to appear before the register, claiming the right to examine him in relation to the validity of a claim of his which had been proved. To this the bankrupt and the assignee objected before the register, on the ground that Jay Cooke & Co. had not proved their debt, and had no standing in court. Jay Cooke & Co. alleged, in reply, that they had filed with the register, on the twenty-third of May, eighteen hundred and seventy, a deposition in proof of their debt, which had been certified by the register in the usual form. This was denied, and it was alleged that protests and affidavits against the claim of Jay Cooke & Co., made by creditors who had proved their debts, had been filed with the register on the eleventh of May, eighteen hundred and seventy. The register sustained the objection made by the assignee, and, at the request of Jay Cooke, the decision was certified to this court.

On the ninth of June, eighteen hundred and seventy, Jay Cooke & Co., Ralli & Fachiri and G. H. & H. Redmond, filed with the register their protest against the claims of thirty-three creditors who had proved their debts before the first meeting of creditors. These protests were objected to by the bankrupt and the assignee on the ground that the protestants had not proved their debts and had no standing in court.

On the twenty-third of June, eighteen hundred and seventy, the day of the adjourned hearing on the discharge, the said protestants moved for an adjournment till June thirtieth, eighteen hundred and seventy. This motion was opposed by the bankrupt, on the ground that the claims of the said protestants had not been proved, and that Jay Cooke & Co. had taken no steps to prove their claims under the order of reference to the register, but had refused, on a requirement to that effect made by the register, to do so, and that all the creditors who had proved their debts, being a majority in number and value of all the creditors, including those in controversy, has signed a written consent to the discharge, and that the bankrupt had, in all other respects, complied with the law, to entitle himself to a discharge. The register decided that he would not adjourn the hearing. Thereupon, at the request of the said protestants, the decision was certified to this court, and the papers touching the subject, including the specifications filed by Reed and Yerks, were transmitted to this court.

On the third of July, eighteen hundred and seventy, Jay Cooke & Co. and Jacobs, filed specifications against a discharge, which were transmitted to this court.

The decision of the register as to the right of Jay Cooke & Co. to examine the assignee as to his debt, and the decision of the register refusing further to adjourn the hearing on the discharge, were reviewed by this court, on a hearing in October, eighteen hundred and seventy. It held, that the claim of Jay Cooke & Co. was duly proved on the twenty-third of May, eighteen hundred and seventy; that the claim of Ralli & Fachiri ought to have appended to it the certificate of the commissioner before whom it was taken, that it was satisfactory to him, and, if such certificate was procured, the claim would be filed *nunc pro tunc*, as of the first of June, eighteen hundred and seventy, and would be regarded as having been duly proved at that time ; that Jay Cooke & Co. were entitled to an order of examination, under section twenty-six of the act, according to form number forty-five ; that the assignee was bound to answer the questions put to him, so far as they related to any matter of examination specified in section twenty-six; that the case would stand for hearing, as to the question of discharge, on the specifications of Jacobs, Jay Cooke & Co., Reed, and Yerks; and that any party might take testimony thereon before the register.

On the seventeenth of November, eighteen hundred and seventy, the bankrupt presented to the circuit judge a petition setting forth the foregoing proceedings and that he was aggrieved by the decisions of this court, and praying the circuit judge to review and reverse such decisions. The circuit judge granted leave to file the petition and made an order requiring Jacobs, Jay Cooke & Co., Yerks, Reed and Ralli & Fachiri, to show cause before him on the nineteenth of November, eighteen hundred and seventy, why the prayer of the petition should not be granted, and directing that in the meantime and until the hearing and determination of the motion on the order, all proceedings under the orders of this court herein should be suspended.

This order stays all proceedings towards a hearing on the specifications against a discharge, and stays such hearing, and, consequently, stays the granting of a discharge, so long as a decision is not made by the circuit judge on a review of the decisions of this court, a review of which is asked. But the twenty-first section of the act provides that proceedings to collect a provable debt shall, on the application of the bankrupt, be stayed, to await the determination of the court in bankruptcy on the question of the discharge, provided there be no unreasonable delay on the part of the bankrupt in endeavoring to obtain his discharge. L. Marcotte & Co. are not parties to the petition of review pending before the circuit judge. They can do nothing to further a decision on such petition, except to make this application to discharge the order of stay granted against them. It is not shown by the bankrupt why the petition of review has not been decided, or whether it has ever been brought to a hearing, and, if it has not, that the failure has been through no fault of his, or what efforts he has made to have a hearing. It is stated, in the petition of L. Marcotte & Co., that the bankrupt is amply able to pay their claim in full. This is not denied by the bankrupt. Of course, he can pay it only out of means acquired since the petition in bankruptcy was filed. I think the unexplained delay since November, eighteen hundred and seventy, on the part of the bankrupt, in procuring a decision on his petition of review, is an unreasonable delay on his part in endeavoring to obtain his discharge, within the intent and meaning of the twenty-first section. The second section provides, that the jurisdiction by petition of review may be exercised by the circuit court, or by any justice thereof, in term time or vacation. It would be a great injustice to permit an order of the circuit judge, which shows, on its face, that he contemplated a stay of only two days till the hearing of the petition of review, and which has now been allowed by the bankrupt to remain as an obstruction for fourteen months, and has operated against L. Marcotte & Co. for three months, to remain any longer as an obstacle to their proceeding to endeavor to collect their claim out of any property which the bankrupt has acquired since his petition in bankruptcy was filed.

So much of the order of October seventeenth, eighteen hundred and seventy-one, as operates as a stay of the proceedings of L. Marcotte & Co. on their judgment, is vacated.

HUGH PORTER, for L. Marcotte & Co.; H. E. & C. B. STOUGHTON, for the bankrupt.—January 27th, 1872.

UNITED STATES DISTRICT COURT—S. D. NEW YORK.

No maritime lien arises for materials furnished, or repairs made to a vessel in her home port, although such vessel is engaged in foreign trade ; hence, neither the shipwright nor material man is entitled to share in the proceeds arising from the sale of the vessel under admiralty process as against a mortgagee or assignee in bankruptcy.

The act of April twenty-fourth, eighteen hundred and sixty-two, of New York, [Laws of 1862, chap. 482,] is unconstitutional and void, so far as it provides for enforcing a maritime contract by proceedings *in rem* against a vessel.

The owner of a vessel became bankrupt and it was sold by proceedings in admiralty, but the amount realized was insufficient to pay the two mortgages against it.

Held, That the first mortgage, covering half the vessel, was to be treated as the first lien on one-half the fund, and that such half must be regarded as composed of two separate funds or quarters, one subject to the first mortgage alone, and one subject first, to the first mortgage, and second, to the second mortgage, which covered three-fourths of the vessel ; that the second mortgage was the first lien on the second half of the proceeds. One-fourth being more than sufficient to pay the first mortgage, the surplus passed to the assignee in bankruptcy, and the remaining three-fourths of the fund went to the payment of the second mortgage.

In re SHIP EDITH. ·

The facts were these : The ship *Edith* was sold by order of the court of admiralty for seamen's wages and towing, and the money arising from her sale paid into court, and, after paying the seamen and the owner of the tug their claims, there remained a large surplus in the registry of the court. Several petitions were filed, praying that the surplus and remnants should be duly marshaled and distributed among the petitioners according to their respective *maritime liens* on the same. The court referred the whole matter to a commissioner to take proof of the matters in the petitions, and to report thereon.

This brought before the commissioner the precise question, " which of the claims presented a maritime lien on the fund in court?" The first petitioner, Bucknam & Co., claims a lien for labor, materials and repairs made on the ship *Edith* in this port.

The testimony before the commissioner shows, that at the time that Bucknam & Co. made the repairs the ship *Edith* was a *domestic vessel in her home port ;* and the commissioner held that their claim was not a *maritime lien.* To this decision Bucknam & Co. excepted.

CHARLES DONOHUE, for Bucknam & Co.; EVERETT P. WHEELER, for Tyler; JOHN SEDGWICK, assignee in bankruptcy, in person.

BLATCHFORD, J.—There is, in the registry of this court, the sum of thirty-one thousand one hundred and seventy-six dollars and eighty-two cents, the net proceeds of the sale of the ship *Edith,* on a sale made of her on the eighth of May, eighteen hundred and seventy-one, under process issued on a decree of this court in a suit *in rem* against her in admiralty. There are four claimants to portions of this fund.

D. Freeman Poole, A. Judson Bucknam and John E. Leech, composing the firm of Bucknam & Co., claim to be paid out of such proceeds the sum of three thousand five hundred and ninety-seven dollars and seventy cents, with interest. Their petition alleges that in July, eighteen hundred and seventy, they, being shipwrights, repaired the vessel in the port of New York, she being, at the time, a domestic vessel, belonging in said port ; that, in making such repairs, they furnished labor and materials to said amount ; and that such amount, with interest, is still due, and is a lien on the vessel, and was so, by the laws of the state of New York, at the time the materials and labor were furnished. The evidence shows that the repairs were made by the order of the master and owners of the vessel, and were made while the vessel was on the water ; that the vessel has always been engaged in foreign trade ; that the lien was "filed" on the twenty-seventh of July, eighteen hundred and seventy ; that thereafter, under the state law, a warrant of seizure for the amount of the claim was issued out of the supreme court of New York against the vessel, under which she was seized by the sheriff ; that, under the same law, a bond was given and the vessel was discharged from custody and from the warrant ; and that a suit on such bond is now pending undetermined in the supreme court of New York.

One Charles Carow, being the owner of the vessel, made and delivered to C. T. Bowring & Co., on the eighteenth June, eighteen hundred and sixty-nine, a mortgage upon the one-half of her as security for the payment of a promissory note for one thousand pounds sterling, and interest of the same date, made by Carow to the order of C. T. Bowring & Co. Such mortgage was recorded in the New York custom-house on the twenty-third of June, eighteen hundred and sixty-nine.

On the eleventh of January, eighteen hundred and seventy, Carow, being the owner of the vessel, made and delivered to Daniel Tyler, to secure an existing indebtedness from Carow to Tyler, a mortgage upon three-fourths of the said vessel. On such mortgage there is due the sum of fifty-five thousand four hundred and twenty-four dollars and forty-six cents, with interest from the first of July, eighteen hundred and seventy. This mortgage was recorded in the New York custom-house on the eleventh of January, eighteen hundred and seventy, and a copy of it was afterwards duly filed in the office of the register of the city and county of New York. The mortgage contains a clause whereby the mortgagor "doth promise, covenant, and agree, for his heirs, executors, and administrators," to and with the mortgagee, "his heirs, executors, administrators and assigns, to warrant and defend the said three-fourths part of said ship Edith, and all the other before-mentioned appurtenances, against all and every person and persons whomsoever;" and a clause that a sale under the mortgage "shall for ever be a perpetual bar, both in law and equity, against" the mortgagor, "his executors, administrators and assigns, and all other persons claiming, or to claim the premises, or any part thereof, by, from, or under them, or either of them."

Carow was, on the twenty-eighth of January, eighteen hundred and seventy-one, adjudged a bankrupt by this court, on a petition for adjudication, filed January thirteenth, eighteen hundred and seventy-one. John Sedgwick was afterwards appointed his assignee.

No objection is made by any of the parties to the payment of the amount due to C. T. Bowring & Co. on the mortgage to them, amounting to five thousand seven hundred and seventy-six dollars and twenty-four cents.

The claim on the part of Tyler is, that the thirty-one thousand one hundred and seventy-six dollars and eighty-two cents should be divided into four equal parts; that the mortgage to C. T. Bowring & Co. should be charged as paid out of one of said four equal parts; and that Tyler should be declared to be entitled to three of said four equal parts. This would distribute the thirty-one thousand one hundred and seventy-six dollars and eighty-two cents as follows: To C. T. Bowring & Co., five thousand seven hundred and seventy-six dollars and twenty-four cents; to the assignee in bankruptcy, two thousand and seventeen dollars and ninety-six cents; to Tyler, twenty-three thousand three hundred and eighty-two dollars and sixty-two cents.

The claim on the part of the assignee in bankruptcy is, that from the thirty-one thousand one hundred and seventy-six dollars and eighty-two cents should be paid the Bowring claim, amounting to five thousand seven hundred and seventy-six dollars and twenty-four cents, and that the balance then left, twenty-five thousand four hundred dollars and fifty-eight cents, should be distributed as follows: one-fourth of it, or six thousand three hundred and fifty dollars and fifteen cents, to the assignee in bankruptcy, and the remaining three-fourths, or nineteen thousand and fifty dollars and forty-three cents, to Tyler.

The claims of the various parties were referred to a commissioner to ascertain and report who are entitled to the said surplus and remnants. He has reported that the thirty-one thousand one hundred and seventy-six dollars and eighty-two cents should be divided into two equal parts of fifteen thousand five hundred and eighty-eight dollars and forty-one cents each; that, taking one of those two parts, namely, fifteen thousand five hundred and eighty-eight dollars and forty-one cents, the Bowring mortgage, five thousand seven hundred and seventy-six dollars and twenty-four cents, should be paid out of it; that the balance thereof, nine thousand eight hundred and twelve dollars and seventeen cents, should be divided into two equal parts, of which one, four thousand nine hundred and six dollars and nine cents, should be paid to the assignee in bankruptcy, and the other, four thousand nine hundred and six dollars and eight cents, should be paid to Tyler; and that the other half of the thirty-one thousand one hundred and seventy-six dollars and eighty-two cents, namely, fifteen thousand five hundred and eighty-eight dollars and forty-one cents should also be paid to Tyler. This division distributes the thirty-one thousand one hundred and seventy-six dollars and eighty-two cents as follows: to C. T. Bowring & Co., five thousand seven hundred and seventy-six dollars and twenty-four cents; to the assignee in bankruptcy, four thousand nine hundred and six dollars and nine cents; and to Tyler, twenty thousand four hundred and ninety-four dollars and forty-nine cents.

The commissioner has also reported that Bucknam & Co. have no lien upon said surplus and remnants, and no legal right to be paid out of the same, in these proceedings, any portion of their said claim.

To this report Bucknam & Co. except, on the grounds (1.) That the report should have been that Bucknam & Co. are entitled to be paid out of the proceeds of the vessel in court; (2.) That the report should have been that Bucknam & Co. have a lien on the fund in court for the amount of their claim; (3.) That Bucknam & Co. should be paid out of the fund.

The assignee in bankruptcy excepts to the report on the grounds: (1.) That the report allows to him out of the surplus, four thousand nine hundred and six dollars and nine cents, whereas it should have allowed to him six thousand three hundred and fifty dollars and fifteen cents; (2.) That it allows to Tyler twenty thousand four hundred and ninety-four dollars and forty-nine cents, whereas it should have allowed to him only nineteen thousand and fifty dollars and forty-three cents.

Tyler excepts to the report on the grounds : (1.) That it reports that the surplus should be divided into two equal parts, and that the Bowring mortgage should be paid out of one of such parts ; (2.) That it reports that the balance of such one of such two equal parts should be equally divided between Tyler and the assignee in bankruptcy ; (3.) That it does not report that said surplus should be divided into four equal parts, that the Bowring mortgage should be charged as paid out of one of such parts, and that Tyler should be declared to be entitled to three of such parts.

(1.) As to the claim of Bucknam & Co. It is contended, for them, that their claim was a maritime lien on the vessel, without regard to the state law ; that, under the state law, they have a lien on the vessel and her proceeds, which this court can and ought to recognise by paying the claim out of the proceeds of the sale of the vessel ; and that, whether they had a lien or not on the vessel, their claim should be paid out of such proceeds.

It is the recognised law of the courts of the United States that a maritime lien does not rise on a contract for materials and supplies furnished to a vessel in her home port, even though such contract may be a maritime contract: The *Belfast*, 7 Wall. 624, 645 ; *Leon* v. *Galceran*, 11 id. 185, 192. It is also a principle recognised by those courts that in respect to a maritime contract for materials and supplies furnished to a vessel in her home port, a state law may lawfully create such liens as it deems proper, not amounting to a regulation of commerce, and may enact, for enforcing such liens, reasonable regulations. The *Belfast*, 7 Wall. 624, 645 ; *Leon* v. *Galceran*, 11 id. 185, 192.

In the present case the materials were supplied and the repairs were made to the vessel in her home port, and no maritime lien arose therefor, although the vessel was engaged in foreign trade.

The statute of New York under which a lien is claimed is the act of April twenty-fourth, eighteen hundred and sixty-two, session laws of eighteen hundred and sixty-two, chapter four hundred and eighty-two. By the first section of that act this debt, having been contracted by the master and owners of the vessel within this state, for work done and materials furnished for repairing the vessel, is made a lien on the vessel, to be preferred to all other liens thereon except mariners' wages. The act provides for filing specifications of the lien, and for the issuing of a warrant to enforce the lien, which is to be a warrant to the sheriff to attach and seize the vessel to satisfy the claim, if established to be a lien on the vessel. The warrant being executed the vessel is to be kept by the sheriff. The warrant may be discharged on the giving of a prescribed bond to the prosecuting creditor, conditioned to pay the amount of all claims which shall be established to be due to the person in whose behalf the warrant was issued, and to have been a subsisting lien on the vessel, pursuant to the provisions of the act, at the time of exhibiting the same. If the warrant is thus discharged, no further proceedings against the vessel seized can be had under the act, founded upon any demand secured by such bond. The bond must be prosecuted within three months after its delivery. If, in an action on the bond, it is found that any sum is due to the plaintiff, which was a subsisting lien on the vessel at the time of exhibiting the same, as provided in the act, judgment is to be rendered that the plaintiff recover the same; but, if in such action it is found that no subsisting lien existed in favor of the plaintiff at the time of exhibiting his claim, judgment is to be rendered against him. If, within a time limited by the act, the creditor who has exhibited his claim has not been satisfied, and the vessel has not been discharged, a warrant is to issue to the sheriff to sell the vessel, and raise a specified amount necessary to satisfy all unsatisfied liens which have been exhibited against the vessel. The proceeds of the sale are, until their distribution, to stand in place of the vessel, and until such distribution any person entitled under the act to enforce a lien against the vessel may enforce the same against such proceeds, in the same manner as is provided in the act for enforcing a lien against the vessel herself, and with like effect. On the distribution of such proceeds, the various claims exhibited, which are found to be subsisting liens on the vessel or her proceeds, according to the provisions of the act, are to be paid out of such proceeds in the order of the delivery of the respective warrants to the sheriff. At any time before final distribution any claim exhibited may be contested in a manner prescribed. When the amount of all the claims which have been exhibited, and which are found to have been subsisting liens on the vessel at the time of exhibiting the same, have been finally determined, the proceeds are to be distributed by the court. Uncontested claims entitled to be paid prior to contested claims may be paid in the order of their respective priorities, notwithstanding such contest; and uncontested claims may be paid after paying all prior uncontested claims, and reserving enough to pay all prior contested claims. Provision is made for discharging the lien on bond after specifications of the lien have been filed, although no warrant to enforce the lien has been issued.

In the case of the steamboat *Josephine*, 39 N. Y. 19, this statute of New York came under consideration, in the court of appeals of New York. In that case a specification of lien was filed by creditors against the steamboat, under the act of eighteen hundred and sixty-two, for supplies furnished by them at New York to the steamboat. During the period covered by the furnishing of the supplies, the steamboat was enrolled at the custom-house in New York, and was engaged in running between the port of New York and state of New Jersey. The court of appeals held that under the decisions of the supreme court of the United States in the *Moses Taylor* 4 Wall. 411, and the *Hine* v. *Trevor*, id. 555, the act of eighteen hundred and sixty-two, to the extent in which it authorized proceedings *in rem* against vessels for causes of action cognizable in the admiralty, invested the courts of New York with admiralty jurisdiction, and was void on the ground, that, under the constitution of the United States, congress had, in fact, and rightfully, given to the district courts of the United States exclusive original cognizance of all civil causes of admiralty and maritime jurisdiction, saving to suitors, in all cases, the right of a common law remedy, where the common law is competent to give it, and that a proceeding *in rem*, as used in the admiralty courts, is not a common law remedy. There can be no doubt that all state legislation providing for the enforcement of a maritime claim or contract in any other manner than by a common law remedy, infringes on the exclusive jurisdiction of the federal courts and violates the constitution of the United States. The contract in the present case, being one for labor and materials furnished by shipwrights in making repairs to a vessel on the water, was a maritime contract. Whether the contract was or not one which the admiralty court would enforce by a proceeding *in rem* against the vessel is of no consequence. *Brookman* v. *Hamill*, 43 N. Y. 554. So far, therefore, as any proceedings *in rem* against the *Edith* were authorized by the act of eighteen hundred and sixty-two, or were taken under that act, they were wholly void.

As the seizure of the vessel under the warrant was void, the bond given to obtain the release of the vessel from custody was also void. *Vose* v. *Cockcroft*, 44 N. Y. 415, 420. It is insisted, however, that the provision of the first section of the act of eighteen hundred and sixty-two, declaring that every debt of the character therein specified shall be a lien on the vessel, is valid, although the provisions for enforcing the lien against the vessel are void. Even if this be assumed, still, the second section of the act provides that the debt shall cease to be a lien at the expiration of six months after the debt was contracted, unless, at the time when the six months shall expire, the vessel shall be absent from the port at which the debt was contracted, in which case the lien shall continue until the expiration of ten days after the vessel shall next return to said port. Such six months, in the present case, expired in January, eighteen hundred and seventy-one, and the debt ceased at that time, at farthest, to be a lien, unless the vessel was at that time absent from the port of New York. The fact of such absence of the vessel is one to be shown affirmatively by the creditor, and no such fact is shown in this case.

· Bucknam & Co. must, therefore, be regarded merely as general creditors ; and the question arises whether, as such, they can be paid the amount of their claim out of these proceeds, as against the mortgagees and the assignee in bankruptcy. In the case of the *Neptune*, 3 Knapp, 94, in the privy council in eighteen hundred and thirty-five, on appeal from the high court of admiralty, the vessel had been sold under a decree in a suit for wages. A surplus remained in the registry. A material-man claimed to be paid out of it for supplies, and a mortgagee claimed the whole of the surplus. The court of admiralty awarded to the material-man the amount of his claim. On appeal the privy council reversed the decree. The vessel was a British vessel, and the supplies were furnished in England. Two questions were considered by the court : (1.) Whether the material-man was entitled to any lien on the proceeds ; (2.) If not, whether the mortgagee was entitled to such proceeds. It was conceded that a material-man without possession had no lien on the vessel itself for supplies furnished in England, and could not prosecute his suit in the court of admiralty against the vessel *in specie*. But a distinction was relied on between proceedings instituted by material-men against the ship *in specie*, and proceedings againstsur plus proceeds remaining in the registry. The principle upon which the court of admiralty had proceeded was, that when a vessel had been sold under process from that court, the balance of the proceeds, after satisfying the immediate object of the sale, was held *in usum jus habentium ;* that by the civil and · maritime law material-men have a lien on the vessel and proceeds ; that although the municipal courts of England had restrained proceedings in the court of admiralty, at the suit of material-men against the vessel itself for supplies furnished in England, no prohibition had ever issued with respect to suits against the proceeds after lawful sale ; that the reasons on which the right of material-men to arrest the ship in such cases had been repudiated were not applicable to the arrest of the proceeds after a lawful sale ; and that, as the vessel was not bonded, and the proceeds had been allowed to come into the registry, they had become subject to the lien of the material-man, from which the vessel *in specie* would have been exempt. The decision of the privy council was, that material-men have no better claim against the proceeds of a vessel in the registry of the court of admiralty than they have against the vessel. The court confirms this observation of Sir Christopher Robinson, in the *Maitland*, 2 Haggard, 253, 255 : "There does not seem to be any solid distinction between original suits and suits against proceeds in cases that are opposed ; whereas, in cases unopposed, the exercise of a judicial discretion by the court in permitting bills of this kind to be paid out of un-claimed proceeds, instead of being indefinitely impounded, may be a sound discretion, and capable of being justified to that extent, notwithstanding the general prohibition." The considerations urged in favor of paying the material-man were all of them overruled on the ground that he had no lien on the proceeds.

In the case of the *New Eagle*, 2 W. Rob. 441, in eighteen hundred and forty-six, there was a contest over proceeds in the registry between mortgagees of the vessel, and a creditor who claimed to be paid for money advanced for the service of the vessel in paying seamen's wages. Dr. Lushington rejected the claim of the creditor and awarded the proceeds to the mortgagees, on the ground that, after the decision of the privy council in the case of the *Neptune*, it was impossible to make a distinction between the proceeds and the vessel itself.

In the United States it is undoubtedly true that where proceeds are rightfully in the possession of a court of admiralty, it is an inherent incident to the jurisdiction of the court to entertain supplemental suits by the parties in interest, to ascertain to whom such proceeds rightfully belong, and to deliver them over to the parties who establish the lawful owner-ship thereof : *Andrews* v. *Wall*, 3 How. 568, 573. But it by no means follows that a general creditor, who has no lien on the thing out of which the proceeds arise, can rightfully claim such proceeds. And although some decisions in the United States express an opinion to that effect, yet no one can be found which maintains the view that a material-man having no lien is to be paid out of the proceeds of a vessel in preference to a mortgagee, or to the assignee in bankruptcy of the person who was the owner of the vessel when the debt was contracted. And that is the present case. There is not enough money to pay the Tyler mortgage in full. As against the assignee in bankruptcy, representing other general creditors of Carow, besides Bucknam & Co., it would be inequitable to permit Bucknam & Co. to obtain a preference in this way over such general creditors. The proceeds cannot be impounded as belonging to Carow, because the title to them has passed to the assignee in bankruptcy, subject only to specific liens on them.

It is by no means clear that the proposition that the lien given by the act of eighteen hundred and sixty-two is valid, although the provisions of that act for enforcing it are void, is a correct one. The proper view would seem to be, that such a lien as is given by the act is, in analogy to the meaning and efficacy of a maritime lien, only a privilege to arrest the vessel for the demand, which privilege constitutes of itself no encumbrance on the vessel, and becomes such only by virtue of an actual attachment of the vessel. The *Globe*, 2 Blatch. C. C. R. 427, 433. On this view, as any attachment of the vessel under the act is void, and the privilege of arrest amounts to nothing, it would follow that the lien given by the first section of the act can never constitute any encumbrance on the vessel or her proceeds.

I must, therefore, pronounce against the payment of the claim of Bucknam & Co. out of the proceeds, and disallow their exceptions.

2. As to the proper mode of distributing the thirty-one thousand one hundred and seventy-six dollars and eighty-two cents among the mortgagees and the assignee in bankruptcy.

The principle governing the rule of distribution adopted

by the commissioner is not stated in his report, but it would seem to be this : Bowring & Co. have a first mortgage, and it is on one-half of the vessel. Tyler has a second mortgage, and it is on three-quarters of the vessel. The Tyler mortgage must be regarded as the first lien on the one-half of the vessel that is not covered by the Bowring mortgage, and, after the Bowring mortgage is paid out of the one-half that is covered by it, the remainder of such one-half must be divided equally between Tyler and the assignee in bankruptcy, on the idea that the parties to the Tyler mortgage intended, by mortgaging generally three-quarters of the vessel after one-half of it had already been mortgaged generally, to cover by the Tyler mortgage, in addition to the one-half not covered by the Bowring mortgage, one-half of what should be left of the one-half covered by the Bowring mortgage after the satisfaction of the Bowring mortgage ; and that, as if Carow had himself paid the Bowring mortgage, Tyler would have covered by his mortgage the one-half not mortgaged to Bowring, and one-half of the one-half mortgaged to Bowring, so, if the Bowring mortgage is paid out of one-half of the proceeds, Tyler must still cover the one-half not mortgaged to Bowring, and one-half of what is left of the one-half of the proceeds out of which the Bowring mortgage is paid.

Both Tyler and the assignee in bankruptcy contest the principle adopted by the commissioner, and each of them claims a different rule of distribution from that adopted by the commissioner, and neither of them assents to the rule proposed by the other of them. The view of the assignee in bankruptcy is, that he has the vessel ; that out of less than one-quarter of her proceeds he discharges the Bowring mortgage ; that then the entire remainder of the proceeds represents the vessel in the state in which the Tyler mortgage attaches to three-quarters thereof ; and that, consequently, three-quarters of such remainder must be given to Tyler and one-quarter to the assignee in bankruptcy. The view of Tyler is, that Bowring & Co. have a first mortgage on two-quarters of the vessel ; that on one of the two quarters covered by the

Bowring mortgage, that mortgage is the sole mortgage ; that
on the other one of the two-quarters covered by the Bowring
mortgage, Tyler has a second mortgage ; that Tyler has a first
and the sole mortgage on the two-quarters not covered by the
Bowring mortgage ; and that it is the right of Tyler to have
the Bowring mortgage satisfied out of that one of the four-
quarters, if sufficient, which is not covered by the Tyler mortgage, so as, if possible, to give to Tyler three-quarters of the
entire proceeds.

The considerations urged on the part of Tyler are, that the
assignee in bankruptcy can only claim what Carow could have
claimed ; that, as the one-quarter not covered by the Tyler
mortgage is sufficient to pay the Bowring mortgage, no part of
the three-quarters which are covered by the Tyler mortgage
can be taken away from Tyler and given to the assignee ; that
such three-quarters are three-quarters of the entire thirty-one
thousand one hundred and seventy-six dollars and eighty-two
cents, and not three-quarters merely of the twenty-five thousand four hundred dollars and fifty-eight cents left after paying the Bowring mortgage out of the thirty-one thousand one
hundred and seventy-six dollars and eighty-two cents ; that
Carow, by his mortgage to Tyler, expressly agrees to warrant
and defend three-fourths of the vessel, that is, three-quarters
of the thirty-one thousand one hundred and seventy-six dollars
and eighty-two cents, against all persons, and therefore cannot, by himself or his assignee, claim any part of such three-
quarters ; that as to him and his assignee, the case must be
treated as if no mortgage to Bowring & Co. had ever existed ;
and that, consequently, as to them, the Bowring mortgage
must be wholly paid, if possible, out of the only one-quarter
which they can claim to hold as against the mortgage to Tyler,
namely, out of the one quarter of the entire thirty-one thousand one hundred and seventy-six dollars and eighty-two cents.
To these considerations it is replied, on the part of the assignee in bankruptcy, that the Tyler mortgage is a mortgage of
three-quarters of the vessel as it stood at the time that mortgage was given, that is, subject to the then existing encum-

brance of the Bowring mortgage ; that the Tyler mortgage is a mortgage of three undivided quarter parts of the vessel, and the Bowring mortgage one of two undivided quarter parts of the vessel, each mortgage affecting every part of the vessel equally with every other part of her ; that the surplus of the two undivided quarters covered by the Bowring mortgage, remaining after satisfying that mortgage, represents, with the other two undivided quarters, the whole vessel, to three-quarters of which aggregate the Tyler mortgage attaches ; and that, as the Tyler mortgage was a mortgage on three undivided quarters of the whole, subject to a prior mortgage on two undivided quarters of the whole, the prior mortgage must be first paid out of two-quarters of the whole, and the remainder of such two-quarters must be added to the other two-quarters, to represent the whole, to three-quarters of which whole the Tyler mortgage attaches.

It seems to me that a proper application of the equitable principles on which a court of admiralty should proceed in distributing these proceeds among these two mortgagees and the assignee in bankruptcy, demands that I should regard the Bowring mortgage as first attaching to two-quarters of the proceeds, and the Tyler mortgage as attaching first to the two-quarters not covered by the Bowring mortgage, and then as being a second mortgage on one of the two-quarters covered by the Bowring mortgage. On this view, as the amount due on the Tyler mortgage is greater than three-quarquarters of the whole proceeds, I think the Bowring mortgage should be regarded as first attaching to two quarters, or fifteen thousand five hundred and eighty-eight dollars and forty-one cents, out of the thirty-one thousand one hundred and seventy-six dollars and eighty-two cents ; that such fifteen thousand five hundred and eighty-eight dollars and forty-one cents should be regarded as made up of two funds, one of them, seven thousand seven hundred and ninety-four dollars and twenty-one cents, subject to the lien of Bowring & Co.'s mortgage alone, and the other of them, seven thousand seven hundred and ninety-four dollars and twenty cents, subject to the lien, first, of Bowring & Co.'s mortgage, and afterwards of Tyler's mortgage : and that the claim of Bowring & Co., five thousand seven hundred and seventy-six dollars and twenty-four cents, should be paid out of the seven thousand seven hundred and ninety-four dollars and twenty-one cents, which is not subject to the lien of Tyler's mortgage, leaving the residue, two thousand and seventeen dollars and ninety-six cents, of that seven thousand seven hun lred and ninety-four dollars and twenty-one cents, to be paid to the assignee in bankruptcy, and the full three-quarters, twenty-three thousand three hundred and eighty-two dollars and sixty-two cents, of the thirty-one thousand one hundred and seventy-six dollars and eighty-two cents, to bo paid to Tyler. This applies to the distribution the familiar principle, that, where there are two funds, and one of them is subject to the lien of one suitor, and the lien of another suitor covers both, the latter suitor will be paid, if possible, out of the fund that is subject only to his own lien. Maclachlan on Merchant Shipping, 601 ; the *Sailor Prince*, 1 Bt. 461, 465.

Independently of this view—which would properly control the distribution in a case where all the fund was to go to mortgagees—I think that neither Carow nor his assignee can, in view of the warranty in the mortgage to Tyler, properly claim any portion of three-quarters of the thirty-one thousand one hundred and seventy-six dollars and eighty-two cents.

A decree will be entered distributing the money in accordance with these views, and disposing of the exceptions of Tyler and of the assignee accordingly.

UNITED STATES CIRCUIT COURT.—S. D. NEW YORK.

A corporation dissolved by a decree of a state court before adjudication. but after the service of an order to show cause, still exists for the purpose of being proceeded against in bankruptcy, as such dissolution does not deprive the district court of its jurisdiction or abate the proceedings.

A cashier is still an officer of the bank for the purpose of being served with an order to show cause, although he has given the keys to the receiver appointed by a state court and has become his clerk and ceases to act as cashier.

Injunction granted restraining the state court receiver from disposing or interfering with the property of the corporation, and from setting up and asserting as against the assignee in bankruptcy, any title to or right of action for any of said property, and enjoins, pending this action, and by final decree, from doing any acts to carry out or effectuate the trusts purporting to be created by his appointment as receiver.

Assignee appointed receiver on giving a stipulation to charge no commissions on such assetts of the receivership as shall pass from the state receivership to the trust represented by the assignee of the bankrupt.

PLATT, Assignee, v. *ARCHER.*

POINTS FOR PLAINTIFF.

First.—The appointment of Mr. Archer as receiver of the property of the bankrupt was equivalent to an assignment, transfer and conveyance by the bankrupt to him, because

1. It vested in him the legal title to the property of the bankrupt, as against the bankrupt. 2 Rev. Stat. N. Y. 460, secs. 67, 68, 71, p. 462, secs. 36, 39 or R. S., 5th ed., Vol. 3, top paging, 763, sec. 44, and top paging, 770, sec. 78 and 79. *In re* Berry, 26 Barb. 55.

2. The bank consented (fol. 105) to his appointment and to all its consequences.

Second.—The taking of the property by the defendant, by authority of the orders appointing him receiver was a taking under legal process, within the meaning of the bankruptcy act. *In re* Bininger, 7 Blatch. 262; *in re* Merchants' Insurance Co., 6 N. B. R. 43.

Third.—The bankruptcy act, in its fourteenth, thirty-fifth, thirty-ninth sections, purports to operate upon not only assignments, conveyances and transfers, but upon legal process issued out of state courts; and in and by those sections it purports to set up a standard or standards by which the validity of such assignments, transfers, conveyances, and legal processes may be measured. It operates upon such acts and processes.

1. By declaring, in section fourteen, that property conveyed in fraud of creditors vests in the assignee.

2. By enacting, in section thirty-five, that conveyances, attachments, sequestrations, seizures, payments, sales, pledges, assignments, transfers and conveyances of a specified description, or made with a specified intent, shall be void, and by providing for the recovery of the property affected thereby, and the transfer of such property to the bankruptcy court, for administration.

3. By furnishing, in section thirty-five, a rule of evidence by which, *prima facie*, the *bona fides* of a sale, judgment, transfer or conveyance, is to be tested.

4. By prescribing, in section thirty-nine, tests of the validity of such payments, conveyances, sales, assignments, transfers and conveyances as are there described, and giving the assignee a right of action for the property affected thereby.

Fourth.—The bankrupt act not only professes to act upon certain transfers of property, and upon certain legal processes, by subjecting them to certain tests of their validity, but also furnishes, in section two, tribunals, viz. : this court and others, to apply those tests in cases where any party, under color of legal process, or of a sale, transfer, or assignment, claims an interest adverse to the assignee, *touching* any property or rights of property of the bankrupt, transferable to or vested in the assignee. This jurisdiction was exercised against a receiver in *Smith* v. *Buchanan*, 8 Blatch. 153.

And the cases in which like jurisdiction has been exercised are collected in an opinion of HILLYER, J., 6 N. B. R. 22.

Fifth.—This court having, therefore, jurisdiction to apply to the legal process, assignment, transfer, conveyance and sale —under which the defendant claims an interest adverse to the assignee touching the property and rights of property of the bankrupt—the tests prescribed by the bankrupt law, the question is, do such legal processes, &c., retain their vitality and validity as against the assignee, when subjected to those tests?

The tests are applied by the inquiry:

1. Under section fourteen, whether these processes were in fraud of creditors?

2. Under section thirty-five, whether they were made to or in favor of a person having reasonable cause to believe the bankrupt to be insolvent or acting in contemplation of insolvency; or to a person having reasonable cause to believe that they were made with a view to prevent the bankrupt's property from coming to its assignee in bankruptcy, or to prevent the same from being distributed under the act, or to defeat, &c., the object of the act; and whether they were made in the usual and ordinary course of business of the debtor?

3. Under section thirty-nine, whether they were made with intent to delay, defraud or hinder creditors or to defeat or delay the operation of the act?

Sixth.—The assignment, transfer and conveyance effected by operation of law in this case to the defendant, vested the property of the bankrupt in the plaintiff upon his appointment, under section fourteen of the bankrupt act, *because such property was thereby conveyed in fraud of creditors, within the meaning of that section.*

Such assignment, transfer, and conveyance are said to have been made under, and the legal process through the medium of which the conveyance was effected, are alleged by the defendant and his advisers to have been authorised by the general law of the state of New York relative to *insolvent corporations.*

Those laws are above referred to; and they, together with continued usage and judicial decisions, constituted, at the time of the passage of the bankrupt law, a partial system of bankruptcy or insolvency as to corporations; that is, they fulfilled so much of the office of a bankrupt law as concerns the distribution of the property of an insolvent corporation.

This system gave the body of the creditors no choice in the selection of a person to execute the trust, but authorised one creditor or the attorney general to force a trustee upon creditors.

The bankrupt act has, within the state of New York, the same operation and effect as if it had been enacted by the legislature of that state. It is *in pari materia* with the statutes last referred to, and may be treated and applied as if it were a state law. As such, it has additional weight as a supersedeas of former legislation, from the fact that the Legislature passed it with the design (avowed in its title) of making the bankrupt system of New York uniform with the bankrupt system of every other state, the same law being enacted in every other state.

The question then arising is, how does the bankrupt law of March second, eighteen hundred and sixty-seven, considered as a law of paramount authority in the state of New York, act upon the assignment impliedly sanctioned and expressly regulated by pre-existing statutes of the same state, the new statute being passed with a view not only to distribute the debtor's property, but to harmonise the insolvent laws of New York with those of other states?

Referring to the words of the bankrupt law, as above quoted, it is probable, if not indisputable, that if any of those words, or similar words, had been used in like statutes in this and other countries, and if so used, they had received a well considered construction, then, when the words were re-enacted, the established construction was enacted with them.

In England, some form of bankrupt law has been in force since before the time of James I.

All the bankrupt acts there passed have provided in substance, that "fraudulent conveyances" should be deemed acts of bankruptcy, and that such conveyances might be set aside as against the assignee in bankruptcy.

Of course, the question soon arose as to what was a fraudulent conveyance within the meaning of those laws; and in determining that question it was held that the term "fraudulent conveyance" (which is synonymous with "conveyance in fraud of creditors," as used in section fourteen of our present bankrupt law; and with "assignment with intent," &c., as used in section thirty-nine) refers not only to conveyances which were covinous and fraudulent at common law and under the statutes of Elizabeth, but also to those which, although not fraudulent and covinous in that sense, become so, when compared with the operation and effect of the bankrupt law. In other words, a conveyance not fraudulent before, might becomes so under the bankrupt law, because contrary to the policy of that law.

Assignments of all a trader's effects, under certain circumstances, were held contrary to the policy, spirit, operation and effect of the bankrupt law, and out of the ordinary course of business, and *therefore* fraudulent. And there was no exception in cases where the assignment was for the benefit of all the creditors of the assignor. Griffith & Thomas' Archbold on Bankruptcy, 119; *Wilson* v. *Day*, 2 Burrow, 830; *Worsley* v. *DeMattos*, 1 Burrow, 467; *Alderson* v. *Taylor*, 4 Burrow, 235; *Linton* v. *Haskett*, 3 Wilson, 47; *Compton* v. *Bedford* 1 W. Blackstone, 362; *Law* v. *Skinner*, 2 W. Blackstone, 996; *Rust* v. *Cooper* 2 Cowp. 629; *Newton* v. *Chandler*, 7 East. 138; *Hassell* v. *Simpson*, 1 Dougl. 92; *Butcher* v. *Easto*, id. 96; *Eckhardt* v. *Wilson*, 8 T. R. 140; *Nunns* v. *Wilmore*, id. 528; *Tappenden* v. *Burgess*, 4 East. 230; *Kittle* v. *Hammond*, Cooke's Bkt. Law, 86; *Hoffman* v. *Pitt*, 5 Esp. 22; *Botcherley* v. *Lancaster*, 1 Ad. & El. 77; *Siebert* v. *Spooner*, 1 M. & W. 714; *Bowker* v. *Bendekin*, 11 M. &. W. 128.

And this has been so well understood in England that the bankrupt acts of George IV., of eighteen hundred and forty-nine and eighteen hundred and sixty-one, specially save voluntary assignments for the benefit of creditors from avoidance, unless proceedings in bankruptcy are commenced within a limited period afterwards; and such assignments are drawn as acts of bankruptcy; and in the costs of bankrupt proceedings allowances are made for the expense of such assignments, when drawn for that purpose. 2 Archbold on Bankruptcy, edition of 1869, sec. 68 of act, also, page 1271 of same volume.

In this country we have had the bankrupt law of eighteen hundred and forty-one.

Its first and second sections provided as follows:

Law of eighteen hundred and forty-one, 6 Stat. at Large, 441.—Sec. 1. " All persons being merchants, &c.,   *   *   shall be liable to become bankrupts   *   *   whenever such person   *   *   shall make any fraudulent conveyance, assignment," &c.

Sec. 2. " All future payments, conveyances, &c., made by any bankrupt, in contemplation of bankruptcy for the purpose of giving a preference ; and all other conveyances or transfers of property made by such bankrupt in contemplation of bankruptcy to any person or persons whatever, not being a *bona fide* creditor or purchaser for a valuable consideration, without notice, shall be deemed utterly void, and a fraud upon this act," &c.

Under these sections, voluntary assignments were held void by judges McLean, Prentiss, Ware, and Conkling, in *Barton* v. *Tower*, 5 L. R. 214, Conkling, J. ; *McLean* v. *Meline*, 3 McLean, 199, McLean, J. ; *McLean* v. *Johnson*, id. 202, McLean, J. ; *Gassett* v. *Morse*, 21 Vermont, Prentiss, J. ; *Jones* v. *Sleeper*, 2 N. Y. Leg. Obs., Ware, J.

In New York there was an insolvent system in force when the case of Hurst, 7 Wend. 241, arose in eighteen hundred and thirty-one. It was there held that a disposition of property for the benefit of creditors, although otherwise untainted with fraud, and not prohibited in terms, was against the policy of the statute and in fraud of the law, and was, therefore, prohibited by necessary implication, and was void. Judge Nelson was a member of the court which decided that case.

All through the cases above quoted, it was held that the motive and intention of an act was to be tested by its natural and necessary consequences, and that the actor is conclusively presumed to intend those consequences ; a fundamental principle which is very strongly stated by Nelson, J., in *Cunningham* v. *Freeborn*, 11 Wend. 240.

Such was, or had been, the state of the law in this country and in England, when the bankrupt law of eighteen hundred and sixty-seven was passed. It used language synonymous with what had thus been construed. If the legislature had intended to except assignments or other insolvency trusts, the exception would have been made expressly.

In view of these authorities, it hardly admits of a doubt that the act of eighteen hundred and sixty-seven, in transferring, by section fourteen, to the assignee in bankruptcy property conveyed "in fraud of creditors," and in nullifying, by section thirty-nine, assignments made with "intent to defraud creditors," meant to include such an assignment as the one now in question, without regard to peculiar features of it arising from the state laws.

There are, however, special inconsistencies between the operation of such an assignment and the operation of the bankrupt law, more glaring than those which existed under the English bankrupt laws.

A review of these inconsistencies fortifies the position, that if the legislature of New York had passed the bankrupt law of eighteen hundred and sixty-seven, it would, by necessary construction, have repealed the system previously in force.

1. Under the law of New York, the trustee is forced upon creditors by one creditor or the attorney-general. Under the act of congress, the creditors force the assignee on the debtor.

2. Under a state law of eighteen hundred and fifty-eight, (Chap. 314, p. 506,) certain rights of action, for instance, to recover property conveyed by the assignor in fraud of creditors, are given to the voluntary assignee. By the fourteenth section of the federal law, which has the same force and effect as if enacted by the state legislature, the same right of action is vested in the assignee in bankruptcy. Which shall prevail?

3. The state law regulates the adjustment of the trustee's

account in a manner varying from that prescribed by the act of congress.

4. The state law postpones the inventory until after choice of trustee is made. But the act of congress makes the petition and inventory simultaneous, in voluntary cases, and in involuntary cases, it makes the inventory and the choice of assignee simultaneous, so that the assignee is chosen in view of a well ascertained responsibility.

5. The right to participate in dividends is determined under the act of congress by one set of tests; under the state law by another.

6. The act of congress remits the administration of bankrupt estates to federal tribunals, whose peculiar duty it is to expound federal law. The state law confines such administration to local tribunals, and withdraws bankrupt estates from all administration under federal law. *In re* Bininger, 7 Blatch. 262.

In these and other particulars the two systems conflict, and upon established principles the last enactment must prevail, not merely because it emanates from a paramount authority, but because, if both systems had the same origin, the two cannot co-exist. *Van Nostrand* v. *Carr*, 30 Md. 128; *in re* Reynolds, 8 R. I. Rep. 485; *Commonwealth* v. *O'Hara*, 6 Am. L. Reg., n. s. 865; *Goodwin* v. *Sharkey*, 5 Abbott's P. R., n. s. 64; *Sturgis* v. *Crowninshield*, 4 Wheat. 122; *Ogden* v. *Saunders*, 12 Wheat. 273; *Ex parte* Eames, 2 Story, 322; *in re* Independent Insurance Company, 6 N. B. R. 261.

Seventh.—Departing from section fourteen and comparing the transaction in question with the general policy and spirit of section thirty-five, and with so much of section thirty-nine as vitiates transfers and legal process made or issued with intent to hinder, delay or defraud creditors, or defeat or delay the operation of the act, the legal process in question is void as against the assignee, and the property affected by it is recoverable by him.

The thirty-fifth section is not wholly borrowed from any other statute of bankruptcy, but as an enactment is in many respect original and peculiar ; although apparently suggested by the language of judicial decisions. It aimed at something which was perhaps not definitely enough indicated by other parts of the enactments. It is such a section as the scope and sphere of federal legislation (designed to sweep away conflicting and hostile local arrangements, and to replace them by uniform methods) would suggest. It is devised for the sake of producing the uniformity which the remaining provisions of the act might have failed to produce. The words are consequently general and comprehensive. They are not confined to abrogating what conflicts with the details or machinery of the law, but they comprehensively remove all that obstructs, impairs, hinders, impedes, defeats, or delays the operation, effect, object or provisions of the act; so that under this section the given transaction cannot be tested without considering, not only the words of the law, but the operation, effect and object of the transaction. And this section was enacted after the courts of England and of the United States had held the necessary effect of a voluntary assignment or transfer to be to impair, impede, hinder, delay and defeat the object of a bankrupt law. *Beattie* v. *Gardner*, 4 N. B. R. 109 ; *Shawhan* v. *Wherritt*, 7 How. 627.

Eighth.—Tested by a close analysis of the words of section thirty-five and section thirty-nine, the legal process in question, and the transfer effected thereby, are void as against the plaintiff.

1. The assignor or debtor must be bankrupt or insolvent, or acting in contemplation of insolvency or bankruptcy. Insolvency is defined *in re* Bininger, 7 Blatch. 262 ; *Toof* v. *Martin*, 6 N. B. R. 49.

"Contemplation of insolvency" therefore needs no definition.

"Contemplation of bankruptcy" was defined in *Buckingham* v. *McLean*, 13 How. 150.

If the appointment of a receiver was an act of bankruptcy, the debtor joining in that act was, because he must have been, in contemplation of bankruptcy as thus defined :

for it knew that such act invited and would sustain an adjudication.

2. As to the grantee, sections thirty-five and thirty-nine require only that he should have "reasonable cause" to believe certain things. And "reasonable cause" is defined by the supreme court of the United States, in *Toof* v. *Martin*, 6 N. B. R. 49.

3. The thing which the grantee must have reasonable cause to believe is that the assignor or debtor is insolvent, or acting in contemplation of insolvency, and that the assignment is made "with a view," to prevent his property from coming to his assignee in bankruptcy, &c.

4. "His assignee" clearly does not mean an assignee already appointed, but means an assignee thereafter to be appointed in bankruptcy. So the meaning is, that the grantee must have reason to believe that the assignment is made in such a way as necessarily to prevent the property from coming to any assignee who may thereafter be appointed. That was clearly the effect in this case.

5. It is also enough, if the grantee has reasonable cause to believe that the assignment is made with a view of preventing the property from being distributed under the act. Certainly it could not be distributed under the act if it was distributed under some other act. In this clause the section gives importance to the *machinery* of the act.

6. It is enough if the grantee has reasonable cause to believe that the assignment is made "with a view" to defeat the object of the act. The object of the act is to establish a uniform system of bankruptcy; that is, to have the property of an insolvent debtor in one state distributed in the same order and proportion, and to the same classes of creditors, and under the supervision of the same class of tribunals and within the same period, as in all other states. But the necessary effect of the assignment was to have the property distributed in different orders and proportions, and to different classes of creditors under the supervision of different tribunals, and within different periods, from those provided in other

states. Another object of the law is to open the federal courts to all creditors without distinction, and give them in those courts a remedy against the debtor's property. This assignment defeats that object by driving the creditor to a state court, unless he can go into a federal court on some peculiar ground of jurisdiction, such as alienage or citizenship in another state.

7. It is also enough if the grantee has reasonable cause to believe that the assignment is made "with a view" to impair, hinder, or delay the "operation and effect" of the act. Here again the section raises the machinery of the act into importance, and sweeps away what obstructs its practical working. The operations of the act are manifold. Its operation on debtors is to compel them to put their property in the control of a federal court, for the purpose of being distributed among creditors who may establish their status as such by proper proof; and such distribution is effected by means of an agent selected by creditors. The assignment in question defeats that operation of the act by promoting a distribution of the property in other methods.

The act operates upon creditors in many beneficial ways, which need not be pointed out in detail. In general it requires them to prove their status as creditors, and to surrender special advantages, and it gives them summary and speedy realization upon their claims. The assignment in question defeats this operation of the act, and hinders, impedes and delays it. No creditor claiming the benefit of the assignment need purge himself as he is required to do by the bankrupt law.

The answer which may be suggested to this objection is that the object of the assignment in question, on its face, appears to be the equal distribution of the property among creditors; and as that is the object of the bankrupt law, the assignment is not at cross purposes with the law. This answer is more plausible than substantial. The words "operation and effect," in the law, refer to the machinery provided by the law; but even if this is not so, yet, taking the whole law together, its ultimate operation and effect is to distribute the property among those who *prove themselves creditors in the federal court* and submit to the conditions there exacted of them; while the ultimate operation and effect of the assignment in question is to distribute the property among those who máy establish their claims in some other way. These are not concurrent, but are substantially inconsistent, trusts. *In re* Hurst, 7 Wend. 241.

7. "In view of" and "with intent to" produce certain specified consequences are phrases referring to a state of mind of which the law does not require proof, but which it conclusively presumes to exist, where the consequences necessarily or naturally flow from the act; and the inquiry which these words suggest is—"What consequences did naturally and necessarily flow from the act?" When these consequences are ascertained, they are conclusively imputed to design; and so conclusive is the inference of the law, that sworn denials of the inferred intent are wholly immaterial. *Cunningham* v. *Freeborn,* 11 Wend. 240; *In re* Bininger, 7 Blatch. 262; *Newman* v. *Cordell,* 43 Barb. 448.

8. The effect of the bankrupt law is to vest in the assignee in bankruptcy property previously conveyed in fraud of creditors. The effect of the assignment, under the law of New York, is to vest a right of action for such property in an assignee selected by one creditor or by the attorney-general. This is a vital difference of the greatest practical consequence.

9. The effect and operation of the bankrupt law is to put the property of the debtor out of the reach of process, while giving the assignee retroactive rights, so as to equalize the distribution of the property as of a period four or six months prior to the proceedings in bankruptcy. This operation and effect is defeated by the making of a voluntary assignment, which, while changing the title to the property, does not at the same time create any agency competent to revoke preferences already carried into effect.

10. The effect and operation of the bankrupt law is to put

the property under the control of the district and circuit courts and the supreme court of the United States. The effect of the voluntary assignment is to leave it within the jurisdiction of the state courts. While there, it is subject to various hazards from which it would be free under the bankrupt law. For instance, it is subject to be swept away by prior lien. It is subject to suit brought to set aside the assignment as fraudulent, and the first suitor in any such proceeding has a preference over the rest.

It is no answer to repeat the phrase—" The only object was to make an equal distribution," &c., when the *effect* is manifestly the contrary.

11. It is also sufficient, if the assignee has reasonable cause to believe that the assignment was made "with a view " to evade any of the provisions of the bankrupt act.

This clause says nothing about the policy, spirit, operation or effect of the law, but refers solely to its provisions, without distinction between the provisions relating to intermediate steps and those effecting final results.

There are provisions of the bankrupt law which are evaded by a distribution of property under a voluntary assignment. All the provisions of the involuntary branch are so evaded. The provisions of the voluntary branch are so evaded—such as those relating to the selection of an assignee, the proving of debts, the surrender of securities, the retroactive rights of an assignee, the compensation of an assignee, &c.

12. It may be suggested, in answer to these points, that the voluntary branches of the law are permissive only, and not imperative, and that it is not expressly made the duty of a debtor to avail himself of that branch. So much may be safely conceded, though in fact the position is unsound. But the fact that a debtor violates no duty by not petitioning, does not give validity to a transfer which the law nullifies. It may be true that the law does not say to the debtor, " You *shall* petition," but it is equally true that it does say, " You shall *not* evade any of the provisions of this act, nor

make any assignment which has the effect to prevent your property from coming to any assignee in bankruptcy hereafter appointed, or to prevent the same from being distributed under this act, or to defeat the object of, or in any way impair, impede, or delay the operation and effect of this act. If you form the wish voluntarily to distribute your property through the medium of a third person, and not directly by your own hand, it must be to such persons as bring themselves within the provisions of this uniform law, and not to such as you may designate; and in other particulars, you must subordinate your wishes to the machinery, object, effect, and provisions herein pointed out and provided." If, then, the debtor does not choose to proceed under the act, he must not proceed in conflict with it. If he is not bound to comply with its provisions, he is bound not to violate them. He must not remove his property out of the reach of process, nor yet convey in fraud of creditors, nor against the policy of the act. If these prohibitions do not create a positive duty they give rise to a necessity which the debtor must submit to.

13. The thirty-fifth section further provides, that if such assignment is not made in the usual and ordinary course of business of the debtor, the fact shall be *prima facie* evidence of fraud; not of fraudulent intent solely, but of fraud intended, consummated, or directly or indirectly produced. Under the English statutes it was constantly held that a voluntary assignment was out of the ordinary course of business; so that the framers of the present bankrupt law have enacted into law what was previously a judicial definition.

14. It may be said, also, that there is no more harm in a debtor making an assignment in trust for his creditors, than in his making the distribution himself. The answer is, that the law does not nullify the latter act, while it does the former. The framers of the law judged of the difference for themselves. The first clause of the thirty-fifth section impliedly permits payment directly to creditors, if not made by way of preference, while the second clause points to pay-

ments and assignments to third persons not creditors, or not acting wholly in their own right as creditors. If, without de-sign to give a preference, the debtor makes a payment di-rectly to a creditor, there are no words in the law to avoid it. The difference between payments and securities directly to creditors, and assignments in trust for creditors, is very dis-tinctly stated in *Cunningham* v. *Freeborn*, 11 Wend. 256; as follows:

"I would hold a debtor in failing circumstances to pay, or give security to, his creditor or creditors, directly, without the intervention of a trustee, who is often the creature of the debtor, without interest or sympathy on behalf of the credi-tor. In this way the creditor would obtain the control of the fund the moment the debtor parted with it, and if favored creditors were preferred, they would be obliged to see to it that they took no more than was a fair security for their debts. They should not be permitted to justify their possession under the cover of trusteeship for others. Each creditor should be his own trustee. If inconvenient for creditors personally to execute the trust, they could appoint a trustee in their place. This modification would have the effect to give the possession and control of the fund, in the first instance, to the creditors, or to a person appointed by them; as the law now stands, the debtor may control the appointment, and a bill in chancery is often necessary to enable the creditor to get possession of the fund. If, in the preference, actual payment was required, or security directly to the person of the creditor or creditors, for his or their debts, and, of course, the immediate control of the property given, the great inducements to these fraudu-lent assignments would be removed. The hope of profit or control of the property by the debtor, after he parted with it, would be extinguished, and he could have no other interest in the preference than to see that it was made. He might still gratify unkind, or worse, feelings, against particular creditors; but he must, at the same time, deny himself the use of the fund of which he deprives them."

This is the language of NELSON, J.

Independently of the authorities above quoted, and treating the question as an original one upon the words, policy and object of the bankrupt law, the following arguments, some of which are repetitions of what has been already said, are submitted as pertinent and controlling:

1. The bankrupt law introduced new elements into the relation of debtor and creditor, so that what was not fraudulent before may be so now.

2. The intent is to be determined by the actual and natural effect.

3. The fourteenth section, in using the words "in fraud of creditors," points the mind not only to what is *intended* to be a fraud, but to what is, *per se*, or consequentially, or technically, or inferentially, a withholding of a right, duty, or advantage due to creditors, under the bankrupt law or otherwise.

4. The reasons assigned by English and American judges in expounding the bankrupt laws which existed prior to eighteen hundred and sixty-seven are applicable now, and are convincing, if not authoritative.

5. The debtor owes to the body of his creditors the duty of yielding them voluntarily every advantage in the distribution of his property which they could obtain by adverse proceedings; and not less than any other does he owe them the duty of yielding them every advantage which the bankrupt law furnishes. When he not only withholds such advantages, but bars the creditors' way to them, he violates a duty created by law; which is another way of saying that he commits a fraud upon the law.

6. By making a voluntary assignment, the debtor withholds privileges, advantages and securities which, by his voluntary act under the bankrupt law, he might bestow; and so he defrauds his creditors.

7. A voluntary assignment is a fraud upon creditors, because, by means of it the debtor is enabled, under our political system, to make a fraudulent use of the bankrupt law. He makes the assignment. That, if valid, takes the property out of the jurisdiction of the federal courts; then he may invoke

the bankrupt law, and, by means of an injunction upon creditor, gets the property out of their reach in the state courts. In that view of it, if the assignment is not a fraud, the bankrupt law is.

8. A denial of an intention to institute voluntary proceedings in bankruptcy is not an affirmation, nor is it, if true, proof of honest intent. It is only a denial of an intention to furnish to creditors the advantages which accrue to them under the bankrupt law. It is consistent with a design to defraud. For instance, a debtor pays a favored creditor in full; he knows that if he goes into bankruptcy within four months he puts that creditor in peril. Therefore, to *defraud the law*, he intends *not* to go into bankruptcy. So as to attachments and other liens.

It is supposed by the plaintiff that the defendant may rely, in opposition to this motion, on *Sedgwick* v. *Place*, and *Sedgwick* v. *Minck*, 1 N. B. R. 204; *Langley* v. *Perry*, 2 N. B. R. 180: Hawkins' Appeal, 2 N. B. R. 122; *Beecher* v. *Bininger*, 7 Blatch. 170. It is therefore submitted.—

Ninth.—That those authorities are not in conflict with the plaintiff's position here.

In *Sedgwick* v. *Place*, 1 N. B. R. 204, the case was heard on a preliminary motion founded on the bill only. Whatever fraud was averred in the bill was denied in the answer, and no proofs were offered in support of the bill. A preliminary motion for an injunction was denied by NELSON, J., solely on the assumption, as he expressly states, that the assignment then in question was untainted with fraud either against creditors or against the bankrupt law.

In some respects, it is difficult to reconcile every sentence of the opinion in *Sedgwick* v. *Place* with judge NELSON'S views expressed in *Cunningham* v. *Freeborn*, 11 Wend. and *Hurst's* case, 7 Wend. As matter of fact, it is true that in *Sedgwick* v. *Place*, when that case was before NELSON, J., no actual argument was had. The papers were submitted to him in the expectation and belief, on the part of counsel on both sides, that he would grant the motion.

In *Sedgwick* v. *Minck*, 1 N. B. R. 204, the assignee sought to deprive creditors of a lien which they had acquired many years before the passage of the bankrupt law. No case within either of sections fourteen, thirty-five, or thirty-nine was made. The decision in that case was clearly right, and was acquiesced in by all parties.

In *Langley* v. *Perry*, 2 N. B. R. 180, the assignment in question was made on May twenty-five, eighteen hundred and sixty-seven, which was before the bankrupt law took effect, and when neither the debtor nor his creditors were able to put the law in motion. Of course an intention to defeat or delay the operation of an inoperative law could not be imputed.

In *Farrin* v. *Crawford*, 2 N. B. R. 181, SWAYNE, J., says, (p. 182) : " I do not mean to impute any intention to defraud or do wrong to either party, *but here are the facts, and the legal result is inevitable.*" He thus recognizes and applies the rule adopted by NELSON, J., in *Cunningham* v. *Freeborn.*

In *Hawkins' Appeal*, 2 N. B. R. 122, no question arose between an assignee in bankruptcy and a voluntary assignee. The question was between creditors of a debtor and the voluntary assignee of the debtor. What the questions were, the report of the case does not disclose. Nor does it appear how creditors, on the settlement of the accounts of a voluntary assignee, in a state court, could avail themselves of the provisions of the bankrupt law. The case is worthy of observation, in that it erroneously states judge NELSON'S decision in *Sedgwick* v. *Place.* Judge NELSON did not dismiss the bill, he only denied a preliminary motion. See judge NELSON's comment on *Sedgwick* v. *Place*, 3 N. B. R. 79.

In *Beecher* v. *Bininger*, 7 Blatch. 170, the questions now arising were not raised at all. The plaintiff in that case, Beecher, did not found his suit either on the fourteenth, thirty-fifth, or thirty-ninth section of the bankrupt law, nor did he attack the process under which the receiver took the property, as fraudulent. His theory was, that by means of the receivership, a trust had been created for the benefit of Clark & Bininger, in a suit in a state court; that the title of

Clark & Bininger to, and their interest in the property had passed to the assignee, and that, therefore, the action in the state court had abated; that the receivers were *functi officiis*, and the assignee had a right to call upon them in this court for an account. On the merits of that theory, the court did not pass then, and has never passed since. It only denied a motion, putting the denial on the ground that, no fraud being alleged, there was no sufficient reason shown for apprehending loss or waste.

On the other hand, see *in re* Smith, 3 N. B. R. 98, 3 N. B. R. 79, letter from judge NELSON; *in re* Pierce & Holbrook, 3 N. B. R. 61; *in re* Randall & Sunderland, 3 N. B. R. 4; *in re* Bininger, 7 Blatch. 262; *Van Nostrand* v. *Carr*, 30 Md. 128; *in re* Reynolds, 8 R. I. R 485; *Dehon* v. *Foster*, 4 Allen 545.

Tenth.—The proper method of obtaining relief against a fraudulent transfer of a bankrupt's property, or against an attempt to take the property out of this jurisdiction, is by bill in equity, fraud being the ground of jurisdiction. Particularly is this so, where a discovery and account is necessary. And the only method of determining conflicting claims of an assignee and an adverse holder of property is by a plenary suit in equity or a formal action at law. *Dehon* v. *Foster*, 4 Allen, 545; *in re* Kerosene Oil Co, 2 N. B. R. 164; *in re* Bonesteel, id. 106; *in re* Ballou, 3 N. B. R. 177; *Smith* v. *Mason*, 6 N. B. R. 1.

Eleventh.—The utmost which the plaintiff needs to do on this motion is to establish three propositions: 1. Color or appearance of superior title, and probability of ultimate recovery. This he has done. 2. Danger of loss or misappropriation. 3. Necessity for this court taking the property into its custody *pendente lite*.

Twelfth.—The defendant is a fraudulent grantee, not merely by construction, but actually so. When he became receiver, the law was too well settled to be misunderstood, that he was becoming a participant in a scheme to defraud the law. He has not only become the trustee under a fraudulent trust, but he has furnished security that he will exe-

cute that trust. The court will presume that he will execute
the trust unless restrained. Hence the necessity and propriety of an injunction. Danger of loss will be presumed to
exist when the property is in the hands of a fraudulent
grantee pledged to devote it to unlawful purposes.

The property is alleged in the bill (fols. 14, 15) to be of
various descriptions, and much of it capable of easy transfer
or alienation. If the defendant is permitted to transfer it
pendente lite, the plaintiff may be compelled to follow it, by a
variety of proceedings, in various courts, into the possession
of numerous purchasers, and thus encounter the evil, so
odious to a court of equity, of multiplicity of suits, and great
diminution of a trust fund in legal expenses.

The defendant's refusal to deliver the property, his claim
of title under a fraudulent conveyance, his refusal to attorn to
this court, his obtaining orders from the state court without
notice to the assignee, all constitute continuing threats to
misappropriate the property, and the case is brought within
the principle of the cases referred in Story, secs. 905 to 908,
918, 953, and of *Onslow* v. ————, 16 Vesey, 173 ; *Douglass* v.
Wiggins, 1 John, ch. 435 ; *Watson* v. *Hunter*, 5 id. 170 ; *Win-
ship* v. *Pitts*, 3 Paige, 259 ; *Frewin* v. *Lewis*, 4 Mylne & Craig,
254 ; *Dehon* v. *Foster*, 4 Allen, 545, 7 Allen, 57 ; *Rector, &c.*
v. *Keech*, 5 Bosw. 691 ; *Galway* v. *S. S. R. Co.*, 13 Abbott's
P. R. 2 ; *Mohawk Co.* v. *Artcher*, 6 Paige, 88 ; *Shaw* v. *Dwight*,
10 Barb. 536 ; *Gillot* v. *Kettle*, 3 Duer, 624 ; *McLane* v. *Lafayette Bank*, 3 McLean, 185 ; *Cropper* v. *Coburn*, 2 Curtis
C. C. R. 465 ; *Raleau* v. *Bernard*, 3 Blatch. 244 ; *McKenzies* v.
Cowing, 4 Cranch's C. C. Rep. 479 ; *Osborn* v. *Bank of U. S.*
9 Wheat. 738 ; *Sawyer* v. *Gill*, 3 Woodbury & M., 97 ; *Bank*
v. *Skelton*, 2 Blatch. 26 ; *St. Luke's Hospital* v. *Barclay*, 3
Blatch. 259 ; *Oreene* v. *Hahberg*, 2 Brock, Marsh 403 ; *Wilson*
v. *Bastable*, 1 Cranch C. C. 394 ; *in re* Mallory, 6 N. B. R. 22.

It is not merely the danger that if the plaintiff recovers,
the property may not be forthcoming, which is to be considered, but danger in a peculiar sense suggested by the
bankrupt law. The danger is, that if the fraudulent grantee

is permitted to execute his trust, the creditors whom the plaintiff represents may lose the benefit of the bankrupt law. Many months must elapse before a final decree can be obtained. Meanwhile, the defendant, by *ex parte* applications in the supreme court, may get authority to pay out a large part of the fund for purposes not authorised by the bankrupt law. A short statute of limitations is running against the plaintiff. If he should undertake to sue parties to whom the bankrupt made prior fraudulent conveyances, he would be met by an assertion of the defendant's title. Nearly two months have now elapsed since the plaintiff was appointed. In another month his duty will be to call a meeting of creditors. If this court takes possession of the fund, it may, *pendente lite*, apply it to the satisfaction of undisputed claims, without injustice. Each party is a trustee, and the *cestui que trust* on both sides are identical, or can be made so, upon compliance with the terms of the bankrupt law. Hence the propriety of a receivership in this suit, through which the fund may, *pendente lite*, go directly to those ultimately entitled to it, and who are the real parties in interest. And an injunction of the kind here asked for necessarily draws after it a receivership. *Osborn* v. *Heyer*, 2 Paige, 342 ; *Bloodgood* v. *Clark*, 4 id. 574; *Mitchell* v. *Bettman*, 25 Barb. 408.

Thirteenth.—The plaintiff, Mr. John H. Platt, asks that he may be appointed receiver, he stipulating to charge no commissions on what may be ultimately transferred from the receivership to the trust represented by himself as plaintiff. This is the course which has been uniformly pursued, for the sake of convenience and economy, in the district court, in like cases.

The plaintiff as assignee is always under the direct control and order of the court, and cannot dispose of the property, even on a final recovery, without leave of the court. In his hands, therefore, the property is in the safest and most economical custody. Any reasons which, in the ordinary exercise of equity jurisdiction, would be valid against the appointment of a party, are inapplicable in cases of this description. The district court acted in that way in *Sedgwick* v. *Place*, 3 N. B. R. 35, 78, and the practice there adopted has been generally followed since, in like case, with the acquiescence of suitors and lawyers, wherever the parties to whom the plaintiff and defendant are accountable, are identical.

F. N. BANGS, of counsel for plaintiff.

BLATCHFORD, J.—On the thirteenth of October, eighteen hundred and seventy-one, the supreme court of New York, in a suit brought by William R. Barr against the Stuyvesant bank, and on a verified complaint and sundry affidavits therein, made an order restraining the bank from exercising any of its corporate franchises, and from collecting or transferring any of its moneys or property until the further order of the court, and appointing the defendant in this suit to be receiver of its property. Such suit was commenced on the twelfth of October. The gravamen of the complaint was, that the bank was insolvent and unable to pay its debts. The bank appeared in the suit by attorney on the twelfth of October, and its counsel consented, in open court, to the making of the order of the thirteenth of October.

On the thirteenth of November, the supreme court, in a suit brought by the people of the state of New York against the bank, and on a summons, a complaint, affidavits, and due notice, counsel for the bank appearing and opposing, made an order enjoining the bank from exercising any of its corporate franchises, and from collecting or transferring any of its moneys or property, and appointing the defendant in this suit to be receiver of its property. The complaint set forth the insolvency of the bank.

On the twenty-third of November, no answer or demurrer having been put in, in the suit brought by Barr, a judgment was entered therein, awarding a perpetual injunction against the bank, and appointing the defendant in this suit to be its receiver, but not dissolving the corporation.

On the twenty-third of December, John Mack filed in the district court of the United States for this district a petition in involuntary bankruptcy against the bank, setting forth, as one of the acts of bankruptcy, the procuring and suffering its property to be taken on legal process by the defendant in this suit, as receiver, with intent to defeat the operation of the bankrupt act. On the filing of the petition, an order to show cause, returnable on the sixth of January, eighteen hundred and seventy-two, was, on the twenty-third of December, issued. The order directed that a copy of the petition and of the order should be served on the president of the bank.

On the twenty-seventh of December, an answer of the bank, in the suit brought by the-people, denying, on information and belief, its insolvency, was sworn to by John Van Orden, who, in the affidavit says that he is " cashier of the Stuyvesant Bank." This answer was subsequently put in in the suit.

On the twenty-eighth of December, on an affidavit of the absence of the president of the bank, and that Van Orden was cashier, an order was made by the district court, that a copy of the petition and of the order to show cause be served on the bank, by serving it on Van Orden, its cashier. Such service was made on Van Orden on the twenty-eighth of December.

On the twenty-ninth of December, in the suit brought by the people, judgment on the answer as frivolous was given against the bank, and it was adjudged that the charter of the bank " is declared to be forfeited, and the said corporation composing the said bank is hereby dissolved," and that the defendant in this suit be continued as receiver, and be appointed receiver of all the property of the bank, and that the bank be enjoined from collecting any debts and transferring any money or property, and from transacting any business whatever.

On the sixth of January, eighteen hundred and seventy-two, on proof of such service of a copy of the petition and order to show cause, on the cashier of the bank, no one appearing in opposition, and the bank being called in open court, and making default in appearing pursuant to the order to show cause, the usual order of adjudication was made by the district court, setting forth that on consideration of the

Platt v. Archer.

proofs, it was found that the facts set forth in the petition were true, and adjudging that the bank became bankrupt within the true intent and meaning of the bankrupt act before the filing of said petition, and declaring and adjudging it bankrupt accordingly, and referring it to a register to take the proceedings required by the act.

At the first meeting of the creditors of the bankrupt, held in pursuance of the warrant issued to the marshal for the choice of assignee, it was resolved by three-fourths in value of the creditors whose claims had been proved, that it was for the general interest of the creditors of the bankrupt, that the estate of the bankrupt should be wound up and settled, and distribution made among the creditors by trustees under the inspection and direction of a committee of creditors, and that the defendant in this suit be nominated as trustee to take, hold and distribute said estate, and that Richard Kelly, the Reverend John Orcutt, and Richard H. Bull, president of the New York Savings Bank, be the committee of creditors under whose direction the said trustee should act; this resolution was duly certified to the district court by the register; the register also certified that the first meeting of creditors was convened on the seventh of February, and was finally closed on the thirteenth of February; that at the meeting votes were cast for assignee, the names of the voters and the amounts of the debts on which they voted, and the name of the person for whom such votes were cast being returned; that there was an opposing interest to the appointment of an assignee by the register in the action of the creditors in nominating a trustee; that no choice of assignee was made by the creditors, and that the register had made no appointment of assignee, believing that such action of the creditors was such an opposing interest as would render his appointing one irregular and void.

On the sixteenth of March, the defendant in this suit, on notice and on affidavits, applied to the district court for confirmation of the action of the creditors in respect to a trustee and a committee. This motion was opposed on affidavits,

and by an order made on the twenty-second of March, the
court denied the motion and appointed the plaintiff in this
suit to be assignee of the estate and effects of the bankrupt.
From the decision rendered by the district judge, it appears
that he was of opinion, on the papers before him, that the
interests of the creditors would not be promoted by the appointment of the defendant in this suit as trustee, and that,
therefore, he declined to confirm such resolution. The principal ground stated for this conclusion was, that as the appointment of the defendant in this suit as receiver by the
state court was one of the grounds on which the bank was
adjudged bankrupt, and he still continued to be such receiver,
and claimed to hold as such receiver what remained in his
hands of the property of the bank which had passed to him,
and had been dealing with the rest as such receiver, and, if
he was to account for it at all to the district court, must account for it as of the day the petition in bankruptcy was filed,
and to a trustee or assignee to be appointed by the district
court; and as it appeared that he did not intend voluntarily
to surrender to any trustee or assignee to be appointed by
the district court the property still in his possession, and did
not intend, if confirmed as trustee by the district court, to
cease acting as receiver, but announced his intention to act
both as receiver and as trustee, and to have his acts authorized by the state court and by the district court, it was not
proper that he should as trustee be plaintiff, and as receiver
be defendant in respect to the matters involved, and he could
not be allowed to occupy the incompatible position of being
a trustee under the bankrupt act, and looking to the state
court as partly the source of his authority, or of holding the
property as receiver under the state laws, and administering
it under the authority or direction of the district court. It
further appears from the decision of the district judge, that
he regarded it as an objection to confirming the proceedings,
that the bank of which Mr. Bull, one of the three persons
named as the committee of creditors, was president, claimed
by its proof of debt to be entitled to a preference under the

statutes of New York, and to be paid in full in priority to others, in a distribution of the assets under the bankrupt act, and that such claim of preference was contested by creditors who were unsecured, and who claimed no preference. The view of the judge was, that the creditors had undertaken to select a committee consisting of three persons, and had thus expressed their desire that the committee should consist of three persons ; that their action under the statute was a unit, and their resolutions must be confirmed as a whole or not at all ; and that it was improper that Mr. Bull should be one of the committee under whose direction the estate of the bankrupt was to be wound up and settled.

The judge regarded the case as having arisen where, under section thirteen of the act, it became the duty of the court to appoint an assignee, the resolution nominating a trustee not being confirmed, and no choice of an assignee having been made by the creditors.

An assignment, in due form under the act, was executed by the district judge to the plaintiff in this suit, on the twenty-second of March, of all the estate which the bankrupt had on the twenty-third of December, eighteen hundred and seventy-one.

On the twenty-third of March the defendant in this suit and Bull and Orcutt filed in this court a petition praying for a review and reversal of the order of adjudication made by the district court, and of the order refusing to confirm the nomination of a trustee and a committee and appointing the plaintiff in this suit to be assignee.

The petition of review sets forth, as objections to the orders : (1.) That the district court had no jurisdiction over the bankrupt, it having been dissolved by a judgment of a competent court before the adjudication. (2.) That it had no jurisdiction over the assets of the bankrupt, they having become vested in a receiver duly appointed by the state court. If it should be held that the district court had such jurisdiction, then it is objected, by the petition, to the order of the twenty-second of March that it refused : (1.) To confirm the resolution nominating the defendant in this suit as trustee. 2.) To confirm the resolution nominat˙ the three ersons as a committee. (3.) To confirm at least two of the committee. If it should be held that the district court had such jurisdiction, and that it was proper for the district judge to refuse to confirm as aforesaid, then it is objected by the petition to the order of the twenty-second of March : (1.) That it appoints the plaintiff in this suit assignee, when less than one-tenth of all the creditors who had proved their claims had voted for him, while more than nine-tenths had voted for the appointment of a trustee. (2.) That the appointment of such assignee was not authorized by law, it having been the duty of the court to direct the bankruptcy to proceed as though no resolution had been passed, and to make all necessary orders for resuming the proceedings, and thereupon to direct that all further proceedings (if any proceedings whatever were, under the circumstances, valid) be remitted to said register, and that an election of a new trustee or assignee thereupon take place. This petition of review has not yet been brought to a hearing before this court.

On the twenty-fifth of April the plaintiff in this suit obtained an order from the state court granting him leave to bring this suit.

The bill in this suit sets out that on the thirteenth of October, eighteen hundred and seventy-one, the Stuyvesant bank was a corporation created by the state of New York and was insolvent ; that it was adjudged a bankrupt by the proceedings before mentioned ; that within four months before the filing of the petition against it, it, being insolvent, made a transfer of its property to the defendant, who then had reasonable cause to believe it to be insolvent, within the thirty-fifth section of the bankrupt act, the transfer being made by means of the order made on that day in the suit brough by Barr ; that the defendant had reasonable cause to believe the bank to be insolvent, and that the transfer was made in fraud of the provisions of said act, and with a view to prevent the property of the bank from coming into the possession of its assignee in bankruptcy and to prevent it from being distributed under said act, and to defeat the object of, and im air, hinder, im de and dela '' eration and effect of, and evade the provisions of said act; that the transfer was not made in the usual and ordinary course of business of the bank; that on the said thirteenth of October, the bank being insolvent, did, with intent, by such disposition of its property, to defeat and delay the operation of said act, and with intent to delay, defraud and hinder its creditors, transfer its property to the defendant in this suit, and procure and suffer its property to be taken by him on legal process; that such legal process consisted in the orders and judgments of the state court, before referred to; that the trust created by said legal processes, and transfer, and appointment of the defendant as receiver, was a trust created in fraud of the creditors of the bankrupt, and the property affected thereby was conveyed by the bankrupt to the defendant in fraud of its creditors, within the meaning of the fourteenth section of the bankrupt act and the transfer was void within the thirty-fifth section, and the legal process was void within the meaning of the thirty-ninth section, and the defendant had reasonable cause to believe that a fraud on the act was intended, and that the said debtor was insolvent; that the defendant has, on demand, refused to give to the plaintiff (whose title is set out) an account and the possession of such property, and claims a title and interest adverse to the plaintiff touching said property; that such property consisted of real, personal and mixed property; that a large proportion of it consisted of claims and choses in action against persons who were indebted to the bankrupt at the time such orders were made by the state court, and that to reduce the same to the possession of the plaintiff by actions at law, or to compel the defendant to respond for the value of the property in actions at law, would require a large number of suits, and a discovery and an accounting by the defendant. The bill prays that said transfer may be decreed to be void as against the plaintiff, and that the said legal processes may be adjudged to be, as against the plaintiff, void, and that the property affected thereby may be adjudged to be vested in the plaintiff, and that the defendant may account for the same, and or the disposition made by him of the same, and of the proceeds thereof, and deliver to the plaintiff so much of such property as remains in his hands, and the proceeds of such of it as he shall have disposed of; and that he be enjoined from disposing of or interfering with said property, and from setting up and asserting, as against the plaintiff, any title to or right of action for any of said property; and that pending this action, and by final decree, he may be enjoined from doing any act to carry out or effectuate the trusts purporting to be created by his appointment as receiver, or from distributing the property affected by such receivership, otherwise than by the permission and direction of this court; and that, pending this action, and by final decree, a receiver of the property transferred to him, or in his possession, and of its proceeds, may be appointed with the usual powers of a receiver in like cases. The plaintiff now moves, on notice, for an injunction, restraining and enjoining the defendant, pending this action, pursuant to the prayer of the bill, and also for the appointment of a receiver, pending this action, pursuant to the prayer of the bill.

It is claimed that the district court had no jurisdiction to adjudge the bank a bankrupt, because the petition and the order to show cause were not served on any one who did or could represent the bank, and that Van Orden was not, at the time of the service, the cashier of the bank. This allegation is made on the ground that on the thirteenth of October Van Orden gave up to the defendant the keys of the bank, and became his clerk on a salary, and ceased to act as cashier, and did not act as cashier from that time prior to the judgment of dissolution. But there was nothing in this which displaced Van Orden from his official relation to the corporation as cashier, as is also apparent from his own oath, on the twenty-seventh of December, that he was then cashier. The corporation was in being on the twenty-eighth of December, when the papers were served on Van Orden, and he was still its cashier for the purpose of being served, as its proper representative, with such papers. If at any time prior to the judgment of dissolution the state court had discharged the receivership and directed the property of the corporation to be restored to its officers, Van Orden would have been a proper officer, as its cashier, to receive the property without any new appointment of him as such.

It is also objected that the bank had no existence when the adjudication was made. But we cannot admit it to be a tenable proposition, that a corporation, subject to the provisions of the bankrupt act, and which has committed an act of bankruptcy, and is in existence when the petition against it is filed, and when the proper papers are serve1 on its proper officer, can oust the jurisdiction of the bankrupt court to proceed on the return day to an adjudication of bankruptcy, because a decree dissolving the corporation has been made after such service and before such return day. The papers having been properly served on an officer of the bank, while the bank was in being, and the bank being called and making default to appear, the order of adjudication is substantially a proceeding *in rem*, and not one *in personam*, the order being that, the facts in the petition, being found to be true, it is adjudged that the bank became bankrupt before the filing of the petition, and is accordingly adjudged bankrupt. The judgment is that the bank became bankrupt before the filing of the petition by having committed acts of bankruptcy set forth in the petition, and which it committed while it was in being, and that it is adjudged bankrupt in respect of the administration of its property, subject to the act, by reason of so having committed such acts of bankruptcy.

Independently of this view, no doctrine can be admitted which would place it in the power of a state or of the courts of a state to render nugatory the operation of the act in respect to such corporations as are subject to it. To concede that what was done in the present case operated to deprive this court of the jurisdiction which attached by the filing of the petition, and the service of the order to show cause, would be to concede that the legislature of the state might lawfully provide by a statute, to be carried into effect by proceeding in its courts, that the institution of proceedings in bankruptcy against an insolvent corporation, and the service of an order to show cause on its officers, should operate to dissolve the corporation; to be followed, as a consequence, by a defeat of the jurisdiction of the bankruptcy court. The authority of congress to pass the bankrupt act is paramount and exclusive, and so is the jurisdiction of the district court thereunder. The thirty-ninth section of the act provides that the debtor, who commits any of the act specified in that section, shall be deemed to have committed an act of bankruptcy, and, subject to the conditions thereinafter prescribed, shall be adjudged a bankrupt. It is not one of those conditions that a corporation debtor, if in being when the petition is filed, and the order to show cause is served, shall continue undissolved until after the adjudication. As respects a corporation proceeded against involuntarily, the proceeding is eminently one *in rem* against its property, as it cannot be discharged from its debts, nor can its members be discharged from their liability as such for its debts, and the proceeding is one solely for the distribution of its assets among its creditors. The prayer of the petition in this case, according to the form prescribed, was that the corporation might be declared a bankrupt, and that a warrant might be issued to take possession of its estate, and that the same might be distributed according to law. Although the assignment to the assignee relates back to the commencement of the proceedings in bankruptcy, as declared by the fourteenth section, yet by the fourteenth, the thirty-fifth and the thirty-ninth sections, the assignee is vested with the title to recover, as assets of the bankrupt, property conveyed or transferred by or out of the bankrupt, in fraud of his creditors, or in fraud of the act, before the filing of the petition in bankruptcy. We are entirely satisfied that the dissolution of the corporation in the present case had no effect to deprive the district court of its jurisdiction.

The suggestion that judgment was pronounced against the corporation without giving it an opportunity of being heard, is answered by the considerations already adverted to. The corporation had all the opportunity of being heard which the district court could or was bound to afford to it. Regarding the proceeding as one *in rem*, there is nothing in the record of the proceedings in the district court to show that the receiver, as claimant of the property, desired to be heard as representing the corporation and such property, and was refused a hearing. In the case of *in re* Independent Insurance Co. 6 N. B. R. 169 and 260, receivers of a dissolved state corporation were admitted to file a plea to the jurisdiction of the bankruptcy court, and such plea was heard on the merits and overruled. In the present case the order of adjudication recites that no one appeared in opposition, and that the bank was called in open court, and came not, but made default to appear. If the receiver had appeared and asked, as representing the bank and its property, to be heard by answering the petition, and been refused leave to do so, a different question would be presented.

Nor do we perceive any force in the position, as applied to this proceeding in bankruptcy, that it abated by the dissolution of the corporation, so as to be incapable of being proceeded with thereafter. The views we have already announced involve the kindred conclusion that the proceedings did not abate.

On the undisputed facts in this case the plaintiff is entitled to the relief he seeks on this motion. In regard to the points raised by the petition of review, respecting the action of the district court in not confirming the resolution of the creditors nominating a trustee and a committee, and in appointing the plaintiff to be assignee, the petition has not been heard before this court, but in view of the suggestion by the defendant that his claim of title as trustee, and the claim of title of the plaintiff as assignee, ought not to be decided until the action of this court on the petition, we have considered those points sufficiently to be able to say that we do not perceive in them anything which ought to constrain us to refrain from granting to the plaintiff any relief which we should otherwise deem it proper to grant.

It is proper that the injunction asked for should issue, and that the plaintiff should be appointed receiver, he stipulating to charge no commission on such assets of his receivership as shall pass therefrom to the trust represented by the assignee of the bankrupt.

Judge WOODRUFF concurs.—May 31, 1872.

UNITED STATES CIRCUIT COURT—E. D. NEW YORK.

On a petition to the circuit court for review of an order of the district court denying the application for removal of an assignee, *Held*, That inasmuch as the petitioner for review has become the sole creditor, an order should be made that the assignee convey the estate of the bankrupt to such assignee as the petitioner and the bankrupt may name, or if they do not agree the matter be referred to the register ; the present assignee to receive all moneys collected by him until his just allowance for commissions and expenses is settled by the districtcourt.

In re SACCHI. *

WOODRUFF, C. J.—The present is an extraordinary appeal to the circuit court. The petitioner for the review of the decision of the district court seeks to remove the assignee in bankruptcy, on the ground of bad faith and mismanagement in his trust, and applies to this court to reverse the order denying his application in the face of the express decision and opinion of the register in bankruptcy, and of the district judge, upon the proofs herein, that the assignee would have been derelict in his duty, if he had not done substantially what he did. Had it been possible for the assignee to obtain these opinions in advance upon these same proofs, counsel would hardly have presumed to say that the assignee was guilty of official misconduct calling for his removal because he acted in accordance with those opinions; and yet the court is asked to condemn him as guilty of official misconduct for doing what both the register and district judge approve. As both of those officers had all the proofs before them which are before me, the claim on this appeal that those proofs show wilful misconduct comes very little short of an attack upon the integrity of the tribunals by whom the proofs were deemed to justify the assignee. Certainly I ought not to impute wilful misconduct and bad faith to the assignee because he drew from the circumstances before him the conclusions which the register and district judge approve.

The question here is not whether in fact there was illegality in the mortgages, the foreclosure of which the assignee re-

* See 6 N. B. R. 398.

sisted, but whether such resistance was fraudulent, malicious, or from unjust motive, and not in good faith for the benefit of the general creditors.

However, I might conclude that upon the whole case the mortgages were valid, that the holders had a right to an early foreclosure, and that delay, while the rents, if any, passed into the hands of the assignee, operates prejudicially to the holders of the mortgages, this would come far short of holding that under circumstances which under the advice of counsel were deemed suspicious—circumstances which the register and district judge have declared suspicious, the assignee was guilty of misconduct calling for his removal because he acted on the suspicion, and sought to bring the inquiry into the proper court for investigation.

But it is not true that had the mortagees seen fit to assert their rights in the mode which was most appropriate, any injustice would have been done to them, nor would unnecessary delay have been permitted to occur to their prejudice.

The purpose and design of the bankrupt law is to bring the property of the bankrupt into the bankrupt court for administration ; and that court is furnished with all needful power to liquidate and settle all liens thereon ; and where there are adverse claims, which it is not appropriate or proper to litigate by summary enquiry and order, provision is made by giving jurisdiction to the district court, concurrently with the circuit court, for that purpose. It is true that state courts have jurisdiction to entertain bills for the foreclosure of mortgages upon the real estate of a bankrupt, and may no doubt properly exercise that jurisdiction, if no objection is made. Special circumstances may sometimes exist in which there is no reason for objection by the assignee, as, for example, when the mortgaged premises are confessedly of less value than the mortgage debt, (*in re* Iron Mountain Co., N. D. New York, Jan., 1872,) and where a foreclosure is pending and the proceedings are nearly completed at the time the proceedings in bankruptcy are commenced, it may sometimes be convenient and economical to suffer the validity of the mortgage

In re Sacchi.

and the amount due to be settled in the state court; but even then, whether to permit a sale by the decree of the state court, or not, will be in the discretion of the court of bankruptcy.

In general mortgagees should not be permitted to pursue the estate of the bankrupt in the state court, but should come to the tribunal which under the federal laws is charged with its administration. No injustice can result from this. If there be doubt whether the mortgaged premises are adequate security for the payment of the debt and interest (when finally adjudged due upon a valid mortgage) the court will recognize the prior lien of the mortgage upon the land and the equitable right of the mortgagee to have the rents separated from the general estate of the bankrupt, by a receivership or otherwise, and not permit them to be applied to the payment of other debts or even to the expenses of the assignee or his fees; and on the obvious ground that he is only entitled to the interest which the bankrupt has in the premises. Nor will any delay be permitted without just reference to the interest of all who are concerned, the mortgagees as well as other creditors.

Nor do I think it doubtful that where no just cause for questioning the validity of the mortgage exists the court in bankruptcy would entertain the summary petition of a mortgagee for the sale of the mortgaged premises, and direct the assignee to make the sale, either free of all liens or subject to the mortgage, as might be deemed judicious. Nor if the assignee disputed the validity of the mortgage is it doubtful that under the jurisdiction declared in the second section of the bankrupt law the mortgagee may proceed by bill in either the district or circuit court.

It is therefore an error to insist that the mortgagee, if not permitted to proceed in the state court, is remediless, or that he must await the pleasure of the assignee and suffer him to collect the rents and income of the mortgaged premises, leaving the interest unpaid. I can see, I think, that it is either misapprehension on this subject or a disregard of these views that led the mortgagees in this case into the state court after the bankruptcy and after the appointment of an assignee, and that the resistance to any withdrawal of the administration from the bankruptcy court, the proper tribunal, has resulted in bitter personal feeling, in great and unnecessary delay, and in large expenses and possible loss, which might have been easily avoided.

It further appears that pending the controversy the petitioner for the review has become the sole creditor of the bankrupt, (other than two prior mortgages of the premises in question,) and that no other property of the bankrupt has come to the assignee, except the mortgaged premises. The bankrupt united in the petition for the substitution of an assignee, to be named by the petitioner as such sole creditor. The assignee, by his counsel, on the argument of this review declared his entire assent to such change. There is therefore no reason why the prayer of the petitioner to that extent should not be granted, the present assignee being allowed, out of any moneys collected, his just and reasonable disbursements, and his commission on the moneys received and paid, or to be paid. But it would not be just or reasonable to allow him, as was suggested on the argument, commissions based upon the speculative idea that, possibly if continued in office and permitted for the mere purpose of earning commissions to litigate the validity of the mortgages against the will of all who are interested in that question, he might establish their invalidity.

The bankrupt law was not enacted for the purpose of enabling assignees to earn fees by unnecessary litigation, when no interest of the parties to be affected thereby requires it, and where, on the contrary, every beneficial interest involved therein forbids it.

Had it, therefore, appeared that, upon the conceded fact that there are no general creditors but the petitioner, and therefore no interest is to be served by further contest respecting the mortgages, (the bankrupt himself uniting in the petition,) the district court had refused to substitute such other assignee, there might have been reason for asking this court to review the decision. But it appears by the decision of the district judge that the petitioner declined to take such substitution unless it proceeded upon other grounds, and this also was conceded on the argument in this court. This, however, does not appear by the order which was made, and which is under review; it ought, I think, to have been made a part of the order, lest it should stand on the record an adjudication that the petitioner was not entitled upon conceded facts to have any part of the relief sought. The mere fact that the petitioner under the advice of his counsel thought himself entitled to a removal of the assignee, on the other ground probably ought not to deprive him of the opportunity to bring the matter to a close without further litigation.

Let an order be made that the assignee convey the estate of the bankrupt to such assignee as the petitioner and the bankrupt may name, or, if they do not agree, that it be referred to register Winslow, to receive the nomination of the petitioner, and if he approve such nomination, then that the assignee convey to the assignee so approved, but reserving to the present assignee all moneys collected by him until his just allowance for his expenses and for his commissions thereon shall be settled in such manner as the district court may direct.

UNITED STATES CIRCUIT COURT—W. D. PENNSYLVANIA.

Unless there is a seizure for rent as provided for in the Pennsylvania statute, the bankrupt act of eighteen hundred and sixty-seven gives the landlord no lien or preference over the bankrupt's other creditors.

Where premises are occupied by the assignee or trustee after adjudication, rent should be paid for the time they are so occupied as part of the administration of the estate.

In re H. L. BUTLER.

Opinion by SAMUEL HARPER, register.

Henry Bockstoce, the claimant, leased to the bankrupt the buildings and premises, No. 127 Liberty street, in the city of Pittsburgh, for a term of five years, from October first, eighteen hundred and sixty-nine, at the rent of one thousand six hundred dollars a year, payable quarterly in advance. He has filed his two separate petitions; one of which shows that the rent due October first, eighteen hundred and seventy, for the months of October, November and December, eighteen hundred and seventy, amounting to four hundred dollars, remains unpaid, and the other showing that the rent due January first, eighteen hundred and seventy-one, for the months of January, February and March, eighteen hundred and seventy-one, of the same amount, also remains unpaid. The claimant prays that the trustee be directed to pay to him the said two amounts in full, in all eight hundred dollars, on the ground that rent is in the nature of a lien, and must be paid in full.

The bankrupt's petition for adjudication was filed January third, eighteen hundred and seventy-one. No distress warrant was issued either before or after.

When rent is in arrear, and a distress warrant is in process of execution when the petition in bankruptcy is filed, it is well settled that the landlord has a good and valid lien, and must be paid in full should the goods on the demised premises be sufficient. This is equally the case should the landlord have a lien for his rent upon the goods on the premises in any other manner. It is also well settled, that if the landlord has not a lien at the time the petition is filed, he cannot acquire one afterwards. *In re* Wynne, 4 N. B. R. 5, decided by CHASE, C. J. Some of the early annotators upon the act of eighteen hundred and sixty-seven have said, that as long as the property remains upon the demised premises it may be distrained. Such writers are in error; because, after petition filed, which is followed by adjudication, the property by operation of law is in the custody of the court, and is not liable to be taken in execution.

When the bankrupt's petition for adjudication was filed there was rent in arrear, but no landlord's warrant had been issued, and there consequently was no lien by distraint. But was there a lien by operation of law? Unless the provisions of section eighty-three, act of sixteenth June, eighteen hundred and thirty-six, Penn. P. L. 777, constitute a lien, there was none. The section is as follows: "The goods and chattels being in or upon any messuage, lands or tenements which are or shall be demised for life, or years, or otherwise, taken by virtue of an execution, and liable to the distress of the landlord, shall be liable for the payment of any sums of money due for rent at the time of taking such goods in execution, provided that such rent shall not exceed one year's rent." Section eighty-four requires the sheriff to pay the rent due out of the proceeds of sale, and section eighty-five provides that proceedings on the execution shall not be stayed without the landlord's consent.

I can find no law upon the Pennsylvania statute book giving the landlord a lien upon the property on the demised premises before proceedings under and by virtue of state law have been commenced, and under which it is seized. The landlord cannot distrain until there is rent due by the terms of the demise, and the lessee is at liberty to remove his property from the premises before the distraint, and the lessor cannot follow it unless there is fraud in the removal. Before the rent falls due by the terms of the lease, the lessor has no lien for his rent, unless the lessee's goods are taken in execution under the provisions of the act of eighteen hundred and thirty-six. To constitute a lien under that act there must be a "taking by virtue of an execution" by a sheriff, coroner or constable. If there be no such taking there can be no lien, for that is the only basis of the landlord's right.

It cannot be contended in this matter that there was such a taking on execution as was contemplated by the act of eighteen hundred and thirty-six. But it is contended, that by a liberal construction of the bankrupt act the provisions of the act of eighteen hundred and thirty-six can be made to apply here, by substituting the assignee for the executive officer of the state courts. To do this, however, would result in making a very motley system out of what to be constitutional must be uniform. If analogies can be drawn from the laws of this state, so can they be from the laws of all other states, and the bankrupt law, which must operate equally and uniformly over the whole Union, would operate as differently as the various systems of the several states. It is clear, upon the authority of *in re* Wynne, *ante,* no lien can be acquired after petition filed by any proceeding instituted in a state court. That case also decides that a distress warrant issued after petition is unwarranted, and cannot create a lien. The property of the bankrupt cannot be seized upon execution, and the landlord cannot obtain a lien in that way, under the act of eighteen hundred and thirty-six. That act is entitled "An act relating to executions," and if the provisions of the section already cited can be engrafted upon the bankrupt act, no good reason can be shown why the entire act should not be incorporated with it. If no lien is created until a seizure ; y virtue of an execution issued in pursuance of the act of eighteen hundred and thirty-six takes place, I cannot see upon what principle it can be said that under the bankrupt act the lessor has a lien when there is no such seizure.

The bankrupt act provides for no preference in favor of the landlord, and no such preference can be recognised in the national courts, unless there be a valid and subsisting lien at the time the petition was filed. The claimant in this matter had no lien at the time the bankrupt's petition was filed, because there was neither a distraint nor a taking by virtue of an execution. And whilst there is nothing in the act of eighteen hundred and sixty-seven which creates a lien for rent, there is a provision which places the lessor on the same common footing as the general body of creditors. The seventh clause of section nineteen provides, that "where the bankrupt is liable to pay rent or other debt falling due at fixed and stated periods, the creditor may prove for a proportionate part thereof up to the time of the bankruptcy, as if the same grew due from day to day and not at such fixed and stated periods." This provision was undoubtedly intended to cover cases where bankruptcy occurs before rent is due by the terms of the demise. If rent is payable quarterly, and bankruptcy intervenes before the end of the quarter, the landlord, in the absence of this provision, could not prove his claim, for nothing would be due or owing to him at the date of the filing of petition. This provision gives him the right to apportion. It is of much importance that this provision should not be lost sight of. It is evidence of the fact that congress had the rights of landlords in view when the act of eighteen hundred and sixty-seven was enacted, and it is equally true that congress did not intend a preference to landlords, unless they have it by the state laws. Where the judgment is not a lien by the state laws it wi l not be treated as a lien by the bankrupt court. *In re* McIntosh, 2 N. B. R. 158; *in re* Cozart, 3 N. B. R. 126. A levy on personal property, not made in conformity with the state laws, was declared void in *Beers et al.* v. *Place et al.* 4 N. B. R. 150.

In re Wynne, *ante*, CHASE, C. J., held that the landlord was entitled to be paid in full, although there was no distress. In deciding the matter he said : " If a lien for rent existed, it was a lien to be discharged by the assignee and enforced in the United States courts of bankruptcy. If it did not exist, it could not be brought into existence by any proceeding whatever. The real question is, were the goods on the premises demised to the bankrupt subject to a lien for rent under the state law when the petition was filed, independently of any proceeding by distress or attachment. Liens are of various descriptions, and may be enforced in different ways ; but we think it sufficient to say here what seems to be well warranted in principle and authority, that whenever the law gives a creditor a right to have a debt satisfied from the proceeds of property, or before the property can be otherwise disposed of, it gives a lien on such property to secure the payment of this debt." Then follows a statement of the law of Virginia, the text of which is as follows : " If after the commencement of any tenancy a lien be obtained or created by deed of trust, mortgage, or otherwise, upon the interest or property in goods on premises leased or rented of any person liable

for the rent, the party having such lien may remove said
goods from the premises on the following terms, and not
otherwise, that is to say, on the terms of paying to the person entitled to the same so much as is in arrear, and securing to him so much as is to become due ; what is so paid or
secured not being more altogether than a year's rent in any
case.   If the goods be taken under legal process, the officer
executing it shall, out of the proceeds of the goods, make
such payment of what is in arrear ; and as to what is to become due, he shall sell a sufficient portion of the goods on a
credit till then, taking from the purchasers bonds with good
security, payable to the person so entitled, and delivering
such bonds to him.   If the goods be not taken under legal
process, such payment and security shall be made and given
before their removal.   Neither this, nor the preceding section, shall effect any lien for taxes, levies or militia fines."
Revised Code of Va. 1860, 169.

In the case before CHASE, C. J., there was another very
important element.   In December, eighteen hundred and
sixty-six, the bankrupt had executed a deed of trust to certain creditors, which was recorded the second day of March,
eighteen hundred and sixty-seven.   The creditors sought to
enforce their lien under the deed of trust and the assignee
resisted ; but the deed of trust was held to be valid, and the
court said : " But these creditors (under the deed of trust)
by no process whatever could appropriate these goods to the
satisfaction of their debts without paying or securing the
year's rent ; and so of process under execution."   The fact
that the lien under the deed of trust, which by the statute of
Virginia was subordinate to the lien for rent, was sustained,
seems to have been the reason for sustaining the landlord's
lien.   But even if there had been no deed of trust, as there
was no execution, the landlord had a lien under the clause
" If the goods be not taken under legal process, such payment and security shall be made and given before their removal."   There is no such provision in the Pennsylvania
statute, but on the contrary, the lessee may remove his goods

at any time before distress or seizure upon execution and the landlord cannot follow them.

In a carefully considered case, *in re* Joslyn *et al.* 3 N. B. R. 118, DRUMMOND, J., held that, "where no distress warrant has been issued prior to the filing of the petition in bankruptcy, the landlord can have no priority or preference over the general creditors." The Illinois statute declares "that in all cases of distress for rent, the person who makes such distress, where the claim is less than one hundred dollars, shall file with a justice of the peace, and where it exceeds one hundred dollars, with the clerk of the circuit court, a copy of the distress warrant and an inventory of the property levied upon, and thereupon the party against whom the distress warrant shall have been issued, shall be duly summoned, and the amount due from him assessed and entered upon the records of the court finding the same, and then the court is to certify to the person or officer making the seizure, the amount so found due, and thereupon the officer is to proceed to sell the property so distrained, and make the amount thus certified to him, and return the certificate so issued to him with an endorsement thereon of his proceedings, which return and certificate shall be filed in the proper court." Bankruptcy intervened between the warrant and certificate and it was held that the proceedings being in the nature of an attachment on mesne process were dissolved and the landlord required to prove his debt as an ordinary creditor.

Under the Pennsylvania statute of eighteen hundred and thirty-six the landlord has no *lien* as against the lessee himself, for as has already been said the latter may remove his goods any time before distraint, but he has a preference as against an execution creditor. The assignment vests in the assignee all the property of bankrupt, with all his rights, and subject to all his duties as they existed on the day the petition in bankruptcy was filed. If the landlord had no lien on the property as against the bankrupt on that day, he has none now as against the assignee, or trustee rather, for the latter's relation to the property is precisely the same as was the

bankru)t's at that time.   That the claimant in this matter
had no lien then as against the bankrupt, he has none now
as against the trustee.   This much is said with reference to the
landlord's rights against the goods on the demised premises.
The rule in Pennsylvania as to his rights against the leasehold estate is different.   Where the landlord reserves the
right to re-enter, he has a lien for arrears of rent which is discharged by the sheriff's sale of the leasehold.   Wood's Appeal,
6 Casey, 274.   Spangler's Appeal, id. 277.   These cases mark
the distinction between the landlord's rights against the
leasehold and his rights against the goods on the premises
sold under an execution.   In the case of a sale of the goods
the landlord has a right to be paid his rent to the date of
levy, whilst out of the proceeds of the leasehold he must be
paid to the date of sale, as his lien continues until discharged
by the sale.   In the one case he has a preference over the
execution creditor merely, in the other he has a lien upon
the leasehold estate.

In this matter the leasehold has not been reduced to
possession by the trustee, but has reverted to the lessor.
The funds in the hands of the trustee arose from the sale of
the goods and chattels.

It will be observed that the second quarter of rents
claimed by the landlord began January first, eighteen hundred and seventy-one, but two days before petition filed,
although by the terms of the lease the rent was due in advance.   I think that, inasmuch as the trustee had possession
of the premises to April first, the estate is liable to pay rent
for that quarter as part of the administration of the estate.
As to the residue of the claim the landlord must prove as an
ordinary creditor.

The parties requested that the matter might be certified
to the judge for his decision.—July 12, 1871.

To Hon. WILSON McCANDLESS, LL. D., Judge.

ı assent to the above.

JOHN BARTON, *attorney for trustee.*

I assent to the ruling of the register as to the second quarter's rent, and dissent to the ruling as to the first quarter's rent.   C. S. FETTERMAN, *attorney for claimant.*

McCANDLESS, J.—The opinion of the register is approved. —August 10, 1871.

The decree of the district court was appealed from to the circuit court, in which, after argument, the following order was made by McKENNAN, C. J.:

And now, to wit: December nineteenth, eighteen hundred and seventy-one, the decree of the district court overruling the exceptions to the opinion of the register is affirmed.

--------●-●--------

UNITED STATES DISTRICT COURT—NEW JERSEY.

The provisions of the bankrupt act confer upon the United States district courts a general superintendence and jurisdiction of all cases and questions arising under the bankrupt act, but this jurisdiction is confined to the court within and for the districts where the proceedings in bankruptcy shall be pending.

An action brought by an assignee in bankruptcy in a district court other than the one in which the proceedings in bankruptcy were pending was dismissed.

An appearance and answer by a defendant does not preclude him from raising the question of jurisdiction.

Courts of bankruptcy are the special creatures of statutory law, and all their jurisdiction is derived from the act which creates them.

JOBBINS, Assignee, v. *MONTAGUE et al.* *

NIXON, J.—This is a bill in equity filed in the district court of the United States, for the district of New Jersey, praying for an injunction and relief.

The complainant is the assignee in bankruptcy of Joseph B. Brauner and Townsend Jackson, of the city of New York, lately composing the firm of J. B. Brauner & Co., and the bill sets out that the said firm were duly adjudicated bankrupts on the twenty-second day of January, eighteen hundred

* See 6 N. B. R. 117.

and seventy, upon a creditors' petition, filed by one Edwin
Saunders, in the district court of the United States, for
the southern district of New York; that the complainant
was duly elected and appointed assignee in bankruptcy of
said bankrupts; was duly qualified; has received from the
register the proper assignments of the bankrupt's estate,
pursuant to the act, and has been ever since acting as such
assignee.

The bill further alleges that on and prior to June fifteen,
eighteen hundred and sixty-nine, Townsend Jackson, one of
the said bankrupts was seized in fee simple of certain lands
and real estate, situate in Jersey City, and state of New Jersey, therein particularly described; that on or about that date,
he, and Martha, his wife, executed and delivered to one Eben-
ezer Montague, of the last mentioned state, a mortgage upon
the said premises, to secure the payment of a bond of the
said Townsend to the said Montague, for the sum of ten
thousand dollars and interest; that the said sum was not due
upon the bond at the date of the execution of the said mortgage; that the same was given by Jackson to Montague, as
the said Montague then well knew, in view and contemplation
of the pecuniary embarrassment in which the affairs of the said
Jackson were then already involved, and for the purpose of
shielding the said property from the just claims of the creditors of the said Jackson. That on or about the twenty-fourth
day of November, eighteen hundred and sixty-nine, the said
Townsend Jackson, being insolvent and bankrupt, and utterly
unable to meet the payment of his debts, with Martha, his
wife, conveyed the said premises, with other property in said
deed specified, to one Benjamin Albertson, in fee simple, professedly for the consideration of fifteen thousand dollars; that
said deed was made in contemplation of bankruptcy, and for
the purpose of delaying, hindering and defrauding the creditors of the said Jackson; that no consideration was in fact
paid by the said Albertson, or if any, the same was grossly
inadequate and designed merely as a cover to the real character of the transaction; and that Albertson then well knew

the circumstances of the said Jackson, and his purpose aforesaid in making the conveyance.

That on or about the twenty-sixth day of February, eighteen hundred and seventy, the complainant, as assignee as aforesaid, filed his bill of complaint in the United States district court for the southern district of New York, for the purpose of setting aside the deed hereinbefore mentioned, and other deeds and conveyances of said Jackson; and of having a receiver appointed for the said property and other property similarly conveyed, and of enjoining the said Jackson, Albertson and others, the grantees of Jackson, who were made parties defendants to said bill, from disposing of the said property and the proceeds thereof; that thereupon an injunction was granted by the court to the foregoing effect, on the twenty-eighth day of February, eighteen hundred and seventy, and duly served upon the said Jackson and Albertson. That on the twenty-third day of September, eighteen hundred and seventy, the complainant was appointed receiver in said cause for the real estate described in said bill, and other property; that on the motion for the appointment of receiver, an affidavit of the said Montague was read in opposition thereto; and that on the eleventh day of October, eighteen hundred and seventy, a copy of the order appointing the complainant receiver was served personally upon the said Montague.

That a few days afterwards, to wit: on the seventeenth of October, eighteen hundred and seventy, Montague filed his bill of complaint in the court of chancery of New Jersey against the said Townsend Jackson, and Martha, his wife, and Benjamin Albertson, and Martha B., his wife, for the foreclosure of the mortgage thereinbefore set forth; that on the seventh day of February, eighteen hundred and seventy-one, a decree by default was taken against the defendants for ten thousand seven hundred and ninety-five dollars and twenty-six cents, principal and interest thereon to that date; that an execution was issued directed to the sheriff of the county of Hudson, commanding him to make sale of the mortgaged premises; that the sheriff had advertised the same in obedience to the said writ, and threatened to.sell on the eleventh day of May, then next ensuing; that the complainant was not made a party to said proceedings in foreclosure, and had no notice thereof, and did not know they were in progress until after the final decree and a few days previous to the time fixed for the sale of the mortgaged premises; that the said proceedings were instituted and carried on by collusion between Montague and Jackson and Albertson, for the purpose of delaying, hindering and defrauding the complainant as assignee and receiver, in the pursuit of his rights in, and remedies against the property mentioned in the said mortgage, and with the intent that, by a sale under the said foreclosure proceedings the said Montague, Jackson, Albertson or some of them might either acquire a defensible title to said property, or realize more money than was justly due on said mortgage, in fraud of the complainant's rights and remedies.

The prayer is, that the said conveyan·ɔ to Albertson may be decreed void and of no effect, as against the complainant and the creditors of the said Jackson; that an account may be taken of the amount, if anything, actually due to Montague upon the said mortgage, and that the complainant may be decreed to be entitled to redeem the mortgaged premises, upon paying or tendering to said Montague the amount so found to be due; that Jackson and Albertson and wife may be restrained from selling, leasing or otherwise disposing of or interfering with the said premises, and Montague from further proceeding in his suit for the foreclosure of his mortgage, or for the sale or possession of the property, and the said sheriff, his deputies and agents, from all proceedings in the execution of the said writ. The bill was filed on the nineteenth of May, eighteen hundred and seventy-one, with a number of affidavits and exhibits in support of its material allegations; and on the same day, upon application of the complainant's solicitor, an injunction was allowed against the defendants according to the prayer of the bill of complaint.

The defendant, Montague, filed his answer June nineteenth, eighteen hundred and seventy-one, substantially denying all the charges of fraud contained in the bill and averring that the mortgage was given to him to secure the payment of ten thousand dollars lent to Jackson in good faith; that the whole sum was advanced by him to Jackson, that only six months' interest had been paid to him thereon, and none of the principal; and that in his proceedings in the court of chancery of New Jersey, for the foreclosure of the said mortgaged premises, he was only pursuing such remedies as the law gave to him for the enforcement of his rights under the mortgage. The case is now before me on the application of the defendant to dissolve the injunction, and his counsel has raised the question of jurisdiction, denying to this court the power in a suit brought by an assignee in bankruptcy, of restraining the defendant from prosecuting his suit in a state court when the bankruptcy proceedings are pending in another district court. If it were a question only affecting the forms of proceeding, I might be inclined to hold that the defendant, by appearance and answer, had waived it, but as it is one of jurisdiction, no voluntary act of the defendant can give such jurisdiction, and it is never too late at any stage of the cause to consider it.

It is a question of great practical importance in the administration of bankrupt's estates, and can only be decided by ascertaining and interpreting the powers vested in the district courts as courts of bankruptcy under the bankrupt act. The first section constitutes the several district courts of the United States, courts of bankruptcy, and original jurisdiction is given to them *in their respective districts* in all matters and proceedings in bankruptcy, and they are authorised to hear and adjudicate upon the same *according to the provisions of the bankrupt act*. This general grant of jurisdiction is followed by a special grant in the subsequent part of the section, extending such jurisdiction to all cases and controversies arising between the bankrupt and any creditor claiming a debt or demand under the bankruptcy; to the collection of the assets of the bankrupt; to the ascertainment and liquidation of liens and other specific claims; to the adjustment of priorities; to the marshaling and disposition of the different funds; and to all acts, matters and things to be done under and in virtue of the bankruptcy, until the final disposition and settlement of the estate and the close of the proceedings in bankruptcy.

The second section grants to the several circuit courts of the United States, " *within and for the districts where the proceedings in bankruptcy shall be pending*," a general superintendence and jurisdiction of all cases and questions arising under the act; and also concurrent jurisdiction with the district courts of "*the same district*" of all suits at law or in equity, which may be brought by the assignee in bankruptcy against any person claiming an adverse interest, or by such person against such assignee, touching any property or rights of property of said bankrupt, transferable to or vested in such assignee. These powers were deemed necessary, in order to a harmonious and efficient administration of the law, and to a satisfactory settlement of the various questions constantly arising in bankruptcy proceedings; but in defining their limits and extent we must not forget that the bankruptcy court is the special creature of statutory law, and that all of its jurisdiction is derived from the act which creates it.

In considering the powers vested in the courts of bankruptcy by the act, two inquiries at once arise.

1. Whether the jurisdiction of the district courts, as courts of bankruptcy, extends territorially beyond their respective districts?

2. Whether the powers conferred may be exercised by any other court than the one in which the bankruptcy proceeding shall be pending?

It is not necessary or proper to answer the first question here and in this case. If the assignee had brought the suit in the district court of the United States, for the southern district of New York, where the proceedings in bankruptcy are pending, it would have arisen there, and probably that

court would have been obliged to examine and settle it. *
But I am concerned with the answer to the second inquiry,
and that I shall proceed to consider.

Bearing in mind that courts of bankruptcy are mere creatures of the statute, and derive all their life and vigor from it;
let it be observed that the original'jurisdiction conferred upon
them, in the first section of the act, in all matters and proceedings in bankruptcy is expressly subject to two limitations.
In the first place such jurisdiction is only given "in their respective districts"; and secondly, they are authorised to hear
and adjudicate only upon such matters and proceedings "according to the provisions of the act."

What do these limitations mean? When the jurisdiction
over bankruptcy matters and proceedings is conferred upon
them "in their respective districts," is it not a fair legal inference that it was meant to be withheld *outside* of these districts? Why was such phrase inserted if such was not the intention of the law making power?

And when they are authorised to hear and adjudicate
upon all matters and proceedings in bankruptcy, "according
to the provisions of the act," are we not, by such a clause,
directed to the eleventh section, which requires every petition in bankruptcy to be filed in the district in which the
debtor has resided or carried on business for the six months
next immediately preceding the time of filing such petition,
or for the longest period during such six months? Is not the
question of residence a jurisdictional fact? If, therefore,
authority is given in the first section to hear and adjudicate
upon all matters and proceedings in bankruptcy, "according
to the provisions of the act," and if the eleventh section limits
the adjudication to the district of the debtor's residence,
whence does another bankrupt court in another district derive
its authority to hear and adjudicate upon such matters and
proceedings?

This interpretation of the first section I think is illustrated
and confirmed by the phraseology of the second section

* See Jobbins v. Montague et al. 6 N. B. R. 117.

The primary design of the second section is to give jurisdiction over bankruptcy matters and proceedings to the circuit court.

It confers upon that court a general superintendence and jurisdiction of all cases and questions arising under the bankrupt act, "within and for the districts *where the proceedings in bankruptcy shall be pending;*" but nowhere else. It also vests in the circuit courts a concurrent jurisdiction with the district courts of the same district of all suits at law or in equity, between the assignee in bankruptcy and any person claiming an adverse interest. It is clear from the language used that the circuit courts have no general superintendence and jurisdiction over cases and questions arising under the bankrupt act, *outside* of the district where the proceedings in bankruptcy are pending. If it was the design of the law to authorise suits in such other districts between the assignee in bankruptcy and persons claiming an adverse interest in the estate, why were such cases, and only such, excluded from the general superintendence and jurisdiction of the circuit courts?

This is not a case of first impression, and I am sustained by respectable authority for such a limitation of the powers of the bankrupt courts.

Mr. Bump, in his valuable treatise on the "Law and Practice of Bankruptcy," chap. xii., speaking of the jurisdiction of the courts, says, "Their jurisdiction over the subject matter only attaches when the cause of action arises from a proceeding in bankruptcy pending before them, and each court only has jurisdiction of those matters that spring out of a case in bankruptcy pending before it.

"If such case is pending in another court, they have no jurisdiction over such matters by virtue of the bankrupt act. The only powers that can be exercised by district courts in such cases, are those which are conferred upon them by other statutes. These principles have been steadily conformed to in practice. Nothing is more common than to find an assignee bringing a suit in a court of bankruptcy against a party who lives in the same district with himself.   No case, however, has yet been reported where he has brought a suit beyond the limits of his own judicial district." p. 177.

BLATCHFORD, J., *in re* Richardson, 2 N. B. R. 74, held, that the act conferred no power upon the district court of the United States for the southern district of New York, as a court of bankruptcy, to grant an injunction to stay proceedings upon suits in the New York state courts against the bankrupts, upon their petition, it appearing that the petitioners had been adjudged bankrupts by the district court of the United States, for the district of Louisiana.   If the law gave them any remedy in such a case, it was either upon application to the court where the proceedings in bankruptcy were pending, or possibly by a proper form of suit in the circuit court, under the general equity powers which that court exercises independently of the bankrupt act.

The reasoning of DILLON, J., in the case of *Markson & Spaulding, assignees,* v. *Heaney,* 4 N. B. R. 165, leads to the same result.   There a bill was filed in the circuit court of the United States for the district of Minnesota, by an assignee in bankruptcy, against a person claiming an adverse interest, to set aside a mortgage as fraudulent in fact and under the bankrupt law, the mortgaged premises being in the state of Indiana, the mortgagee residing in Minnesota, and the proceedings in bankruptcy pending in the district court of Kansas.

The court refused the injunction asked for, holding that in such a case the circuit court of Minnesota had no bankruptcy jurisdiction, because the bankruptcy proceedings were pending in another district.

The precise question now before me arose in the district court of the United States for the district of Massachusetts, in the case of *Sherman et al.* v. *Bingham et al.* 5 N. B. R. 34.

'   That was an action of assumpsit, brought by assignees to receive money alleged to have been paid by the bankrupts to the defendants by way of preference.   The proceedings in bankruptcy were pending in the district court of Rhode Island, and suit was commenced by the assignees in the district court of Massachusetts. Upon a plea to the jurisdiction, and after argument and consideration, LOWELL, J., held that the district court of Massachusetts, as a bankruptcy court, had no jurisdiction in that case, or in any case where the proceedings in bankruptcy had begun and were pending in another district.

Thus, the construction of the bankrupt act and the authority of adjudged cases, constrain me in the present case to dissolve the injunction and dismiss the bill for want of jurisdiction. I should be glad to have reached a different result, for. I can readily 'see that the denial to the bankruptcy courts of the jurisdiction here claimed impairs their efficiency, and may lead to difficulty and embarrassment in the administration of bankrupt's estates. This argument, however, is rather to be addressed to the congress on an application to enlarge their jurisdiction, than to the courts to induce the exercise of doubtful powers. If my view of the extent and scope of the authority conferred upon the courts is too narrow, the complainant has his remedy by appeal, and I shall not regret, but rather rejoice, if the superior courts can see their way clear to give a wider and less literal construction to the provisions of the act.

UNITED STATES DISTRICT COURT—S. D. NEW YORK.

It is not the intention of the forty-third section of the bankrupt act of eighteen hundred and sixty-seven, that the will of three-fourths in value of the creditors whose claims have been proved, is to control those creditors who do not vote in favor of a resolution passed under that section, unless the court sees that the interests of the latter will be promoted by carrying the resolutions into effect. Application to confirm the resolution denied, the costs to be paid out of the estate.

In re T. H. VETTERLEIN et al.

BLATCHFORD, J.—The forty-third section of the bankrupt act, in providing that the court shall confirm a resolution passed under that section, if it shall appear to it that the resolution was duly passed, and that the interests of the creditors will be promoted thereby, refers to the interest of all the creditors, and its design is to put it in the power of the court to protect the interests of those who do not vote in favor of the resolution. The will of three-fourths in value of the creditors whose claims have been proved is not to control in respect to the claims of those who do not vote in favor of the resolution, unless the court sees that the interests of the latter will be promoted by carrying the resolution into effect. The twenty-second section of the act provides that a creditor to have his demand allowed must make a deposition setting forth among other things that no agreement has been made by him to sell or dispose of his claim, or to receive any consideration whereby any action on his part in the proceedings under the act shall be in any way affected, influenced or controlled, and that no claim shall be allowed unless all the statements set forth in the deposition shall appear to be true. The twenty-ninth section of the act provides that no discharge shall be granted, or, if granted, be valid, if the bankrupt, or any person in his behalf, has influenced the action of any creditor at any stage of the proceedings by any pecuniary consideration or obligation. In the present case it appears that every one of the creditors who has signed the resolution appointing the trustee and the committee has made an agreement to sell his claim to the trustee and to receive a consideration for voting in favor of the resolution. Each has already received from the assignee a dividend of sixteen per cent. By an agreement signed by each, the person named as trustee is, as soon as three-fourths in value of the creditors shall have signed the agreement, to deposit in the hands of the trustee enough money to pay to each signer nineteen per cent. more ; and attorneys designated are to vote on behalf of such signers for such person as trustee ; and when such person is appointed trustee and the assignee has conveyed all the estate to the trustee and been discharged, the assignee is to pay to the signers the nineteen per cent. out of the deposits ; and such payment is to operate as an assignment of the claims of the signers to such person as the trustee shall name. By a contemporaneous agreement between the trustee and the bankrupts, certain real estate conveyed by the sons of the bankrupts and the wife of one of them to a person named by the trustee is to be sold and its proceeds and other moneys in the hands of such person are to be paid to the trustee; and the claims of the said signers are to remain as security to the trustee for said moneys advanced by him until the same and the sum of twelve thousand five hundred dollars as a compensation for his services as trustee shall be reimbursed to him, and after the bankruptcy proceedings are superseded and the trustee is paid such advances and compensation he is to convey to the bankrupts all that remains of the estate. Certainly this court can give no sanction to such an arrangement. As well might the bankrupts themselves be appointed trustees. A person who is to hold the estate under such a private trust is not a proper person to be appointed trustee. The forty-third section provides that the trustee shall proceed to wind up and settle the estate under the direction and inspection of the committee of the creditors for the equal benefit of all the creditors. This trustee has obligated himself, by a private agreement, to wind up the estate for his own benefit and that of the signing creditors, to the exclusion of the non-signing creditors. Moreover, but a single person is named as a committee, and he is one who has signed the agreement referred to, and will thereby cease to be a creditor the moment the trustee takes the estate and the nineteen per cent. is paid. A trustee who, after his appointment, should enter into such obligations and arrangements as those shown to have been entered into in advance by this trustee, would be removed by any court of equity. The interests of the non-signing creditors are deliberately sacrificed by the arrangements entered into. Under them the trustee has obligated himself to use the estate to reimburse to himself his advances and to pay his compensation of twelve thousand five hundred dollars, and to turn over the rest to the bankrupts. The money put into the hands of the assignee it is expressly agreed shall be used to pay the creditors who sign. No others can receive the nineteen per cent. Those who have not signed appeal to the court not to sanction such a proceeding. The proposed trustee resides in Philadelphia, and if the estate should pass into his hands he would hold it without having given security, and free from the control of any committee or of this court.

The application to confirm the resolution is denied, with costs to the opposing creditors, to be paid by the assignee out of the estate.

———•♦•———

UNITED STATES DISTRICT COURT—S. D. NEW YORK.

A debtor in failing circumstances attempted to make a compromise with his creditors of twenty-five per cent., but they rejected this offer and threatened him with proceedings in bankruptcy. At this time he represented that he had several promissory notes amounting to over nine hundred dollars. Some days after this a petition in bankruptcy was filed against him, and the order to show cause, together with the injunction served some two days later. The bankrupt swore that at the time of the service of the injunction he had sold the notes and spent most of the proceeds.

Testimony was taken, and at the close, the register, to whom the proceedings had been referred, decided that an order should be entered directing the bankrupt within five days to hand over to said assignee the amount of the notes, with interest from the date of the adjudication, or in default thereof, an attachment issue against him as for a contempt, which order was duly approved by the judge.

In re KEMPNER.

I, the undersigned, register in charge of the above entitled matter, do hereby certify that since the filing of my last certificate I have been further attended by counsel for the respective parties, and have taken further evidence, which is hereto subjoined.

And I further certify that in my judgment the case, as now presented, is one that calls upon the court to hold the bankrupt for the full value of the notes in question.

The facts are as follows : on Friday, the twenty-fourth day of March, eighteen hundred and seventy-one, the bankrupt called his creditors together with a view of effecting a com-

In re Kempner.

promise. He made a statement of his debts and property, and proposed to pay his creditors twenty-five cents on a dollar of their respective claims in full satisfaction thereof. His creditors indignantly rejected the offer and threatened him with proceedings in bankruptcy. At this meeting he represented himself as being in possession, among other things, of six promissory notes, amounting in all to nine hundred and twenty-three dollars, the proceeds of the sale of the stock in trade of his store in New Haven, which he sold out to his brother about a month before. This meeting was adjourned to the following day, Saturday, twenty-fifth of March. On that day others of his creditors attended, when he made the same statement, representing himself as still in possession of said notes, and urged the creditors to accept of the compromise he had offered on the previous day. These creditors also rejected the offer, expressed dissatisfaction, and threatened him with bankruptcy proceedings. These statements, as to what occurred on Saturday, are in great part denied by the bankrupt, although they are positively sworn to by *five* of the creditors. The petition against the bankrupt was filed on Saturday, the twenty-fifth, and an injunction was at the same time issued forbidding all interference with his property, which with the order to show cause was served on the bankrupt on Monday the twenty-seventh.

The bankrupt swears that at the time of the service of these papers, he had sold the notes in question, at a discount of ninety dollars, to one Henry Jacobs, and had spent all the proceeds of such sale, save about two hundred dollars.

Under the circumstances of this case, I think the burden of showing that the notes or money for which they were sold, were not in the possession and under the control of the bankrupt at the time the assignee takes title, the time of the filing of the petition, and even up to the time of the service of the injunction and order to show cause upon him, is on the bankrupt and not on the assignee. On Friday he knew of his insolvency, and offers his creditors twenty-five cents on a dollar, in settlement of their claims. They refuse to take it, and threaten him with bankruptcy proceedings. It is true he denies that any such threat was made, but his denial cannot prevail against the positive testimony of the five witnesses to the contrary. If then, after that period, he places these notes beyond the reach of the assignee, with intent to do so, he commits a felony under the forty-fourth section of the act. The law will not *presume* that such a felonious act was committed, but benevolently presumes the contrary. This presumption then must be overcome by evidence. The bankrupt fails to overcome it; without pausing to inquire whether a court will hear a party charge himself with a felony, the testimony taken together satisfies me that the bankrupt did not part with that money previous to the service of the order and injunction in bankruptcy. He was a man of small means and undoubtedly of economical habits; his rent was one hundred and sixteen dollars and sixty-six cents a month, but he underlet a part of his house, (for ninety-three dollars.) His business could not possibly have supplied him with the means of an affluent or even of a generous livelihood. He says of his business in answer to question thirty-four, " *I did business on a very small scale.*" This is the reason he assigns for keeping no books, or what would seem, from his testimony, to be equivalent to none ; and this was probably true, for he sold his New Haven store for one thousand four hundred dollars. The whole amount of his debts when he stopped business was only about eleven thousand or twelve thousand dollars, and his assets amounted to about two thousand seven hundred or three thousand dollars. They would pay nominally exactly thirty-two and one-half cents on a dollar of his debts, (see answer to question fifty-eight.) These notes comprised one-third of his assets, (really nearly all of them as the result shows;) that he should have got rid of this sum between Saturday *afternoon* and Monday, at the hour the order was served upon him, can be accounted for only upon the hypothesis that he was endeavoring to hide it in anticipation of such service, to keep it from his assignee. But that he should have used it in payment of debts, paying one hundred cents on a dollar, is contradicted by his whole course of conduct; a man who labors strenuously to obtain a compromise on Friday and Saturday by the payment of twenty-five cents on a dollar, and is expecting to succeed in this compromise up to the moment the bankruptcy papers are served upon him, (fol. 72,) would be likely to use nearly all his available means during those few hours in paying one hundred cents on a dollar of his debts. He does not seem to have been very much pressed for money during the month previous, for he had received five hundred dollars cash upon the sale of the New Haven store. His account of the use to which he put that five hundred dollars is not very satisfactory. (See answer to question eight.) I can't think, therefore, that with this sum in his hands, his family expenses had, during that month, run far behind hand, if, indeed, he was so anxious to pay them as he would have us believe. But his attempt to account for the manner in which he disposed of the proceeds of those notes is even more unsatisfactory. In answer to the question (number twelve,) "What became of the cash?" he says, I used it up for my family purposes, gas, rent, shoemakers and cutters.

Question, (No. 13.) Can you give any statement of these amounts you paid?

A. I cannot except a doctor's bill for about nineteen or twenty dollars; I don't remember; I have the bill I think." This testimony was given on the twenty-ninth of June, only three months after the events of which he was speaking, and the bills of which he speaks, though repeatedly called for, have never been produced except two—the doctor's bill, (Exhibit B,) bearing date twenty-seventh of March, though it does not appear, on the face of the bill at least, when it was paid. But this bill is not produced till July twenty-eight, and then he says of it, (answer forty-seven,) "I got this bill from the doctor since the last examination." The other paper is a receipt for one hundred and sixteen dollars and sixty-seven cents, for the rent in advance of house No. 147 West Twenty-fifth street, (in which he did not then reside; fol. 67,) for the month of May following. It appears by this receipt that this money was paid on the sixteenth of March, and there is nothing in the testimony to contradict it. The bankrupt's attention is called to it, and he says, (answer 46,) "This receipt for rent was made in my presence, most likely on the day it bears date." Clearly this rent was not paid from the proceeds of the sale of the notes, which sale took place more than ten days afterwards. This fact is finally acknowledged in his testimony of December eleven, (fol. 86,) "There is no further allusion to any payment for gas," and as to the "shoemakers and cutters," referred to in that answer, he says, in answer to the question, (No. 24,) "How much did you pay for shoemaker's bills?" "I don't remember." Question, (25,) "How much did you pay for cutter's bills?" Answer. "I don't remember." Question, (26.) "Do your books show what you paid for these two bills?" Answer. "I don't know; I suppose not." Notwithstanding this uncertainty as to the entries in his books, he seems to have been his own bookkeeper, for he says he kept none; and when further pressed as to what sums he had paid out of the proceeds of the sale of the notes for rent, (Question No. 27,) he says, "I paid two months' rent at one hundred and sixteen dollars and sixty-six cents per month." Though at a subsequent sitting, (fol. 67,) he admits that he paid but one. At the next sitting his testimony is as follows: (fol. 32.) "I paid McCollum, I think his name is John; he lives at the Fifth Avenue hotel; I can't tell when I paid him, but I know I paid him the rent, one hundred and sixteen dollars and sixty-six cents a month; I paid him for one month. I could not say whether it was Monday, Tuesday or Wednesday of the week after I got this money of Jacobs that I so paid him. This was for the rent of the house where I lived. This was in advance. This sum I paid him was for the rent of the house for the month next following the payment to him, (April.) *But of this money I got of Jacobs I paid two months' rent, both times for a month in advance.* Rent was payable on the first of the month. He always came after it to my house; I always paid him in advance; he is now paid up in full; I owe him nothing."

It is clear that this rent was not the rent referred to in the receipt, Exhibit A. For that was for the house he was to remove into on the first of May, (fol. 67,) and was in advance for that month and was paid to E. R. Roberts & Co., agents for Mary A. Nicholson. This was for the house he *then* lived in, (fol. 67.) These two months' rent were not paid at the same time, for he says, "both times were for a month in advance." * * "I always paid him in advance," and hence could not have *both* been paid from the money received of Jacobs. If it was "always paid in advance," he paid the March rent in February, and as he left the house the first of May, there was but one month's (April,) payable. But as he admits that he "could not say whether it was Monday, Tuesday or Wednesday of the week after I got this money of Jacobs that I so paid him, and as the order and injunction was served on Monday, it would not seem worth while to attempt to bring this payment within the subject of the present inquiry. But what would, in the absence of all the foregoing testimony, be conclusive on this subject, is the testimony of McCollum, taken by the assignee, on the eighteenth of December. His name is not "John" as the bankrupt suggested, but George W., and it would seem a little strange that the bankrupt should have been ignorant of the christian name of his landlord, especially as "He always came after it (rent) to my house;" and it suggests the possibility that he did not desire to have him called. Yet, there can be no doubt of the man. Indeed the bankrupt does not suggest any doubt upon this point. McCollum testifies that the bankrupt owed him one hundred and sixteen dollars and sixty-seven cents on the first day of April, eighteen hundred and seventy-one, for rent of house 248 West Thirty-sixth street. That on Tuesday, April six, he went to his store to collect it, found it had failed, and that other parties were in possession; bankrupt not there. He went to his house; found him out, called the next morning again, Friday, April seven; did not see him; went again Saturday evening following; found him in. He demanded the rent; Kempner replies that he had failed;

had not a dollar in the world to pay him with, except what he had received from the tenants up stairs, which was about fifty dollars. But finally the bankrupt proposes that if one hundred dollars would be received in full he would try and *borrow* it; McCollum assents to this, and Kempner "went down stairs and brought up a gentleman who handed me one hundred dollars, and I gave a receipt for the month of April." The witness continues, "since the twenty-fifth of March I have received no rent of Kempner except this one hundred dollars. The rent for the month of March I received on the first week, or in the first fifteen days of March." There is no attempt to contradict this witness, but if his statement is true, there is no escaping the conclusion that the bankrupt has committed the most wilful perjury; and this should on the maxim *falsus in uno, alsus in omnibus*, dispose of his whole property.

The allegation that the bankrupt paid out some part of the money in question to his shoemakers, or men called "teams," does not seem to be any better supported. It was for the services of these men for the week ending Saturday, March twenty-fifth, that these alleged payments were made. But it appears that his store or shop was taken possession of by the city marshal, and two men put in charge, on Monday of that week, (March twentieth.) It would not seem very probable that he continued his "teams" at work, in all respects as though nothing had occurred. He says, (fol. 29,) that his teams were in the habit of earning from two hundred to three hundred dollars a week; at two hundred and fifty dollars a week his disbursements for labor alone would be thirteen thousand dollars a year. This certainly does not tally with the accounts he gives of his business when excusing himself for not keeping books. In question (34) he says, " I did business on a very small scale;" nor yet does it tally with the state of his affairs when he attempted to compromise with his creditors; when his debts were eleven thousand or twelve thousand dollars, and his assets about two thousand seven hundred dollars. When he offers himself as a witness in his own behalf, and is examined by his own counsel, he asserts, (fol. 65,) that "on that Saturday (twenty-fifth) I paid out to shoemakers, cutters and employees about two hundred and fifty dollars; I think it was more." But when he is inquired of by the assignee's counsel how he ascertained the amount paid to the shoemakers? he answers, (fol. 73,) " more by belief than by knowledge; I know I paid them, and I know they worked through the week. I have not refreshed my memory by any entries or memorandum." But it would be difficult to believe that if his disbursements for labor were from two hundred to three hundred dollars a week, he kept no more satisfactory account of it on paper than some of his answers would indicate. Take the following for example, "I kept no cash book," (fol. 13.)

Q. In what did you make your cash entries? A. I made them loosely on pieces of paper.

Q. Have you no statement now of the cash you received and paid out while you were in business? A. No, sir; I have not.

Q. Do your books show any account of these transactions from the time you sold out the store to your brother? (fol. 17.) A. I don't know anything about it.

Q. Can you refer to any entries in your books which will show a single payment to any of your creditors from this money? A. I don't know.

Q. How much did you pay for your shoemaker's bills? (fol. 20.) A. I don't remember.

Q. How much did you pay for cutter's bills? A. I don't remember.

Q. Do your books show what you paid for these two bills? A. I don't know; I suppose not.

Q. During that time, (the time he had carried on business in New York,) had you had no cash book? (fol. 23.) A. No more than I have stated; I might sometimes have marked down something, but nothing regular; I did business on a very small scale.

Men who keep no books, but trust wholly to their memories, ought to have and generally do have very good memories. But this man is unable to assist the assignee to the means of contradicting him, by recalling to memory the names of one single one of his employees, either the servants of his family, to whom he swears he paid sixty or seventy dollars, (this amount would indicate that they had been sufficiently long in his family to have found out their names,) or the shoemakers, cutters, &c., who compose his teams. Pressed repeatedly on this point, he recalls the name of his cutter, "Meyer," (fol. 30 ;) has "no doubt that it is in the book where he lives, a book I kept for work," (fol. 31.) But this book the assignee is unable to get possession of. Yet the assignee finds this "Meyer," (he testifies as "Meyer Hecter,"(and obtains his testimony, (fol. 95 and 96.) This man contradicts him flatly, as to working after the city marshal took possession. He asserts, (fol. 96) what is in keeping with every probability, that the city marshal took possession of his stock on Monday, March twentieth, and that Kempner paid him off in full (twenty-one dollars) the Saturday before. "I stopped working on the Monday after the marshal came in ; he paid me nothing after this twenty-one dollars ; I did no work, and went away after the marshal came in ; Kempner discharged me at that time ; there was no other cutter then ; I was the only cutter ; there was a stock fitter of the name of Schmidt ; *he left at the time I did.*" There was no attempt to contradict this man on the part of the bankrupt, by way of cross-examination or otherwise ; nor was there any attempt to corroborate by him anything that had been previously asserted by the bankrupt concerning the continuance of the work after the marshal took possession.

The fact, if it be one, (fol. 66,) that he paid out of the money in question sixty or seventy dollars to his domestic servants, and forty dollars to the nurse who attended his wife in her last confinement, was not remembered by him when he testifies on the twenty-ninth of June, (fol. 16.) On the fifth day of July, however, he is able to say, "I have no doubt I paid my servant girl out of this money I got of Jacobs, I had no other money." But he only recalls the fact that he paid his domestic servants sixty or seventy dollars out of the money in question, when he is testifying in his own behalf, on the twenty-sixth of July. When asked, (June twenty-ninth,) "How much did you pay for servants' wages?" he answers, "I don't know, sir; my wife is sick and I can't keep things so closely as I did." Yet he swears that he gave none of this money to his wife, (fol. 22.)

There does not seem to be any credible evidence that he parted with a shilling of the money he got from Jacobs, if indeed he received any money from him, prior to the service of the orders in bankruptcy upon him. The whole case, with the evidence and surrounding circumstances, points unmistakably in my judgment to the conclusion that the bankrupt, failing to effect a compromise with his creditors, and having been by them threatened with proceedings in bankruptcy, if indeed such proceedings had not been already inaugurated, colluded with Jacobs to keep the notes in question from the assignee, and appropriate the same to his or their own use. The bankrupt, in his testimony, develops no such character as would make such a hypothesis improbable. For he is contradicted in almost every point upon which witnesses have spoken, in one by five witnesses. The character attributed to him by his creditors both at the meetings on the twenty-fourth and twenty-fifth of March, in promptly rejecting his offer of a compromise, and threatening him with bankruptcy, as well as by obtaining an injunction against such disposition of his property at the time of filing their petition, is also consistent with such a hypothesis. Merchants toward their brother merchants who are unfortunate, yet honest and fair, are almost uniformly not only just but generous. But, however little weight may be given to this, nothing can be claimed from these circumstances that tends to corroborate the bankrupt's statements.

Again, the testimony touching the sale of these notes is altogether unsatisfactory. It is proved by five witnesses, and must be accepted as the truth, that he stated at the meeting of the few creditors that came together on Saturday, that he still had these notes in his possession. His *sworn* statements, however, are as follows: (fol. 26.)

Q. When was the first time that you saw Mr. Jacobs about the sale of the notes to him? A. The day of the meeting of the creditors, Friday, twenty-fourth of March.

Q. Where did you see him; was it at his house? A. Yes, we were neighbors and I saw him Friday afternoon on the day of the meeting, or rather in the evening. I showed him the notes; but I am not sure that I had the notes in my pocket when I called at his house. I think I handed him the notes the next morning. I handed him the notes the next morning at his house and he handed me the money. I believe he gave me some part of the money in checks and some in bills—on reflection he paid me all money. He told me to wait a little while and he went out and got the money. This was all the examination he made of the notes. He said, "Mr. Kempner, I don't know your brother, but if you say the notes are good I will take them." I did not endorse them. * * * This was Saturday morning; I keep Saturday as the Sabbath.

This is his recollection of an important occurrence that took place but three months before. He called Friday afternoon—no it was Friday evening. He showed him the notes—no he is not sure that he had them in his pocket. He gave me some part of the money in checks and some in bills—no he paid me all money. Truth does not report itself with such uncertainty.

Jacobs (at fol. 58) gives his narrative. Kempner represented himself as "very hard pressed." He had never seen the maker of the notes, yet he takes them without inquiry or endorsement, and pays down their face in cash less ninety dollars. He thinks it was all done in twenty-four hours. He thinks he had the notes over night. He does not generally do business on Saturdays, but he paid for these notes on that day (he can't say whether before or after sundown) as soon as he came, from money he had in the house (he had sold some stocks that day.) Afterwards he thinks it may have been somewhere about noon that he handed him the money; he had been away from his house—somewhere in Eight avenue that morning—before he paid the money.

In this short narrative he differs from Kempner in several particulars. Kempner, says, "he told me to wait a little while, and he went out and got the money." Jacobs, says, "I had the money in the house; I had sold some stocks that day and had the money in the house; I am positive of that. The next day as soon as he came I gave him the money." Kempner, says, "I am not sure that I had the notes in my pocket when I called at his house, (Friday,) I think I handed him the notes the next morning—I handed him the notes the next morning." Jacobs, says, "He gave me the notes on Friday afternoon—I am most sure it was on Friday I had the notes in my possession. I think I had them over night." It is scarcely possible that this man, who spoke of the bankrupt as "merely a friend of mine," was ignorant of his true condition, and that under those circumstances he would have advanced eight hundred and fifty dollars or thereabouts, at one time, upon security of which he was utterly ignorant, for the mere chance of making ninety dollars.

I regard the bankrupt as utterly discredited, and, although it may seem a harsh remedy to order him to hand over that money, yet it is the mildest of the three remedies to which the assignee may obviously have recourse.

I therefore recommend that an order be entered directing said bankrupt, within five days, to hand over to said assignee the sum of nine hundred and twenty-three dollars and interest thereon, since the twenty-fifth day of March, eighteen hundred and seventy-one, and the costs of these proceedings to be adjusted by the register in charge, or that an attachment issue against him as for a contempt.

I. T. WILLIAMS, *Register.*

BLATCHFORD, J.—Let an order be entered in conformity to the register's certificate.

In re Stephens.

UNITED STATES DISTRICT COURT—W. D. WISCONSIN. ·

A and B were copartners on and prior to March thirty-first, eighteen hundred and seventy ; on that day the firm was dissolved, having an indebtedness of eleven thousand dollars to third parties, and ten thousand dollars to B for the capital stock. The assets amounted to some nineteen thousand dollars ; six thousand of which was real estate, and the balance consisted of the stock of merchandise, notes and accounts. A had no property except some six hundred dollars and his homestead.

At the dissolution, A bought B's interest in the firm property, except the real estate, and gave B his notes for seven thousand dollars, secured by a chattel mortgage on the stock then on hand, and thereafter to be acquired. A also agreed to pay the firm's liabilities, and B took the real estate at a valuation of six thousand dollars.

It was agreed that the mortgage *was not* to be filed until March thirty-first, eighteen hundred and seventy-one. On the twenty-first of March, eighteen hundred and seventy-one, A transferred his stock, notes and accounts, worth some twelve thousand dollars to B, in payment of the seven thousand dollar notes, B agreeing to pay the firm debts, which were about five thousand dollars. A was adjudged a bankrupt, and his assignee filed his petition praying the court to compel B to surrender his preference.

The court granted a stay of proceedings on the prayer of B, to allow him to surrender his preference, which he did, and filed claims against the estate of A for the seven thousand dollars due him. and also five thousand dollars of firm debts. *Held*, that under the facts of the case, the seven thousand dollars was a fraud as against the creditors of A, and that B should be allowed to prove for the five thousand dollars only.

In re E. R. STEPHENS.

On and prior to March thirty-first, eighteen hundred and seventy, E. R. Stephens and Satterlee Warden were copartners in mercantile business at Darlington, in said district. On that day the firm dissolved. The firm then owed to third parties eleven thousand dollars, and to Warden for capital in the business fifteen thousand dollars ; and had assets of the value of nineteen thousand seven hundred and fifty dollars, six thousand dollars of which was real estate, and the balance consisted of the stock of merchandise, notes and accounts. Stephens had no capital in the business, and had individual property not exceeding six hundred dollars, except his homestead. S. & W. settled on that day, and S. bought W's interest in the firm property, except the real estate, and gave to W. his notes for seven thousand dollars, secured by a chattel mortgage on the stock then on hand, and thereafter to be acquired. S. also agreed to pay the eleven thousand dollars of firm debts, and W. took the real estate of the firm at six thousand dollars. By agreement between S. & W., the chattel mortgage was not filed until March thirty, eighteen hundred and seventy-one. S. continued the business alone until March twenty-one, eighteen hundred and seventy-one, when he transferred his stock of merchandise and notes and accounts, valued at twelve thousand dollars, to W., in payment of the seven thousand dollars due to W.; W. at the same time agreeing to pay the firm debts, which were about five thousand dollars.

S. was adjudicated a bankrupt, and proceedings commenced by assignee on petition to compel W. to surrender preference. Testimony was taken, and on the argument W. asked to have proceedings stayed that he might surrender, which was granted by the court, and W. thereupon surrendered the property to the assignee; and then filed claims against the bankrupt's estate for the seven thousand dollars, for which he had the notes and mortgage of S.; and for the five thousand dollars of firm debts, which he, W., had agreed to pay. From March thirty-one, eighteen hundred and seventy, to March twenty-one, eighteen hundred and seventy-one, Stephens contracted other debts in his business to the amount of seven thousand dollars, which are now unpaid.

P. A. ORTON, Jr., for assignee; H. S. ORTON, tor Warden.

HOPKINS, J.—This is a motion on behalf of the assignee in bankruptcy to expunge certain debts proven by Satterlee Warden against the bankrupt's estate, on the ground: FIRST. That he had received a preference by way of payment from the bankrupt, which he had not wholly surrendered; and, SECOND. That the debts were void as arising out of a transaction between the parties entered into to defraud the creditors of the bankrupt.

At the conclusion of the argument, I announced that I regarded the transfer of the property by the bankrupt to Mr. Warden on the twentieth of March, eighteen hundred and seventy-one, in payment of these claims as clearly creating a preference within the meaning of the bankrupt law, and a plain violation of its provisions. I further stated that I thought the testimony showed that he had surrendered to the assignee all the property he had received of the bankrupt upon said debts before filing the proof of his claims, although he did not do so until after the testimony had been taken on proceedings to recover it. But upon the question as to the effect of the surrender at that time, as well as several other matters discussed, I took the case under consideration, and after a careful examination of the whole case, I have come to the conclusion that Mr. Warden, by the surrender of the property that he took in payment of these claims of the bankrupt, released himself from the penalty prescribed in the thirty-ninth section of the act.

I fail to see any reason for a distinction between sections thirty-five and thirty-nine in that respect. The attempt to maintain a distinction between voluntary and involuntary proceedings fails to commend itself to my judgment.

A full surrender of a fraudulent preference by a creditor is a complete condonation of that offence as I understand the provisions of section twenty-three. That section is not limited in its operation to cases of voluntary proceedings.

The preference is what the law denounces, the intent of the act being to secure an equal distribution of the estate of a bankrupt among all his creditors, and if a creditor voluntarily yields a preference he may have acquired or attempted to acquire, and surrenders all the property, so that it does not in any manner interrupt the equal distribution required by the act; the party is restored to his rights as they stood before the preference. If a creditor having received preference, refuses to surrender, and a suit is prosecuted against him by the assignee for the property or money unlawfully received as a preference, and a recovery is had against him, he cannot then surrender and receive the benefits of that section. He is then by section thirty-nine forbidden the privilege of proving his debt or receiving any dividend; and it may be a matter of discretion with the court whether a party should be allowed to surrender after suit brought, and particularly after the testimony is taken, and the defendant becomes satisfied it is enough to defeat him. I don't think the spirit of the act would warrant a practice of the kind. A party should not be allowed to experiment and speculate upon the ability of the assignee to prove a case against him, and when he sees he has succeeded, then to plead guilty and surrender, and take the benefit of section twenty-three. Such a practice ought not to be tolerated, and hereafter, except under very peculiar circumstances I shall not allow a party guilty of a fraudulent preference to surrender after suit brought and prove his debt under sections two and three, if on examination I should conclude I had the power to prevent. I shall expect a party to elect, and after having elected, shall hold him to his election. But in this case, he did surrender, and I think he is therefore relieved from the penalty imposed by the bankrupt act. I adopt the construction given to that part of the act. *In re Scott, et al.* 4 N. B. R. 139; *Tonkin* v. *Trewartha*, id. 13; and *in re* Kepp, 3 id. 190; *in re* Montgomery, id. 97; and *in re* Davidson, id. 106. So if the case of the assignee rested wholly upon the bankrupt act, the motion would be denied. But a question of far more importance and difficulty is presented, that is, whether the transaction between Warden and the bankrupt on the thirtieth of March, eighteen hundred and seventy, was not intended to defraud the subsequent creditors of Stephens, and hence void at common law, and according to the general doctrine of courts of equity; and it is claimed that if so, I should so find, that that fraud is not conditional, but inherent in the transaction, and renders all the promises of Stephens made with Warden upon such transaction void, and and that no court will lend its aid to enforce them or either of them. That the case will then fall within the principle of the maxim *ex turpi causa, non oritur actio*. *Nelles* v. *Clark*, 20 Wend. 24, and cases cited.

In order to rightly understand my conclusions on this point it will be necessary to briefly state some of the facts established by the evidence. Stephens and Warden were

In re Stephens.

partners in the mercantile business at Darlington, commencing sometime in eighteen hundred and sixty-five. Warden was the man of means, Stephens the active man, although both attended to the business some. The business was not successful, and before March eighteen hundred and seventy, Stephens had withdrawn and used up all his capital, and the company was .owing Warden fifteen thousand dollars, and their other liabilities were a little over ten thousand dollars. On the thirty-first of March, eighteen hundred and seventy, an inventory was completed, which showed that the firm nominally had assets equal to the debts or nearly so, but they were not equal in actual value to the firm liabilities by several thousand dollars. Stephens had but very little property except his homestead. The firm was then insolvent, although Mr. Warden was perfectly good, and able to pay all the liabilities. On that day they dissolved, and Warden transferred his interest in the firm assets to Stephens, except the real estate, which Warden took at six thousand dollars, and applied towards the amount the firm owed him; Stephens agreed to pay all the firm debts to third parties, and gave his notes for seven thousand dollars to Warden, that being the balance due him, which he secured by chattel mortgage upon the goods then in the store, and upon all such as he might *afterwards acquire* until the payment of that debt. It was agreed, however, that the chattel mortgage was not to be filed, for the alleged reason that if it was it would prevent Stephens buying any more goods upon credit.

It must have been known to Mr. Warden that Mr. Stephens was insolvent, and that he could not pay out of the stock the indebtedness assumed by him; and the case fails to disclose any ground for a belief upon the part of Warden of the ability of Stephens to go on long with the business. It had been unsuccessful with the credit his name had given to it, and in the light of the testimony no court could find that Mr. Warden believed that Stephens would be able to continue long, and the taking of the chattel mortgage to secure the debts to him shows that he meant to keep a control of the stock and goods, so that he could at any time secure himself by taking possession. In view of these facts I am forced to the conclusion that it was a scheme on the part of Warden and Stephens to clothe Stephens with the apparent ownership of the property, and send him out to obtain goods on credit from parties ignorant of the condition of his affairs and of the security to Warden, and thus enable him to obtain the means with which to pay the balance due to Warden, which in any other way he would be unable to do. Warden must have known such would be the probable result of Stephen's undertaking, and when he consented to keep his mortgage off the record he must be held to have done so with a view of enabling Stephens to obtain credit that he ought not to have, and to obtain property that he could not pay for, and which, according to the terms of his mortgage, was incumbered by it as soon as placed in the store.

I must upon these facts hold that the design of the parties was to defraud the subsequent creditors of Stephens, and therefore that the notes given to Warden and the chattel mortgage were absolutely void as to the subsequent creditors of Stephens, and that the proof of claim filed therefor must be stricken out. This, I find, was a fraud upon the subsequent creditors, and this case should be treated as if they were the parties contesting it. The assignee, in objecting, is in reality acting in their interest. The parties entered into this arrangement for the real purpose of casting upon the subsequent creditors the hazards of Stephen's success in continuing the business, all the property he could get was they supposed, covered by this mortgage to Warden, so that Warden would be secured any way.

Suppose the subsequent creditors, instead of proceeding in bankruptcy, had proceeded by attachment, and taken this property, and Warden had commenced his action to recover it back upon his mortgage, can it be possible that upon the facts as proven in this court, that a court or jury would hesitate a moment in finding that this scheme was devised to defraud Stephens' subsequent creditors. The facts constitute fraud—fraud *in fact*.   *Case* v. *Phelps*, 5 N. B. R. 452; *Stillman* v. *Ashdonn*, 2 Atk. 481; *Reade* v. *Livingston*, 3 John Ch. 481; *Parrish et al.* v. *Murphree et al.* 13 How. 99.   In the latter case, McLEAN, J., in delivering the opinion of the court, says, "The statute designed to prohibit frauds by protecting the rights of creditors.   If the facts and circumstances show a fraudulent intent, the conveyance is void against all creditors past and future."

The taking of the mortgage which expressly covers the goods Stephens might *afterwards acquire* as well as those he then had, and keeping it from the records for the express purpose of enabling him to acquire more upon credit, in view of his pecuniary situation and the known hazardous nature of the business he was engaged in, are sufficient to warrant and authorise any court to find that Mr. Warden was acting in bad faith towards the parties that might, in ignorance of his claim, sell him goods on credit, and I know of no principle of law or equity that would allow him to hold such property as against the creditors thus deceived, or to share with them in its distribution.

The subsequent conduct of the parties is in harmony with this construction.   When the crisis came we find Warden taking all the property and accounts to pay his debts and the balance of the firm debts without making any provisions for subsequent creditors.   It was insisted by the counsel for the assignee that the claims proven by Warden, as company debts, should be excluded upon the same ground, as the contract of dissolution embraced them as well as the payment of his individual debts, but I think they are distinguishable.

Mr. Warden's right to prove them does not rest wholly on the agreement made by Stephens at that time; if it did, I think they would be based on the same grounds.   But he had no claim until he had paid the debt, and when he paid them he had the right to claim contribution of Stephens, independent of the agreement and the right to prove them, and have them allowed to the extent of his right to contribution, and as between the parties in the case he would be entitled to the whole sum paid, as he had largely overpaid his portion, and the company and Mr. Stephens as one of the members, were owing him a much larger amount than these claims. He stands on his rights as partner to be reimbursed for his advancements, and can recover independent of the agreement, and if the agreement was void it cannot be said to merge his original claim, nor set up if void, by Stephens or those representing him, as a defence to such original claim. *Meshke* v. *Van Dorn*, 16 Wis. 320, 225; *Terreal* v. *Sharen*, 1 Saunders, 295; *The Queen* v. *Seuel*, 7 Modern, 119; *Vilas* v. *Jones*, 1 Com. 276; *Johnson* v. *Johnson*, 11 Mass. 359. Again there was no contract made to defraud existing creditors; the fraudulent part of the agreement related to the effort of Warden to get his pay at the expense of future creditors, and only that part should be held void that was fraudulent.

The debt of Doty & Judge, supposed to be one thousand dollars, should be excluded, as the proof is defective in not stating the amount paid therefor by Warden. But as it is probable under the rule above adopted, Mr. Warden may withdraw that proof and perfect it according to the facts.

The claim proven at three hundred and four dollars and twenty-five cents, contains items that have accrued since the filing of petition, and for insurance which is not provable. From the testimony I cannot find that there is due but the charge for cash twenty-two dollars, loaned to Stephens to go to Kansas. I do not see that a claim against Stephens is established for the balance of these items; and that claim is disallowed except as to the twenty-two dollars loaned to Stephens to go to Kansas. All the other claims are allowed as proven, except the seven thousand dollar claim upon Stephen's notes to Warden hereinbefore mentioned.

A suggestion was made by me on the argument, in relation to a mortgage given by Stephens to Warden, to secure certain notes endorsed by Warden, to the effect that a release of that portion of the property not embraced in the homestead set off, might entitle Mr. Warden to prove those claims. On further reflection I am inclined to think that in order to be allowed to prove these claims, he should discharge the mortgage absolutely. *In re* Stephens, 5. N. B. R. 298. I think, to be allowed to prove a debt unlawfully preferred, the party must surrender the unlawful preference wholly, wipe out the security entirely.

UNITED STATES DISTRICT COURT—S. D. NEW YORK.

An assignee in bankruptcy applied to the United States district court, and obtained an injunction to restrain the sale of property under the decree of foreclosure in a mortgage, after the proceedings had reached a stage where, substantially, all the expenses, except those which would attend the sale of the property, had been incurred. Sometime thereafter he applied for leave to dissolve the injunction and sell the property. *Held*, That the petition must be dismissed, with costs to the assignee, for the reason that he had not applied at the commencement of the foreclosure suit for a stay of proceedings. Injunction dissolved.

In re H. BRINKMAN.

BLATCHFORD, J.—I think the most advisable course, in this matter, is to deny the prayer of the assignee's petition for leave to sell the real estate and to dissolve the injunction granted by the order of July thirty-first, eighteen hundred and seventy-one, and vacate that order, and allow the property to be sold under the decree of foreclosure in the state court. The assignee in bankruptcy, having been a party to that suit, was instrumental in placing that suit in the position in which it was on the thirty-first of July, eighteen hundred and seventy-one, when he, for the first time, applied to this court to stay the sale under the decree in that suit, which was to take place three days afterwards. It is quite apparent from the testimony on the reference, under the assignee's petition, that there was no good reason for applying to this court to stay the foreclosure proceedings. They had reached a stage where, substantially, all the expenses, except those which would attend any sale of the property, even by this court, had been incurred in reaching a decree in the foreclosure suit and incurred by the action of the assignee, while a party to such suit, in suffering proceedings to go on without applying to this court to restrain them. It will become a question for consideration hereafter, whether the assignee ought not to be charged personally with liability for the amount of those expenses, and be compelled to refund them to the estate after they shall have been paid out of the proceeds of the land to the plaintiff in the suit, as being a waste, committed by him, of the estate. At present the petition must be dismissed, with costs to be paid by the assignee personally, and not out of the estate, and the injunction must be dissolved.—February 22, 1872.

UNITED STATES DISTRICT COURT—N. D. ILLINOIS.

An alleged bankrupt, during the pendency of bankruptcy proceedings and while under an injunction from the United States District Court prohibiting him from selling or disposing of any of his property, sold certain promissory notes belonging to him. He was finally adjudged a bankrupt. *Held*, That the purchaser acquires no title to the notes in question, as he took with constructive notice at least and cannot claim to be an innocent purchaser for value. That the adjudication relates back to the time of the filing of the petition, and the assignee may recover the notes or their value from the purchaser. The payment of the notes having been guaranteed the court orders that the assignee preserve the notes and guaranties thereon intact, that they may be used as evidence if required in proceedings by the purchaser against the guarantor.

In re J. J. LAKE.

BLODGETT, J.—This is a proceeding by petition on the part of the assignee of John J. Lake to compel the respondents, Commerford and Lawrence, to deliver to him certain promissory notes alleged to belong to the bankrupt's estate.

The admitted facts are that on the twenty-fourth of July, eighteen hundred and sixty-eight, certain creditors of said Lake filed a petition in this court, charging him with acts of bankruptcy, and the usual rule was entered requiring him to show cause why he should not be adjudged a bankrupt. At the same time an injunction was issued restraining Lake from selling, encumbering or otherwise disposing of his property, or any part thereof, until the further order of the court. Lake filed a denial of the acts of bankruptcy charged, and demanded a jury trial, and the case stood at issue and for trial on this denial, and the injunction remained in full force

In re Lake.

on the twelfth of October, eighteen hundred and sixty-eight, on which day Lake, who resided in Livingston county, called on the respondents who were and are bankers residing and doing business at Morris in Grundy county, and offered to sell them three promissory notes for the sum of five hundred dollars each, dated the thirteenth of July, eighteen hundred and sixty-eight, made by one Charles G. Peters, payable to said Lake, and secured by a mortgage on a tract of land in Livingston county, which Lake had conveyed to Peters. Lake was a stranger to respondents, but he was accompanied by one Clarke, who was well known to them, and in good financial credit. Lake being a stranger, respondents refused to buy the notes of him unless Clarke would guaranty the payment thereof. The negotiation finally resulted in respondents purchasing the notes for the sum of twelve hundred dollars, Lake endorsing them, and Clarke placing his name thereon as guarantor and Lake assigning the mortgage by which the notes were secured to respondents. Upon the trial of the case made by the petition and denial, Lake was found guilty of the acts of bankruptcy, and adjudged a bankrupt by the court. An assignee was duly elected, and the estate of the bankrupt conveyed to him. The assignee now claims these notes as part of the property of the estate.

By the fourteenth section of the bankrupt act all the property and rights and interest in property which the bankrupt had at the time of the filing of the petition pass to the assignee, and the title of the assignee relates back to the time of the filing of the petition.

The filing of the petition praying the adjudication in bankruptcy is notice to all the world, and all persons dealing with the person thus charged do so at their peril. No person can by dealing with a debtor thus situated acquire any title to his property as against his assignee in bankruptcy if the proceeding ripens into judgment of bankruptcy. *In re* Gregg, 3 N. B. R. 131; *ex parte* Vogel, 2 id. 138; *in re* Wynne, 4 id. 5.

But it is contended that negotiablepaper forms an exception to this rule, and that the *bona fide* purchaser of such paper will be protected, although a petition in bankruptcy may be pending against the seller of such paper, and the counsel for respondents have presented an exceedingly ingenious and plausable argument in support of this proposition, relying mainly upon a class of cases where it has been held that bank notes, bills of exchange and promissory notes, even when stolen or obtained from the owners by actual fraud, could not be recovered if they had passed to *bona fide* purchasers for value without notice. To my mind, however, the difficulty in applying this principle of law to the case before the court arises from the fact that the respondents cannot be said to be *bona fide* holders without notice. All the parties to the transaction were domiciled in this district, and the transaction took place within the district. The proceedings in bankruptcy were then pending, and the bankrupt, Lake, was then under an injunction from this court prohibiting him from selling or disposing of any of his property. The respondents are concluded by the notice thus given them by the records of this court, and it does not lie in their mouths to say they are innocent purchasers.

The rule relied upon by the attorney for respondents arises from the policy of the law in favor of protecting commercial transactions in negotiable or commercial paper made in due course of business, without fraud and for value paid. But an equally inexorable rule requires that all persons shall be held to take notice of judicial proceedings pending in courts having general jurisdiction over them.

The decree will be that respondents be required to deliver the notes in question to Lake's assignee within ten days.

It was also urged that inasmuch as these notes bear Clarke's guaranty of payment to respondents, some order should be made enabling them to avail themselves of it; but as Clarke is not before the court, I think the most the court can do at present is to require the assignee to preserve the notes and guaranties thereon intact for a reasonable time at least, so that they may be used as evidence hereafter, if required in any proceedings by respondents against Clarke.

UNITED STATES DISTRICT COURT—WASHINGTON TERRITORY.

An attachment issued out of the state court is dissolved from the date of the filing of the petition where an order of adjudication is subsequently granted.

Costs that accrued under such attachment, prior to the filing of the petition in bankruptcy, are not a valid lien on the property unless incurred at defendant's request.

In setting apart for the use of the bankrupt exempt property, the assignee is not obliged to designate articles on which there is no lien.

An assignee is chargeable personally with costs of the proceedings where he files a petition to have an attachment dissolved which covers property that has already been set apart by him as exempt.

In re C. H. PRESTON. *

In the matter of the petition of Geo. N. McConaha, assignee of the estate of C. H. Preston, bankrupt, praying that a sale made by Stretch, sheriff of Snohomish county, be set aside.

On a hearing before his honor, judge Green, it was agreed by counsel that a statement of facts be prepared and submitted for his honor's decision, as a special case under the statute. The following statement of facts is herewith submitted and agreed to by the assignee and defendant's counsel:

FIRST. That on the twentieth day of February, eighteen hundred and seventy-one, one-half interest in six work oxen was attached by Benjamin Stretch, sheriff of Snohomish county, in a suit brought by J. P. White, plaintiff, *v.* C. H. Preston, defendant. The one-half interest in said cattle was the property of the defendant in the suit. Preston and the defendant, Henry Mills, owned the other half interest.

SECOND. That, on the fourth day of March, eighteen hundred and seventy-one, an order was made by the Hon. O. Jacobs, commanding the sale of said property by said sheriff, (for the reason that the same was expensive to keep;) and further ordered that the amount arising from said sale be deposited in the office of the clerk of the United States district court for the third judicial district, viz., L. B. Andrews.

* See 5 N. B. R. 293.

THIRD. That said Stretch, in accordance with the provisions of said order, sold said property on the twentieth day of March, eighteen hundred and seventy-one, to Henry Mills, and deposited the money in the clerk's hands as directed.

FOURTH. That on the eighteenth day of March, eighteen hundred and seventy-one, said C. H. Preston filed his petition in bankruptcy against himself with the clerk of the supreme court, at Olympia, and on the twenty-fourth day of March, eighteen hundred and seventy-one, was adjudged as bankrupt.

FIFTH. That the transcript of the said petition of C. H. Preston was filed with the clerk of the third judicial district, twenty-fourth day of March, eighteen hundred and seventy-one.

SIXTH. That, on the twentieth day of March, when said property was sold by said sheriff Stretch, he had not had notice that said Preston had filed his petition in bankruptcy, Two hundred dollars was the amount realized from such sale, and was a fair price for the property sold.

SEVENTH. The property in question has been set aside by the assignee, George N. McConaha, as exempt under the provisions of the bankrupt law.

Question 1st. Whether the filing of the bankrupt petition in the supreme court at Olympia, on the eighteenth March, dissolved the attachment and rendered null and void the sale and all proceedings subsequent at that date, or whether, under the whole circumstances of the case, the court will hold it valid.

Question 2d. Whether or not the costs that accrued under the attachment, prior to the filing of bankrupt petition in the supreme court, are a valid lien upon the property in controversy, or upon the money arising from the sale thereof? If a valid lien, is it to be enforced in the bankrupt court? Or has the sheriff a right to retain the property or money until his costs are paid?

Question 3d. Was the petition filed so as to work a dissolution of the attachment until the transcript was filed with the clerk of the district court and the fifty dollars paid as security for register's fees?

The judge is to pass upon the regularity of the proceedings in this matter thus far; if regular, then the costs to abide the final result, otherwise to be paid by plaintiff.

No right of appeal is waived by either party.

G. N. McCONAHA, assignee; McGILVRA & BAXTER for defendants; A. N. MERRICK for bankrupt.

GREEN, J.—Under this special case, submitted to me on the twentieth day of June, eighteen hundred and seventy-one, it is assumed that the attachment proceedings were regular up to the time of the commencement of proceedings in bankruptcy; and that at the commencement of the latter proceedings the attachment suit had not proceeded to judgment.

I answer to the first question, that the attachment was dissolved from the date to which the assignment in bankruptcy relates—that is, from the time of the commencement of bankruptcy proceedings. The operation of the assignment in reference to the attachment was, not to avoid it *ab initio*, but to arrest all proceedings under it; to dissolve it as of the date of the filing of the petition in the supreme court; to leave untouched all previously accrued rights; to prevent the subsequent accrument of rights, under the attachment. From the date of the dissolution of the attachment the sheriff or other person having then actual possession of the attached property became divested of all official relation to that property, and became a simple bailee thereof to the use of the person by virtue of the bankrupt act entitled to the same. If he afterwards, by sale or in any other way, disposed of the property, otherwise than to transfer the bankrupt's estate in the same to him to whom by the bankrupt law it fell, his act had no official character, and needed to make it valid the ratification of the person having title under the law. The court will not in this proceeding hold it valid, but suggests that in order to such validity it would need such a ratification. Such ratification does not appear.

In re Preston.

Coming to the first part of the second question: An alleged debtor cannot personally be compelled to pay costs, except of his own making, until he has been adjudged a debtor or costs have been adjudged against him. And until such judgment, of course costs not made at his instance cannot be collected out of his general property as a debt owing from him to the officer.

Section nineteen of the bankrupt law contains an exhaustive enumeration of all claims that may be proved against the bankrupt's estate or any part of it. The enumeration comprises only claims owing by the bankrupt to creditors. No other kind of claim—no charge on specific property unless to secure a personal debt from the bankrupt, is good against the unexcepted articles in court; and it is just to conclude that what could not be enforced against an article if in court, cannot be a charge against it out of court, excepted by the assignee. Excepted articles have at least that measure of exemption that they would have if subject to distribution.

Section twenty agrees with section nineteen; recognizes mortgages or pledges of real or personal estate, and liens, "for the securing of debts owing to the creditor from the bankrupt," as good charges on the bankrupt's estate, and by implication rejects all other charges. The sheriff here has no lien answering the description of the law. His costs were at plaintiff's instance, and do not properly before judgment constitute a debt owing from the bankrupt defendant to the officer, (in fact they cannot even after judgment properly be said to,) and such costs could not anywhere, it is believed, before judgment, be collected by the officer against the defendant, unless, through the specific property attached. It would, indeed, be unjust to allow the sheriff to satisfy his costs out of the property of the bankrupt defendant in attachment, when those costs were incurred at the request of plaintiff, and when the suit being summarily superseded, the law creates no presumption in favor of the title of plaintiff to costs as against the defendant. Where a suit is thus superseded, the law creates no presumption in favor of either party. It might very well be, that defendant in the attachment suit would, if permitted, have been able to prove himself unindebted. How inequitable, in such a case, would be a diminution of the assets of the bankrupt, by the necessarily considerable expenses of an attachment certainly groundless, possibly malicious!

It is to be noted that, under the laws of this territory, if the attaching plaintiff should fail in his attachment suit, the defendant would be entitled to a restoration of all his property attached, without diminution and subject to no lien growing out of the suit.

From these considerations, I am of opinion that the costs that accrued under the attachment prior to the filing of the bankrupt's petition are not a valid lien upon the property in controversy; unless, indeed, some of those costs were incurred at defendant's request, in which case there might be a lien for so much thereof so long as the sheriff retained the property. A release, voluntarily, of the property would be an abandonment of any lien upon it.

And this brings me to the second part of this question : The sheriff parted with the goods at his peril; his lien on them, if any he had, was lost when he let them go. Nothing less than the consent of the person entitled at the time of sale to the property could have made the sale good, and preserved the lien to take effect on the proceeds. The sale, without approval of the person legally entitled, cannot be regarded as good by this court, notwithstanding the purchaser had no actual notice of the dissolution of the attachment, and paid full value for the goods. The commencement of bankruptcy proceedings was notice to all the world of such dissolution. As the sheriff parted with the very goods attached, he could have no lien surviving, unless he sold by consent of the owner.

But supposing the sale valid by consent of the proper party, I think that even then no lien could be enforced here. The property sold had been set apart by the assignee as exempt. Goods of that kind might, under readily supposable circumstances, lawfully be exempted. To the action of the assignee no exception was taken. I assume, therefore, his action in that behalf to be good.

One object of the law is to place all the estate of the bankrupt in such a posture and so far in the control of.the bankrupt court, that that court can fully and exclusively determine what is to be left to the bankrupt, and freely dispose of and distribute among the creditors the remainder. The estate of the bankrupt might be all personal property, and every article be subject to a lien to secure a debt owing to one or another creditor. By the operation of the law, no such lien, except at the option of its holder, would be extinguished. Every such lien would constitute for the person holding it a special property in the thing covered by the lien, be a part of that person's estate, possibly the most valuable part, and for the law to divest it might be to make one bankrupt in the endeavor to relieve another.

The designation of the assignee does not, then, on the one hand, operate to divest any such lien, because that would be inequitable as we have just seen, and the bankrupt law accords the designation no such operation.

On the other hand, the assignee is not obliged to designate articles on which are no lien; if he were, the bankrupt might have nothing exempted. Besides, the assignee is not a judicial officer to determine the question of lien or no lien. If the assignee should make such a designation of excepted articles as would by reason of the encumbrances on those articles be worthless, or insufficient to fulfil the beneficent design of the law in making exemption, I think the bankrupt could obtain redress by excepting to the determination of the assignee, and that such would be his proper remedy. His appeal from the assignee to the court would bring before the court the whole question of the existence and amount of the liens.

But the question not being brought before the court by that mode, the bankrupt is remitted to such rights and

In re Preston.

remedies in the excepted property as any other man not a bankrupt has in his own property—with this exception, that this bankruptcy court will protect him in the enjoyment of his exempt property against all acts and claims contrary to the bankrupt law. Taking the designation of the assignee to be good, it follows that in contemplation of law the articles excepted never passed to the assignee and are not now and never have been in the possession of the court. The exemption, as well as the assignment, relates back to the filing of the petition. The excepted articles, in contemplation of law, remain the property of the bankrupt subject to all legal encumbrances. A lien on articles so excepted cannot be enforced in the bankruptcy court, because that court has not possession of the articles the lien effects. It has sent them beyond, or rather declined to receive them within, its jurisdiction, and would need to obtain jurisdiction by setting aside the action of the assignee before it could enforce the lien. Only such liens as are on property in the possession of the court will be enforced by it.

The lien the sheriff claims here cannot, as the case stands, be enforced in this court.

Question the third is answered by referring to sections thirty-eight and forty-seven of the bankrupt act. Section thirty-eight makes the filing of a petition for adjudication in bankruptcy upon which an order may be issued the commencement of proceedings under the act. Section forty-seven makes the fifty dollars deposit as security for register's fees merely an act preliminary to the issue of the warrant. An order of adjudication having issued, the time of filing the petition in the supreme court is the date of the dissolution of the attachment.

As to the regularity of the proceedings herein, I am of opinion that the petition filed by the assignee was improperly filed by him, inasmuch as he, having exempted the property attached was not interested in the subject matter of the petition. The special case, though not in all respects formal, is, taken together with the petition, sufficiently intelligible, and presents, by agreement of parties interested, question properly determinable by this court.

The costs incident to the petition of the assignee, and all costs in this proceeding accrued prior to the filing of the special case, will be paid by the assignee personally; the remainder will abide the further order of the court.

———•••———

UNITED STATES DISTRICT COURT—S. D. NEW YORK.

A subpœna to appear and answer a bill in equity cannot be served at the last place of abode as in the case of an order to show cause under section forty of the bankrupt act, or at the last usual place of abode as in form number fifty-seven in bankruptcy, but must be left at the existing present dwelling house, or the existing, present, usual, customary place of abode of the defendant.

There is no irregularity in making the subpœna returnable on the first Tuesday of the month instead of the first Monday, as the equity rules provide that the subpœna shall be returnable on a rule day; and that the first Monday of every month shall be a rule day. The spirit of general order thirty-two and the equity rules were sufficiently complied with in this case.

Motion granted setting aside the order *pro confesso*, and denied in respect to setting aside the subpœna. Application to have a receiver appointed denied.

HYSLOP, *Assignee*, v. HOPPOCK *et al.*

BLATCHFORD, J.—The bill in this case was filed on the fifth day of October, eighteen hundred and seventy-one. The prayer of the bill is that a conveyance made by Ely Hoppock, the bankrupt, November fifteenth, eighteen hundred and sixty-seven, of a lot of land on Thirteenth street, in the city of New York, to one Samuel Cary, and a conveyance made by said Hoppock, October fourth, eighteen hundred and sixty-seven, of a lease of a lot of land on Fourteenth street, in said city, to one Walter Barnes, and which lease was assigned by said Barnes on the same day to Caroline Hoppock the wife of the bankrupt, and assigned by her November fifteenth, eighteen hundred and sixty-seven, to said Barnes, and assigned on the same day, by the said Barnes and said bankrupt to said Cary, and the properties covered by which conveyances, lease and assignments were devised and bequeathed by said Cary by his last will and testament, made November twenty-ninth, eighteen hundred and seventy, to said Caroline Hoppock, may be decreed to have been fraudulent and void as against the creditors of the said bankrupt, and that such properties and the proceeds thereof and the right of action therefor may be decreed to have vested in the plaintiff, and that the defendant, Brown, who is alleged to be receiving the rents of the properties may be decreed to account to the plaintiff for such rents from the first of May, eighteen hundred and seventy-one, and that the bankrupt and his wife may be enjoined from parting with or encumbering the properties, and from receiving the rents thereof, and that the plaintiff may be appointed receiver of such rents.

On the filing of the bill, a subpœna to appear and answer was issued on the fifth of October, eighteen hundred and seventy-one, returnable on the first Tuesday of November, eighteen hundred and seventy-one, and directed to the defendants. On the sixth of October, eighteen hundred and seventy-one, the marshal, in writing, deputed Charles L. Clarke to serve the subpœna. In an affidavit sworn to by Mr. Clarke on the seventh of October, eighteen hundred and seventy-one, and filed on the ninth of November, eighteen hundred and seventy-one, and annexed to the subpœna, he deposes that on the sixth day of October, eighteen hundred and seventy-one, he served the annexed subpœna on Ely Hoppock and Caroline Hoppock, his wife, two of the defendants therein, by leaving copies thereof, for each of the defendants, at the dwelling house or usual place of abode of the said Ely Hoppock and Caroline, his wife, to wit: number 38 West Fourteenth street, in the city of New York, with a free white person, a member or resident in the family. This service purported to be made under the provisions of rule thirteen in equity, which is: "The service of all subpœnas shall be by delivery of a copy thereof by the officer serving the same to the defendant personally, or, in case of husband and

wife, to the husband personally, or by leaving a copy thereof
at the dwelling house or usual place of abode of each defendant, with some free white person who is a member or
resident in the family." On such service a rule was entered
on the ninth of November, eighteen hundred and seventy-
one, taking the bill as confessed against the defendants, Ely
Hoppock and Caroline, his wife, for want of an appearance.
Those defendants now come into court without appearing
generally in the cause and move the court that the order *pro
confesso*, and the subpœna and its alleged service and the
affidavit thereof, and all subsequent proceedings of the plaintiff on the subpœna and order be set aside, on the grounds,
among others: (1.) That the subpœna was not made returnable on a rule day, but was made returnable on the first
Tuesday of the month; (2.) That the place mentioned in the
affidavit of service, 38 West Fourteenth street, was not the
dwelling house or usual place of abode of the defendants or
either of them.

It is satisfactorily shown by affidavits that neither of the
two defendants has been personally served with a subpœna;
that 38 West Fourteenth street, in the city of New York,
was not, on the sixth of October, eighteen hundred and
seventy-one, the dwelling house or usual place of abode of
either of them, and that 38 West Fourteenth Street, in the
city of New York, has not been the dwelling house or usual
place of abode of either of them, since the thirtieth day of
April, eighteen hundred and sixty-eight. Where the dwelling
house or usual place of abode of the defendants has been
since June, eighteen hundred and sixty-eight, or is now, is not
shown, but it would seem to be indicated that it is now in
Canada, if anywhere. Although the bankrupt may have fled
from the jurisdiction of this court in bankruptcy to avoid the
consequences of frauds committed by him on his creditors,
and although his wife, the recipient of the benefits of such
frauds, may have accompanied him in his flight, and although
he and she may be hiding just over the lines in Canada, and
venturing into this state at Niagara Falls, only for the pur-

pose of making an affidavit for the purposes of this motion, yet this court, sitting in equity for the purposes of this suit, has acquired no jurisdiction of the persons of the defendants by such service of the subpœna as has been made. This court cannot, in the evidence, hold that 38 West Fourteenth Street, in the city of New York, has been at any time since the thirtieth of April, eighteen hundred and sixty-eight, the dwelling house or usual place of abode of either of the defendants. The rule does not permit the service to be made by leaving the subpœna at the "last" place of abode, as in the case of an order to show cause under section forty of the bankrupt act, or at the "last usual" place of abode, as in form number fifty-seven in bankruptcy, but it is to be left at the existing, present, dwelling house, or the existing, present, usual, customary place of abode. I cannot hold that 38 West Fourteenth Street, in the city of New York, was on the sixth of October, eighteen hundred and seventy-one, the dwelling house of the defendants or either of them, or the usual place of abode of them or either of them, in the face of the facts shown that neither of them has occupied the house 38 West Fourteenth Street as a dwelling house or place of abode since the thirtieth of April, eighteen hundred and sixty-eight, although it is not shown where any dwelling house or place of abode is situated which is now occupied by the bankrupt, or which has been occupied by him since the thirtieth of April, eighteen hundred and sixty-eight, or where any dwelling house or place of abode is situated which is now occupied by his wife, or which has been occupied by her since the twenty-fifth of May, eighteen hundred and sixty-eight. The question is one of the jurisdiction which this court, as a court sitting in equity in this suit, has acquired over the persons of the defendants in this suit by process issued and served therein.

I see no irregularity in making the subpœna in this case returnable on the first Tuesday of the month, and not on the first Monday. There is a new term of this court on the first Tuesday of each month. There are but two or three terms of each circuit court in the year, and hence the general equity rules provide that the subpœna shall be returnable on a rule day; that the first Monday of every month shall be a rule day; and that the return day of the subpœna shall be the next rule day, or the next rule day but one occurring after twenty days from the time of issuing the subpœna. General order number thirty-two in bankruptcy provides that " in proceedings in equity instituted for the purpose of carrying into effect the provisions of the bankrupt act, or of enforcing the rights and remedies given by it, the rules of equity practice established by the supreme court of the United States shall be followed as nearly as may be." I think the spirit of this general order and of those rules was sufficiently complied with in this case, in respect to the return day of the subpœna.

The motion must, therefore, be granted in respect to seting aside the order *pro confesso*, and the alleged service of the subpœna, and the affidavit of such service, and all subsequent proceedings of the plaintiff on the subpœna and order, and denied in respect to setting aside the subpœna.

The plaintiff also moves that he may be appointed receiver of the rents and profits of the said properties. Inasmuch as Mrs. Hoppock is the person alleged to hold the properties adversely to the plaintiff, and she has not been served with process, and the defendant Brown is not alleged to have acted otherwise than as agent for others in receiving the ren's, the motion for a receiver must be denied.

AMOS G. HULL for plaintiff; CHARLES TRACY for Hoppock and wife.—January 10, 1872.

UNITED STATES DISTRICT COURT—S. D. NEW YORK.

The service of a subpœna to appear and answer a bill in equity is regulated by an act of congress, and if the defendants do not reside within the district the district court has no power to obtain jurisdiction over their persons by any service of process made otherwise than in accordance with rule thirteen. Application to have service made by publication or personal service on the son of defendant denied.

HYSLOP, *Assignee*, v. HOPPOCK *et al.*

BLATCHFORD, J.—The bill in this case was filed October fifth, eighteen hundred and seventy-one, to set aside certain conveyances of real estate, as fraudulent as against the creditors of Ely Hoppock, the bankrupt. A subpœna to appear and answer was issued, but cannot be served on the defendants Ely Hoppock and his wife, by reason of their continued absence from the jurisdiction of this court. Enquiry has been made at their last place of abode, but they cannot be found so as to be served on the subpœna, and it is alleged that they have gone out of the state, or otherwise absconded to avoid the service of the process of this court. It is stated that they are in the receipt of the rents of the property and ought to be affected by the bill, and that their son, as their agent, receives the rents and transmits the same to them monthly. On these facts the plaintiff asks that an order be made directing said defendants to appear at a day to be named and answered in the bill, and that such order be served by publication or otherwise, or that an order for the service of the subpœna upon the son of the defendants for them, and that such service be deemed good service on them, and that thereupon an order be made directing an appearance to be entered for said defendants.

The ground on which this application is made is, that where the service of the subpœna cannot be made by ordinary means, a resort may be had to extraordinary means, such as service at the last place of abode, or on some other person, and that by statute in England such substituted service on a receiver of rents is allowed.

I regard this whole subject, so far as service of the subpœna in this suit is concerned, as regulated by act of congress and by the rules established by the supreme court. Under the eleventh section of the act of September twenty-fourth, seventeen hundred and eighty-nine, (1 Stat. at Large, 79,) if the defendants are inhabitants of the United States, this suit cannot be brought against them by any original process in any other district than that whereof they are inhabitants, or in which they shall be found at the time of serving the process. If they are inhabitants of the United States and of this district, or are found within this district, the subpœna may, by rule thirteen in equity, be served on them personally, or the husband personally for the wife, or by leaving a copy at the dwelling house or usual place of abode of each of them in this district, with some free white person who is a member or resident in the family. If they are not inhabitants of this district, and are not found within this district, I know of no statute conferring on this court the power of obtaining jurisdiction over their persons in this suit, by any service of process made otherwise than in accordance with rule thirteen, or the power to make any one of the orders applied for. In the absence of any statute, or any rule having the force of a statute, conferring such power, I must refuse the application.

UNITED STATES DISTRICT COURT—MAINE.

S was adjudged a bankrupt by the district court of the United States for the district of Maine, of which he was a citizen, and P was appointed his assignee, also residing in same district. The assignee filed his bill in equity in the same court to recover certain preferences of the respondent, who resided in and was a citizen of Massachusetts, and had no property in this district, and was not found here. The subpœna was served on respondent in Massachusetts, who appeared to object to the jurisdiction of this court. *Held*, That the court did not have jurisdiction to proceed against the respondent.

PAINE, *Assignee*, v. *CALDWELL*.

A. W. Paine, *pro se*, contended that the bill was sustainable by virtue of the provisions of the bankrupt act, the first section of which gives to the district court original jurisdiction in all matters and proceedings in bankruptcy, extending to "all cases and controversies arising between the bankrupt and the creditor, to *the collection of all the assets of the bankrupt* * * * and to all its acts, matters and things to be done under and by virtue of the bankruptcy, until the final distribution and settlement of the estate, and close of proceedings in bankruptcy." The second section also giving concurrent jurisdiction with the circuit court, "of all suits at law or in equity, which may or shall be brought by the assignee, * * *against any person claiming an adverse interest,* * * touching any property or rights of property of the bankrupt, &c. The studied manner in which these sections are framed to include every cause of action, without limitation, seems to leave no doubt of the intention of congress to embrace claims such as now involved.

The clause providing for such, "*jurisdiction in their respective districts*" in the first section means very clearly the same as the similiar clause in the section, which provides that said "courts of the United States, within and for the districts where the proceedings in bankruptcy shall be pending," shall have the jurisdiction mentioned, the whole tenor of which seems to add force to the argument, adduced from the other language already cited, to limit the right of the assignee in all suits to that district where the proceedings in bankruptcy shall be pending." These clauses do not in any way limit the right of action to any cause short of "*all cases*" in the first section, and "*any person*" in the second. When the statute has failed to make such limitations, there is no warrant for the court to do it.

Consistent with the construction have been all the decisions thus far known to have been made on this subject under the act. What seems to be conclusive on the point in issue is the uniform rule which the courts have established, that the assignee cannot maintain suit in any other of the district courts, except only in that "where the proceedings in bankruptcy shall be pending." The converse would seem to allow as matter of course, *in re* Richardson, 2 N. B. R. 74; *Markson & Spaulding* v. *Heaney*, 4 N. B. R. 165; *Shearman* v. *Bing-*

ham et al. 5 N. B. R. 34; *in re* Penn. *et al.*, id. 30; see also Bump's 3 ed. 162 to 182, and 244 to 256.

The general language of the act, which by its unmistakable language gives the jurisdiction claimed, can only be ruled away on the supposition that congress might not intend to give the assignee any remedy against parties out of the district, or that they forgot to provide for it. Both hypotheses are inadmissible. The language must then control, and if thereby any inconvenience or hardship results, congress and not the court must furnish the remedy. Attention was also called to the fact stated in the bill, that the money sued for, having been collected on an execution recovered in the state court of Maine within the district, by an authorised attorney of that court, the court would sustain their jurisdiction by the service made upon the attorney, and the case of *Marco* v. *Low*, 55 Me. 549, and cases therein referred to was cited.

Fox, J.—The question presented is one of jurisdiction. Can the district court sustain a bill in equity brought by an assignee in bankruptcy in this district, against a citizen of Massachusetts not found in this district, and who has no property therein, the bill being instituted to recover back the amount received from a preference in fraud of the act by the respondent obtaining a judgment against the bankrupt before the supreme court of this state, and collecting the same within four months of the commencement of proceedings in bankruptcy, the bankrupt being known by the respondent to be insolvent? Service of the subpœna was made on the respondent in Massachusetts, and he appears to object to the jurisdiction of the court.

By the judiciary act it was provided " that no person shall be arrested in one district for trial in another, in any civil cause before the circuit or district court, and no civil action shall be brought before either the circuit or district courts, against an inhabitant of the United States, by any original process in any other district than that whereof he is an inhabitant, or shall be found at the time of serving the writ."

Paine v. Caldwell.

In *Picquet* v. *Swan*, 5 Mason, 35, STORY, J., in a very elaborate opinion announced as the result of his examination, "that by the general provisions of the laws of the United States, the circuit courts could issue no process beyond the limits of their districts, and that independent of positive legislation, the process can only be served upon persons within the same district." In *Toland* v. *Sprague*, 12 Pet. 327, the supreme court held that merely by an attachment on trustee process of the estate of a defendant who resided in Gibraltar, the circuit court did not acquire jurisdiction over the party ; that the circuit court of each district sits within and for that district, and is bounded by its local limits, and that whatever may be the extent of their jurisdiction over the subject matter of suits, in respect to persons and property, it can only be exercised within the limits of the district. Congress has not in terms authorised any original civil process to run into any other district, with the single exception of subpœnas for witnesses, and the court say, " we think that the opinion of the legislature is thus manifested to be that the process of a circuit court cannot be served without that district in which it is established, without the special authority of law therefor." In *Herndon* v. *Ridgeway*, 17 How. 424, the supreme court decided that the district court of Mississippi, which probably had the jurisdiction of a circuit court, could not entertain a bill to compel parties to interplead who are not found in the district ; that jurisdiction over parties is acquired only by service of process within the state or by a voluntary appearance.

These authorities are conclusive that this court, prior to the passage of the bankrupt act, did not have the jurisdiction claimed for it, and I do not understand it to be very strenuously contended by the complainant in his learned argument, that the district court derived the authority from the judiciary act, or any other law of congress than the bankrupt act itself. He argues that this authority is found in the first and second section of the act, conferring, as he says, on this court exclusive jurisdiction in all matters pertaining to the estate of the bankrupt, subject to a concurrent jurisdiction in certain matters with the district court under the provisions of the second section. For the purpose of this inquiry it may be conceded that the district court in which the proceedings in bankruptcy are originated has within its district exclusive jurisdiction over the estate of the bankrupt, although many of the state courts, under the present as well as the former act, have sustained actions brought by assignees for the recovery of debts due to the estate, as well as for the conversion of property by transfers in fraud of the bankrupt act. *Vide Beals* v. *Quinn*, 101 Mass. 262 ; *Forbes* v. *Howe*, 102 Mass. 428 ; *Peiper* v. *Harmer*, 5 N. B. R. 252.

This concession does not control or even afford us much ·aid in reaching a conclusion upon the question now before us, as. the claim here is not that the district court has exclusive jurisdiction of bankrupt matters *within* its own district, but that it is not limited by its own district, and may extend beyond its territorial limits, and by its procees bring before it parties from the most remote state in the Union.

Such authority should be conferred by positive, direct legislation, and cannot be derived from inferences or implication, or from any general indefinite expressions found in the law.

The first section of the bankrupt law confers and defines the jurisdiction of the district court, " that the several district courts of the United States, be, and they are hereby constituted courts of bankruptcy, and they shall have original jurisdiction *in their respective districts*, in all matters and proceedings in bankruptcy." In the opinion of the court the words "in their respective districts," found in this provision of the act, are not without effect. They must receive their usual, ordinary signification, and it is believed, manifest a purpose and intent in congress to restrict and limit the authority and jurisdiction of the district courts in bankruptcy within their own districts, in accordance with the practice as it then was, and not to confer upon them a jurisdiction throughout the United States, in utter conflict with all prior legislation, and the settled policy of congress.

The jurisdiction in bankruptcy is conferred on the district courts by the expression that they shall have original jurisdiction *in their respective districts*. This is the grant; by it alone has it jurisdiction and authority, and whilst its authority does extend to all matters in bankruptcy, and there is no limit to the subject matter over which the court has jurisdiction, it is expressly confined and restricted, in its exercise, to the limits of its own territory, and enjoys no other or greater power or authority outside of its own district than it had before the bankrupt act was passed; and it seems necessary to utterly reject and expunge from the provision these words of limitation prescribing its own district as the bounds and extent of its jurisdiction, before it can be declared that by this grant a jurisdiction is bestowed on the court co-extensive with the Union.

It is said that these words do not limit the jurisdiction, but only require that the court shall act within its own district; that in the exercise of its jurisdiction it has control over all matters and proceedings in bankruptcy, and after a specific enumeration of certain matters, that the first section of the act declares " that the jurisdiction shall extend to all matters and things to be done under and by virtue of the bankruptcy, until the final distribution and settlement of the estate and the close of proceedings in bankruptcy." This language must be taken in connection with that before cited, and is controlled by it, and cannot be considered as extending the jurisdiction of the court beyond its district. If the construction put by the court upon the grant to the district courts, " of original jurisdiction in their respective districts" is erroneous, I am still of opinion that this language, broad and comprehensive as it is, extending its jurisdiction to all matters and things to be done under the bankruptcy, should not be held to authorise it to summon before it parties from without its district. If congress had intended to grant such unlimited authority to the district courts, as to authorise this court sitting in Maine, to issue its process and summon before it a citizen of California or Oregon, it is believed that clear, positive, unambiguous language would have been employed, (by an express grant,) manifesting beyond all question that such was the intent, and not by any general uncertain legislation have authorised a practice in utter conflict with the policy of all prior legislation. The language employed in the first section was proper and necessary to confer on the district court full and complete jurisdiction over the estate of the bankrupt. It is none too broad and comprehensive in its relation to the subject matter, and there does not appear to be any occasion for giving to it a construction which will extend the jurisdiction of the courts so much beyond their well established boundaries.

In repeated instances it will be found that general language of this nature has been employed by congress in conferring upon the federal courts jurisdiction, and in every instance have the courts held, notwithstanding the generality of the language, that they were restricted to their own respective districts. In *Picquet* v. *Swan*, 5 Mason, 35, before cited, STORY, J., says, "The process acts have prescribed the forms of process and modes of service to be according to the state jurisprudence; but they do not appear to me to be intended to enlarge the sphere of jurisdiction of the circuit courts. I cannot judicially say that the phraseology of the process acts ought to receive a more extensive interpretation, so as to break down or interfere with the policy of the judiciary acts, founded as it seems to me on principles of public law, public convenience and immutable justice."

In *Toland* v. *Sprague*, *ubi supra*, it was claimed that congress having adopted the forms of writs and modes of process in the several states, had thereby authorised the circuit court of Massachusetts to take jurisdiction by trustee process against a non-resident, not found in the district; but the supreme court held that the acts of congress adopting the state process, adopt the form and mode of service only as far as the persons are rightfully within the reach of such process, and did not intend to enlarge the sphere of the jurisdiction of the courts.

The case of *ex parte* Graham, 3 Wash. C. C. 456, was a writ of *habeas corpus* to discharge from imprisonment the petitioner, who had been arrested in Pennsylvania on a warrant against him in a prize cause, issued by the circuit court of Massachusetts. WASHINGTON, J., p. 458, says " the question here turns upcn the authority of the district or circuit courts of one district to issue its process into any other district to compel the appearance of a person residing or found within the latter jurisdiction before the court from which the process issued, or to stand committed for any alleged contempt of that court. It is admitted that these courts, in the exercise of their common law and equity jurisdiction, have no authority generally to issue process into another district, except in cases where such authority has been specially bestowed by some law of the United States. The provisions of the act of seventeen hundred and eighty-nine appear manifestly to circumscribe the jurisdiction of the courts, as to the person of the defendant, by the limits òf the district where the suit is brought, and that the process of these courts was considered by the legislature to be bounded by the same limits, is obvious from the subsequeut acts passed. It has been argued that these restraints are incompatible with the essential jurisdiction of an admiralty court, more especially in prize causes. The distinction which is contended for has not, and it is confidently believed cannot be shown. It is true that the ninth section of the judiciary act gives to the district court exclusive original jurisdiction of all civil causes of admiralty and maritime jurisdiction without limitation, and it is not less true that the eleventh section of the act gives to the circuit courts original jurisdiction of all suits of a civil nature at common law and equity where an alien is a party, or the suit is between a citizen of the state, equally unlimited, except as to the amount. But the jurisdiction of these courts, though unlimited as to the subject matter of which they have cognizance, by any express declaration of the legislature, is nevertheless limited in point of locality, as well by the general principles of law, which our courts acknowledge as rules of decision, as by the express provisions of the eleventh section. As to the first, it will be acknowledged that there is no law of congress which limits the jurisdiction of the courts by the nature of the suits of which they have cognizance; by what law then is it, that actions of ejectment, dower, &c., can be brought only in the district where the land lies? If the defendant be served with process in the district where the suit was brought, neither the eleventh section or any other provision in the act of congress has restrained the jurisdiction of the court in the supposed cases. The only answer to the question is, that the want of jurisdiction is the result of certain general principles of law acting upon the particular subject. In like manner the jurisdiction of these courts when sitting in admiralty or prizes causes is limited by the general principles which apply to courts of admiralty in England and the United States, as well as in other countries, though bounded only by the nature of the causes over which they are to decide, and not in any respect by place; it is neverthe ess essential to the exercise of the jurisdiction by any particular court, that the person or thing against whom or which the court proceeds, should be within the jurisdiction of such court, &c."

This extract from the opinion of that learned judge, sets forth so clearly by illustration and argument, that the authority now claimed for the district court does not exist, that I have preferred to present it at length in the very words of the court, rather than in any way detract from its effect by any abridgment of it. The judiciary act gave to the district court exclusive original cognizance of all civil causes of admiralty and maritime jurisdiction, without qualification or limitation of any kind. This language was as comprehensive as any to be found in the bankrupt law, and yet the court had no doubt that its jurisdiction was limited and bounded by the locality of the district, and this decision should control the result of the present suit.

It is argued, that if the district court does not possess this power and authority, an assignee is without remedy to enforce his claims in behalf of the estate against non-residents of his district, and not found therein; but such, I apprehend, will not prove to be the case, as it is shown that the state courts are ready to exercise jurisdiction over their own citizens in suits against them in behalf of assignees in bankruptcy, and in most cases the authority of the circuit court, in the district where the delinquent resides could be appealed to by the assignee, as he would ordinarily be a citizen of another state, and if these should not afford the needed redress, congress could very easily supply the deficiency by conferring on the several district courts authority to sustain suits by assignees from other districts, ancillary to the original proceedings in bankruptcy.

I am satisfied that the authority here claimed for the district courts to issue their process against parties in remote districts would be attended with the most dangerous consequences, and would frequently prove an instrument of oppression and extortion; and if it did exist and was frequently called into exercise, would soon overthrow the bankrupt act. Assignees having nothing personally at risk, as the expenses would ordinarily be a charge upon the estate, would, I have no doubt, very frequently institute proceedings in their own districts against citizens of other remote districts, with whom the bankrupt may at some time have had dealings, trusting to the defendant's willingness to pay a considerable amount in the way of compromise, rather than be subjected to the expense and vexations of a protracted law suit, at a distance and in a place where he may be a stranger and unknown, and in which if he proved successful he would necessarily incur large expenditures which are not recompensed in any taxation of costs. In some instances the defendant might be arrested by the marshal of the district where he resides and thrown into prison, and there detained a long time to await the result of a controversy in a distant district, and to which he was debarred from giving his personal attendance by reason of his imprisonment. The whole proceeding in the exercise of such a jurisdiction would be attended with difficulties which as WASHINGTON, J., in the case before cited, says, "nothing but an act of congress can remove." I hold in the language of STORY, J., that this limitation of the jurisdiction of the court "is founded in principles of public law, public convenience and immutable justice," and I trust the day may never come when any such baneful authority will be conferred on this or any other court.

No decision has been cited sustaining the position of the complainant, and the opinion of BENEDICT, J., *in re* Hirsch, 2 N. B. R. 1, is apparently against it. In *Markson & Spaulding* v. *Heaney*, 4 N. B. R. 167, DILLON, J., alludes to the point but refrains from giving any opinion upon it.

The bill sets forth that the fraudulent preference obtained by defendant was by means of a judgment recovered by him against the bankrupt before the supreme judicial court of the state, and which was paid within four months of the commencement of the bankruptcy proceedings. Service in the present suit was made of the subpœna on the attorney who acted for the defendant in obtaining this judgment, and it is argued that the respondent having resorted to and availed himself of the courts in Maine to obtain this fraudulent judgment, continues subject to the authority of the courts in this state, including the district court in bankruptcy, and cannot withdraw from the state with the fruits of his judgment, without remaining amenable to the courts in any ulterior proceedings arising from his original suit. The complainant relies on *Marco* v. *Low*, 55 Me. 549, in which it was decided that the supreme court of Maine could, as a court of equity, enjoin the respondent from further prosecuting in that court as a court of law, a suit in favor of the respondent, against the complainant, notwithstanding the respondent may not have resided or personally been within the state since the commencement of the bill.

With that decision I entirely concur, and the principle on which it rests has been repeatedly sustained by the federal courts. In *Freeman* v. *Howe*, 24 How. 460, it is thus stated in the opinion of the court, "the principle is, that a bill filed on the equity side of the court to restrain or regulate judgment or suits at law *in the same court,* and thereby prevent injustice, or an inequitable advantage under mesne or final process is not an original suit, but ancillary and dependent, supplementary merely to the orginial suit out of which it had arisen, and is maintained without reference to the citizenship or residence of the parties."

So STORY, J.. in *Dunlap* v. *Stetson,* 4 Mason, 360, says, " such suits are not original and are properly sustainable, *in that court* which gave the original judgment, and has it completely under its control." This jurisdiction attaches only to the court in which the original suit is or was pending, and the present is the first attempt, so far as the court is advised, in which it was claimed that a citizen of another state, who has recovered in a state court an inequitable judgment, thereby conferred on the federal courts in the district in which the judgment was recovered jurisdiction over him with authority to sustain a bill in equity against him in behalf of the defendant in the original suit, although not found in the district, and afford such redress as equity and good conscience might ordinarily require if the original suit had been instituted in the federal court instead of the state court.

Bill dismissed without costs.—February, 1872.

UNITED STATES DISTRICT COURT—RHODE ISLAND.

An assignee in bankruptcy can proceed against an adverse claimant of property only by action at law or plenary bill in equity; but whether an adverse claimant may not proceed against an assignee by mere petition, *quære?* Rulings in *Barlow* v. *Peckham,* 5 N. B. R. 72, and *in re* Masterson, 4 N. B. R. 180, reconsidered and qualified, and rulings in *Knight* v. *Cheney,* 5 N. B. R. 305, and *Smith* v. *Mason,* 6 N. B. R. 1, and *in re* Evans, Lowell's Dec. 526, commented upon.

FERGUSON et ux v. *PECKHAM, Assignee, et al.*

The petitioners having a valid mortgage upon certain property of a bankrupt of which the assignee held possession, by petition sought to obtain an order from the court that the assignee make sale of simply his right of redemption in said

property. The petition was opposed on various grounds,
and dismissed for reasons assigned; the only point of much ·
interest being that which is presented and treated of in the
concluding portion of the court's opinion, as follows:

KNOWLES, J.—I deem it advisable in this connection to
notice more pointedly than I yet have done one objection
urged by the learned counsel of the respondents. That was,
that the court could not consistently entertain the motion
under consideration, because in *Birtow* v. *Peckham*, 5 N. B.
R. 72, it had ruled, and *in re* Masterson, 4 N. B. R. 180, had
assumed that only by a suit in equity, or by action at law,
can a controversy between an assignee and a claimant of an
adverse interest be brought to the consideration of the court.
This objection, it may be conceded, seems to be well taken,
but I find it unnecessary here to consider its pertinence or validity.   It suffices to say, that the ruling referred to (in October,
eighteen hundred and seventy) was intended and believed to
be in entire conformity with that of justice Clifford, in *Knight*
v. *Cheney*, as orally announced in September, eighteen hundred
and seventy, in a brief communication to counsel and parties,
informing them of his judgment in that case, and of his purpose at a more convenient season to commit to writing and
place on file his opinion *in extenso* upon the questions involved.   As it was not noticed by myself or others, that in
that communication any distinction was recognized between a
petition by an assignee against an adverse claimant, and a
petition by such a claimant against an assignee, the court in
its opinion recognized no distinction.   By suit in equity or
action at law, said the court, expressly or impliedly, and not
by petition, must such parties respectively assert their antagonist rights and claims.   But herein it seems the court
acted under a misapprehension of the scope of the rulings of
justice Clifford, for it appears that in his opinion in *Knight*
v. *Cheney*, 5 B. N. R. 305, as written and published in October,
eighteen hundred and seventy-one, he restricts his reasonings
and language to the case on hand, (that of a petitioning as-

signee against an adverse claimant,) adjudging that by action at law or suit in equity, must an assignee proceed against an adverse claimant, studiously avoiding any expression of his views respecting the right of an adverse claimant to proceed by simple petition against an assignee. Indeed, for aught that is expressed in his opinion as printed, (of implications I here say nothing,) or in the opinion in *Smith* v. *Mason*, 6 N. B. R. 1, (supreme court, December, eighteen hundred and seventy,) their author may hereafter without inconsistency assent to the views of the learned judge of the Massachusetts district, *in re* Evans, Lowell's Dec. 526, (uttered in January, eighteen hundred and seventy-one, but not printed, it is believed, until May, eighteen hundred and seventy-two,) lucidly expressed as follows:

"It is said to have been decided by Mr. Justice Clifford, sitting in the district of Rhode Island, that actions by assignees against persons 'claiming an adverse interest,' should be by regular suits at law or in equity, as the facts may require, and not by summary petitions in the court of bankruptcy. I suppose this decision is to be taken subject to the qualifications of sections six and twenty-five of the statute, the first of which gives power to any persons who choose to submit to the jurisdiction to take the opinion of the district court on a case stated; and the latter gives the court of bankruptcy power to order the sale of property in the actual possession of the assignee, who is to hold the proceeds instead of the property, subject to all lawful claims and liens. And I may add, that on general principles the assignee, who is an officer of the bankrupt court, may be proceeded against by summary petition in respect to any fund in his hands, if the opposing party choose to proceed in that way, though the assignee himself has no right to take similar action against third persons. The decision to which I refer has not been written out; but I take it to be the law, that subject to the exceptions which I have referred to, the assignee must bring his action."

LOWELL, J., it is here seen, adopts and follows the rulings

of justice Clifford, (as did the supreme court in *Smith* v. *Mason,* in December, eighteen hundred and seventy,) restrictive of the rights of an assignee, while in unmistakable terms he accords to an adverse claimant a right of election of remedies, as between the simple petition and summary proceedings on the one hand, and a regular suit at law or in equity on the other.

I add, in conclusion, as due to myself and to litigants in this district, that my rulings in *Barstow* v. *Peckham,* and in other cases, if any, are here retracted so far as in conflict with those of my brother of the Massachusetts district, as above quoted, mine having been made under a misapprehension as to the scope of justice Clifford's decision, rather than as the conclusions of my own judgment as a judicial officer. Under a decision of the supreme court coinciding with that of justice Clifford, I must, of course, continue to hold that an assignee cannot by summary petition prosecute his claims against an adverse claimant; but whether an adverse claimant may or can prosecute his claims against an assignee by such petition, as held by LOWELL, J., is a question upon which I reserve my opinion, until it shall again arise, and shall have been as it never yet has been in my hearing, fully argued by opposing counsel.

To an argument in support of the doctrine that under the provisions of the bankrupt act an adverse claimant is entitled to an election of remedies not accorded to his antagonist assignee, it will be a gratification to listen at any time; as it will also be to learn by what "general principles" affecting the question at issue, the special provisions of that act in regard to the *jurisdiction* in bankruptcy of the federal courts, are to be held to be controlled, limited or qualified.

WINGATE HAYS, for petitioners; JAMES TILLINGHAST and ABRAHAM PAYNE, for respondents.—May 12, 187

UNITED STATES DISTRICT COURT—W. D. WISCONSIN.

Bankrupts made application for their discharge and took the testimony of the assignee, who swore that at the time he took possession of the estate it was worth fourteen thousand dollars, which was more than fifty per cent. of the debts of said bankrupts, as set forth in their schedule.

The evidence further shows that the assignee offered the real estate at public sale, but was unable to obtain a bid upon it for the reason that it was heavily encumbered. and was at that time advertised for sale under a mortgage foreclosure suit. The assignee collected some twelve thousand two hundred dollars. Unsecured claims to amount of fourteen thousand dollars have been proved, of which six thousand five hundred dollars were contracted prior to January first, eighteen hundred and sixty-nine, and seven thousand five hundred dollars subsequent to that date.

On the part of the bankrupts it was claimed that a discharge should be granted from all their debts, for the reason that they had shown that at the time their estate passed into the hands of the assignee, it was worth fifty per cent. of the claims proved

Held, That the word assets must be construed to mean money received by the assignee, and that bankrupts are only entitled to receive a discharge from their debts contracted prior to January first, eighteen hundred and sixtynine.

In re G. & J. J. VAN RIPER.

I, the undersigned register, do hereby certify that in the course of proceedings before me, at the hearing on the petition of said bankrupts for their discharge, the said bankrupts appeared before me, and took and subscribed the oath required by section twenty-nine of the bankrupt act, and that no appearance was entered by any creditor in opposition to the application for discharge. That upon motion of Messrs. Atwell & Tryon, attorneys for the said bankrupts, the assignee of the said bankrupts' estate was sworn and examined before me; he testified that at the time he took possession of the said estate, consisting of real and personal property, it was, in his judgment, worth the sum of fourteen thousand dollars, whether above encumbrances or not, is not stated; this sum is more than fifty per centum of the whole of the debts of the said bankrupts, as set forth by them in their schedules annexed to their petition for adjudication.

From a report heretofore made by the said assignee, it appears that he offered the real estate at public sale, but was unable to obtain a bid therefor, for the reason that it was heavily encumbered by mortgage, and was at the same time advertised for sale under and by virtue of a decree in chancery, in a suit brought to foreclose the equity of redemption in said mortgage ; that at the foreclosure sale, the property was sold for less than the amount due on the mortgage, and that he, the assignee, never received anything for the real estate. In his said deposition the assignee states that he considers the real estate was worth twelve thousand dollars of the above sum of fourteen thousand dollars, at the time he was appointed assignee.

The assignee further reports that he has realized the gross sum of two thousand two hundred and thirteen dollars and fourteen cents, from the sale of personal property, and collection of accounts belonging to the joint estate of the bankrupt's and the sum of fifty dollars from the individual estate of Jacob J. Van Riper ; this is all that he received. He may collect a few hundred dollars more, but this is contingent upon a suit which he has brought to recover certain property which he claims belongs to the estate of the bankrupts.

Unsecured claims amounting to fourteen thousand three hundred and eighty-two dollars and thirty-three cents, have been proved and allowed against the joint estate of said bankrupts, (upon all of which they are liable as principal debtors,) and a dividend of ten per cent. has been declared and paid thereon. Of said claims, six thousand seven hundred and thirty-nine dollars and sixty-two cents were contracted prior to January first, eighteen hundred and sixty-nine, and the sum of seven thousand six hundred and forty-two dollars and seventy-one cents subsequent to that date. A claim of four hundred and seventy dollars and forty-four cents has also been proved and allowed against the individual estate of Jacob J. Van Riper. No dividend has been declared on this claim.

The written assent of creditors, contemplated by the provisions of section thirty-three of the bankrupt act, has never been filed by the bankrupts.

The said bankrupts, by their said attorneys, claimed that

they were entitled to a full discharge from *all* their debts, for the reason that by the said deposition of the said assignee, it is shown that at the time their estate or "assets" passed into the hands of the assignee, the said estate or "assets" (or the value thereof) were "equal *to*" fifty per centum of the claims subsequently proved, upon which they were liable as principal debtors, and which claims or debts were contracted subsequent to the first day of January, eighteen hundred and sixty-nine; that if upon an appraisal of the estate or "assets," their value is found to be "equal to" fifty per centum of debts proved, then, by virtue of the amendments of July twenty-seventh, eighteen hundred and sixty-eight, and July fourteenth, eighteen hundred and seventy, of section thirty-three of the bankrupt act, whereby, among other changes, the words "equal to" were substituted for the word "pay" contained in the original act, the court should grant a full discharge without requiring the assent of a majority of creditors to be filed. The determination of this point rests entirely upon the construction to be placed on the word "assets," as used in s id section thirty-three; whether it is to be taken in its most comprehensive sense, meaning the entire estate and effects, (or the appraised value thereof,) as they come to the hands of the assignee, or the proceeds or money received upon a sale of such estate and effects. If, as claimed by the bankrupts, it means the whole estate and effects of whatsoever nature, before being reduced to money, then I think the position assumed by them is correct, and that a full discharge should be granted. Their "assets" in such case were "equal to" fifty per centum of claims proved, and the bankrupts have complied with the requirements of section thirty-three as amended. But it seems to me that their definition of the word "assets" is one that cannot be maintained. What sum the estate or "assets" may be appraised at, is by no means a true criterion of their value, or rather what they are "equal to;" there may be as many differing opinions as to the value of a given piece of property, as the number of individuals whose judgment is sought. The true test as to value, (when that value is to be used to pay creditors,) is the amount the property will bring upon a sale by the assignee, in accordance with the requirements of the law and general orders; what it produces in money with which to pay dividends to creditors and costs of proceedings, money being the only thing with which such payments can be made.

The supreme court of the United States have placed an interpretation upon the word "assets," as used in reference to the granting of a discharge to bankrupts, which shows clearly that they hold the meaning to be money received. Section twenty-nine provides that if "*no assets*" have come to the hands of the assignee, the bankrupt may apply for a discharge, &c. Form number thirty-five, of forms promulgated by the supreme court, is headed "assignee's return where there are no assets," and consists of a certificate by the assignee that "he has neither received nor paid any *moneys* on account of the estate." In the following cases the same meaning has been applied to the term "no assets." *In re* Hughes, 1 N. B. R. 9; *in re* Dodge, 1 N. B. R. 115; *in re* Solis, 3 N. B. R. 186. In the cases cited, the assignees had in their possession certain notes, accounts and claims against others in favor of the bankrupts, upon which *no money* had been received; although it was thought something would eventually be realized therefrom, it was held that there were *no assets* in the hands of the assignee, at the time of the application for discharge. Taking this to be the true interpretation, it therefore follows that at the time the assignee in the case now presented testified that the "assets" were worth fourteen thousand dollars, he would, had the bankrupts then applied for a discharge, (assuming sufficient time had elapsed therefor,) have been required to make "assignee's return where there are no assets," *i. e.*, that he had neither received (assets) nor paid any money, (assets,) &c., &c., notwithstanding the fact that he held property which in his judgment was worth the sum of fourteen thousand dollars. As shown by the report of the assignee, this property when sold brought the sum of two thousand two hundred and thirty-two dollars and fourteen cents, being considerably less than fifty per centum of claims proved.

In re Freiderick, 3 N. B. R. 117, an application was made for the appointment of appraisers to ascertain the value of "assets" of the bankrupt, it being claimed by him that the value of said "assets" or estate, was "equal to" fifty per centum of provable claims. The application was denied by the court, and it was held that "the plain and obvious meaning of 'assets' in this section (thirty-three) was the *proceeds* of the debtor's property which are applicable to the payment of his debts." And further, that since the amendment, the section is to be construed as if it read, "the *proceeds* of the bankrupt's property in the hands of the assignee, and subject to be divided among his creditors, must be equal to fifty per centum," &c.

This same construction was repeated *in re* Graham, 5 N. B. R. 155. BLATCHFORD, J., *in re* Webb *v.* Taylor, 3 N. B. R. 177, concurs in the decision *in re* Freiderick.

In re Kahley, 6 N. B. R. 189, a *sum* exceeding fifty per centum of debts proven, was received by the assignee from bankrupt's estate, but after payment of costs and expenses of proceedings in bankruptcy, the dividend to creditors was not "equal to" fifty per centum of such debts. Discharge was granted to the bankrupt, it being held that the question of discharge should be governed by the gross amount or sum received by the assignee, (when equal to fifty per centum of claims proven,) and not by the percentage of dividend to creditors. While the court dissents from the views expressed *in re* Freiderick, the decision certainly does not go to the length claimed by the bankrupts *in re* Van Riper.

It is held that by the amendment of section thirty-three, the word "assets" should now receive its ordinary signification, which is as comprehensive as "estate" or "effects;" that the right to a discharge should be based upon the "gross value" of the bankrupts' "assets." I understand the words "gross *value*" as here used, to signify the gross amount or sum of *money* received upon a sale of the bankrupt's estate and effects, for upon page one hundred and ninety-two, the

In re Van Riper.

judge says, "The clear intention of the amendment, to my mind, was to relieve the bankrupt of the costs and expenses of the proceedings. If his estate *realized a sum* equal to fifty per centum of claims proven, he should be discharged, whether it was paid to creditors or absorbed by costs and expenses." And on page one hundred and ninety-three, "in section forty-seven, it is stated "that if sufficient "*assets*" for the payment of fees," &c., showing that it (the word asset) may be used, and is used as meaning the estate, applicable alike to the payment of debts and expenses." Unless *money* can be realized from the "estate," "effects" or "assets," then there is nothing belonging to the bankrupts' estate, whether called estate or assets, applicable to the payment of fees. I do not understand the decision *in re* Kahley, to go further than to assert the rule that the question of discharge shall be determined by the gross amount of *money* realized, without regard to the disposition that may be made of such amount.

Upon a careful examination of the whole question, and of the proceedings in the above bankruptcy, I am led to the conclusion that the said bankrupts, George Van Riper and Jacob J. Van Riper, are *not* entitled to a discharge from *all* their debts, and therefore certify and report, that they have in all things conformed to their duty under the bankrupt act, respecting their debts contracted prior to the first day of January, A. D., eighteen hundred and sixty-nine, and that they are entitled, under the provisions of said act, to receive a discharge from their debts contracted prior to said first day of January, and which existed on the sixth day of June, A. D., eighteen hundred and seventy. *In re* Seay, 4 N. B. R. 82.

J. DAVIDSON BURNS, *Register.*

WITHEY, J.—The rulings of the register are approved. I fully concur in the opinions expressed, and direct decrees to be entered in conformity thereto.

UNITED STATES SUPREME COURT—UTAH TERRITORY.

When creditors have proved their claims under a voluntary petition in bankruptcy they thereby waive the right to insist on going back of this and proceeding under an involuntary petition. Motion to dismiss previous petition filed against bankrupts granted.

A creditor holding collaterals is entitled to have his claim referred to the register for investigation, and the assignee is not justified in rejecting it until proofs have been taken and the matter fully inquired into.

When the bankrupts made an agreement with a party to pay him for certain services, the benefits of which services would accrue to the other creditors, such claim is entitled to preference.

In re J. F. NOUNNAN & CO.

On the twenty-third of April, eighteen hundred and sixty-nine, H. P. Kimball, creditor of Joseph F. Nounnan & Co., filed a petition, praying an adjudication in involuntary bankruptcy against them. On the third of May, an order was issued by the court, requiring the bankrupts to show cause, etc. Also, on the eleventh of May following, David Kimball filed his petition against the firm, upon which like proceedings were had as those under the first petition, and the parties rested without further or other proceedings therein. On the ninth day of June, eighteen hundred and seventy, the said bankrupts, under the firm name of Joseph F. Nounnan & Co., filed in court their voluntary petition to be adjudged bankrupts, but no schedules accompanied the voluntary petition; the record simply states that voluntary petition was filed, but makes no mention of any schedules therewith. The report of the register states that there is, among the papers, certain papers, marked schedules A, B, C, D, E, F; that said paper A is incomplete in this, that forms four and five are wanting, and that they are not signed by the petitioners, and that there is no oath attached thereto as prescribed by law; that schedule B is incomplete in this, that forms one, two, four, five and six are wanting, and that form three is not signed, and there is no oath attached to the same as prescribed by law; that schedule C is incomplete in this, that forms one, two and five are wanting, and there is no signature or oath attached to the other forms as prescribed by law; that schedules C and D of Joseph F. Nounnan are incomplete in this, forms three, four and six wanting, not signed, no oath attached and no duplicate of the same on file as prescribed by law. Schedule E, of Joseph M. Orr, is incomplete in this, forms one, two, three and five are wanting, and they are not signed, and no oath attached thereto. Schedule F, of Joseph M. Orr is incomplete in this, forms three and four are wanting and not signed, and no oath attached, and no duplicate, and none of the aforesaid schedules have been filed as required by law.

An order of reference and a warrant to the messenger was issued by the court. On the tenth day of June, eighteen hundred and seventy, the register issued the warrants on the personal appearance of the bankrupts. On the twenty-second of June, the creditors met for the proof of debts and the choice of an assignee, and they elected Benjamin G. Reybold as assignee, who, upon notice, filed his bond and accepted the trust.

At the time of the filing the first petition, the assets of the bankrupts rested upon a claim or debt against the Union Pacific Railroad Co., then unsettled, and it appears that Nounnan & Co., on July seventeenth, eighteen hundred and sixty-nine, prior to the commencement of proceedings in bankruptcy under the voluntary petition of themselves, and about three months after the commencement of proceedings on the petition of creditors against them, made a certain contract with Charles L. Stevenson, a surveyor, to perform certain services, and to make out and deliver them his professional opinion of the value of certain work therein specified, to be used in evidence in the suit then pending against the railroad company, which said agreement is as follows

"Articles of agreement made and entered into this seventeenth day of July, eighteen hundred and sixty-nine, by and between C. L. Stevenson, of Corinne, Utah, party of the first part, and Joseph F. Nounnan and J. M. Orr, parties doing business under the name and style of Joseph F. Nounnan & Co., of Salt Lake City, party of the second part, witnesseth:

"That whereas the said party of the first part, in capacity of a civil engineer, has this day bound himself to accompany a party of men selected by the said second party, for the purpose of measuring and re-classing the work the said second party performed last year, under a certain contract made with S. B. Reed, superintendent and engineer of construction of the Union Pacific Railroad Co., dated at Salt Lake City, May twentieth, eighteen hundred and sixty-eight, and then there, as an engineer and expert in such matters, to give his professional opinion of the value of the work performed by the said second party under their said contract with S. B. Reed, superintendent and engineer, as aforesaid;

"Now, therefore, this agreement witnesseth : That for and in consideration of the foregoing things to be done and performed by the first party, the said second party hereby agrees to pay to the said first party one hundred dollars cash, the receipt whereof is hereby acknowledged, and the further sum of twenty-five hundred dollars on the recovery of their suit against the Union Pacific Railroad Co. It is further mutually agreed by and between the parties hereto, that all expenses incurred by the said first party in carrying out this agreement, either now or at any future period during the pending of said suit against the said Union Pacific Railroad Co., shall be paid by said second party.

In witness whereof we have hereunto affixed our names and seals the day and year above written.

"C. L. STEVENSON.
" Witness   " J. F. NOUNNAN & Co."
"THOS. H. BATES.
" J. H. NOUNNAN.
"THOS. HUBBARD."   [Stamp, 10 cts.]

Stevenson made the surveys and estimates, and wrote up his opinion in a certain book, produced in evidence, but he neglected to deliver the opinion or report to the firm, and kept it in his own possession to the time his evidence was taken in support of this application, though prior to the disposal of the above suit he permitted the firm to examine the book for the purpose of the suit. The time spent by Stevenson under the agreement was from the twenty-first of July to the twentieth of August following. Stevenson also claimed, under what he alleges was a verbal agreement between Nounnan & Co. and himself, that they, on condition that he remained in Salt Lake City until he gave in his testimony in regard to the controversy with the railroad company, would pay his and his family's expenses during such detention, under which agreement he alleges he remained in Salt Lake City from August first, eighteen hundred and sixty-nine, to June first, eighteen hundred and seventy, at an expense on that account of one thousand nine hundred dollars, less three hundred and twelve dollars, for which he puts in another claim of extra service, all of which he claimed should be paid in full and in preference to other creditors. These allegations rested on his sole testimony, whilst Nounnan & Co. state they never made any verbal agreement with him, and that their firm is not indebted to Stevenson on any matter excepting on the written agreement.

Also Mr. Thomas J. Almy, a creditor, who has received collateral security for his claim, petitioned that he be substituted in place of the former petitioners, H. P. Kimball and D. Kimball, or that Joseph F. Nounnan & Co. be declared involuntary bankrupts on the first petitions instead of on his own voluntary petition, on the ground of irregularity in the proceedings.

Certain motions herein having been argued before associate justices Hawley and Strickland, and they having disagreed in their conclusions, the matter came up for re-argument before the full bench, on January fourth, eighteen hundred and seventy-one. It was shown to the court that David P. Kimball and Heber P. Kimball filed their petition April twenty-third, eighteen hundred and sixty-nine, and their amended petition May eleventh, eighteen hundred and sixty-nine, praying that Joseph F. Nounnan & Co., (the above named Nounnan and Orr,) be declared bankrupts, &c.; that afterwards, before adjudication, by agreement with the Kimballs and by the acquiescence of the other creditors of Joseph F. Nounnan & Co., they prosecuted a claim against the Union Pacific Railroad Co.; that they employed, by agreement in writing, Stevenson, an engineer, to make certain surveys and measurements of portions of the Union Pacific Railroad involved in the litigation; that Joseph F. Nounnan & Co. recovered from the railroad company the sum of ninety-five thousand dollars; that Joseph F. Nounnan & Co. then filed their own petition in bankruptcy, June ninth, eighteen hundred and seventy; *that the Kimballs and all other creditors* taking no further steps under the first two petitions, or either of them, came in and proved their claims under the third or voluntary petition; that an assignee was chosen under the last named petition; that Joseph F. Nounnan & Co. paid over to the assignee for the benefit of the creditors, the ninety-five thousand dollars recovered from the railroad company, and that *that* sum was nearly or quite all the assets of the bankrupts.

The argument came up on the following motions:

1. On the part of Stevenson, that he be allowed the stipulated price for his services, and that his demand be preferred.

2. On the part of the Kimballs, that their petitions of April twenty-third, and May eleventh, eighteen hundred and sixty-nine, be dismissed.

3. On the part of Thomas J. Almy, a creditor, that he be substituted in the place and stead of the Kimballs, as petitioning creditor, &c.; or that a hearing be had upon the first and second petitions, &c.; or that the three petitions be combined and a hearing had, &c.

4. On the part of the assignee, that Almy's claim be rejected on the ground that Almy had received certain collateral security therefor, which he had sold.

MR. KIRKPATRICK for Stevenson; MR. MARSHALL for the Kimballs; MR. ALMY in person; MR. MAXWELL and MR. ROBERTSON for the assignee.

McKEAN, C. J.—In very important particulars this case differs from any reported case, and the court, in deciding the questions raised, must therefore make, rather than follow precedents. I have reached the following conclusions:

First. All the creditors having proved their claims, and other proceedings having been taken under the third or voluntary petition, filed June ninth, eighteen hundred and seventy, the creditors thereby waived the right now to insist on going back and proceeding under the first two petitions, or either of them. The petition of Thomas J. Almy should therefore be denied.

Second. The motion to dismiss the petitions of the Kimballs, filed April twenty-third and May eleventh, eighteen hundred and sixty-nine, should be granted.

Third. The petition of the assignee that Almy's claim be rejected, cannot be allowed. But that claim should be referred to the register to examine and report thereon.

Fourth. The bankrupts and the creditors have had, or are to have, the full benefit of Stevenson's services, and he should be held to have substantially complied with the terms of his contract.

Fifth. The nature of Stevenson's services and the circumstances under which they were rendered, entitle him to be placed among the preferred creditors.

Sixth. The court is not necessarilly bound by contract between Stevenson and Joseph F. Nounnan & Co., as to the amount of Stevenson's compensation—other creditors are interested in that question. But taking all the proofs into consideration, Stevenson should be allowed the amount stipulated in the written contract, less the amount already paid, and his claim to such amount should be preferred.

The subsequent opinion and order of court of McKean, C. J., concurred in by Strickland, J., delivered May twelfth, eighteen hundred and seventy-one, is as follows:

Present.—McKean, C. J. and Strickland, J.

On reading and filing affidavits and other papers herein, and after listening to the arguments of counsel for all parties in interest, it is ordered: First. That the sum of eight thousand dollars be reserved by the assignee to await the further action of the court upon the claim of Thomas J. Almy

SECOND. That the said claim of Thomas J. Almy be again referred to the register to further examine into and report thereon.

THIRD. That the claim of the First National Bank of Utah be made preferred, and paid as follows, to wit: The sum of one thousand five hundred dollars, with interest thereon from the nineteenth day of April, eighteen hundred and seventy, at ten per centum per annum; and the further sum of two thousand five hundred dollars, with interest thereon from the first day of July, eighteen hundred and seventy, at two per centum per month.

FOURTH. That the claims of Feramorz Little be made preferred claims, and paid as follows, to wit: The sum of one thousand one hundred and sixty-four dollars, with interest thereon from the twenty-sixth day of January, eighteen hundred and seventy, at two per centum per month, and the further sum of four hundred and ten dollars and fifty cents, without interest.

FIFTH. That the claims of John W. Kerr for money advances, for interest thereon for services in aid of the arbitration between the bankrupt and the Union Pacific Railroad Company, be allowed to the amount of six thousand one hundred dollars only, and that the same be preferred.

SIXTH. That the claim of A. Blair, arbitrator, for one thousand six hundred and sixty dollars be allowed and preferred.

SEVENTH. That the claim of Thomas H. Bates be allowed to the amount of five thousand dollars only, and that the same be preferred.

EIGHTH. That the claim of Walker Brothers for three thousand four hundred and ten dollars be allowed and preferred.

NINTH. That the claim of Kahn Brothers, for five hundred and ninety-eight dollars be allowed and preferred.

TENTH. The motion to set aside the election of assignee is overruled.

Justice Hawley was not present, and did not participate in the deliberations of the court at this sitting.

UNITED STATES DISTRICT COURT—KENTUCKY.

In proceedings in bankruptcy commenced after January first, eighteen hundred and sixty-nine, where it does not appear either that the bankrupt's assets are equal to fifty per cent. of the claims proved against him on which he is liable as principal debtor, or that the requisite number of his creditors have assented to his discharge, a discharge from debts contracted prior to January first, eighteen hundred and sixty-nine, only, will be granted although the bankrupt shows that his assets equal fifty per cent. of the claims proved against his estate that were contracted subsequent to January first, eighteen hundred and sixty-nine.

In re J. L. SHOWER.

BALLARD, J.—On the twelfth day of October, eighteen hundred and seventy, John L. Shower filed his petition to be adjudged a bankrupt. He now applies to be discharged from all debts, from those which were contracted on or after January first, eighteen hundred and sixty-nine, as well as from those contracted prior to that date.

In support of this application he shows assets equal to fifty per centum of such claims proved against his estate as were contracted on or after the first of January, eighteen hundred and sixty-nine, but fails to show that his assets are equal to fifty per centum of *all* the claims proved against his estate on which he is liable as principal debtor.

It is indisputable that the application must be granted so far as it seeks a discharge from the debts contracted prior to January first, eighteen hundred and sixty-nine, but I do not agree with the register that upon the facts shown, any discharge can be granted from the debts contracted on or after that date. The only provisions of the statute which relate to the subject are to be found in the second clause of the thirty-third section of the act of March second, eighteen hundred and sixty-seven, (14 Stat. at Large,) in the amendment of July twenty-seventh, eighteen hundred and sixty-eight, (15 Stat. at Large, 227) and in the further amendment of July fourteenth, eighteen hundred and seventy. (16 Stat. at Large, 276.)

Let us now bring the provisions of these several statutes

together, and after learning the meaning of the original act, as amended by the act of July, eighteen hundred and sixty-eight, endeavor to ascertain how this meaning is modified by the act of July, eighteen hundred and seventy. The second clause of the thirty-third section of the act of March second, eighteen hundred and sixty-seven, provides, "And in all proceedings in bankruptcy commenced after one year from the time this act shall go into operation, no discharge shall be granted to a debtor whose assets do not pay more than fifty per centum of the claims against his estate, unless the assent in writing of a majority in number and value of his creditors who have proved their claims is filed in the case at or before the time of application for a discharge."

I believe it has been universally held, that this provision of the act went into operation on the first day of June, eighteen hundred and sixty-seven. The act of July twenty-seventh, eighteen hundred and sixty-eight, provides that said clause be so amended as to read as follows: " In all proceedings of bankruptcy commenced after the first of January, eighteen hundred and sixty-nine, no discharge shall be granted to a debtor whose assets shall not be equal to fifty per centum of the claims proved against his estate, upon which he shall be liable as principal debtor, unless the assent in writing of a majority in number and value of his creditors to whom he shall have become liable as principal debtor, and who shall have proved their claims, be filed in the case, at or before the time of the hearing of the application for a discharge."

This amendment effected several changes.

FIRST. Under the original act, the bankrupt could not obtain a discharge upon showing simply that he had conformed to his duty, unless the proceedings by or against him were commenced on or before the first day of June, eighteen hundred and sixty-eight. By the amendment he may obtain his discharge upon showing such conformity, if the proceedings were commenced on or before the first of January, eighteen hundred and sixty-nine.

SECOND. Under the old law, in proceedings commenced after the first of June, eighteen hundred and sixty-eight, the bankrupt could obtain no discharge, unless his assets paid fifty per centum of all claims against his estate, whether owing by him as principal debtor or otherwise; by the amendment, in proceedings commenced after the first of January, eighteen hundred and sixty-nine, he is entitled to his discharge, if his assets are equal to fifty per centum of the claims proved, upon which he is liable as principal debtor.

THIRD. By the original act, if the bankrupt, in asking for a discharge, relied upon the assent of his creditors, he was obliged to file such assent in the case at or before the application for discharge; by the amendment, the assent may be filed at or before the time of the hearing of the application.

Under the original act of March second, eighteen hundred and sixty-seven, and the amendment of July twenty-eighth, eighteen hundred and sixty-eight, the bankrupt was entitled to a discharge from his debts, no matter when the debts were contracted, but he was not entitled to such discharge unless proceedings were commenced within a given time. His right to a discharge did not depend upon the date of his debts, but upon the date of the proceedings. If the proceedings were commenced before the given date, he was either entitled to a discharge from all his debts, (except those expressly excepted,) or he was not entitled to a discharge from any. If the proceedings were commenced by or against him after the first of January, eighteen hundred and sixty-nine, he could be discharged from no debts, no matter when contracted, unless his assets were equal to fifty per centum of the claims proved against him, upon which he was liable as principal debtor, or unless the assent in writing of a majority in number and value of his creditors, to whom he was liable as principal, and who had proved their claims, was filed in the case at or before the hearing of the application.

We come now to consider the amendment of the fourteenth of July, eighteen hundred and seventy, (16 Stat. at Large, 276.) That amendment provides, "That the provisions of the second clause of the thirty-third section, as amended by the first section of an act in amendment thereof, approved July twenty-seventh, eighteen hundred and sixty-eight, shall not apply to those debts from which the bankrupt seeks a dis- charge, which were contracted prior to January first, eighteen hundred and sixty-nine." We have just seen that under the provisions of the second clause of the thirty-third section, as amended by the act of July twenty-seventh, eighteen hundred and sixty-eight, the bankrupt could not, in proceedings com- menced after January first, eighteen hundred and sixty-nine, if he did not rely on the assent of creditors, obtain a dis- charge from any of his debts, unless his assets were equal to fifty per centum of the claims proved against him, upon which he was liable as principal. This amendment declares that the provisions of said second clause shall not apply to debts from which the bankrupt seeks a discharge, which were con- tracted prior to January first, eighteen hundred and sixty- nine, but it leaves those provisions to apply in full force to debts from which he seeks a discharge, which were contracted after that time. The effect, then, of this last amendment is, that in proceedings commenced after January first, eighteen hundred and sixty-nine, the bankrupt will, upon showing only general conformity, be discharged from all debts contracted prior to January first, eighteen hundred and sixty-nine, but will not be discharged from any contracted on or after that time, without showing either that his assets are equal to fifty per centum of the claims proved against his estate, upon which he shall be liable as principal, or that his creditors have assented.

The demand that the assets shall equal fifty per centum of the claims proved makes no reference to the time when the claims were contract d. There is nothing whatever in the 'language of the demand to distinguish between claims con- tracted before and claims contracted after the first of Jan- uary, eighteen hundred and sixty-nine. One class is as prov- able against the estate of the bankrupt as the other, and therefore when the statute says that the bankrupt shall not

be discharged from his debts contracted on or after the first
of January, eighteen hundred and sixty-nine, unless his
assets shall be equal to fifty per centum of the claims proved
against his estate, it is impossible to reject in the computation
the claims proved which were contracted before the first of
January, eighteen hundred and sixty-nine.

The assent must be equal to fifty per centum of all the
claims proved on which the bankrupt is liable as principal,
including as well those contracted prior to January, eighteen
hundred and sixty-nine as those contracted afterwards.
Under the act of eighteen hundred and sixty-eight, the bankrupt in proceedings commenced after January first, eighteen
hundred and sixty-nine, could not be discharged from any of
his debts, no matter when contracted, unless his assets bore
a given relation to the claims proved, upon which he was liable as principal, or unless he exhibited the assent of his creditors.   Under the act of eighteen hundred and seventy, he
will be discharged from all debts contracted before the first
of January, eighteen hundred and sixty-nine, though he has
no assets, and though he obtain no assent of creditors. but he
cannot be discharged from any debt contracted since, unless
he comply with the demands of the act of eighteen hundred
and sixty-eight—that is, he must, I repeat, either show that
his assets are equal to fifty per centum of all claims proved
on which he is liable as principal, or he must exhibit the
assent of creditors.   Let me, if possible, make this matter
still plainer.   The universal rule of construction is to read
every statute which has been amended, as if the amendments
were incorporated with the original act.   Now if we incorporate into the second clause of the thirty-third section of
the bankruptcy act of March second, eighteen hundred and
sixty-seven, the provisions contained in the amendatory act
of July twenty-seventh, eighteen hundred and sixty-eight, and
of July fourteenth, eighteen hundred and seventy, it will read
as follows :   " In all proceedings in bankruptcy commenced
after the first of January, eighteen hundred and sixty-nine,
no discharge shall be granted to a debtor from debts con-

tracted on or after the first of January, eighteen hundred and sixty-nine, whose assets shall not equal fifty per centum of the claims proved against his estate, upon which he shall be liable as principal debtor, unless the assent in writing of a majority in number and value of his creditors, to whom he shall have become liable as principal debtor, and who have proved their claims, be filed in the case, at or before the time of hearing of the application for discharge."

If this be the reading of the statute, and that it is seems to me to be undeniable, there seems to be no ground for the claim of the bankrupt. It seems to be as plain as language can be that he cannot be discharged from debts contracted since, though he is entitled to be discharged from the debts contracted prior to January first, eighteen hundred and sixty-nine, because his proceedings were commenced after that time and his assets are not equal to fifty per centum of claims proved against his estate on which he is liable as principal debtor, and there is no pretense that any of his creditors have assented to his discharge. Whether or not a bankrupt will be discharged from debts contracted after January first, eighteen hundred and sixty-nine, upon filing the assent of creditors whose debts were contracted before that time and which have been proved, if they constitute all of the debts proven or a majority in number and value, is a question not directly presented in this case. The conclusion at which I have arrived on the question before me seems to furnish a ready answer; but it is not proper that it should be either answered or discussed until it arises.

I have heretofore prescribed four forms of discharge : one applicable to cases in which the proceedings were commenced prior to January first, eighteen hundred and sixty-nine ; a second, to cases commenced after that date, in which cases it does not appear either that the assets are equal to fifty per centum of the claims proved, &c., or that the creditors have assented ; a third, to cases commenced after that date in which it does appear that the assets equal fifty per centum, &c., and a fourth, to cases commenced after that date in which the assent of creditors is filed. In this case, as the proceedings were commenced after the first of January, eighteen hundred and sixty-nine, and as it does not appear either that his assets are equal to fifty per centum of the claims proved against his estate on which he is liable as principal debtor, or that any of his creditors have assented to his discharge, a discharge of the second class will be granted.

Accordingly, it is considered that, whereas John L. Shower has been duly adjudicated a bankrupt, under the act of congress establishing a uniform system of bankruptcy throughout the United States, and appears to have conformed to all the requirements of law in that behalf,

It is therefore ordered by the court, that said John L. Shower be forever discharged from all debts and claims which by said act are made provable against his estate, and which existed on the twelfth day of October, eighteen hundred and seventy, on which day the petition for adjudication was filed by him, excepting such debts as were contracted on or after the first day of January, eighteen hundred and sixty-nine, and such, if any, as are excepted from the operation of a discharge in bankruptcy.

[END OF VOLUME VI.]

GENERAL ORDERS IN BANKRUPTCY.

In pursuance of the tenth section of the act entitled "An act to establish a uniform system of bankruptcy throughout the United States," approved March second, eighteen hundred and sixty-seven, the justices of the supreme court of the United States have framed the following general orders, which shall constitute the rules of practice and procedure in bankruptcy in the district courts of the United States.

DECEMBER TERM, 1871.

The general orders in bankruptcy, heretofore established by this court, are so amended as to read as follows:

I.

DUTIES OF CLERKS OF DISTRICT COURTS.

The clerks of the several district courts shall enter upon each petition in bankruptcy the day and the hour of the day upon which the same shall be filed; and shall also make a similar note upon every subsequent paper filed with them, except such papers as have been filed before the register, and so endorsed by him; and the papers in each case shall be kept in a file by themselves. No paper shall be taken from the files for any purpose except by order of the court. Every paper shall have endorsed upon it a brief statement of its character. The clerks shall keep a docket, in which the cases shall be entered and numbered in the order in which they are commenced; and the number of each case shall be endorsed on every paper. The docket shall be so arranged that a brief memorandum of every proceeding in each case shall be entered therein, in a manner convenient for reference, and shall at all times be open for public inspection. The clerks shall also keep separate minute-books for the record of proceedings in bankruptcy, in which shall be entered a minute of all the proceedings in each case, either of the court or of a register of the court, under their respective dates.

II.

PROCESS.

All process, summons and subpœnas shall issue out of the court under the seal thereof, and be tested by the clerk; and blanks, with the signature of the clerk and seal of the court, may, upon application, be furnished to the registers.

III.

APPEARANCE.

Proceedings in bankruptcy may be conducted by the bankrupt in person in his own behalf, or by a petitioning or opposing creditor; but a creditor will only be allowed to manage before the court his individual interest. Either party may appear and conduct the proceedings by attorney who shall be an attorney or counselor atuhorised to practice in the circuit or district court. The name of the attorney or counselor, with his place of residence and business, shall be entered upon the docket, with the date of the entry. All papers or proceedings offered by an attorney to be filed, shall be endorsed as above required; and orders granted on motion shall containthe name of the party or attorney making the motion. Notices and orders which are not, by the act or by these rules, required to be served on the party personally, may be served upon his attorney.

IV.

COMMENCEMENT OF PROCEEDINGS.

Upon the filing of a petition in case of voluntary bankruptcy, or as soon as any adjudication of bankruptcy is made upon a petition filed in case of involuntary bankruptcy, the petition shall be referred to one of the registers in such manner as the district court shall direct, and the petitioner shall furnish the register with a copy of the papers in the case, and thereafter all the proceedings required by the act shall be had before him, except such as are required by the act to be had in the district court, or by special order of the district judge, unless some other register is directed to act in the case.

The order designating the register to act upon any petition shall name a day upon which the bankrupt shall attend before the register, from which date he shall be subject to the orders of the court in all matters relating to his bankruptcy, and may receive from the register a protection against arrest, to continue until the final adjudication on his application for a discharge, unless suspended or vacated by order of the court.

A copy of the order shall forthwith be sent by mail to the register, or be delivered to him personally, by the clerk or other officer of the court.

V.

REGISTERS.

The time when and the place where the registers shall act upon the matters arising under the several cases referred to them, shall be fixed by special order of the district court, or by the register acting under the authority of a general order, in each case, made by the district court; and at such times and places the registers may perform the acts which they are empowered to do by the act, and conduct proceedings in relation to the following matters, when uncontested, viz. : making adjudication of bankruptcy on petition of the debtor; directing, unless otherwise ordered by the court, the newspapers in which the notice shall be published by the messenger ; administering oaths ; receiving the surrender of a bankrupt ; granting protection thereon ; giving requisite direction for notices, advertisements and other ministerial proceedings ; taking proofs of claims ; ordering payment of rates and taxes, and salary or wages of persons in the employment of the assignee ; ordering amendments, or inspection, or copies, or extracts of any proceedings ; taking accounts of proceeds of securities held by any creditor ; taking evidence concerning expenses and charges against the bankrupt's estate ; auditing and passing accounts of assignees ; proceedings for the declaration and payment of dividends, and taxing costs in any of the proceedings, all of which shall be subject to the control of the court.

VI.

DISPATCH OF BUSINESS.

Every register, in performing the duties required of him under the act, and by these orders, or by orders of the district court, shall use all reasonable dispatch, and shall not adjourn the business but for good cause shown. Six hours' session shall constitute a day's sitting if the business requires ; and when there is time to complete the proceedings in progress within the day, the party obtaining any adjournment or postponement thereof may be charged, if the court think proper, with all the costs incurred in consequence of the delay.

VII.

EXAMINATION AND FILING OF PAPERS.

It shall be the duty of the register to examine the bankrupt's petition and schedules filed therewith, and to certify whether the same are correct in form; or, if deficient, in what respect they are so; and the court may allow amendments to be made in the petition and schedules upon the application of the petitioner, upon proper cause shown, at any time prior to the discharge of the bankrupt. The register shall endorse upon each paper filed with him the time of filing, and at the close of the last examination of the bankrupt, the register having charge of the case shall file all the papers relating thereto in the office of the clerk of the district court, and these papers, together with those on file in the clerk's office, and the entries in the minute-book, shall constitute the record in each case; and the clerk shall cause the papers in each case to be bound together.

VIII.

ORDERS BY THE REGISTER.

Whenever an order is made by a register in any proceeding in which notice is given to either party before the order can be made, the fact that the notice was given, and the substance of the evidence of the manner in which it was given, shall be recited in the preamble to the order, and the fact also stated that no adverse interest was represented at the time and place appointed for the hearing of the matter upon such notice; and whenever an order is made where adverse interests are represented before the register, the fact shall be stated that the opposing parties consented thereto, or that the adverse interest represented made no opposition to the granting of such order.

IX.

NOTIFICATION TO ASSIGNEE OF HIS APPOINTMENT.

It shall be the duty of the register, immediately upon the appointment of an assignee, as prescribed in sections twelve and thirteen of the act, (should he not be present at such meeting,) to notify him, by personal or mail service, of his appointment; and in such notification the assignee so appointed shall be required to give notice forthwith to the register of his acceptance or rejection of the trust.

X.

TESTIMONY, HOW TAKEN.

The examination of witnesses before a register in bankruptcy may be conducted by the party in person or by his counsel or attorney, and the witnesses shall be subject to examination and cross-examination, which shall be had in conformity with the mode now adopted in courts of law. The depositions upon such examination shall be taken down in writing by the register in the form of narrative, unless he determines that the examination shall be by question and answer in special instances, and when completed shall be read over to the witness and signed by him in the presence of the register. Any question or questions which may be objected to shall be noted by the register upon the deposition, but he shall not have power to decide on the competency, materiality or relevancy of the question; and the court shall have power to deal with the costs of incompetent, immaterial or irrelevant depositions, or parts of them, as may be just. In case of refusal of a witness to attend, or to testify before a register, the same proceedings may be had as are now authorised with respect to witnesses to be produced on examination before an examiner of any of the courts of the United States on written interrogatories.

XI.

MINUTES BEFORE REGISTER, FILING, ETC.

A memorandum made of each act performed by a register shall be in suitable form, to be entered upon the minute-book of the court, and shall be forwarded to the clerk of the court not later than by mail the next day after the act has been performed. Whenever an issue is raised before the register in any proceedings, either of fact or law, he shall cause the same to be stated in writing in the manner required by the fourth and sixth sections of the act, and certify the same forthwith to the district judge for his decision. The pendency of the issue undecided before a judge shall not necessarily suspend or delay other proceedings before the register or court in the case.

XII.

ACCOUNTS FOR SERVICES OF REGISTER AND MARSHAL.

Every register shall keep an accurate account of his traveling and incidental expenses, and those of any clerk or other officer attending him in the performance of his duties in any case or number of cases which may be referred to him; and shall make return of the same under oath, with proper vouchers, (when vouchers can be procured,) on the first Tuesday in each month; and the marshal shall make his return, under oath, of his actual and necessary expenses in the service of every warrant addressed to him, and for custody of property, publication of notices and other services, and other actual and necessary expenses paid by him, with vouchers therefore whenever practicable, and also with a statement that the amounts charged by him are just and reasonable.

XIII.

MARSHAL AS MESSENGER.

It shall be the duty of the marshal as messenger to take possession of the property of the bankrupt, and to prepare, within three days from the time of taking such possession, a complete inventory of all the property, and to return it as soon as completed. The day of filing the petition and the value of the assets as appearing in schedule B shall be stated. The time for making the inventory and return may be enlarged, under proper circumstances, by special order of the district court: [*Provided, however,* That if any goods or effects so taken into possession as the property of the bankrupt shall be claimed by or in behalf of any other person, the marshal shall forthwith notify the petitioning creditor of such claim, and may, within five days after so giving notice of such claim, deliver them to the claimant or his agent, unless the petitioning creditor or party at whose instance possession is taken shall, by bond with sufficient sureties, to be approved by the marshal, indemnify the marshal for the taking and detention of such goods and effects, and the expenses of defending against all claims thereto; and, in case of such indemnity, the marshal shall retain possession of such goods and effects, and proceed in relation thereto as if no such claim had been made: *And provided further,* That in case the petitioning creditor claims that any property not in the possession of the bankrupt belongs to him, and should be taken by the marshal, the marshal shall not be bound to take possession of the same, unless indemnified in like manner.] He shall also, in case the bankrupt is absent or cannot be found, prepare a schedule of the names and residences of his creditors, and the amount due to each, from the books or other papers of the bankrupt that may be seized by him under his warrant, and from any other sources of information; but all statements upon which his return shall be made shall be in writing, and sworn to by the parties making them, before one of the registers in bankruptcy of the court, or a commissioner of the courts of the United States. In cases of voluntary bankruptcy, the marshal may appoint special deputies to act, as he may designate, in one or more cases, as messengers, for the purpose of causing the notices to be published and served as required in the eleventh section of the act, and for no other purpose. In giving the notices required by the third subdivision of the eleventh section of the act, it shall be sufficient to give the names, residences and amount of the debts (in figures) due the several creditors, so far as known, and no more.

XIV.

PETITIONS AND AMENDMENTS.

All petitions, and the schedules filed therewith, shall be printed or written out plainly, and without abbreviation or interlineation, except where such abbreviation and interlineation may be for the purpose of reference; and whenever any amendments are allowed, they shall be written and signed by the petitioner on a separate paper, in the same manner as the original schedules were signed and verified; and if the amendments are made to different schedules, the amendments to each schedule shall be made separately, with proper reference to the schedule proposed to be amended, and each amendment shall be verified by the oath of the petitioner in the same manner as the original schedules.

XV.

PRIORITY OF ACTIONS (INVOLUNTARY BANKRUPTCY.)

Whenever two or more petitions shall be filed by creditors against a common debtor, alleging separate acts of bankruptcy committed by said debtor on different days within six months prior to the filing of said petitions, and the debtor shall appear and show cause against an adjudication of bankruptcy against him on the petitions, that petition shall be first heard and tried which alleges the commission of the earliest act of bankruptcy; and in case the several acts of bankruptcy are alleged in the different petitions to have been committed on the same day, the court before which the same are pending may order them to be consolidated, and proceed to a hearing as upon one petition; and if an adjudication of bankruptcy be made upon either petition, or for the commission of a single act of bankruptcy, it shall not be necessary to proceed to a hearing upon the remaining petitions, unless proceedings be taken by the debtor for the purpose of causing such adjudication to be annulled or vacated.

XVI.

FILING PETITIONS IN DIFFERENT DISTRICTS.

In case two or more petitions shall be filed against the same individual in different districts, the first hearing shall be had in the district in which the debtor has his domicile, and such petition may be amended by inserting an allegation of an act of bankruptcy committed at an earlier date than that first alleged, if such earlier act is charged in either of the other petitions; and in case of two or more petitions against the same firm in different courts, each having jurisdiction over the case, the petition first filed shall be first heard, and may be amended by the insertion of an allegation of an earlier act of bankruptcy than that first alleged, if such earlier act is charged in either of the other petitions, and, in either case, the proceedings upon the other petitions may be stayed until an adjudication is made upon the petition first heard; and the court which makes the first adjudication of bankruptcy shall retain jurisdiction over all proceedings therein until the same shall be closed. In case two or more petitions for adjudication of bankruptcy shall be filed in different districts by different members of the same copartnership for an adjudication of the bankruptcy of said copartnership, the court in which the petition is first filed having jurisdiction shall take and retain jurisdiction over all proceedings in such bankruptcy until the same shall be closed; and if such petitions shall be filed in the same district, action shall be first had upon the one first filed.

XVII.

CONCERNING REDEMPTIONS OF PROPERTY AND COMPOUNDING CLAIMS.

Whenever it may be deemed for the benefit of the estate of a bankrupt to redeem and discharge any mortgage or other pledge, or deposit, or lien upon any property. real or personal, or to relieve said property from any conditional contract, and to tender performance of the conditions thereof, or to compound any debts or other claims or securities due or belonging to the estate of the bankrupt, the assignee, or the bankrupt, or any creditor who has proved his debt, may file his petition therefor in the office of the clerk of the district court;

and thereupon the court shall appoint a suitable time and place for the hearing thereof, notice of which shall be given in some newspaper, to be designated by the court, at least ten days before the hearing, so that all creditors and other persons interested may appear and show cause, if any they have, why an order should not be passed by the court upon the petition authorising such act on the part of the assignee.

XVIII.

PROCEEDINGS IN CASE OF COPARTNERSHIPS.

In case one or more members of a copartnership refuse to join in a petition to have the firm declared bankrupt, the parties refusing shall be entitled to resist the prayer of the petition in the same manner as if the petition had been filed by a creditor of the partnership, and notice of the filing of the petition shall be given to him in the same manner as provided by law and by these rules in the case of a debtor petitioned against; and he shall have the right to appear at the time fixed by the court for the hearing of the petition, and to make proof, if he can, that the copartnership is not insolvent, or has not committed an act of bankruptcy, and to take all other defenses which any debtor proceeded against is entitled to take by the provisions of the act; and in case an adjudication of bankruptcy is made upon the petition, such copartner shall be required to furnish to the marshal, as messenger, a schedule of his debts and an inventory of his property, in the same manner as is required by the act in cases of debtors against whom adjudication of bankruptcy shall be made.

XIX.

DUTIES OF ASSIGNEES.

The assignee shall, immediately on entering upon his duties, prepare a complete inventory of all the property of the bankrupt that comes into his possession; and all sales of the same shall be by public auction, unless otherwise ordered by the court. Every assignee shall keep full, exact, and regular books of account of all receipts, payments, and expenditures of money by him, and shall make report to the court, within twenty days after receiving the deed of assignment, of the articles set off to the bankrupt by him, according to the provisions of the fourteenth section of the act, with the estimated value of each article, and any creditor may take exceptions to the determination of the assignee within twenty days after the filing of the report. The register may require the exceptions to be argued before him, and shall certify them to the court for final determination at the request of either party. At the expiration of three months from the date of the adjudication of bankruptcy, the assignee shall file with the register a report, which shall exhibit just and true accounts of all his receipts and payments, verified by his oath ; and he shall also file at the same time a statement of the whole estate of the bankrupt as then ascertained, of the property recovered and of the property outstanding, specifying the cause of its being outstanding, and also what debts or claims are yet undetermined. The register may, if he shall judge it expedient, order that the second general meeting of creditors be called. Similar reports and statements shall be made, and similar proceedings had thereon, at the expiration of each successive period of three months. The substance of each monthly return of the assignee shall be sent by the register to any creditor who shall · request it and pay the fee provided for notices to creditors. In case the assignee shall neglect to file any report or statement which it is made his duty to file or make by the bankrupt act, or any general order in bankruptcy, within five days after the same shall be due, it shall be the duty of the register to make an order requiring the assignee to show cause before the court, at a time specified in the order, why he should not be removed from office. The register shall cause a copy of the order to be served upon the assignee at least seven days before the time fixed for the hearing, and proof of the service thereof to be delivered to the clerk.

XX.

COMPOSITION WITH CREDITORS (ARBITRATION.)

Whenever an assignee shall make application to the court for authority to submit a controversy arising in the settlement of demands against the bankrupt's estate, or of debts due to it, to the determination of arbitrators, or for authority to compound and settle such controversy by agreement with the other party, the subject-matter of the controversy and the reasons why the assignee thinks it proper and most for the interest of the creditors that it should be settled by arbitration or otherwise, shall be set forth clearly and distinctly in the application ; and the court, upon examination of the same, may immediately proceed to take testimony and make an order thereon, or may direct the assignee to give notice of the application, either by publication or by mail, or both, to the creditors who have proved their claims to appear and show cause, on a day to be named in the order and notice, why the application should not be granted, and may make such order thereon as may be just and proper.

XXI.

DISPOSAL OF PROPERTY BY ASSIGNEE.

In making sales of personal property, the assignee shall give at least ten days' notice of the time and place of the sale, and of the articles to be sold, by advertisement in one or more newspapers, to be designated by the court or by a register, and by posted handbills or otherwise, as he may think best for the interest of the estate, or as the court may order, and he shall give like notice of the sale of any real estate at least twenty days before such sale. Upon his application to the court, and for good cause shown, the assignee may be authorised to sell any specified portion of the bankrupt's estate at private sale; in which case he shall keep an accurate account of each article sold, and the price received therefor, and to whom sold; which account he shall file with his report, at the first meeting of creditors after the sale. The court, by order in special cases, may dispense with newspaper and handbill advertisements. In making sale of the franchise of a corporation, it may be offered in fractional parts or in certain numbers of shares, corresponding to the number of shares in the bankrupt corporation. And in making the sale of the real estate of a bankrupt, the assignee shall, unless otherwise ordered by the court, offer the same in lots or parcels, if it exists in separate parcels, in such manner as may be for the interest of the creditors of the estate.

XXII.

PERISHABLE PROPERTY.

In all cases where goods or other articles come into possession of the messenger or assignee which are perishable, or liable to deterioration in value, the court may, upon application, in its discretion, order the same to be sold, and the proceeds deposited in court.

XXIII.

SERVICE OF NOTICE.

The notice provided by the eighteenth section of the act shall be served by the marshal or his deputy, and notices to the creditors of the time and place of meeting provided by the section shall be given through the mail by letter, signed by the clerk of the court.

Every envelope containing a notice sent by the clerk or messenger shall have printed on it a direction to the postmaster at the place to which it is sent to return the same within ten days unless called for.

XXIV.

OPPOSITION TO DISCHARGE.

A creditor opposing the application of a bankrupt for discharge shall enter his appearance in opposition thereto on the day when the creditors are required to show cause, and shall file his specification of the grounds of his opposition, in writing, within ten days thereafter, unless the time shall be enlarged by order of the district court in the case, and the court shall thereupon make an order as to the entry of said case for trial on the docket of the district court, and the time within which the same shall be heard and decided.

XXV.

SECOND AND THIRD MEETING OF CREDITORS.

Whenever any bankrupt shall apply for his discharge, within three months from the date of his being adjudged a bankrupt, under the provisions of the twenty-ninth section of the act, the court may direct that the second and third meetings of creditors of said bankrupt required by the twenty-seventh and twenty-eighth sections of said act shall be had on the day which may be fixed in the order of notice for the creditors to appear and show cause why a discharge should not be granted such bankrupt; and the notices of such meeting shall be sufficient if it be added to the notice to show cause, that the second and third meetings of said creditors shall be had before the register upon the same day that cause may be shown against the discharge, or upon some previous days or day.

XXVI.

APPEALS.

Appeals in equity from the district to the circuit court, and from the circuit to the supreme court of the United States, shall be regulated by the rules governing appeals in equity in the courts of the United States. Any supposed creditor who takes an appeal to the circuit court from the decision of the district court rejecting his claim, in whole or in part, according to the provision of the eighth section of the act, shall give notice of his intention to enter the appeal within ten days from the entry of the final decision of the district court upon his claim; and he shall file his appeal in the clerk's office of the circuit court within ten days thereafter, setting forth a statement in writing of his claim in the manner prescribed by said section; and the assignee shall plead or answer thereto in like manner within ten days after the statement shall be filed. Every issue thereon shall be made up in the court, and the cause placed upon the docket thereof, and shall be heard and decided in the same manner as other actions at law.

XXVII.

IMPRISONED DEBTOR.

If at the time of preferring his petition the debtor shall be imprisoned, the court, upon his application, may order him to be produced upon *habeas corpus* by the jailor, or any officer in whose custody he may be, before the register, for the purpose of testifying in any matter relating to his bankruptcy; and if committed after the filing of his petition upon process in any civil action founded upon a claim provable in bankruptcy, the court may, upon like application, discharge him from such imprisonment. If the petitioner, during the pendency of the proceedings in bankruptcy, be arrested or imprisoned upon process in any civil action, the district court, upon his application, may issue a writ of *habeas corpus* to bring him before the court, to ascertain whether such process has been issued for the collection of any claim provable in bankruptcy, and, if so provable, he shall be discharged; if not, he shall be remanded to the custody in which he may lawfully be. Before granting the order for discharge, the court shall cause notice to be served upon the creditor, or his attorney, so as to give him an opportunity of appearing and being heard before the granting of the order.

XXVIII.

DEPOSIT AND PAYMENT OF MONEYS.

The district court in each district shall designate certain national anks, if there are any within the judicial district, or if there are none, then some other safe depository, in which all moneys received by assignees or paid into court in the course of any proceedings in bankruptcy shall be deposited; and every assignee and the clerk of said court shall deposit all sums received by them, severally, on account of any bankrupt's estate, in one designated depository; and every clerk shall make a report to the court of the funds received by him, and of deposits made by him, on the first Monday of every month. On the first day of each month the assignee shall file a report with the register, stating whether any collections, deposits or payments have been made by him during the preceding month, and if any, he shall state the gross amount of each. The register shall enter such reports upon a book to be kept by him for that purpose, in which a separate account shall be kept with each estate; and he shall also enter therein the amount, the date, and the expressed purpose of each check countersigned by him. No moneys so deposited shall be drawn from such depos.tory unless upon a check, or warrant, signed by the clerk of the court, or by an assignee, and countersigned by the judge of the court, or one of the regis- t rs designated for that purpose, stating the date, the sum, and the account for which it is drawn; and an entry of the substance of such check or warrant, with the date thereof, the sum drawn for, and the account for which it is drawn, shall be forthwith made in a book kept for that purpose by the assignee or the clerk; and all checks and drafts shall be entered in the order of time in which they are drawn, and shall be numbered in the case of each estate. A copy of this rule shall be furnished to the depository so designated, and also the name of any register authorised to countersign said checks.

XXIX.

PREPAYMENT OR SECURITY OF FEES.

The fees of the register, marshal, and clerk shall be paid or secured in all cases before they shall be compelled to per- form the duties required of them by the parties requiring such service; and in the case of witnesses their fees shall be tendered or paid at the time of the service of the summons or subpœna, and shall include their traveling expenses to and from the place at which they may be summoned to attend. The court may order the whole, or such portion of the fees and costs in each case to be paid out of the fund in court in such case as shall seem just.

The funds deposited with the register, marshal, and clerk shall, in all cases where they come out of the bankrupt's estate, be considered as a part of such estate, and the assignee shall be charged therewith, and shall not be allowed for any disbursements therefrom, except upon the production of proper vouchers from such officers, respectively, given after the due allowance of their respective bills.

XXX.

AS TO FEES AND COSTS.

In addition to the fees expressly allowed by the bankrupt act, there shall be allowed the following: To the clerks: For every copy of any paper in proceedings in bankruptcy, twenty-five cents for certifying the same, and ten cents in addition for each folio of one hundred words. For each notice required to be sent by mail, when signed by the clerk, ten cents; to be prepaid by the party required to give the notice.

To the registers: Affidavits to any petition, schedule, or other proceedings in bankruptcy, except proof of debt by a creditor or his agent, for each oath and certifying the same, twenty-five cents.

For examining petition and schedules and certifying to their correctness, three dollars.

For notification to assignee of his appointment, fifty cents. For assignment of bankrupt's effects, one dollar. For order to assignee directing publication of his appointment, fifty cents. For order for examination of the bankrupt or his wife, one dollar.

Summons or subpœna for witness, twenty-five cents. For taking examination of bankrupt or his wife, or any witness, under section twenty-six, and for each examination in proof of debt under section twenty-two, twenty cents for each folio, and one dollar for each hour actually engaged; and for certifying each affidavit or deposition in proof of debt as satisfactory, twenty-five cents.

The fees paid by creditors for establishing their debts as above, shall be entitled to priority of payment under section twenty-eight.

For computation of dividends, five dollars, and ten cents for each creditor to whom a dividend is declared. For every certificate of question to the district court or judge, under the fourth and sixth sections of the act, one dollar, which may be increased in any case by order of the judge.

When the proceedings are not conducted in the usual office of the register, the traveling and incidental expenses of the register, and of any clerk or other officer attending him, shall be allowed, and five dollars for each day employed in going, attending, and returning, and such expenses and fees shall be apportioned among the cases as provided in section five.

No other allowance shall be made for clerk-hire.

For each notice which the register may be required to send to creditors, fifteen cents, which shall include postage and stationery.

For each memorandum sent by the register to the clerk, ten cents for each folio, and fifteen cents for the certificate.

No fees shall be allowed to the register except those hereinbefore enumerated.

The fifty dollars deposited, under rule forty-seven, with

the clerk for the register, shall be delivered by the clerk to the register to whom the case is referred.

Ten days before the day fixed for the consideration of the assignee's final account, or at any other time fixed by the court on its own motion, or on the application of any person interested, the clerk, marshal, and register shall file with a master commissioner of the court, or some other fit person who shall be appointed by the court for that purpose as a standing auditor, a statement of fees, including prospective fees for final distribution, which shall exhibit, by items, each service and the fee charged for it, and the amount received. Said auditor shall tax each fee-bill, allowing none but such as are provided for by the statute or by these rules, which taxation shall be conclusive, reserving to the party interested exceptions to the report, which shall be decided by the court.

The reasonable compensation of the master or auditor for taxing these fee-bills, not exceeding ten dollars in any one case of bankruptcy, shall be paid out of any funds in the hands of the assignee, and if there be no such funds, by the clerk, marshal, and register, in proportion to the amount of their bills so taxed and allowed.

Any money received by either of the officers mentioned in excess of lawful fees or compensation, shall be ordered by the judge to be paid into court, and such order may be enforced, if necessary, by attachment as for contempt.

No bankrupt's discharge shall be refused or delayed by reason of the non-payment of any fees except the fee for his certificate of discharge.

XXXI.

COSTS IN CONTESTED ADJUDICATIONS.

In cases of involuntary bankruptcy, where the debtor resists an adjudication, and the court, after hearing, shall adjudge the debtor a bankrupt, the petitioning creditor shall recover, to be paid out of the fund, the same costs that are allowed by law to a party recovering in a suit in equity; and in case the petition shall be dismissed, the debtor may recover like costs from the petitioner.

XXXII.

AS TO FORMS AND SCHEDULES.

The several forms specified in the schedules annexed to these orders for the several purposes therein stated shall be observed and used, with such alterations as may be necessary to suit the circumstances of any particular case. In all cases where, by the provisions of the act, a special order is required to be made in any proceeding, or in any case instituted under the act in a district court of the United States, such order shall be framed by the court to suit the circumstances of the particular case; and the forms hereby prescribed shall be followed as nearly as may be, and so far as the same are applicable to the circumstances requiring such special order. In proceedings in equity, instituted for the purpose of carrying into effect the provisions of the act, or for enforcing the rights and remedies given by it, the rules of equity practice established by the supreme court of the United States shall be followed as nearly as may be. In proceedings at law, instituted for the same purpose, the rules of the circuit court regulating the practice and procedure in cases at law shall be followed as nearly as may be. But the court, as the judge thereof, may, by special rule in any case, vary the time allowed for return of process, for appearance and pleading, and for taking testimony and publication, and may otherwise modify the rules for the preparation of any particular case so as to facilitate a speedy hearing.

XXXIII.

OMISSIONS AND AMENDMENTS.

Whenever a debtor shall omit to state in the schedules annexed to his petition any of the facts required to be stated concerning his debts or his property, he shall state, either in its appropriate place in the schedules or in a separate affidavit to be filed with the petition, the reason for the omission, with such particularity as will enable the court to determine whether to admit the schedules as sufficient, or to require the debtor to make further efforts to complete the same according to the requirements of the law; and in making any application for amendment to the schedules, the debtor shall state under oath the substance of the matters proposed to be included in the amendment, and the reasons why the same had not been incorporated in his schedules as originally filed, or as previously amended. In like manner, he may correct any statement made during the course of his examination.

XXXIV.

PROOF OF DEBTS.

Depositions to prove claims against a bankrupt's estate shall be correctly entitled in the court and in the cause.

When made to prove a debt due to a copartnership, it must appear on oath that the deponent is member of the creditor firm ; when made by an agent, the reason the deposition is not made by the claimant in person must be stated ; and when made to prove a debt due to a corporation, and the corporation has no such officer as cashier or treasurer, the deposition may be made by the officer whose duties most nearly correspond to those of cashier or treasurer. Depositions to prove debts existing in open account shall state when the debt became or will become due ; and if it consists of items maturing at different dates the average due date shall be stated ; in default of which it shall not be necessary to compute interest upon it. All such depositions shall contain an averment that no note has been received for such account nor any judgment rendered thereon. Proofs of debts received by any assignee shall be delivered to the register to whom the cause is referred. The register may decline to file any deposition until the fee for filing the same is paid. When a proof of debt is sent by mail to the register, and it shall be accompanied by the fee for filing it, and the fee for sending a notice to a creditor, the register shall acknowledge the receipt of it, and state the amount at which he has entered it, and if it shall be insufficient or unsatisfactory to the register he shall state the reason.

Any creditor may file with the register a request that all notices to which he may be entitled shall be addressed to him at any place, to be designated by the post office box or street number, as he may appoint, and thereafter and until some other designation shall be made by such creditor, all notices shall be so addressed ; and in other cases notices shall be addressed as specified in the proof of debt.

Claims which have been assigned before proof shall be supported by a deposition of the owner at the time of the commencement of proceedings, setting forth the true consideration of the debt, and that it is entirely unsecured, or if secured, such deposition shall set forth the security, as is required in proving secured claims.

Upon filing with the register satisfactory proof of the assignment of a claim proved and entered on the register's docket, the register shall immediately give notice by mail, to the original claimant, of the filing of such proof of assignment.

And if no objection be entered within ten days, he shall make an order subrogating the assignee to the original claimant.

If objection be made within the time specified. or within

such further time as may be granted for that purpose, the register shall certify the objection into court for determination. The claims for persons contingently liable for the bankrupt may be proved in the name of the creditor, when known by the party contingently liable.

When the name of the creditor is unknown, such claims may be proved in the name of the party contingently liable ; but no dividend shall be paid upon such claim, except upon satisfactory proof that it will diminish, *pro tanto*, the original debt. The execution of any letter of attorney to represent a creditor, or of an assignment of claim after proof, or of the consent of a creditor to a bankrupt's discharge, may be proved or acknowledged before a register in bankruptcy, or a United States circuit court commissioner. When executed on behalf of a copartnership, or of a corporation, the person executing the instrument shall make oath that he is a member of the firm, or duly authorised officer of the corporation, on whose behalf he acts.

When the party executing is not personally known to the officer taking the proof or acknowledgement, his identity shall be established by satisfactory proof.

When the assignee or any creditor shall desire the re-examination of any claim filed against the bankrupt's estate, he may apply by petition to the register to whom the cause is referred, for an order for such re-examination; and thereupon the register shall make an order fixing a time for hearing the petition, of which due notice shall be given by mail, addressed to the creditor.

At the time appointed, the register shall take the examination of the creditor, and of any witnesses that may be called by either party; and if it shall appear from such examination that the claim ought to be expunged or diminished, the register, if no objection be made, may order accordingly. If objection be made, the register shall require the parties then, or within a time to be fixed for that purpose, to form an issue to be certified into court for determination.

If the petitioner is in default in making up said issue, the petition shall be dismissed; if the creditor whose claim is re-examined is in default in making said issue, the claim may be diminished or expunged by the register.

All orders thus made by the register may be reviewed by the court on special petition, and upon showing satisfactory cause for such review.

INDEX.

ACT OF BANKRUPTCY.

1. Payment of wages to employees, though made in the regular course of business, is an act of bankruptcy if done in contemplation of insolvency; for although the law prefers an employee to the amount of fifty dollars, this preference must be secured by and through the proceedings in bankruptcy, and not outside of them or independent of and in spite of the act.—*In re* Kenyon & Fenton, 238.

2. A person cannot commit an act of bankruptcy while insane; but if when *sane* he has committed such an act, he may be made bankrupt upon a petition *in invitum*, after he has become *insane*. Whether he can obtain a discharge, *quære.*—*In re* Pratt, 276.

See ASSIGNMENT, 3; JURISDICTION, 2; RENT, 1.

ACTION.

1. Creditors who have received more than the amount stipulated in the composition deed, without the knowledge of the other creditors, are not thereby barred from bringing an action against the debtor on their original obligation, when such action is brought on the ground that the composition deed was fraudulently procured.—*Elfelt et al.* v. *Snow et al,.* 57.

2. A petition was filed by a creditor to restrain the assignee in bankruptcy from prosecuting a certain action of law in the supreme court of New York state, to recover the payment of money made contrary to the provisions of the thirty-ninth section of the bankrupt act, claiming to recover back the amount so paid. *Held,* That said act is the law of the state courts as well as of the national tribunals; and if by virtue of that act the state court has no jurisdiction in the action brought against the petitioners, it will so decide upon proper plea, and that no reason appears to compel the assignee to resort to the national tribunals instead of those of the State.—*In re* Central Bank, 207.

ADJUDICATION.

1. The application of creditors other than the petitioning creditors in a bankruptcy proceeding for an order annulling the adjudication on the ground that there was an agreement of compromise preceding the commencement of bankruptcy proceedings, to which agreement the petitioning creditor was a party, must be denied.—*In re* Bush, 179.

2. The proceeding by a petitioning creditor to force his debtor into bank-

ruptcy is a proceeding *inter partes* like an ordinary action at law or suit in equity, and until the adjudication is had, they are the only parties.   No outside creditor has a right to resist the adjudication, or to ask that it be annulled.—*Id.*

3. Where the district judge for the southern district of New York privately signed the form of an adjudication of bankruptcy, on the first day of March, and endorsed on the same the words and figures "Filed March 1st, 1871, S. B.," and on the second day of March granted a re-argument of the application of the petitioning creditor in another district for leave to intervene and oppose an adjudication in this district, and at such re-argument on the third day of March, a certified copy of an adjudication made in such other district on the second day of March having been produced and read, the district judge produced the paper which had been signed by him on the first of March, but which, during the interval, had been in the sole knowledge and possession of the said judge, and had neither been entered with the clerk nor promulgated as an adjudication of the court, *Held,* That the said paper operated as an adjudication only as of the time when it was so produced in court, and promulgated, to wit, as of the third of March, and that the adjudication which was regularly made and entered in the other district on the second of March, took precedence as the earlier adjudication.—*In re* Boston, Hartford and Erie R. R. Co.

See INJUNCTION, 1, 2 ; LIEN, 3 ; PURCHASER OF NOTES, SECURED DEBT.

AGENT.

1. When an agent is sent by an insolvent debtor to compromise with creditors, and some of them, through him, return different terms than those submitted, such agent does not thereby become that of such creditors, but remains the agent of the debtor, and his knowledges, mistakes and acts are those of his principal—the insolvent. The same effect would be produced if he were deemed the *common* agent of both parties.—*Curran et al.* v. *Munger et al.*, 33.

AMENDMENT.—See COMMERCIAL PAPER, 3 ; DISTRICT COURT, 3 ; SUSPENSION OF PAYMENT.

APPEAL.

1. A court should not do indirectly what it has no power to do directly, therefore, when a petition has been dismissed in the United States circuit court, the parties considering themselves aggrieved by such decision cannot apply to the United States district court for a re-hearing of the original decree, that they may, on an adverse decision being re-entered, again have the right to appeal to the circuit court, as this would be an attempt to extend the time fixed by the statute within which an appeal can be allowed.—*In re* Troy Woolen Co., 16.

2. An assignee obtained an order of the district court, requiring the bankrupt and certain other parties to deliver to him property belonging to said bankrupt. From this order an appeal was taken to the United States circuit court, in form and manner prescribed by the eighth section of the bankrupt act. The assignee moved to dismiss the appeal on the ground that the proceedings in the district court were summary, and could only be reviewed by summary petition, and, therefore, not a case for an appeal under the eighth section of the bankrupt act. *Held,* That although the appeal might be irregular, the district court

had jurisdiction, and from the evidence was justified in making the decree appealed from. Decree affirmed with costs.—*Samson, Assignee,* v. *Blake et al.,* 401.

See JUDGMENT, 2.

ASSETS.

1. The term assets in the thirty-third section of the bankrupt act as amended July fourteenth, eighteen hundred and seventy, is not used to express the net balance to be distributed among the creditors, but means the entire estate of the bankrupt, irrespective of the use to which it may be appropriated by the court. Hence, where the estate was originally sufficient to pay fifty per cent. of the debts proved, but a large part has been wasted by litigation, the bankrupt is entitled to his discharge without the assent of his creditors.—*In re* Kabley *et al.,* 189. .

2. Bankrupts made application for their discharge and took the testimony of the assignee, who swore that at the time he took possession of the estate it was worth fourteen thousand dollars, which was more than fifty per cent. of the debts of said bankrupts, as set forth in their schedule. The evidence further shows that the assignee offered the real estate at public sale, but was unable to obtain a bid upon it for the reason that it was heavily encumbered, and was at that time advertised for sale under a mortgage foreclosure suit. The assignee collected some twelve thousand two hundred dollars. Unsecured claims to amount of fourteen thousand dollars have been proved, of which six thousand five hundred dollars were contracted prior to January first, eighteen hundred and sixty-nine, and seven thousand five hundred dollars subsequent to that date. On the part of the bankrupts it was claimed that a discharge should be granted from all their debts, for the reason that they had shown that at the time their estate passed into the hands of the assignee it was worth fifty per cent. of the claims proved. *Held,* That the word assets must be construed to mean money received by the assignee, and that bankrupts are only entitled to receive a discharge from their debts contracted prior to January first, eighteen hundred and sixty-nine.—*In re* G. & J. J. Van Riper, 573.

ASSIGNEE.

1. In the absence of fraud, the assignee takes only such rights and interests as the bankrupt himself had or could assert at the time of his bankruptcy, and consequently they are affected with all the equities which would affect the bankrupt himself if he were asserting those rights and interests.—*In re* Dow, 10

2. An assignee is an officer of the court and acts subject to its orders. The bankrupt is entitled to a certificate of the assignee giving the names and residence of the creditors who have proven their claims, as per form, in order to enable him to move the court for an order to show cause why he should not be discharged, &c. The register has the power to make such an order and it is the duty of the assignee to obey it. Motions to compel an assignee to do his duty are properly made before the register.—*In re* Blaisdell *et al.,* 78.

3. It is not essential to the title of the assignee that the assignment to him by the register should be recorded within six months from its date. The title of the assignee takes effect by relation, from the commencement of the proceed-

ings in bankruptcy, and the recording is not required for the mere purpose of
giving notice to purchasers.—*Davis* v. *Anderson et al.*, 145.

4. The assignee in bankruptcy can claim only such interest and right in any
property as the bankrupt could have claimed at the filing of the petition by or
against him. Hence, where the bankrupt has made conveyances by which his
books of account pass to an assignee of his own selection, the assignee in bankruptcy cannot claim them until such conveyances are shown to have been
fraudulent and void. To obtain possession of such books an assignee must
proceed by a bill in equity or action at law, in which the validity of said conveyances can be tested, and not by simple petition.—*Rogers, Assignee,* v. *Winsor*, 247.

5. An assignee is not at liberty to charge the assets of the estate in his hands
for professional and clerical services rendered him in the execution of his trust
until the same shall have been first duly allowed by the court.—*In re* Noyes,
277.

6. Before incurring expenses for professional services and clerk hire, an
• assignee must apply to court for proper authority ; if, however, he has incurred
and paid such expenses, or demands compensation beyond what he is entitled
to by section twenty-eight of the bankrupt law, he must accompany his final
account with a separate and distinct application for an allowance of the charges,
and submit to such examination and furnish such proofs as may be required
touching the necessity of such disbursements and services.—*Id.*

7. The assignee has a right to recover from the judgment creditor, (a bank,)
although it has given no receipt to the sheriff, but only a certificate of deposit.—*Trader's National Bank of Chicago* v. *Campbell*, 313.

8. An assignee has the right to proceed against a creditor in the federal court
for the proceeds of a sale on an execution issued out of a state court, where the
judgment on which it is founded is alleged to be in fraud of the bankrupt act.—
Id.

9. A, who was insolvent at the time, wrote to his brother-in-law, B, at St.
Louis, to come and buy him out. In response to this letter, B came to the
residence of A, and arranged to take the whole of his stock at twenty-five per
cent. below cost. B, leaving the stock in possession of A. during his absence,
went to Chillicothe, Missouri, and offered to sell the whole stock to C, at twenty
per cent. below cost. Thereupon, B and C went together to the residence of
of A; C examined, paid for and shipped the goods away. The assignee in
bankruptcy sued C for the goods and recovered a verdict, which was set aside
on appeal and the case remanded. On the second trial he obtained a judgment
from which defendant again appealed. This time, however, the judgment
was affirmed. Defendant then appealed to the United States court, on the
ground that the jury were improperly charged. *Held*, That the charge was perfectly proper, as the judge of the court below had distinctly informed the jury
that notice of the fraud or participation in it, on the part of the defendant, was
essential to the recovery on the part of the assignee. Judgment affirmed.—
Babbitt, Assignee, v. *Walbrun & Co.*, 359.

10. Assignees under the state law cannot receive allowance for attorneys
fees, nor compensation for their own services where the debtor has been adjudged a bankrupt.—*In re* Cohn, 379.

11. A petition was filed against an assignee in bankruptcy to have him re-

moved for the reason that he attacked two mortgages upon the bankrupt's property without sufficient cause, and that he delayed a sale of the property for the purpose of obtaining the rents in order to spend them in litigation. *Held*, That the assignee was fully justified in his attack upon the mortgages, and that there was no evidence to show that he ever collected any rents, or how much he spent in litigation. Petition dismissed, with costs to be paid out of the fund.— *In re* Sacchi, 398.

12. Injunction granted restraining the state court receiver from disposing or interfering with the property of the corporation, and from setting up and asserting as against the assignee in bankruptcy any title to or right of action for any of said property, and enjoins, pending this action, and by final decree, from doing any acts to carry or effectuate the trusts purporting to be created by his appointment as receiver. Assignee appointed receiver on giving a stipulation to charge no commissions on such assets of the receivership as shall pass from the state receivership to the trust represented by the assignee of the bankrupt.— *Platt, Assignee*, v. *Archer*, 465.

13. On a petition to the circuit court for the review of an order of the district court denying the application for the removal of an assignee, *Held*, That inasmuch as the petitioner for review has become the sole creditor, an order should be made that the assignee convey the estate of the bankrupt to such assignee as the petitioner and the bankrupt may name, or if they do not agree the matter be referred to the register ; the present assignee to receive all moneys collected by him until his just allowance for commissions and expense is settled by the district court.— *In re* Sacchi, 497.

14. In setting apart for the use of the bankrupt exempt property, the assignee is not obliged to designate articles on which there is no lien. An assignee is chargeable personally with costs of the proceedings where he files a petition to have an attachment dissolved which covers property that has already been set apart by him as exempt.— *In re* Preston, 545.

15. An assignee in bankruptcy can proceed against an adverse claimant of property only by action at law or plenary bill in equity ; but whether an adverse claimant may not proceed against an assignee by mere petition, *quære ?* Rulings in *Barlow* v. *Peckham*, 5 N. B. R. 72, and *in re* Masterson, 4 N. B. R. 180, reconsidered and qualified, and rulings in *Knight* v. *Cheney*, 5 N. B. R. 305, and *Smith* v. *Mason*, 6 N. B. R. 1, and *in re* Evans, Lowell's Dec. 526, commented upon.— *Ferguson et ux* v. *Peckham, Assignee, et al.*, 569.

See ACTION, 2 ; MEETING OF CREDITORS. 2 ; POSSESSION OF FUNDS.

ASSIGNMENT.

1. If assignments of policies of insurance belonging to a bankrupt prior to his adjudication, are valid, they can be maintained as against the assignee, to be appointed in bankruptcy proceedings, and if they are not legal and binding, they should not be made so as against non-assenting creditors, by the dismissal of proceedings after the expiration of the time allowed to dissenting creditors to commence proceedings in order to avoid a preference has elapsed.— *In re* Bush, 179.

2. A debtor made an assignment of his stock in trade and notes of hand to one of his creditors within six weeks of the filing of a petition in bankruptcy against the debtor. Assignment held void under section thirty-five of the

bankrupt act ; and assignee in bankruptcy entitled to recover from the preferred creditor the value of the goods and notes thus transferred to him.—*North, Assignee,* v. *House et al.,* 365.

3. A finding himself unable to meet his liabilities, compromised with all his creditors, except B, whom he proposed to pay in full if he would give a large extension of time ; to this B agreed, and received, as security, an assignment of two judgments, and also a deed for a lot, which together were supposed to exceed in value the amount of B's claim. At the time of this transfer an agreement was entered into, in effect that whatever was paid on the judgments should be credited on the claim, and the lot was to be returned within twelve months from the date of the transfer, providing the indebtedness was all liquidated. The claim was not paid, however, and more than six months after the assignment a petition in bankruptcy was filed against A by B, alleging that he had made a disposition of his property out of his usual and ordinary course of business, with intent to hinder and delay his creditors. *Held,* 1. That B's claim was an existing indebtedness provable in bankruptcy. 2. That A made a disposition of his property with the intent to delay, hinder and defraud his creditors, and that he had committed an act of bankruptcy.—*Ecfort & Petring* v. *Greely,* 433.

See FRAUDULENT CONVEYANCE, 1.

ATTACHMENT.

1. An attachment issued out of the state court is dissolved from the date of the filing of the petition where an order of adjudication is subsequently granted. Costs that accrued under such attachment, prior to the filing of the petition in bankruptcy, are not a valid lien on the property unless incurred at defendant's request.—*In re* Preston, 545.

BANKRUPT ACT.

1. It was not the intent or purpose of the bankrupt law to abrogate state statutes of limitation, and such is not its effect. Whether congress has power to do so. *Quære.*—*In re* Cornwall, 305

2. SECTION 43.—A creditor who claims a preference, which preference is contested by the other creditors, is an improper person to be one of the committee selected according to section forty-three of the bankrupt act.—*In re* The Stuyvesant Bank, 272.

See RECEIVER.

BILL IN EQUITY.—See ASSIGNEE, 4.

BOOKS OF ACCOUNT.—See ASSIGNEE, 4.

CARRYING ON BUSINESS.

1. "Carrying on business," within the meaning of the eleventh section of the bankrupt law, as applied to a railroad corporation, does not mean the conduct of such transactions as are merely collateral or incidental to the purpose for which the corporation is created, whether they are conducted by agents or officers, and although an office is continously kept for the purpose.—*In re* Alabama & Chattanooga R. R. Co., 107.

CLAIM.

1. A sent certain notes to B, which were endorsed by C, to be discounted and the proceeds placed to his (A's) credit. He drew against them by certain drafts in favor of C, which B failed to pay. C was subsequently adjudged a bankrupt, and B sought to prove his claim against the bankrupt for the notes sent to him by A, but the assignee refused to allow it. On the petition of B to review the action of the assignee in refusing to allow the claim to be proved, the court held, that inasmuch as the drafts were not paid, B had no right to retain the notes, and, therefore, there was a failure of consideration. Claim rejected. —*In re* Howard, Cole & Co., 372.

2. When a creditor presents his claim for probate, he at once subjects himself and his claim to the power and jurisdiction of the court, and becomes subject to its orders within the provisions of the bankrupt act ; among which is the provision that the court may examine such creditor concerning the debt sought to be proved. He is, therefore, so examined as a party to the proceedings, and is in no sense a "witness ;" hence the refusal of the assignee to pay witness fees under such circumstances must be sustained.—*In re* Paddock, 396.

COMMERCIAL PAPER.

1. The negotiable paper of a firm of manufacturers is commercial paper within the meaning of the act, regardless of the purpose for which it was given.—*In re* Kenyon & Fenton, 238.

2. When a man enters the commercial community as a merchant, trader, banker, broker, manufacturer or miner, he assumes all the responsibilities which attach to his calling. One of these is to take care of his commercial paper, whether made before or after he commenced business ; hence, if obligations, given before but falling due after he engaged in business, are allowed to remain unpaid for fourteen days after maturity, the maker can be adjudged a bankrupt.—*In re* Carter, 299.

3. Under the thirty-ninth section of the bankrupt act, as amended by the act of July fourteenth, eighteen hundred and seventy, providing for putting into involuntary bankruptcy a person " who, being a banker, broker, merchant, trader, manufacturer or miner, has fraudulently stopped payment, or who has stopped or suspended and not resumed payment of his commercial paper within a period of fourteen days," a person who is not a banker, broker, merchant, trader, manufacturer or miner. is liable to be put into involuntary bankruptcy, if he has stopped or suspended and not resumed payment of his commercial paper within a period of fourteen days.—*In re* the Hercules Mutual Life Assurance Society, 338.

4. Under the section, as so amended, a person cannot be put into involuntary bankruptcy for the fraudulent stoppage of payment, unless he is a banker, broker, merchant, trader, manufacturer or miner ; but if he is one of those classes, he may, for the fraudulent stoppage of the payment of his debts, be put into bankruptcy at once, without waiting fourteen days, and without his stoppage being a stoppage of the payment of commercial paper.—*Id.*

5. Under the section, as so amended, "commercial paper" means bills of exchange, promissory notes, bank checks and other negotiable instruments for

the payment of money, which, by their form and on their face, purport to be such instruments as are by the law merchant recognized as falling under the designation of "commercial paper."—*Id.*

6. The clause in the thirty-ninth section, in regard to the stoppage of the payment of commercial paper, ought not to be used to enable a creditor to collect an ordinary debt on commercial paper, where there has been no stoppage or suspension of payment of the commercial paper of the debtor. Such stoppage or suspension has not taken place, when a sufficient excuse is shown why the paper was not paid.—*Id.*

7. Even though the suspension may have continued for fourteen days, yet a *bona fide* denial of liability on the paper is such an adequate legal excuse that a person ought not to be adjudged a bankrupt solely for suspending for fourteen days on the paper, even though, on investigation, the bankruptcy court may be of opinion that, in fact, the debtor was liable on the paper.—*Id.*

8. A debtor may, under certain circumstances, be considered as really having suspended payment generally of his commercial paper, although but a single piece of paper is shown to have lain over unpaid for fourteen days. Petition dismissed with costs.—*Id.*

COMPENSATION.—See Assignee, 5, 6, 10.·

COMPROMISE.—See Adjudication, 1 ; Agent, 1 ; Assignment, 3 ; Injunction, 3 ; Payment by Debtor.

CONTEMPT.—See Discharge. 3 ; Injunction, 3 ; Register, 4.

CONVEYANCE.

1. The word conveyance in the bankrupt act is a generic term, including all proceedings to dispose of or encumber property in derogation of the equality of creditors, with intent by such disposition either to defeat or delay the operation of the act ; hence it includes mortgages on real estate which, if given contrary to the provisions of the thirty-ninth section, are void, and deprives the mortgagee of all right to prove his claim in bankruptcy, even though he should be willing to surrender his rights under the mortgage.— *Bingham* v. *Frost and* v. *Williams*, 130.

2. Land conveyed in fraud of creditors passes to the assignee in bankruptcy of the grantor by virtue of section fourteen of the act, though conveyed more than six months before the bankruptcy, and is not within section thirty-five.— *Pratt, Jr.*, v. *Curtis et al.*, 139.

3. In Massachusetts a voluntary conveyance to a wife or child of the grantor by a person much indebted is *prima facie* fraudulent as to existing creditors. If such a deed is set aside by existing creditors, it seems that the land or its proceeds are assets for creditors generally. If it should be assets only for a certain class of creditors, yet the assignee is the proper plaintiff to impeach the deed.—*Id.*

4. Where a debtor whose property exceeds in value all that he owes, for the purpose of paying all his debts and of securing to himself a maintenance in the future, conveys all his property to another upon an agreement that the

latter should pay all such debts and support the grantor for the residue of his life, such conveyance is not *per se* fraudulent or void as against creditors, nor an act of bankruptcy.—*In re* Cornwall, 305.

CORPORATION.

1. Upon a petition in bankrupt y against the Boston, Hartford and Erie Railroad Company, it appears that the company owned a railroad situated partly in Connecticut and partly in Massachusetts; that a company by that name was first chartered by Connecticut, with power to purchase and complete any railroads running through parts of both states, on the line between Boston and Hartford; that such purchases were made; that subsequently the Boston, Hartford and Erie Railroad Company was, by an act of the Massachusetts legislature, declared to be a corporation within that state; and that the road in both states was owned by the same stockholders, conducted by the same directors and subject to the same debts, in the same manner as if it were wholly within one state. *Held,* That—whether this company were one corporation or two corporations chartered by different states, but united, and having in all respects a common interest, or an anomalous body, not precisely answering either of their descriptions—upon the filing of the creditor's petition in the district court of the district where the principal office and place of business of the road was situated, that court acquired exclusive jurisdiction over proceedings in bankruptcy against it, which could not be affected by a petition subsequently filed by another creditor in another distrtict.—*In re* Boston, Hartford and Erie R. R. Co., 209.

2. If the company be regarded as composed of two corporations, the case would be governed by the spirit if not by the letter of sections thirty-six and thirty-seven of the bankrupt act and general order sixteen, relating to partnerships, and to joint stock companies. In the absence of any such provisions in the act, the same rule would be deducible from the practice of courts of equity in analogous cases, where different parties apply to different tribunals, existing under the same general jurisdiction, for the distribution of the same funds.—*Id.*

3. As the same debtor, in substance, was before both courts, the title of the assignees appointed under the petition first filed would cover all the assets owned by the bankrupt at the time of the filing of that petition, and it would therefore be useless to proceed upon any petition subsequently filed in another district, since there would be no assets left to be reached by it.—*Id.*

4. In this case, after the filing of a petition in bankruptcy against the company in Massachusetts, another creditor filed another petition against it in Connecticut, under a collusive agreement with the company that no defence should be made to the proceeding. The creditor who had petitioned in Massachusetts thereupon filed an application in the district court in Connecticut, stating the prior proceedings by himself and the collusion, and praying for leave to come in and defend. The court found this application insufficient in its force, and proceeded to an adjudication of bankruptcy, and the appointment of assignees, who were the same previously chosen in Massachusetts. *Held,* On a petition of review to the circuit court, that the application was legally sufficient; that no adjudication should have been granted; but that, under the circumstance

of the case, it was sufficient, without reversing the decree, to order a stay of any further proceedings.—*Id.*

5. The proper course for the court in Connecticut would have been to admit the intervening creditor as a defendant, and then to stay further proceedings until the court in Massachusetts had made some adjudication on the petition then pending. Nor could an adjudication in bankruptcy then made necessarily require the Connecticut court to dismiss the second petition. It might be advisable to continue it in that court to fall back upon, if the Massachusetts decree should, for any reason not applicable to the Connecticut proceedings, prove unavailing or erroneous.—*Id.*

6. A corporation that has been dissolved by a decree of a state court, and a receiver appointed, still exists for the purpose of being proceeded against in bankruptcy; hence, an adjudication is valid if the corporation by answer admits the acts of bankruptcy alleged against it, although the receiver may not have been a party to the answer or given his assent to such adjudication. No power exists to wrest from the jurisdiction of the courts in bankruptcy the assets of such bankrupt individuals and corporations as are within the scope of the provisions of the United States bankrupt act.—*In re* Independent Insurance Co., 260.

7. A corporation, incorporated for the transaction of the business of life insurance, and not inhibited from borrowing money for the legitimate purposes of its business, and from giving notes, as evidence of such indebtedness, may, although not expressly authorized to do so, borrow money for use in its legitimate business, and give a time engagement to pay the debt.—*In re* Hercules Mutual Life Assurance Society, 338.

8. A corporation dissolved by a decree of a state court before adjudication, but after the service of an order to show cause, still exists for the purpose of being proceeded against in bankruptcy, as such dissolution does not deprive the district court of its jurisdiction or abate the proceedings.—*Platt, Assignee,* v. *Archer,* 465.

9. A cashier is still an officer of the bank for the purpose of being served with an order to show cause, although he has given the keys to the receiver appointed by a state court and has become his clerk and ceases to act as cashier.—*Id.*

See CARRYING ON BUSINESS; JURISDICTION, 6, 7.

CREDITOR.

1. A and B were copartners in trade, but A owned most all of the property put into the firm, in his own individual right, and at the time of the formation of the partnership was in debt to some extent. This property was all he was worth, and his individual debts were contracted on the strength of this property. The firm carried on business several years, when the bulk of copartnership property was sold out under a deed of trust given by the firm to secure firm indebtedness, but no formal dissolution took place. A short time afterwards A filed his voluntary petition in bankruptcy; at this time the copartnership assets consisted of some personal property and a few outstanding accounts from which the assignee realized nothing. *Held,* That the individual and copartnership creditors should share equally.—*In re* Goedde & Co., 295.

DISCHARGE.

1. A discharge, unless impeached for fraud, is a bar to the continuance of a suit on a claim which was provable under the bankrupt law.—*Humble & Co. v. Carson*, 84.

2. A sued B in assumpsit on a promissory note. Defendant pleaded his discharge in bankruptcy in bar. Plaintiff replied that he ought not to be barred, for the reason that the defendant's schedule of indebtedness did not contain a statement of his debt, and that plaintiff had no notice of the proceedings in bankruptcy. *Held*, The omission of a creditor's name from the schedule of indebtedness of a bankrupt is not sufficient ground for annulling and setting aside a discharge, unless such omission is shown to have been fraudulent.— *Symonds* v. *Barnes*, 377.

3. On the return of an order to show cause why the bankrupt should not be attached for contempt in disobeying an order requiring him to appear and be examined under section twenty-six of the bankrupt act, he put in an answer that he was fully discharged before the issuing of the order, and therefore not subject to the orders of the court. *Held*, That after a discharge has been granted, the power or means to discover assets by the examination of the bankrupt, under section twenty-six, no longer remains, and that the power of examination will not be revived until the discharge has been set aside. Proceedings for contempt discharged.—*In re* G. C. Jones, 386.

4. UNREASONABLE DELAY IN APPLYING FOR.—A filed his petition in bankruptcy on the thirtieth day of October, eighteen hundred and sixty-nine. and on the twelfth day of May, eighteen hundred and seventy, filed his application for a discharge. On the fifteenth of June, eighteen hundred and seventy-one, B, one of his creditors, commenced an action in a state court, to recover for goods delivered to A, shortly before the filing of his petition in bankruptcy. A filed an offer in writing to allow judgment to be entered for the amount claimed with costs, and then presented his petition to the United States district court of that district, stating that the debt to B arose prior to the filing of his petition in bankruptcy, and that it was a provable debt, and praying that he might be allowed to take judgment for the amount claimed, and that further proceedings in the action might be stayed to await the determination of the court on the question of his discharge, whereupon an order to that effect was granted. On application of B, to discharge the order of stay, on the ground that there had been unreasonable delay on the part of the bankrupt in endeavoring to obtain his discharge, *Held*, That there had been unreasonable delay, for the reason that the bankrupt had, on the seventeenth day of November, eighteen hundred and seventy, presented his petition to the circuit court. to review a decision of the district court, on questions arising in reference to a discharge, returnable on the nineteenth, with a stay of proceedings on such decision, and there was no evidence to show why he had not, for fourteen months, brought the matter to a hearing. Order entered vacating the stay of proceedings.—*In re* W. Belden, 443.

5. In proceedings in bankruptcy commenced after January first, eighteen hundred and sixty-nine, where it does not appear either that the bankrupt's assets are equal to fifty per cent. of the claims proved against him on which he is liable as principal debtor, or that the requisite number of his creditors

have assented to his discharge, a discharge from debts contracted prior to January first, eighteen hundred and sixty-nine, only, will be granted, although the bankrupt shows that his assets equal fifty per cent. of the claims proved against his estate that were contracted subsequent to January first, eighteen hundred and sixty-nine.—*In re* J. L. Shower, 586.

See AFSETS ; ASSIGNEE, 2 ; DISTRICT COURT, 2.

DISMISSAL OF PROCEEDINGS.—See APPEAL, 1, 2 ; ASSIGNEE, 11 ; ASSIGN-MENT, 1 ; COMMERCIAL PAPER, 8 ; CORPORATION, 5 ; FRAUD, 2 ; INJUNCTION, 3 ; JUDGMENT, 2 ; JURISDICTION, 8 ; PETITION, 1, 2 ; SALE, 3 ; SETTING ASIDE JUDGMENT.

DISTRICT COURT.

1. The United States district court has ample power to restrain a claimant of a lien, obtained by collusion with the bankrupt, from proceeding elsewhere to enforce his lien, and this power may be summarily exercised without a formal suit. When necessary, for the protection of the bankrupt's estate, or in further-ance of justice, an order once made may be revoked.—*Samson, Assignee,* v. *Clark & Burton*, 403.

2. An assignee applied by petition to the district court to compel the return to him of certain property of the bankrupt, which had been taken from his pos-session by the sheriff, by virtue of a writ of replevin, issued in the name of A against D. A appeared, and without objection to the form of proceedings, answered the petition, denying that the property was ever the property of the bankrupt. A trial was had, and the court adjudged that D had no title or interest, but that the property belonged to the bankrupt's estate. A then brought his petition of review in the circuit court. The assignee moved to dis-miss it on the ground that the value of the property in question was not suffi-cient to give the court jurisdiction ; that the petition alleges no error of law, assigns no specific error, in fact. *Held,* That in summary proceedings there is nothing in the law to limit the jurisdiction of the court, on review, to the value of the property in controversy ; that the neglect to assign any specific error was one that might be cured by amendment, and no delay should happen to the creditors through mere defect in the formal procedings. The power of review is given the court as a court of equity, and on appeal it is not bound to reverse on strictly legal grounds, if satisfied that the facts are correctly found and that no injustice has been done. The declarations of the bankrupt were admissible as evidence, as the declarations of a co-conspirator in the attempt to defraud and as part of the *res gestæ.* Decree affirmed, with costs.—*Samson, Assignee,* v. *Blake et al.*, 410.

3. The district court sitting in bankruptcy has a right to recall a final decree granting a discharge to a bankrupt upon application made during the term of court at which the decree was passed. *It seems* that the court has the power to do this after the term has ended. This power will be exercised in a case in which counsel opposing the discharge was prevented by a sudden and overpowering accident from being present at the hearing, if it shall be made to appear that the opposing creditors were in fact prevented by the accident from presenting their case, and if they believe they had, and have, a good case upon the merits, showing fraud in the bankrupt.—*In re* Dupee, 89.

EVIDENCE.

1. An exemplified copy of an examination of the debtor, taken under the laws of the state of New York, under supplemental proceedings upon a judgment, was offered, for the purpose of proving admissions of the debtor. *Held*, That under the act of congress approved May twenty-sixth, seventeen hundred and ninety, such copy was proper evidence, such examination being "judicial proceedings" within the meaning of said act.—*In re* Rooney, 163.

EXAMINATION.

1. The examination of witnesses orally before the court is no ground for reversal of an order. Order affirmed.—*Samson, Assignee,* v. *Clark & Burton,* 403. Of BANKRUPT.—See DISCHARGE, 3.

EXECUTION.—See ASSIGNEE, 8; FRAUDULENT CONVEYANCE, 1; INJUNCTION, 2; JUDGMENT, 1; SALE, 1.

EXEMPTION.

1. An exemption, in accordance with the provisions of the fourteenth section of the present bankrupt act, cannot be allowed to an individual partner out of the partnership estate, as such exemption can only be allowed in case there is a surplus after paying the partnership creditors.—*In re* J. S. & J. Price, 400.

FALSE REPRESENTATIONS.

A debtor cannot be allowed to have the benefit of a composition with his creditors which was confessedly procured by the false representations of his agent, upon the ground that the agent was ignorant of the truth and made the representations in good faith.—*Elfelt et al.* v. *Snow et al.*, 57.

FRAUD.

1. When proceedings were pending in bankruptcy, and a preferred creditor and the insolvent settle the petitioning creditor's debt and employ the attorney who conducts such proceedings to compromise with the other creditors, authorising him to pay some one price and others another, and it appears that such discrimination was in fact made, such scheme is *prima facie* fraudulent, and the burden is upon the actors to show that all the creditors consented to such preferences; it will not be presumed. But if any one creditor does not consent it is a fraud upon him, although all the others are satisfied.—*Curran et al.* v. *Munger et al.*, 33.

2. When a bill made a purchaser from the trustees under the voluntary deed a party defendant, without sufficient allegations that he knew of or partook in the fraud, the bill was dismissed as to him, but retained as to the other defendants, who were the parties to the voluntary settlement.—*Pratt, Jr.,* v. *Curtis et al.*, 139.

A and B were copartners on and prior to March 31st, eighteen hundred and seventy; on that day the firm was dissolved, having an indebtedness of eleven thousand dollars to third parties, and ten thousand dollars to B for the capital stock. The assets amounted to some nineteen thousand dollars : six thousand of which was real estate, and the balance consisted of the stock of merchandise, notes and accounts. A had no property except some six hundred dollars and his homestead. At the dissolution, A bought B's interest in the firm property, except the real estate, and gave B his notes for seven thousand dollars, secured by a chattel mortgage on the stock then on hand, and thereafter to be acquired. A also agreed to pay the firm's liabilities, and B took the real estate at a valuation of six thousand dollars. It was agreed that the mortgage was not to be filed until March thirty-first, eighteen hundred and seventy-one. On the twenty-first of March, eighteen hundred and seventy-one, A transferred his stock, notes and accounts, worth some twelve thousand dollars, to B, in payment of the seven thousand dollar notes, B agreeing to pay the firm debts, which were were about five thousand dollars. A was adjudged a bankrupt, and his assignee filed his petition praying the court to compel B to surrender his preference. The court granted a stay of proceedings on the prayer of B, to allow him to surrender his preference, which he did, and filed claims against the estate of A for the seven thousand dollars due him, and also five thousand dollars of firm debts. *Held*, That under the facts of the case, the seven thousand dollars was a fraud as against the creditors of A, and that B should be allowed to prove for the five thousand dollars only.—*In re E. R. Stephens*, 533.

See CONVEYANCE, 2, 3, 4 ; DISTRICT COURT, 2 ; IMPRISONMENT ; PAYMENT BY DEBTOR.

FRAUDULENT CONVEYANCE.

1. Where the bankrupt fraudulently conveyed his lands to avoid a judgment, a purchaser under the judgment and a sale made under execution after proceedings in bankruptcy commenced, cannot defend on the ground that the assignee did not commence suit to set aside the execution, sale and deed within two years after the assignment. No cause of action accrued to the assignee against such purchaser until he acquired his title under the judgment and execution sale.—*Davis* v. *Anderson et al.*, 145.

2. That clause of section forty-four of the United States bankrupt act of eighteen hundred and sixty-seven, which punishes by imprisonment any fraudulent disposition of the goods of a debtor, obtained on credit and remaining unpaid for, within three months next before the commencement of proceedings in bankruptcy, is constitutional and valid. Motion in arrest of judgment on this ground denied, and defendant sentenced to one year's imprisonment.— *United States* v. *Pusey*, 284.

3. A transfer by an insolvent debtor with a view to secure his property, or any part of it, to one creditor, and thus prevent an equal distribution among all his creditors, is a transfer in fraud of the bankrupt act.—*Toof et al.* v. *Martin*, 49.

4. A debtor made a transfer of real estate to his brother-in-law, who on the same day re-conveyed the property to the wife of the debtor. *Held*, That the transfer took place at the time of the actual execution and delivery of the deeds, and not at their date, and was therefore within the six months limited by the act.—*In re* Rooney, 163.

FRAUDULENT PREFERENCE.

1. A confession of judgment entered before the first day of June, eighteen hundred and sixty-seven, but after the enactment of the bankrupt law, is a

fraudulent preference, when both parties knew of the insolvency of the debtor. —*Traders National Bank of Chicago* v. *Campbell, Assignee*, 353.

2. Receiving money in its capacity as a bank from collections due the bankrupt, by the creditor, and handing the same to the sheriff, who applies it to the payment of the bank's judgment, is a fraudulent preference ; so too, taking a check from the bankrupt for the amount on deposit and crediting the amount of the check on the bankrupt's note the day before taking judgment is a preference, and void, hence the question of set.off does not arise.—*Id.*

INJUNCTION.

1. An injunction granted under section forty of the bankrupt act does not extend beyond the adjudication. Hence any proceedings to punish parties for contempt in violating an injunction after adjudication, must be dismissed with costs.—*In re* Moses, 181.

2. An injunction was granted on an order to show case before adjudication in bankruptcy had taken place, to restrain the sheriff and all other persons from selling the property of the alleged bankrupt, on a judgment obtained by default in a suit brought in the state court. The sheriff moved to dissolve the injunction on the following grounds :—First, that said injunction is not addressed to any person, therefore does not include the sheriff and judgment creditor. Second, that the court has exceeded its just power, and cannot lawfully restrain the judgment creditor from selling the property in question, the judgment not being impeachable for fraud or as preference under the bankrupt act, the judgment having been docketed before the filing of the petition. *Held*, First, when the injunction was served upon the sheriff and judgment creditor, it plainly apprised them of what they were restrained from doing, and the fact that they were not named in the order can make no substantial difference. Second, that neither the judgment nor the levy of execution divests the alleged bankrupt of his property, and he would be bound to include such estate in his inventory if adjudged a bankrupt ; and further, that the bankruptcy court may, in the exercise of a lawful jurisdiction, restrain by injunction the sale of property under an execution issued from a state court, even before the commencement of proceedings in bankruptcy.—*In re* Lady Bryan Mining Co., 252.

3. A debtor in failing circumstances attempted to make a compromise with his creditors of twenty-five per cent., but they rejected this offer and threatened him with proceedings in bankruptcy. At this time he represented that he had several promissory notes amounting to over nine hundred dollars. Some days after this a petition in bankruptcy was filed against him, and the order to show cause, together with the injunction served some two days later. The bankrupt swore that at the time of the service of the injunction he had sold the notes and spent most of the proceeds. Testimony was taken, and at the close, the register, to whom the proceedings had been referred, decided that an order should be entered directing the bankrupt within five days to hand over to said assignee the amount of the notes, with interest from the day of the adjudication, or in default thereof, an attachment issue against him as for a contempt, which order was duly approved by the judge.—*In re* Kempner, 521.

3. An assignee in bankruptcy applied to the United States district court, and obtained an injunction to restrain the sale of property under the decree of

foreclosure in a mortgage, after the proceedings had reached a stage where, substantially, all the expenses, except those which would attend the sale of the property, had been incurred. Sometime thereafter he applied for leave to dissolve the injunction and sell the property. *Held,* That the petition must be dismissed, with costs to the assignee, for the reason that he had not applied at the commencement of the foreclosure suit for a stay of proceedings. Injunction dissolved.—*In re* Brinkman, 541.

See PURCHASER OF NOTES ; SERVING SUBPŒNA.

INSANITY. —See ACT OF BANKRUPTCY.

INSOLVENCY.

1. By insolvency, as used in the bankrupt act, when applied to traders and merchants, is meant inability of a party to pay his debts as they become due in the ordinary course of business.— *Toof et al* v. *Martin,* 49.

See PREFERENCE ; REASONABLE CAUSE.

INSURANCE.—See LIEN.

JUDGMENT.

1. The United States district court sitting in bankruptcy has power to enjoin the sheriff of a state court, or parties litigant therein, from proceeding to sell property levied upon by virtue of a writ of execution issued out of such court upon a judgment obtained therein before proceedings in bankruptcy were commenced.—*In re* Mallory, 22.

2. A gave his bond to the United States as security for a certain claim against a vessel. The cause was tried and a decision adverse to the United States rendered. Additional evidence was produced in the circuit court, on appeal, and the decision of the district court was reversed, and a decree of condemnation rendere on the twenty-seventh of May, eighteen hundred and seventy. While proceedings were pending in the circuit court, A filed his petition in bankruptcy, and was, on the thirtieth day of June, eighteen hundred and sixty-nine, discharged from all his debts dischargable under the bankrupt act. On the eighth of June, eighteen hundred and seventy, the circuit court overruled A's plea of discharge in bar of the claim, and gave judgment against him on the release bond. On the twenty-first of April, eighteen hundred and seventy-one, the secretary of the treasury, for a valuable consideration, transferred the judgment to B, who, on the twenty-seventh of May, eighteen hundred and seventy-one, filed a petition to set aside A's discharge. *Held,* That when the United States elected to take judgment upon the bond they parted with all right to prove it as a debt due and payable from the bankrupt at the time of the adjudication of bankruptcy, and as a debt to be proved against the estate ; that it is *res judicata* that this debt is not affected by the discharge, as the judgment is subsisting and operative. Exception sustained and the petition dismissed.—*In re* Mansfield, 388.

JURISDICTION.

1. When the revisory jurisdiction of the circuit court is invoked over the decision of the district court upon a question of fact, the burden of proof is on the

petitioner for review to show cause in the decision, and he must also show that the evidence cannot support the finding.—*In re* Dow, 10.

2. The object and intent of the United States bankrupt act of eighteen hundred and sixty-seven is to place the administration of the affairs of insolvent persons and corporations exclusively under the jurisdiction of the federal courts. Hence, the appointment of a receiver for an insolvent insurance company by a state court is an act of bankruptcy, being a "taking on legal process" within the meaning of the thirty-ninth section of said act; the United States courts sitting in bankruptcy having in such cases exclusive jurisdiction over the property.—*In re* Merchant's Insurance Co., 43.

3. A railroad company incorporated by the laws of a state for constructing, maintaining and operating a railroad, cannot be proceeded against in bankruptcy in a district court without the state or states where its railroad is to be built, maintained and operated, on the petition of a creditor charging an act of bankruptcy. Allegation and proof that such company kept an office in said district for six months next preceding the filing of the petition, where its officers acted, its board of directors met, and where it contracted debts, made loans, purchases and payments, does not give such court jurisdiction.—*In re* Alabama and Chattanooga R. R. Co., 107.

4. The business of a railroad company, in the sense of the act, can only be carried on where the railroad is or is to be constructed, maintained and operated; hence, the district court of the United States for the southern district of New York has no jurisdiction to adjudge an Alabama railroad corporation a bankrupt on such a petition by a creditor.—*Id.*

5. The district court has jurisdiction of a bill in equity by an assignee in bankruptcy to set aside a conveyance of land alleged to be fraudulent as to creditors, although there may be concurrent remedy at law.—*Pratt, Jr.,* v. *Curtis et al.*, 139.

6. A decree of a state court dissolving an insurance company incorporated under the laws of the state, and appointing receivers to take and distribute the property of the company, and enjoining the latter from the further prosecution of its business, which decree was founded upon the insolvency of the corporation, does not take away the jurisdiction of the district court of the United States to adjudge the corporation bankrupt. The state laws do not extend to all the matters arising in bankruptcy, such as preferences and property out of the state, and even if it be granted that the state courts have concurrent jurisdiction of an insolvent corporation, they have not full jurisdiction of the subject matter.—*In re* Independent Insurance Co., 169.

7. On review of a motion in the United States court to appoint a receiver to take possession of the property of a corporation already ordered to be delivered to a receiver appointed by a state court. *Held,* That the jurisdiction of the two courts was concurrent; that the jurisdiction of the state court was first invoked and asserted, consequently no court of concurrent jurisdiction can or ought to interfere with it. Motion continued, to allow the defendants to set up the facts in regard to the proceedings of the chancery court of Sumter county by formal answer.—*Blake* v. *The Alabama and Chattanooga R. R. Co. et al.*, 331.

8. The provisions of the bankrupt act confer upon the United States district courts a general superintendence and jurisdiction of all cases and questions

arising under the bankrupt act, but this jurisdiction is confined to the court within and for the district where the proceedings in bankruptcy shall be pending. An action brought by an assignee in bankruptcy in a district court other than the one in which the proceedings in bankruptcy were pending was dismissed. An appearance and answer by a defendant does not preclude him from raising the question of jurisdiction. Courts of bankruptcy are the special creatures of statutory law, and all their jurisdiction is derived from the act which creates them.—*Jobbins* v. *Montague et al.*, 509.

9. S was adjudged a bankrupt by the district court of the United States for the district of Maine, of which he was a citizen, and P was appointed his assignee, also residing in same district. The assignee filed his bill in equity in the same court to recover certain preferences of the respondent, who resided in and was a citizen of Massachusetts, and had no property in this district, and was not found here. The subpœna was served on respondent in Massachusetts, who appeared to. object to the jurisdiction of this court. *Held*, That the court did not have jurisdiction to proceed against the respondent.—*Paine, Assignee,* v. *Caldwell*, 558.

See CLAIM, 2; CORPORATION, 1, 2; DISTRICT COURT, 3.

KNOWLEDGE OF INSOLVENCY.

1. When a debtor and a preferred creditor know of the insolvency, but erroneously suppose all other creditors have compromised for thirty-five cents in time paper, a transfer so securing the creditor as to create a preference financially is an act of bankruptcy. If insolvency is once known all parties act at their peril, when such condition actually exists, whether known or unknown. —*Curran et al.* v. *Munger et al.*, 33.

LIEN.

creditor who has his debt secured by a valid trust deed containing a covenant to insure the buildings erected on the property to their full insurable value, has a clear and specific lien upon the proceeds of the insurance, to the exclusion of the general creditors in case of a loss by fire. The fact that the policies were not regularly assigned makes no difference, as in equity the assignment is executed the moment the insurance is effected ; nor is the case altered on account of the clause in the said deed allowing the insurance company to be selected by the party loaning the money, because an insurance having been effected to the insurable value of the property the creditor has no power to insure further.—*In re* Sands Ale Brewing Co., 101.

2. After the filing of a petition in bankruptcy no valid lien can be acquired upon property of the bankrupt by proceedings in a state court ; and an assignee is not bound to go into a state court to defend such a suit, the action being a nullity as to him.—*Stuart, Assignee,* v. *Hines et al.*, 416.

3. A sheriff who levies upon property by virtue of an order to sell under a mortgage foreclosure suit, before the debtor is adjudicated a bankrupt, has a valid lien and may sell the property after the adjudication. Injunction to restrain purchaser from meddling with the property refused, but leave given the assignee to redeem it within three months if he thinks it worth more than the mortgage debt, interest and costs.—*Goddard, Assignee,* v. *Weaver*, 448.

4. No maritime lien arises for materials furnished, or repairs made to a vessel in her home port, although such vessel is engaged in foreign trade; hence, neither the shipwright nor material man is entitled to share in the proceeds arising from the sale of the vessel under admiralty process as against a mortgagee or assignee in bankruptcy. The act of April twenty-fourth, eighteen hundred and sixty-two, of New York, [Laws of 1862, chap. 482,] is unconstitutional and void, so far as it provides for enforcing a maritime contract by proceedings *in r. m* against a vessel.—*In re* Ship Edith, 449.

See RENT, 3.

LIMITATION, STATUTES OF.—See BANKRUPT ACT ; CREDITOR, 3 ; DEBT, 2.

MANUFACTURERS.

1. The publishers of a daily paper and proprietors of a book and job printing office are manufacturers within the meaning of the bankrupt act.—*In re* Kenyon & Fenton, 238.

MEETINGS OF CREDITORS.

1. A third meeting of creditors—not being a final meeting—should not be called except for cause shown, and if the register be satisfied that no such cause exists, he is justified in refusing to grant the order for such a meeting.— *In re* Clark & Bininger, 194.

2. There can be only one first meeting of creditors and all adjournments are but continuance of the same, and if there appear any opposition or opposing interest to the appointment of a particular assignee, at any stage of the meeting, such opposition is to be considered as continuing until the termination of such first meeting, whether upon the day first appointed or any other day to which such meeting might be continued, unless it affirmatively appeared that such opposition was withdrawn. In such cases it is the duty of the register to report the facts and return the matter for the action of the court.—*In re* Norton, 297.

See REGISTER, 2, 3.

MORTGAGE.

1. A mortgage executed in a state having no statute on the subject of record, or if record is not required between the parties, will not be defeated by the proviso in the fourteenth section of the United States bankrupt act of eighteen hundred and sixty-seven in relation to recording.—*In re* Dow, 10.

• 2. A creditor who accepts a chattel mortgage with a view to obtain a preference, having reasonable cause to believe at the time that a fraud on the act was intended and that his debtor was insolvent, will not be allowed to prove his debt in bankruptcy, and likewise loses the lien of his mortgage.—*Bingham* v. *Richmond & Gibbs*, 127.

3. A creditor advanced money to his debtor, within four months of proceedings in bankruptcy, and took a mortgage of the debtor's stock in trade, first, as security therefor ; secondly, included in the same mortgage, another (antecedent) debt due to himself, which was secured by a prior mortgage on the same property, held by and given to the bankrupt's (debtor's) former copartner ; and, thirdly, for convenience, and to save writing an additional mortgage, an over-

due note taken up and held by the endorser, by whose request it was inserted in the mortgage. Subsequent to proceedings in bankruptcy, the stock in trade was sold, with the consent of the several mortgagees, who proved their claims before the register as secured debts, and joined with the assignee in submitting to the register their rights under the mortgage. The register held that the mortgage was void as against the assignee, because intended to secure a pre-existing debt, &c.—the overdue note—according to the principle of the decision in *Denny* v. *Dana*, 2 Cush. 160. *Held*, On appeal by the mortgagee, (the endorser withdrawing therefrom and surrendering all rights under the mortgage,) that the mortgage could be severed and sustained in part, and denied as to the rest. The court also disapproved the mode of presenting the case. It should be presented by a petition of the mortgagee against the funds in court. —*In re* Stowe, *ex parte* Godfrey, 429.

4. The owner of a vessel became bankrupt and it was sold by proceedings in admiralty, but the amount realized was insufficient to pay the two mortgages against it. *Held*, That the first mortgage, covering half the vessel, was to be treated as the first lien on one-half the fund, and that such half must be regarded as composed of two separate funds or quarters, one subject to the first mortgage alone, and one subject first, to the first mortgage, and second, to the second mortgage, which covered three-fourths of the vessel; that the second mortgage was the first lien on the second half of the proceeds. One-fourth being more than sufficient to pay the first mortgage, the surplus passed to the assignee in bankruptcy, and the remaining three-fourths of the fund went to the payment of the second mortgage.—*In re* Ship Edith, 449.

See CONVEYANCE, 1 ; LIEN, 3 ; ORDINARY COURSE OF BUSINESS ; PROOF OF DEBT, 1.

OFFSET.

1. A creditor of an insolvent who has reasonable ground to believe him to be such, can assign his demand to a debtor of the insolvent whose debt is not yet payable, so as to enable the latter to offset the demand so assigned to him against the debt due from him to the insolvent, the latter debt having become due and payable at the time the offset is claimed.—*In re* City Bank of Savings, Loan and Discount, 71.

ORDER TO SHOW CAUSE.

1. The order to show cause, as required by section forty of the bankrupt act, may be served personally outside the district in which the petition is filed by any one authorised by the solicitor for the petitioner to make it. This rule is not altered where one or more of several partners file their petition in bankruptcy, in which several members of the partnership refuse to join : the parties so refusing may be proceeded against as involuntary bankrupts, and the order to show cause may be served on them outside the territorial jurisdiction of the court, and by a person duly authorised by the solicitor for the petitioner.— *Stuart, Assignee,* v. *Hines et al.*, 416.

See CORPORATION 8, 9 ; INJUNCTION, 2.

ORDINARY COURSE OF BUSINESS.

1. It is not "out of the usual and ordinary course of business," for a corporation engaged in manufacture and which owns mortgages yet to become due, and desires to realize money thereon for use in its regular business, to sell such mortgages for their cash value. Hence a transfer made under such a state of circumstances will be adjudged valid as against the assignee in bankruptcy.— *Judson* v. *Kelty et al.*, 165.

See INSOLVENCY.

PAYMENT BY DEBTOR.

1. A debtor who seeks to make a composition of his debts by the payment of a part only of what he owes, is not bound to make any representations concerning his assets or resources ; but he must act in good faith, and if he does make any such representations, he must make them truly or he will be guilty of fraud.—*Elfelt et al.* v. *Snow et al.*, 57.

PARTNER.—See EXEMPTION ; ORDER TO SHOW CAUSE ; PROOF OF DEBT, 1.

PETITION.

1. On a motion to dismiss a petition in bankruptcy for the reason that it was not signed or sworn to by the petitioning creditors or either of them. *Held*, That the general attorneys or creditors cannot make, sign and verify for such creditors a valid petition, as the debtor must be adjudged a bankrupt on the petition of one or more of his creditors, and not on that of their agent or attorney. Petition dismissed, and all orders made thereunder vacated.—*In re* Butterfield, 257.

2. Where a petition is dismissed the debtor is entitled to receive by law the attorney's fees on a hearing in equity, twenty dollars. No fee can be taxed for petitioner's attorney.—*Dundore* v. *Coates & Bros.*, 304.

3. A petition to enjoin a party from making use of a certain agreement which he holds is not a formal suit but a summary proceeding. —*Samson, Assignee,* v. *Clark & Burton,* 403.

POSSESSION OF FUNDS.

1. Where a party lays claim to a certain fund, the possession of the depositary is his possession, provided his claim is just and legal ; therefore, if the assignee in bankruptcy would divest him of the possession and control of the fund in question, he must do it by a suit at law or in equity, as provided in the third clause of the second section of the bankrupt act.—*Smith* v. *Moson,* 1.

PREFERENCE.

1. The transfer by a debtor of a large portion of his property, while he is insolvent, to one creditor, without making provision for an equal distribution of its proceeds to all his creditors, necessarily operates as a preference to him, and must be taken as conclusive evidence that a preference was intended, unless the debtor can show that he was at the time ignorant of his insolvency, and that his affairs were such that he could reasonably expect to pay all his debts. The burden of proof is upon him in such a case, and not upon the assignee or contestant in bankruptcy.—*Toof et al.* v. *Martin,* 49.

See BANKRUPT ACT, SEC. 43 ; KNOWLEDGE OF INSOLVENCY, 1.

PROOF OF DEBT.

1. An agreement between two traders to unite their stocks in trade as the capital of a partnership to be formed between them, and to convert the separate business debts of either into joint debts of the firm, will not entitle a separate creditor who has not acceded in any way to the arrangement before bankruptcy, to prove his claim as a joint creditor of the firm against the partnership estate.—*In re* Isaacs & Cohn, 92.

2. There is nothing illegal in endeavoring to produce all the claims against the estate of a bankrupt for the purpose of staying the bankruptcy proceedings altogether ; failing in this, the purchaser should nevertheless be allowed to prove the claims purchased as though he were an original creditor.—*In re* Pease *et al.*, 173.

3. Creditors of bankrupt having security, whether by judgment, mortgage, or otherwise, must prove their debts against the bankrupt and foreclose their liens under the authority of the court in bankruptcy, or they may not only be barred of their debt, but may also lose the benefit of their securities.—*Davis* v. *Anderson et al.*, 145.

4. When written objections to a proof of debt are filed with the register and testimony is taken thereon, it is his duty, if requested by either party, to certify the same to the district judge for decision, even though no proof whatever be offered tending to invalidate the debt so proved.—*In re* Clark & Bininger, 202.

5. A petition in involuntary bankruptcy is not a mere suit *inter partes*, but rather partakes of the nature of a proceeding *in rem*, in which any actual creditor has a direct interest. If a third party, claiming to be a creditor of the respondent, seeks to intervene in such a proceeding, it is not an indispensable pre-requisite to his admission that he should have proved his debt in the ordinary form ; provided he can satisfy the court that he is in fact a creditor, and that his purpose is a meritorious one.—*In re* Boston, Hartford & Erie Railroad Co., 209.

6. When creditors have proved their claims under a voluntary petition in bankruptcy they thereby waive the right to insist on going back of this and proceeding under an involuntary petition. Motion to dismiss previous petition filed against bankrupts granted. A creditor holding collaterals is entitled to have his claim referred to the register for investigation, and the assignee is not justified in rejecting it until proofs have been taken and the matter fully inquired into. When the bankrupts made an agreement with a party to pay him for certain services, the benefits of which services would accrue to the other creditors, such claim is entitled to preference.—*In re* Nounnan & Co., 579.

PURCHASE OF NOTES

1. An alleged bankrupt, during the pendency of bankruptcy proceedings, and while under an injunction from the United States District Court prohibiting him from selling or disposing of any of his property, sold certain promissory notes belonging to him. He was finally adjudged a bankrupt. *Held*, That the purchaser acquires no title to the notes in question, as he took with constructive notice at least, and cannot claim to be an innocent purchaser for value. That the adjudication relates back to the time of the filing of the

petition, and the assignee may recover the notes or their value from the purchaser. The payment of the notes having been guaranteed, the court orders that the assignee preserve the notes and guaranties thereon intact, that they may be used as evidence if required in proceedings by the purchaser against the guarantor.—*In re* Lake, 542.

REASONABLE CAUSE.

1. A creditor has reasonable cause to believe a debtor, who is a . trader, to be insolvent, when such a state of facts is brought to the creditor's notice respecting the affairs and pecuniary condition of the debtor as would lead a prudent business man to the conclusion that he is unable to meet his obligations as they mature in the ordinary course of business.—*Toof et al.* v. *Martin*, 49.

See MORTGAGE, 2 ; OFFSET.

RECEIVER.

1. A receiver appointed under an order of a state court cannot be one of the trustees appointed under section forty-three of the bankrupt act, for the reason that he must account, if at all, as receiver, to a trustee or assignee to be appointed by the United States district court, for the property as it stood at the date of the commencement of bankruptcy proceedings, and it is not proper that he should, as trustee, be plaintiff, and as receiver be defendant. It appearing, furthermore, that the receiver does not intend, voluntarily, to surrender his receivership, when appointed a trustee by the court, but expects to have his acts as receiver and trustee confirmed by the respective courts, this court decides that his position is one of incompatibility, for if he is to be trustee under the bankrupt act, he must look to this court alone for authority and direction. For the same reason a receiver cannot be appointed assignee although three-fourths in value of the creditors whose claims were proven nominated him as trustee.—*In re* Stuyvesant Bank, 272.

REGISTER.

1. The register in charge has power to order the assignee to furnish him with all necessary information as to funds in his hands.—*In re* Clark & Bininger, 194.

2. A register has power so to audit and pass the accounts of an assignee at a second meeting called only under the twenty-seventh section of the act, as to bind the creditors, even though no notice had been given under the twenty-eighth section or otherwise, that such accounting would be had, and though such accounts be not filed until the hour of the meeting. If the creditors omit to attend such meeting, or fail to object to such accounts, it is the duty of the register to direct their payment. The provision in section twenty-eight, for auditing and passing the accounts of the assignee at the meeting for the final dividend, cannot be regarded as in any manner implying that such accounts of the assignee as are presented at the second general meeting of creditors shall not then be audited and passed by the register.—*In re* Clark & Bininger, 197.

3. When the register gave notice at the second meeting of creditors called only under the twenty-seventh section of the act, that the accounts of the

assignee filed at such meeting would not be audited or passed at such meeting, as no notice of such auditing or passing had been given to creditors, and as the amounts had not been on file ten days, as required by the twenty-eighth section of the act. *Held,* On an application by the assignee to the district judge to compel the register to order the payment of such accounts, that the register was right in refusing to make such order. —*In re* Clark & Bininger, 204.

4. A register may order bankrupts to hand over to his custodian funds in their hands. Disobedience to such an order adjudged a contempt, for which an attachment was issued from the court. —*In re* F. & A. Speyer, 255.

See ASSIGNEE, 2; MEETINGS OF CREDITORS, 1, 2 ; MORTGAGE, 3 ; PROOF OF DEBT, 2.

RENT.

1. The payment of rent in full by an insolvent corporation, in order to prevent the forfeiture of a valuable lease, is a technical act of bankruptcy.—*In re* Merchants' Insurance Co., 43.

2. A landlord's right to rent, against the bankrupt's estate, expires on the day of adjudication. If the assignee occupy the premises after that day, he, and not the estate, is liable for the rent ; when, however, his occupancy is for the benefit of the estate, he will be credited by the rent he is obliged to pay — *In re* Webb & Co., 302.

3. Unless there is a seizure for rent as provided for in the Pennsylvania statute, the bankrupt act of eighteen hundred and sixty-seven gives the landlord no lien or preference over the bankrupt's other creditors. Where premises are occupied by the assignee or trustee after adjudication, rent should be paid for the time they are so occupied as part of the administration of the estate.— *In re* Butler, 501.

REPLEVIN.—See DISTRICT COURT, 3.

RETURN OF GOODS.

1. A contracted with B for the sale of certain scales, payment to be made by B's note on their delivery and after they were set up. They were delivered but not set up according to contract, and B's note was not given. Soon after this B was declared bankrupt. A petitioned to have his goods returned, which was granted, and an order entered according.—*In re* Pusey, 40.

REVIEW, PETITION FOR.—See DEMURRER, 1.

SALE.

1. A sale of the debtor's land by virtue of an execution issued and levied after the filing of the petition in bankruptcy will not pass the title to the land as against the assignee, although the judgment was entered and the lien created prior to the bankruptcy.—*Davis* v. *Anderson et al.*, 145.

2. The bankrupt court may order a sale of the bankrupt's property free and clear of encumbrances, and the secured creditor will then have his remedy only against the fund in court. If the secured creditor fails to prove his debt and proceeds against the fund, he does so at his peril.—*Id.*

3. A consigned goods to B with orders to sell them and take negotiable notes

payable to his order. B sold the goods to C, taking negotiable notes payable to himself instead of to A. At the time of the sale, C was accommodation endorser for B to a large amount. B discounted the notes above mentioned and paid the proceeds to C, to apply towards taking up the notes on which C was endorser. B was insolvent at that time, and shortly thereafter was adjudged a bankrupt. His assignee brought suit and recovered the amount thus paid to C on the ground that he, C, had reasonable cause to believe B was insolvent when he received the money. A filed a bill in equity to recover the money in the hands of the assignee, claiming that as it never belonged either to B or C, he ought to be allowed to assert his right to it. The court held that it was not *shown* that the money paid to C by B was the product of the sale of A's goods, that although the bill alleges the whole of it was thus derived, and the allegation is not denied by the answer, the allegation is not on this account to be taken as true; that it is only an allegation of some fact which is presumed to be within the knowledge of the party answering, that can be taken as true, simply because it is not denied. The court further held that the fund having been recovered not in virtue of any right in the complainant personally, but in virtue of the rights of the bankrupt's creditors generally, and in virtue of the clear legal right of all the creditors, under the bankrupt law, it must be distributed among them generally and not given to one. Bill dismissed with costs.—*While* v. *Jones*, 175.

4. An assignee acting under an order of court directing him to sell the goods of a bankrupt for the highest price he could obtain above a certain minimum specified, must comply with the order, and if it is made to appear to the court that he has not obtained the highest price offered, the sale will be set aside and the assignee directed to refund the amount received, and hold the sale open for higher offers until a day specified, when it shall be closed for the highest offer in cash received up to that time. Costs and attorney's fees of ten dollars ordered to be paid out of the funds belonging to the estate of the bankrupt.—*In re* Ryan & Griffin, 235.

SECURED DEBT.

1. A debt wholly or in part secured, either by levy under an execution, by pledge of personal property or mortgage upon real estate, will sustain a petition for an adjudication of bankruptcy. The better practice is, when the debt is *fully* secured, to waive the security in the petition, but this is not necessary to its support.—*In re* Stansell, 183.

SERVING SUBPŒNA.

1. There is nothing in the general orders in bankruptcy, or in the rules in equity prescribed by the supreme court, which authorises a marshal to serve a subpœna to appear and answer in an equity suit at a place outside of the territorial limit of the district for which he is appointed. Service of subpœna and injunction set aside for irregularity.—*Jobbins* v. *Montogue et al.*, 117.

SETTING ASIDE JUDGMENT.

1. Granting a second trial has the effect of setting aside a judgment previously rendered. Case dismissed without prejudice, leaving the party to their remedy under the bankrupt law. Costs to be paid by plaintiffs.—*Humble & Co.* v. *Carson*, 84.

STATE COURT.—See Action ; Corporation, 6, 8 ; Jurisdiction, 6, 7 ; Lien, 2 ; Receiver.

STATUTES OF LIMITATION.

1. Where a debt is barred by the statute of limitations, a promise by the debtor to pay it when able has been regarded as a conditional promise, and not to operate as a revival entitling the creditor to sue until ability to pay appears ; but where there is a present debt a promise to pay it when able does not destroy or postpone the right of the creditor to sue, nor does it in anywise hinder or prevent the running of the statute.—*In re* Cornwall, 305.

2. Nor does a promise to deposit the money in a savings bank, to the account of the creditor, convert the relation of the parties into that of trustee and *cestui que trust,* so as to prevent the running of the statute.—*Id.*

STAY OF PROCEEDINGS.—See Corporation, 4 ; Discharge, 4 ; Proof of Debt, 2.

STRANGERS.—See Voluntary Appearance.

SUBPŒNA.

1. A subpœna to appear and answer a bill in equity cannot be served at the last place of abode as in the case of an order to show cause under section forty of the bankrupt act; or at the last usual place of abode as in form number fifty-seven in bankruptcy, but must be left at the existing present dwelling house or the existing, present, usual, customary place of abode of the defendant. There is no irregularity in making the subpœna returnable on the first Tuesday of the month instead of the first Monday, as the equity rules provide that the subpœna shall be returnable on a rule day ; and that the first Monday of every month shall be a rule day. The spirit of general order thirty-two and the equity rules were sufficiently complied with in this case. Motion granted setting aside the order *pro confesso,* and denied in respect to setting aside the subpœna. Application to have a receiver appointed denied.—*Hyslop, Assignee,* v. *Hoppock et al.,* 552.

2. The service of a subpœna to appear and answer a bill in equity is regulated by an act of congress, and if the defendants do not reside within the district, the district court has no power to obtain jurisdiction over their persons by any service of process made otherwise than in accordance with rule thirteen. Application to have service made by publication or personal service on the son of defendant denied.—*Hyslop, Assignee,* v. *Hoppock et al.,* 557.

SUSPENSION OF PAYMENT.

1. A suspension of payment of commercial paper for fourteen days under section thirty-nine, before the amendment of July fourteenth, eighteen hundred and seventy, was *per se* an act of bankruptcy. The omission to pay such paper for fourteen days, subsequent to that amendment, is a suspension within its meaning, although the paper fell due and was dishonored before its passage.—*Baldwin et al.* v. *Wilder et al.,* 85.

TRUSTEE.

1. A was residuary legatee of B, and took the real estate subject to the payment of a certain sum to C in trust for the benefit of three of B's children, to be paid at the expiration of three years from B's death. A enjoyed the possession of this real estate some thirty years, became insolvent, was adjudicated a bankrupt in January, eighteen hundred and seventy-one, and the estate in question was sold by his assignee. C did not receive the sum which was to have been paid to him by A according to the terms of the will. On the question of distribution the court held, that A was not an express or direct trustee, and that the statutory bar was a complete defence to any claim for the amount to have been paid to C as trustee.—*In re* O'Neale, 425

See STATUTE OF LIMITATIONS.

TWO YEARS.

1. The limitation of two years in section two of the bankrupt act applies only to property held adversely to the bankrupt and his assignee.—*Davis v. Anderson et al.*, 145.

VOLUNTARY APPEARANCE.

1. Strangers to the proceedings in bankruptcy not served with process and who have not voluntarily appeared and become parties to such a litigation, cannot be compelled to come into court under a petition for a rule to show cause, as the third clause of the second section of the said act affords the assignee a convenient, constitutional and sufficient remedy to contest every adverse claim made by any person to any property or rights of property transferable to or vested in such assignee. Cause remanded for further proceedings in conformity to the opinion of this court.—*Smith v. Mason*, 1.

WAGES.—See ACT OF BANKRUPTCY.

WANT OF NOTICE.

1. Want of notice to a bankrupt is a formal objection, well taken—as the bankrupt has an interest in the continuance of proceedings which may result in his discharge.—*In re* Bush, 179.

WITNESS.—See CLAIM, 2.

Lightning Source UK Ltd.
Milton Keynes UK
UKHW012012121218
333853UK00007B/459/P